CHILTON BOOK COMPANY

REPAIR & TUNE-UP GUIDE

CUTLASS
1970 to
1987

All U.S. and Canadian models of rear wheel drive
Cutlass • Cutlass Supreme • F-85 • 4-4-2

President LAWRENCE A. FORNASIERI
Vice President and General Manager JOHN P. KUSHNERICK
Editor-in-Chief Editor KERRY A. FREEMAN, S.A.E.
Senior Editor RICHARD J. RIVELE, S.A.E.
Editor MARTIN J. GUNTHER

CHILTON BOOK COMPANY
Radnor, Pennsylvania
19089

SAFETY NOTICE

Proper service and repair procedures are vital to the safe, reliable operation of all motor vehicles, as well as the personal safety of those performing repairs. This book outlines procedures for servicing and repairing vehicles using safe, effective methods. The procedures contain many NOTES, CAUTIONS and WARNINGS which should be followed along with standard safety procedures to eliminate the possibility of personal injury or improper service which could damage the vehicle or compromise its safety.

It is important to note that repair procedures and techniques, tools and parts for servicing motor vehicles, as well as the skill and experience of the individual performing the work vary widely. It is not possible to anticipate all of the conceivable ways or conditions under which vehicles may be serviced, or to provide cautions as to all of the possible hazards that may result. Standard and accepted safety precautions and equipment should be used during cutting, grinding, chiseling, prying, or any other process that can cause material removal or projectiles.

Some procedures require the use of tools specially designed for a specific purpose. Before substituting another tool or procedure, you must be completely satisfied that neither your personal safety, nor the performance of the vehicle will be endangered.

Although the information in this guide is based on industry sources and is as complete as possible at the time of publication, the possibility exists that the manufacturer made later changes which could not be included here. While striving for total accuracy, Chilton Book Company cannot assume responsibility for any errors, changes, or omissions that may occur in the compilation of this data.

PART NUMBERS

Part numbers listed in this reference are not recommendations by Chilton for any product by brand name. They are references that can be used with interchange manuals and aftermarket supplier catalogs to locate each brand supplier's discrete part number.

SPECIAL TOOLS

Special tools are recommended by the vehicle manufacturer to perform their specific job. Use has been kept to a minimum, but where absolutely necessary, they are referred to in the text by the part number of the tool manufacturer. These tools can be purchased, under the appropriate part number, from the Service Tool Division, Kent-Moore Corporation, 29784 Little Mack, Roseville, MI 48066-2298, or an equivalent tool can be purchased locally from a tool supplier or parts outlet. Before substituting any tool for the one recommended, read the SAFETY NOTICE at the top of this page.

ACKNOWLEDGMENTS

The Chilton Book Company expresses its appreciation to the General Motors Corporation, Detroit, Michigan for their generous assistance.

Information has been selected from shop manuals, owners manuals, service bulletins, and technical training manuals.

Copyright © 1987 by Chilton Book Company
All Rights Reserved
Published in Radnor, Pennsylvania 19089 by Chilton Book Company

Manufactured in the United States of America
1234567890   6543210987

Chilton's Repair & Tune-Up Guide: Cutlass 1970–87
ISBN 0-8019-7753-3 pbk.
Library of Congress Catalog Card No. 86-47775

CONTENTS

1 General Information and Maintenance

1 How to use this Book
2 Tools and Equipment
8 Routine Maintenance and Lubrication

2 Tune-Up and Performance Maintenance

39 Tune-Up Procedures
40 Tune-Up Specifications
45 Troubleshooting

3 Engine and Engine Overhaul

64 Engine Electrical
65 Engine Troubleshooting
73 Engine Mechanical
78 Engine Specifications

4 Emission Controls and Fuel System

135 Emission Control System and Service
152 Fuel System Service

5 Chassis Electrical

188 Accessory Service
193 Instruments Panel Service
194 Lights, Fuses and Flashers

6 Drive Train

200 Manual Transmission
203 Clutch
204 Automatic Transmission
210 Driveshaft and U-Joints
218 Rear Axle

7 Suspension and Steering

220 Suspension
225 Steering

8 Brakes

245 Front Disc Brakes
250 Front Drum Brakes
251 Rear Drum Brakes
254 Brake Specifications

9 Body and Trim

259 Exterior
267 Interior

10

279 Mechanic's Data
281 Glossary
287 Abbreviations
289 Index

154 Chilton's Fuel Economy and Tune-Up Tips

266 Chilton's Body Repair Tips

Quick Reference Specifications For Your Vehicle

Fill in this chart with the most commonly used specifications for your vehicle. Specifications can be found in Chapters 1 through 3 or on the tune-up decal under the hood of the vehicle.

 Tune-Up

Firing Order_____

Spark Plugs:

    Type_____

    Gap (in.)_____

Torque (ft. lbs.)_____

Idle Speed (rpm)_____

Ignition Timing (°)_____

    Vacuum or Electronic Advance (Connected/Disconnected)_____

Valve Clearance (in.)

    Intake_____   Exhaust_____

Capacities

Engine Oil Type (API Rating)_____

    With Filter Change (qts)_____

    Without Filter Change (qts)_____

Cooling System (qts)_____

Manual Transmission (pts)_____

    Type_____

Automatic Transmission (pts)_____

    Type_____

Front Differential (pts)_____

    Type_____

Rear Differential (pts)_____

    Type_____

Transfer Case (pts)_____

    Type_____

FREQUENTLY REPLACED PARTS

Use these spaces to record the part numbers of frequently replaced parts.

PCV VALVE	OIL FILTER	AIR FILTER	FUEL FILTER
Type_____	Type_____	Type_____	Type_____
Part No._____	Part No._____	Part No._____	Part No._____

General Information
and Maintenance

HOW TO USE THIS BOOK

Chilton's Repair & Tune-Up Guide for the Cutlass is intended to help you learn more about the inner workings of your vehicle and save you money on its upkeep and operation.

The first two chapters will be the most used, since they contain maintenance and tune-up information and procedures. Studies have shown that a properly tuned and maintained car can get at least 10% better gas mileage than an out-of-tune car. The other chapters deal with the more complex systems of your car. Operating systems from engine through brakes are covered to the extent that the average do-it-yourselfer becomes mechanically involved. This book will not explain such things as rebuilding the differential for the simple reason that the expertise required and the investment in special tools make this task uneconomical. It will give you detailed instructions to help you change your own brake pads and shoes, replace points and plugs, and do many more jobs that will save you money, give you personal satisfaction, and help you avoid expensive problems.

A secondary purpose of this book is a reference for owners who want to understand their car and/or their mechanics better. In this case, no tools at all are required.

Before removing any bolts, read through the entire procedure. This will give you the overall view of what tools and supplies will be required. There is nothing more frustrating than having to walk to the bus stop on Monday morning because you were short one bolt on Sunday afternoon. So read ahead and plan ahead. Each operation should be approached logically and all procedures thoroughly understood before attempting any work.

All chapters contain adjustments, maintenance, removal and installation procedures, and repair or overhaul procedures. When repair is not considered practical, we tell you how to remove the part and then how to install the new or rebuilt replacement. In this way, you at least save the labor costs. Backyard repair of such components as the alternator is just not practical.

Two basic mechanic's rules should be mentioned here. One, whenever the left side of the car or engine is referred to, it is meant to specify the driver's side of the car. Conversely, the right side of the car means the passenger's side. Secondly, most screws and bolts are removed by turning counterclockwise, and tightened by turning clockwise.

Safety is always the most important rule. Constantly be aware of the dangers involved in working on an automobile and take the proper precautions. (See the section in this chapter, Servicing Your Vehicle Safely and the SAFETY NOTICE on the acknowledgment page).

Pay attention to the instructions provided. There are 3 common mistakes in mechanical work:

1. Incorrect order of assembly, disassembly or adjustment. When taking something apart or putting it together, doing things in the wrong order usually justs costs you extra time; however, it CAN break something. Read the entire procedure before beginning disassembly. Do everything in the order in which the instructions say you should do it, even if you can't immediately see a reason for it. When you're taking apart something that is very intricate (for example, a carburetor), you might want to draw a picture of how it looks when assembled at one point in order to make sure you get everything back in its proper position. (We will supply exploded view whenever possible). When making adjustments, especially tune-up adjustments, do them in order; often, one adjustment affects another, and you cannot ex-

pect even satisfactory results unless each adjustment is made only when it cannot be changed by any other.

2. Overtorquing (or undertorquing). While it is more common for overtorquing to cause damage, undertorquing can cause a fastener to vibrate loose causing serious damage. Especially when dealing with aluminum parts, pay attention to torque specifications and utilize a torque wrench in assembly. If a torque figure is not available, remember that if you are using the right tool to do the job, you will probably not have to strain yourself to get a fastener tight enough. The pitch of most threads is so slight that the tension you put on the wrench will be multiplied many, many times in actual force on what you are tightening. A good example of how critical torque is, can be seen in the case of spark plug installation, especially where you are putting the plug into an aluminum cylinder head. Too little torque can fail to crush the gasket, causing leakage of combustion gases and consequent overheating of the plug and engine parts. Too much torque can damage the threads, or distort the plug, which changes the spark gap.

There are many commercial products available for ensuring that fasteners won't come loose, even if they are not torqued just right (a very common brand is Loctite®). If you're worried about getting something together tight enough to hold, but loose enough to avoid mechanical damage during assembly, one of these products might offer substantial insurance. Read the label on the package and make sure the product is compatible with the materials, fluids, etc. involved before choosing one.

3. Crossthreading. This occurs when a part such as a bolt is screwed unto a nut or casting at the wrong angle and forced. Cross threading is more likely to occur if access is difficult. It helps to clean and lubricate fasteners, and to start threading with the part to be installed going straight in. Then, start the bolt, spark plug, etc. with you fingers. If you encounter resistance, unscrew the part and start over again at a different angle until it can be inserted and turned several turns without much effort. Keep in mind that many parts, especially spark plugs, use tapered threads so that gentle turning will automatically bring the part you're threading to the proper angle if you don't force it or resist a change in angle. Don't put a wrench on the part until it's been turned a couple of turns by hand. If you suddenly encounter resistance, and the part has not seated fully, don't force it. Pull it back out and make sure it's clean and threading properly.

Always take you time and be patient; once you have some experience, working on your car will become an enjoyable hobby.

TOOLS AND EQUIPMENT

Naturally, without the proper tools and equipment it is impossible to properly service you vehicle. It would be impossible to catalog each tool that you would need to perform each or any operation in this book. It would also be unwise for the amateur to rush out and buy any expensive set of tools on the theory that he may need one or more of them at some time.

The best approach is to proceed slowly, gathering together a good quality set of those tools that are used most frequently. Don't be misled by the low cost of bargain tools. It is far better to spend a little more for better quality. Forged wrenches, 10 or 12 point sockets and fine tooth ratchets are by far preferable to their less expensive counterparts. As any good mechanic can tell you, there are few worse experiences than trying to work on a car or truck with bad tools. Your monetary savings will be far outweighed by frustration and mangled knuckles.

Begin accumulating those tools that are used most frequently; those associated with routine maintenance and tune-up.

In addition to the normal assortment of screwdrivers and pliers you should have the following tools for routine maintenance jobs:

1. SAE (or Metric) or SAE/Metric wrenches/sockets and combination open end/box end wrenches in sizes from ⅛″ (3mm) to ¾″ (19mm); and a spark plug socket (¹³⁄₁₆″ or ⅝″ depending on plug type).

If possible, buy various length socket drive extensions. One break in this department is that the metric sockets available in the U.S. will all fit the ratchet handles and extensions you may already have (¼″, ⅜″, and ½″ drive).

2. Jackstands for support.

3. Oil filter wrench.

4. Oil filler spout for pouring oil.

5. Grease gun for chassis lubrication.

6. Hydrometer for checking the battery.

7. A container for draining oil.

8. Many rags for wiping up the inevitable mess.

In addition to the above items there are several others that are not absolutely necessary but handy to have around. These include oil dry, a transmission funnel and the usual supply of lubricants, antifreeze and fluids, although these can be purchased as needed. This is a basic list for routine maintenance, but only your personal needs and desire can accurately determine you list of tools.

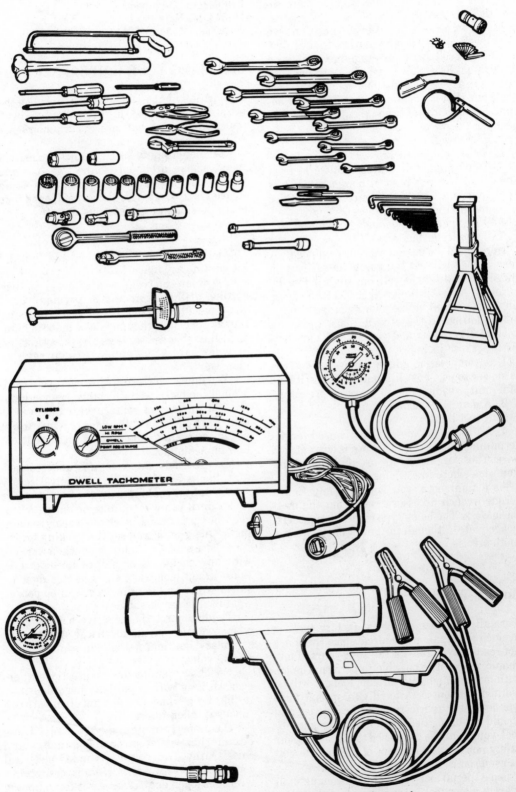

This basic collection of hand tools will handle most service needs

The second list of tools is for tune-ups. While the tools involved here are slightly more sophisticated, they need not be ourtageously expensive. There are several inexpensive tach/dwell meters on the market that are every bit as good for the average mechanic as a $100.00 professional model. Just be sure that it goes to at least 1,200-1,500 rpm on the tach scale and that it works on 4, 6 or 8 cylinder engines. A basic list of tune-up equipment could include:

1. Tach-dwell meter.
2. Spark plug wrench.
3. Timing light (a DC light that works from the car's battery is best, although a AC light that plugs into 110V house current will suffice at some sacrifice in brightness).
4. Wire spark plug gauge/adjusting tools.
5. Set of feeler blades

Here again, be guided by your own needs. A feeler blade will set the points as easily as a dwell meter will read well, but slightly less accurately. And since you will need a tachometer anyway . . . well, make your own decision.

In addition to these basic tools, there are several other tools and gauges you may find useful. These include:

1. A compression gauge. The screw-in type is slower to use, but eliminates the possibility of a faulty reading due to escaping pressure.
2. A manifold vacuum gauge.
3. A test light.
4. An induction meter. This is used for determining whether or not there is current in a wire. These are handy for use if a wire is broken somewhere in a wiring harness.

As a final note, you will probably find a torque wrench necessary for all but the most basic work. The beam type models are perfectly adequate, although the newer click type are more precise.

Special Tools

Normally, the use of special factory tools is avoided for repair procedures, since these are not readily available for the do-it-yourself mechanic. When it is possible to perform the job with more commonly available tools, it will be pointed out, but occasionally, a special tools was designed to perform a specific function and should be used. Before substituting another tool, you should be convinced that neither your safety nor the performance of the vehicle will be compromised.

Some special tools are available commercially from major tool manufacturers. Others can be purchased from your car dealer or from:

Service Tool Division
Kent-Moore Corporation
29784 Little Mack
Roseville, MI 48066-2290

SERVICING YOUR CAR SAFELY

It is virtually impossible to anticipate all of the hazards involved with automotive maintenance and service, but care and common sense will prevent most accidents.

The rules of safety for mechanics range from "don't smoke around gasoline," to "use the proper tool for the job." The trick to avoiding injuries is to develop safe work habits and take every possible precaution.

Dos

• Do keep a fire extinguisher and first aid kit within easy reach.

• Do wear safety glasses or goggles when cutting, drilling, grinding or prying, even if you have 20-20 vision. If you wear gasses for the sake of vision, they should be made of hardened glass that can serve also as safety glasses, or wear safety goggles over you regular glasses.

• Do shield you eyes whenever you work around the battery. Batteries contain sulphuric acid. In case of contact with the eyes or skin, flush the area with water or a mixture of water and baking soda and get medical attention immediately.

• Do use safety stands for any undercar service. Jacks are for raising vehicles; safety stands are for making sure the vehicle stays raised until you want it to come down. Whenever the car is raised, block the wheels remaining on the ground and set the parking brake.

• Do use adequate ventilation when working with any chemicals or hazardous materials. Like carbon monoxide, the asbestos dust resulting from brake lining wear can be poisonous in sufficient quantities.

• Do disconnect the negative battery cable when working on the electrical system. The secondary ignition system can contain up to 40,000 volts.

• Do follow manufacturer's directions whenever working with potentially hazardous materials. Both brake fluid and antifreeze are poisonous if taken internally.

• Do properly maintain your tools. Loose hammerheads, mushroomed punches and chisels, frayed or poorly grounded electrical cords, excessively worn screwdrivers, spread wrenches (open end), cracked sockets, slipping ratchets, or faulty droplight sockets can cause accidents.

• Likewise, keep you tools clean; a greasy wrench can slip off a bolt head, ruining the bolt and often ruining you knuckles in the process.

• Do use the proper size and type of tool for the job being done.

• Do when possible, pull on a wrench handle rather than push on it, and adjust your stance to prevent a fall.

• Do be sure that adjustable wrenches are tightly closed on the nut or bolt and pulled so that the face is on the side of the fixed jaw.

• So select a wrench or socket that fits the nut or bolt. The wrench or socket should sit straight, not cocked.

• Do strike squarely with a hammer; avoid glancing blows.

• Do set the parking brake and block the drive wheels if the work requires the engine running.

Always use support stands when working under your car

Don'ts

• Don't run the engine in a garage or anywhere else without proper ventilation-EVER! Carbon monoxide is poisonous; it takes a long time to leave the human body and you can build up a deadly supply of it in your system by simply breathing in a little every day. You may not realize you are slowly poisoning yourself. Always use power vents, windows, fans or open garage doors.

• Don't work around moving parts while wearing a necktie or other loose clothing. Short sleeves are much safer than long, loose sleeves; hard-toed shoes with neoprene soles protect your toes and give a better grip on slippery surfaces. Jewelry such as watches, fancy belt buckles, beads or body adornment of any kind is not safe working around a car. Long hair should be tied back under a hat or cap.

• Don't use pockets for toolboxes. A fall or bump can drive a screwdriver deep into you body. Even a wiping cloth hanging from the back pocket can wrap around a spinning shaft or fan.

• Don't smoke when working around gasoline, cleaning solvent or other flammable material.

• Don't smoke when working around the battery. When the battery is being charged, it gives off explosive hydrogen gas.

• Don't use gasoline to wash your hands; there are excellent soaps available. Gasoline may contain lead, and lead can enter the body through a cut, accumulating in the body until you are very ill. Gasoline also removes all the natural oils from the skin so that bone dry hands will suck up oil and grease.

• Don't service the air conditioning system unless you are equipped with the necessary tools and training. The refrigerant, R-12, is extremely cold when compressed, and when released into the air will instantly freeze any surface it contacts, including your eyes. Although the refrigerant is normally non-toxic, R-12 becomes a deadly poisonous gas in the presence of an open flame. One good whiff of the vapors from burning refrigerant can be fatal.

• Don't use screwdrivers for anything other than driving screws! A screwdriver used as a prying tool can snap when you least expect it, causing injuries. At the very least, you'll ruin a good screwdriver.

• Don't use a bumper jack (that little ratchet, scissors, or pantograph jack supplied with the car) for anything other than changing a flat! These jacks are only intended for emergency use out on the road; they are NOT designed as a maintenance tool. If you are serious about maintaining you car yourself, invest in a hydraulic floor jack of at least 1½ ton capacity, and at least two sturdy jackstands.

SERIAL NUMBER IDENTIFICATION

Vehicle Identification Number (VIN)

It is important for servicing and ordering parts to be certain of the vehicle and engine identification. The VIN (vehicle identification number) is a 13 digit number (through 1980) or 17 digit number (1981 and later) visible through the windshield on the driver's side of the dash

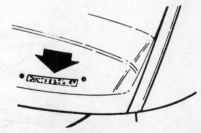

Vehicle identification number (VIN) located on the driver's side of the dash

Thirteen digit Vehicle Identification Number (VIN)

Seventeen digit Vehicle Identification Number (VIN)

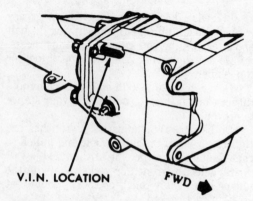

V.I.N. LOCATION   FWD ➤

Manual transmission serial number location

and contains the vehicle and engine identification codes.

Engine Serial Number Location

On all V8 engines and the V6 231 engine through 1979, the serial number is found on a pad at the front right or left hand side of the cylinder block, just below the cylinder head. On the 1980 and later V6 231, and the 1984 and later V6 diesel engine, the serial number is found on the left rear of the block.

Transmission Serial Number Location

A transmission serial number is stamped on a plate which is attached to either the right or left side of the transmission case on all automatic transmissions. On manual transmissions, the serial number is stamped on a pad on the top right side of the case.

Rear Axle

The code for the rear axle is stamped on the right side of the axle housing tube.

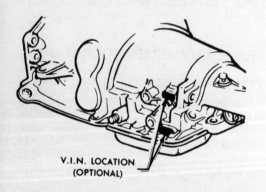

V.I.N. LOCATION
(OPTIONAL)

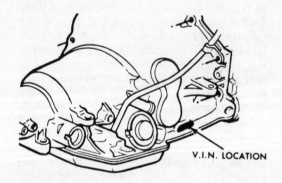

V.I.N. LOCATION

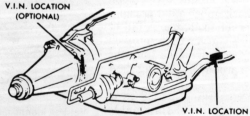

V.I.N. LOCATION
(OPTIONAL)

V.I.N. LOCATION

Various optional serial number locations on the Turbo Hydra-Matic transmissions

Thirteen digit Vehicle Identification Number (VIN)

(The 6th digit indicated the model year, and the 5th digit identifies the factory installed engine.)

Model Year Code		Engine Code					
Code	Year	Code	Displacement Cu. in.	Liters	Cyl.	Fuel Delivery	Eng. Mfg.
3	1973	D	250	4.1	6	1 bbl.	Chev
		H	350	5.7	8	2 bbl	Olds
		K	350	5.7	8	4 bbl.	Olds
		M	350	5.7	8	4 bbl. (DE)	Olds
		T	455	7.5	8	4 bbl.	Olds
		U	455	7.5	8	4 bbl.	Olds
		V	455	7.5	8	4 bbl.	Olds
4	1974	D	250	4.1	6	1 bbl.	Chev
		K	350	5.7	8	4 bbl.	Olds
		M	350	5.7	8	4 bbl. (DE)	Olds
		T	455	7.5	8	4 bbl.	Olds
		U	455	7.5	8	4 bbl.	Olds
5	1975	C	231	3.8	6	2 bbl.	Buick
		D	250	4.1	6	1 bbl.	Chev
		F	260	4.3	8	2 bbl.	Olds.
		K	350	5.7	8	4 bbl.	Olds
		T	455	7.5	8	4 bbl.	Olds
		U	455	7.5	8	4 bbl.	Olds
6	1976	C	231	3.8	6	2 bbl.	Buick
		D	250	4.1	6	1 bbl.	Chev
		F	260	4.3	8	2 bbl.	Olds
		H	350	5.7	8	2 bbl.	Olds
		R	350	5.7	8	4 bbl.	Olds
		T	455	7.5	8	4 bbl.	Olds
7	1977	C	231	3.8	6	2 bbl.	Buick
		F	260	4.3	8	2 bbl.	Olds
		U	305	5.0	8	2 bbl.	Chev
		L	350	5.7	8	4 bbl.	Chev
		R	350	5.7	8	4 bbl.	Olds
		K	403	6.6	8	4 bbl.	Olds
8	1978	A	231	3.8	6	2 bbl.	Buick
		F	260	4.3	8	2 bbl.	Olds
		U	305	5.0	8	2 bbl.	Chev
		H	305	5.0	8	4 bbl.	Chev
		L	350	5.7	8	4 bbl.	Chev
		R	350	5.7	8	4 bbl.	Olds
		N	350	5.7	8	Diesel	Olds
		K	403	6.6	8	4 bbl.	Olds
9	1979	A	231	3.8	6	2 bbl.	Buick
		2	231	3.8	6	2 bbl.	Buick
		F	260	4.3	8	2 bbl.	Olds
		P	260	4.3	8	Diesel	Olds
		G	305	5.0	8	2 bbl.	Chev
		H	305	5.0	8	4 bbl.	Chev
		L	350	5.7	8	4 bbl.	Chev
		R	350	5.7	8	4 bbl.	Olds
		N	350	5.7	8	Diesel	Olds
		K	403	6.6	8	4 bbl.	Olds
A	1980	A	231	3.8	6	2 bbl.	Buick
		2	231	3.8	6	2 bbl.	Buick
		F	260	4.3	8	2 bbl.	Buick
		P	260	4.3	8	Diesel	Olds
		G	305	5.0	8	2 bbl.	Chev
		H	305	5.0	8	4 bbl.	Chev
		L	350	5.7	8	4 bbl.	Chev
		R	350	5.7	8	4 bbl.	Olds
		N	350	5.7	8	Diesel	Olds

Seventeen digit Vehicle Identification Number (VIN)

(The 10th digit indicates the model year and the 8th digit identifies the factory installed engine)

Model Year Code		Engine Code					
Code	Year	Code	Displacement Cu. in.	Liters	Cyl.	Fuel Delivery	Eng. Mfg.
B	1981	A	231	3.8	6	2 bbl.	Buick
		F	260	4.3	8	2 bbl.	Olds
		H	305	5.0	8	4 bbl.	Chev
		Y	307	5.0	8	4 bbl.	Olds
		L	350	5.7	8	4 bbl.	Chev
		N	350	5.7	8	Diesel	Olds
C	1982	A	231	3.8	6	2 bbl.	Buick
		8	260	4.3	8	2 bbl.	Olds
		V	263	4.3	6	Diesel	Olds
		J	267	4.4	8	2 bbl.	Chev
		Y	307	5.0	8	4 bbl.	Olds
		N	350	5.7	8	Diesel	Olds
D	1983	A	231	3.8	6	2 bbl.	Buick
		V	263	4.3	6	Diesel	Olds
		Y	307	5.0	8	4 bbl.	Olds
		N	350	5.7	8	Diesel	Olds
E	1984	A	231	3.8	6	2 bbl.	Buick
		V	263	4.3	6	Diesel	Olds
		Y	307	5.0	8	4 bbl.	Olds
		N	350	5.7	8	Diesel	Olds
F	1985	A	231	3.8	6	2 bbl.	Buick
		V	263	4.3	6	Diesel	Olds
		Y	307	5.0	8	4 bbl.	Olds
		Q	307	5.0	8	4 bbl.	Olds
		N	350	5.7	8	Diesel	Olds
G	1986	A	231	3.8	6	2 bbl.	Buick
		Y	307	5.0	8	4 bbl.	Olds
		9	307	5.0	8	4 bbl.	Olds
H	1987	A	231	3.8	6	2 bbl.	Buick
		Y	307	5.0	8	4 bbl.	Olds
		9	307	5.0	8	4 bbl.	Olds

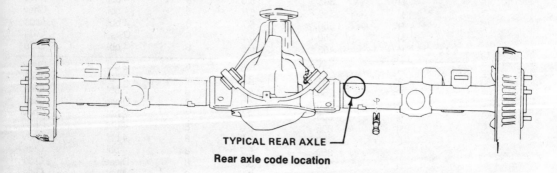

TYPICAL REAR AXLE

Rear axle code location

ROUTINE MAINTENANCE

Air Cleaner

The air cleaner has a dual purpose. It not only filters the air going to the carburetor, but also acts as a flame arrester if the engine should backfire through the carburetor. If an engine maintenance procedure requires the tempo- rary removal of the air cleaner, remove it; oth- erwise, never run the engine without it. Oper- ating a car without its air cleaner result in some throaty sounds from the carburetor giv- ing the impression of increased power but will only cause trouble. Unfiltered air to the carbu- retor will eventually result in a dirty, ineffi- cient carburetor and engine. A dirty carburetor increases the chances of carburetor backfire and, without the protection of an air cleaner, fire becomes a probable danger. The air cleaner assembly consists of the air cleaner itself, which is the large metal container that fits over the carburetor, the element contained within, and the flame arrester located in the base of the air cleaner. The air filter should be inspected at its first 12,00 miles, rechecked every 6,000 miles thereafter, and replace at 30,000 mile intervals. Inspections and replacements should be more frequent if the car is op-

Using a clean rag or paper towel, wipe out the inside of the air cleaner

Unscrew the wing nut and remove the cover

Remove and discard the old filter

Check the small crankcase breather

erated in a dirty, dusty environment. When inspecting the element, look for dust leaks, holes or an overly dirty appearance. If the element is excessively dirty, it may cause a reduction in clean air intake. If air has trouble getting through a dirty element, the carburetor fuel mixture will become richer (more gas, less air), the idle will be rougher, and the exhaust smoke will be noticeably black. To check the effectiveness of your paper element, remove the air cleaner assembly and, if the idle increases, then the element is restricting airflow and should be replaced. The flame arrester, located at the base of the carburetor, should be cleaned in solvent (kerosene) once every 12,000 miles.

Positive Crankcase Ventilation (PCV) Valve

LOCATION

6-Cyl. Inline & V6 Engines

The PCV valve is located in the right hand valve cover on 6 cylinder inline and V6 engines through 1980. On 1981 and later engines, it is located in the rear of the intake manifold.

V8 Engines

The PCV valve is located in one of the valve covers depending on the engine. Replace the PCV valve every 30,000 miles. The PCV filter, located in the air cleaner, is replaced when the air cleaner element is replaced.

For further details on PCV valve operation see Chapter 4.

Evaporative Emissions Control System

This system, standard since 1970, eliminates the release of unburned fuel vapors into the atmosphere. The only periodic maintenance required is an occasional check of the connecting lines of the system for kinks or other damage and deterioration. Lines should only be replaced with quality fuel line or special hose marked EVAP. Every 24 months/30,000 miles the filter in the bottom of the carbon canister which is located in the engine compartment should be removed and replaced.

For further details on the Evaporative Emission Control System please refer to Chapter 4.

Battery

SPECIFIC GRAVITY TEST

Except Maintenance Free Batteries

At least once a year, check the specific gravity of the battery. It should be between 1.20 and 1.26 at room temperature.

The specific gravity can be checked with the use of an hydrometer, an inexpensive instrument available from many sources, including

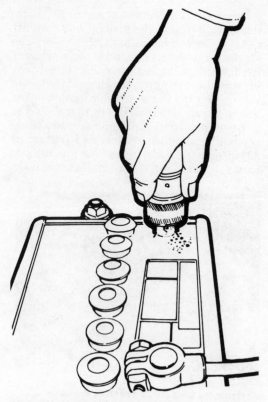

Clean the post with a wire brush, or a terminal cleaner made for the purpose (shown)

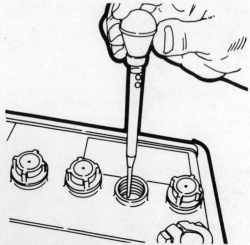

Specific gravity can be checked with an hydrometer

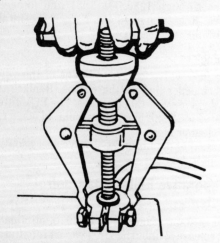

Pullers make clamp removal easier

Clean the inside of the clamps with a wire brush or the special tool shown

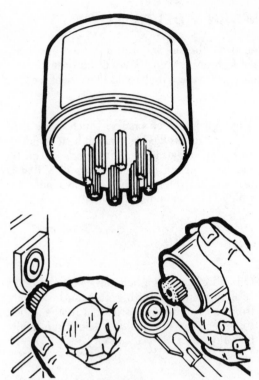

Special tools are also available for cleaning the posts and clamps on side terminal batteries

auto parts stores. The hydrometer has a squeeze bulb at one end and a nozzle at the other. Battery electrolyte is sucked into the hydrometer until the float is lifted from its seat. The specific gravity is then read by noting the position of the float. Generally, if after charging, the specific gravity between any two cells varies more than 50 points (0.050), the battery is bad and should be replaced.

It is not possible to check the specific gravity in this manner on sealed (maintenance free) batteries. Instead, the indicator built into the top of the case must be relied on to display any signs of battery deterioration. If the indicator is dark, the battery can be assumed to be OK. If the indicator is light, the specific gravity is low, and the battery should be charged or replaced.

CLEANING CABLES AND CLAMPS

Once a year, the battery terminals and the cable clamps should be cleaned. Loosen the clamps and remove the cables, negative cable first. On batteries with posts on top, the use of a puller specially made for the purpose is recommended. These are inexpensive, and available in auto parts stores. Side terminal battery cables are secured with a bolt.

Clean the cable clamps and the battery ter-minal with a wire brush, until all corrosion, grease, etc. is removed and the metal is shiny. It is especially important to clean the inside of the clamp thoroughly, since a small deposit of foreign material or oxidation will prevent a sound electrical connection and inhibit either starting or charging. Special tools are available for cleaning these parts, one type for conventional batteries and another type for side terminal batteries.

Before installing the cables, loosen the battery holddown clamp or strap, remove the battery and check the battery tray. Clear it of any debris, and check it for soundness. Rust should be wire brushed away, and the metal given a coat of anti-rust paint. Replace the battery and tighten the holddown clamp or strap securely, but be careful not to overtighten, which will crack the battery case.

After the clamps and terminals are clean, reinstall the cables, negative cable last; do not hammer on the clamps to install. Tighten the clamps securely, but do not distort them. Give the clamps and terminals a thin external coat of grease after installation, to retard corrosion.

Check the cables at the same time that the terminals are cleaned. If the cable insulation is cracked or broken, or if the ends are frayed, the cable should be replace with a new cable of the same length and gauge.

NOTE: *Keep flame or sparks away from the battery; it gives off explosive hydrogen gas. Battery electrolyte contains sulphuric acid. If you should splash any on your skin or in your eyes, flush the affected area with plenty of clear water; if it lands in your eyes, get medical help immediately.*

REPLACEMENT

When it becomes necessary to replace the battery, select a battery with a rating equal to or greater then the battery originally installed. Deterioration, embrittlement and just plain aging of the battery cables, starter motor, and associated wires makes the battery's job harder in successive years. The slow increase in electrical resistance over time makes it prudent to install a new battery with a greater capacity than the old. Details on battery removal and installation are covered in Chapter 3.

Belts
TENSION CHECKING AND ADJUSTMENT

Check the drive belts every 7,500 miles or six months for evidence of wear such as cracking, fraying, and incorrect tension. Determine belt tension at a point halfway between the pulleys by pressing on the belt with moderate thumb pressure. If the distance between the pulleys

HOW TO SPOT WORN V-BELTS

V-Belts are vital to efficient engine operation—they drive the fan, water pump and other accessories. They require little maintenance (occasional tightening) but they will not last forever. Slipping or failure of the V-belt will lead to overheating. If your V-belt looks like any of these, it should be replaced.

This belt has deep cracks, which cause it to flex. Too much flexing leads to heat build-up and premature failure. These cracks can be caused by using the belt on a pulley that is too small. Notched belts are available for small diameter pulleys.

Cracking or weathering

Oil and grease on a belt can cause the belt's rubber compounds to soften and separate from the reinforcing cords that hold the belt together. The belt will first slip, then finally fail altogether.

Softening (grease and oil)

Glazing is caused by a belt that is slipping. A slipping belt can cause a run-down battery, erratic power steering, overheating or poor accessory performance. The more the belt slips, the more glazing will be built up on the surface of the belt. The more the belt is glazed, the more it will slip. If the glazing is light, tighten the belt.

Glazing

The cover of this belt is worn off and is peeling away. The reinforcing cords will begin to wear and the belt will shortly break. When the belt cover wears in spots or has a rough jagged appearance, check the pulley grooves for roughness.

Worn cover

This belt is on the verge of breaking and leaving you stranded. The layers of the belt are separating and the reinforcing cords are exposed. It's just a matter of time before it breaks completely.

Separation

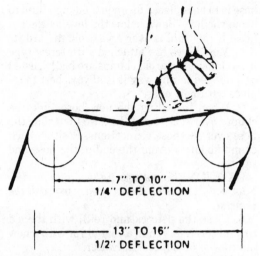

7" TO 10"
1/4" DEFLECTION

13" TO 16"
1/2" DEFLECTION

A gauge is recommended, but you can check belt tension with thumb pressure

Slip the new belt over the pulley

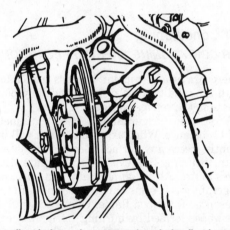

To adjust belt tension or to replace belts, first loosen the component's mounting and adjusting bolts slightly

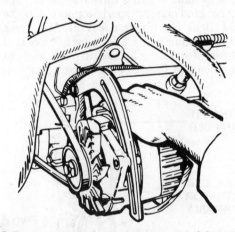

Pull outward on the component and tighten the mounting bolts

(measured from the center of each pulley) is $^{13}/_{16}$" (20.6mm), the belt should deflect ½" (13mm) at the halfway point or ¼" (6mm) if the distance is 7-10" (178-254mm). If the deflection is found to be too much or too little, loosen the mounting bolts and make the adjustments.

Before you attempt to adjust any of your engine's belts, you should take an old rag soaked in solvent and clean the mounting bolts of any road grime which has accumulated there. On some of the harder-to-reach bolts, an application of penetrating oil will make them easier to loosen. When you're adjusting belts, especially on late model V8's with air conditioning and power steering, it would be especially helpful to have a variety of socket extensions and universals to get to those hard-to-reach bolts.

NOTE: *When adjusting the air pump belt, if you are using a pry bar, make sure that you pry against the cast iron end cover and not against the aluminum housing. Excessive force on the housing itself will damage it.*

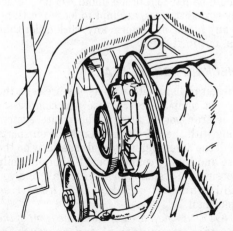

Push the component toward the engine and slip off the belt

Early Fuel Evaporation (EFE) Valve
CHECKING

This is a more effective form of heat riser which is vacuum actuated. It is used on all models built in 1975 and later. It heats incoming mixture during the engine warm-up process, utilizing a ribbed heat exchanger of thin metal that is located in the intake manifold. This preheating allows the choke to open more rapidly, thus reducing emissions. Problems in this system might be indicated by poor engine operation during warm-up.

This valve should be checked initially at 6 months/7,500 miles, and thereafter, at 18 months/22,500 mile intervals.

To check, move the valve through its full stroke by hand, making sure that the linkage does not bind and is properly connected. If the valve sticks, free it with a solvent. Also check that all vacuum hoses are properly connected and free of cracks or breaks. Replace hoses or broken or bent linkage parts as necessary.

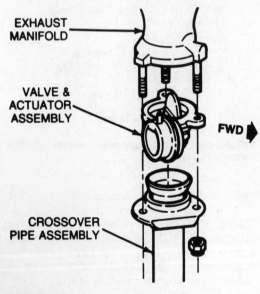

EXHAUST MANIFOLD

VALVE & ACTUATOR ASSEMBLY

FWD ➡

CROSSOVER PIPE ASSEMBLY

Typical EFE valve

Hoses
HOSE REPLACEMENT

1. Remove the radiator cap.
2. Drain the coolant from the radiator by opening the radiator petcock, if so equipped, or by disconnecting the lower radiator hose. If your car is equipped with a petcock it might be a good idea to squirt a little penetrating oil on it first.
3. To replace the bottom hose drain all the coolant from the radiator but if only the top hose is to be replaced drain just enough fluid to bring the level down below the level of the top hose. If the fluid is over a year old discard it.
4. Most hoses are attached with screw type hose clamps. If the old clamps are badly rusted or damaged in any way it is always best to replace with new ones.
5. When installing the new hose slide the clamps over each end of the hose then slide the hose over the hose connections. Position each clamp about ¼" from the end of the hose and tighten.
CAUTION: *Do not over tighten at the radiator connections as it is very easy to crush the metal.*
6. Close the petcock and refill with the old coolant if it is less than a year old or with a new mixture of 50/50, coolant/water.
7. Start the engine and idle it for 15 minutes with the radiator cap off and check for leaks. Add coolant if necessary and install the radiator cap.

Air Conditioning
AIR CONDITIONING SAFETY PRECAUTIONS

There are two particular hazards associated with air conditioning systems and they both relate to the refrigerant gas.

First, the refrigerant gas is an extremely cold substance. When exposed to air, it will instantly freeze any surface it comes in contact with, including your eyes. The other hazard relates to fire. Although normally non-toxic, refrigerant gas becomes highly poisonous in the presence of an open flame. One good whiff of the vapor formed by burning refrigerant can be fatal. Keep all forms of fire (including cigarettes) will clear of the air conditioning system.

Any repair work to an air conditioning system should be left to a professional. Do not, under any circumstances, attempt to loosen or tighten any fitting or perform any work other than that outlined here.

CHECKING FOR OIL LEAKS

Refrigerant leaks show up as oily areas on the various components because the compressor oil is transported around the entire system along with the refrigerant. Look for oil sports on all the hoses and lines, and especially on the hose and tubing connections. If there are oily deposits, the system may have a leak, and you should have it checked by a qualified repairman.

NOTE: *A small area of oil on the front of the compressor is normal and no cause for alarm.*

HOW TO SPOT BAD HOSES

Both the upper and lower radiator hoses are called upon to perform difficult jobs in an inhospitable environment. They are subject to nearly 18 psi at under hood temperatures often over 280°F., and must circulate nearly 7500 gallons of coolant an hour—3 good reasons to have good hoses.

Swollen hose

A good test for any hose is to feel it for soft or spongy spots. Frequently these will appear as swollen areas of the hose. The most likely cause is oil soaking. This hose could burst at any time, when hot or under pressure.

Cracked hose

Cracked hoses can usually be seen but feel the hoses to be sure they have not hardened; a prime cause of cracking. This hose has cracked down to the reinforcing cords and could split at any of the cracks.

Frayed hose end (due to weak clamp)

Weakened clamps frequently are the cause of hose and cooling system failure. The connection between the pipe and hose has deteriorated enough to allow coolant to escape when the engine is hot.

Debris in cooling system

Debris, rust and scale in the cooling system can cause the inside of a hose to weaken. This can usually be felt on the outside of the hose as soft or thinner areas.

CHECK THE COMPRESSOR BELT

Refer to the section in this chapter on Drive Belts.

KEEP THE CONDENSER CLEAR

Periodically inspect the front of the condenser for bent fins or foreign material (dirt, bugs, leaves, etc.) If any cooling fins are bent, straighten them carefully with needlenosed pliers. You can remove any debris with a stiff bristle brush or hose.

OPERATE THE A/C SYSTEM PERIODICALLY

A lot of A/C problems can be avoided by simply running the air conditioner at least once a week, regardless of the season. Simply let the system run for at least 5 minutes a week (even in the winter), and you'll keep the internal parts lubricated as well as preventing the hoses from hardening.

REFRIGERANT LEVEL CHECK

There are two ways to check refrigerant level, depending on how your model is equipped.

With Sight Glass

The first order of business when checking the sight glass is to find the sight glass. It will either be in the head of the receiver/drier, or in one of the metal lines leading from the top of the receiver/drier. Once you've found it, wipe it clean and proceed as follows:

1. With the engine and the air conditioning system running, look for the flow of refrigerant through the sight glass. If the air conditioner is working properly, you'll be able to see a continuous flow of clear refrigerant through the sight glass, with perhaps an occasional bubble at very high temperatures.

2. Cycle the air conditioner on and off to make sure what you are seeing is clear refrigerant. Since the refrigerant is clear, it is possible to mistake a completely discharged system for one that if fully charged. Turn the system off and watch the sight glass. If there is refrigerant in the system, you'll see bubbles during the off cycle. If you observe no bubbles when the system is running, and the air flow from the unit in the car is delivering cold air, everything is OK.

3. If you observe bubbles in the sight glass while the system is operating, the system is low on refrigerant. Have it checked by an professional.

4. Oil streaks in the sight glass are an indication of trouble. Most of the time, if you see oil in the sight glass, it will appear as a series of streaks, although occasionally it may be a sol-

id stream of oil. In either case, it means that part of the charge has been lost.

Without Sight Glass

On vehicles that are not equipped with sight glasses, it is necessary to feel the temperature difference in the inlet and outlet lines at the receiver/drier to gauge the refrigerant level. Use the following procedure:

1. Locate the receiver/drier. It will generally be up front near the condenser. It is shaped like a small fire extinguisher and will always have two lines connected to it. One line goes to the expansion valve and the other goes to the condenser.

2. With the engine and the air conditioner running, hold a line in each hand and gauge their relative temperatures. If they are both the same approximate temperature, the system is correctly charged.

3. If the line from the expansion valve to the receiver/drier is a lot colder than the line from the receiver/drier to the condenser, then the system is overcharged. It should be noted that this is an extremely rare condition.

4. If the line that leads from the

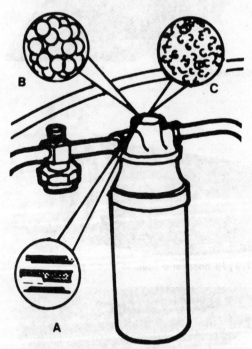

Oil streaks (A), constant bubbles (B) or faom (C) indicate there is not enough refrigerant in the system. Occasional bubbles during initial operation is normal. A clear sight glass indicates a proper charge of refrigerant or no refrigerant at all, which can be determined by the presence of cold air at the outlets in the car. If the glass is clouded with a milky white substance, have the receiver/drier checked professionally

Troubleshooting Basic Air Conditioning Problems

Problem	Cause	Solution
There's little or no air coming from the vents (and you're sure it's on)	• The A/C fuse is blown • Broken or loose wires or connections • The on/off switch is defective	• Check and/or replace fuse • Check and/or repair connections • Replace switch
The air coming from the vents is not cool enough	• Windows and air vent wings open • The compressor belt is slipping • Heater is on • Condenser is clogged with debris • Refrigerant has escaped through a leak in the system • Receiver/drier is plugged	• Close windows and vent wings • Tighten or replace compressor belt • Shut heater off • Clean the condenser • Check system • Service system
The air has an odor	• Vacuum system is disrupted • Odor producing substances on the evaporator case • Condensation has collected in the bottom of the evaporator housing	• Have the system checked/repaired • Clean the evaporator case • Clean the evaporator housing drains
System is noisy or vibrating	• Compressor belt or mountings loose • Air in the system	• Tighten or replace belt; tighten mounting bolts • Have the system serviced

Sight glass condition
  Constant bubbles, foam or oil streaks
  Clear sight glass, but no cold air
  Clear sight glass, but air is cold
  Clouded with milky fluid
	• Undercharged system
	• No refrigerant at all
	• System is OK
	• Receiver drier is leaking dessicant
		• Charge the system
		• Check and charge the system
		• Have system checked

Large difference in temperature of lines	• System undercharged	• Charge and leak test the system
Compressor noise	• Broken valves • Overcharged • Incorrect oil level • Piston slap • Broken rings • Drive belt pulley bolts are loose	• Replace the valve plate • Discharge, evacuate and install the correct charge • Isolate the compressor and check the oil level. Correct as necessary. • Replace the compressor • Replace the compressor • Tighten with the correct torque specification
Excessive vibration	• Incorrect belt tension • Clutch loose • Overcharged • Pulley is misaligned	• Adjust the belt tension • Tighten the clutch • Discharge, evacuate and install the correct charge • Align the pulley
Condensation dripping in the passenger compartment	• Drain hose plugged or improperly positioned • Insulation removed or improperly installed	• Clean the drain hose and check for proper installation • Replace the insulation on the expansion valve and hoses
Frozen evaporator coil	• Faulty thermostat • Thermostat capillary tube improperly installed • Thermostat not adjusted properly	• Replace the thermostat • Install the capillary tube correctly • Adjust the thermostat
Low side low—high side low	• System refrigerant is low • Expansion valve is restricted	• Evacuate, leak test and charge the system • Replace the expansion valve
Low side high—high side low	• Internal leak in the compressor—worn	• Remove the compressor cylinder head and inspect the compressor. Replace the valve plate assembly if necessary. If the compressor pistons, rings or

Troubleshooting Basic Air Conditioning Problems (cont.)

Problem	Cause	Solution
Low side high—high side low (cont.)		cylinders are excessively worn or scored replace the compressor
	• Cylinder head gasket is leaking	• Install a replacement cylinder head gasket
	• Expansion valve is defective	• Replace the expansion valve
	• Drive belt slipping	• Adjust the belt tension
Low side high—high side high	• Condenser fins obstructed	• Clean the condenser fins
	• Air in the system	• Evacuate, leak test and charge the system
	• Expansion valve is defective	• Replace the expansion valve
	• Loose or worn fan belts	• Adjust or replace the belts as necessary
Low side low—high side high	• Expansion valve is defective	• Replace the expansion valve
	• Restriction in the refrigerant hose	• Check the hose for kinks—replace if necessary
	• Restriction in the receiver/drier	• Replace the receiver/drier
	• Restriction in the condenser	• Replace the condenser
Low side and high side normal (inadequate cooling)	• Air in the system	• Evacuate, leak test and charge the system
	• Moisture in the system	• Evacuate, leak test and charge the system

receiver/drier to the condenser is a lot colder than the other line, the system is under charged.

5. If the system is undercharged or overcharged, have it checked by a professional air conditioning mechanic.

NOTE: *This book contains checking and charging procedures for your Cutlass air conditioning system. More comprehensive testing, diagnosis and service procedures may be found in CHILTON'S GUIDE TO AIR CONDITIONING SERVICE AND REPAIR, book part number 7580, available at your local retailer.*

Windshield Wipers

Intense heat from the sun, snow and ice, road oils, and the chemicals used in windshield washer solvents combine to deteriorate the rubber wiper refills. The refills should be replaced about twice a year or whenever the blades begin to streak or chatter.

WIPER REFILL REPLACEMENT

Normally, if the wipers are not cleaning the windshield properly, only the refill has to be replaced. The blade and arm usually require replacement only in the event of damage. It is not necessary (except on new Tridon® refills) to remove the arm or the blade to replace the refill (rubber part), though you may have to position the arm higher on the glass. You can do this by turning the ignition switch on and op-erating the wipers. When they are positioned where they are accessible, turn the ignition switch off.

There are several types of refills and your vehicle could have any kind, since aftermarket blades and arms may not use exactly the same type refill as the original equipment.

Most Anco® styles use a release button that is pushed down to allow the refill to slide out of the yoke jaws. The new refill slides in and locks in place.

The Trico® style is unlocked at one end by squeezing 2 metal tabs, and the refill is slid out of the frame jaws. When the new refill is installed, the tabs will click into place, locking the refill. Some Trico® refills are removed by locating where the metal backing strip or the refill is wider. Insert a small screwdriver blade between the frame and metal backing strip. Press down to release the refill from the retaining tab.

The polycarbonate type is held in place by a locking lever that is pushed downward out of the groove in the arm to free the refill. When the new refill is installed, it will lock in place automatically.

The Tridon® refill has a plastic backing strip with a notch about an inch from the end. Hold the blade (frame) on a hard surface so that the frame is tightly bowed. Grip the tip of the backing strip and pull up while twisting counterclockwise. The backing strip will snap out of the retaining tab. Do this for the remaining tabs until the refill is free of the arm. The length of these refills is molded into the end

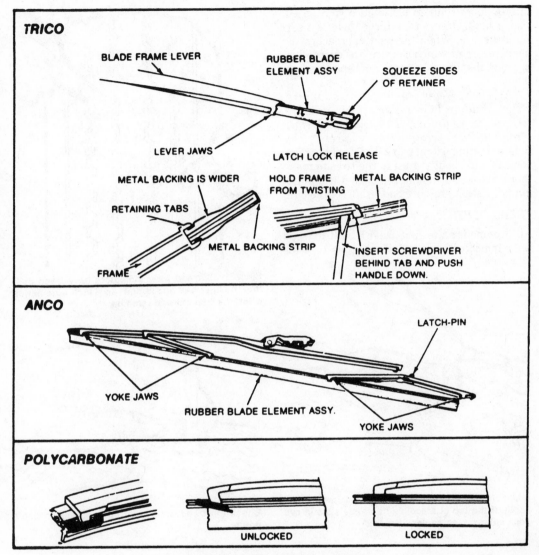

The three types of wiper blade retention

and they should be replace with identical types.

No matter which type of refill you use, be sure that all of the frame claws engage the refill. Before operating the wipers, be sure that no part of the metal frame is contacting the windshield.

Tires

INFLATION PRESSURE

Tire inflation is the most ignored item of auto maintenance. Gasoline mileage can drop as much as 0.8% for every 1 pound per square inch (psi) of under inflation.

Two items should be permanent fixture in every glove compartment; a tire pressure gauge and a tread depth gauge. Check the tire air pressure (including the spare) regularly with a pocket type gauge. Kicking the tires won't tell you a thing, and the gauge on the service station air hose is notoriously inaccurate.

The tire pressures recommended for you car are usually found on a Tire Placard, located on the driver's door or the glove compartment door. Ideally, inflation pressure should be checked when the tires are cool. When the air becomes heated it expands and the pressure increases. Every 10° rise (or drop) in temperature means a difference of 1 psi, which also explains why the tire appears to lose air on a very cold night. When it is impossible to check the tires cold, allow for pressure build-up due to heat. If the hot pressure exceeds the cold pressure by more than 15 psi, reduce your speed, load or both. Otherwise internal heat is created in the tire. When the heat approaches the temperature at which the tire was cured, during manufacture, the tread can separate from the body.

CAUTION: *Never counteract excessive pressure build-up by bleeding off air pressure (letting some air out). This will only further raise the tire operating temperature.*

Before starting a long trip with lots of luggage, you can add about 2-4 psi to the tires to make them run cooler, but never exceed the maximum inflation pressure on the side of the tire.

TREAD DEPTH

All tires made since 1968, have 8 built-in tread wear indicator bars that show up as ½″ wide

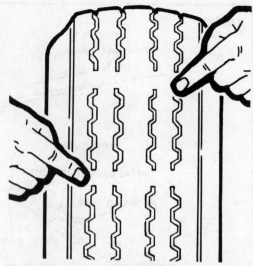

Since 1968, tread wear indicators have been built into the tire tread and appear as ½ inch wide bands when ¹/₁₆ inch of tread remains

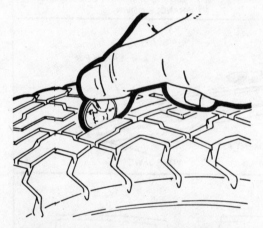

A Lincoln penny can be used to approximate tread depth. If the top of Lincoln's head is visible in two adjacent grooves, replace the tire

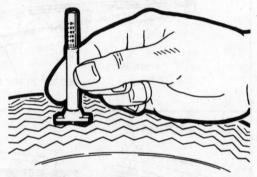

Check the tread depth with an inexpensive depth gauge

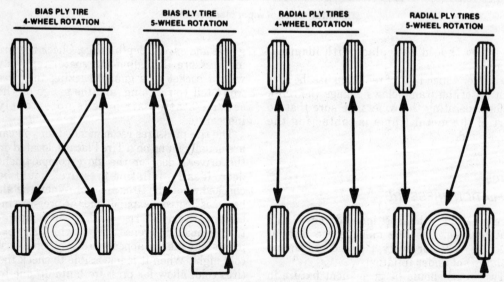

Tire rotation patterns

smooth bands across the tire when $^1\!/_{16}"$ (1.6mm) of tread remains. The appearance of tread wear indicators means that the tires should be replaced. In fact, many states have laws prohibiting the use of tires with less than $^1\!/_{16}"$ (1.6mm) tread.

You can check you won tread depth with an inexpensive gauge or by using a Lincoln head penny. Slip the Lincoln penny into several tread grooves. If you can see the top of Lincoln's head in 2 adjacent grooves, the tires have less than $^1\!/_{16}"$ (1.6mm) tread left and should be replaced. You can measure snow tires in the same manner by using the tails side of the Lincoln penny. If you can see the top of the Lincoln memorial, its's time to replace the snow tires.

TIRE ROTATION

Tire wear can be equalized by switching the position of the tires about every 6000 miles. Including a conventional spare in the rotation pattern can give up to 20% more tire life.

Troubleshooting Basic Wheel Problems

Problem	Cause	Solution
The car's front end vibrates at high speed	• The wheels are out of balance • Wheels are out of alignment	• Have wheels balanced • Have wheel alignment checked/adjusted
Car pulls to either side	• Wheels are out of alignment • Unequal tire pressure • Different size tires or wheels	• Have wheel alignment checked/adjusted • Check/adjust tire pressure • Change tires or wheels to same size
The car's wheel(s) wobbles	• Loose wheel lug nuts • Wheels out of balance • Damaged wheel • Wheels are out of alignment • Worn or damaged ball joint • Excessive play in the steering linkage (usually due to worn parts) • Defective shock absorber	• Tighten wheel lug nuts • Have tires balanced • Raise car and spin the wheel. If the wheel is bent, it should be replaced • Have wheel alignment checked/adjusted • Check ball joints • Check steering linkage • Check shock absorbers
Tires wear unevenly or prematurely	• Incorrect wheel size • Wheels are out of balance • Wheels are out of alignment	• Check if wheel and tire size are compatible • Have wheels balanced • Have wheel alignment checked/adjusted

Troubleshooting Basic Tire Problems

Problem	Cause	Solution
The car's front end vibrates at high speeds and the steering wheel shakes	• Wheels out of balance • Front end needs aligning	• Have wheels balanced • Have front end alignment checked
The car pulls to one side while cruising	• Unequal tire pressure (car will usually pull to the low side) • Mismatched tires • Front end needs aligning	• Check/adjust tire pressure • Be sure tires are of the same type and size • Have front end alignment checked
Abnormal, excessive or uneven tire wear See "How to Read Tire Wear"	• Infrequent tire rotation • Improper tire pressure • Sudden stops/starts or high speed on curves	• Rotate tires more frequently to equalize wear • Check/adjust pressure • Correct driving habits
Tire squeals	• Improper tire pressure • Front end needs aligning	• Check/adjust tire pressure • Have front end alignment checked

CAUTION: *Do not include the new SpaceSaver® or temporary spare tires in the rotation pattern.*

There are certain exceptions to tire rotation, however. Studded snow tires should not be rotated, and radials should be kept on the same sire of the car (maintain the same direction of rotation). The belts on radial tires get set in a pattern. If the direction of rotation is reversed, it can cause rough ride and vibration.

NOTE: *When radials or studded snows are taken off the car, mark them, so you can maintain the same direction of rotation.*

TIRE STORAGE

Store the tires at proper inflation pressures if they are mounted on wheels. All tires should be kept in a cool, dry place. If they are stored in the garage or basement, do not let them stand on a concrete floor; set them on strips of wood.

Fuel Filter

REPLACEMENT

Gasoline Engine

The fuel filter is located behind the fuel inlet connection on the carburetor. 1976 and later fuel filter incorporate a check valve and are not interchangeable with earlier years. Replace the fuel filter every 15, 000 miles, or sooner if engine flooding is a problem.

1. Using an open-end wrench (preferably a line or flare nut wrench), disconnect the fuel line connection from the larger fuel filter nut. You will have to hod the other nut with a

Tire Size Comparison Chart

"Letter" sizes			Inch Sizes	Metric-inch Sizes		
"60 Series"	"70 Series"	"78 Series"	1965–77	"60 Series"	"70 Series"	"80 Series"
		Y78-12	5.50-12, 5.60-12	165/60-12	165/70-12	155-12
			6.00-12			
		W78-13	5.20-13	165/60-13	145/70-13	135-13
		Y78-13	5.60-13	175/60-13	155/70-13	145-13
			6.15-13	185/60-13	165/70-13	155-13, P155/80-13
A60-13	A70-13	A78-13	6.40-13	195/60-13	175/70-13	165-13
B60-13	B70-13	B78-13	6.70-13	205/60-13	185/70-13	175-13
			6.90-13			
C60-13	C70-13	C78-13	7.00-13	215/60-13	195/70-13	185-13
D60-13	D70-13	D78-13	7.25-13			
E60-13	E70-13	E78-13	7.75-13			195-13
			5.20-14	165/60-14	145/70-14	135-14
			5.60-14	175/60-14	155/70-14	145-14
			5.90-14			
A60-14	A70-14	A78-14	6.15-14	185/60-14	165/70-14	155-14
	B70-14	B78-14	6.45-14	195/60-14	175/70-14	165-14
	C70-14	C78-14	6.95-14	205/60-14	185/70-14	175-14
D60-14	D70-14	D78-14				
E60-14	E70-14	E78-14	7.35-14	215/60-14	195/70-14	185-14
F60-14	F70-14	F78-14, F83-14	7.75-14	225/60-14	200/70-14	195-14
G60-14	G70-14	G77-14, G78-14	8.25-14	235/60-14	205/70-14	205-14
H60-14	H70-14	H78-14	8.55-14	245/60-14	215/70-14	215-14
J60-14	J70-14	J78-14	8.85-14	255/60-14	225/70-14	225-14
L60-14	L70-14		9.15-14	265/60-14	235/70-14	
	A70-15	A78-15	5.60-15	185/60-15	165/70-15	155-15
B60-15	B70-15	B78-15	6.35-15	195/60-15	175/70-15	165-15
C60-15	C70-15	C78-15	6.85-15	205/60-15	185/70-15	175-15
	D70-15	D78-15				
E60-15	E70-15	E78-15	7.35-15	215/60-15	195/70-15	185-15
F60-15	F70-15	F78-15	7.75-15	225/60-15	205/70-15	195-15
G60-15	G70-15	G78-15	8.15-15/8.25-15	235/60-15	215/70-15	205-15
H60-15	H70-15	H78-15	8.45-15/8.55-15	245/60-15	225/70-15	215-15
J60-15	J70-15	J78-15	8.85-15/8.90-15	255/60-15	235/70-15	225-15
	K70-15		9.00-15	265/60-15	245/70-15	230-15
L60-15	L70-15	L78-15, L84-15	9.15-15			235-15
	M70-15	M78-15				255-15
		N78-15				

Note: Every size tire is not listed and many size comparisons are approximate, based on load ratings. Wider tires than those supplied new with the vehicle, should always be checked for clearance.

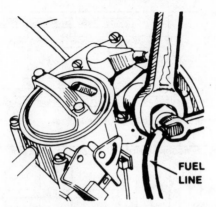

The fuel filter is located behind the large fuel line inlet nut on the carburetor

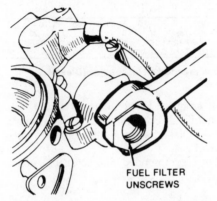

Remove the retaining nut and the filter will pop out under spring pressure

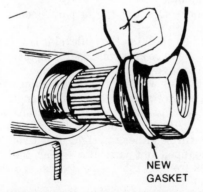

Install the new filter and spring. Certain early models use a bronze filter element, but most are made of paper

wrench to keep it from turning. Most of the time these units are quite difficult to remove. It is a good idea to apply a lot of penetrating oil to the threads and then tap the nut lightly with a hammer.

2. Once you have the fuel line disconnected from the carburetor, remove the larger nut

from the carburetor with a box-end wrench or socket.

3. Remove the filter element and spring from the carburetor.

4. Check the element for dirt blockage by blowing through the fuel inlet end. If the element is good, air should pass through easily.

5. Once you have checked and/or replaced the filter, reinstall the carburetor nut and the fuel line. Be careful not to strip the threads on the fuel line

Diesel Engines

On diesel engines the fuel filter is located at the back of the engine above the intake manifold between the mechanical fuel pump and the injection pump. The filter should be replaced at least every 30,000 miles. Disconnect the fuel lines from the filter, replace with a new filter and reconnect the fuel lines.

FLUIDS AND LUBRICANTS

Fuel Recommendations

Most gasoline engines from 1975 are designed to use only unleaded gasoline. Unleaded gasoline must be used for proper emission control system operation. Its use will also minimize spark plug fouling and extend engine oil life. Using leaded gasoline can damage the emission control system and could result in loss of emission warranty coverage.

The use of a fuel too low in octane (a measurement of anti-knock quality) will result in spark knock. Since many factors such as altitude, terrain, air temperature and humidity affect operating efficiency, knocking may result even though the recommended fuel is being used. If persistent knocking occurs, it may be necessary to switch to a higher grade of fuel. Continuous or heavy knocking may result in engine damage.

NOTE: *Your engine's fuel requirement can change with time, mainly due to carbon buildup, which will in turn change the compression ratio. If you engine pings, knocks, or runs on, switch to a higher grade of fuel. Sometimes just changing brands will cure the problem. If it becomes necessary to retard the timing from the specifications, don't change it more than a few degrees. Retarded timing will reduce power output and fuel mileage, in addition to increasing the engine temperature.*

All diesel engines in temperatures above 20°F (-7°C), are to use Number 2 diesel fuel. In temperatures below 20°F (-7°C) Number 1 diesel fuel is recommended. In some areas of the country, a combination of Number 1 and Number 2 diesel fuel is available and is recommended for winter use.

The reason that Number 2 diesel fuel is not recommended for cold weather operation is, at temperatures below 5°F (-15°C), paraffin wax flakes form that thicken the fuel and block the fuel filter.

OPERATION IN FOREIGN COUNTRIES

If you plan to drive your car outside the United States or Canada, there is a possibility that fuels will be too low in anti-knock quality and could produce engine damage. Send to Oldsmobile's Owner Relations Department the Vehicle Identification Number, compression ratio of your engine and the countries in which you plan to operate and they will send you details of adjustments or modifications that can be made to you engine. It is also wise to consult with local authorities upon arrival in a foreign country to determine the best fuels available.

Engine

OIL RECOMMENDATION

The SAE (Society of Automotive Engineers) grade number indicates the viscosity of the engine oil and thus its ability to lubricate at a given temperature. The lower the SAE grade number, the lighter the oil; the lower the viscosity, the easier it is to crank the engine in cold weather.

Oil viscosities should be chosen from those oils recommended for the lowest anticipated temperatures during the oil change in interval.

Multi-viscosity oils (10W-30, 20W-50 etc.) offer the important advantage of being adaptable to temperature extremes. They allow easy starting at low temperatures, yet they give good protection at high speeds and engine temperatures. This is a decided advantage in changeable climates or in long distance touring.

The API (American Petroleum Institute) designation indicates the classification of engine oil used under certain given operating conditions.

Use only oils with the API service designation SF, SF/CC or SF/CD for gasoline engines and for diesel engines use only SF/CC and SF/CD. Oils of this type perform a variety of functions inside the engine in addition to their basic function as a lubricant. Through a balanced system of metallic detergents and polymeric dispersants, the oil prevents the formation of high and low temperature deposits and also keeps sludge and particles of dirt in suspension. Acids, particularly sulfuric acid, as

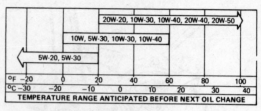

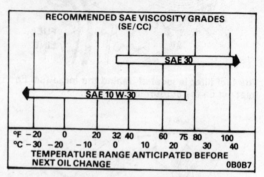

Recommended oil viscosities (Gas)

Recommended oil viscosities (Diesel)

well as other by-products of combustion, are neutralized. Both the SAE grade number and the API designation can be found on top of the oil can.

For recommended oil viscosities, refer to the charts.

OIL LEVEL CHECK

Every time you stop for fuel, check the engine oil as follows:

1. Make sure the car is parked on level ground.

2. When checking the oil level it is best for the engine to be at normal operating temperature, although checking the oil immediately after stopping will lead to a false reading. Wait a few minutes after turning off the engine to allow the oil to drain back into the crankcase.

3. Open the hood and locate the dipstick which will be either the right or left side depending upon you particular engine. Pull the dipstick from its tube, wipe it clean and then reinsert it.

4. Pull the dipstick out again and, holding it horizontally, read the oil level. The oil should be between the FULL and ADD marks on the dipstick. If the oil is below the ADD mark, add oil of the proper viscosity through the capped opening in the top of the cylinder head cover. See the Oil and Fuel Recommendations chart in this chapter for the proper viscosity and rating of oil to use.

5. Replace the dipstick and check the oil level again after adding any oil. Be careful not to overfill the crankcase. Approximately one

quart of oil will raise the level from the ADD mark to the FULL mark. Excess oil will generally be consumed at an accelerated rate.

CHANGING OIL AND FILTER

Change your oil according to the Maintenance Interval Chart shown in this chapter.

The mileage figures given are recommended intervals assuming normal driving and conditions. If your car is used under dusty, polluted or off-road conditions, change the oil filter more often than specified. The same goes for cars driven in Stop-and-go traffic or only for short distances at a time. Always drain the engine oil after the engine has been running long enough to bring it up to normal operating temperature. Hot oil will flow easier and more contaminants will be removed along with the oil than if it were drained cold. To change the oil and filter:

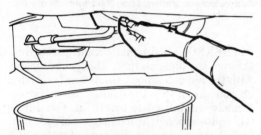

By keeping inward pressure on the plug as you unscrew it, oil won't escape past the threads

1. Run the engine until it reaches normal operating temperature.

2. Jack up the front of the car and support it on safety stands.

3. Slide a drain pan of at least 6 quarts capacity under the oil pan.

4. Loosen the drain plug. Turn the plug out by hand. By keeping an inward pressure on the plug as you unscrew it, oil won't escape past the threads and you can remove it without being burned by hot oil.

5. Allow the oil to drain completely and then install the drain plug. Don't overtighten the plug, or you'll be buying a new pan or a trick replacement plug for stripped threads.

6. Using a strap wrench, remove the oil filter. Keep in mind that it's holding about one quart of dirty, hot oil.

7. Empty the old filter into the drain pan and dispose of the filter.

8. Using a clean rag, wipe off the filter adapter on the engine block. Be sure that the rag doesn't leave any lint which could clog an oil passage.

9. Coat the rubber gasket on the filter with fresh oil. Spin it onto the engine by hand; when the gasket touches the adapter surface, give it another ½-¾ turn. No more, or you'll squash the gasket and it will leak.

10. Refill the engine with the correct amount of fresh oil. See the Capacities chart.

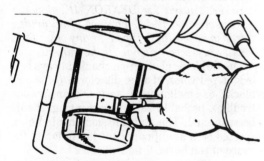

Remove the oil filter with a strap wrench

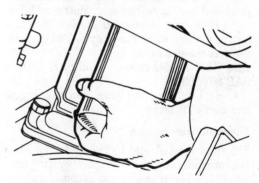

Install the new oil filter by hand

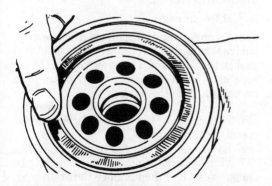

Coat the new oil filter gasket with clean oil

Add oil through the capped opening in the cylinder head cover

11. Check the oil level on the dipstick. It is normal for the level to be a bit above the full mark. Start the engine and allow it to idle for a few minutes.

CAUTION: *Do not run the engine above idle speed until it has built up oil pressure, indicated when the oil light goes out.*

12. Shut off the engine, allow the oil to drain for a minute, and check the oil level. Check around the filter and drain plug for any leaks, and correct as necessary.

Transmission

FLUID RECOMMENDATIONS

In all manual transmissions use only standard GL-5 hypoid gear oil-SAE 80W or SAE 80W/90. All automatic transmissions use only DEXRON®II automatic transmission fluid.

LEVEL CHECK

Manual Transmission

1. With the car parked on a level surface, remove the filler plug from the side of the transmission housing.

2. If the lubricant begins to trickle out of the hole, there is enough and you need not go any further. Otherwise, carefully insert your finger (watch out for sharp threads) and check to see if the oil is up to the edge of the hole.

3. If not, add oil through the hole until the level is at the edge of the hole. Most gear lubricants come in a plastic squeeze bottle with a nozzle; making additions simple. You can also use a common kitchen baster. Use only standard GL-5 hypoid-type gear oil-SAE 80W or SAE 80W/90.

4. Replace the filler plug, run the engine and check for leaks.

Automatic Transmission

The fluid level should be checked only when the transmission is hot (normal operating temperature). The transmission is considered hot after about 20 miles of highway driving.

1. Park the car on a level surface with the engine idling. Shift the transmission into Neutral and set the parking brake.

2. Remove the dipstick, wipe it clean and then reinsert it firmly. Be sure that it has been pushed all the way in. Remove the dipstick again and check the fluid level while holding it horizontally. With the engine running, the fluid level should be between the second notch and the FULL HOT line. If the fluid must be checked when it is cool, the level should be between the first and second notches.

3. If the fluid level is below the second notch (engine hot) or the first notch (engine cold),

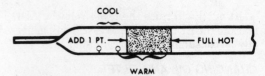

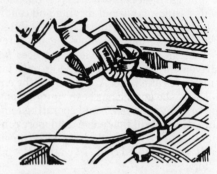

Automatic transmission dipstick marks; the proper level is within the shaded area

Add automatic transmission fluid through the dipstick tube

add DEXRON®II automatic transmission fluid through the dipstick tube. This is easily done with the aid of a funnel. Check the level often as you are filling the transmission. Be extremely careful not to overfill it. Overfilling will cause slippage, seal damage and overheating. Approximately one pint of automatic transmission fluid will raise the fluid level from one notch/line to the other.

NOTE: *Always use DEXRON®II automatic transmission fluid. The use of automatic transmission fluid Type F or any other fluid will cause severe damage to the transmission.*

The fluid on the dipstick should always be a bright red color. If it is discolored (brown or black), or smells burnt, serious transmission troubles, probably due to overheating, should be suspected. The transmission should be inspected by a qualified technician to locate the cause of the burnt fluid.

DRAIN AND REFILL

Manual Transmission

There is no recommended interval for the manual transmission but it is always a good idea to change the fluid if you have purchased the car used or if it has been driven in water high enough to reach the axles.

1. The oil must be hot before it is drained. Drive the car until the engine reaches normal operating temperature.

2. Remove the filler plug to provide a vent.

3. Place a large container underneath the transmission and then remove the drain plug.

4. Allow the oil to drain completely. Clean

off the drain plug and replace it; tighten it until it is just snug.

5. Fill the transmission with the proper lubricant as detailed earlier in this chapter. Refer to the Capacities chart for the correct amount of lubricant.

6. When the oil level is up to the edge of the filler hole, replace the filler plug. Drive the car for a few minutes, stop, and check for any leaks.

Automatic Transmission

1. The fluid should be changed with the engine warm. Raise the car in the air and support it with jackstands.

2. Place a large pan under the transmission. Remove all the front and side bolts. Loosen the rear bolts about four turns. Pry or tap the pan loose and let it drain.

3. Remove the pan and the gasket. Clean the pan thoroughly with solvent and air dry it. Be very careful not to get any lint from rags in the pan.

4. The transmission will be equipped either with a replaceable filter or a strainer which must be cleaned. Turbo 400 transmissions will have a filter. All others may have either a filter or a strainer.

5. Remove the strainer-to-valve body screws, the strainer and the gasket. On the 400 transmission, remove the filter retaining bolt, filter, and intake pipe O-ring. If there is a strainer, clean it in solvent and air dry it.

6. Install the new filter or cleaned strainer with a new gasket. On the Turbo 400, install a new intake pipe O-ring along with a new filter.

7. Install the pan with a new gasket. Tighten the bolts evenly to 10-13 ft.lb.

8. Lower the car and add five pints of DEXRON®II automatic transmission fluid through the dipstick tube.

9. Start the engine and let it idle in Park. Do not race the engine. Shift through each of the gears, then shift back to Park. Check the fluid level on the dipstick. The fluid level will probably be one pint low. Add fluid as necessary. Do not overfill the transmission.

10. Drive the car long enough to thoroughly warm up the transmission. Recheck the fluid level and add fluid as necessary.

Coolant

FLUID RECOMMENDATIONS

Check the coolant level in the radiator at every oil change. If the coolant level is low, refill the radiator with 50/50 solution of antifreeze (ethylene glycol) and water. Every 2 years or 30,000 miles drain, flush and refill the cooling system.

LEVEL CHECK

Once a month, the engine coolant level should be checked. This is quickly accomplished by observing the level of coolant in the recovery tank, which is the translucent tank mounted to the right or left of the radiator, and connected to the radiator filler neck by a length of hose. As long as coolant is visible in the tank between the Full Cold and Full Hot marks the coolant level is OK.

If coolant is needed, a 50/50 mix of ethylene glycol base antifreeze and clear water should always be used for additions, both winter and summer. This is imperative on cars with air conditioning; without the antifreeze, the heater core could freeze when the air conditioning is used. Add coolant to the recovery tank through the capped opening; make additions only when the engine is cool.

DRAIN SYSTEM, FLUSH AND REFILL

The cooling system should be drained, flushed and refilled every two years or 30,000 miles, according to the manufacturer's recommendations. However, many mechanics prefer to change the coolant every year; it is cheap insurance against corrosion, overheating or freezing.

1. Remove the radiator cap when the engine is cool.

CAUTION: *To avoid injury when working with a hot engine, cover the radiator cap with a thick cloth. Wear a heavy glove to protect your hand. Turn the radiator cap slowly to the first stop, and allow all the pressure to vent (indicted when the hissing noise stops). When the pressure has been released, press down and remove the cap the rest of the way.*

2. The heater should be turned on to its maximum heat position, so that the core is flushed out.

3. Shut off the engine and open the drain cock in the bottom of the radiator. Drain the radiator.

4. Close the drain cock and fill the system with clear water. A cooling system flushing additive can be added, if desired.

5. Run the engine until it is hot again.

6. Drain the system, then flush with water until it runs clear.

7. Clean out the coolant recovery tank: remove the cap leaving the hoses in place. Remove the tank and drain it of any coolant. Clean it out with soap and water, empty it, and install it.

8. Close the drain cock and fill the radiator with a 50/50 mix of ethylene glycol base antifreeze and water to the base of the radiator filler neck. Fill the coolant recovery tank with the

same mixture to the Full Hot mark. Install the recovery tank cap.

9. Run the engine until the upper radiator hose is hot again (radiator cap still off). With the engine idling, add the 50/50 mix of antifreeze and water to the radiator until the level reaches the bottom of the filler neck. Shut off the engine and install the radiator cap, aligning the arrows with the overflow tube. Turn off the heater.

Master Cylinder

FLUID RECOMMENDATION AND LEVEL CHECK

The brake master cylinder is located under the hood, in the left rear section of the engine compartment. It is divided into two sections (reservoirs) and the fluid must be kept within ¼" of the top edge of both reservoirs. The level should be checked at least every 7,500 miles.

NOTE: *Any sudden decrease in the level of fluid indicates a possible leak in the system and should be checked out immediately.*

To check the fluid level, simply pry off the retaining bar and then lift off the top cover of the master cylinder. When making additions of brake fluid, use only fresh, uncontaminated

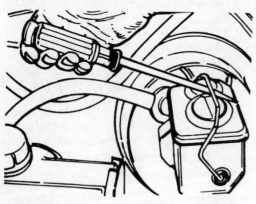

Pry the retaining bail from the master cylinder reservoir cap to check the fluid level

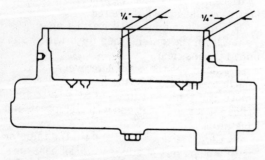

The fluid level in the master cylinder reservoir should be within ¼ in. of the top edge

brake fluid which meets or exceeds DOT 3 standards. Be careful not to spill any brake fluid on painted surfaces, as it eats paint. Do not allow the brake fluid container or the master cylinder reservoir to remain open any longer than necessary; brake fluid absorbs moisture from the air, reducing its effectiveness and causing corrosion in the lines.

NOTE: *The reservoir cover on some later models (1978 and later) may be without a retaining bail. If so, simply pry the cover off with your fingers.*

Power Steering Pump

FLUID RECOMMENDATION AND LEVEL CHECK

Power steering fluid level should be checked at least once every 7,500 miles. To prevent possible overfilling, check the fluid level only when the fluid has warmed to operating temperatures and the wheels are turned straight ahead. If the level is low, fill the pump reservoir with DEXRON®II Automatic Transmission Fluid. 1977 and later cars require GM power steering fluid, until the fluid level measures full on the reservoir dipstick. Low fluid level usually produces a moaning sound as the wheels are turned (especially when standing still or parking) and increases steering wheel effort.

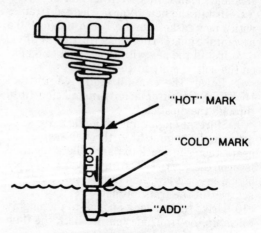

"HOT" MARK

"COLD" MARK

"ADD"

Use the dipstick to check the power steering fluid

Chassis Greasing

There are only two areas which require regular chassis greasing: the front suspension components and the steering linkage. These parts should be greased every 12 months or 7,500 miles (12,000 Km.) with an EP grease meeting G.M. specification 6031M.

If you choose to do this job yourself, you will need to purchase a hand operated grease gun, if you do not own one already, and a long flexible extension hose to reach the various grease fittings. You will also need a cartridge of the appropriate grease.

Press the fitting on the grease gun hose onto the grease fitting on the suspension or steering linkage component. Pump a few shots of grease into the fitting, until the rubber boot on the joint begins to expand, indicating that the joint if full. Remove the gun from the fitting. Be careful not to overfill the joints, which will rupture the rubber boots, allowing the entry of dirt. You can keep the grease fittings clean by covering them with a small square of tin foil.

Chassis and Body Lubrication

Every 12 months or 7,500 miles (12,000 km.), the various linkages and hinges on the chassis and body should be lubricated, as follows:

TRANSMISSION SHIFT LINKAGE

Lubricate the manual transmission shift linkage contact points with the EP grease used for chassis greasing, which should meet G.M. specification 6031M. The automatic transmission linkage should be lubricated with clean engine oil.

HOOD LATCH AND HINGES

Clean the latch surfaces and apply clean engine oil to the latch pilot bolts and the spring anchor. Use the engine oil to lubricate the hood hinges as well. Use a chassis grease to lubricate all the pivot points in the latch release mechanism.

DOOR HINGES

The gas tank filler door, car door, and trunk link hinges should be wiped clean and lubricated with clean engine oil. Silicone spray also works well on these parts, but must be applied more often. Use engine oil to lubricate the trunk or hatch lock mechanism and the lock bolt and striker. The door lock cylinders can be lubricated easily with a shot of silicone spray or one of the many dry penetrating lubricants commercially available.

PARKING BRAKE LINKAGE

Use chassis grease on the parking brake cable where it contact the guides, links, levers, and pulleys. The grease should be a water resistant one for durability under the car.

ACCELERATOR LINKAGE

Lubricate the carburetor stud, carburetor lever, and the accelerator pedal lever at the support inside the car with clean engine oil.

Wheel Bearings

The bearings should be repacked every 30,000 miles. After repacking, the bearings must be adjusted properly. See Chapter 8 for procedures.

PUSHING

This is the last recommended method of starting a car and should be used only in an extreme case. Chances of body damage are high, so be sure that the pushcar's bumper does not override your bumper. If you car has an automatic transmission it cannot be push started. In an emergency, you can start a manual transmission car by pushing. With the bumpers evenly matched, get in your car, switch on the ignition, and place the gearshift in Second or Third gear—do not engage the clutch. Start off slowly. When the speed of the car reaches about 15-20 mph, release the clutch.

JACKING

There are certain safety precautions which should be observed when jacking the vehicle. They are as follows:

1. Always jack the car on a level surface.

2. Set the parking brake if the front wheels are to be raised. This will keep the car from rolling backward off the jack.

3. If the rear wheels are to be raised, block the front wheels to keep the car from rolling forward.

4. Block the wheel diagonally opposite the one which is being raised.

5. If the vehicle is being raised in order to work underneath it, support it with jackstands. Do not place the jackstands against the sheet metal panels beneath the car or they will become distorted.

The service operations in this book often require that one end or the other, or both, of the car is raised and safely supported. The ideal method, of course, would be a hydraulic hoist. Since this is beyond both the resource and requirement of the do-it-yourselfer, a small hydraulic, screw or scissors jack will suffice for the procedures in this guide. Two sturdy jackstands should be acquired if you intend to work under the car at any time. An alternate method of raising the car would be drive-on ramps. These are available commercially or can be fabricated from heavy boards or steel. Be sure to block the wheels when using ramps. Never use concrete blocks to support the car.

JUMP STARTING A DEAD BATTERY

The chemical reaction in a battery produces explosive hydrogen gas. This is the safe way to jump start a dead battery, reducing the chances of an accidental spark that could cause an explosion.

Jump Starting Precautions

1. Be sure both batteries are of the same voltage.
2. Be sure both batteries are of the same polarity (have the same grounded terminal).
3. Be sure the vehicles are not touching.
4. Be sure the vent cap holes are not obstructed.
5. Do not smoke or allow sparks around the battery.
6. In cold weather, check for frozen electrolyte in the battery.
7. Do not allow electrolyte on your skin or clothing.
8. Be sure the electrolyte is not frozen.

Jump Starting Procedure

1. Determine voltages of the two batteries; they must be the same.
2. Bring the starting vehicle close (they must not touch) so that the batteries can be reached easily.
3. Turn off all accessories and both engines. Put both cars in Neutral or Park and set the handbrake.
4. Cover the cell caps with a rag—do not cover terminals.
5. If the terminals on the run-down battery are heavily corroded, clean them.
6. Identify the positive and negative posts on both batteries and connect the cables in the order shown.
7. Start the engine of the starting vehicle and run it at fast idle. Try to start the car with the dead battery. Crank it for no more than 10 seconds at a time and let it cool off for 20 seconds in between tries.
8. If it doesn't start in 3 tries, there is something else wrong.
9. Disconnect the cables in the reverse order.
10. Replace the cell covers and dispose of the rags.

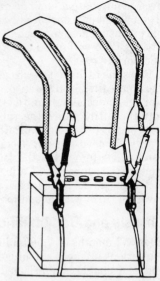

Side terminal batteries occasionally pose a problem when connecting jumper cables. There frequently isn't enough room to clamp the cables without touching sheet metal. Side terminal adaptors are available to alleviate this problem and should be removed after use.

NOTE: *When jump starting a diesel engine vehicle with charging equipment, be sure equipment used is 12 volt and negative ground. Do Not use 24 volt charging equipment. Using such equipment can cause serious damage to the electrical system or electronic parts.*

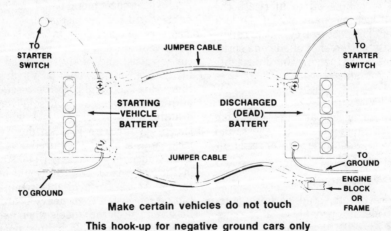

TO STARTER SWITCH

JUMPER CABLE

TO STARTER SWITCH

STARTING VEHICLE BATTERY

DISCHARGED (DEAD) BATTERY

JUMPER CABLE

TO GROUND

ENGINE BLOCK OR FRAME

TO GROUND

Make certain vehicles do not touch

This hook-up for negative ground cars only

Maintenance Intervals in Thousands of Miles*

Item	'70	'71	'72	'73	'74	'75	'76	'77	'78	'79-'80	'81-'87
Clean air cleaner element or oil bath	12	12	12	12	12	15	—	—	—	—	—
Replace air cleaner element	24	24	12 six/24 V8	12 six/24 V8	12 six/24 V8	15 six/30 V8	30	30	30	30	30
Replace or clean air cleaner PCV element or flame arrestor	12	12	24	24	24	30	30	30	30	30	30
Replace PCV valve	12/12 mo	24/24 mo	24/24 mo	24/24 mo	24/24 mo	30/24 mo	30/24 mo	30	30	30	30
Replace evaporative canister filter	12/12 mo	12/12 mo	24/24 mo	24/24 mo	24/24 mo	30/24 mo	30/24 mo	30	30/24 mo	30/24 mo	30/24 mo
Lubricate heat riser if sticking	as needed	as needed	6/4 mo	6/4 mo	12/12 mo	8/6 mo	8/6 mo	12	12	12	12
Rotate tires	6	as needed	as needed	as needed	as needed	8/15 radial	as needed	8①	6②	6②	6②
Replace fuel filter	24	24	24/24 mo	12/12 mo	12/12 mo	12/12 mo	15/12 mo	15	15/12 mo	15/12 mo	15
Change engine oil and filter	6/4 mo	6/4 mo	6/4 mo	6/4 mo	6/4 mo	7/6 mo	7/6 mo	7/12 mo	7/12 mo	7/12 mo	7/12 mo
Change automatic transmission fluid and filter	24	24	24	24	24	30	60	60	60	100	100
Check manual transmission, and axle fluid levels	6	6/4 mo	6/4 mo	6/4 mo	6/4 mo	8/6 mo	8/6 mo	7	7	7	7
Grease chassis	6	6	6	6	6/4 mo	8/6 mo	8/6 mo	8/12 mo	7/12 mo	7/12 mo	7/12 mo
Grease front wheel bearings	30	30	30	30	24	30	30 2WD/12 4WD	30	30	30	30
Change engine coolant	24 mo	24 mo	24 mo	24 mo	24 mo	30/24 mo	30/24 mo	30/24 mo	30/24 mo	30	30

*Minimum intervals for a car driven the average 12,000 miles per year under ideal conditions. Intervals given only in thousands of miles can be roughly converted to months: 12,000 mi=12 mo. Halve service intervals for severe use such as trailer towing or off-road driving. If both miles and months are given, use whichever interval elapses first.

① 15,000 miles for radial tires

② 12,000 miles for radial tires

Capacities

| Year | Engine No. Cyl Displacement (Cu in.) | Engine Crankcase Add 1 qt For New Filter | Transmission Pts to Refill After Drawing | | | Drive Axle (pts) | Gasoline Tank (gals) | Cooling System (qts) | |
| | | | Manual | | Auto-matic ● | | | | |
			3-Speed	4/5-Speed				With Heater	With A/C
'70	6-250 Chev.	4	3.5	—	6	3.7	20②	12.2	12.2
	8-350 Olds.	4	3.5	2.25	6	3.7	20②	15.2	15.7
	8-455 Olds.	4	3.5	2.25	6	3.7	20②	17.5	18
	8-455 4-4-2	4	5	2.25	6	3.7	20	16.2	17.2
'71	6-250 Chev.	4	3.5	—	6	4.25	20③	12.2	12.2
	8-350 Olds.	4	3.5	2.25	6	4.25	20③	15.2	15.7
	8-455 Olds.	4	3.5	—	6	4.25	20③	17.5	18
	8-455 4-4-2	4	4.5	2.5	6	4.25	20	16.2	17.2
'72	8-350 Olds.	4	3.5	2.25	6	4.25①	20②	15.2	15.7
	8-455 Olds.	4	—	—	6	4.25①	23	17	17.5
'73	8-350 Olds.	4	3.5	2.25	6	4.25①④	22	15.9⑥	16⑥
	8-455 Olds.	4	—	2.25	6	4.25①④	22	17.0⑦	18⑦
'74	8-350 Olds.	4	—	—	6	4.25④	22	20.0	20.0
	8-455 Olds.	4	—	—	6	5.50	22	21.0⑧	21.5⑧
'75	6-250 Chev.	4	3.5	—	6	4.25	22	17.0⑬	17.0
	8-260 Olds.	4	3.5	—	6	4.25	22	23.5	23.5⑧
	8-350 Olds.	4	—	—	6	4.25④	22	20.0	22.5
	8-455 Olds.	4	—	—	6	5.50	22	21.0⑧	21.5⑧
'76–'77	6-231 Buick	4	—	3⑭	6	3.5	18.5	13.5	14
	6-250 Chev.	4	—	—	6	4.25	22	17	17
	8-260 Olds.	4	—	3.5	6	4.25	22	23.5	26
	8-350, 403 Olds.	4	—	—	6	4.25④	22	20	22.5
	8-455 Olds.	4	—	—	6	5.4	22	21.0⑧	21.5⑧
'78	6-231 Buick	4	3.5	3.5	6	3.5	18.0⑨	12.0	12.0
	8-260 Olds.	4	—	3.5	6	3.5	18.0⑨	16.25	16.25
	8-305 Chev.	4	—	3.5	6	3.5	18.0⑨	15.5	15.5
	8-350 Chev.	4	—	—	6	3.5	18.0⑨	15.5	16.25
'79–'80	6-231 Buick	4	3.5	3.0	6	3.5	18.2	13.3	13.3
	8-260 Olds.	4	—	3.5	6	3.5	18.2	16.25⑩	16.25⑩
	8-260 Diesel	7⑤	—	3.5	6	3.5	19.75	19.75	19.75
	8-305 Chev.	4	—	3.0	6	3.5	18.2	15.5	15.5
	8-350 Olds.	4	—	—	6	3.5	18.2	15	15.25
	8-350 Diesel	7⑤	—	—	6	3.5	18.2	17.5	17.5
'81	6-231 Buick	4	3	—	⑪	3.5	18.0	13.0	13.0⑬
	8-260 Olds.	4	—	—	⑫	3.5	18.0	15.9	15.5⑭
	8-307 Olds.	4	—	—	8	3.5	18.0	14.9	15.6
	8-350 Diesel	7	—	—	6.5	3.5	19.75	17.4	17.3
	6-231 Buick	4	3	—	⑪	3.5	18.0	13.0	13.0⑬

Capacities (cont.)

Year	Engine No. Cyl Displacement (Cu in.)	Engine Crankcase Add 1 qt For New Filter	Transmission Pts to Refill After Drawing			Drive Axle (pts)	Gasoline Tank (gals)	Cooling System (qts)	
			Manual		Auto-matic ●			With Heater	With A/C
			3-Speed	4/5-Speed					
'81	8-260 Olds.	4	—	—	⑫	3.5	18.0	15.9	15.5⑭
	8-307 Olds.	4	—	—	8	3.5	18.0	14.9	15.6
	8-350 Diesel	7	—	—	6.5	3.5	19.75	17.4	17.3
'82	6-231 Buick	4	—	—	⑮	3.5	18.0	13.0	13.0⑬
	8-260 Olds.	4	—	—	6.3	3.5	18.0	15.9	15.5⑭
	6-263 Diesel	6⑤	—	—	7	3.5	19.75	14.5	15.3
	8-267 Chev.*	4	—	—	6	3.5	18.0	15.5	15.5
	8-305 Chev.*	4	—	—	6	3.5	18.0	15.5	15.5
	8-307 Olds.	4	—	—	8	3.5	18.0	14.9	15.6
	8-350 Diesel	7⑤	—	—	6.3	3.5	19.75	17.4	17.3
'83	6-231 Buick	4	—	—	6	3.5	18.2	13.3	13.3
	6-263 Diesel	6⑤	—	—	6	3.5	19.8	12.9	12.9
	8-307 Olds.	4	—	—	6	3.5	18.2	15.5	15.5
	8-350 Diesel	7⑤	—	—	6	3.5	19.8	18.0	18.0
'84–'85	6-231 Buick	4	—	—	6	3.5	19.8	13.3	13.3
	6-263 Diesel	6⑤	—	—	6	3.5	19.8	12.9	12.9
	8-307 Olds.	4	—	—	6	3.5	18.2	15.5	15.5
	8-350 Diesel	7⑤	—	—	6	3.5	19.8	18.0	18.0
'86–'87	6-231 Buick	4	—	—	7	3.5	18.0	13.5	13.5
	8-307 Olds.	4	—	—	7	3.5	18.0	15.5	15.5

*Canada only
● Does not include Torque Converter
① Limited Slip: 5.4
② Sta. Wgn.: 23
③ Sta. Wgn.: 22
④ Sta. Wgn.: 5.5
⑤ Includes mandatory filter change
⑥ W/Heavy Duty cooling: 21.0
⑦ W/Heavy Duty cooling: 22.0
⑧ W/Heavy Duty cooling: 23.5
⑨ Sta. Wgn.: 18.25
⑩ 1980 W/AC: 15.9; W/O/AC: 16.6
⑪ Exc. Sta. Wgn.: 6.5
 Sta. Wgn. w/2.73: 1 rear axle (TH-M200C): 7.0
 Sta. Wgn. w/3.23: 1 rear axle (TH-M250C): 8.0
⑫ Exc. Sta. Wgn.: 6.5
 Sta. Wgn.: 7.0
⑬ W/Heavy Duty cooling: 13.6
⑭ W/Heavy Duty cooling: 16.6
⑮ W/TH-M250C: 8.0
 W/TH-M350C: 6.3

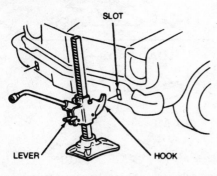

SLOT

LEVER   HOOK

FRONT

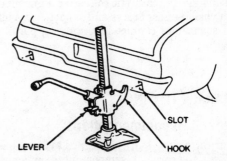

SLOT

LEVER   HOOK

REAR

Some early models have jacking slots in the bumpers

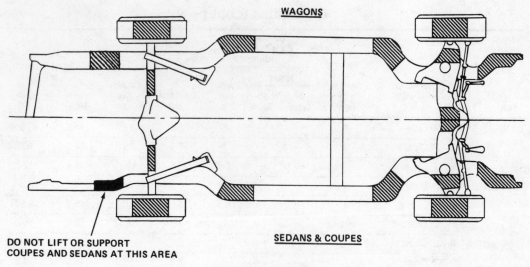

WAGONS

SEDANS & COUPES

DO NOT LIFT OR SUPPORT
COUPES AND SEDANS AT THIS AREA

Vehicle lifting points

Do not work beneath a vehicle supported only by a tire changing jack. Always use jack stands which are properly positioned under the car

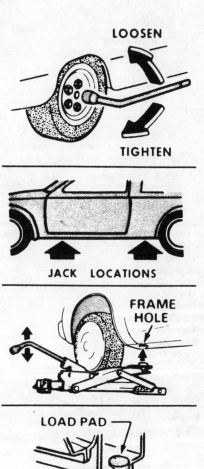

LOOSEN

TIGHTEN

JACK LOCATIONS

FRAME HOLE

LOAD PAD

FRAME

JACK

Later models use a scissors jack that fits into frame holes on both sides of the car

They may break if the lead is not evenly distributed.

Regardless of the method of jacking or hoisting the car, there are only certain areas of the undercarriage and suspension you can safely use to support it. See the illustration, and make sure that only the shaded areas are used. In addition, be especially careful that you do not damage the catalytic converter. Remember that various cross braces and supports on a left can sometimes contact low hanging parts of the car.

TRAILER TOWING

General Recommendations

Your car was primarily designed to carry passengers and cargo. It is important to remember that towing a trailer will place additional loads on your vehicle's engine, drive train, steering, braking and other systems. However, if you find it necessary to tow a trailer, using the proper equipment is a must.

Local laws may require specific equipment such as trailer brakes or fender mounted mirrors. Check your local laws.

Trailer Weight

The weight of the trailer is the most important factor. A good weight-to-horsepower ratio is about 35:1, 35 lbs. of GCW (Gross Combined Weight) for every horsepower your engine develops. Multiply the engine's rated horsepower by 35 and subtract the weight of the car passengers and luggage. The result is the approximate ideal maximum weight you should tow, although a a numerically higher axle ratio can help compensate for heavier weight.

Hitch Weight

Figure the hitch weight to select a proper hitch. Hitch weight is usually 9–11% of the trailer gross weight and should be measured with the trailer loaded. Hitches fall into three types: those that mount on the frame and rear bumper or the bolt-on or weld-on distribution type used for larger trailers. Axle mounted or clamp-on bumper hitches should never be used.

Check the gross weight rating of your trailer. Tongue weight is usually figured as 10% of gross trailer weight. Therefore, a trailer with a maximum gross weight of 2,000 lb. will have a maximum tongue weight of 200 lb. Class I trailers fall into this category. Class II trailers are those with a gross weight rating of 2,000-3,500 lb., while Class III trailers fall into the 3,500-6,000 lb. category. Class IV trailers are those over 6,000 lb. and are for use with fifth wheel trucks, only.

When you've determined the hitch that you'll need, follow the manufacturer's installation instructions, exactly, especially when it comes to fastener torques. The hitch will subjected to a lot of stress and good hitches come with hardened bolts. Never substitute an inferior bolt for a hardened bolt.

Cooling
ENGINE

One of the most common, if not THE most common, problems associated with trailer towing is engine overheating.

If you have a standard cooling system, without an expansion tank, you'll definitely need to get an aftermarket expansion tank kit, preferably one with at least a 2 quart capacity. These kits are easily installed on the radiator's overflow hose, and come with a pressure cap designed for expansion tanks.

Another helpful accessory is a Flex Fan. These fan are large diameter units are designed to provide more airflow at low speeds, with blades that have deeply cupped surfaces. The blades then flex, or flatten out, at high speed, when less cooling air is needed. These fans are far lighter in weight than stock fans, requiring less horsepower to drive them. Also, they are far quieter than stock fans.

If you do decide to replace your stock fan with a flex fan, note that if your car has a fan clutch, a spacer between the flex fan and water pump hub will be needed.

Aftermarket engine oil coolers are helpful for prolonging engine oil life and reducing overall engine temperatures. Both of these factors increase engine life.

While not absolutely necessary in towing Class I and some Class II trailers, they are recommended for heavier Class II and all Class III towing.

Engine oil cooler systems consist of an adapter, screwed on in place of the oil filter, a remote filter mounting and a multi-tube, finned heat exchanger, which is mounted in front of the radiator or air conditioning condenser.

TRANSMISSION

An automatic transmission is usually recommended for trailer towing. Modern automatics have proven reliable and, of course, easy to operate, in trailer towing.

The increased load of a trailer, however, causes an increase in the temperature of the automatic transmission fluid. Heat is the worst enemy of an automatic transmission. As the temperature of the fluid increases, the life of the fluid decreases.

It is essential, therefore, that you install an automatic transmission cooler.

The cooler, which consists of a multi-tube, finned heat exchanger, is usually installed in front of the radiator or air conditioning compressor, and hooked inline with the transmission cooler tank inlet line. Follow the cooler manufacturer's installation instructions.

Select a cooler of at least adequate capacity, based upon the combined gross weights of the car and trailer.

Cooler manufacturers recommend that you use an aftermarket cooler in addition to, and not instead of, the present cooling tank in your radiator. If you do want to use it in place of the radiator cooling tank, get a cooler at least two sizes larger than normally necessary.

NOTE: *A transmission cooler can, sometimes, cause slow or harsh shifting in the transmission during cold weather, until the fluid has a chance to come up to normal operating temperature. Some coolers can be purchased with or retrofitted with a temperature bypass valve which will allow fluid flow through the cooler only when the fluid has reached operating temperature, or above.*

Handling A Trailer

Towing a trailer with ease and safety requires a certain amount of experience. It's a good idea to learn the feel of a trailer by practicing turning, stopping and backing in an open area such as an empty parking lot.

HOW TO BUY A USED CAR

Many people believe that a two or three year old, or older, car is a better buy than a new one. This may be true. The new car suffers the heaviest depreciation in the first few years, but is not old enough to present a lot of costly repairs. Whatever the age of the used car you want to buy, this section and a little patience will help you select one that should be safe and dependable.

Shopping Tips

1. First, decide what model you want and how much you want to spend.
2. Check the used car lots and your local newspaper ads. Privately owned cars are usually less expensive, however, you will not get a warranty that, in most cases, comes with a used car purchased from a dealer.
3. Never shop at night. The glare of the lights makes it easy to miss defects in the paint and faults in the body caused by accident or rust repair.
4. Once you've found a car that you're interested in, try to get the name and phone number of the previous owner. Contact that person for details about the car. If he or she refuses information about the car, shop elsewhere. A private seller can tell you about the car and its maintenance history, but there are few laws requiring honesty from private citizens who are selling used vehicles. There are laws forbidding the tampering with or turning back a vehicle's odometer mileage reading. These laws apply to both a private seller as well commercial dealers. The law also requires that the seller, or anyone transferring ownership of a vehicle, must provide the buyer with a signed statement indicating the mileage on the odometer at the time of transfer.

5. Write down the year, model and serial number of the car before you buy it. Then, dial 1-800-424-9393, the toll-free number of the National Highway Traffic Safety Administration, and ask if the car has ever been included on any manufacturer's recall list. If so, make sure the necessary repairs were made.

6. Use the Used Car Checklist in this section, and check all the items on the used car that you are considering. Some items are more important than others. You've already determined how much money you can afford for repairs, and, depending on the price of the car, you should consider doing some of the needed repairs yourself. Beware, however, of trouble in areas involving operation, safety or emissions. Problems in the Used Car Checklist are arranged as follows:

1–8: Two or more problems in this segment indicate a lack of maintenance. You should reconsider your selection.

9–13: Indicates a lack of proper care, however, these can usually be corrected with a tune-up or relatively simple parts replacement.

14–17: Problems in the engine or transmission can be very expensive. Walk away from any car with problems in these areas.

7. If you are satisfied with the apparent condition of the car, take it to an independent diagnostic center or mechanic for a complete checkout. If your state has a state inspection program, have it inspected immediately before purchase, or specify on the invoice that purchase is conditional on the car's passing a state inspection.

8. Road test the car. Refer to the Road Test Checklist in this section. If your original evaluation, and the road test agree, the rest is up to you.

Used Car Checklist

NOTE: *The numbers on the illustration correspond to the numbers in this checklist.*

1. *Mileage:* Average mileage is about 12,000 miles per year. More than average may indicate hard usage. Catalytic converter equipped models may need converter service beyond the 50,000 mile mark.

2. *Paint:* Check around the tailpipe, molding and windows for overspray, indicating that the car has been repainted.

3. *Rust:* Check fenders, doors, rocker panels, window moldings, wheelwells, flooring

and in the bed, for signs of rust. Any rust at all will be a problem. There is no way to stop the spread of rust, except to replace the part or panel.

4. *Body Appearance:* Check the moldings, bumpers, grille, vinyl roof, glass, doors, tail gate and body panels for overall condition. Check for misalignment, loose holddown clips, ripples, scratches in the glass, rips or patches in the top. Mismatched paint, welding in the bed, severe misalignment of body panels or ripples may indicate crash work.

5. *Leaks:* Get down under the car and take a good look. There are no normal leaks, other than water from the air conditioning condenser drain tube.

6. *Tires:* Check the tire air pressure. A common trick is to pump the tires up hard to make the car roll more easily. Check the tread wear and the spare tire condition. Uneven wear is a sign that the front end is, or was, out of alignment. See the Troubleshooting Chart for indications of treadwear.

7. *Shock Absorbers:* Check the shocks by forcing downward sharply on each corner of the car. Good shocks will not allow the car to rebound more than twice after you let go.

8. *Interior:* Check the entire interior. You're looking for an interior condition that agrees with the overall condition of the car. Reasonable wear can be expected, but be suspicious of new seatcovers on sagging seats, new pedal pads, and worn armrests. These indicate an attempt to cover up hard usage. Pull back the carpets and/or mats and look for signs of water leaks or flooding. Look for missing hardware, door handles, control knobs, etc. Check lights and signal operations. Make sure that all accessories, such as air conditioner, heater, radio, etc., work. Air conditioning, especially automatic temperature control units, can be very expensive to repair. Check the operation of the windshield wipers.

9. *Belts and Hoses:* Open the hood and check all belts and hoses for wear, cracks, or weak spots. Check around hose connections for stains, indicating leaks.

10. *Battery:* Low electrolyte level, corroded terminals and/or a cracked battery case, indicate a lack of maintenance.

11. *Radiator:* Look for corrosion or rust in the coolant, indicating a lack of maintenance.

12. *Air Filter:* A dirty air filter element indicates a lack of maintenance.

13. *Spark Plug Wires:* Check the wires for cracks, burned spots or wear. Worn wires will have to be replaced.

14. *Oil Level:* If the level is low, chances are that the engine either uses an excessive amount of oil, or leaks. If the oil on the dipstick appears foamy or tan in color, a leakage of coolant into the oil is indicated. Stop here, and go elsewhere for your car. If the oil appears thin or has the smell of gasoline, stop here and go elsewhere for your car.

15. *Automatic Transmission:* Pull the transmission dipstick out when the engine is running in PARK. If the fluid is hot, the dipstick should read FULL. If the fluid is cold, the level will show about one pint low. The fluid itself should be bright red and translucent, with no burned odor. Fluid that is brown or black and has a burned odor is a sign that the transmission needs major repairs.

16. *Exhaust:* Check the color of the exhaust smoke. Blue smoke indicates excessive oil usage, usually due to major internal engine problems. Black smoke can indicate burned valves or carburetor problems. Check the exhaust system for leaks. A leaky system is dangerous and expensive to replace.

17. *Spark Plugs:* Remove one of the spark plugs. An engine in good condition will have spark plugs with a light tan or gray deposit on the electrodes. See the color Tune-Up section for a complete analysis of spark plug condition.

Road Test Check List

1. *Engine Performance:* The car should have good accelerator response, whether cold or warm, with adequate power and smooth acceleration through the gears.

2. *Brakes:* Brakes should provide quick, firm stops, with no squealing, pulling or fade.

3. *Steering: Sure control with no binding, harshness or looseness, and no shimmy in the wheel should be encountered. Noise or vibration from the steering wheel means trouble.*

4. *Clutch:* Clutch action should be quick and smooth with easy engagement of the transmission.

5. *Manual Transmission:* The transmission should shift smoothly and crisply with easy change of gears. No clashing and grinding should be evident. The transmission should not stick in gear, nor should there be any gear whine evident at road speed.

6. *Automatic Transmission:* The transmission should shift rapidly and smoothly, with no noise, hesitation or slipping. The transmission should not shift back and forth, but should stay in gear until an upshift or downshift is needed.

7. *Differential:* No noise or thumps should be present. No external leakage should be present.

8. *Driveshaft, Universal Joints:* Vibration

and noise could mean driveshaft problems. Clicking at low speed or coast conditions means worn U-joints.

9. *Suspension:* Try hitting bumps at different speeds. A car that bounces has weak shock absorbers. Clunks mean worn bushings or ball joints.

10. *Frame:* Wet the tires and drive in a straight line. Tracks should show two straight lines, not four. Four tire tracks indicates a frame bent by collision damage. If the tires can't be wet for this purpose, have a friend drive along behind you and see if the car appears to be traveling in a straight line.

Tune-Up and Performance Maintenance

2

TUNE-UP PROCEDURES

In order to extract the full measure of performance and economy from you car's engine it is essential that it be properly tuned at regular intervals. Although the tune-up intervals for the newer models have been stretched to limits which would have been thought impossible a few years ago, periodic maintenance is till required. A regularly scheduled tune-up will keep your car's engine running smoothly and will prevent the annoying minor breakdowns and poor performance associated with an untuned engine.

A complete tune-up should be performed at the interval specified in the Maintenance Intervals chart in Chapter One. This interval should be halved if the car is operated under severe conditions, such as trailer towing, prolonged idling, continual stop and start driving, or if starting and running problems are noticed. It is assumed that the routine maintenance described in the first chapter has been kept up, as this will have a decided effect on the results of a tune-up. All of the applicable steps should be followed in order, as the result is a cumulative one.

If the specifications on the tune-up label in the engine compartment disagree with the Tune-Up Specifications chart in this chapter, the figures on the sticker must be used. The label often reflects changes made during the production run.

Spark Plugs

Spark plugs ignite the air and fuel mixtu001823the cylinder as the piston reaches the top of the compression stroke. The controlled explosion that results forces the piston down, turning the crankshaft and the rest of the drive train.

The average life of a sparkplug is 22,000-30,000 miles, on models equipped with HEI. Part of the reason for this extraordinarily long like is the exclusive use of unleaded fuel, which reduce the amount of deposits within the combustion chamber and on the spark plug electrodes themselves, compared with the deposits left by the leaded gasoline used in the past. An additional contribution to long like is make by the HEI (High Energy Ignition) System, which fires the spark plugs with over 35,000 volts of electricity. The high voltage serves to deep the electrodes clear, and because it is a cleaner blast of electricity than that produced by conventional breaker-point ignitions, the electrodes suffer less pitting and wear.

Nevertheless, the like of a spark plug is dependent on a number of factors, including the mechanical condition of the engine, driving conditions, and the driver's habits.

When you remove the plugs, check the condition of the electrodes; they are a good indicator of the internal state of the engine. Since the spark plug wires must be checked every 15,000 miles, the spark plugs can be removed and examined at the same time. This will allow you to keep an eye on the mechanical status of the engine.

A small deposit of light tan or rust-red material on a spark plug that has been used for any period of time is to be considered normal. Any other color, or abnormal amounts of wear or deposits, indicates that there is something amiss in the engine.

The gap between the center electrode and the side or ground electrode can be expected to increase not more than 0.001″ every 1,000 miles under normal conditions.

When a spark plug is functioning normally or, more accurately, when the plug is installed in an engine that is functioning properly, the plugs can be taken out, cleaned, regapped, and reinstalled in the engine without doing the engine any harm.

Tune-Up Specifications

When analyzing compression test results, look for uniformity among cylinders rather than specific pressures.

Year	Engine No. Cyl Displacement (cu in.)	hp	Spark Plugs Orig Type	Gap (in.)	Distributor Point Dwell (deg)	Point Gap (in.)	Ignition Timing (deg) ▲ Man Trans ①	Auto Trans	Intake Valve Opens ■(deg)●	Fuel Pump Pressure (psi)	Idle Speed (rpm) ▲ Man Trans●	Auto Trans●
'70	6-250 Chev.	155	R-46T	.035	31–34	.019	TDC	4B	16	4–5	830–750	630–600
	8-350 Olds.	250	R-46S	.030	28–32	.016	10B	10B	16	5.5–6.5	750	575
	8-350 Olds.	310	R-45S	.030	28–32	.016	10B	10B	16	5.5–6.5	650	575
	8-350 (W31) Olds.	325	R-43S	.030	28–32	.016	14B	14B	40	5.5–6.5	750	625
	8-455 Olds.	320	R-45S	.030	28–32	.016	—	8B	20	5.5–6.5	—	575
	8-455 Olds.	365③	R-44S	.030	28–32	.016	—	12½	20	5.5–6.5	—	600
	8-455 Olds.	365④	R-45S	.030	28–32	.016	—	8B	24	5.5–6.5	—	575
	8-455 Olds.	365⑤	R-44S	.030	28–32	.016	12B	12B	24②	5.5–6.5	700	650
	8-455 (W30) Olds.	370⑤	R-44S	.030	28–32	.016	8B	8B	56	5.5–6.5	700	650
'71	6-250 Chev.	145	R-46TS	.035	31–34	.019	4B	4B	16	4–5	600⑧	575⑧
	8-350 Olds.	240	R-46S	.040	28–32	.016	10B	10B	14	5.5–6.5	750	600
	8-350 Olds.	260	R-45S⑥	.040	28–32	.016	10B	12B	14②	5.5–6.5	750	600
	8-455 Olds.	270	R-46S	.040	28–32	.016	—	8B	20	5.5–6.5	—	600
	8-455 Olds.	320	R-46S	.040	28–32	.016	—	8B	20	5.5–6.5	—	600
	8-455 Olds.	340	R-45S	.040	28–32	.016	10B	10B	24②	5.5–6.5	750	600
	8-455 (W30) Olds.	350	R-45S	.040	28–32	.06	12B	10B	56	5.5–6.5	765	600
'72	8-350 Olds.	160	R-46S	.040	28–32	.016	8B	8B(6B)	16(22)	5.5–6.5	750	650/550
	8-350 Olds.	180	R-46S	.040	28–32	.016	8B	12B	16(22)	5.5–6.5	750	600
	8-455 Olds.	250	R-46S	.040	28–32	.016	10B	8B	30⑦	5.5–6.5	750	600
	8-455 Olds.	270	R-46S	.040	28–32	.016	10B	8B	30⑦	5.5–6.5	750	600
	8-455 Olds.	300	R-45S	.040	28–32	.016	12B	10B	56	5.5–6.5	750	650

Year	Engine	HP	Spark Plug	Gap	Dwell	Point Gap	Timing	Timing		Fuel Pump Pressure		Idle Speed	Idle Speed
'73	8-350	160	R-46S	.040	30	.016	—	14B	22	5.5-6.5	22	—	650/550
	8-350 Olds.	180	R-46S	.040	30	.016	—	12B	22	5.5-6.5	22	—	650/550
	8-350 Olds.	180	R-45S	.040	30	.016	—	12B	22	5.5-6.5	22	1000/600	—
	8-455 Olds.	225	R-45S	.040	30	.016	10B	8B	28	5.5-6.5	28	1000/750	650/550
'74	8-350 Olds.	160, 180	R-46S	.040	30	.016	—	12B	22	5.5-6.5	22	—	650/550
	8-350 Olds.	200	R-46S	.040	30	.016	—	14B	22	5.5-6.5	22	—	650/550
	8-455 Olds.	210	R-46S	.040	30	.06	—	8B	22	5.5-6.5	22	—	650/550
'75	8-455 Olds.	230	R-46SX	.080	Electronic		—	8B	22	5.5-6.5	22	—	650/550
	6-250 Chev.	100	R-46TX	.060	Electronic		10B	10B	16	4-5	16	800/425	600/425
	8-260 Olds.	110	R-46SX	.080	Electronic		16B	18B(16B)	22	5.5-6.5	22	750	650/550
	8-350 Olds.	170	R-46SX	.080	Electronic		—	20B	16	5.5-6.5	16	—	600/650
	8-455 Olds.	190	R-46SX	.080	Electronic		—	16B	20	5.5-6.5	20	—	650/550(600)
'76	6-250 Chev.	105	R-46TS	.035	Electronic		6B	10B	16	4-5	16	850/425	550(600)/425
	8-260 Olds.	110	R-46SX	.080	Electronic		16B(14B)	18B(16B)[9]	14	5.5-6.5	14	750	650[10]/550
	8-350 Olds.	170	R-46SX	.080	Electronic		—	20B[11]	16	5.5-6.5	16	—	650[10]/550(600)
	8-455 Olds.	190	R-46SX	.080	Electronic		—	16B	20	5.5-6.5	20	—	650[10]/550(600)
'77	6-231 Buick	105	R-46TSX	.060	Electronic		12B	12B	17	5.5-6.5	17	800/600	800/600
	8-260 Olds.	110	R-46SZ	.060	Electronic		16B @ 1100	16B @ 1100	14	5-6	14	750	650/550
	8-350 Olds.	170	R-46SZ	.060	Electronic		—	20B @ 1100	16	6-7	16	—	700/600
	8-403 Olds.	185	R-46SZ	.060	Electronic		—	20B[16] @ 1100	20	6-7	20	—	650/550
'78	6-231 Buick	105	R-46TSX	.060	Electronic		15B	15B	17	5-6	17	800	600
	8-260 Olds.	110	R-46SZ	.060	Electronic		18B	20B[15]	14	5-6	14	800	500[14]
	8-305 Chev.	145	R-45TS	.045	Electronic		4B	[12]	28	7-9	28	600	500[13]
	8-305 Chev.	160	R-45TS	.045	Electronic		—	4B	28	7-9	28	—	500
	8-350 Chev.	170	R-45TS	.045	Electronic		—	8B	28	7-9	28	—	600(500)
'79	6-231 Olds.	115	R-46TSX	.060	Electronic		15B	15B	17	4-5	17	800/600	670/550(600)[13]
	8-260 Olds.	110	R-46SZ	.060	Electronic		18B	20B[16]	14	5.5-6.5	14	800-650	625/550[20]
	8-260 Olds.	Diesel	—	—		—	—	5B[17]	16	8-12[16]	16	660/575	650/590

Tune-Up Specifications (cont.)

When analyzing compression test results, look for uniformity among cylinders rather than specific pressures.

Year	Engine No. Cyl Displacement (cu in.)	hp	Spark Plugs Orig Type	Gap (in.)	Distributor Point Dwell (deg)	Point Gap (in.)	Ignition Timing (deg)▲ Man Trans[1]	Auto Trans	Intake Valve Opens ■(deg)●	Fuel Pump Pressure (psi)	Idle Speed (rpm)▲ Man Trans●	Auto Trans●
'79	8-305 Chev.	145	R-45TS	.045	Electronic	—	4B	4B[18]	28	7.5–9.0	700/600	600(650)/500(600)
	8-305 Chev.	160	R-44TS	.045	Electronic	—	4B	4B[19]	28	7.5–9.0	700	600/500[21]
	8-350 Chev.	160	R-45TS	.045	Electronic	—	—	8B	28	7.5–9.0	—	650(600)/600(500)
	8-350 Olds.	Diesel	—	—	—	—	—	5B[17]	16	8–12[16]	—	650/575
'80	6-231 Buick	110	[20]	[20]	Electronic	—	15B @ 800	15B @ 550	16	3–4.5	800	550
	8-260 Olds.	Alt.	R46SX	.080	Electronic	—	—	20B @ 1100[23]	14	5.5–6.5	—	500
	8-260 Olds.	Diesel	—	—	—	—	—	[22]	16	5.5–6.5[16]	—	600
	8-305 Chev.	155	R45TS	.045	Electronic	—	—	4B	28	7.5–9.0	—	500
	8-350 Olds.	Diesel	—	—	—	—	—	[22]	16	5.5–6.5	—	600
'81 USA Models	6-231 Buick	All	R-45TS8	.080	Electronic	—	15B	15B	16	3.0–4.5	—	[22]
	8-260 Olds.	All	R-46SX	.080	Electronic	—	—	18B @ 1100	14	5.5–6.5	—	[22]
	8-307 Olds.	All	R-46SX	.080	Electronic	—	—	15B @ 1100	20	6.0–7.5	[22]	[22]
	8-350 Olds.	Diesel	—	—	—	—	—	6B	16	5.5–6.5	—	600
'81 Canada Models	6-231 Buick	All	R-45TS	.045	Electronic	—	15B	15B	16	3.0–4.5	—	650
	8-305 Chev.	All	R-45TS	.045	Electronic	—	—	4B	28	7.5–9.0	—	500
	8-350 Olds.	Diesel	—	—	—	—	—	6B	16	5.5–6.5	—	600
'82 USA Models	6-231 Buick	All	R-45TS8	.080	Electronic	—	—	15B	16	3.0–4.5	—	[22]
	8-260 Olds.	All	R-46SX	.080	Electronic	—	—	20B @ 1100	14	5.5–6.5	—	[22]
	6-263 Olds.	Diesel	—	—	—	—	—	6A @ 1300	—	—	—	650
	8-307 Olds.	All	R-46SX	.080	Electronic	—	—	20B @ 1100	14	5.5–6.5	—	[22]
	8-350 Olds.	Diesel	—	—	—	—	—	4A @ 1250	16	5.5–6.5	—	600
'82 Canada	6-231 Buick		R-45TS8	.080	Electronic	—	—	15B	16	3.0–4.5	—	550

'83–'85	8-305 Chev.		R-45TS	.045	Electronic	—	10B	28	7.5–9.0	500
	6-231 Buick	—	R45TX	.040	Electronic	—	㉒	16	4.25–5.75	㉒
	8-307 Olds.	—	R46SX	.080	Electronic	—	㉒	—	6.0–7.5	㉒
'86–'87	6-231 Buick	110	R-45TSX	.060	Electronic	—	㉒	—	5.5–7.0	㉒
	8-307 Olds.	All	FR3LS6	.060	Electronic	—	㉒	—	6.0–7.5	㉒

▲ See text for procedure

■ All figures Before Top Dead Center

● Figure in parentheses indicated California engine. Where two idle speed figures appear separated by a slash, the second is with the idle speed solenoid disconnected.

① Set V8 timing through 1974 at 1100 rpm without A/C and at 850 rpm with A/C. See sticker for timing rpm on later models.

② Figure is 30 degrees for manual transmission

③ Cutlass

④ Vista Cruiser

⑤ 442

⑥ R-46S for automatic transmission

⑦ Figure is 44 degrees for manual transmission

⑧ Without A/C
  550—automatic transmission
  500—manual transmission

⑨ A/C on and compressor clutch wires disconnected

⑩ 22B with 2.4:1 axle

⑪ 49 states: 4B
  Calif.: 6B
  High Altitude: 8B

⑫ High Altitude: 600

⑬ High Altitude, except Sta. Wgn.: 550

⑭ Calif., except Sta, Wgn.: 18B @ 1100

⑮ Nozzle opening pressure: 1800 psi

⑯ Static

⑰ Calif.: 2B

⑱ High Altitude: 8B

⑲ High Altitude: 650/550

⑳ High Altitude: 650/600

㉑ See Underhood Specifications sticker

㉒ Sta. Wgn.: 18B @ 1100
  M.T.: R45TS; gap: .040
  A.T. exc. Calif.: R45TS; gap: .040
  A.T. Calif.: R45TSX; gap:.060

B Before Top Dead Center

TDC Top Dead Center

— Not applicable

NA Not Available

NOTE: *The underhood specifications sticker often reflects tune-up specification changes made in production. Sticker figures must be used if they disagree with those in this chart.*

Diesel Tune-Up Specifications

Year	Engine No. of cyl. Displacement Manufacture	Fuel Pump Pressure (psi)	Compression Pressure (psi) ②	Intake Valve Opens (°B.T.D.C.)	Idle speed (rpm)
'81–'85	8-350 Olds	5.5–6.5	275 minimum	16	①
'82–'85	6-263 Olds	5.8–8.7	275 minimum	16	①

NOTE: The underhood specifications sticker often reflects tune-up specification changes made in production. Sticker figures must be used if they disagree with those in this chart.

B.T.D.C—Before top dead center (No. 1 cylinder)

① See the underhood specifications sticker

② The lower cylinder reading must not be less than 70% of the highest cylinder reading.

When, and if, a plug fouls and begins to misfire, you will have to investigate, correct the cause of the fouling, and either clean or replace the plug.

There are several reasons why a spark plug will foul and you can learn which is at fault by just looking at the plug. A few of the most common reasons for plug fouling, and a description of the fouled plug's appearance, are listed in the color insert section of this book, which also offers solutions to the problems.

Spark plugs suitable for use in you car's engine are offered in a number of different heat ranges. The amount of heat which the plug absorbs is determined by the length of the lower insulator. The longer the insulator, the hotter the plug will operate; the shorter the insulator, the cooler it will operate. A spark plug that absorbs (or retains) little heat and remains too cool will accumulate deposits of oil and carbon, because it is not hot enough to burn them off. This leads to fouling and consequent misfiring. A spark plug that absorbs too much heat will have no deposits, but the electrodes will burn away quickly and, in some cases preignition may result. Preignition occurs when the spark plug tips get so hot that they ignite the fuel/mixture before the actual spark fires. This premature ignition will usually cause a pinging sound under conditions of low speed and heavy load. In severe cases, the heat may become high enough to start the fuel/air mixture burning throughout the combustion chamber rather than just to the front of the plug. In this case, the resultant explosion (detonation) will be strong enough to damage pistons, rings, and valves.

In most cases the factory recommended heat range is correct; it is chosen to perform will under a wide range of operating conditions. However, it most of your driving is long distance, high speed travel, you may want to install a spark plug one step colder than standard. If most of your driving is of the short trip variety, when the engine may not always reach operating temperature, a hotter plug may help burn off the deposits normally accumulated under those conditions.

REMOVAL

1. Number the wires with pieces of adhesive tape so that you won't cross them when you replace them.

2. The spark plug boots have large grips to aid in removal. Grasp the wire by the rubber boot and twist the boot ½ turn in either direction to break the tight seal between the boot and the plug. Then twist and pull on the boot to remove the wire from the spark plug. Do not pull on the wire itself or you will damage the carbon cord conductor.

3. Use a ⅝" spark plug socket to loosen all of the plugs about two turns. A universal joint installed at the socket end of the extension will ease the process.

NOTE: *If removal of the plugs is difficult, apply a few drops of penetrating oil or silicone spray to the area around the base of the plug, and allow it a few minutes to work.*

4. If compressed air is available, apply it to the area around the spark plug holes. Otherwise, use a rag or a brush to clean the area. Be careful not to allow any foreign material to drop into the spark plug holes.

5. Remove the plugs by unscrewing them the rest of the way.

INSPECTION

Check the plugs for deposits and wear. If they are not going to be replaced, clean the plugs

```
        1 2 3   4   5
        ‾ ‾ ‾   ‾   ‾
        R 4 5   T S X
```

1 — R--INDICATES RESISTOR-TYPE PLUG.
2 — "4" INDICATES 14 mm THREADS.
3 — HEAT RANGE
4 — TS--TAPERED SEAT.
      S--EXTENDED TIP
5 — SPECIAL GAP

Spark plug coding using a AC-R45TSX as an example

Troubleshooting Engine Performance

Problem	Cause	Solution
Hard starting (engine cranks normally)	• Binding linkage, choke valve or choke piston	• Repair as necessary
	• Restricted choke vacuum diaphragm	• Clean passages
	• Improper fuel level	• Adjust float level
	• Dirty, worn or faulty needle valve and seat	• Repair as necessary
	• Float sticking	• Repair as necessary
	• Faulty fuel pump	• Replace fuel pump
	• Incorrect choke cover adjustment	• Adjust choke cover
	• Inadequate choke unloader adjustment	• Adjust choke unloader
	• Faulty ignition coil	• Test and replace as necessary
	• Improper spark plug gap	• Adjust gap
	• Incorrect ignition timing	• Adjust timing
	• Incorrect valve timing	• Check valve timing; repair as necessary
Rough idle or stalling	• Incorrect curb or fast idle speed	• Adjust curb or fast idle speed
	• Incorrect ignition timing	• Adjust timing to specification
	• Improper feedback system operation	• Refer to Chapter 4
	• Improper fast idle cam adjustment	• Adjust fast idle cam
	• Faulty EGR valve operation	• Test EGR system and replace as necessary
	• Faulty PCV valve air flow	• Test PCV valve and replace as necessary
	• Choke binding	• Locate and eliminate binding condition
	• Faulty TAC vacuum motor or valve	• Repair as necessary
	• Air leak into manifold vacuum	• Inspect manifold vacuum connections and repair as necessary
	• Improper fuel level	• Adjust fuel level
	• Faulty distributor rotor or cap	• Replace rotor or cap
	• Improperly seated valves	• Test cylinder compression, repair as necessary
	• Incorrect ignition wiring	• Inspect wiring and correct as necessary
	• Faulty ignition coil	• Test coil and replace as necessary
	• Restricted air vent or idle passages	• Clean passages
	• Restricted air cleaner	• Clean or replace air cleaner filler element
	• Faulty choke vacuum diaphragm	• Repair as necessary
Faulty low-speed operation	• Restricted idle transfer slots	• Clean transfer slots
	• Restricted idle air vents and passages	• Clean air vents and passages
	• Restricted air cleaner	• Clean or replace air cleaner filter element
	• Improper fuel level	• Adjust fuel level
	• Faulty spark plugs	• Clean or replace spark plugs
	• Dirty, corroded, or loose ignition secondary circuit wire connections	• Clean or tighten secondary circuit wire connections
	• Improper feedback system operation	• Refer to Chapter 4
	• Faulty ignition coil high voltage wire	• Replace ignition coil high voltage wire
	• Faulty distributor cap	• Replace cap
Faulty acceleration	• Improper accelerator pump stroke	• Adjust accelerator pump stroke
	• Incorrect ignition timing	• Adjust timing
	• Inoperative pump discharge check ball or needle	• Clean or replace as necessary
	• Worn or damaged pump diaphragm or piston	• Replace diaphragm or piston

Troubleshooting Engine Performance (cont.)

Problem	Cause	Solution
Faulty acceleration (cont.)	• Leaking carburetor main body cover gasket	• Replace gasket
	• Engine cold and choke set too lean	• Adjust choke cover
	• Improper metering rod adjustment (BBD Model carburetor)	• Adjust metering rod
	• Faulty spark plug(s)	• Clean or replace spark plug(s)
	• Improperly seated valves	• Test cylinder compression, repair as necessary
	• Faulty ignition coil	• Test coil and replace as necessary
	• Improper feedback system operation	• Refer to Chapter 4
Faulty high speed operation	• Incorrect ignition timing	• Adjust timing
	• Faulty distributor centrifugal advance mechanism	• Check centrifugal advance mechanism and repair as necessary
	• Faulty distributor vacuum advance mechanism	• Check vacuum advance mechanism and repair as necessary
	• Low fuel pump volume	• Replace fuel pump
	• Wrong spark plug air gap or wrong plug	• Adjust air gap or install correct plug
	• Faulty choke operation	• Adjust choke cover
	• Partially restricted exhaust manifold, exhaust pipe, catalytic converter, muffler, or tailpipe	• Eliminate restriction
	• Restricted vacuum passages	• Clean passages
	• Improper size or restricted main jet	• Clean or replace as necessary
	• Restricted air cleaner	• Clean or replace filter element as necessary
	• Faulty distributor rotor or cap	• Replace rotor or cap
	• Faulty ignition coil	• Test coil and replace as necessary
	• Improperly seated valve(s)	• Test cylinder compression, repair as necessary
	• Faulty valve spring(s)	• Inspect and test valve spring tension, replace as necessary
	• Incorrect valve timing	• Check valve timing and repair as necessary
	• Intake manifold restricted	• Remove restriction or replace manifold
	• Worn distributor shaft	• Replace shaft
	• Improper feedback system operation	• Refer to Chapter 4
Misfire at all speeds	• Faulty spark plug(s)	• Clean or replace spark plug(s)
	• Faulty spark plug wire(s)	• Replace as necessary
	• Faulty distributor cap or rotor	• Replace cap or rotor
	• Faulty ignition coil	• Test coil and replace as necessary
	• Primary ignition circuit shorted or open intermittently	• Troubleshoot primary circuit and repair as necessary
	• Improperly seated valve(s)	• Test cylinder compression, repair as necessary
	• Faulty hydraulic tappet(s)	• Clean or replace tappet(s)
	• Improper feedback system operation	• Refer to Chapter 4
	• Faulty valve spring(s)	• Inspect and test valve spring tension, repair as necessary
	• Worn camshaft lobes	• Replace camshaft
	• Air leak into manifold	• Check manifold vacuum and repair as necessary
	• Improper carburetor adjustment	• Adjust carburetor
	• Fuel pump volume or pressure low	• Replace fuel pump
	• Blown cylinder head gasket	• Replace gasket
	• Intake or exhaust manifold passage(s) restricted	• Pass chain through passage(s) and repair as necessary
	• Incorrect trigger wheel installed in distributor	• Install correct trigger wheel

Troubleshooting Engine Performance (cont.)

Problem	Cause	Solution
Power not up to normal	• Incorrect ignition timing	• Adjust timing
	• Faulty distributor rotor	• Replace rotor
	• Trigger wheel loose on shaft	• Reposition or replace trigger wheel
	• Incorrect spark plug gap	• Adjust gap
	• Faulty fuel pump	• Replace fuel pump
	• Incorrect valve timing	• Check valve timing and repair as necessary
	• Faulty ignition coil	• Test coil and replace as necessary
	• Faulty ignition wires	• Test wires and replace as necessary
	• Improperly seated valves	• Test cylinder compression and repair as necessary
	• Blown cylinder head gasket	• Replace gasket
	• Leaking piston rings	• Test compression and repair as necessary
	• Worn distributor shaft	• Replace shaft
	• Improper feedback system operation	• Refer to Chapter 4
Intake backfire	• Improper ignition timing	• Adjust timing
	• Faulty accelerator pump discharge	• Repair as necessary
	• Defective EGR CTO valve	• Replace EGR CTO valve
	• Defective TAC vacuum motor or valve	• Repair as necessary
	• Lean air/fuel mixture	• Check float level or manifold vacuum for air leak. Remove sediment from bowl
Exhaust backfire	• Air leak into manifold vacuum	• Check manifold vacuum and repair as necessary
	• Faulty air injection diverter valve	• Test diverter valve and replace as necessary
	• Exhaust leak	• Locate and eliminate leak
Ping or spark knock	• Incorrect ignition timing	• Adjust timing
	• Distributor centrifugal or vacuum advance malfunction	• Inspect advance mechanism and repair as necessary
	• Excessive combustion chamber deposits	• Remove with combustion chamber cleaner
	• Air leak into manifold vacuum	• Check manifold vacuum and repair as necessary
	• Excessively high compression	• Test compression and repair as necessary
	• Fuel octane rating excessively low	• Try alternate fuel source
	• Sharp edges in combustion chamber	• Grind smooth
	• EGR valve not functioning properly	• Test EGR system and replace as necessary
Surging (at cruising to top speeds)	• Low carburetor fuel level	• Adjust fuel level
	• Low fuel pump pressure or volume	• Replace fuel pump
	• Metering rod(s) not adjusted properly (BBD Model Carburetor)	• Adjust metering rod
	• Improper PCV valve air flow	• Test PCV valve and replace as necessary
	• Air leak into manifold vacuum	• Check manifold vacuum and repair as necessary
	• Incorrect spark advance	• Test and replace as necessary
	• Restricted main jet(s)	• Clean main jet(s)
	• Undersize main jet(s)	• Replace main jet(s)
	• Restricted air vents	• Clean air vents
	• Restricted fuel filter	• Replace fuel filter
	• Restricted air cleaner	• Clean or replace air cleaner filter element
	• EGR valve not functioning properly	• Test EGR system and replace as necessary
	• Improper feedback system operation	• Refer to Chapter 4

Check the spark plug gap with a wire feeler gauge

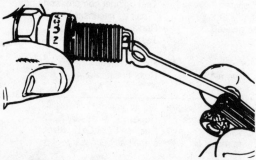

Adjust the electrode gap by bending the side electrode

thoroughly. Remember that any kind of deposit will decrease the efficiency of the plug. Plugs can be cleaned on a spark plug cleaning machine, which can sometimes be found in service stations, or you can do an acceptable job of cleaning with a stiff brush. If the plugs are cleaned, the electrodes must be filed flat. Use an ignition points file, not an emery board or the like, which will leave deposits. The electrodes must be filed perfectly flat with sharp edges; rounded edges reduce the spark plug voltage by as much as 50%.

Check the spark plug gap before installation. The ground electrode must be parallel to the center electrode and the specified size wire gauge should pass through the gap with a slight drag. Always check the gap on new plugs, too; they are not always correctly set at the factory. Do not use a flat feeler gauge when measuring the gap, because the reading will be inaccurate. Wire gapping tools usually have a bending tool attached. Use that to adjust the side electrode until the proper distance is obtained. Also, be careful not to bend the side electrode too far or too often; it may weaken and break off within the engine, requiring removal of the cylinder head to retrieve it.

INSTALLATION

1. Lubricate the threads of the spark plugs with a drop of oil or a shot of silicone spray. In-

stall the plugs and tighten them hand tight. Take care not to cross-thread them.

2. Tighten the spark plugs with a socket. Do not apply the same amount of force you would use for a bolt; just snug them in. These spark plugs do not use gaskets, and over-tightening will make future removal difficult. If a torque wrench is available, tighten to 7-15 ft.lb.

NOTE: *While over-tightening the spark plug is to be avoided, under-tightening is just as bad. If combustion gases leak past the threads, the spark plug will overheat and rapid electrode wear will result.*

3. Install the wires on their respective plugs. Make sure the wires are firmly connected. You will be able to feel them click into place. Spark plug wiring is shown in the firing order diagrams if you get into trouble.

CHECKING AND REPLACING SPARK PLUG WIRES

Every 15,000 miles, inspect the spark plug wires for burns, cuts, or breaks in the insulation. Check the boots and the nipples on the distributor cap. Replace any damaged wiring.

Every 45,000 miles or so, the resistance of the wires should be checked with an ohmmeter. Wires with excessive resistance will cause misfiring, and may make the engine difficult to start in damp weather. Generally, the useful life of the cables is 45,000-60,000 miles.

To check resistance, remove the distributor cap, leaving the wires in place. Connect one lead of an ohmmeter to an electrode within the cap; connect the other lead to the corresponding spark plug terminal (remove it from the spark plug for this test). Replace any wire which shows a resistance over 30,000 ohms. The following chart gives resistance values as a function of length. Generally speaking, however, resistance should not be considered the outer limit of acceptability.

- 0-15 inches: 3,000-10,000Ω
- 15-25 inches: 4,000-15,000Ω
- 25-35 inches: 6,000-20,000Ω
- Over 35 inches: 25,000Ω

It should be remembered that resistance is also a function of length; the longer the wire, the greater the resistance. Thus, if the wires on you car are longer than the factory originals, resistance will be higher, quite possibly outside these limits.

When installing new wires, replace them one at a time to avoid mixups. Start by replacing the longest one first. Install the boot firmly over the spark plug. Route the wire over the same path as the original. Insert the nipple firmly onto the tower on the distributor cap, then install the cap cover and latches to secure the wires.

FIRING ORDERS

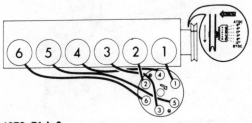

1970–71 L-6

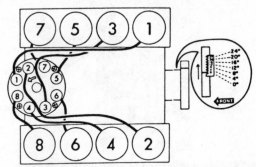

1975 and later—8-260, 307, 350, 403, 455 Oldsmobile built engines

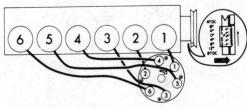

1975 and later L-6

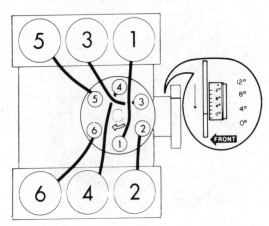

V6

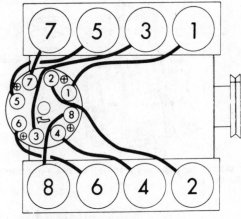

V8 Chevrolet built engines

Breaker Points and Condenser
REMOVAL AND REPLACEMENT

NOTE: *Always replace the points and condenser as a unit.*

Six Cylinder

NOTE: *The HEI (High Energy Ignition) used on some 1974 and all 1975 and later models requires no distributor maintenance other than checking the condition of the cap and wires. There are no points to wear out or adjust.*

1. Remove the distributor cap from the distributor and place it out of the way.

2. Remove the rotor.

3. Make a note of the wire connections and then remove the wires from the contact point terminal.

4. Remove the mounting screws and lift the point set condenser from the breaker plate.

5. Clean the breaker plate.

6. Install a new points set onto the breaker plate.

7. Install a new condenser and connect the

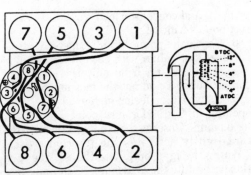

1970–74 V8

6-250 distributor caps are retained by screws

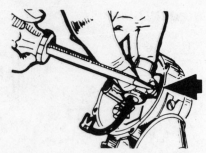

The condenser is held in place by a screw and clamp

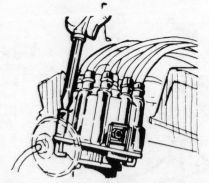

V8 distributor caps are retained by push-and-turn latches

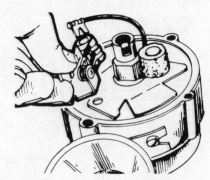

Install the point set on the breaker plate, then attach the wires

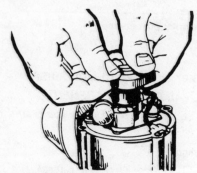

Pull the 6-250 rotor straight up to remove

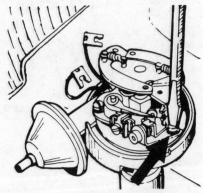

The points on all models are retained by screws; a magnetic or clamping type screwdriver can aid in avoiding dropping them

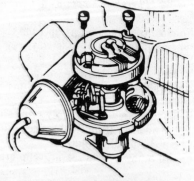

The V8 rotor is held on by two screws

primary and condenser lead wires to the contact point terminal.

8. Check the points for alignment. Contact surfaces must align with each other. If alignment is necessary, bend only the stationary contact support and not the movable one.

9. Using a flat feeler gauge, set the point opening at 0.019″ for new points, 0.016″ for used points. Observe the points while an assistant lightly activates the ignition switch. Turning the ignition key to the START position will rotate the distributor shaft and cause the points to open and close. When the points

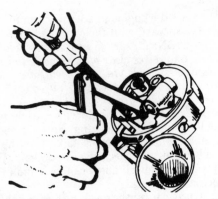

Use a screwdriver to spread or narrow the point gap on the 6-250

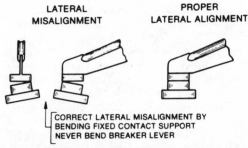

LATERAL MISALIGNMENT   PROPER LATERAL ALIGNMENT

CORRECT LATERAL MISALIGNMENT BY BENDING FIXED CONTACT SUPPORT NEVER BEND BREAKER LEVER

Check the points for proper alignment after installation

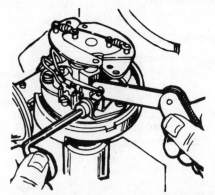

Use an Allen wrench to adjust the point gap on the V8

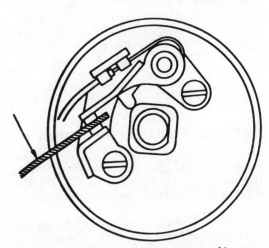

The arrow points to the feeler gauge used to measure point gap

open completely (this occurs when the rubbing block is resting on the high point of the cam lobe), TURN THE IGNITION KEY OFF and check the space between the open points. This space or gap should be 0.019" for new points. If

not, slightly loosen the point set mounting screw and, using a screwdriver to move the point support, adjust the gap until correct. Tighten the mounting screw.

10. Install the rotor and distributor cap.

11. Start the engine, check the dwell angle and then the ignition timing.

V8 Engines

NOTE: *The HEI (High Energy Ignition) used on some 1974 and all 1975 and later models requires no distributor maintenance other than checking the condition of the cap and wires. There are no points to wear out or adjust.*

Point alignment is preset at the factory and requires no adjustment. Point sets using the push-in type wiring terminal should be used on these distributors equipped with an R.F.I. (radio frequency interference) shield (1970-74). Points using a lockscrew type terminal may short out due to the shield contacting the screw.

1. Remove the distributor cap and rotor. The distributor is in the rear of small V8s, and in the front of the 455.

2. Remove the two attaching screws and remove the static shield.

3. Remove the two wiring terminals from the retainer.

4. Remove the mounting screws and lift out the points and condenser.

5. Install the new points and condenser and tighten the mounting screws.

6. Install the primary and condenser wires in the retainer. (Some people find it easier to reverse the above two steps and hook up the wires before they install the new points).

7. Check the cam lubricator to make sure it is not dry or worn out. It is supposed to be replaced every 12 months or 12,000 miles. Adjust it so that it just touches the cam lobes. Additional grease should not be applied to the lubricator.

8. Bump the engine over until the points are on the high side of the cam and check the point

gap. Adjust them to an initial setting of 0.016″. You'll need a ⅛″ allen wrench or a flexible adjusting tool.

9. Replace the static shield. If you leave it off, you won't be able to hear your radio.

10. Install the rotor, making sure the round peg goes in the round hole and the square peg goes in the square hole. Install the distributor cap.

11. Start the engine and check the point dwell and the ignition timing. On the 455 motor, it is impossible to set the dwell adjusting tool. These are available at any auto parts store. On the smaller V8s with the distributor in the back, it is possible to set the dwell with a short allen wrench, but it is much easier if you have the dwell adjusting tool.

Dwell Angle

Dwell angle is the amount of time (measured in degrees of distributor cam rotation) that the contact points in the distributor remain closed. Initial point gap determines dwell angle. If the points are set too wide, they open gradually and dwell angle (the time they remain closed) is small. This wide gap causes excessive arching at the points, and, because of this, point burning. This small dwell doesn't give the coil sufficient time to build up maximum energy and so coil output decreases. If the points are set too close, the dwell is increased, but the points may bounce at higher speeds and the idle becomes rough and starting is made harder. The wider the point opening, the smaller the dwell, and the smaller the point gap, the larger the dwell. Thus, a point gap of 0.019″ on a V8 engine might produce a dwell of 28°, while a gap of 0.016″ might produce a dwell of 34°. Adjusting the dwell by making the initial point gap setting with a feeler gauge is sufficient to get the car started, but a finer adjustment should be made. To make this adjustment, you need a dwell meter.

Dwell angle is permanently set electronically on HEI distributors, requiring no adjustment or checking.

ADJUSTMENT
6-Cylinder

1. Install the new points as outlined earlier.
2. Connect the dwell meter by hooking up one lead (usually black) to a good ground somewhere on the engine; connect the other lead (usually red) to the coil primary post. This is the one with the small wire that leads to the distributor.
3. If the dwell meter has a set line, adjust the meter needle until it rests on the line.

4. Start the engine and let it warm up. The dwell is checked with the engine idling.
   CAUTION: *Be sure to keep fingers, clothes, tools and wires clear of the engine fan. The transmission should be in Neutral or Park, parking brake set, and running in a well-ventilated area.*

5. Check the dwell angle with the engine at an idle. If it needs adjusting, shut the engine off, and readjust the point gap. Start the engine back up and check the dwell again. Both point gap and dwell angle can be found in the specifications chart.

6. Once you get the dwell correct, set the ignition timing. Remember that changing the dwell changes the ignition timing although changing the timing does not affect the dwell angle. Therefore, dwell angle adjustment must always be done before timing adjustment.

V8 Engines

1. After installing the points, hook up the dwell meter by connecting one lead (usually black) to a good ground and the other lead (usually red) to the distributor side of the coil If the dwell meter has a set line, adjust the needle until it rests on the line.

2. Start the engine and let it warm up. The engine should be idling at normal operating temperature when the dwell is set.

3. Raise the adjusting window on the distributor cap and insert a ⅛″ allen wrench into the adjusting screw. Better yet, use a long-handled flexible adjusting tool.

4. Turn the adjusting screw until the specified dwell angle is obtained on the dwell meter. On 455 motors, it is easier and safer to shut the engine off while you are making the adjustment.

5. Once the dwell is correct, adjust the ignition timing.

High Energy Ignition (HEI) System

The General Motors HEI system is a pulse-triggered, transistor-controlled, inductive discharge ignition system. The engine HEI system is contained within the distributor cap.

The distributor, in addition to housing the mechanical and vacuum advance mechanisms, contains the ignition coil (except on some inline six engines), the electronic control module, and the magnetic triggering device. The magnetic pick-up assembly contains a permanent magnet, a pole piece with internal teeth, and a pick-up coil (not to be confused with the ignition coil).

For 1981, an HEI distributor with Electronic Spark Timing is used (for more information on

EST, refer to Chapter 4). This system uses a one piece distributor with the ignition coil mounted in the distributor cap, similar to 1980.

All Spark timing changes in the 1981 distributors are done electronically by the Electronic Control Module (ECM) which monitors information from various engine sensors, computes the desired spark timing and then signals the distributor to change the timing accordingly. No vacuum or mechanical advance systems are used whatsoever.

In the HEI system, as in other electronic ignition systems, the breaker points have been replace with an electronic switch-a transistor-which is located within the control module. The switching transistor performs the same function the points did in a conventional ignition system; it simply turns coil primary current on and off at the correct time. Essen-

tially then, electronic and conventional ignition system operated on the same principle.

The module which houses the switching transistor is controlled (turned on and off) by a magnetically generated impulse induced in the pick-up coil. When the teeth of the rotating timber align with the teeth of the pole piece, the induced voltage in the pick-up coil signals the electronic module to open the coil primary circuit. The primary current then decreases, and a high voltage is induced in the ignition coil secondary windings which is then directed through the rotor and high voltage leads (spark plug wires) to fire the spark plugs.

In essence then, the pick-up coil module system simply replaces the conventional breaker points and condenser. The condenser found within the distributor is for radio suppression purposes only and has nothing to do with the ignition process. The module automatically

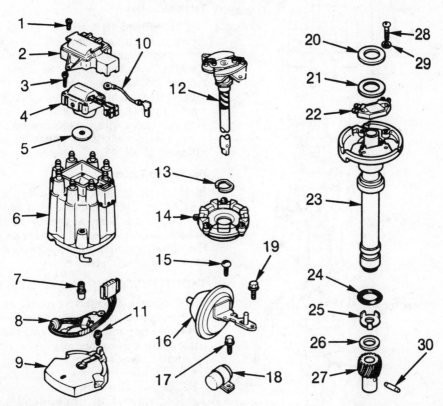

1. Cap cover attaching screw	11. Rotor screw	22. Module
2. Distributor cap cover	12. Distributor mainshaft	23. Distributor housing
3. Coil attaching screw	13. Pole piece and plate retainer	24. Housing stem washer
4. Distributor coil	14. Distributor pole piece and plate	25. Shaft spacer washer
5. Coil to distributor cap seal	15. Vacuum control attaching screw	26. Shaft thrust washer
6. Distributor cap	16. Distributor vacuum control	27. Distributor drive gear
7. Resistor brush	17, 18. Capacitor and attaching screw	28. Module attaching screw
8. Module coil harness	19. Vacuum control attaching screw	29. Washer
9. Distributor rotor	20. Felt washer	30. Gear attaching pin
10. Distributor ground lead	21. Distributor housing seal	

HEI Integral coil electronic ignition distributor

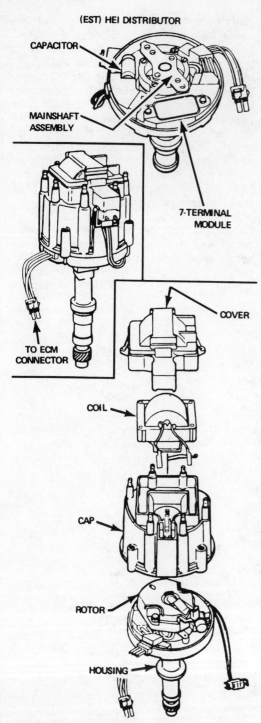

(EST) HEI DISTRIBUTOR

CAPACITOR

MAINSHAFT ASSEMBLY

7-TERMINAL MODULE

TO ECM CONNECTOR

COVER

COIL

CAP

ROTOR

HOUSING

HEI EST distributor components—1981 and later (note absence of vacuum advance unit)

controls the dwell period, increasing it with increasing engine speed. Since dwell is automatically controlled, it cannot be adjusted. The module itself is non-adjustable and non-repairable and must be replace if found defective.

HEI SYSTEM PRECAUTIONS

Before going on to troubleshooting, it might be a good idea to take note of the following precautions:

Timing Light Use

Inductive pick-up timing lights are the best kind to use with HEI. Timing lights which connect between the spark plug and the spark plug wire occasionally (not always) give false readings.

Spark Plug Wires

The plug wires used with HEI systems are of a different construction than conventional wires. When replacing them, make sure you get the correct wires, since conventional wires won't carry the voltage. Also, handle them careful to avoid cracking or splitting them and never pierce them.

Tachometer Use

Not all tachometers will operate or indicate correctly when used on a HEI system. While some tachometers may give a reading, this does not necessarily mean the reading is correct. In addition, some tachometers hook up differently from others. If you can't figure out whether or not your tachometers will work on your car, check with the tachometer manufacturer. Dwell readings, of course, have no significance at all.

HEI System Testers

Instruments designed specifically for testing HEI systems are available from several tool manufacturers. Some of these will even test the module itself. However, the tests given in the following section will require only an ohmmeter and a voltmeter.

TROUBLESHOOTING THE HEI SYSTEM

The symptoms of a defective component within the HEI system are exactly the same as those you would encounter in a conventional system. Some of these symptoms are:
- Hard or No Starting
- Rough Idle
- Poor Fuel Economy
- Engine misses under load or while accelerating

If you suspect a problem in you ignition system, there are certain preliminary checks which you should carry out before you begin to check the electronic portions of the system. First, it is extremely important to make sure the vehicle battery is in a good state of charge. A defective or poorly charged battery will cause the various components of the ignition system to read incorrectly when they are being tested. Second, make sure all wiring connections are clean and tight, not only at the battery, but also at the distributor cap, ignition coil and at the electronic control module.

Since the only change between electronic and conventional ignition systems is in the distributor component area, it is imperative to check the secondary ignition circuit first. If the secondary circuit checks out properly, then the engine condition is probably not the fault of the ignition system. To check the secondary ignition system, perform a simple spark test. Remove one of the plug wires and insert some sort of extension in the plug socket. An old spark plug with the ground electrode removed make a good extension. Hold the wire and extension about ¼" away from the block and crank the engine.

CAUTION: *Its a good idea to wear heavy gloves at this time.*

If a normal spark occurs, then the problem is most likely not in the ignition system. Check for fuel system problems, or fouled spark plugs.

If, however, their is no spark or a weak spark, then further ignition system testing will have to be done. Troubleshooting techniques fall into two categories, depending on the nature of the problem. The categories are (1) Engine cranks, but won't start or (2) Engine runs, but runs rough or cuts out. To begin with, let's consider the first case.

Engine Fails to Start

If the engine won't start, perform a spark test as described earlier. This will narrow the problem area down considerably. If no spark occurs, check for the presence of normal battery voltage at the battery (BAT) terminal in the distributor cap. The ignition switch must be in the on position for this test. Either a voltmeter or a test light may be used for this test. Connect the test light wire to ground and the probe end at the BAT terminal at the distributor. If the light comes on, you have voltage to the distributor. If the light fails to come on, this indicates an open circuit in the ignition primary wiring leading to the distributor. In this case, you will have to check wiring continuity back to the ignition switch using a test light. If there is battery voltage at the BAT terminal, but no spark at the plugs, then the problem lies within the distributor assembly. Go on to the distributor components test section.

Engine Runs, But Runs Rough or Cuts Out

1. Make sure the plug wires are in good shape first. There should be no obvious cracks or breads. You can check the plug wires with

HEI Plug Wire Resistance Chart

Wire Length	Minimum	Maximum
0–15 inches	3000 ohms	10,000 ohms
15–25 inches	4000 ohms	15,000 ohms
25–35 inches	6000 ohms	20,000 ohms
Over 35 inches		25,000 ohms

an ohmmeter, but do not pierce the wires with a probe. Check the chart for the correct plug wire resistance.

2. If the plug wires are OK, remove the cap assembly and check for moisture, cracks, chips or carbon tracks, or any other high voltage leaks or failures. Replace the cap if any defects are found. Make sure the timer wheel rotates when the engine is cranked. If everything is all right so far, go on to the distributor components test section following.

DISTRIBUTOR COMPONENTS TESTING

If the trouble has been narrowed down to the units within the distributor, the following tests can help pinpoint the defective component. An ohmmeter with both high and low ranges should be used. These tests are made with the cap assembly removed. and the battery wire disconnected. If a tachometer is connected to the TACH terminal, disconnect it before making these tests.

1. Connect a ohmmeter between the TACH and BAT terminals in the distributor cap. The primary coil resistance should be less than one ohm.

2. To check the coil secondary resistance, connect an ohmmeter between the rotor button and the BAT terminal. Note the reading. Connect the ohmmeter between the rotor button and the TACH terminal. Note the reading. The resistance in both cases should be between 6,000 and 30,000 ohms. Be sure to test between the rotor button and both the BAT and TACH terminals.

3. Replace the coil only if the readings in Step 1 and Step 2 are infinite.

NOTE: *These resistance checks will not disclose shorted coil windings. This condition can only be detected with scope analysis or a suitably designed coil tester. If these instruments are unavailable, replace the coil with a known good coil as a final coil test.*

4. To test the pick-up coil, first disconnect the white and green module leads. Set the ohmmeter on the high scale and connect it between a ground and either the white or green lead. Any resistance measurement less than

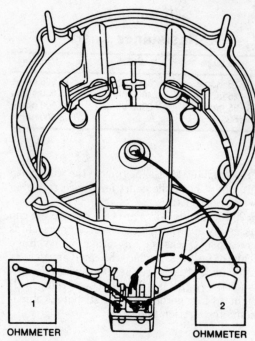

Ohmmeter 1 shows the primary coil resistance connection. Ohmmeter 2 shows the secondary resistance connection (1980 shown, most models similar)

infinity requires replacement of the pick-up coil.

5. Pick-up coil continuity is tested by connecting the ohmmeter (on low range) between the white and green leads. Normal resistance is between 650 and 850 ohms, or 500 and 1500 ohms on 1977 and later models. Move the vacuum advance arm while performing this test. This will detect any break in coil continuity. Such a condition can cause intermittent misfiring. Replace the pick-up coil if the reading is outside the specified limits.

6. If no defects have been found at this time, and you still have a problem, then the module will have to be checked. If you do not have access to a module tester, the only possible alternative is a substitution test. If the module fails the substitution test, replace it.

HEI SYSTEM MAINTENANCE

Except for periodic checks of the spark plug wires, and an occasional check of the distributor cap for cracks (see Steps 1 and 2 under Engine Runs, But Runs Rough or Cuts Out for details), no maintenance is required on the HEI system. No periodic lubrication is necessary; engine oil lubricates the lower bushing, and an oil-filled reservoir lubricates the upper bushing.

COMPONENT REPLACEMENT

Integral Ignition Coil

1. Disconnect the feed and module wire terminal connectors from the distributor cap.
2. Remove the ignition set retainer.
3. Remove the 4 coil cover-to-distributor cap screws and coil cover.
4. Remove the 4 coil-to-distributor cap screws.
5. Using a blunt drift, press the coil wire spade terminals up out of the distributor cap.
6. Lift the coil up out of the distributor cap.
7. Remove and clean the coil spring, rubber seal washer and coil cavity of the distributor cap.
8. Coat the rubber seal with a dielectric lubricant furnished in the replacement ignition coil package.
9. Reverse the above procedures to install.

Distributor Cap

1. Remove the feed and module wire terminal connectors from the distributor cap.
2. Remove the retainer and spark plug wires from the cap.
3. Depress and release the 4 distributor cap-to-housing retainers and lift off the cap assembly.
4. Remove the 4 coil cover screws and cover.
5. Using a finger or a blunt drift, push the spade terminals up out of the distributor cap.
6. Remove all 4 coil screws and lift the coil, coil spring and rubber seal washer out of the cap coil cavity.
7. Using a new distributor cap, reverse the above procedures to assemble being sure to clean and lubricate the rubber seal washer with dielectric lubricant.

Rotor

1. Disconnect the feed and module wire connectors from the distributor.
2. Depress and release the 4 distributor cap-to-housing retainers and lift off the cap assembly.
3. Remove the two rotor attaching screws and rotor.
4. Reverse the above procedure to install.

Vacuum Advance

1. Remove the distributor cap and rotor as previously described.
2. Disconnect the vacuum hose from the vacuum advance unit.
3. Remove the two vacuum advance retaining screws, pull the advance unit outward, rotate and disengage the operating rod from its tang.
4. Reverse the above procedure to install.

Module

1. Remove the distributor cap and rotor as previously described.

2. Disconnect the harness connector and pick-up coil spade connectors from the module. Be careful not to damage the wires when removing the connector.

3. Remove the two screws and module from the distributor housing.

4. Coat the bottom of the new module with electric lubricant supplied with the new module. Reverse the above procedure to install.

HEI SYSTEM TACHOMETER HOOKUP

There is a terminal marked TACH on the distributor cap. Connect one tachometer lead to this terminal and the other lead to a ground. On some tachometers, the leads must be connected to the TACH terminal and to the battery positive terminal.

CAUTION: *Never ground the TACH terminal; serious module and ignition coil damage will result. If their is any doubt as to the correct tachometer hookup, check with the tachometer manufacturer.*

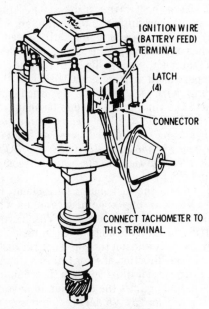

IGNITION WIRE
(BATTERY FEED)
TERMINAL

LATCH
(4)

CONNECTOR

CONNECT TACHOMETER TO
THIS TERMINAL

Tachometer connection for the HEI system

Tachometer Hook-Up-Diesel Engine

A magnetic pickup tachometer is necessary because of the lack of an ignition system. The tachometer probe is inserted into the hole in the timing indicator.

Ignition Timing

Ignition timing is the measurement, in degrees of crankshaft rotation, of the point at which the spark plugs fire in each of the cylinders. It is measured in degrees before or after Top Dead Center (TDC) of the compression stroke.

Because it takes a fraction of a second for the spark plug to ignite the mixture in the cylinder, the spark plug must fire a little before the piston reaches TDC. Otherwise, the mixture will not be completely ignited as the piston passes TDC and the full power of the explosion will not be used by the engine.

The timing measurement is given in degrees of crankshaft rotation before the piston reaches TDC (BTDC). If the setting for the ignition timing is 5° BTDC, the spark plug must fire 5° before each piston reaches TDC. This only holds true, however, when the engine is at idle speed.

As the engine speed increases, the pistons go faster. The spark plugs have to ignite the fuel even sooner if it is to be completely ignited when the piston reaches TDC. To do this, the distributor has two means to advance the timing of the spark as the engine speed increases. This is accomplished by centrifugal weights within the distributor, and a vacuum diaphragm mounted on the side of the distributor.

If the ignition is set too far advanced (BTDC), the ignition and expansion of the fuel in the cylinder will occur too soon and tend to force the piston down while it is still traveling up. This causes engine ping. If the ignition spark is set too far retarded, after TDC (ATDC), the piston will have already passed TDC and started on its way down when the fuel is ignited. This will cause the piston to be forced down for only a portion of its travel. This will result in poor engine performance and lack of power.

Timing marks consist of a notch on the rim of the crankshaft pulley and a scale of degrees attached to the front of the engine. The notch corresponds to the position of the piston in the number 1 cylinder. A stroboscropic (dynamic) timing light is used, which is hooked into the circuit of the No. 1 cylinder spark plug. Every time the spark plug fires, the timing light flashes. By aiming the timing light at the timing marks, the exact position of the piston within the cylinder can be read, since the stroboscropic flash makes the mark on the pulley appear to be standing still. Proper timing is indicated when the notch is aligned with the correct number on the scale.

There are three basic types of timing lights available. The first is a simple neon bulb with two wire connections (one for the spark plug and one for the plug wire, connecting the light in series). This type of light is quite dim, and must be held closely to the marks to be seen,

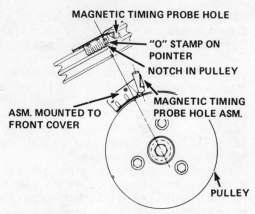

MAGNETIC TIMING PROBE HOLE

"O" STAMP ON POINTER

NOTCH IN PULLEY

ASM. MOUNTED TO FRONT COVER

MAGNETIC TIMING PROBE HOLE ASM.

PULLEY

Magnetic timing probe hole (diesel engines)

but it is quite inexpensive. The second type of light operates from the car's battery. Two alligator clips connect to the battery terminals, while a third wire connects to the spark plug with a adapter. This type of light is more expensive, but the xenon bulb provides a nice bright flash which can even be seen in sunlight. The third type replace the battery source with 110 volt house current. Some timing lights have other functions built into them, such as dwell meters, tachometers, or remote starting switches. These are convenient, in that they reduce the tangle of wires under the hood, but may duplicate the functions of tools you already have.

If your car has electronic ignition, you should use a timing light with an inductive pickup. This pickup simply clamps onto the NO.1 spark plug wire, eliminating the adapter. It is not susceptible to crossfiring or false triggering, which may occur with a conventional light, due to the greater voltages produce by electronic ignition.

CHECKING AND ADJUSTMENT

1. Warm the engine to normal operating temperature. Shut off the engine and connect the timing light to the No. 1 spark plug (left front). do not, under any circumstances, pierce a wire to hook up a light.

2. Clean off the timing marks and mark the pulley or damper notch and the timing scale with white chalk or paint. The timing notch on the damper or pulley can be elusive. Bump the engine around with the starter or turn the crankshaft with a wrench on the front pulley bolt to get it to an accessible position.

3. Disconnect and plug the vacuum advance hose at the distributor, to prevent any distributor advance. The vacuum line is the rubber hose connected to the metal cone-shaped canister on the side of the distributor. A short screw,

pencil, or a golf tee can be used to plug the hose.

NOTE: *1981 and later models with Electronic Spark Timing have no vacuum advance, therefore you may skip the previous step, but you must disconnect the four terminal EST connector before going on.*

4. Start the engine and adjust the idle speed to the specified in the Tune-Up Specifications chart. Some cars require that the timing be set with the transmission in Neutral. You can disconnect the idle solenoid, if any, to get the speed down. Otherwise, adjust the idle speed screw. This is to prevent any centrifugal advance of timing in the distributor.

On HEI systems, the tachometer connects to the TACH terminal on the distributor. Some tachometers must connect to the TACH terminal and to the positive battery terminal. Some tachometers won't work at all with HEI. Consult the tachometer manufacturer if the instructions supplied with the unit do not give the proper connection.

CAUTION: *Never ground the HEI TACH terminal; serious system damage will result, including module burnout.*

5. Aim the timing light at the timing marks. Be careful not to touch the fan, which may appear to be standing still. Keep you clothes and hair, and the light's wires clear of the fan, belt, and pulleys. If the pulley or damper notch isn't aligned with the proper timing mark (see the Tune-Up Specifications chart), the timing will have to be adjusted.

NOTE: *TDC or Top Dead Center corresponds to 0; BTDC, or Before Top Dead Center, may be shown as BEFORE; A, or ATDC, or After Top Dead Center, may be shown as AFTER.*

6. Loosen the distributor base clamp locknut. You can buy special wrenches which make this task a lot easier on V8s. Turn the distributor slowly to adjust the timing, holding it by the body and not the cap. Turn the distributor in the direction of rotor rotation (found in the Firing Order illustration in this chapter) to retard, and against the direction to advance.

NOTE: *The 231 V6 engine has two timing marks on the crankshaft pulley. One timing mark is 1/8" wide and the other, four inches away, is 1/16" wide. The smaller mark is used for setting the timing with a hand-held timing light. The larger mark is used with the magnetic probe and is only of use to a dealer or garage. Make sure you set the timing using the smaller mark.*

7. Tighten the locknut. Check the timing, in case the distributor moved as you tightened it.

8. Replace the distributor vacuum hose, if removed. Correct the idle speed.

9. Shut off the engine and disconnect the light.

Valve Lash

Hydraulic valve lifters rarely require adjustment, and are not adjusted as part of a normal tune-up. The valves on most engines cannot be adjusted. If there is excessive clearance in the valve train, look for worn push rods, rocker arms, valve springs or collapsed or stuck lifters. Chevrolet engines require initial lash adjustment whenever rocker arms are removed. (See Chapter Three)

Idle Speed and Mixture Adjustment

NOTE: *For idle speed adjustments on the diesel engines refer to the Diesel Engine Fuel System in Chapter 4.*

1970 1 bbl.

1. Remove the air cleaner and run the engine until it reaches normal operating temperature.

2. Apply the parking brake and set blocks in front and in back of the wheels.

3. Make sure that the choke plate is fully open, and the fast idle cam follower is off the cam. If the car has an air conditioner, make sure it is off.

4. Disconnect the air vacuum hose from the base of the carburetor and plug the fitting. Disconnect the vacuum advance hose from the distributor and plug the end of the hose. Plug the carburetor hot idle compensator.

5. If the car has an automatic transmission, place the selector lever in Drive. If the car has a manual transmission, put it in neutral.

6. Make sure that the solenoid wire is connected, and the throttle stop screw is not touching the throttle lever.

7. Adjust the idle mixture to obtain the highest possible rpm. Then adjust the throttle solenoid plunger to obtain an idle speed 25 rpm above the higher of the two idle speeds listed in the tune-up specifications chart.

8. Turn the idle mixture screw inward to lower the idle speed to the correct rpm.

9. The lower idle speed is adjusted next. Disconnect the solenoid wire and adjust the throttle stop screw to obtain the lower of the two idle speeds shown in the chart.

10. Re-connect all the hoses and replace the air cleaner.

1971 and 1975-76 1 bbl.

NOTE: *1971 and some later models are equipped with a Combination Emission Control (CEC) solenoid. This solenoid does not function as an idle speed solenoid, and*

should not be adjusted during a routing carburetor adjustment.

1. Set the parking brake and block the drive wheels.

2. Start the engine and run it to normal operating temperature. Make sure that the choke is fully open before you make any adjustments.

3. You can set the idle solenoid with the air cleaner removed, but Oldsmobile states that the air cleaner must be in place to set the idle mixture.

4. Disconnect the fuel tank hose from the vapor canister, and disconnect the EGR valve hose.

5. Disconnect the distributor vacuum hoses from the CEC solenoid and plug the hose leading to the carburetor.

6. Make sure the air conditioner is turned off if the car has one, and that the dwell and timing are correct. If the car has an automatic transmission, it should be in Drive. Manual transmission cars should be in neutral.

7. Connect a tachometer to the engine if you haven't already.

8. On 1971 models, set the correct idle speed by turning the idle speed adjusting screw. Since this carburetor has a CEC solenoid instead of a throttle solenoid, no other adjustment is possible. The idle mixture is set the same as later model carburetors.

9. On later model carburetors (75-76), turn the throttle stop solenoid inward or outward to obtain the higher of the two idle speeds listed in the tune-up chart.

10. Disconnect the solenoid wire and insert a 1/8" allen wrench into the end of the solenoid to obtain the lower of the two listed idle speeds. If the car is equipped with an automatic transmission, this adjustment should be made with the transmission in Park.

11. To set the idle mixture, increase the idle speed to about 1,000 rpm over the specified setting and then cut the tab off the limiter cap. Turn the mixture screw counterclockwise until the maximum possible rpm is reached. Then reset the idle speed to 100 rpm over the specified (with the idle speed screw, not the mixture screw).

12. Turn the idle mixture screw clockwise until the idle speed reaches the specified setting.

NOTE: *Idle mixture is set at the factory, which is why the mixture screws are capped. If you richen the mixture, you alter the emission levels. Normally, idle mixture does not need adjusting. If, however, you adjust your idle mixture, you should take your car to a dealership or a garage where the emission level can be checked with a CO meter.*

1970-74 2 bbl.

1. After making sure that the dwell and timing are correct, remove the air cleaner and disconnect and plug the air cleaner hose at the intake manifold.

2. Start the engine and let it warm up. Make sure the choke is open and the air conditioner if off. Set the parking brake and block the drive wheels.

3. Disconnect the hoses from the vapor canister and plug them. Disconnect the EGR valve hose if the car has an EGR valve and plug it. 1973 and later cars will have an EGR valve.

4. Disconnect the vacuum advance line from the distributor and plug it.

5. On models with a throttle solenoid or vacuum actuator, turn the solenoid plunger inward or outward to obtain the higher of the two idle speeds listed in the tune-up chart. After this adjustment has been made, disconnect the electric lead from the solenoid or the vacuum hose from the vacuum actuator. Plug the vacuum hose after disconnecting it. If the car is equipped with an automatic transmission, place the transmission in Park. Adjust the throttle stop screw to obtain an idle speed which corresponds with the lower of the two idle speeds listed in the tune-up specifications chart.

6. To adjust the idle mixture, turn the engine off and turn the idle mixture screws inward until they are lightly seated.

7. Back out the mixture screws six full turns and then start the engine.

8. With the engine running, adjust the screws equally to obtain the highest possible idle speed.

NOTE: *Idle mixture screws have been preset at the factory and capped. Remove the caps only in the case of major overhaul, throttle body removal, or when all other possible causes of poor idle condition have been thoroughly checked. If you find it necessary to adjust the idle mixture, have the CO concentration checked by a dealer or garage with a CO meter.*

9. Reset the idle speed to specifications with the idle speed screw or the idle solenoid.

10. Install new idle limiter caps.

1970-74 4 bbl.

1. After marking sure that the dwell and timing are correct, remove the air cleaner and disconnect and plug the air cleaner hose at the intake manifold.

2. Start the engine and let it warm up. Make sure the choke is open and the air conditioner is off. Set the parking brake and block the wheels.

3. On 1973-74 models, disconnect and plug the vapor canister hoses. Disconnect the EGR valve and plug the hose on all models.

4. Disconnect and plug the distributor vacuum hose at the distributor.

5. On models without a throttle solenoid or vacuum actuator, turn the idle speed adjusting screw inward or outward to obtain the idle speed listed in the specifications.

6. On models with a throttle solenoid or vacuum actuator, turn the solenoid plunger inward or outward to obtain the higher of the two idle speeds listed in the specifications. After this adjustment has been made, disconnect the electric lead from the solenoid or the vacuum hose from the vacuum actuator. Plug the vacuum hose after disconnecting it. On models with an automatic transmission, place the transmission in Park. Adjust the throttle stop screw to obtain an idle speed which corresponds to the lower of the two idle speeds listed in the specifications.

7. To adjust the idle mixture, shut the engine off, break the tabs off the limiter caps and turn the idle mixture screws inward until they are lightly seated.

NOTE: *Idle mixture screws have been preset at the factory and capped. Remove the caps only in the case of major overhaul, throttle body removal, or when all other possible causes of poor idle condition have been thoroughly checked. If you find it necessary to adjust the idle mixture, have the CO concentration checked by a dealer or garage with a CO meter.*

8. Back out the idle mixture screws six full turns, then start the engine and adjust the screws equally to obtain the highest possible idle.

9. If necessary, reset the idle speed to specifications with the idle speed screw or the idle solenoid.

10. Install new idle limiter caps.

1975-76 V6 and V8

NOTE: *Idle speed and mixture must be set with the engine at normal operating temperature, the air conditioner OFF, the air cleaner on, and the transmission in Drive.*

1. Set the parking brake and block the wheels.

2. Disconnect the evaporative emission hose at the air cleaner. Disconnect and plug the distributor vacuum line at the distributor. Disconnect and plug the EGR vacuum line at the EGR valve on all 1976 V6s.

3. Adjust the idle speed to that specification in the Tune Up Specifications chart. First adjust the idle speed screw with the solenoid disconnect to get the lower speed, then adjust the

solenoid screw with the solenoid connect to get the higher speed on models so equipped. If there is no solenoid, adjust he idle speed with the idle speed screw.

4. Cut the tabs off the mixture screw caps then turn them out to obtain the maximum idle speed.

5. Using the solenoid screw (if equipped), or the idle speed screw, adjust the idle speed to the higher speed specified on the underhood sticker, which is usually 60-100 rpm above the normal idle speed.

6. Turn in the mixture screws equally until the engine returns to the normal idle speed. On the V6, reset the idle speed with the solenoid deenergized, if necessary.

7. Reconnect all the hoses removed in Step 2.

1977

NOTE: *Engines produced by several GM divisions are used. The vehicle emission control information sticker in the engine compartment should be checked for the individual engine specifications.*

1. With the engine at normal operating temperature, set the parking brake and block the wheels.

2. Remove the air cleaner to gain access to the idle air screws, but leave the vacuum lines connected.

3. Disconnect and plug the other vacuum lines as indicated by the emission control sticker.

4. Connect a tachometer and timing light to the engine, and if necessary, adjust the ignition timing to specifications. Disconnect the vacuum advance line, if directed by the instructions on the emission control sticker.

5. Carefully remove the idle mixture screw limiter caps. Lightly seat the screws by turning them into the carburetor base, and then back the screws out equally until the engine will run without stalling.

6. If the car has automatic transmission, place the selector lever in Drive.

7. Back out the idle mixture screws, 1/8 of a turn at a time, until the maximum idle speed is obtained.

8. Adjust the engine idle speed to 25-50 rpm over the specified low rpm setting. Repeat step 7, if necessary.

NOTE: *Two idle speed adjustments are normally required. One is the normal rpm setting, controlled by the adjustment of the electric solenoid screw, and the second adjustment, or low setting, is controlled by a screw on the carburetor throttle shaft lever. If the car has air conditioning, the solenoid may be used as an idle speed up control. To deter-*

mine the type used, turn the air conditioning on; if the engine idle speed increases, the solenoid is used as a speedup device. The idle speed setting is then adjusted by the screw on the throttle shaft lever.*

9. Turn each screw in, 1/8 of a turn at a time, until the idle speed reaches the specified idle rpm.

10. Reset the idle speed.

11. Connect all the vacuum lines and install the air cleaner. Recheck the idle speed and correct as necessary.

Idle Speed

1978 2 GC, 2 GE Carburetor

1. Run the engine to normal operating temperature. Make sure that the choke is fully opened, set the parking brake, block the drive wheels, turn the air conditioning Off and connect a tachometer to the engine according to the manufacturer's instructions.

2. Disconnect and plug the vacuum hoses at the vapor canister and EGR valve.

3. Place the transmission in Park (AT) or Neutral (MT).

4. Disconnect and plug the vacuum advance hose at the distributor. Set the ignition timing.

5. Reconnect the vacuum advance hose and turn the idle speed screw to obtain the specified rpm.

6. Connect all hoses and remove the tachometer.

1978-80 M2ME/M2MC/E2ME-210 Carburetor

1. Run the engine to normal operating temperature.

2. Make sure that the choke is fully opened, set the parking brake, block the wheels, connect a tachometer to the engine according to the manufacturer's instructions, disconnect the compressor clutch wire, turn the A/C Off, place the transmission in Drive, and disconnect and plug the vacuum advance hose at the distributor.

NOTE: *If instructions on car's underhood sticker differ from these, follow underhood sticker.*

3. Set the ignition timing, if necessary.

4. Reconnect the vacuum advance hose.

5. Disconnect the purge hose at the vapor canister.

6. On cars without A/C: set the idle speed by turning the idle screw to obtain the specified rpm. On cars with A/C: set the idle speed screw to the specified rpm. Turn the A/C on. Open the throttle momentarily to extend the solenoid plunger, then adjust the solenoid screw to obtain the solenoid idle speed shown on the underhood sticker. Turn the A/C off.

7. Connect all hoses, and remove the tachometer.

1978-80 M4MC-M4ME Carburetor

1. Run the engine to normal operating temperature.

2. Make sure that the choke is fully opened, turn the A/C Off, set the parking brake and block the wheels.

3. Connect a tachometer to the engine according to the manufacturer's instructions.

4. Disconnect the purge hose from the vapor canister. On the 350, plug the purge hose.

5. Disconnect and plug the EGR vacuum hose at the valve. Disconnect and plug the vacuum advance hose.

6. Place the transmission in Park.

7. Check and adjust the timing.

8. Reconnect the vacuum advance hose.

9. Place the transmission in Drive.

NOTE: *If instructions on the underhood sticker differ from these, follow underhood sticker.*

10. On cars without A/C: Turn the idle speed screw to obtain the specified rpm.

On cars with A/C: Turn the idle speed screw to set the specified curb idle speed. Turn the A/C ON and disconnect the compressor clutch wire. Open the throttle momentarily to extend the solenoid plunger. Adjust the solenoid screw to obtain the solenoid idle speed shown on the underhood sticker. Reconnect the compressor clutch and turn the A/C Off.

11. Reconnect all hoses and remove the tachometer.

1981 and Later.

Most 1981 and later models are equipped with an Idle Speed Control (ISC) mounted on the float bowl. Idle speeds are computer controlled and the ICS should not be adjusted.

On some V8 models an Idle Load Compensator (ILC) is mounted on the float bowl to control the curb idle speed. The ILC is adjusted at the factory and capped to prevent readjustment. If an idle problem is suspected on either

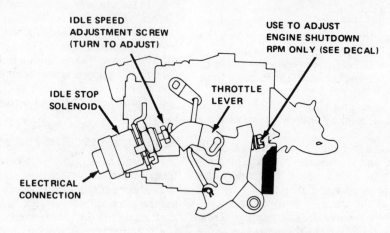

IDLE SPEED ADJUSTMENT SCREW (TURN TO ADJUST)

USE TO ADJUST ENGINE SHUTDOWN RPM ONLY (SEE DECAL)

IDLE STOP SOLENOID

THROTTLE LEVER

ELECTRICAL CONNECTION

(MODELS NOT EQUIPPED WITH A/C)

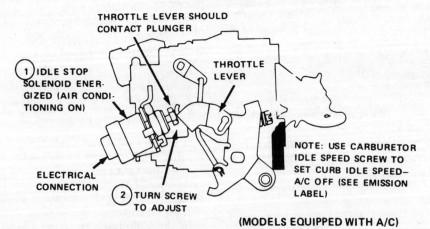

THROTTLE LEVER SHOULD CONTACT PLUNGER

1 IDLE STOP SOLENOID ENERGIZED (AIR CONDITIONING ON)

THROTTLE LEVER

ELECTRICAL CONNECTION

2 TURN SCREW TO ADJUST

NOTE: USE CARBURETOR IDLE SPEED SCREW TO SET CURB IDLE SPEED— A/C OFF (SEE EMISSION LABEL)

(MODELS EQUIPPED WITH A/C)

Typical 2 bbl idle speed adjustment locations

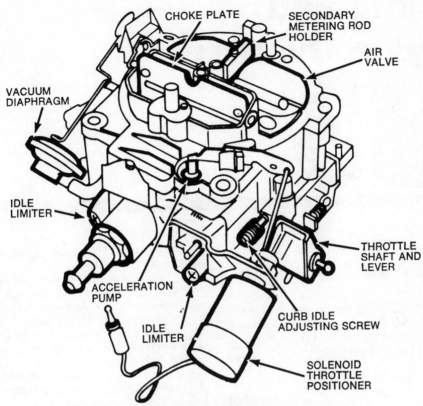

CHOKE PLATE

SECONDARY
METERING ROD
HOLDER

AIR
VALVE

VACUUM
DIAPHRAGM

IDLE
LIMITER

THROTTLE
SHAFT AND
LEVER

ACCELERATION
PUMP

IDLE
LIMITER

CURB IDLE
ADJUSTING SCREW

SOLENOID
THROTTLE
POSITIONER

Typical 4 bbl idle speed adjustment locations

of the above systems it is recommended that it be corrected by a qualified technician.

On cars that do not include either an ISC or ILC, but are equipped with air conditioning, an idle speed solenoid is used to maintain idle speed. For adjustment of these models refer to the 1978-80 adjustment procedures.

NOTE: *The underhood sticker specifies which idle system your car is equipped with.*

Idle Mixture Adjustment

1978-80

Changes in the carburetors for 1978-80 cars have made the adjustment of idle mixture im-possible without the use of a propane enrich-ment system not available to the general pub-lic. Backing out the mixture screw, of itself, will have little or no effect on the mixture. Most 1979 and later carburetors have mixture screws concealed by staked-in plugs. Mixture adjustments are possible only during carbure-tor overhaul.

1981 and Later

On these models the air/fuel mixture is con-trolled by the electronic control module of the computer command control system. No adjust-ment should be attempted.

Engine and Engine Overhaul

3

ENGINE ELECTRICAL

Understanding the Engine Electrical System

The engine electrical system can be broken down into three separate and distinct systems-(1) the starting system; (2) the charging system; (3) the ignition system.

BATTERY AND STARTING SYSTEM

The battery is the first link in the chain of mechanisms which work together to provide cranking of the automobile engine. In most modern cars, the battery is a lead-acid electro--chemical device consisting of six two-volt (2 V) subsections connected in series so the unit is capable of producing approximately 12 V of electrical pressure. Each subsection, or cell, consists of a series of positive and negative plates held a short distance apart in a solution of sulfuric acid and water. The two types of plates are of dissimilar metals. This causes a chemical reaction to be set up, and it is this re-action which produces current flow from the battery when its positive and negative terminals are connected to an electrical appliance such as a lamp or motor. The continued transfer of electrons would eventually convert the sulfuric acid in the electrolyte to water, and make the two plates identical in chemical composition. As electrical energy is removed from the battery, its voltage output tends to drop. Thus, measuring battery voltage and battery electrolyte composition are two ways of checking the ability of the unit to supply power. During the starting of the engine, electrical energy is removed from the battery. However, if the charging circuit is in good condition and the operating conditions are normal, the power removed from the battery will be replaced by the generator (or alternator) which will force electrons back through the battery, reversing the normal flow, and restoring the battery to its original chemical state.

The battery and starting motor are linked by very heavy electrical cables designed to minimize resistance to the flow of current. Generally, the major power supply cable that leaves the battery goes directly to the starter, while other electrical system needs are supplied by a smaller cable. During the starter operation, power flows from the battery to the starter and is grounded through the car's frame and the battery's negative ground strap.

The starting motor is specially designed, direct current electric motor capable of producing a very great amount of power for its size. One thing that allows the motor to produce a great deal of power is its tremendous rotating speed. It drives the engine through a tiny pinion gear (attached to the starter's armature), which drives the very large flywheel ring gear at a greatly reduced speed. Another factor allowing it to produce so much power is that only intermittent operation is required of it. Thus, little allowance for air circulation is required, and the windings can be built into a very small space.

The starter solenoid is a magnetic device which employs the small current supplied by the starting switch circuit of the ignition switch. This magnetic action moves a plunger which mechanically engages the starter and electrically closes the heavy switch which connect it to the battery. The starting switch circuit consists of the starting switch contained within the ignition switch, a transmission neutral safety switch or clutch pedal switch, and the wiring necessary to connect these with the starter solenoid or relay.

A pinion, which is a small gear, is mounted to a one-way drive clutch. This clutch is splined to the starter armature shaft. When the ignition switch is moved to the start position, the solenoid plunger slides the pinion toward the flywheel ring gear via a collar and spring. If the teeth on the pinion and flywheel match properly, the pinion will engage the flywheel immediately. If the gear teeth butt one another, the spring will be compressed and will force the gears to mesh as soon as the starter turns far enough to allow them to do so. As the solenoid plunger reaches the end of its travel, it closes the contacts that connect the battery and starter and then the engine is cranked.

As soon as the engine starts, the flywheel ring gear begins turning fast enough to drive the pinion at an extremely high rate of speed. At this point, the one-way clutch begins allowing the pinion to spin faster than the starter shaft so that the starter will not operate at excessive speed. When the ignition switch is released from the starter position, the solenoid is de-energized, and a spring contained within the solenoid assembly pulls the gear out of the mesh and interrupts the current flow to the starter.

Some starters employ a separate relay, mounted away from the starter, to switch the motor and solenoid current on and off. The relay thus replaced the solenoid electrical switch, but does not eliminate the need for a solenoid mounted on the starter used to mechanically engage the starter drive gears. The relay is used to reduce the amount of current the starting switch must carry.

THE CHARGING SYSTEM

The automobile charging system provides electrical power for operation of the vehicle's ignition and starting systems and all the electrical

Troubleshooting Basic Starting System Problems

Problem	Cause	Solution
Starter motor rotates engine slowly	• Battery charge low or battery defective	• Charge or replace battery
	• Defective circuit between battery and starter motor	• Clean and tighten, or replace cables
	• Low load current	• Bench-test starter motor. Inspect for worn brushes and weak brush springs.
	• High load current	• Bench-test starter motor. Check engine for friction, drag or coolant in cylinders. Check ring gear-to-pinion gear clearance.
Starter motor will not rotate engine	• Battery charge low or battery defective	• Charge or replace battery
	• Faulty solenoid	• Check solenoid ground. Repair or replace as necessary.
	• Damage drive pinion gear or ring gear	• Replace damaged gear(s)
	• Starter motor engagement weak	• Bench-test starter motor
	• Starter motor rotates slowly with high load current	• Inspect drive yoke pull-down and point gap, check for worn end bushings, check ring gear clearance
	• Engine seized	• Repair engine
Starter motor drive will not engage (solenoid known to be good)	• Defective contact point assembly	• Repair or replace contact point assembly
	• Inadequate contact point assembly ground	• Repair connection at ground screw
	• Defective hold-in coil	• Replace field winding assembly
Starter motor drive will not disengage	• Starter motor loose on flywheel housing	• Tighten mounting bolts
	• Worn drive end busing	• Replace bushing
	• Damaged ring gear teeth	• Replace ring gear or driveplate
	• Drive yoke return spring broken or missing	• Replace spring
Starter motor drive disengages prematurely	• Weak drive assembly thrust spring	• Replace drive mechanism
	• Hold-in coil defective	• Replace field winding assembly
Low load current	• Worn brushes	• Replace brushes
	• Weak brush springs	• Replace springs

accessories. The battery serves as an electrical surge or storage tank, storing (in chemical form) the energy originally produced by the engine-driven generator. The system also provides a means of regulating generator output to protect the battery from being overcharged and to avoid excessive voltage to the accessories.

The storage battery is a chemical device incorporating parallel lead plates in a tank containing a sulfuric acid-water solution. Adjacent plates are slightly dissimilar, and the chemical reaction of the two dissimilar plates produces electrical energy when the battery is connected to a lead such as the starter motor. The chemical reaction is reversible, so that when the generator is producing a voltage (electrical pressure) greater then that produced by the battery, electricity is forced into the battery, and the battery is returned to its fully charged state.

The vehicle's generator is driven mechanically, through V belts, by the engine crankshaft. It consists of two coils of fine wire, one stationary (the stator), and one movable (the rotor). The rotor may also be known as the armature and consists of fine wire wrapped around an iron core which is mounted on a shaft. The electricity which flows through the two coils of wire provided initially by the battery in some cases) creates an intense magnetic field around both rotor and stator, and the interaction between the two diodes creates

voltage, allowing the generator to power the accessories and change the battery.

There are two types of generators; the earlier is the direct current (DC) type. The current produced by the DC generator is generated in the armature and carried off the spinning armature by stationary brushes contacting the commutator. The commutator is a series of smooth metal contact plates on the end of the armature. The commutator plates, which are separated from one another by a very short gap, are connected to the armature circuits so that current will flow in one direction only in the wires carrying the generator output. The generator stator consists of two stationary coils of wire which draw some of the output current of the generator to form a powerful magnetic field and create the interaction of fields which generates the voltage. The generator field is wired in series with the regulator.

Newer automobiles use alternating current generators or alternators because they are more efficient, can be rotated at higher speeds, and have fewer brush problems. In an alternator, the field rotates while all the current produced passes only through the stator windings. The brushes bear against continuous slip rings rather than a commutator. This causes the current produced to periodically reverse the direction of its flow. Diodes (electrical one-way switches) block the flow of current from traveling in the wrong direction. A series of diodes is wires together to permit the alternating flow

Troubleshooting Basic Charging System Problems

Problem	Cause	Solution
Noisy alternator	· Loose mountings · Loose drive pulley · Worn bearings · Brush noise · Internal circuits shorted (High pitched whine)	· Tighten mounting bolts · Tighten pulley · Replace alternator · Replace alternator · Replace alternator
Squeal when starting engine or accelerating	· Glazed or loose belt	· Replace or adjust belt
Indicator light remains on or ammeter indicates discharge (engine running)	· Broken fan belt · Broken or disconnected wires · Internal alternator problems · Defective voltage regulator	· Install belt · Repair or connect wiring · Replace alternator · Replace voltage regulator
Car light bulbs continually burn out—battery needs water continually	· Alternator/regulator overcharging	· Replace voltage regulator/alternator
Car lights flare on acceleration	· Battery low · Internal alternator/regulator problems	· Charge or replace battery · Replace alternator/regulator
Low voltage output (alternator light flickers continually or ammeter needle wanders)	· Loose or worn belt · Dirty or corroded connections · Internal alternator/regulator problems	· Replace or adjust belt · Clean or replace connections · Replace alternator or regulator

of the stator to be converted to a pulsating, but unidirectional flow at the alternator output. The alternator's field is wired in series with the voltage regulator.

The regulator consists of several circuits. Each circuit had a core, or magnetic coil of wire, which operates a switch. Each switch is connected to ground through one or more resistors. The coil of wire responds directly to system voltage. When the voltage reaches the required level, the magnetic field created by the winding of wire closes the switch and inserts a resistance into the generator field circuit, thus reducing the output. The contacts of the switch cycle open and close many times each second to precisely control voltage.

While alternators are self-limiting as far as maximum current is concerned, DC generators employ a current regulating circuit which responds directly to the total amount of current flowing through the generator circuit rather than to the output voltage. The current regulator is similar to the voltage regulator except that all system current must flow through the energizing coil on its way to the various accessories.

SAFETY PRECAUTIONS

Observing these precautions will ensure safe handling of the electrical system components, and will avoid damage to the vehicle's electrical system:

a. Be absolutely sure of the polarity of a booster battery before making connections. Connect the cables positive to positive, and negative to negative. Connect positive cables first and then make the last connection to a ground on the body of the booster vehicle so that arcing cannot ignite hydrogen gas that may have accumulated near the battery. Even momentary connection of a booster battery with the polarity reserved will damage alternator diodes.

b. Disconnect both vehicle battery cables before attempting to charge a battery.

c. Never ground the alternator or generator output or battery terminal. Be cautious when using metal too around a battery to avoid creating a short circuit between the terminals.

d. Never ground the field circuit between the alternator and regulator.

e. Never run an alternator or generator without load unless the field circuit is disconnected.

f. Never attempt to polarize an alternator.

g. Keep the regulator cover in place when taking voltage and current limiter readings.

h. Use insulated tools when adjusting the regulator.

i. Whenever DC generator-to regulator wires have been disconnected, the generator must be repolarized. To do this with an externally grounded, light duty generator, momentarily place a jumper wire between the battery terminal and the generator terminal of the regulator. With an internally grounded heavy duty unit, disconnect the wire to the regulator field terminal and touch the regulator battery terminal with it.

Distributor

REMOVAL AND INSTALLATION

1. Disconnect the ground cable from the battery.

2. Tag and disconnect the feed and module terminal connectors from the distributor cap.

3. Disconnect the hose at the vacuum advance (models equipped).

4. Depress and release the distributor cap-to-housing retainers and lift off the cap assembly.

5. Using crayon or chalk, make locating marks on the rotor and module and on the distributor housing and engine for installation purposes.

6. Loosen and remove the distributor clamp bolt and clamp, lift the distributor out of the engine. Noting the relative position of the rotor and module alignment marks, make a second mark on the rotor to align it with the mark on the module.

7. With a new O-ring on the distributor housing and the second mark on the rotor aligned with the mark on the module, install the distributor, taking care to align the mark on the housing with the one on the engine. It may be necessary to lift the distributor and turn the rotor slightly to align the gears and the oil pump driveshaft.

8. With the respective marks aligned, install the clamp and bolt finger-tight.

9. Install and secure the distributor cap.

10. Connect the feed and module connectors to the distributor cap.

11. Connect a timing light to the engine and plug the vacuum hose.

12. Connect the ground cable to the battery.

13. Start the engine and set the timing.

14. Turn the engine off and tighten the distributor clamp bolt. Disconnect the timing light and unplug and connect the hose to the vacuum advance.

NOTE: To avoid confusion, replace spark plug wires one at a time.

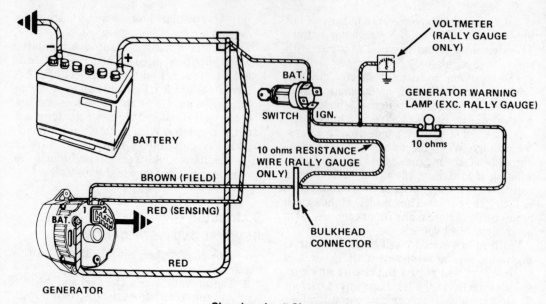

Charging circuit SI system

Alternator

ALTERNATOR PRECAUTIONS

1. Always observe proper polarity of the battery connections; be especially careful when jump-starting the car.

2. Never ground or short out any alternator or alternator regulator terminals.

3. Never operate the alternator with any of its or the battery's leads disconnected.

4. Always remove the battery or disconnect its output lead while charging it.

5. Always disconnect the battery ground cable when replacing any electrical component.

6. Never subject the alternator to excessive heat or dampness. If you are steam-cleaning the engine, cover the alternator.

7. Never use arc-welding equipment with the alternator connected.

ALTERNATOR TESTING

Two types of alternator/regulator combinations have been used on Cutlasses. From 1970-72, an alternator with external regulator was used on Standard Cutlasses. 1973 and later models use an alternator with the regulator incorporated. 4-4-2 models have used the integral regulator alternator since 1970. While several charging system tests are given here, alternator repair procedures are not. Because of their complexity, it is recommended that you take you alternator to a qualified repair man if it is defective.

Preliminary Charging System Tests

1. If you suspect a defect in your charging system, first perform these general checks before going on to more specific tests.

2. Check the condition of the alternator belt and tighten if necessary.

Alternator Output Test

ALTERNATOR WITH EXTERNAL REGULATOR

1. You will need a tachometer and a voltmeter for this test. You will also need a jumper wire.

2. Connect the tachometer to the engine.

3. Disconnect the wiring harness at the voltage regulator. With a jumper wire, connect the F: wire to the number three wire in the wire harness plug.

4. Connect a voltmeter across the battery terminals, the positive voltmeter lead to the positive battery terminal and the negative lead to the negative terminal. Note the reading.

5. Start the engine and let it idle.

6. Gradually raise the engine speed to 1,500-2,000 rpm. The reading on the voltmeter should increase on to two volts over the initial reading. If there is no increase in the reading, the alternator is defective and must be repaired, If the increase is greater than two volts, then the regulator is defective and must be adjusted or replaced. (See voltage adjustment in the regulator section).

ALTERNATOR WITH INTEGRAL REGULATOR

1. You will need a ammeter for this test.

2. Disconnect the battery ground cable.

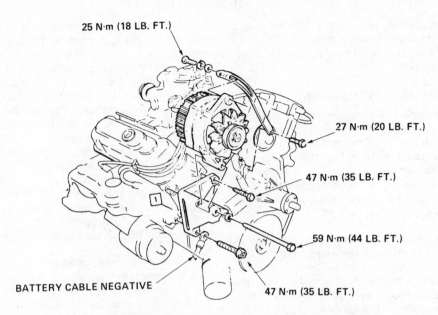

25 N·m (18 LB. FT.)

27 N·m (20 LB. FT.)

47 N·m (35 LB. FT.)

59 N·m (44 LB. FT.)

BATTERY CABLE NEGATIVE

47 N·m (35 LB. FT.)

Typical alternator mounting-Buick built engines

3. Disconnect the wire from the battery terminal on the alternator.

4. Connect the ammeter negative lead to the battery terminal wire removed in step three, and connect the ammeter positive lead to the battery terminal on the alternator.

5. Reconnect the battery ground cable and turn on all electrical accessories. If the battery is fully charged, disconnect the coil wire and bump the starter a few times to partially discharge it.

6. Start the engine and run it until you obtain a maximum current reading on the ammeter.

7. If the current is within ten amps of the rated output of the alternator, the alternator is working properly. If the current is not within ten amps, insert a screwdriver in the test hole in the end frame of the alternator and ground the tab in the test hole against the side of the hole.

8. If the current is now within ten amps of

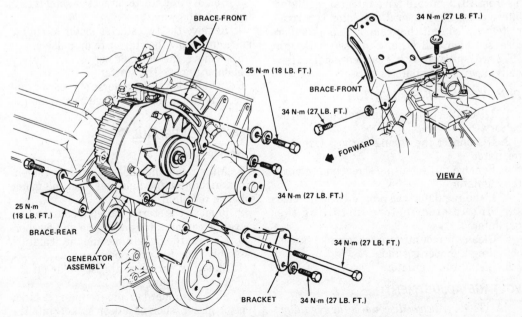

BRACE-FRONT

34 N·m (27 LB. FT.)

25 N·m (18 LB. FT.)

BRACE-FRONT

34 N·m (27 LB. FT.)

FORWARD

VIEW A

25 N·m (18 LB. FT.)

BRACE-REAR

34 N·m (27 LB. FT.)

GENERATOR ASSEMBLY

34 N·m (27 LB. FT.)

BRACKET   34 N·m (27 LB. FT.)

Typical alternator mounting—Chevrolet built engines

the rated output, remove the alternator and have the voltage regulator replaced. If it is still below ten amps of rated output, have the alternator repaired.

REMOVAL AND INSTALLATION

1. Disconnect the battery ground cable.
2. L6 engines have their alternators mounted on the left side. V8 engines have their alternator mounted high on the right-hand side, unless the car is equipped with power steering and air-conditioning, in which case the alternator is mounted low on the left-hand side. V6 alternators are mounted on the right-hand side.
3. Disconnect all wiring to the alternator, noting the locations of the wires. You may find it helpful to mark the wires.
4. Loosen the alternator adjusting bolt and slide the alternator over until you can remove the drive belt. On cars equipped with air-conditioning and/or power steering, it may be necessary to loosen one or the other to gain access to the alternator. If addition, it is sometimes far easier to work from underneath the car.
5. Remove the alternator mounting bolts and remove the alternator.
6. Installation is the reverse order of removal. When adjusting the belts, make sure you have ¼-½″ of play at the belt's mid-point.

Regulator

The regulator is an integral part of the alternator on 1973 and later Cutlasses. 4-4-2 models from 1970 onward have integral regulator alternators. The integral regulator is a completely sealed unit that cannot be adjusted or disassembled. All other Cutlasses through 1972 are equipped with a conventional, externally mounted regulator.

REMOVAL AND INSTALLATION

1. Disconnect the ground cable from the battery.
2. Disconnect the wiring harness from the regulator.
3. Remove the mounting screw and remove the regulator.
4. If the regulator has a base gasket, make sure it's in place before installing the regulator.
5. Clean the mounting areas to make sure of obtaining a proper ground.
6. Install the regulator.

VOLTAGE ADJUSTMENT

CAUTION: *Always disconnect the regulator before removing or installing the cover in order to prevent damage by short-circuiting.*

1. Before adjusting the regulator, make sure the battery is in good condition and fully charged.
2. The voltage regulator setting is dependent on ambient temperature. While not strictly necessary, it is helpful to know the underhood temperature. The accompanying chart will give you the different voltage settings at varying temperatures.
3. Connect a voltmeter across the battery terminals. Connect a tachometer to the engine.
4. Start the engine and run it for approximately fifteen minutes at 1,200 rpm. The lights and accessories must be turned off.
5. After the warm-up period, cycle the regulator by shutting off the engine and restarting it.
6. With the engine running at approximately 2,200 rpm, note the voltage reading. The allowable range is from 13.0 to 15.0 volts depending upon underhood temperatures.
7. If the regulator needs adjusting, remove the cover and adjust the voltage by turning the adjusting screw.

NOTE: *The spring holder should remain against the heat of the screw after the adjustment is made. This prevents the setting from varying.*

Starter

REMOVAL AND INSTALLATION

1. Disconnect the negative battery cable at the battery.
2. Raise the car and support it with jack stands.
3. Remove any starter braces or shields that may be in the way.
4. Remove the two starter motor to engine bolts, and allow the starter to drop down.
5. Remove the solenoid wires and battery cable and remove the starter.
6. Installation is the reverse of removal. Replace any shims that may have been removed.

STARTER OVERHAUL

Drive Replacement

1. After removing the starter from the engine, disconnect the field coil from the motor solenoid terminal.
2. Remove the starter through bolts and remove the commutator end frame and washer.
3. Remove the field frame and the armature assembly from the drive housing.
4. Slide the two-piece thrust collar off the end of the armature shaft.
5. Slide a standard ½″ pipe coupling or other type of spacer (such as a deep socket) into the shaft so that the end of the coupling butts against the edge of the retainer.

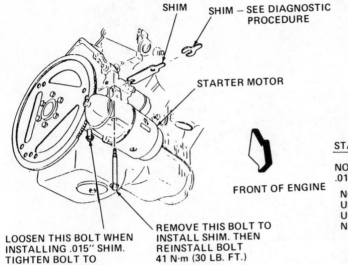

SHIM   SHIM — SEE DIAGNOSTIC PROCEDURE

STARTER MOTOR

FRONT OF ENGINE

LOOSEN THIS BOLT WHEN INSTALLING .015" SHIM. TIGHTEN BOLT TO 41 N·m (30 LB. FT.)

REMOVE THIS BOLT TO INSTALL SHIM. THEN REINSTALL BOLT 41 N·m (30 LB. FT.)

STARTER NOISE REPAIR PROCEDURE

NOISE DURING CRANKING . . . USE .015" SHIM ON OUTBOARD PAD.

NOISE AFTER ENGINE FIRES . . . USE .015" SHIMS ONE AT A TIME UNTIL NOISE IS CORRECTED. USE NO MORE THAN 4 SHIMS.

Typical starter motor mounting—Buick and Chevrolet built engines

6. Tap the end of the coupling with a hammer, driving the retainer off the snapring.

7. Remove the snapring from the groove in the armature shaft.

8. Slide the retainer and clutch from the armature shaft.

9. To reassemble, reverse the above procedure.

10. During reassembly, be sure to slide the snapring, after it has been forced onto the armature shaft, past the grease groove to the snapring groove.

11. To reinstall the snapring retainer, sue

two paris of pliers at the same time, on opposite sides of the armature shaft, and grip the retainer and thrust collar and squeeze until the retainer is forced over the snapring.

Brush Replacement

1. After removing the starter from the engine, disconnect the field coil from the motor solenoid terminal.

2. Remove the starter through bolts and remove the commutator end frame and washer.

3. Remove the field frame and the armature assembly from the drive housing.

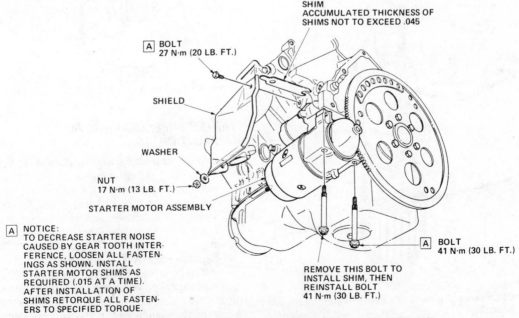

SHIM ACCUMULATED THICKNESS OF SHIMS NOT TO EXCEED .045

[A] BOLT 27 N·m (20 LB. FT.)

SHIELD

WASHER

NUT 17 N·m (13 LB. FT.)

STARTER MOTOR ASSEMBLY

[A] NOTICE: TO DECREASE STARTER NOISE CAUSED BY GEAR TOOTH INTERFERENCE, LOOSEN ALL FASTENINGS AS SHOWN. INSTALL STARTER MOTOR SHIMS AS REQUIRED (.015 AT A TIME). AFTER INSTALLATION OF SHIMS RETORQUE ALL FASTENERS TO SPECIFIED TORQUE.

REMOVE THIS BOLT TO INSTALL SHIM, THEN REINSTALL BOLT 41 N·m (30 LB. FT.)

[A] BOLT 41 N·m (30 LB. FT.)

Typical starter motor mounting—Oldsmobile built engines (350, 403)

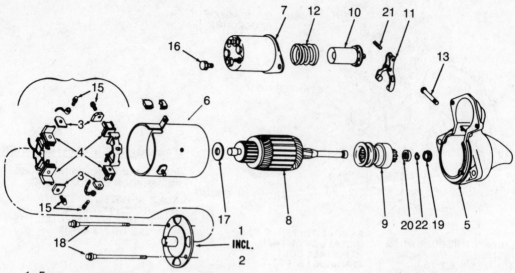

1. Frame—commutator end
2. Brush and holder pkg.
3. Brush
4. Brush holder
5. Housing—drive end
6. Frame and field asm.
7. Solenoid switch
8. Armature

9. Drive asm.
10. Plunger
11. Shift lever
12. Plunger return springer
13. Shift lever shaft
14. Lock washer
15. Screw—brush attaching
16. Screw—field lead to switch

17. Washer—brake
18. Thru bolt
19. Pinion stop collar
20. Thrust collar
21. Plunger pin
22. Pinion stop retainer ring
23. Lever shaft retaining ring

Disassembled view of starter motor

4. Remove the brush holder pivot pin which positions one insulated and one grounded brush.

5. Remove the brush springs.

6. Remove the brushes.

7. Installation is in the reverse order of removal.

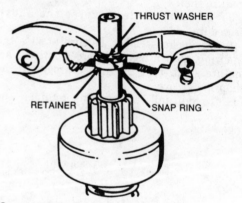

Snap ring installation

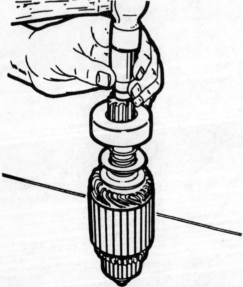

Use a piece of pipe to drive the retainer toward the snap ring

STARTER SOLENOID REMOVAL AND INSTALLATION

1. Remove the screw and washer from the motor connector strap terminal.

2. Remove the two screws which retain the solenoid housing to the end frame assembly.

3. Twist the solenoid clockwise to remove the flange key from the keyway slot in the housing.

4. Remove the solenoid assembly.

5. With the solenoid return spring installed on the plunger, position the solenoid body on the drive housing and turn it counterclockwise to engage the flange key in the keyway slot.

6. Install the two screws which retain the solenoid housing to the end frame.

Battery

REMOVAL AND INSTALLATION

1. Disconnect the battery ground cable at the battery. Disconnect the positive cable at the battery.

2. Unfasten the battery hold-down clamps.

3. Remove the battery.

CAUTION: *Exercise extreme care in handling the battery. Remember it is filled with a highly corrosive acid.*

4. Installation is in the reverse order of removal.

ENGINE MECHANICAL

Gasoline Engine

REMOVAL AND INSTALLATION

In the process of removing the engine you will come across a number of steps which call for the removal of a separate component or system, i.e. Disconnect the exhaust system or Remove the radiator. In all of these instances, a detailed removal procedure can be found elsewhere in the chapter, or in some cases, in another chapter which deals with the specific component in question.

NOTE: *Refer to the vehicle and engine identification chart at the beginning of chapter 1 to determine the type and manufacturer of the engine used in your vehicle.*

1. Scribe marks at the hood hinges and the hinge brackets. Remove the hood.

2. Disconnect the battery and drain the coolant.

CAUTION: *When draining the coolant, keep in mind that cats and dogs are attracted by the ethylene glycol antifreeze, and are quite likely to drink any that is left in an uncovered container or in puddles on the ground. This will prove fatal in sufficient quantity. Always drain the coolant into a sealable container. Coolant should be reused unless it is contaminated or several years old.*

3. Remove the air cleaner.

4. On cars with air conditioning (A/C), disconnect the compressor ground wire from the bracket. Remove the electrical connector from the compressor. Remove the compressor and position the compressor out of the way. Do not disconnect any hoses.

CAUTION: *If the compressor refrigerant lines do not have enough slack to position the compressor out of the way without disconnecting the refrigerant lines, the air conditioning system will have to be discharged by a trained air conditioning specialist. Under no conditions should an untrained person attempt to disconnect the air conditioning refrigerant lines. These lines contain pressurized Freon*, which can be extremely dangerous.*

5. Remove the fan blade, pulley, and belts.

6. Disconnect the radiator and heater hoses. Remove the radiator and shroud assembly.

7. Remove the power steering pump and move it out of the way. Do not disconnect any hoses.

8. Remove the fuel pump hoses and plug them.

9. Disconnect the vapor emission lines, from the carburetor, the vacuum supply hose from the carburetor to the vacuum manifold, and the power brake vacuum hoses, if equipped.

10. Disconnect the throttle linkage at the carburetor.

11. Disconnect the oil and coolant switches.

12. Disconnect the engine-to-body ground strap.

13. Raise the car and disconnect the starter wires.

14. Disconnect the pipes from the exhaust manifold and support the exhaust system.

15. On Oldsmobile-built engines:

   a. Remove the torque converter cover and the converter-to-flywheel retaining bolts.

   b. Remove the engine mounting bolts.

   c. Remove the three engine-to transmission bolts from the right side.

   d. Remove the starter motor.

   e. Lower the car and support the transmission with a floor jack.

   f. Remove the three engine-to-transmission bolts from the left side and remove the engine.

16. On Chevrolet and Buick-built engines:

   a. Remove the flywheel and converter cover.

   b. On cars with automatic transmission, remove the flywheel-to-converter attaching bolts. Matchmark the converter to the flywheel. On all automatic transmission models, remove the engine-to transmission attaching bolts. On manual transmission models, disconnect the driveshaft, the shaft linkage, the clutch equalizer shaft and the transmission mount.

   c. Remove the motor mount fasteners and the cruise control bracket, if so equipped.

   d. Lower the car and support the transmission, except for models with manual transmissions.

   e. Raise the engine slightly so the engine mount through bolts can be removed. On models with manual transmissions, remove the engine and transmission as a unit.

17. Install the engine in the reverse order of removal. Note that there are dowel pins in the block that have matching holes in the bellhousing. These dowel pins must be in almost perfect alignment before the engine will go together with the transmission. See Manual Transmission, Removal and Installation for clutch alignment procedures.

Diesel Engine

REMOVAL AND INSTALLATION

1. Drain the cooling system.
CAUTION: *When draining the coolant, keep in mind that cats and dogs are attracted by the ethylene glycol antifreeze, and are quite likely to drink any that is left in an uncovered container or in puddles on the ground. This will prove fatal in sufficient quantity. Always drain the coolant into a sealable container. Coolant should be reused unless it is contaminated or several years old.*
2. Remove the air cleaner.
3. Mark the hood-to-hinge position and remove the hood.
4. Disconnect the ground cables from the batteries.
5. Disconnect the ground wires at the fender panels and the ground strap at the cowl.
6. Disconnect the radiator hoses, cooler lines, heater hoses, vacuum hoses, power steering pump hoses, air conditioning compressor (hoses attached), fuel inlet hose and all attaching wiring.
7. Remove the bellcrank clip.
8. Disconnect the throttle and transmission cables.
9. Remove the radiator.
10. Raise and support the car.
11. Disconnect the exhaust pipes at the manifold.
12. Remove the torque converter cover and the three bolts holding the converter to the flywheel.
13. Remove the engine mount bolts.
14. Remove the three right side transmission-to-engine bolts. Remove the starter.
15. Lower the car and attach a hoist to the engine.
16. Slightly raise the transmission with a jack.
17. Remove the three left side transmission-to-engine bolts and remove the engine.
18. Installation is the reverse of removal. Converter cover bolts are torqued to 40 ft.lb.

Engine Overhaul Tips

Most engine overhaul procedures are fairly standard. In addition to specific parts replacement procedures and complete specifications for your individual engine, this chapter also is a guide to accept rebuilding procedures. Examples of standard rebuilding practice are shown and should be used along with specific details concerning your particular engine.

Competent and accurate machine shop services will ensure maximum performance, reliability and engine life.

In most instances it is more profitable for the do-it-yourself mechanic to remove, clean and inspect the component, buy the necessary parts and deliver these to a shop for actual machine work.

On the other hand, much of the rebuilding work (crankshaft, block, bearings, piston rods, and other components) is well within the scope of the do-it-yourself mechanic.

TOOLS

The tools required for an engine overhaul or parts replacement will depend on the depth of your involvement. With a few exceptions, they will be the tools found in a mechanic's tool kit (see Chapter 1). More in-depth work will require any or all of the following:
• a dial indicator (reading in thousandths) mounted on a universal base
• micrometers and telescope gauges
• jaw and screw-type pullers
• scraper
• valve spring compressor
• ring groove cleaner
• piston ring expander and compressor
• ridge reamer
• cylinder hone or glaze breaker
• Plastigage®
• engine stand
The use of most of these tools is illustrated in this chapter. Many can be rented for a one-time use from a local parts jobber or tool supply house specializing in automotive work.

Occasionally, the use of special tools is called for. See the information on Special Tools and Safety Notice in the front of this book before substituting another tool.

INSPECTION TECHNIQUES

Procedures and specifications are given in this chapter for inspecting, cleaning and assessing the wear limits of most major components. Other procedures such as Magnaflux® and Zyglo® can be used to locate material flaws and stress cracks. Magnaflux® is a magnetic process applicable only to ferrous materials. The Zyglo® process coats the material with a fluorescent dye penetrant and can be used on any material Check for suspected surface cracks can be more readily made using spot check dye. The dye is sprayed onto the suspected area, wiped off and the area sprayed with a developer. Cracks will show up brightly.

OVERHAUL TIPS

Aluminum has become extremely popular for use in engines, due to its low weight. Observe the following precautions when handling aluminum parts:

• Never hot tank aluminum parts (the caustic hot tank solution will eat the aluminum.

• Remove all aluminum parts (identification tag, etc.) from engine parts prior to the tanking.

• Always coat threads lightly with engine oil or antiseize compounds before installation, to prevent seizure.

• Never overtorque bolts or spark plugs especially in aluminum threads.

Stripped threads in any component can be repaired using any of several commercial repair kits (Heli-Coil®, Microdot®, Keenserts®, etc.).

When assembling the engine, any parts that will be frictional contact must be prelubed to provide lubrication at initial start-up. Any product specifically formulated for this purpose can be used, but engine oil is not recommended as a prelube.

When semi-permanent (locked, but removable) installation of bolts or nuts is desired, threads should be cleaned and coated with Loctite® or other similar, commercial non-hardening sealant.

REPAIRING DAMAGED THREADS

Several methods of repairing damaged threads are available. Heli-Coil® (shown here), Keenserts® and Microdot® are among the most widely used. All involve basically the same principle—drilling out stripped threads, tapping the hole and installing a prewound insert—making welding, plugging and oversize fasteners unnecessary.

Two types of thread repair inserts are usually supplied: a standard type for most Inch Coarse, Inch Fine, Metric Course and Metric Fine thread sizes and a spark lug type to fit

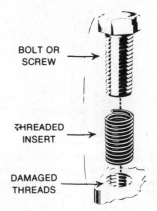

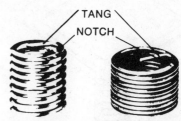

Damaged bolt holes can be repaired with thread repair inserts

Standard thread repair insert (left) and spark plug thread insert (right)

most spark plug port sizes. Consult the individual manufacturer's catalog to determine exact applications. Typical thread repair kits will contain a selection of prewound threaded inserts, a tap (corresponding to the outside diameter threads of the insert) and an installation tool. Spark plug inserts usually differ because they require a tap equipped with pilot threads and a combined reamer/tap section. Most manufacturers also supply blister-packed thread repair inserts separately in addition to a master kit containing a variety of taps and inserts plus installation tools.

Before effecting a repair to a threaded hole, remove any snapped, broken or damaged bolts or studs. Penetrating oil can be used to free frozen threads. The offending item can be removed with locking pliers or with a screw or stud extractor. After the hole is clear, the thread can be repaired, as follows:

Drill out the damaged threads with specified drill. Drill completely through the hole or to the bottom of a blind hole

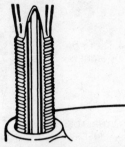

With the tap supplied, tap the hole to receive the thread insert. Keep the tap well oiled and back it out frequently to avoid clogging the threads

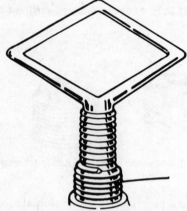

Screw the threaded insert onto the installation tool until the tang engages the slot. Screw the insert into the tapped hole until it is ¼–½ turn below the top surface, After installation break off the tang with a hammer and punch

Checking Engine Compression

A noticeable lack of engine power, excessive oil consumption and/or poor fuel mileage measured over an extended period are all indicators of internal engine war. Worn piston rings, scored or worn cylinder bores, blown head gaskets, sticking or burnt valves and worn valve seats are all possible culprits here. A check of each cylinder's compression will help you locate the problems.

As mentioned in the Tools and Equipment section of Chapter 1, a screw-in type compression gauge is more accurate that the type you simply hold against the spark plug hole, although it takes slightly longer to use. It's worth it to obtain a more accurate reading. Follow the procedures below.

Gasoline Engines

1. Warm up the engine to normal operating temperature.
2. Remove all spark plugs.
3. Disconnect the high tension lead from the ignition coil.

The screw-in type compression gauge is more accurate

4. On fully open the throttle either by operating the carburetor throttle linkage by hand or by having an assistant floor the accelerator pedal.
5. Screw the compression gauge into the no.1 spark plug hole until the fitting is snug. NOTE: *Be careful not to crossthread the plug hole. On aluminum cylinder heads use extra care, as the threads in these heads are easily ruined.*
6. Ask an assistant to depress the accelerator pedal fully on both carbureted and fuel injected vehicles. Then, while you read the compression gauge, ask the assistant to crank the engine two or three times in short bursts using the ignition switch.
7. Read the compression gauge at the end of each series of cranks, and record the highest of these readings. Repeat this procedure for each of the engine's cylinders. Compare the highest reading of each cylinder to the compression pressure specification in the Tune-Up Specifications chart in Chapter 2. The specs in this chart are maximum values.

A cylinder's compression pressure is usually acceptable if it is not less than 80% of maximum. The difference between any two cylinders should be no more than 12–14 pounds.

8. If a cylinder is unusually low, pour a tablespoon of clean engine oil into the cylinder through the spark plug hole and repeat the compression test. If the compression comes up after adding the oil, it appears that the cylinder's piston rings or bore are damaged or worn. If the pressure remains low, the valves may not be seating properly (a valve job is needed), or the head gasket may be blown near that cylinder. If compression in any two adjacent cylinders is low, and if the addition of oil doesn't help the compression, there is leakage past the head gasket. Oil and coolant water in the combustion chamber can result from this problem. There may be evidence of water droplets on the engine dipstick when a head gasket has blown.

Standard Torque Specifications and Fastener Markings

In the absence of specific torques, the following chart can be used as a guide to the maximum safe torque of a particular size/grade of fastener.
- There is no torque difference for fine or coarse threads.
- Torque values are based on clean, dry threads. Reduce the value by 10% if threads are oiled prior to assembly.
- The torque required for aluminum components or fasteners is considerably less.

U.S. Bolts

SAE Grade Number	1 or 2			5			6 or 7		
Number of lines always 2 less than the grade number.									
Bolt Size (Inches)—(Thread)	Maximum Torque			Maximum Torque			Maximum Torque		
	Ft./Lbs.	Kgm	Nm	Ft./Lbs.	Kgm	Nm	Ft./Lbs.	Kgm	Nm
¼—20	5	0.7	6.8	8	1.1	10.8	10	1.4	13.5
—28	6	0.8	8.1	10	1.4	13.6			
⁵/₁₆—18	11	1.5	14.9	17	2.3	23.0	19	2.6	25.8
—24	13	1.8	17.6	19	2.6	25.7			
³/₈—16	18	2.5	24.4	31	4.3	42.0	34	4.7	46.0
—24	20	2.75	27.1	35	4.8	47.5			
⁷/₁₆—14	28	3.8	37.0	49	6.8	66.4	55	7.6	74.5
—20	30	4.2	40.7	55	7.6	74.5			
½—13	39	5.4	52.8	75	10.4	101.7	85	11.75	115.2
—20	41	5.7	55.6	85	11.7	115.2			
⁹/₁₆—12	51	7.0	69.2	110	15.2	149.1	120	16.6	162.7
—18	55	7.6	74.5	120	16.6	162.7			
⅝—11	83	11.5	112.5	150	20.7	203.3	167	23.0	226.5
—18	95	13.1	128.8	170	23.5	230.5			
¾—10	105	14.5	142.3	270	37.3	366.0	280	38.7	379.6
—16	115	15.9	155.9	295	40.8	400.0			
⅞—9	160	22.1	216.9	395	54.6	535.5	440	60.9	596.5
—14	175	24.2	237.2	435	60.1	589.7			
1—8	236	32.5	318.6	590	81.6	799.9	660	91.3	894.8
—14	250	34.6	338.9	660	91.3	849.8			

Metric Bolts

Relative Strength Marking	4.6, 4.8			8.8		
Bolt Markings						
Bolt Size Thread Size x Pitch (mm)	Maximum Torque			Maximum Torque		
	Ft./Lbs.	Kgm	Nm	Ft./Lbs.	Kgm	Nm
6 x 1.0	2–3	.2–.4	3–4	3–6	.4–.8	5–8
8 x 1.25	6–8	.8–1	8–12	9–14	1.2–1.9	13–19
10 x 1.25	12–17	1.5–2.3	16–23	20–29	2.7–4.0	27–39
12 x 1.25	21–32	2.9–4.4	29–43	35–53	4.8–7.3	47–72
14 x 1.5	35–52	4.8–7.1	48–70	57–85	7.8–11.7	77–110
16 x 1.5	51–77	7.0–10.6	67–100	90–120	12.4–16.5	130–160
18 x 1.5	74–110	10.2–15.1	100–150	130–170	17.9–23.4	180–230
20 x 1.5	110–140	15.1–19.3	150–190	190–240	26.2–46.9	160–320
22 x 1.5	150–190	22.0–26.2	200–260	250–320	34.5–44.1	340–430
24 x 1.5	190–240	26.2–46.9	260–320	310–410	42.7–56.5	420–550

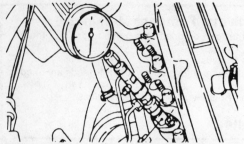

Diesel engines require a special compression gauge adaptor

Diesel Engines

Checking cylinder compression on diesel engines is basically the same procedure as on gasoline engines except for the following:

1. A special compression gauge adaptor suitable for diesel engines (because these engines have much greater compression pressures) must be used.

2. Remove the injector tubes and remove the injectors from each cylinder.

NOTE: *Don't forget to remove the washer underneath each injector. Otherwise, it may get lost when the engine is cranked.*

3. When fitting the compression gauge adaptor to the cylinder head, make sure the bleeder of the gauge (if equipped) is closed.

4. When reinstalling the injector assemblies, install new washers underneath each injector.

Rocker Arm (Valve) Cover

NOTE: *Some engines are assembled using RTV (Room Temperature Vulcanizing) silicone sealant in place of rocker arm cover gasket. If the engine was assembled using RTV,*

General Engine Specifications

Year	Engine No. Cyl Displacement (cu in.)	Carburetor Type	Horsepower @ rpm■	Torque @ rpm (ft. lbs.)■	Bore x Stroke (in.)	Compression Ratio	Oil Pressure @ 2000 rpm
'70	6-250	1 bbl	155 @ 4200	240 @ 2000	3.875 x 3.530	8.50:1	30—45
	8-350	2 bbl	250 @ 4400	355 @ 2600	4.057 x 3.385	9.00:1	30—45
	8-350	4 bbl	310 @ 4800	390 @ 3200	4.057 x 3.385	10.25:1	30—45
	8-350 (W31)	4 bbl	325 @ 5400	360 @ 3600	4.057 x 3.385	10.50:1	30—45
	8-455	2 bbl	320 @ 4200	500 @ 2400	4.126 x 4.250	10.25:1	30—45
	8-455	4 bbl	365 @ 5000	500 @ 3200	4.126 x 4.250	10.50:1	35—50
	8-455 (W30)	4 bbl	370 @ 5200	500 @ 3600	4.126 x 4.250	10.50:1	35—50
'71	6-250	1 bbl	145 @ 4200	230 @ 2000	3.875 x 3.530	8.00:1	30—45
	8-350	2 bbl	240 @ 4200	350 @ 2400	4.057 x 3.385	8.50:1	30—45
	8-350	4 bbl	260 @ 4600	360 @ 3200	4.057 x 3.385	8.50:1	30—45
	8-455	2 bbl	280 @ 4000	445 @ 2000	4.126 x 4.250	8.50:1	30—45
	8-455	4 bbl	320 @ 4400	460 @ 2800	4.126 x 4.250	8.50:1	30—45
	8-455	4 bbl	340 @ 4600	460 @ 3200	4.126 x 4.250	8.50:1	30—50
	8-455 (W30	4 bbl	350 @ 4700	460 @ 3200	4.126 x 4.250	8.50:1	30—50
'72	8-350	2 bbl	160 @ 4000	275 @ 2400	4.057 x 3.385	8.50:1	30—45
	8-350 ①	2 bbl	175 @ 4000	295 @ 2600	4.057 x 3.385	8.50:1	30—45
	8-350	4 bbl	180 @ 4000	275 @ 2800	4.057 x 3.385	8.50:1	30—45
	8-350 ①	4 bbl	200 @ 4400	300 @ 3200	4.057 x 3.385	8.50:1	30—45
	8-455	4 bbl	225 @ 3600	360 @ 2600	4.126 x 4.250	8.50:1	30—50
	8-455 ①	4 bbl	250 @ 4200	370 @ 2800	4.126 x 4.250	8.50:1	30—50
	8-455	4 bbl	270 @ 4400	370 @ 3200	4.126 x 4.250	8.50:1	30—50
	8-455 (W30)	4 bbl	300 @ 4700	410 @ 3200	4.126 x 4.250	8.50:1	30—50

General Engine Specifications (cont.)

Year	Engine No. Cyl Displacement (cu in.)	Carburetor Type	Horsepower @ rpm ■	Torque @ rpm (ft. lbs.) ■	Bore x Stroke (in.)	Compression Ratio	Oil Pressure @ 2000 rpm
'73	8-350	2 bbl	160 @ 3800	275 @ 2400	4.057 x 3.385	8.50:1	30—45
	8-350	4 bbl	180 @ 3800	275 @ 2800	4.057 x 3.385	8.50:1	30—45
	8-455	4 bbl	225 @ 3600	360 @ 2600	4.126 x 4.250	8.50:1	30—50
	8-455	4 bbl	250 @ 4000	370 @ 2800	4.126 x 4.250	8.50:1	30—50
'74	8-350	4-bbl	160 @ 3800	275 @ 2400	4.057 x 3.385	8.50:1	30—45
	8-350	4 bbl	180 @ 3800	275 @ 2800	4.057 x 3.385	8.50:1	30—45
	8-350 ①	4 bbl	200 @ 4200	300 @ 3200	4.057 x 3.385	8.50:1	30—45
	8-455	4 bbl	210 @ 3600	350 @ 2400	4.126 x 4.250	8.50:1	30—50
	8-455 ①	4 bbl	230 @ 4000	370 @ 2800	4.126 x 4.250	8.50:1	30—50
'75	6-250	1 bbl	100 @ 3600	175 @ 1600	3.875 x 3.530	8.50:1	36—41
	8-260	2 bbl	110 @ 3400	205 @ 1600	3.550 x 3.385	8.50:1	30—45
	8-350	4 bbl	160 @ 3800	275 @ 2400	4.057 x 3.385	8.50:1	30—45
	8-455	4 bbl	190 @ 3400	350 @ 2400	4.126 x 4.250	8.50:1	30—45
'76—'77	6-231	2 bbl	105 @ 3400	185 @ 2000	3.800 x 3.400	8.00:1	37 ②
	6-250	1 bbl	105 @ 3800	185 @ 1200	3.875 x 3.530	8.25:1	36—41
	8-260	2 bbl	110 @ 3400	205 @ 1600	3.660 x 3.385	8.00:1	30—45
	8-350	4 bbl	170 @ 3800	275 @ 2400	4.057 x 3.385	8.50:1	30—45
	8-403	4 bbl	185 @ 3600	320 @ 2200	4.351 x 3.385	8.50:1	30—45
	8-455	4 bbl	190 @ 3400	350 @ 2000	4.126 x 4.250	8.50:1	30—45
'78	6-231	2 bbl	105 @ 3400	185 @ 2000	3.800 x 3.400	8.0:1	37
	8-260	2 bbl	100 @ 3400	205 @ 1800	3.500 x 3.385	7.5:1	40
	8-305	2 bbl	145 @ 3800	245 @ 2400	3.736 x 3.480	8.5:1	40
	8-305	4 bbl	160 @ 4000	265 @ 2200	3.736 x 3.480	8.5:1	40
	8-350	4 bbl	170 @ 3800	270 @ 2400	4.000 x 3.480	8.5:1	40
	8-350	4 bbl	170 @ 3800	275 @ 2000	4.057 x 3.385	8.0:1	40
	8-350	Diesel	120 @ 3600	220 @ 1800	4.057 x 3.385	22.0:1	40
	8-403	4 bbl	185 @ 3600	320 @ 2200	4.351 x 3.385	8.0:1	40
'79—'80	6-231	2 bbl	115 @ 3800	190 @ 2000	3.800 x 3.400	8.0:1	37
	8-260	2 bbl	110 @ 3400	205 @ 1800	3.500 x 3.385	7.5:1	40
	8-260	Diesel	90 @ 3600	170 @ 2200	3.500 x 3.385	22.5:1	40
	8-305	2 bbl	145 @ 3800	245 @ 2400	3.736 x 3.480	8.5:1	40
	8-305	4 bbl	160 @ 4000	235 @ 2400	3.736 x 3.480	8.5:1	40
	8-350	4 bbl	160 @ 3800	260 @ 2400	4.000 x 3.480	8.5:1	40
	8-350	4 bbl	170 @ 3800	275 @ 2000	4.057 x 3.385	8.0:1	40
	8-350	Diesel	120 @ 3600	220 @ 2200	4.057 x 3.385	22.5:1	40
	8-403	4 bbl	185 @ 3600	320 @ 2200	4.351 x 3.385	8.0:1	40
'81 USA Models	6-231	2 bbl	110 @ 3800	190 @ 1600	3.800 x 3.400	8.0:1	37
	8-260	2 bbl	105 @ 3600	205 @ 1800	3.500 x 3.385	7.5:1	40
	8-307	4 bbl	148 @ 3800	250 @ 2400	3.800 x 3.385	8.0:1	40
	8-350	Diesel	125 @ 3600	225 @ 1600	4.057 x 3.385	22.5:1	40

General Engine Specifications (cont.)

Year	Engine No. Cyl Displacement (cu in.)	Carburetor Type	Horsepower @ rpm■	Torque @ rpm (ft. lbs.)■	Bore x Stroke (in.)	Compression Ratio	Oil Pressure @ 2000 rpm
'81 Canada Models	6-231	2 bbl	115 @ 3800	190 @ 2000	3.800 x 3.400	8.0:1	37
	8-305	4 bbl	155 @ 4000	240 @ 1600	3.736 x 3.480	8.5:1	40
	8-350	Diesel	125 @ 3600	225 @ 1600	4.057 x 3.385	22.5:1	40
'82 USA Models	6-231	2 bbl	110 @ 3800	190 @ 1600	3.800 x 3.400	8.0:1	37
	8-260	2 bbl	105 @ 3600	205 @ 1800	3.500 x 3.385	7.5:1	40
	6-263	Diesel	85 @ 3600	165 @ 1600	4.057 x 3.385	21.6:1	40
	8-307	4 bbl	140 @ 3600	240 @ 1600	3.800 x 3.385	8.0:1	40
	8-350	Diesel	105 @ 3200	200 @ 1600	4.057 x 3.385	22.5:1	48
'81 Canada Models	6-231	2 bbl	110 @ 3800	190 @ 1600	3.800 x 3.400	8.0:1	37
	8-267	4 bbl	120 @ 3600	215 @ 2000	3.500 x 3.480	8.3:1	40
	8-305	4 bbl	155 @ 4000	240 @ 1600	3.736 x 3.480	8.5:1	40
'83	6-231	2 bbl	110 @ 3800	190 @ 1600	3.800 x 3.400	8.0:1	37
	6-263	Diesel	85 @ 3600	165 @ 1600	4.057 x 3.385	21.6:1	40
	8-307	4 bbl	148 @ 3800	250 @ 2400	3.800 x 3.385	8.0:1	40 ③
	8-350	Diesel	125 @ 3600	225 @ 1600	4.057 x 3.385	22.5:1	40 ④
'84–'85	6-231	2 bbl	110 @ 3800	190 @ 1600	3.800 x 3.400	8.0:1	37
	6-263	Diesel	85 @ 3600	165 @ 1600	4.057 x 3.385	21.6:1	40
	8-307	4 bbl	148 @ 3800	250 @ 2400	3.800 x 3.385	8.0:1	40 ③
	8-307	4 bbl	180 @ 4000	245 @ 3200	3.800 x 3.385	8.0:1	40 ③
	8-350	Diesel	125 @ 3600	225 @ 1600	4.057 x 3.385	22.5:1	40 ④
'86–'87	6-231	2 bbl	110 @ 3800	190 @ 1600	3.800 x 3.400	8.0:1	37 ④
	8-307	4 bbl	140 @ 3200	255 @ 2000	3.800 x 3.385	7.99:1	40 ③
	8-307	4 bbl	170 @ 4000	250 @ 2600	3.800 x 3.385	7.99:1	40 ③

■Beginning 1972, horsepower and torque are SAE net figures. They are measured at the rear of the transmission with all accessories installed and operating. Since the figures vary when a given engine is installed in different models. Some are representative rather than exact.
① Dual exhaust
② @ 2500 rpm
③ 1500 rpm
④ 2400 rpm

Valve Specifications

Year	Engine No. Cyl. Displacement (cu in.)	Seat Angle (deg)	Face Angle (deg)	Spring Test Pressure (lbs. @ in.)	Spring Installed Height (in.)	Stem to Guide Clearance (in.)		Stem Diameter (in.)	
						Intake	Exhaust	Intake	Exhaust
'70	6-250	46	45	186 @ 1.27	1²¹⁄₃₂	.0010–.0027	.0010–.0027	.3414	.3414
	8-350	45	46	187 @ 1.27	1²¹⁄₃₂	.0010–.0027	.0015–.0032	.3429	.3424
	8-455	45	46	187 @ 1.27	1²¹⁄₃₂	.0010–.0027	.0015–.0032	.3429	.3424
	8-455 4-4-2	①	④	187 @ 1.27 ⑤	1²¹⁄₃₂	.0010–.0027	.0015–.0032	.3429	.3424
'71	6-250	46	45	186 @ 1.27	1²¹⁄₃₂	.0010–.0027	.0010–.0027	.3414	.3414
	8-350	45	46	187 @ 1.27	1²¹⁄₃₂	.0010–.0027	.0015–.0032	.3424	.3424
	8-455	45	46	187 @ 1.27	1²¹⁄₃₂	.0010–.0027	.0015–.0032	.3424	.3424
	8-455 4-4-2	①	④	184 @ 1.27 ⑤	1²¹⁄₃₂	.0010–.0027	.0015–.0032	.3429	.3424

Valve Specifications (cont.)

Year	Engine No. Cyl. Displacement (cu in.)	Seat Angle (deg)	Face Angle (deg)	Spring Test Pressure (lbs. @ in.)	Spring Installed Height (in.)	Stem to Guide Clearance (in.) Intake	Stem to Guide Clearance (in.) Exhaust	Stem Diameter (in.) Intake	Stem Diameter (in.) Exhaust
'72	8-350	[6]	[7]	187 @ 1.27	1 21/32	.0010–.0027	.0015–.0032	.3429	.3424
	8-350 Calif.	45	46	198 @ 1.23	1 21/32	.0010–.0027	.0015–.0032	.3429	.3424
	8-455 98	[6]	46	187 @ 1.27	1 21/32	.0010–.0027	.0015–.0032	.3429	.3424
	8-455	[1]	[4]	206 @ 1.19	1 21/32	.0010–.0027	.0015–.0032	.3429	.3424
'73	8-350	[2]	[12]	187 @ 1.27	1 21/32	.0010–.0027	.0015–.0032	.3429	.3424
	8-455	[2]	[12]	187 @ 1.27	1 21/32	.0010–.0027	.0015–.0032	.3429	.3424
	8-455 Cutlass M.T.	[10]	[11]	206 @ 1.19	1 21/32	.0010–.0027	.0015–.0032	.3429	.3424
'74	8-350	[2]	[12]	187 @ 1.27	1 21/32	.0010–.0027	.0015–.0032	.3429	.3424
	8-455	[2]	[12]	187 @ 1.27	1 21/32	.0010–.0027	.0015–.0032	.3429	.3424
'75	6-250	46	45	186 @ 1.27	1 21/32	.0010–.0027	.0015–.0032	.3413	.3414
	8-260	[2]	[12]	186 @ 1.27	1 47/64	.0010–.0027	.0015–.0032	.3427	.3424
	8-350	[2]	[12]	187 @ 1.27	1 21/32	.0010–.0027	.0015–.0032	.3429	.3424
	8-455	[2]	[12]	187 @ 1.27	1 21/32	.0010–.0027	.0015–.0032	.3429	.3424
'76–'77	6-231	45	45	168 @ 1.33	1 47/64	.0015–.0032	.0015–.0032	.3408	.3408
	6-250	46	45	175 @ 1.26	1 21/32	.0010–.0027	.0015–.0032	.3413	.3414
	8-260	[2]	[12]	187 @ 1.27	1 47/64	.0010–.0027	.0015–.0032	.3428	.3423
	8-350, 403	[3]	[12]	187 @ 1.27	1 21/32	.0010–.0027	.0015–.0032	.3429	.3424
	8-455	[2]	[12]	187 @ 1.27	1 21/32	.0010–.0027	.0015–.0032	.3429	.3424
'78	6-231 Buick	45	45	168 @ 1.327	1 47/64	.0015–.0032	.0015–.0032	.3405–.3412	.3405–.3412
	8-260 Olds.	[2]	[12]	187 @ 1.270	1 47/64	.0010–.0027	.0015–.0032	.3425–.3432	.3420–.3427
	8-305 Chev.	46	45	200 @ 1.160 [8]	[9]	.0010–.0037	.0010–.0037	.3414	.3414
	8-350 Chev.	46	45	200 @ 1.160 [8]	[9]	.0010–.0037	.0010–.0037	.3414	.3414
	8-350 Olds.	[2]	[12]	187 @ 1.270	1 47/64	.0010–.0027	.0015–.0032	.3425–.3432	.3420–.3427
	8-350 Diesel	[2]	[12]	151 @ 1.300	1 47/64	.0010–.0027	.0015–.0032	.3425–.3432	.3420–.3427
	8-403 Olds.	[2]	[12]	187 @ 1.270	1 47/64	.0010–.0027	.0015–.0032	.3425–.3432	.3420–.3427
'79–'80	6-231 Buick	45	45	168 @ 1.327	1 47/64	.0015–.0032	.0015–.0032	.3405–.3412	.3405–.3412
	8-260 Olds.	[2]	[12]	187 @ 1.270	1 47/64	.0010–.0027	.0015–.0032	.3425–.3432	.3420–.3427
	8-260 Diesel	[2]	[12]	151 @ 1.300	1 47/64	.0010–.0027	.0015–.0032	.3425–.3432	.3420–.3427
	8-305 Chev.	46	45	200 @ 1.160	[2]	.0010–.0037	.0010–.0037	.3414	.3414
	8-350 Chev.	46	45	200 @ 1.160	[9]	.0010–.0037	.0010–.0037	.3414	.3414
	8-350 Olds.	[2]	[12]	187 @ 1.270	1 47/64	.0010–.0027	.0015–.0032	.3425–.3432	.3420–.3427
	8-350 Diesel	[2]	[12]	151 @ 1.300	1 47/64	.0010–.0027	.0015–.0032	.3425–.3432	.3420–.3427
	8-403 Olds.	[2]	[12]	187 @ 1.270	1 47/64	.0010–.0027	.0015–.0032	.3425–.3452	.3420–.3427

Valve Specifications (cont.)

Year	Engine No. Cyl. Displacement (cu in.)	Seat Angle (deg)	Face Angle (deg)	Spring Test Pressure (lbs. @ in.)	Spring Installed Height (in.)	Stem to Guide Clearance (in.)		Stem Diameter (in.)	
						Intake	Exhaust	Intake	Exhaust
'81	6-231 Buick	45	45	164 @ 1.340 ⑬	1.727	.0015–.0035	.0015–.0032	.3402–.3412	.3405–.3412
	8-260 Olds.	②	⑫	187 @ 1.270	1.670	.0010–.0027	.0015–.0032	.3425–.3432	.3420–.3427
	8-305 ⑭ Chev.	46	45	200 @ 1.250	1.700	.0010–.0027	.0010–.0027	.3414	.3414
	8-307 Olds.	②	⑫	187 @ 1.270	1.670	.0010–.0027	.0015–.0032	.3425–.3432	.3420–.3427
	8-350 ⑭ Chev.	46	45	200 @ 1.250	1.700	.0010–.0027	.0010–.0027	.3414	.3414
	8-350 Olds. D	②	⑫	210 @ 1.220	1.670	.0010–.0027	.0015–.0032	.3425–.3432	.3420–.3427
'82	6-231 Buick	45	45	220 @ 1.340	1.727	.0015–.0035	.0015–.0032	.3401–.3412	.3405–.3412
	8-260 Olds.	②	⑫	187 @ 1.270	1.670	.0010–.0027	.0015–.0032	.3425–.3432	.3420–.3427
	6-263 Olds. D	②	⑫	210 @ 1.220	1.670	.0010–.0027	.0015–.0032	.3425–.3432	.3420–.3427
	8-267 Chev.	46	45	200 @ 1.250	1.700	.0010–.0027	.0010–.0027	.3414	.3414
	8-305 Chev.	46	45	200 @ 1.250	1.700	.0010–.0027	.0010–.0027	.3414	.3414
	8-307 Olds.	②	⑫	187 @ 1.270	1.670	.0010–.0027	.0015–.0032	.3425–.3432	.3420–.3427
	8-350 Olds. D	②	⑫	210 @ 1.220	1.670	.0010–.0027	.0015–.0032	.3425–.3432	.3420–.3427
'83–'85	6-231 Buick	45	45	210 @ 1.340	1²³⁄₃₂	.0015–.0035	.0015–.0032	.3407	.3409
	6-263 Olds.	②	⑫	210 @ 1.220	1⁴³⁄₆₄	.0010–.0027	.0015–.0032	.3429	.3429
	8-307 Olds ⑮	②	⑫	180 @ 1.270	1⁴³⁄₆₄	.0010–.0027	.0010–.0032	.3429	.3429
	8-307 Olds ⑭	②	⑫	203 @ 1.220	1⁴³⁄₆₄	.0010–.0027	.0010–.0032	.3429	.3429
	8-350 Olds.	②	⑫	210 @ 1.220	1⁴³⁄₆₄	.0010–.0027	.0015–.0032	.3429	.3429
'86–'87	6-231 Buick	45	45	182 @ 1.34	1⁴⁷⁄₆₄	.0015–.0035	.0015–.0032	.3401–.3412	.3405–.3412
	8-307 Olds ⑮	⑰	⑱	187 @ 1.270	1.670	.0010–.0027	.0010–.0032	.3425–.3432	.3420–.3427
	8-307 Olds. ⑯	⑰	⑱	210 @ 1.220	1.670	.0010–.0027	.0010–.0032	.3425–.3432	.3420–.3427

① Intake 30°, exhaust 45°
② Intake 45°, exhaust 31°
④ Intake 30°, exhaust 46°
⑤ With air induction—302 @ 1.17
⑥ Intake 45°, exhaust 30°
⑦ Intake 46°, exhaust 30°
⑧ Intake 200 @ 1.25
⑨ Intake: 1²³⁄₃₂
   Exhaust 1¹⁹⁄₃₂
⑩ Intake 31°, exhaust 45°
⑪ Intake 30°, exhaust 44°
⑫ Intake 44°, exhaust 30°
⑬ Exhaust 182 @ 1.340
⑭ Canada Only
⑮ VIN-Y
⑯ VIN-9
⑰ Intake 45°, exhaust 60°
⑱ Intake 46°, exhaust 59°

never use a gasket when reassembling. Conversely, if the engine was assembled using a rocker arm cover gasket, never replace it with RTV. When using RTV, an ⅛" bead is sufficient. Always run the bead on the inside of the bolt holes.

REMOVAL AND INSTALLATION

Gasoline Engines

1. Remove the air cleaner if necessary.
2. Disconnect the PCV valve from the valve cover.
3. Disconnect the spark plug wires and move away from the valve cover.
4. Remove any accessory mounting brackets as necessary that may be in the way.
5. Remove the valve cover to cylinder head attaching screws and remove the valve cover.
6. Before reinstalling the valve cover, thoroughly clean the cover gasket surface and install a new gasket or RTV (Room Temperature Vulcanizing) sealer.

Diesel Engines

1. Remove the injection pump and lines as outlined in Chapter 4.
2. If removing the right valve cover on the V6 engine, disconnect the crankcase ventilation system pipes, grommets, filter and crankcase depression regulator valve.
3. Remove the valve cover to cylinder head attaching screws.
4. Remove any accessory mounting brackets that may be in the way, then remove the valve cover.
5. Before installing the valve cover make sure the valve cover and head gasket surfaces are thoroughly clean.
6. Apply RTV sealer or equivalent to the valve cover, then install the cover and retaining screws.
7. The remainder of installation is the reverse of removal.

Rocker Arm and Shaft

REMOVAL AND INSTALLATION

Buick Built Engines

1. Remove the rocker arm covers.
2. Remove the rocker arm shaft assembly bolts.
3. Remove the rocker arm shaft assembly.
4. To remove the rocker arms from the shaft, the nylon arm retainers must be removed. They can be removed with a pair of water pump pliers, or they can be broken by hitting them below the head with a chisel.
5. Remove the rocker arms from the shaft. Make sure you keep them in order. Also note that the external rib on each arm points away

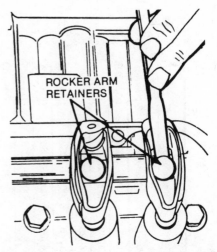

Removing nylon rocker arm retainers—Buick built engines

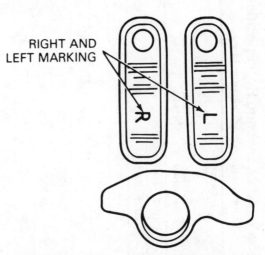

Replacement rocker arm identification—Buick built engines

Position of rocker arms on shaft—Buick built engines

Crankshaft and Connecting Rod Specifications
All measurements are given in inches

Year	Engine No. Cyl Displacement (cu in.)	Crankshaft				Connecting Rod		
		Main Brg Journal Dia	Main Brg Oil Clearance	Shaft End-Play	Thrust on No.	Journal Diameter	Oil Clearance	Side Clearance
'70–'73	6-250	2.3004	.003–.0029	.002–.006	7	1.999–2.000	.0007–.0027	.007–.016
	8-350	2.4990[6]	.0005–.0021[1]	.004–.008	3	2.1238–2.1248	.0004–.0033[7]	[4]
	8-455	2.9998	.0005–.0021[2]	.004–.008	3	2.4988–2.4998	.004–.0033	[4][5]
'74	8-350	2.4990[9]	.0005–.0021[1]	.004–.008	3	2.1238–2.1248	.0004–.0033	.006–.020
	8-455	2.9998	.0005–.0021[2]	.004–.008	3	2.4988–2.4998	.0004–.0033	.006–.020
'75–'77	6-231	2.4995	.0004–.0015	.004–.008	2	2.0000	.0005–.0026	.006–.027
	6-250	2.2988	.0035[8]	.002–.006	7	1.999–2.000	.0035	.009–.014
	8-260	2.4990[9]	.0005–.0021[1]	.004–.008	3	2.1238–2.1248	.0004–.0033	.006–.020
	8-350, 403	2.4990[9]	.0005–.0021[1]	.004–.008	3	2.1238–2.1248	.0004–.0033	.006–.020
	8-455	2.9998	.0005–.0021[2]	.004–.008	3	2.4988–2.4998	.0004–.0033	.006–.020
'78	6-231 Buick	2.4995	.0003–.0017	.004–.008	2	2.2487–2.2495	.0005–.0026	.006–.027
	8-260 Olds.	2.4985–2.4995[10]	.0005–.0021[11]	.0035–.0135	3	2.1238–2.1248	.004–.0033	.006–.020
	8-305 Chev.	[12]	.0035 max[13]	.002–.006	3	2.1990–2.2000	.003 max	.008–.014
	8-350 Chev.	[12]	.0035 max[13]	.002–.006	3	2.1990–2.2000	.003 max	.008–.014
	8-350 Olds.	2.4985–2.4995[10]	.0005–.0021[11]	.0035–.0135	3	2.1238–2.1248	.0004–.0033	.006–.020
	8-260, 350 Diesel	2.9993–3.0003	.0005–.0021[11]	.0035–.0135	3	2.1238–2.1248	.0005–.0026	.006–.020
	8-403 Olds.	2.4985–2.4995[10]	.0005–.0021[11]	.0035–.0135	3	2.1238–2.1248	.0004–.0033	.006–.020
'79–'80	6-173 Chev.	2.494	.0005–.0015	.002–.0079	3	2.000	.0005–.0020	.006–.017
	6-231 Buick	2.4995	.0003–.0017	.004–.008	2	2.2487–2.2495	.0005.0026	.006–.027
	8-260 Olds.	2.4985–2.4995[10]	.0005–.0021[11]	.0035–.0135	3	2.1238–2.1248	.0004–.0033	.006–.020
	8-305 Chev.	[12]	.0035 max[13]	.002–.006	3	2.1238–2.1248	.0004–.0033	.006–.020
	8-307 Olds.	2.4990–2.4995[14]	.0005–.0021[11]	.0035–.0135	3	2.1238–2.1248	.0004–.0033	.006–.020
	8-350 Chev.	[12]	.00356 max[13]	.002–.006	3	2.1990–2.2000	.003 max	.008–.014

Year	Engine	Main Brg Journal Dia.	Main Brg Oil Clearance	Shaft End-Play	Thrust on No.	Rod Journal Dia.	Rod Oil Clearance	Rod Side Clearance
'81	8-260 350, Diesel	2.9993–3.0003	.0005–.0021	.0035–.0135	3	2.1238–2.1248	.0005–.0026	.006–.020
	8-403 Olds.	2.4985–2.4995 ⑩	.0005–.0021 ⑪	.0035–.0135	3	2.1238–2.1248	.0004–.0033	.006–.020
	6-231 Buick	2.4990–2.4995	.0003–.0018	.0030–.0090	3	2.2487–2.2495	.0005–.0026	.006–.027
	8-260 Olds.	2.4990–2.4995 ⑭	.0005–.0021 ⑪	.0035–.0135	3	2.1238–2.1248	.0004–.0033	.006–.020
	8-305 Chev.	⑫	⑮	.0020–.0060	3	2.0986–2.0998	.0013–.0035	.006–.014
	8-307 Olds.	2.4990–2.4995 ⑭	.0005–.0021 ⑪	.0035–.0135	3	2.1238–2.1248	.0004–.0033	.006–.020
	8-350 Chev.	⑫	⑮	.0020–.0060	3	2.0986–2.0998	.0013–.0035	.006–.014
	8-350 Olds. D	2.9993–3.0003	.0005–.0021 ⑪	.0035–.0135	3	2.1238–2.1248	.0005–.0026	.006–.020
'82	6-231 Buick	2.4990–2.4995	.0003–.0018	.0030–.0090	3	2.2487–2.2495	.0005–.0026	.006–.023
	8-260 Olds.	2.4990–2.4995 ⑭	.0005–.0021 ⑪	.0035–.0135	3	2.1238–2.1248	.0004–.0033	.006–.020
	6-263 Olds. D	2.9993–3.0003	⑯	.0035–.0135	4	2.2490–2.2510	.0003–.0025	.0082–.0214
	8-267 Chev.	⑫	⑮	.0020–.0060	3	2.0986–2.0998	.0013–.0035	.006–.014
	8-305 Chev.	⑫	⑮	.0020–.0060	3	2.0986–2.0998	.0013–.0035	.006–.014
	8-307 Olds.	2.4990–2.4995 ⑭	.0005–.0021 ⑪	.0035–.0135	3	2.1238–2.1248	.0004–.0033	.006–.020
	8-350 Olds. D	2.9993–3.0003	.0005–.0021 ⑰	.0035–.0135	3	2.1238–2.1248	.0005–.0026	.006–.020
'83–'85	6-231 Buick	2.4995	.0003–.0018	.011–.003	2	2.2487–2.2495	.0005–.0026	.006–.015
	6-263 Olds. D	2.9993–3.003	.0005–.0021 ⑯	.0035–.0135	3	2.2490–2.2510	.0005–.0026	.006–.020
	8-307 Olds.	2.4990–2.4995 ⑭	.0005–.0021 ⑪	.0035–.0135	3	2.1238–2.1248	.0004–.0033	.006–.020
	8-350 Olds. D	2.9993–3.0003	.0005–.0021 ⑰	.0035–.0135	3	2.2495–2.2500	.0005–.0026	.006–.020
'86–'87	6-231	2.4995	.0003–.0018	.003–.011	2	2.2487–2.2495	.0005–.0026	.003–.015
	8-307	2.4985–2.4995 ⑩	.0005–.0021 ⑪	.0035–.0135	3	2.1238–2.1248	.0004–.0033	.006–.020

C: Chevrolet Built
D: Diesel
① No. 5—.0015–.0031
② No. 5—.0020–.0034
④ 1970—.002–.013; 1971—.002–.011; 1972–73—.006–.020
⑤ 1970–73W-30—.002–.021
⑥ 1973—2.50 in.
⑦ 1973—.0005–.0026
⑧ No.1—.0020 in. max
⑨ No. 1—2.4993 in.
⑩ #1:2.4988–2.4998
⑪ #5: .0015–.0031

⑫ #1: 2.4484–2.4493
　 #2, 3, 4: 2.4481–2.4490
　 #5: 2.4479–2.4488
⑬ #1.0020 max
⑭ #1: 2.4993–2.4998
⑮ #1: .0008–.0020
　 #2, 3, 4: .0011–.0023
　 #5: .0017–.0032
⑯ #1, 2, 3: .0005–.0021
　 #4: .0020–.0034
⑰ #5: .0020–.0034

Piston and Ring Specifications

Year	Engine	Piston-Bore Clearance	Ring Side Clearance			Ring Gap		
			Top Compression	Bottom Compression	Oil Control	Top Compression	Bottom Compression	Oil Control
1975–87	6-231 B	.0013–.0035	.0030–.0050	.0030–.0050	.0–.0035	.010–.020①	.010–.020①	.015–.035⑲
1970–76	6-250 C	.0025 max.	.0012–.0027	.0012–.0032	.0–.0050	.010–.020	.010–.020	.015–.055
1975–82	8-260 O	.0010–.0020⑨	.0020–.0040	.0020–.0040	.005–.011	.010–.023②	.010–.023②	.015–.055③
1979–80	8-260 OD	.0050–.0060	.0040–.0060	.0018–.0038	.0010–.0050	.012–.022	.010–.020	.015–.055
1982–85	6-263 OD	.0030–.0040	.0050–.0070	.0030–.0050	.0010–.0050	.015–.025	.015–.025	.001–.005
1982*	8-267 C	.0007–.0017	.0012–.0032	.0012–.0032	.0020–.0070	.010–.020	.010–.025	.015–.055
1972–82	8-305④ C	.0007–.0017	.0012–.0042⑫	.0012–.0042⑫	.0020–.0080⑬	.010–.030⑭	.010–.035⑮	.015–.065⑯
1981–87	8-307 O	.0008–.0018⑰	.0020–.0040⑱	.0020–.0040⑱	.0010–.0050	.009–.019	.009–.019	.015–.055⑩
1977–82	8-350④ C	.0007–.0017	.0012–.0042⑫	.0012–.0042⑫	.0020–.0080⑬	.010–.030⑭	.010–.035⑮	.015–.065⑯
1970–74	8-350 O	.0010–.0020	.0020–.0040	.0020–.0040	.0010–.0050	.010–.023	.010–.023	.015–.055
1975–82	8-350 O	.0010–.0020	.0020–.0040	.0020–.0040	.001–.005	⑤	⑤	.015–.055⑪
1978–85	8-350 OD	.0050–.0060⑦	.0050–.00070	.0018–.0038⑧	.0010–.0050	.015–.025	.015–.025	.015–.055
1977–79	8-403 O	.0010–.0020	.0020–.0040	.0020–.0040	.015–.055	⑥	⑥	.015–.055
1970–76	8-455 O	.0010–.0020	.0020–.0040	.0020–.0040	.0020–.0080	.010–.023	.010–.023	.015–.055

C: Chevrolet built
D: Diesel
O: Oldsmobile built
B: Buick built
*Canada only

① 1979–82: .013–.023
② 1979–82: .010–.020 except those with Sealed Power rings
1979–82 with Sealed Power rings: .009–.019
③ 1979–82 with Muskegon rings: .010–.035
④ 1981–82, with 8-305, 350 used in Canadian Cutlass models only
⑤ 1975–78: .010–.023
1979–82 except those with Sealed Power rings: .013–.023
1979–82 with Sealed Power rings: .010–.020
⑥ 1977–78: .010–.023
1979 except those with Sealed Power rings: .010–.020
1979 with Sealed Power rings: .009–.019

⑦ 1982: .0030–.0040
⑧ 1982: .0030–.0050
⑨ 1981–82: .0008–.0018
⑩ with TRW rings: .010–.025
⑪ Canada: .015–.035
⑫ Canada: .0012–.0032
⑬ Canada: .0020–.0070
⑭ Canada: .010–.020
⑮ Canada: .010–.025
⑯ Canada: .0156–.055
⑰ 1986–87: .00075–.00175
⑱ 1986–87: .0018–.0038
⑲ 1986–87: .015–.055

Torque Specifications
All readings in ft. lbs.

Year	Engine	Cylinder Head Bolts	Rod Bearing Bolts	Main Bearing Bolts	Crankshaft Damper or Pulley Bolt	Flywheel to Crankshaft Bolts	Manifold Intake	Manifold Exhaust
'70–'72	6-250	95	35	65	Press fit	60	25	30
	8-All	80	42	120 ②	160 min	③	35	25
'73–'74	8-All	85	42	120 ②	160 min	③	40	25
'75	6-250	95	35	65	Press fit	60	①	④
	8-260, 350, 455	85	42	120 ②	200–310	③	40	25
'76–'77	6-231	80	40	115	175	60	45	25
	6-250	95	35	65	Press fit	60	①	②
	8-260, 350, 403, 455	85	42	120 ②	200–310	③	40	25
'78–'80	6-231 Buick	80	40	100	225	60	45	25
	8-260 Olds.	85 ⑤	42	②	200–310	③	40 ⑤	25
	8-305 Chev	65	45	70	60	60	30	20
	8-350 Buick	80	40	100	225	60	45	25
	8-350 Chev.	65	45	70	60	60	30	④
	8-350 Olds.	130 ③	42	②	200–310	60	40 ⑤	25
	8-260 350 Diesel	130 ⑤	42	120	200–310	60	40 ⑤	25
	8-403 Olds.	130 ⑤	42	②	200–310	60	40 ⑤	25
'81	6-231 Buick	80	40	100	225	60	45	25
	8-260 Olds.	85	42	②	200–310	60	40	25
	8-305 Chev.	65	45	70	60	60	30	20
	8-307 Olds.	130	42	②	200–310	60	40	25
	8-350 Olds. Diesel	130	42	120	200–310	60	40	25
'82–'85	6-231 Buick	80	40	100	225	60	45	25
	8-260 Olds.	85	42	②	200–310	60	40	25
	6-263 Olds. Diesel	⑤	42	107	160–350	48	41	29
	8-267 Chev.	65	45	70	60	60	30	20
	8-305 Chev.	65	45	70	60	60	30	20
	8-307 Olds.	130	42	②	200–310	60	40	25
	8-350 Olds. Diesel	130	42	120	200–310	60	40	25
'86–'87	6-231 Buick	80	45	100	200	60	45	20
	8-307 Olds.	125	42	②	200–310	60	40	25

① Intake manifold integral with cylinder head
② 8-260, 8-307, 8-350: Torque to 80 ft. lbs. on No. 1, 2, 3, 4 and 120 ft. lbs. on No. 5
③ A.T. 60 ft. lbs.; M.T. 90 ft. lbs.
④ Inner bolts—30 ft. lbs.; outer bolts—20 ft. lbs. minimum
⑤ #5, 6, 11, 12, 12, 14: 59 ft. lb.
   All others: 142 ft. lb.
⑦ Clean and dip entire bolt in engine oil before tightening to obtain a correct torque reading

Troubleshooting Engine Mechanical Problems

Problem	Cause	Solution
External oil leaks	• Fuel pump gasket broken or improperly seated	• Replace gasket
	• Cylinder head cover RTV sealant broken or improperly seated	• Replace sealant; inspect cylinder head cover sealant flange and cylinder head sealant surface for distortion and cracks
	• Oil filler cap leaking or missing	• Replace cap
	• Oil filter gasket broken or improperly seated	• Replace oil filter
	• Oil pan side gasket broken, improperly seated or opening in RTV sealant	• Replace gasket or repair opening in sealant; inspect oil pan gasket flange for distortion
	• Oil pan front oil seal broken or improperly seated	• Replace seal; inspect timing case cover and oil pan seal flange for distortion
	• Oil pan rear oil seal broken or improperly seated	• Replace seal; inspect oil pan rear oil seal flange; inspect rear main bearing cap for cracks, plugged oil return channels, or distortion in seal groove
	• Timing case cover oil seal broken or improperly seated	• Replace seal
	• Excess oil pressure because of restricted PCV valve	• Replace PCV valve
	• Oil pan drain plug loose or has stripped threads	• Repair as necessary and tighten
	• Rear oil gallery plug loose	• Use appropriate sealant on gallery plug and tighten
	• Rear camshaft plug loose or improperly seated	• Seat camshaft plug or replace and seal, as necessary
	• Distributor base gasket damaged	• Replace gasket
Excessive oil consumption	• Oil level too high	• Drain oil to specified level
	• Oil with wrong viscosity being used	• Replace with specified oil
	• PCV valve stuck closed	• Replace PCV valve
	• Valve stem oil deflectors (or seals) are damaged, missing, or incorrect type	• Replace valve stem oil deflectors
	• Valve stems or valve guides worn	• Measure stem-to-guide clearance and repair as necessary
	• Poorly fitted or missing valve cover baffles	• Replace valve cover
	• Piston rings broken or missing	• Replace broken or missing rings
	• Scuffed piston	• Replace piston
	• Incorrect piston ring gap	• Measure ring gap, repair as necessary
	• Piston rings sticking or excessively loose in grooves	• Measure ring side clearance, repair as necessary
	• Compression rings installed upside down	• Repair as necessary
	• Cylinder walls worn, scored, or glazed	• Repair as necessary
	• Piston ring gaps not properly staggered	• Repair as necessary
	• Excessive main or connecting rod bearing clearance	• Measure bearing clearance, repair as necessary
No oil pressure	• Low oil level	• Add oil to correct level
	• Oil pressure gauge, warning lamp or sending unit inaccurate	• Replace oil pressure gauge or warning lamp
	• Oil pump malfunction	• Replace oil pump
	• Oil pressure relief valve sticking	• Remove and inspect oil pressure relief valve assembly
	• Oil passages on pressure side of pump obstructed	• Inspect oil passages for obstruction

Troubleshooting Engine Mechanical Problems (cont.)

Problem	Cause	Solution
No oil pressure (cont.)	• Oil pickup screen or tube obstructed	• Inspect oil pickup for obstruction
	• Loose oil inlet tube	• Tighten or seal inlet tube
Low oil pressure	• Low oil level	• Add oil to correct level
	• Inaccurate gauge, warning lamp or sending unit	• Replace oil pressure gauge or warning lamp
	• Oil excessively thin because of dilution, poor quality, or improper grade	• Drain and refill crankcase with recommended oil
	• Excessive oil temperature	• Correct cause of overheating engine
	• Oil pressure relief spring weak or sticking	• Remove and inspect oil pressure relief valve assembly
	• Oil inlet tube and screen assembly has restriction or air leak	• Remove and inspect oil inlet tube and screen assembly. (Fill inlet tube with lacquer thinner to locate leaks.)
	• Excessive oil pump clearance	• Measure clearances
	• Excessive main, rod, or camshaft bearing clearance	• Measure bearing clearances, repair as necessary
High oil pressure	• Improper oil viscosity	• Drain and refill crankcase with correct viscosity oil
	• Oil pressure gauge or sending unit inaccurate	• Replace oil pressure gauge
	• Oil pressure relief valve sticking closed	• Remove and inspect oil pressure relief valve assembly
Main bearing noise	• Insufficient oil supply	• Inspect for low oil level and low oil pressure
	• Main bearing clearance excessive	• Measure main bearing clearance, repair as necessary
	• Bearing insert missing	• Replace missing insert
	• Crankshaft end play excessive	• Measure end play, repair as necessary
	• Improperly tightened main bearing cap bolts	• Tighten bolts with specified torque
	• Loose flywheel or drive plate	• Tighten flywheel or drive plate attaching bolts
	• Loose or damaged vibration damper	• Repair as necessary
Connecting rod bearing noise	• Insufficient oil supply	• Inspect for low oil level and low oil pressure
	• Carbon build-up on piston	• Remove carbon from piston crown
	• Bearing clearance excessive or bearing missing	• Measure clearance, repair as necessary
	• Crankshaft connecting rod journal out-of-round	• Measure journal dimensions, repair or replace as necessary
	• Misaligned connecting rod or cap	• Repair as necessary
	• Connecting rod bolts tightened improperly	• Tighten bolts with specified torque
Piston noise	• Piston-to-cylinder wall clearance excessive (scuffed piston)	• Measure clearance and examine piston
	• Cylinder walls excessively tapered or out-of-round	• Measure cylinder wall dimensions, rebore cylinder
	• Piston ring broken	• Replace all rings on piston
	• Loose or seized piston pin	• Measure piston-to-pin clearance, repair as necessary
	• Connecting rods misaligned	• Measure rod alignment, straighten or replace
	• Piston ring side clearance excessively loose or tight	• Measure ring side clearance, repair as necessary
	• Carbon build-up on piston is excessive	• Remove carbon from piston

Troubleshooting Engine Mechanical Problems (cont.)

Problem	Cause	Solution
Valve actuating component noise	• Insufficient oil supply	• Check for: (a) Low oil level (b) Low oil pressure (c) Plugged push rods (d) Wrong hydraulic tappets (e) Restricted oil gallery (f) Excessive tappet to bore clearance
	• Push rods worn or bent	• Replace worn or bent push rods
	• Rocker arms or pivots worn	• Replace worn rocker arms or pivots
	• Foreign objects or chips in hydraulic tappets	• Clean tappets
	• Excessive tappet leak-down	• Replace valve tappet
	• Tappet face worn	• Replace tappet; inspect corresponding cam lobe for wear
	• Broken or cocked valve springs	• Properly seat cocked springs; replace broken springs
	• Stem-to-guide clearance excessive	• Measure stem-to-guide clearance, repair as required
	• Valve bent	• Replace valve
	• Loose rocker arms	• Tighten bolts with specified torque
	• Valve seat runout excessive	• Regrind valve seat/valves
	• Missing valve lock	• Install valve lock
	• Push rod rubbing or contacting cylinder head	• Remove cylinder head and remove obstruction in head
	• Excessive engine oil (four-cylinder engine)	• Correct oil level

Troubleshooting the Cooling System

Problem	Cause	Solution
High temperature gauge indication—overheating	• Coolant level low	• Replenish coolant
	• Fan belt loose	• Adjust fan belt tension
	• Radiator hose(s) collapsed	• Replace hose(s)
	• Radiator airflow blocked	• Remove restriction (bug screen, fog lamps, etc.)
	• Faulty radiator cap	• Replace radiator cap
	• Ignition timing incorrect	• Adjust ignition timing
	• Idle speed low	• Adjust idle speed
	• Air trapped in cooling system	• Purge air
	• Heavy traffic driving	• Operate at fast idle in neutral intermittently to cool engine
	• Incorrect cooling system component(s) installed	• Install proper component(s)
	• Faulty thermostat	• Replace thermostat
	• Water pump shaft broken or impeller loose	• Replace water pump
	• Radiator tubes clogged	• Flush radiator
	• Cooling system clogged	• Flush system
	• Casting flash in cooling passages	• Repair or replace as necessary. Flash may be visible by removing cooling system components or removing core plugs.
	• Brakes dragging	• Repair brakes
	• Excessive engine friction	• Repair engine
	• Antifreeze concentration over 68%	• Lower antifreeze concentration percentage

Troubleshooting the Cooling System (cont.)

Problem	Cause	Solution
High temperature gauge indication— overheating (cont.)	• Missing air seals • Faulty gauge or sending unit • Loss of coolant flow caused by leakage or foaming • Viscous fan drive failed	• Replace air seals • Repair or replace faulty component • Repair or replace leaking component, replace coolant • Replace unit
Low temperature indication— undercooling	• Thermostat stuck open • Faulty gauge or sending unit	• Replace thermostat • Repair or replace faulty component
Coolant loss—boilover	• Overfilled cooling system • Quick shutdown after hard (hot) run • Air in system resulting in occasional "burping" of coolant • Insufficient antifreeze allowing coolant boiling point to be too low • Antifreeze deteriorated because of age or contamination • Leaks due to loose hose clamps, loose nuts, bolts, drain plugs, faulty hoses, or defective radiator • Faulty head gasket • Cracked head, manifold, or block • Faulty radiator cap	• Reduce coolant level to proper specification • Allow engine to run at fast idle prior to shutdown • Purge system • Add antifreeze to raise boiling point • Replace coolant • Pressure test system to locate source of leak(s) then repair as necessary • Replace head gasket • Replace as necessary • Replace cap
Coolant entry into crankcase or cylinder(s)	• Faulty head gasket • Crack in head, manifold or block	• Replace head gasket • Replace as necessary
Coolant recovery system inoperative	• Coolant level low • Leak in system • Pressure cap not tight or seal missing, or leaking • Pressure cap defective • Overflow tube clogged or leaking • Recovery bottle vent restricted	• Replenish coolant to FULL mark • Pressure test to isolate leak and repair as necessary • Repair as necessary • Replace cap • Repair as necessary • Remove restriction
Noise	• Fan contacting shroud • Loose water pump impeller • Glazed fan belt • Loose fan belt • Rough surface on drive pulley • Water pump bearing worn • Belt alignment	• Reposition shroud and inspect engine mounts • Replace pump • Apply silicone or replace belt • Adjust fan belt tension • Replace pulley • Remove belt to isolate. Replace pump. • Check pulley alignment. Repair as necessary.
No coolant flow through heater core	• Restricted return inlet in water pump • Heater hose collapsed or restricted • Restricted heater core • Restricted outlet in thermostat housing • Intake manifold bypass hole in cylinder head restricted • Faulty heater control valve • Intake manifold coolant passage restricted	• Remove restriction • Remove restriction or replace hose • Remove restriction or replace core • Remove flash or restriction • Remove restriction • Replace valve • Remove restriction or replace intake manifold

NOTE: *Immediately after shutdown, the engine enters a condition known as heat soak. This is caused by the cooling system being inoperative while engine temperature is still high. If coolant temperature rises above boiling point, expansion and pressure may push some coolant out of the radiator overflow tube. If this does not occur frequently it is considered normal.*

Troubleshooting the Serpentine Drive Belt

Problem	Cause	Solution
Tension sheeting fabric failure (woven fabric on outside circumference of belt has cracked or separated from body of belt)	• Grooved or backside idler pulley diameters are less than minimum recommended • Tension sheeting contacting (rubbing) stationary object • Excessive heat causing woven fabric to age • Tension sheeting splice has fractured	• Replace pulley(s) not conforming to specification • Correct rubbing condition • Replace belt • Replace belt
Noise (objectional squeal, squeak, or rumble is heard or felt while drive belt is in operation)	• Belt slippage • Bearing noise • Belt misalignment • Belt-to-pulley mismatch • Driven component inducing vibration • System resonant frequency inducing vibration	• Adjust belt • Locate and repair • Align belt/pulley(s) • Install correct belt • Locate defective driven component and repair • Vary belt tension within specifications. Replace belt.
Rib chunking (one or more ribs has separated from belt body)	• Foreign objects imbedded in pulley grooves • Installation damage • Drive loads in excess of design specifications • Insufficient internal belt adhesion	• Remove foreign objects from pulley grooves • Replace belt • Adjust belt tension • Replace belt
Rib or belt wear (belt ribs contact bottom of pulley grooves)	• Pulley(s) misaligned • Mismatch of belt and pulley groove widths • Abrasive environment • Rusted pulley(s) • Sharp or jagged pulley groove tips • Rubber deteriorated	• Align pulley(s) • Replace belt • Replace belt • Clean rust from pulley(s) • Replace pulley • Replace belt
Longitudinal belt cracking (cracks between two ribs)	• Belt has mistracked from pulley groove • Pulley groove tip has worn away rubber-to-tensile member	• Replace belt • Replace belt
Belt slips	• Belt slipping because of insufficient tension • Belt or pulley subjected to substance (belt dressing, oil, ethylene glycol) that has reduced friction • Driven component bearing failure • Belt glazed and hardened from heat and excessive slippage	• Adjust tension • Replace belt and clean pulleys • Replace faulty component bearing • Replace belt
"Groove jumping" (belt does not maintain correct position on pulley, or turns over and/or runs off pulleys)	• Insufficient belt tension • Pulley(s) not within design tolerance • Foreign object(s) in grooves • Excessive belt speed • Pulley misalignment • Belt-to-pulley profile mismatched • Belt cordline is distorted	• Adjust belt tension • Replace pulley(s) • Remove foreign objects from grooves • Avoid excessive engine acceleration • Align pulley(s) • Install correct belt • Replace belt
Belt broken (Note: identify and correct problem before replacement belt is installed)	• Excessive tension • Tensile members damaged during belt installation • Belt turnover • Severe pulley misalignment • Bracket, pulley, or bearing failure	• Replace belt and adjust tension to specification • Replace belt • Replace belt • Align pulley(s) • Replace defective component and belt

Troubleshooting the Serpentine Drive Belt (cont.)

Problem	Cause	Solution
Cord edge failure (tensile member exposed at edges of belt or separated from belt body)	• Excessive tension • Drive pulley misalignment • Belt contacting stationary object • Pulley irregularities • Improper pulley construction • Insufficient adhesion between tensile member and rubber matrix	• Adjust belt tension • Align pulley • Correct as necessary • Replace pulley • Replace pulley • Replace belt and adjust tension to specifications
Sporadic rib cracking (multiple cracks in belt ribs at random intervals)	• Ribbed pulley(s) diameter less than minimum specification • Backside bend flat pulley(s) diameter less than minimum • Excessive heat condition causing rubber to harden • Excessive belt thickness • Belt overcured • Excessive tension	• Replace pulley(s) • Replace pulley(s) • Correct heat condition as necessary • Replace belt • Replace belt • Adjust belt tension

from the rocker arm shaft bolt located between each pair of rocker arms.

6. If you are installing new rocker arms, note that the replacement rocker arms are marked **R** and **L** for right and left side installation. Do not interchange them.

7. Install the rocker arms on the shaft and lubricate them with oil.

Rocker Arm

REMOVAL AND INSTALLATION

L-6 Engine

1. Remove the valve cover.

2. The rocker arms are individually mounted. Remove the attaching nut from each rocker arm and lift the rocker arm nut, ball, and the rocker arm from the cylinder head. Keep all the assemblies in order so they can be installed in their original location.

3. Install the rocker arms and balls on their studs after coating the wear points with white grease.

4. Make sure the pushrod is installed in the lifter and the end of the rocker arms, and tighten the rocker arm attaching nut fingertight.

5. Adjust the valves. (See the valve adjustment section.)

V8 Chevrolet Built Engines

1. Remove the valve cover(s).

2. Remove the rocker arm nut and rocker arm ball.

3. Lift the rocker arm off the rocker arm stud. Always keep the rocker arm assemblies together and assemble them on the same stud.

4. Remove the pushrod from its bore. Make sure the rods are returned to their original bores, with the same end in the block.

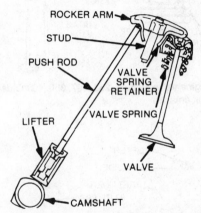

Engine valve system-Chevrolet built engines

5. Reverse the removal procedure to install the rocker arms. Tighten the rocker arm ball retaining nut to 20 ft.lb.

263 (Diesel), 350, 403 (Gas and Diesel) Oldsmobile Engines

NOTE: *If only the rocker arms on the diesels have been removed, Bleed-down, but not disassembly of the lifters will be necessary. See Valve Lifter Bleed-down.*

1. Remove the valve covers.

2. The rocker arms are removed in paris for each cylinder. Remove the two bolts that attach the rocker arm pivot to the cylinder head. Remove the two rocker arms.

3. Repeat the procedure for each pair of rocker arms. Keep them in order for proper reassembly.

4. To install the rocker arms, it is necessary to ensure that the lifters are off the am lobe and that the valves are closed.

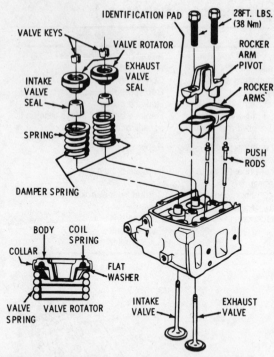

Engine valve system, 260, 307, 350, 403 Oldsmobile built engines

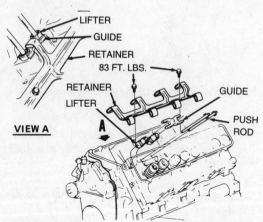

Valve lifter guides and retainer, 1985 and later 307 (code y) engine

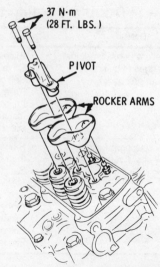

Rocker arms and pivots—263 Oldsmobile built diesel engine

Diesel Valve Lifter Bleed-Down

If the intake manifold or head has been removed, removal, disassembly, reassembly and bleed-down of the lifter will be necessary. This procedure requires the use of special tools not available to the general public. Therefore, we won't cover it here. If only the rocker arms have been removed. or loosened, the bleed-down procedure is much simpler, but still quite complicated. Proceed as follows:

1. Before installing any removed rocker arms, rotate the engine crankshaft to a position of the No.1 cylinder being 32 degrees before top dead center. This is 2 inches counterclockwise from the 0 mark on the timing scale, measured along the rim of the pulley. If only a right side rocker arm was loosened or removed, remove the No.1 cylinder glow plug to determine if the position of the piston is correct. Compression pressure as the piston rises will assure that you're right.

2. If a left side rocker arm was loosened or removed, rotate the crankshaft until the No.5 cylinder intake valve pushrod ball is 7mm (0.28″) above the No.5 cylinder exhaust valve pushrod ball.

NOTE: *Use only hand wrenches to torque the rocker pivot balls.*

3. If removed, install the No.5 cylinder pivot and rocker arms. Torque the bolts alternately between the intake and exhaust valves until the valve begins to open, then stop!

4. Install the rest of the rocker arms, except the No.3 exhaust valve, if removed.

5. If removed, install, but do not torque, the No.3 valve pivots beyond the point at which the valve would be fully open. This point is in-

5. To do this, attach a remote starter to the engine or have an assistant bump the engine over until the valves are closed for each cylinder.

6. With the valves for each cylinder closed, install the paired rocker arms. Lubricate all pivot and rocker arm wear points with white grease before installation. Torque the retaining bolts to 25 ft.lb.

7. Reinstall the valve covers with new gaskets.

dicated by a strong resistance while still turning the pivot retaining bolts. If you go beyond this point, the pushrods will be bent. Torque the bolts SLOWLY to allow the lifter to bleed down.

6. Torque the No.5 cylinder pivot bolt slowly. Do not go beyond the point at which the valve would be fully open. This is indicated as described above.

7. DO NOT TURN THE CRANKSHAFT FOR 45 MINUTES AFTER THE ABOVE PROCEDURE HAS BEEN COMPLETED.

8. Finish assembling the engine.

Thermostat
REMOVAL AND INSTALLATION

CAUTION: *When draining the coolant, keep in mind that cats and dogs are attracted by the ethylene glycol antifreeze, and are quite likely to drink any that is left in an uncovered container or in puddles on the ground. This will prove fatal in sufficient quantity. Always drain the coolant into a sealable container. Coolant should be reused unless it is contaminated or several years old.*

To replace the thermostat, drain the cooling system below the level of the thermostat and remove the two bolts holding the water neck in place. Remove the water neck and the thermostat will lift out. Clean the mating surfaces of both the water neck and the intake manifold. Use a new gasket when installing the thermostat. If only RTV sealant was used from the factory, use only RTV sealant during assembly.

NOTE: *The spring of the thermostat must be installed toward the engine.*

Intake Manifold
REMOVAL AND INSTALLATION

L-6 Engine

1975 and later L-6 engines are equipped with an intake manifold which is integral with the cylinder head and cannot be removed. Earlier inline six engines use a combined intake/exhaust manifold. Both are removed together.

1. Remove the air cleaner assembly.

2. Disconnect the throttle linkage at the carburetor. Detach the fuel lines and vacuum lines from the carburetor.

3. Remove the PCV valve and hose from the valve cover. Disconnect the air supply hose from the check valve on the air injection manifold, if so equipped.

4. Unbolt the exhaust manifold from the exhaust pipe. Spray the threads with a rust penetrant first.

5. Unbolt the manifold bolts and clamps.

6. Remove the manifold assembly. If you wish to separate the manifold, remove the single bolt and two nuts at the center of the assembly.

7. Installation is in the reverse order of removal. Use new gaskets and make sure the ports are free of any debris.

Buick Built Engines

1. Disconnect the negative battery cable and drain the radiator.

CAUTION: *When draining the coolant, keep in mind that cats and dogs are attracted by the ethylene glycol antifreeze, and are quite likely to drink any that is left in an uncovered container or in puddles on the ground. This will prove fatal in sufficient quantity. Always drain the coolant into a sealable container. Coolant should be reused unless it is contaminated or several years old.*

2. Remove the air cleaner.

3. Disconnect the upper radiator hose and the heater hose at the manifold.

4. Disconnect the accelerator linkage at the carburetor and the linkage bracket at the manifold. Remove the cruise control chain, if so equipped.

5. Remove the fuel line from the carburetor and the booster vacuum pipe from the manifold.

6. On 1976 models, disconnect the choke pipe at the choke housing.

7. Disconnect and label the transmission vacuum modulator line, idle stop solenoid wire (if so equipped), distributor wires and the temperature sending unit wire.

8. Disconnect and mark the vacuum hoses at the distributor and the carburetor.

9. Disconnect the coolant bypass hose at the manifold.

10. On six cylinder models, remove the dis-

Intake manifold torque sequence—Buick built engines

TORX® head bolt

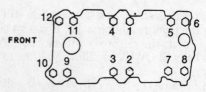

Intake manifold torque sequence—267, 305 and 350 Chevrolet built engines

tributor cap and wires to gain access to the Torx head bolt. Remove the bolt.

11. Remove the throttle linkage springs. On 1976 models, remove the spark plug wires.

12. Remove the A/C compressor top bracket, if so equipped.

13. Remove the manifold.

14. Use a new gasket to install. Use sealer on the end of the rubber gasket seals. Carefully guide the manifold onto the engine block dowel pin. Observe Turbocharger Precautions given with the previous Turbocharger information. Tighten the bolts in the proper order. Installation is the reverse of removal steps.

V8 Chevrolet Built Engines.

1. Drain the cooling system.

CAUTION: *When draining the coolant, keep in mind that cats and dogs are attracted by the ethylene glycol antifreeze, and are quite likely to drink any that is left in an uncovered container or in puddles on the ground. This will prove fatal in sufficient quantity. Always drain the coolant into a sealable container. Coolant should be reused unless it is contaminated or several years old.*

2. Remove the air cleaner.

3. Disconnect the battery ground.

4. Disconnect the upper radiator hose and the heater hose at the manifold.

5. Disconnect all linkage and hoses attached to the manifold and/or carburetor.

6. Remove the distributor, mark the rotor position with chalk on the distributor body, then remove the distributor.

7. Remove the air cleaner bracket, air pump and bracket, accelerator return spring and bracket and accelerator bellcrank.

8. Remove the alternator upper mounting bracket.

9. Unbolt and remove the manifold.

V8 Oldsmobile Built Gasoline Engines

1. Remove the carburetor air cleaner, drain the radiator.

CAUTION: *When draining the coolant, keep in mind that cats and dogs are attracted by the ethylene glycol antifreeze, and are quite likely to drink any that is left in an uncovered container or in puddles on the ground. This will prove fatal in sufficient quantity. Always drain the coolant into a sealable container. Coolant should be reused unless it is contaminated or several years old.*

2. Disconnect the upper radiator hose, bypass hose, and heater hose from the manifold.

3. Disconnect the throttle linkage, vacuum and gas lines from the carburetor.

4. Remove the generator and air conditioning compressor brackets if necessary.

CAUTION: *Do not disconnect the A/C lines. Personal injury could result.*

5. Disconnect the temperature gauge wire. Remove the oil filler tube on 455 engines.

6. Remove the intake manifold bolts and re-

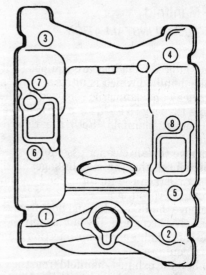

Intake manifold torque sequence—263 diesel engine

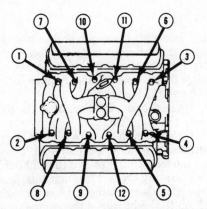

Intake manifold torque sequence, 260, 307, 350, 403 Oldsmobile built gasoline and diesel engines

move the manifold with the carburetor attached.

7. Install in the reverse order of removal, tightening the bolts first to 15 ft.lb., then to the figure specified in the torque chart, in the sequence illustrated. Coat all gasket surfaces with sealer.

263 and 350 Oldsmobile Built Diesel Engines.

NOTE: *See Diesel Valve Lifter bleed-down.*
1. Remove the air cleaner.
2. Drain the radiator. Loosen the upper by-pass hose clamp, remove the thermostat housing bolts, and remove the housing and the thermostat from the intake manifold.

CAUTION: *When draining the coolant, keep in mind that cats and dogs are attracted by the ethylene glycol antifreeze, and are quite likely to drink any that is left in an uncovered container or in puddles on the ground. This will prove fatal in sufficient quantity. Always drain the coolant into a sealable container. Coolant should be reused unless it is contaminated or several years old.*

3. Remove the breather pipes from the rocker covers and the air crossover. Remove the air crossover.
4. Disconnect the throttle rod and the return spring. If equipped with cruise control, remove the servo.
5. Remove the hairpin clip at the bellcrank and disconnect the cables. Remove the throttle cable from the bracket on the manifold; position the cable away from the engine. Disconnect and label any wiring as necessary.
6. Remove the alternator bracket if necessary. On the 350 cu. in. engine, if equipped with air conditioning, remove the compressor mounting bolts and move the compressor aside, without disconnecting any of the hoses. Remove the compressor mounting bracket from the intake manifold.

7. Disconnect the fuel line from the pump and the fuel filter. Remove the fuel filter and bracket.
8. Remove the fuel injection pump and lines. See above for procedures.
9. Disconnect and remove the vacuum pump or oil pump drive assembly from the rear of the engine.
10. Remove the intake manifold drain tube.
11. Remove the intake manifold bolts and remove the manifold. Remove the adapter seal. Remove the injection pump adapter.
12. Clean the mating surfaces of the cylinder heads and the intake manifold using a putty knife.
13. Coat both sides of the gasket surface that seal the intake manifold to the cylinder heads with G.M. sealer No.1050026 or the equivalent. Position the intake manifold gaskets on the cylinder heads. Install the end seals, making sure that the ends are positioned under the cylinder heads.
14. Carefully lower the intake manifold into place on the engine.
15. Clean the intake manifold bolts thoroughly, then dip them in clean engine oil. Install the bolts and on the 350 V8 tighten to 15 ft.lb. in the sequence shown. Next, tighten all the bolts to 30 ft.lb., in sequence. On the 263 V6 eng. tighten to 15 ft.lb. in the sequence shown, then retorque to 41 ft.lb.
16. Install the intake manifold drain tube and clamp.
17. Install injection pump adapter. See Injection Pump Adapter, Adapter Seal and New Adapter Timing Mark Removal and Installation in Chapter 4. If a new adapter is not being used, skip steps 4 and 9.
18. Install the fuel injection pump. See Diesel Engine, under Fuel System, above for procedures.
19. Install the vacuum pump or coil pump drive assembly.

CAUTION: *Do Not operate the engine without vacuum pump/oil pump assembly in place as this assembly drives the engine oil pump.*

20. Install the remaining components as they were removed. For throttle rod and transmission cable adjustments, see Diesel Engine, Fuel Injection Pump removal and installation, steps 22 and 27, in Chapter 4.

Exhaust Manifold
REMOVAL AND INSTALLATION
L6 Engine

Up until 1975, the exhaust manifold is removed with the intake manifold. See the section on intake manifold removal. For 1975 and later models, see the following procedure.

1. Remove the air cleaner.

2. If equipped with power steering, remove the power steering pump and bracket. Leave the pump hoses connected and set the pump out of the way.

3. If so equipped, remove the air pump bracket.

4. Remvoe the EFE valve bracket.

5. Remove the throttle linkage and throttle return springs.

6. Unbolt the exhaust manifold from the exhaust pipe. Spray the threads with rust penetrant first.

7. Remove the manifold bolts and remove the exhaust manifold.

8. To install, clean and oil all the manifold-to-head bolts.

9. When installing the manifold, torque the bolts in stages to the specified torque in the proper sequence.

10. The rest of installation is in the reverse order of removal.

Buick Built Engines

1. Jack up the car and support on axle stands.

2. Disconnect the exhaust crossover pipe from the manifolds on both sides of the engine and lower it. On the V6, disconnect the choke pipe if you are working on the right side, the EFE line if you are working on the left side.

3. If equipped with manual transmission, remove the equalizer shaft. Disconnect the turbocharger, if so equipped.

4. Remove the exhaust manifold-to-cylinder head bolts.

5. Remove the manifold from beneath the car.

6. Reverse the above to install. Always use the bolt locks.

V8 Chevrolet Built Engines

LEFT SIDE

1. Disconnect the battery ground cable and raise the car. Disconnect the exhaust pipe at the manifold.

2. Remove the front manifold to exhaust pipe flange stud, and then remove the rear spark plug shield; lower the car.

3. Remove the air conditioning compressor and set it aside. DO NOT disconnect any air conditioning lines.

4. Disconnect and label the spark plug wires and their holder, the temperature sending unit lead and the dipstick.

5. Remove the attaching bolts and remove the manifold.

6. To install, reverse the removal procedure.

RIGHT SIDE

1. Disconnect the ground cable, and remove the fan shroud upper bolts and loosen the fan shroud. Remove the air cleaner intake pipe. If equipped with an air pump, remove the air injector manifold assembly.

2. Raise the car and disconnect the exhaust pipe at the manifold.

3. On some models, there will not be enough clearance to remove the manifold. If so, perform the following: Remove the right side engine mounting bracket through bolt, and loosen the left side mounting bracket through bolt. Jack up the right side of the engine, reinstall the right side through bolt, and lower the engine until the through bolt is resting on the mounting bracket.

4. Remove the rear spark plug shield bolt.

5. Lower the car and remove the spark plug wires (label them first), air cleaner heat stove pipe, and the air cleaner intake pipe. Remove the rear spark plug shield.

6. Remove the manifold to engine bolts, and remove the manifold, the EFE valve and the vacuum can.

7. To install, reverse the removal procedure.

350, 403 Oldsmobile Built Gasoline Engines through 1977

1. Disconnect the negative battery cable and remove the air cleaner.

2. Remove the alternator and the alternator bracket.

3. Raise the car and support it with jackstands.

4. If the car is equipped with a crossover pipe, remove the bolts from the exhaust manifold flanges and remove the crossover pipe.

5. On cars equipped with air-conditioning, it will be necessary to remove the right front wheel to gain access to the right-hand manifold through the opening in the inner fender panel.

6. If the car is equipped with hot-air shrouds, remove them from the manifolds.

7. Unbolt the exhaust pipes from the exhaust manifolds. Spray the manifold studs with a penetrating lubricant first.

8. Remove the bolts which attach the manifolds to the cylinder heads, and remove the manifolds.

9. Installation is in the reverse order of removal.

V8 Oldsmobile Built Gasoline Engines

RIGHT SIDE

1. Raise and support the car on jackstands.

2. Disconnect the exhaust crossover pipe.

3. Disconnect the exhaust pipe.

4. Unbolt and remove the manifold.

5. Installation is the reverse of removal.

LEFT SIDE

1. Raise and support the car on jackstands.

2. Disconnect the crossover pipe.

3. Lower the car.

4. Disconnect the steering intermediate shaft.

5. Remove the heat shroud.

6. Unbolt and remove the manifold.

7. Installation is the reverse of removal.

263 and 350 Oldsmobile Built Diesel Engines

1. Drain the cooling system.

CAUTION: *When draining the coolant, keep in mind that cats and dogs are attracted by the ethylene glycol antifreeze, and are quite likely to drink any that is left in an uncovered container or in puddles on the ground. This will prove fatal in sufficient quantity. Always drain the coolant into a sealable container. Coolant should be reused unless it is contaminated or several years old.*

2. Remove the air cleaner.

3. Disconnect the upper radiator hose and thermostat bypass hose from the water outlet.

4. Disconnect the heater inlet hose and the AC vacuum line from the water valve.

5. Remove the crankcase ventilation pipes from the air crossover (V6) or valve covers (V8).

6. Remove the fuel pump and immediately cap all pipe openings.

7. Remove the fuel injection pump.

8. Disconnect all wiring and remaining hoses from the manifold.

9. Remove the cruise control servo.

10. Remove the intermediate pump adapter.

11. Unbolt and remove the manifold and adapter seal.

12. Clean all gasket surfaces thoroughly.

13. Coat both sides of the new gaskets with sealer.

14. Position the gasket on the engine. Install the end seals making sure that their ends are under the heads.

NOTE: *The seals and their mating surfaces must be dry. Apply a bead of RTV silicone sealer at the ends of the seals.*

15. Position the intake manifold on the engine and connect the thermostat bypass hose. Dip the bolts in oil and torque them in sequence to 15 ft. lb. Then, retorque them in sequence to 40 ft. lb.

16. Install all other parts in reverse order of removal. Apply chassis lube to the seal area of the intake manifold and pump adapter.

Radiator

REMOVAL AND INSTALLATION

Through 1976

1. Drain the radiator and disconnect the upper and lower radiator hoses. Disconnect the transmission fluid cooler lines, if so equipped.

CAUTION: *When draining the coolant, keep in mind that cats and dogs are attracted by the ethylene glycol antifreeze, and are quite likely to drink any that is left in an uncovered container or in puddles on the ground. This will prove fatal in sufficient quantity. Always drain the coolant into a sealable container. Coolant should be reused unless it is contaminated or several years old.*

2. Disconnect the coolant recovery hose.

3. Remove the fan shroud-to-radiator screws. Lift the shroud out of the clips and hang the shroud over the fan.

4. Remove the radiator upper mounting panel.

5. Remove the radiator. Reverse to install.

1977 and Later

1. Refer to steps 1-2 of the above procedure.

2. On 1978 and later models, remove the fan blade and the fan clutch.

3. Remove the fan housing attaching screws and lift out the shroud.

On models which have the fan shroud stapled together, remove the staples, then remove the upper shroud half. During assembly, the shroud halves must be drilled and bolted together.

NOTE: *Some air conditioned models have a high-pressure A/C line which runs across the top of the upper radiator shroud. It is not necessary to remove the line in order to remove the shroud. If the A/C line is clamped to the shroud, disconnect the clamp. Carefully slide the upper shroud half out from under the A/C line, toward the passenger side of the vehicle (fan removed).*

4. Remove the radiator. Reverse to install.

Water Pump

REMOVAL AND INSTALLATION

All Engines

1. Drain the cooling system. Remove the fan shroud, if necessary for clearance.

CAUTION: *When draining the coolant, keep in mind that cats and dogs are attracted by the ethylene glycol antifreeze, and are quite likely to drink any that is left in an uncovered container or in puddles on the ground. This will prove fatal in sufficient quantity. Always drain the coolant into a sealable container.*

Coolant should be reused unless it is contaminated or several years old.

2. Loosen the belt or belts, then remove the fan blades and pulley or pulleys from the hub on the water pump shaft. Remove the belt or belts.

3. Disconnect the hose from the water pump inlet and the heater hose from the nipple. Remove the bolts, then remove the pump and gasket from the timing case cover or engine block. To install the pump:

1. Install the pump assembly with a new gasket. Bolts and lock washers must be torqued evenly.

2. Connect the radiator hose to the pump inlet and the heater hose to the nipple. Fill the cooling system and check all points of possible coolant leaks.

3. Install the fan pulley or pulleys and the fan blade. Install the belt or belts and adjust for correct tension.

Cylinder Head

REMOVAL AND INSTALLATION

Inline Six Cylinder

1. Drain the cooling system and remove the air cleaner. Disconnect the PCV hose.

CAUTION: *When draining the coolant, keep in mind that cats and dogs are attracted by the ethylene glycol antifreeze, and are quite likely to drink any that is left in an uncovered container or in puddles on the ground. This will prove fatal in sufficient quantity. Always drain the coolant into a sealable container. Coolant should be reused unless it is contaminated or several years old.*

2. Disconnect the throttle linkage at the carburetor. Disconnect the fuel line at the carburetor. Disconnect the vacuum line to the distributor.

3. Remove the top radiator hose. Remove the battery ground strap. Disconnect the wires from the temperature sending unit.

4. Disconnect the wires from the coil and remove the coil Remove the spark plug wires from the plugs.

5. Disconnect the exhaust pipe at the manifold flange. On 1970-74 engines, the intake and exhaust manifolds are removed as a unit. On 1975-76 engines, the intake manifold is integral with the head and cannot be removed.

6. Remove the manifold bolts and remove the manifold or manifolds.

7. Remove the rocker arm cover. Mark and remove the rocker arms. Mark and remove the pushrods. It is important to mark them as they must go back in their correct place.

8. Remove the cylinder head bolts. You'll probably need a breaker bar as they are under a lot of torque.

9. Remove the cylinder head. It may be necessary to tap the head lightly with a hammer to break the seal. Don't pry between the head and the block as you may gouge one or the other. Remove the manifold gasket. Generally speaking, it is necessary to scrape the top of the engine block and the cylinder head to remove the gasket.

10. To install the cylinder head, first place a new head gasket over the dowel pins in the top of the block.

NOTE: *Different types of head gaskets are available. If you are using a steel-asbestos composition gasket, do not use gasket sealer.*

11. Lower the cylinder head carefully into place over the dowel pins and the gasket.

12. Clean and oil the cylinder head bolts, install them and run them down snug.

13. Tighten the head bolts in three stages in the correct sequences. The final torque should be 90 to 95 foot pounds.

14. Install the pushrods in their correct openings, making sure they are seated in their lifter sockets.

15. Install the rocker arms in their correct position. Tighten the rocker arm nuts until all pushrod play is taken up.

16. Install the manifold or manifolds, using new gaskets. Torque the manifold to the specified torque.

17. Install the upper radiator hose. Install the coil and coil wires.

18. Install the fuel line, vacuum line, and throttle linkage. Install the ground strap.

19. Connect the exhaust pipe to the exhaust manifold.

20. Adjust the valves. (See the valve adjustment section.) Install the rocker arm cover, using a new gasket. Install the air cleaner.

Buick Built Engines

1. Disconnect the battery.

2. Drain the coolant.

CAUTION: *When draining the coolant, keep in mind that cats and dogs are attracted by the ethylene glycol antifreeze, and are quite likely to drink any that is left in an uncovered container or in puddles on the ground. This will prove fatal in sufficient quantity. Always drain the coolant into a sealable container.*

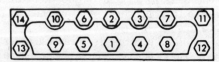

6-250 cylinder head torque sequence

Coolant should be reused unless it is contaminated or several years old.

3. Remove the air cleaner.

4. Remove the air conditioning compressor, but do not disconnect any lines. Disconnect the AIR hose at the check valve. Remove the turbocharger assembly, if so equipped.

5. Remove the intake manifold.

6. When removing the right cylinder head, loosen the alternator belt, disconnect the wiring and remove the alternator. If equipped with A/C, remove the compressor from the mounting bracket and position it out of the way. Do not disconnect any of the hoses.

7. When removing the left cylinder head, remove the dipstick, power steering pump and air pump if so equipped.

8. Disconnect and label the plug wires.

9. Disconnect exhaust manifold from the head being removed.

10. Remove the rocker arm cover and rocker shaft assembly. Lift out the push rods. Be extremely careful to avoid getting dirt into the valve lifters. Keep the pushrods in order; they must be returned to their original positions.

11. Remove the cylinder head bolts.

12. Remove the cylinder head and gasket.

13. Reverse the above steps to install. Torque the head bolts to specifications in three steps.

likely to drink any that is left in an uncovered container or in puddles on the ground. This will prove fatal in sufficient quantity. Always drain the coolant into a sealable container. Coolant should be reused unless it is contaminated or several years old.

2. Disconnect:
• battery
• radiator and heater hose from manifold.
• throttle linkage
• fuel line
• coil wires
• temperature sending unit
• power brake hose, distributor vacuum hose, and crankcase vent hoses.

3. Remove:
• distributor, marking position
• alternator upper bracket
• coil and bracket
• manifold attaching bolts.
• intake manifold and carburetor.

4. Remove:
• rocker arm covers
• rocker arm nuts, balls, rocker arms, and pushrods. These items must be replaced in their original locations.

5. Remove cylinder head bolts, cylinder head, and gaskets. Reverse procedure to install. Tighten head bolts evenly to the specified torque. On engines having steel gasket, use sealer on both sides. No sealer should be used on steel-asbestos gaskets. Adjust the valve lash.

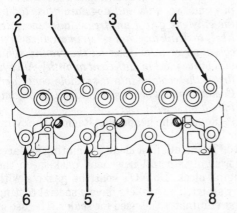

Cylinder head torque sequence—V6 Buick built engines

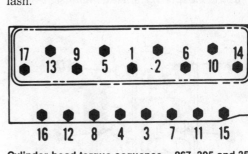

Cylinder head torque sequence—267, 305 and 350 Chevrolet built engines

V8 Oldsmobile Built Gasoline Engine

1. Drain the cooling system.

CAUTION: *When draining the coolant, keep in mind that cats and dogs are attracted by the ethylene glycol antifreeze, and are quite likely to drink any that is left in an uncovered container or in puddles on the ground. This will prove fatal in sufficient quantity. Always drain the coolant into a sealable container. Coolant should be reused unless it is contaminated or several years old.*

2. Remove the intake manifold and carburetor as an assembly.

V8 Chevrolet Built Engines

NOTE: *The engine should be overnight cold before the cylinder head is removed to prevent warpage.*

CAUTION: *Do not discharge the compressor or disconnect the A/C lines. Personal injury could result.*

1. Drain coolant. Remove the air cleaner.

CAUTION: *When draining the coolant, keep in mind that cats and dogs are attracted by the ethylene glycol antifreeze, and are quite*

3. Remove exhaust manifolds.

4. Loosen or remove any accessory brackets which interfere.

5. Remove the valve cover. Loosen any accessory brackets which are in the way.

6. Remove the battery ground strap from the cylinder head.

7. Remove rocker arm bolts, pivots, rocker arms and pushrods. Scribe the pivots and identify the rocker arms and pushrods so that they may be installed in their original locations.

NOTE: *On cars with the 455 engine and air-conditioning, it may be necessary to disconnect the right motor mount and jack up the right front corner of the engine to remove the number eight pushrod. If the car is equipped with power brakes, it may be necessary to disconnect the booster and turn it sideways to remove the number seven pushrod.*

8. Remove cylinder head bolts and cylinder head(s).

9. Install in the reverse order of removal. It is recommended that the head gasket be coated on both sides with sealer. Dip head bolts in oil before installing. Tighten all head bolts in the correct sequence to 60-70 ft.lb., then again is sequence to the specified torque. See Specifications at the beginning of this section for correct head bolt torque. Retorque the bolts after engine is warmed up.

NOTE: *In 1981 and later models the head gaskets must be installed without sealer.*

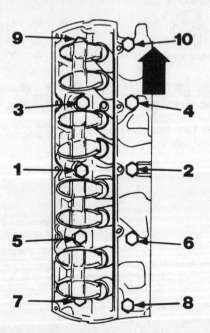

Cylinder head torque sequence, 260, 307, 350, 403 Oldsmobile built engines

263, and 350 Oldsmobile Built Diesel Engines

NOTE: *See diesel valve lifter bleed down procedure.*

1. Remove the intake manifold, using the procedure outlined above.

2. Remove the rocker arm cover(s), after removing any accessory brackets which interfere with cover removal.

3. Disconnect and label the flow plug wiring.

4. If the right cylinder head is being removed, remove the ground strap from the head.

5. Remove the rocker arm bolts, the bridged pivots, the rocker arms, and the pushrods, keeping all the parts in order so that they can be returned to their original positions. It is a good practice to number or mark the parts to avoid interchanging them.

6. Remove the fuel return lines from the nozzles.

7. Remove the exhaust manifold(s), using the procedure outlines above.

8. Remove the engine block drain plug on the side of the engine from which the cylinder head is being removed. On V6s, remove the pipe-thread plugs covering the upper cylinder head bolts.

CAUTION: *When draining the coolant, keep in mind that cats and dogs are attracted by the ethylene glycol antifreeze, and are quite likely to drink any that is left in an uncovered container or in puddles on the ground. This will prove fatal in sufficient quantity. Always drain the coolant into a sealable container. Coolant should be reused unless it is contaminated or several years old.*

9. Remove the head bolts. Remove the cylinder head.

10. To install, first clean the mating surfaces thoroughly. Install new head gaskets on the engine block. Do NOT coat the gaskets with any sealer. The gaskets have a special coating that eliminates the need for sealer. The use of sealer will interfere with this coating and cause leaks. Install cylinder head onto the block.

11. Clean the had bolts (and pipe-thread plugs-V6s) thoroughly. On the V8, dip the bolts in clean engine oil and install into the cylinder head until the heads of the bolts lightly contact the cylinder block. On V6s, coat the plug threads, bolt threads and the area under the bolt threads with sealer/lubricant part No. 1052080 or equivalent.

NOTE: *The correct sealer must be used or coolant leads and bolt torque loss will result.*

12. On the V8, tighten the bolts, in the sequence illustrated, to 100 ft.lb. When all bolts

have been tightened to this figure, begin the tightening sequence again, and torque all bolts to 130 ft.lb.

13. On V6s, tighten all head bolts in sequence to the following torques:
- all except bolts 5, 6, 11, 12, 13 and 14 — 100 ft.lb.
- bolts 5, 6, 11, 12, 13, and 14 — 41 ft.lb.
- all bolts except 5, 6, 11, 12, 13, and 14 — 142 ft.lb.
- bolts 5, 6, 11, 12, 13, and 14 — 59 ft.lb.

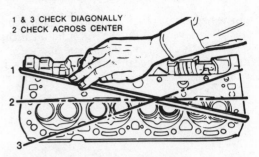

1 & 3 CHECK DIAGONALLY
2 CHECK ACROSS CENTER

Check the cylinder head for warpage

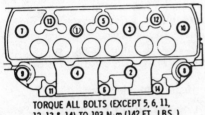

TORQUE ALL BOLTS (EXCEPT 5, 6, 11, 12, 13 & 14) TO 193 N·m (142 FT. LBS.). NUMBERS 5, 6, 11, 12, 13 & 14 TORQUE TO 80 N·m (59 FT. LBS.).

Cylinder head torque sequence—263 Diesel engine (V6)

CLEANING AND INSPECTION

Chip carbon away from the valve heads, combustion chambers, and ports, using a chisel made of hardwood. Remove the remaining deposits with a stiff wire brush.

NOTE: *Be sure that the deposits are actually removed, rather than burnished.*

Have the cylinder head (cast iron only) hot-tanked to remove grease, corrosions, and scale from the water passages.

CAUTION: *Do not hot-tank aluminum parts. Clean the remaining cylinder head parts in an engine cleaning solvent. Do not remove the protective coating from the springs.*

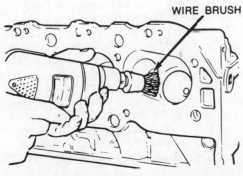

WIRE BRUSH

Remove the carbon from the cylinder head with a wire brush and electric drill

RESURFACING

NOTE: *Cylinder head resurfacing should be performed by a competent machine shop.*
Place a straight-edge across the gasket surface of the cylinder head. Using feeler gauges, determine the clearance at the center of the straightedge. If warpage exceeds 0.003″ in a 6″ span, or 0.006″ over the total length, the cylinder head must be resurfaced.

NOTE: *If warpage exceeds the manufacturer's maximum tolerance for material removal, the cylinder head must be replaced.*
When milling the cylinder heads of V-type engines, the intake manifold mounting position is altered, and must be corrected by milling the manifold flange a proportionate amount.

Valves and Springs

NOTE: *All valve reconditioning procedures should be performed by a competent machine shop.*
The equivalents of the special tools mentioned in the following procedures may be used.

BUICK BUILT ENGINES

Removal and Installation and Reconditioning

1. Remove cylinder head. Place on a clean surface.
2. Using suitable spring compressor, such as J-8062, compress valve spring and remove valve spring cap key. Release tool and remove spring and cap.
3. Remove valve seals from intake valve guides. Seals must be discarded. Remove valves. Place valves in numerical order so that they can be reinstalled in original location.
4. Remove all carbon from combustion chambers, piston heads, and valves. When using scrapers or wire brushes for removing carbon, avoid scratching valve seats and valve faces. A soft wire brush is suitable for this purpose.
5. Clean carbon and gum deposits from valve guide bores. Use Reamer J-8101.
6. Inspect valve faces and seats for pits,

burned sports or other evidences of poor seating. If a valve head must be ground until the outer edge is sharp in order to true up the face, discard the valve because the sharp edge will run too hot. 45 degrees is the correct angle for valve faces.

7. If valve stem has too much clearance in its guide, the guide should be reamed using 0.006" and 0.010" reamer.

8. True up valve seats to 45 degrees. Cutting a valve seat results in lowering the valve spring pressure and increases the width of the seat. The nominal width of the intake valve seat is $\frac{1}{16}$". If the intake valve seat is over $\frac{5}{64}$" wide after truing up it should be narrowed to specified width by the use of 20 degree and 70 degree stones. The nominal width of the exhaust valve seat is $\frac{3}{32}$". If the exhaust valve is over $\frac{7}{64}$" wide after truing, it should be narrowed to the specified width Use 20 degree and 70 degree stones to narrow the valve seats to the specified widths.

Improper hydraulic valve lifter operation may result if valve and seat have been refinished enough to allow the end of the valve stem to raise approximately 0.050" above normal position. In this case it will be necessary to grind off end of the valve stem or replace parts.

9. Lightly lap the valves into seats with the fine grinding compound. The refacing and re-seating operations should leave the refinished surfaces smooth and true so that a minimum of lapping is required. Excessive lapping will groove the valve face preventing a good seat when hot.

New valves should not be lapped under any condition as the 0.0004" to 0.0015" nickel-plated surface on the exhausts will be removed.

10. Test valves for concentricity with seats and for tight seating. The usual test is to coat the valve face lightly with Prussian blue, or equivalent, and turn the valve against seat. If the valve face is concentric with the valve stem a mark will be made all around the face, which if the face is not concentric with the stem, a mark will be made on only one side of the face. Next, coat the valve seat lightly with Prussian blue, or equivalent. Rotate the valve against the seat to determine if the valve seat is concentric with the valve guide, and if the valve is seating all the way around. Both of these tests are necessary to prove that a proper seat is being obtained.

11. Remove any burrs from valve stem with a fine stone and polish with crocus cloth.

12. Lubricate valve stems and guides with engine oil and reinstall valves.

13. Install new intake valve seals. Do not install exhaust valve guide seals.

a. Start valve seal carefully over valve stem. Push seal down until to touches top of guide.

b. Use installation tool J-22509 to push seal over valve guide until upper inside surface of seal touches top of guide.

NOTE: *COMPRESS SPRINGS ONLY ENOUGH TO INSTALL KEEPERS. EXCESS COMPRESSION CAN CAUSE SPRING RETAINER TO DAMAGE VALVE SEAL*

14. Install intake valve springs on the 350 cu. in. with closely-wound coil toward the cylinder head. Exhaust valve springs on the 350 engine and all valve springs for V-6 engine, may be installed with either end up.

15. Reinstall valve spring, cap and cap retainer, using same equipment used for removal.

16. Install cylinder head.

CHEVROLET BUILT ENGINES

Removal and Reconditioning

1. With cylinder head removed, remove valve rocker arm nuts, balls and rocker arms (if not previously done).

2. Using Tool J-8062, compress the valve springs and remove valve keys. Release the compressor tool and remove rotators or spring caps, oil shedders, springs and damper assembly. Then remove oil seals.

3. Remove valves from cylinder head and place them in a rack in their proper sequence so that they can be assembled in their original positions.

4. Inspect the valves for burned heads, cracked faces or damaged stems.

Excessive valve stem to bore clearance will cause excessive oil consumption and may cause valve breakage. Insufficient clearance will result in noisy and sticky functioning of the valve and disturb engine smoothness.

5. Measure valve stem clearance as follows: Clamp a dial indictor on one side of the cylinder head rocker arm cover gasket rail, locating the indictor so that movement of the valve stem from side to side (crosswise to the head) will cause a direct movement of the indictor stem. The indictor stem must contact the side of the valve stem just above the valve guide. With the valve head dropped about $\frac{1}{16}$" off the valve seat; move the stem of the valve from side to side using light pressure to obtain a clearance reading. If clearance exceeds specifications it will be necessary to ream valve guides for oversize valves. Service valves are available in standard, 0.003", 0.015" and 0.030" oversize.

6. Check valve spring tension with Tool J-8056 spring tester.

Springs should be compressed to the specified height and checked against the specifications chart. Springs should be replaced is not within 10 lbs. 44N of the specified load (without dampers).

7. Inspect rocker arm studs for wear or damage.

Rocker arm studs that have damaged threads or are loose in cylinder heads should be replaced with new studs available in 0.003″ and 0.013″ oversize. Studs may be installed after reaming the holes as follows:

a. Remove old stud by placing Tool J-5802-1 over the stud, installing nut and flat washer and removing stud by turning nut.

b. Ream hole for oversize stud using Tool J-5715 for 0.003″ oversize or Tool J-6036 for 0.013″ oversize. Do not attempt to install an oversize stud without reaming stud hole.

c. Coat press-fit area of stud with hypoid axle lubricant. Install new stud, using Tool J-6880 as a guide. Gauge should bottom on head.

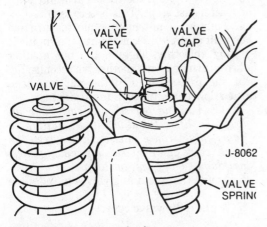

Removing valve key and valve cap

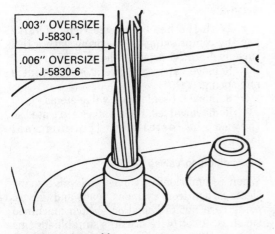

Reaming valve guide

8. Valves with oversize stems are available (see specifications). To ream the valve guide bores for oversize valves use Tool Set J-5830.

9. Reconditioning the valve seats is very important, because the seating of the valves must be perfect for the engine to deliver the power and performance built into it.

10. Another important factor is the cooling of the valve heads. Good contact between each valve and its seat in the head is essential to insure that the heat in the valve head will be properly carried away.

Several different types of equipment are available for reseating valve seats. The recommendations from the manufacturer of the equipment being used should be carefully followed to attain proper results.

It is important that valve seat concentricity be measured. Valve seats should be concentric to within 0.002″ total indicator reading.

Installation

1. Insert a valve in the proper port.

2. Assemble the valve spring and related parts as follows:

a. Set the valve spring (with damper) oil shedder and valve cap or rotator in place.

b. Compress the spring with Tool J-8062.

c. Install oil seal in the lower groove of the stem, making sure that the seal is flat and not twisted.

d. Install the valve locks and release the compressor tool, making sure that the locks seat properly in the upper groove of the valve stem.

3. Install the remaining valves.

4. Check each valve stem oil seal by placing Valve Seal Leak Detector (Tool J-23994) over the end of the valve stem and against the cap. Operate the vacuum pump and make sure no air leaks past the seal.

5. Check the installed height of the valve springs, using a narrow thin scale. A cutaway scale will help. Measure form the top of the shim or the spring seat to the top of the oil shedder. If this is found to exceed the specified height, install a valve spring seat shim approximately $\frac{1}{16}$″ thick, At no time should the spring be shimmed to give an installed height under the minimum specified.

Valve Adjustment-V8 Engines

NOTE: *Whenever new components are being installed, coat bearing surfaces of rocker arms and rocker arm balls with Molykote® or equivalent or damage to parts could occur.*

1. Install push rods. Be sure push rods seat in lifter sockets.

2. Install rocker arms, rocker arm balls and

rocker arm nuts. Tighten rocker arm nuts until all lash is eliminated.

3. Adjust valves when lifter is on base circle of camshaft lobe as follows:

a. Crank engine until mark on torsional damper lines up with center or **0** mark on the timing tab fastened to the crankcase front cover and the engine is in the number 1 firing position. This may be determined by placing fingers on the number 1 valves as the mark on the damper comes near the **0** mark on the crankcase front cover. If the valves are not moving, the engine is in the number 1 firing position. If the valves move as the mark comes up to the timing tab, the engine is in number 6 firing position and should be turned over one more time to reach the number 1 position.

b. With the engine in the number 1 firing position as determined above, the following valves may be adjusted.
- Exhaust-1, 3, 4, 8
- Intake-1, 2, 5, 7

c. Back out adjusting nut until lash is felt at the push rod then turn in adjusting nut until all lash is removed. This can be determined by checking push rod side play while turning adjusting nut. When play has been removed, turn adjusting nut in one full additional turn (to center lifter plunger).

d. Crank the engine one revolution until the pointer **0** mark and torsional damper mark are again in alignment. This is number 6 firing position. With the engine in this position the following valves may be adjusted.
- Exhaust-2, 5, 6, 7
- Intake-3, 4, 6, 8

4. Install rocker arm covers as previously outlined.

5. Start engine and adjust carburetor idle speed.

L6 Preliminary Adjustment

1. After rocker arm or cylinder head disassembly, proceed as follows:

2. Remove the valve cover if it is not already removed.

3. Remove the distributor cap and crank the engine until the rotor points at number one plug terminal in the cap. It is easier to do this if you mark the location of number one plug wire before you remove the cap. The points should be open and timing marks should be aligned.

4. With the engine in the number one firing position, adjust: Intake numbers 1, 2, 4, Exhaust numbers 1, 3, 5.

5. The adjustment is performed as follows: Turn the adjusting nut until all lash is removed from this particular valve train. This can be determined by checking pushrod sideplay while tuning the adjusting nut. When all play has been removed, turn the adjusting nut one more turn. This will place the lifter plunger in the center of its travel.

6. Crank the engine over until number six cylinder is in the firing position. At this point, you can adjust the following valves: Intake numbers 3, 5, and 6; exhaust numbers 2, 4, and 6.

7. After the engine is running, readjust the valves following the procedure under Engine Running.

L6 Engine Running Adjustment

1. Run the engine until normal operating temperature is attained. Remove the valve cover. To prevent oil splashing, install oil deflector clips, which are available at auto supply stores.

2. With the engine at idle, back off the rocker arm nut until the rocker arm begins to clatter.

3. Slowly tighten the rocker arm nut until the clatter just stops. This is zero lash.

4. Tighten the nut another quarter turn and then wait about ten seconds until the engine is running smoothly. Tighten the nut another quarter turn and wait another ten seconds. Repeat the procedure until the nut has been turned down one full turn from zero lash.

NOTE: *Pausing ten seconds each time allows the lifter to adjust itself. Failing to pause might cause interference between the intake valve and the piston top causing internal damage and bent pushrods.*

5. Adjust the remaining valves in the same manner.

6. Replace the valve cover.

OLDSMOBILE BUILT ENGINES

Removal

1. With the head removed remove valve keys by compressing valve spring with a tool such as J-5892-1 or equivalent.

2. Remove valve spring rotator or retainers and springs.

3. Remove oil seals from valve stems.

4. Remove valves. Keep valves separated so they can be installed in their original locations.

Reconditioning Valves

When reconditioning valves and valve seats, clean carbon from cylinder heads and valves, using care not to gouge or scratch machined surfaces. A soft wire brush is suitable for this purpose. Whenever valves are replaced, or new valves installed, the valve seats must be reconditioned.

Narrow the valve seats to the specified width. This operation is done by grinding the portside with a 30 degree stone to lower the seat and a 60 degree stone to raise the seat. See chart for valve seat width.

Intake valve seats are induction hardened and must be ground, not cut.

Valve Seal Identification

Intake:
Std.-.005″ O.S.   Gray Colored
.010″-.013″ O.S.   Orange Colored
Exhaust:
Std.-.005″ O.S.   Ivory Colored
.010″-.013″ O.S.   Blue Colored

If valve guide bores are worn excessively, they can be reamed oversize. This will require replacement of the valves with oversize valves (stems). The guide bores should be reamed before grinding the valve seats. Valve clearance is guide bore should be 0.0015″ to 0.0032″ (exhaust) or 0.001″ to 0.0027″ for the intake valve.

Measuring Valve Stem Height

Whenever a new valve is installed, or after grinding valves, it will be necessary to measure valve stem height as follows:

VALVE SPRING COMPRESSOR
TOOLS J-5892-1

Removing valve spring—Oldsmobile built engines

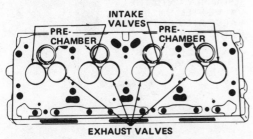

Valve location, 260, 307, 350, 403 Oldsmobile built engines

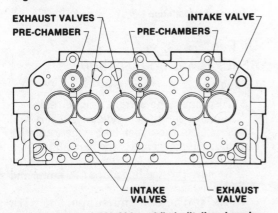

Valve location—263 Oldsmobile built diesel engine

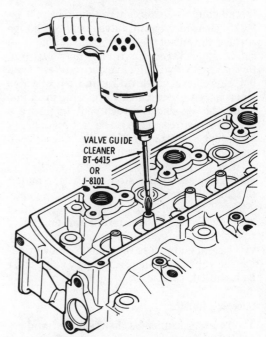

VALVE GUIDE
CLEANER
BT-6415
OR
J-8101

Cleaning valve guide bores—263 diesel shown

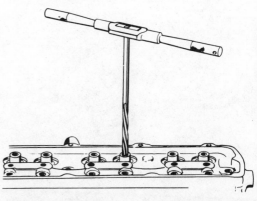

Reaming valve guide bores—350 Oldsmobile built engine shown

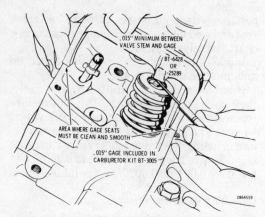

Measuring valve stem height—Oldsmobile built engines

Install gauge J-25289. There should be at least 0.015" clearance on all valves between gauge surface and end of the valve stem. (Valve stem can be gauged with or without the valve rotator on the valve.) If clearance is less then 0.015", remove valve and grind tip of valve stems as required on a valve refacing machine, using the Vee-block attachment to insure a smooth 90 degree end. Also be certain to break sharp edge on ground valve tip. Observe an original valve to determine chamfer.

After all valve keys have been installed on valves, tap each valve stem end with a mallet to seat valve rotators and keys. Using gauge J-25289 re-gauge all valves between valve stem and gauge (0.015" minimum) and valve rotator and gauge (0.030" minimum). If any valve stem end is less then 0.005" above rotator, the valve is too short and a new valve must be installed.

Checking Rotators

The rotators cannot be disassembled and require replacement only when they fail to rotate the valve.

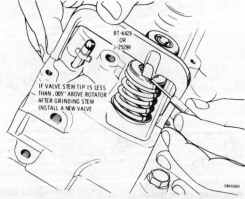

Measuring rotor height—Oldsmobile built engines

Rotator action can be checked by applying a daub of paint across the top of the body and down the collar. Run engine approximately 1,500 rpm. There should appear to be motion between the body and collar; the body will appear to walk around the collar. Rotator action can be either clockwise or counterclockwise. Sometimes, on removal and reinstallation, the direction of rotation will change but this does not matter so long as it rotates.

Any time the valves are removed for service, the tips should be inspected for improper pattern which could indicate valve rotator malfunction.

Installation

1. Install valves in their respective guides.
2. Install new oil seals over valve stem, using Tool J-22315 (350) or Tool J2651 (263). Position seals down as far as possible on valve stem. The seals will correctly position themselves when the engine is started. Inspect seal for cracks after installation.
3. Position valve springs over valve stems.
4. Install valve rotators, then compress spring with a tool such as J-22891, and install valve stem keys.
5. Check valve springs and keys to be sure they are properly seated.

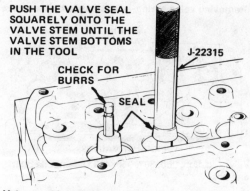

Valve seal installation—

Oil Pan
REMOVAL AND INSTALLATION
L-6 Engine

1. Disconnect the battery ground cable.
2. Remove the upper radiator support and the bracket to the upper hose. One cars with air-conditioning, remove the fan and clutch assembly.
3. Remove the fuel line at the fuel pump and the starter leads at the starter.
4. Raise the car and support it with jackstands. Drain the oil.

5. Remove the front motor mount bracket to motor mount bolts.

6. Remove the flywheel cover and the starter. Disconnect the automatic transmission linkage, if so equipped.

7. Disconnect the exhaust pipe at the manifold.

8. Position the timing mark in the six o'clock position.

9. Raise the engine with a jack at the crankshaft damper and remove the right engine mount with bracket.

10. Remove the oil pan attaching bolts and the oil pan. It may be necessary to raise the engine further to get the pan out. Be careful not to damage any cowl-mounted parts.

11. Installation is in the reverse order of removal.

Buick Built Engines

1. Raise the car and drain the oil.

2. Remove the flywheel cover.

3. Remove the exhaust crossover pipe.

4. Remove the oil pan attaching bolts and remove the oil pan.

V8 Chevrolet Built Engines

1. Disconnect battery ground cable.

2. Remove distributor cap.

3. Remove radiator upper mounting panel or fan shroud.

4. Remove fan.

5. Drain engine oil.

6. Disconnect exhaust or crossover pipes.

7. Remove converter housing underpan and splash shield. On cars with manual transmission, remove the starter, then remove the flywheel cover.

8. Rotate crankshaft until timing mark on torsional damper is at 6:00 o'clock position.

9. Remove front engine mount through bolts.

10. Raise engine and insert blocks under engine mounts.

11. Remove oil pan.

12. Installation is the reverse of removal.

V8 Oldsmobile Built Gasoline Engines Except 455

1. Remove the distributor cap and align the rotor to No. 1 firing position. On 1978 and later models, align the timing marks so No. 1 is at top dead center.

2. Disconnect the battery ground cable and remove the dipstick.

3. Remove the upper radiator support and the fan shroud attaching screws.

4. Raise the car and drain the oil.

5. Remove the flywheel cover.

6. Remove the starter motor assembly.

7. Disconnect the exhaust pipes and the crossover pipe.

8. Disconnect the engine mounts and raise the front of the engine as far as possible.

9. Remove the oil pan attaching bolts and remove the pan.

10. Coat both sides of the new gasket with sealer when installing. Installation is the reverse of removal. Torque the attaching bolts to 10 ft.lb.

Oldsmobile Built 455 V8 Engine

1. Disconnect the negative battery cable. Unbolt the fan shroud.

2. Raise the car and support it with jackstands. Drain the oil.

3. Remove the driveshaft. Disconnect the exhaust pipes and starter.

4. Support the rear of the engine and remove the flywheel housing inspection cover.

5. Disconnect the modulator line, speedometer cable, transmission oil cooler lines, and shaft linkage. Remove the transmission crossmember.

6. Remove the transmission.

7. Remove the flywheel and raise the front of the engine.

8. Remove the right engine mount and raise the engine about two inches. Install a wedge to hold the engine in position.

9. Loosen the left engine mount-to-block bolts enough to allow for the removal of the oil pan bolts.

10. Remove the oil pan bolts, free the pan from the block and disconnect the oil pump.

11. Remove the oil pan and the oil pump.

12. To install, clean all the gasket surfaces and apply sealer to both sides of the pan gasket. Install the gasket on the block. Install the front and rear rubber seals.

13. Hold the oil pan in the approximate position and install the oil pump, tightening the bolts to 35 ft.lb.

14. Install the oil pan. Install the flywheel.

15. Remove the edge holding the engine on the right side and install the engine mount.

16. Lower the front of the engine on the right side and install the engine mount.

17. Install the transmission crossmember and remove the support from the rear of the engine.

18. Connect the modulator line, speedometer cable, oil cooler lines, and transmission linkage.

19. Install the starter and connect the exhaust pipes.

20. Install the driveshaft.

21. Lower the car and fill the crankcase.

22. Install the fan shroud and connect the battery cable.

263 and 350 Oldsmobile Built Diesel Engines

1. On V8s, remove the vacuum pump and drive (with A/C) or the oil pump drive (without A/C). On V6s, remove the oil pump drive and vacuum pump.

2. Disconnect the batteries and remove the dipstick.

3. Remove the upper radiator support and fan shroud.

4. Raise and support the car. Drain the oil.

5. Remove the flywheel cover.

6. Disconnect the exhaust and crossover pipes.

7. Remove the oil cooler lines at the filter base.

8. Remove the starter assembly. Support the engine with a jack.

9. Remove the engine mounts from the block.

10. Raise the front of the engine mounts from the block.

11. Raise the front of the engine and remove the oil pan.

12. Installation is the reverse of removal.

Oil Pump

REMOVAL AND INSTALLATION

L-6 Engine

1. Remove the oil pan.

2. Remove the two flange mounting bolts, the pick-up pipe bolt, then remove the pump and screen together.

3. To install, align the oil pump drive shafts to match with the distributor tang and position the flange over the distributor lower bushing. Install the pump mounting bolts.

4. Install the oil pan.

Buick Built Engines

The oil pump is located in the timing chain cover and is connected by a drilled passage to the oil screen housing and pipe assembly in the oil pan. All oil is discharged from the pump to the oil pump cover assembly, on which the oil filter is mounted.

1. To remove the oil pump cover and gears, first remove the oil filter.

2. Remove the screws which attach the oil pump cover assembly to the timing chain cover.

3. Remove the cover assembly and slide out the oil pump gears. Clean the gears and inspect them for any obvious defects such as chipping or scoring.

4. Remove the oil pressure relief valve cap, spring and valve. Clean them and inspect them for wear or scoring. Check the relief valve spring to see that it is not worn on its side or collapsed. Replace the spring if it seems questionable.

5. Check the relief valve for a correct fit in its bore. It should be an easy slip fit and no more. If any perceptible shake can be felt, the valve and/or the cover should be replaced.

6. To install, lubricate the pressure relief valve and spring and place them in the cover. Install the cap and the gasket. Torque the cap to 35 ft.lb.

7. Pack the oil pump gear cavity full of petroleum jelly. Do not use gear lube. Reinstall the oil pump gears so that the petroleum jelly is forced into every cavity of the gear pocket, and between the gear teeth. There must be no air spaces. This step is very important. Unless the pump is packed, it may not begin to pump oil as soon as the engine is started.

8. Install the cover assembly using a new gasket and sealer. Tighten the screws to 10 ft. lbs.

9. Install the oil filter.

All V8 Engines

1. Remove the oil pan.

2. Remove the attaching bolts, and then remove the pump and drive shaft extension.

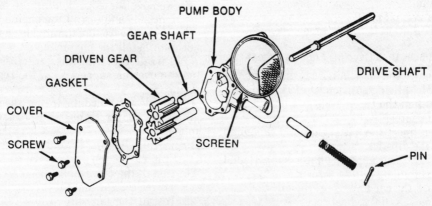

Typical oil pump assembly

3. To install, insert the drive shaft extension through the opening in the main bearing cap until the shaft mates with the distributor drive gear. You may have to turn the drive shaft extension one way or the other to get the two to mesh.

4. Position the pump on the cap and install the attaching bolts. Torque the bolts to 35 ft. lbs.

5. Reinstall the oil pan.

Timing Chain, Cover Oil Seal and Cover

REMOVAL AND INSTALLATION

L6 Engine

NOTE: *Align engine to No. 1 cylinder at TDC before cam gear installation. The L6 engine camshaft is gear-driven. The removal of the timing gear requires removal of the camshaft. After the camshaft is removed, place the camshaft and gear in an arbor press and remove the gear from the cam. Installation is in the reverse order of removal. The clearance between the camshaft and the thrust plate should be 0.001-0.005" Refer to camshaft removal and installation section.*

1. Drain the engine coolant, remove the radiator hoses, and remove the radiator.

CAUTION: *When draining the coolant, keep in mind that cats and dogs are attracted by the ethylene glycol antifreeze, and are quite likely to drink any that is left in an uncovered container or in puddles on the ground. This will prove fatal in sufficient quantity. Always drain the coolant into a sealable container. Coolant should be reused unless it is contaminated or several years old.*

2. Remove the fan belt and any accessory belts. Remove the fan pulley.

3. A harmonic balancer puller is necessary to pull the balancer. Install the puller and remove the balancer.

4. Remove the two screws which attach the oil pan to the front cover. Remove the screws which attach the front cover to the block. Do not remove the cover yet.

5. Before the front cover is removed, it is necessary to cut the oil pan front seal. Pull the cover forward slightly.

6. Using a sharp knife or razor knife, cut the oil pan front seal flush with the cylinder block on both sides of the cover.

7. Remove the front cover and the attached portion of oil pan front seal. Remove the front cover gasket from the block.

8. To install the front cover, first obtain an oil pan front seal. Cut the tabs from the new seal.

9. Install the seal in the front cover, pressing the tops into the holes provided in the cover. Coat the mating area of the front cover with a room temperature vulcanizing sealer first.

10. Coat the new front cover gasket with sealer and install it on the cover.

11. Apply a bead of RTV sealer to the joint formed at the oil pan and cylinder block.

12. Install the front cover.

13. Install the harmonic balancer. Make sure the front cover seal is positioned evenly around the balancer. If you do not have access to a balancer installation tool (and you probably don't), you can either fabricate one using the illustration as a guide, or you can tap the balancer on using a brass or plastic mallet. If you use the last method, make sure the balancer goes on evenly.

14. The rest of the installation is in the reverse order of removal.

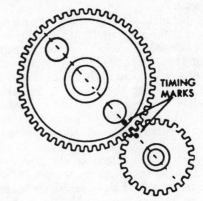

6-250 timing gear alignment

Buick Built Engines

1. Drain the cooling system.

CAUTION: *When draining the coolant, keep in mind that cats and dogs are attracted by the ethylene glycol antifreeze, and are quite likely to drink any that is left in an uncovered container or in puddles on the ground. This will prove fatal in sufficient quantity. Always drain the coolant into a sealable container. Coolant should be reused unless it is contaminated or several years old.*

2. Remove the radiator, fan, pulley and belt.

3. Remove the fuel pump and alternator, if necessary to remove cover.

4. Remove the distributor. If the timing chain and sprockets will not be disturbed, note the position of the distributor for installation in the same position.

5. Remove the thermostat bypass hose.

6. Remove the harmonic balancer.

7. Remove the timing chain-to-crankcase bolts.

8. Remove the oil pan-to-timing chain cover bolts and remove the timing chain cover.

9. Using a punch, drive out the old seal and the shedder toward the rear of the seal.

10. Coil the new packing around the opening so the ends are at the top. Drive in the shedder using a punch. Properly size the packing by rotating a hammer handle around the packing until the balancer hub can be inserted through the opening.

11. Align the timing marks on the sprockets.

12. Remove the camshaft sprocket bolt without changing the position of the sprocket. On the V6, remove the oil pan.

13. Remove the front crankshaft oil slinger.

14. On the V6, remove the camshaft sprocket bolts.

15. Using the two large screwdrivers, carefully pry the camshaft sprocket and the crankshaft sprocket forward until they are free. Remove the sprockets and the chain.

To install:

1. Make sure, with sprockets temporarily installed, that No. 1 piston is at top dead center and the camshaft sprocket O-mark is straight down on the centerline of both shafts.

2. Remove the camshaft sprocket and assemble the timing chain on both sprockets. Then slide the sprockets-and-chain assembly on the shafts with the O-marks in their closest together position and on a centerline with the sprocket hubs.

3. Assemble the slinger on the crankshaft with I.D. against the sprocket, (concave side toward the front of engine). Install the oil pan, if removed.

4. On the V6, install the camshaft sprocket bolts.

5. Install the distributor drive gear.

6. Install the drive gear and eccentric bolt and retaining washer. Torque to 40-55 ft.lb.

7. Install the timing case cover. Install a new seal by lightly tapping it in place. The lip of the seal faces inward. Pay particular attention to the following points.

a. Remove the oil pump cover and pack the space around the oil pump gears completely full of petroleum jelly. There must be

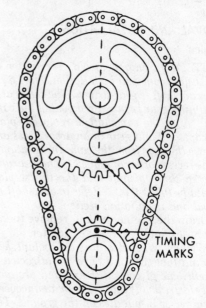

Valve timing marks—Buick built engines

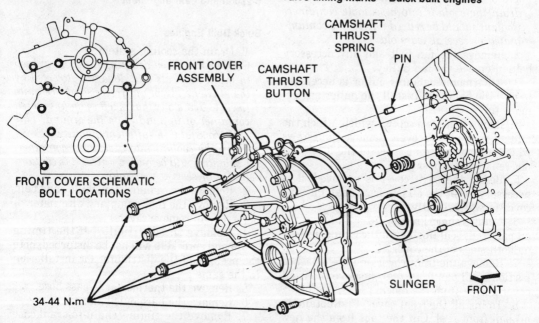

Timing chain cover—Buick built engines

no air space left inside the pump. Reinstall the pump cover using a new gasket.

b. The gasket surface of the block and timing chain cover must be clean and smooth. Use a new gasket correctly positioned.

c. Install the chain cover being certain the dowel pins engage the dowel pin holes before starting the attaching bolts.

d. Lube the bolt threads before installation and install them.

e. If the car has power steering the front pump bracket should be installed at this time.

f. Lube the O.D. of the harmonic balancer hub before installation to prevent damage to the seal when starting the engine.

Timing Front Cover

REMOVAL AND INSTALLATION

V8 Chevrolet Built Engines

NOTE: *If the timing chain is to be replaced, position the engine to align the timing marks at TDC (0 on the scale) with the No. 1 cylinder on its compression stroke (valves closed). DO NOT rotate the cam or crankshaft while the chain is removed.*

1. Drain and remove radiator.

CAUTION: *When draining the coolant, keep in mind that cats and dogs are attracted by the ethylene glycol antifreeze, and are quite likely to drink any that is left in an uncovered container or in puddles on the ground. This will prove fatal in sufficient quantity. Always drain the coolant into a sealable container. Coolant should be reused unless it is contaminated or several years old.*

2. Remove the fan belt and accessory drive belts. Remove the crankshaft pulley.

3. Remove harmonic balancer, using a puller.

NOTE: *The outer ring (weight) of the harmonic balancer is bonded to the hub with rubber. The balancer must be removed with a puller which acts on the inner hub only. Pulling on the outer portion of the balancer will break the rubber bond or destroy the tuning of the torsional damper.*

4. Remove the water pump. If the oil pan isn't to be removed, cut the pan seal off flush with the block.

5. Remove timing gear cover attaching screws, and cover and bracket.

6. Clean all the gasket mounting surfaces.

7. Apply a bead of silicone sealer to the oil pan-to-cylinder block joint.

8. Install a centering tool in the crankshaft snout hole in the front cover and install the cover.

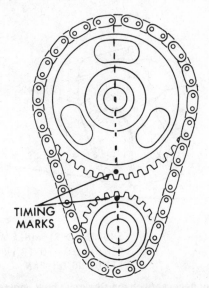

Valve timing marks—Chevrolet built engines

Cutting the oil pan front seal—Chevrolet built engines

9. Install the front cover bolts finger tight, remove the centering tool and tighten the cover bolts. Install the harmonic balancer, pulley, water pump, belts, radiator, and all other parts.

CAUTION: *The engines use a harmonic balancer. Breakage may occur if the balancer is hammered back onto the crankshaft. A special installation tool is necessary.*

NOTE: *When replacing the crankshaft damper, it has been found that lightly polishing the crankshaft damper with crocus cloth will greatly ease replacement. This procedure will also assist in any future removals, as it is sometimes difficult to pull a damper even with a puller. Be sure that the polishing is not overdone, or the damper will wobble on the crankshaft.*

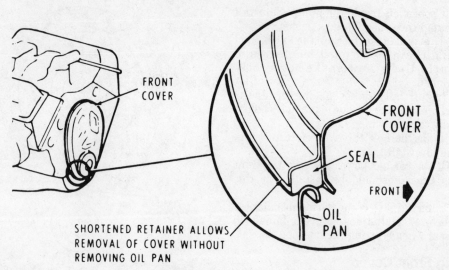

SHORTENED RETAINER ALLOWS
REMOVAL OF COVER WITHOUT
REMOVING OIL PAN

It is not necessary on the Chevrolet built engines to remove or lower the pan to remove the timing cover. The seal retainer is shortened enough to clear the pan

V8 Oldsmobile Built Gasoline Engines

1. Drain the coolant. Disconnect the radiator hose and the bypass hose. Remove the fan, belts and pulley.

CAUTION: *When draining the coolant, keep in mind that cats and dogs are attracted by the ethylene glycol antifreeze, and are quite likely to drink any that is left in an uncovered container or in puddles on the ground. This will prove fatal in sufficient quantity. Always drain the coolant into a sealable container. Coolant should be reused unless it is contaminated or several years old.*

2. Remove the vibration damper and crankshaft pulley.

3. Drain the oil and remove the oil pan.

4. Remove the front cover attaching bolts and remove the cover, timing indicator and water pump from the front of the engine.

5. On 1977 and later models, grind a chamfer on the end of each dowel pin as illustrated. When install the dowel pins, they must be inserted chamfered end first. Trim about ⅛" from each end of the new front pan seal and trim any excess material from the front edge of the oil pan gasket. Be sure all mating surfaces are clean.

6. Install in the reverse order of removal using a new gasket with sealing compound. Tighten self-tapping water pump attaching screws to 13 ft.lb., $\frac{5}{16}$" front cover attaching bolts to 25 ft.lb. and the four bottom bolts (cov-

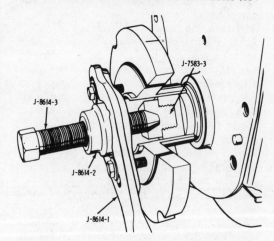

Removing the balancer—Oldsmobile built V8 engines

Chamfer the alignment pin—Oldsmobile built engines

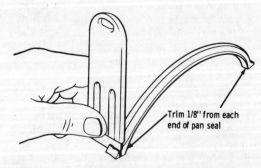

Trim 1/8" from each end of pan seal

Trimming the oil pan seals—Oldsmobile built engines

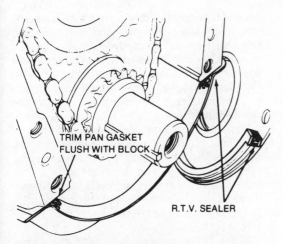

Applying sealer and trimming the pan gasket—Oldsmobile built engines

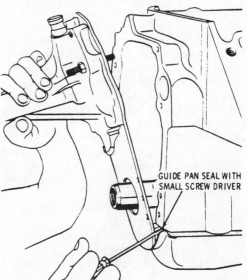

Installing the front cover—Oldsmobile built engines

er plate) to 35 ft.lb. Torque the pulley hub bolt to 310 ft.lb. Crankshaft pulley bolts should be torqued to 10 ft.lb. Tighten the fan bolts to 20 ft.lb.

263 and 350 Oldsmobile Built Diesel Engines

1. Drain the cooling system and disconnect the radiator hoses.

CAUTION: *When draining the coolant, keep in mind that cats and dogs are attracted by the ethylene glycol antifreeze, and are quite likely to drink any that is left in an uncovered container or in puddles on the ground. This will prove fatal in sufficient quantity. Always drain the coolant into a sealable container. Coolant should be reused unless it is contaminated or several years old.*

2. Remove all belts, fan and pulley, crank-

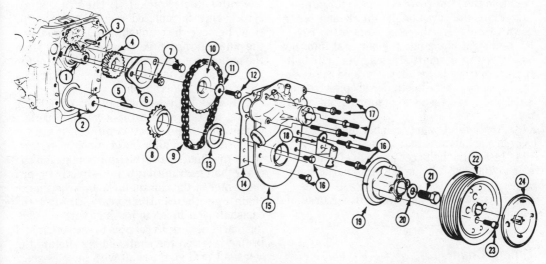

1. Camshaft	9. Timing chain
2. Crankshaft	10. Camshaft sprocket
3. Camshaft sprocket key	11. Washer
4. Injection pump drive gear	12. 87 N·m (65 ft. lbs.)
5. Crankshaft sprocket key	13. Slinger
6. Front camshaft bearing retainer	14. Gasket
7. 65 N·m (48 ft. lbs.)	15. Front cover
8. Crankshaft sprocket	16. 55 N·m (41 ft. lbs.)

17. 28 N·m (21 ft. lbs.)
18. Probe holder (rpm counter)
19. Crankshaft balancer
20. Washer
21. 217–475 N·m (160–350 ft. lbs.)
22. Pulley assembly
23. 40 N·m (30 ft. lbs.)
24. Cover

Engine front cover and timing chain assembly—263 Oldsmobile built diesel engine

shaft pulley and balancer, using a balancer puller.

CAUTION: *The use of any other type of puller, such as a universal claw type which pulls on the outside of the hub, can destroy the balancer. The outside ring of the balancer is bonded in rubber to the hub. Pulling on the outside will break the bond. The timing mark is on the outside ring. If it is suspected that the bond is broken, check that the center of the keyway is 16 degrees from the center of the timing slot. In addition, there are chiseled aligning marks between the weight and the hub.*

3. Unbolt and remove the cover, timing indicator and water pump.

4. It may be necessary to grind a flat on the cover for gripping purposes.

5. Grind a chamfer on one end of each dowel pin.

6. Cut the excess material from the front end of the oil pan gasket on each side of the block.

7. Clean the block, oil pan and front cover mating surfaces with solvent.

8. Trim about ⅛″ off each end of a new front pan seal.

9. Install a new front cover gasket on the block and a new seal in the front cover.

10. Apply sealer to the gasket around the coolant holes.

11. Apply sealer to the block at the junction of the pan and front cover. On V6, apply R.T.V. sealer on the front cover oil pan seal retainer.

12. Place the cover on the block and press down to compress the seal. Rotate the cover left and right and guide the pan seal into the cavity using a small screwdriver. Oil bolt threads and heads, install two to hold the cover in place, then install both dowels pins (chamfered end first). Install remaining front cover bolts.

13. Apply a lubricant, compatible with rubber, on the balancer seal surface.

14. Install the balancer and bolt. Torque the bolt to 200-300 ft.lb. on V8, 160-350 ft.lb. on V6.

15. Install all other parts in reverse of removal.

Timing Chain
REMOVAL AND INSTALLATION
V8 Chevrolet Built Engines

All Chevrolet V8 engines are equipped with a timing chain. To replace the chain, remove the crankcase front cover. This will allow access to the timing chain. Crank the engine until the marks punched on both sprockets are closest to one another and in line between the shaft centers. Take out the three bolts that hold the camshaft sprocket to the camshaft. This sprocket is a light press fit on the camshaft and will come off readily. It is located by a dowel. The chain comes off with the camshaft sprocket. A gear puller will be required to remove the crankshaft sprocket.

Without disturbing the position of the engine, mount the new crank sprocket on the shaft, then mount the chain over the camshaft sprocket. Arrange the camshaft sprocket in such a way that the timing marks will line up between the shaft centers and the camshaft locating dowel will enter the dowel hole in the cam sprocket.

Place the cam sprocket, with the chain mounted over it, in position on the front of the camshaft and pull up with the three bolts that hold it to the camshaft.

After the sprockets are in place, turn the engine two full revolutions to make certain that the timing marks are in correct alignment between the shaft centers.

V8 Oldsmobile Built Engines

1. Remove the timing case cover and take off the camshaft gear.

NOTE: *The fuel pump operating cam is bolted to the front of the camshaft sprocket and the sprocket is located on the camshaft by means of a dowel.*

2. Remove the oil slinger, timing chain, and the camshaft sprocket. If the crankshaft sprocket is to be replaced, remove it also at this time. Remove the crankshaft key before using the puller. If the key can not be removed, align the puller so it does not overlap the end of the key, as the keyway is only machined part of the way into the crankshaft gear.

3. Reinstall the crankshaft sprocket being careful to start it with the keyway in perfect alignment since it is rather difficult to correct for misalignment after the gear has been started on the shaft. Turn the timing mark on the crankshaft gear until it points directly toward the center of the camshaft. Mount the timing chain over the camshaft gear and start the camshaft gear up on to its shaft with the timing marks as close as possible to each other and in line between the shaft centers. Rotate the camshaft to align the shaft with the new gear.

4. Install the fuel pump eccentric with the flat side toward the rear.

5. Drive the key in with a hammer until it bottoms.

6. Install the oil slinger.

NOTE: *Any time the timing chain and gears are replaced on the diesel engine it will be necessary to retime the engine. Refer to the*

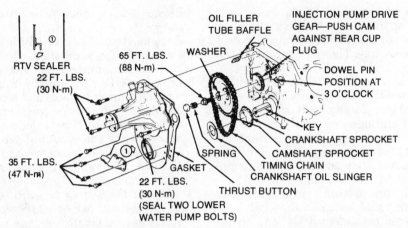

OIL FILLER
TUBE BAFFLE

INJECTION PUMP DRIVE
GEAR—PUSH CAM
AGAINST REAR CUP
PLUG

65 FT. LBS.
(88 N-m)

WASHER

RTV SEALER
22 FT. LBS.
(30 N-m)

DOWEL PIN
POSITION AT
3 O'CLOCK

KEY
CRANKSHAFT SPROCKET
CAMSHAFT SPROCKET
TIMING CHAIN
CRANKSHAFT OIL SLINGER

35 FT. LBS.
(47 N-m)

SPRING
GASKET

22 FT. LBS.
(30 N-m)
(SEAL TWO LOWER
WATER PUMP BOLTS)

THRUST BUTTON

Engine front cover and timing chain assembly—350 Oldsmobile built diesel engine

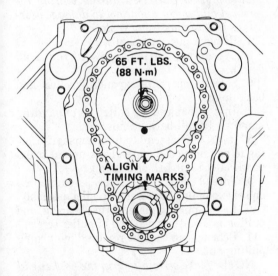

65 FT. LBS.
(88 N·m)

ALIGN
TIMING MARKS

Timing mark alignment—Oldsmobile built engines

paragraph on Diesel Engine Injection Timing.

263 Oldsmobile Built Diesel Engines

1. Remove the front cover. See above for procedure. Remove the valve covers.

2. Loosen all rocker arm pivot bolts evenly so that lash exists between the rocker arms and valves. It is not necessary to completely remove the rocket arms unless related service is being performed.

3. Remove the crankshaft oil slinger and the camshaft sprocket bolt and washer.

4. Remove the timing chain, camshaft and crankshaft sprockets. If the crankshaft sprocket is a tight fit on the crankshaft use an appropriate puller to remove it.

5. If the camshaft sprocket-to-cam key comes out with the camshaft sprocket, remove the front camshaft bearing retainer and install

the key into the injection pump drive gear. Install the bearing retainer.

6. Install the key in the crankshaft, if removed.

7. Install the camshaft sprocket, crankshaft sprocket and the timing chain together, align the timing marks on the camshaft and the crankshaft. Tighten the camshaft sprocket bolt to 64 ft.lb.

8. Install the oil slinger and the remaining parts of the front cover assembly.

9. After installing the front cover, bleed down the valve lifters as instructed in Diesel Engine, Rocker Arm Replacement, above.

10. Remaining installation is the reverse of removal. Sealant is used in place of valve cover gaskets.

Camshaft and Bearings

L-6 Engine

REMOVAL AND INSTALLATION

1. Remove the grille. Remove the radiator hoses and remove the radiator.

2. Remove the timing gear cover.

3. Remove the valve cover and gasket, loosen all the rocker arm nuts, and pivot the rocker arms clear of the pushrods.

4. Remove the distributor and the fuel pump.

5. Remove the pushrods. Remove the coil and then remove the side cover. Remove the valve lifters.

6. Remove the two camshaft thrust plate retaining screws by working through the holes in the camshaft gear.

7. Remove the camshaft and gear assembly by pulling it out through the front of the block.

8. If either the camshaft or the camshaft gear is being renewed, the gear must be pressed off the camshaft. The replacement

parts must be assembled in the same way. When placing the gear on the camshaft, press the gear onto the shaft until it bottoms against the gear spacer ring. The end clearance of the thrust plate should be 0.001 to 0.005"

9. Pre-lube the camshaft lobes with either engine oil or STP®, and then install the camshaft assembly in the engine. Be careful not to damage the bearings.

10. Turn the crankshaft and the camshaft gears so that the timing marks align. Push the camshaft into position and install and torque the thrust plate bolts to 7 ft.lb.

11. Check camshaft and crankshaft gear run-out with a dial indicator. Camshaft gear run-out should not exceed 0.004" and crankshaft gear run-out should not be above 0.003"

12. Using a dial indicator, check the backlash at several points between the camshaft and crankshaft gear teeth. Backlash should be 0.004-0.006"

13. Install the timing gear cover. Install the harmonic balancer.

14. Install the valve lifters and the pushrods. Install the side cover. Install the coil and the fuel pump.

15. Install the distributor and set the timing. Pivot the rocker arms over the pushrods and adjust the valves.

16. Install the radiator, hoses and grille.

Buick Built Engines

REMOVAL

1. Complete steps 1 through 8 under Timing Chain, Cover Oil Seal, & Cover Removal and Installation, above. Skip steps 9 and 10, complete steps 11 through 15.

NOTE: *If equipped with air conditioning, unbolt the condenser and position it out of the way. If this is not possible, have a mechanic*

discharge the system. Never attempt to discharge the system yourself.

2. Remove the hydraulic lifters, keeping them in order for installation.

3. Slide the camshaft forward, out of the bearing bores. Do this carefully, to avoid damage to the bearing surfaces and bearings.

NOTE: *Slightly scored camshaft bearings will be satisfactory if the surfaces of camshaft journals are polished and bearings are cleaned up to remove burrs, and the fit of shaft in bearings is free and within the specification.*

Should the bearing be galled beyond repair, the bearing will have to be replaced. Replacement camshaft bearings may be installed with Tool OTC 817, or equivalent. Care must be exercised during bearing removal and installation, not to damage bearings that are not being replaced.

4. Remove the crankshaft.

5. Assembly puller screw to required length.

6. Select proper size expanding collect and back-up nut.

7. Install expanding collet on expanding mandrel. Install back-up nut.

8. Insert this assembly into camshaft bearing to be removed. Tighten back-up nut to expand collet to fit I.D. of bearing.

9. Thread end of puller screw assembly into end of expanding mandrel and collet assembly.

10. Install pulling plate, thrust bearing, and pulling nut on threaded end of puller screw.

11. Bearing can then be removed by turning pulling nut.

NOTE: *Make certain to grip the ⅝" hex end of the puller screw with a wrench to keep it from rotating when the pulling nut is turned. Failure to do this will result in the locking up*

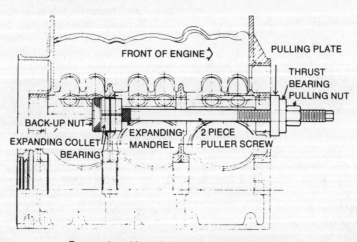

Removal and installation of camshaft bearings

of all threads in the pulling assembly and possible over expansion of the collet.

12. Repeat the above procedure to remove any other bearings, except the front bearing, which may be pulled from the rear of the engine.

NOTE: *When removing rear cam bearing, it is necessary to remove welch plug at the back of cam bore. However, if only the front bearing is being replaced it is not necessary to remove the engine or welch plug. The front bearing can be removed by using a spacer between the pulling plate and the cylinder block.*

INSTALLATION

1. Assemble puller screw to required length.
2. Select proper size expanding collet and back-up nut.
3. Install expanding collet on expanding mandrel.
4. Install back-up nut.
5. Place new camshaft bearing on collet and GENTLY hand tighten back-up nut to expand collet to fit bearing. Do not over tighten back-up nut. A loose sliding fit between collet and bearing surface is adequate. This will provide just enough clearance to allow for the collapse which will occur when the new bearing is pulled into the engine block.
6. Slide mandrel assembly and bearing into bearing bore as far as it will go without force.
7. Thread end of puller screw onto the end of the mandrel. Make certain to align oil holes in bearing and block properly. One of the collet separation lines may be used as a reference point.
8. Install pulling plate, thrust bearing and pulling nut on threaded end of puller screw.
9. Install bearing in the same manner as described in Step 11 and 12.

NOTE: *When installing rear cam bearing, install new welch plug at back of cam bore. Coat O.D. of plug with nonhardening sealer before installation.*

10. The remainder of the installation is the reverse of removal. Clean all gasket surfaces thoroughly and use new gaskets. Lubricate the camshaft lobes with heavy oil before installation, and be careful not to contact any of the bearings with the cam lobes. Make sure that the camshaft timing marks are aligned with the crankshaft marks. See installation steps under Timing Chain, Cover Oil Seal, & Cover Removal and Installation.

V8 Chevrolet Built Engines

MEASURING LOBE LIFT

1. With the rocker arms removed, position indicator with ball socket adapter (Tool

J-8520) on push rod. Make sure push rod is in the lifter socket.

2. Rotate the crankshaft slowly in the direction of rotation until the lifter is on the heel of the cam lobe. At this point, the push rod will be in its lowest position.
3. Set dial indicator on zero, then rotate the crankshaft slowly, or attach an auxiliary starter switch and bump the engine over, until the push rod is in fully raised position.

CAUTION: *Whenever the engine is cranked remotely at the starter, with a special jumper cable or other means, the distributor primary lead must be disconnected from the coil.*

4. Compare the total lift recorded from the dial indicator with specifications.
5. If camshaft readings for all lobes are within specifications, remove dial indicator assembly.
6. Install and adjust valve mechanism as outlined.

REMOVAL

1. Remove valve lifters as previously outlined.
2. Remove crankcase from cover as previously outlined.
3. Remove grille.
4. Remove fuel pump push rod.
5. Complete camshaft removal as follows: Sprocket is a light fit on camshaft. If sprocket does not come off easily a light blow on the lower edge of the sprocket (with a plastic mallet) should dislodge the sprocket.
6. Install two $5/16''$-18 x 4″ bolts in camshaft bolt holes then remove camshaft.

NOTE: *All camshaft journals are the same diameter and care must be used in removing camshaft to avoid damage to bearings.*

The camshaft bearing journals should be measured with a micrometer for an out-of-round condition. If the journals exceed 0.001″ out-of-round, the camshaft should be replaced.

Camshaft bearings can be replaced while engine is disassembled for overhaul, or without complete disassembly of the engine. To replace bearings without complete disassembly remove the camshaft and crankshaft leaving cylinder heads attached and pistons in place. Before removing crankshaft, tape threads of connecting rod bolts to prevent damage to crankshaft. Fasten connecting rods against sides of engine so they will not be in the way while replacing camshaft bearings.

7. With camshaft and crankshaft removed, drive camshaft rear plug from cylinder block.
8. Using Tool Set J-6098 or equivalent with nut and thrust washer installed to end of

threads, index pilot in camshaft front bearing and install puller screw through pilot.

9. Install remover and install tool with shoulder toward bearing, making sure a sufficient amount of threads are engaged.

10. Using two wrenches, hold puller screw while turning nut. When bearing has been pulled from bore, remove remover and installer tool and bearing from puller screw.

11. Remove remaining bearings (except front and rear) in the same manner. It will be necessary to index pilot in camshaft rear bearing to remove the rear intermediate bearing.

12. Assemble remover and installer tool on driver handle and remove camshaft front and rear bearings by driving towards center of cylinder block.

INSTALLATION

NOTE: *The camshaft front and rear bearings should be installed first. These bearings will act as guides for the pilot and center the remaining bearings being pulled into place.*

1. Assemble remover and installer tool on driver handle and install camshaft front and rear bearings by driving towards center of cylinder block.

2. Using Tool set J-6098, with nut then thrust washer installed to end of threads, index pilot in camshaft front bearing and install puller screw through pilot.

3. Index camshaft bearing in bore (with oil hole aligned as outlined below), then install remover and installer tool on puller screw with shoulder toward bearing.

NOTE: *Number one cam bearing oil hole must be positioned so that oil holes are equi--distant from 6 o'clock position. Number two through number four bearing oil holes must be positioned at 5 o'clock position (toward left side of engine and at a position even with bottom of cylinder bore). Number five bearing oil hole must be in 12 o'clock position.*

4. Using two wrenches, hold puller screw while turning nut. After bearing has been pulled into bore, remove the remover and installer tool from puller screw and check alignment of oil hole in camshaft bearing.

5. Install remaining bearings in the same manner. It will be necessary to index pilot in the camshaft rear bearing to install the rear intermediate bearing.

6. Install a new camshaft rear plug.

Plug should be installed flush to $\frac{1}{32}$" deep and be parallel with rear surface of cylinder block.

NOTE: *Whenever a new camshaft is installed coat camshaft lobes with Molykote® or its equivalent. Also whenever a new camshaft*

is installed, replacement of all valve lifters is recommended to insure durability of the camshaft lobes and lifter feet.

7. Lubricate camshaft journals with engine oil and install camshaft.

8. Install timing chain on camshaft sprocket. Hold the sprocket vertically with the chain hanging down, and align marks on camshaft and crankshaft sprockets.

9. Align dowel in camshaft with dowel hole in camshaft sprocket then install sprocket on camshaft.

10. Draw the camshaft sprocket onto camshaft using the mounting bolts. Torque to specifications.

11. Lubricate timing chain with engine oil.

12. Install fuel pump push rod.

13. Install grille.

14. Install crankcase front cover.

15. Install valve lifters.

V8 Oldsmobile Built Gasoline Engines

CAUTION: *All Oldsmobile V8s require discharging of the air conditioning for camshaft removal. This should not be attempted by anyone who lacks the skill and experience to do so, as contact with the refrigerant can cause serious personal injury.*

REMOVAL

1. Disconnect the battery.

2. Drain and remove the radiator.

CAUTION: *When draining the coolant, keep in mind that cats and dogs are attracted by the ethylene glycol antifreeze, and are quite likely to drink any that is left in an uncovered container or in puddles on the ground. This will prove fatal in sufficient quantity. Always drain the coolant into a sealable container. Coolant should be reused unless it is contaminated or several years old.*

3. Disconnect the fuel line at the fuel pump. Remove the pump on 1978 and later models.

4. Disconnect the throttle cable and the air cleaner.

5. Remove the alternator belt, loosen the alternator bolts, and move the alternator to one side.

6. Remove the power steering pump from its brackets and move it out of the way.

7. Remove the air conditioning compressor from its brackets and move the compressor out of the way without disconnecting the lines.

8. Disconnect the hoses from the water pump.

9. Disconnect the electrical and vacuum connections.

10. Mark the distributor as to location in the block. Remove the distributor.

On 1977 and later models, remove the crankshaft pulley and the hub attaching bolt. Remove the crankshaft hub. Skip to Step 19.

11. Raise the car and drain the oil pan.

12. Remove the exhaust crossover pipe and starter motor.

13. Disconnect the exhaust pipe at the manifold.

14. Remove the harmonic balancer and pulley.

15. Support the engine and remove the front motor mounts.

16. Remove the flywheel inspection cover.

17. Remove the engine oil pan.

18. Support the engine by placing wooden blocks between the exhaust manifolds and the front crossmember.

19. Remove the engine front cover.

20. Remove the valve covers.

21. Remove the intake manifold, oil filler pipe, and temperature sending switch.

22. Mark the lifters, pushrods, and rocker arms as to location so that they may be installed in the same position. Remove these parts.

23. If the car is equipped with air conditioning, discharge the A/C system and remove the condenser. See CAUTION above.

24. Remove the fuel pump eccentric, camshaft gear, oil slinger, and timing chain.

25. Carefully remove the camshaft from the engine.

NOTE: *The camshaft bearings must be replaced in complete sets. All bearings must be removed before any can be installed. No. 1 bearing must be removed first, then No. 2, then 3, 4, and 5. When installing the bearings, No. 5 must be installed first, then 4, 3, 2 and 1.*

Camshaft Bearing Remover and Installer Set BT-6409 is an available tool. The set can be used to remove cam bearings with the engine either in or out of the car. To replace bearings with engine in car, proceed as follows:

26. Install No. 1 Cam Bearing Remover and Installer BT-6409-1 on Handle J-8092 and drive out front cam bearing.

27. Place Pilot BT-6409-6 on Driver Bt-6409-7 and install No. 2 Cam Bearing Tool BT-6409-2 on driver and drive out No. 2 bearing.

28. Remove No.3 and 4 bearings in the same manner, using BT-6409-3 and BT-6409-4 removers.

NOTE: *Each cam bearing is a different diameter and the correct sequence must be used for both removal and installation.*

29. To remove No. 5 bearing with engine in chassis, use puller BT-6409-8.

INSTALLATION

NOTE: *To aid aligning bearings with oil passages, place each bearing in the front bore with tapered edge toward block and align the oil hole in the bearing with the center of the oil slot in the bore. Mark top of bearing. When installing the bearings the mark will act as a guide.*

1. Place new No. 5 bearing on BT-6409-5 and drive bearing in until the last white line on the driver is flush with the front face of the pilot.

2. Use BT-6409-9 to check oil hole opening.

3. Remove BT-6409-5 Installer and install BT-6409-4. Place No. 4 bearing on installer and drive in until the next to last white line on driver is flush with pilot.

4. Follow the same procedure to install No. 3 and No. 2.

5. Install Tool BT-6409-1 on Handle J-8092 and place No. 1 bearing on installer. Drive bearing in until white line on Installer BT-6409 is flush with front face of block.

6. Use BT-6409-9 to check all oil hole openings. Wire must enter hole or the bearing will not receive sufficient lubrication.

7. Inspect the shaft for signs of excessive wear or damage.

8. Liberally coat camshaft and bearings with heavy engine oil or engine assembly lubricant and insert the cam into the engine.

9. Align the timing marks on the camshaft and crankshaft gears. See Timing Chain Replacement and Valve Timing for details.

10. Install the distributor using the locating marks made during removal. If any problems are encountered, see Distributor Installation.

11. To install, reverse the removal procedure but pay attention to the following points:

   a. Install the timing indicator before installing the power steering pump bracket.

   b. Install the flywheel inspection cover after installing the starter.

   c. Replace the engine oil and radiator coolant.

Camshaft

263 and 350 Oldsmobile Built Diesel Engines

REMOVAL AND INSTALLATION

Removal of the camshaft requires removal of the injection pump drive and driven gears, remove of the intake manifold, disassembly of the valve lifters, and re-timing of the injection pump.

NOTE: *The air conditioning, if equipped, must be discharged by a professional technician and the condenser removed.*

1. Disconnect the negative battery cables. Drain the coolant. Remove the radiator.

CAUTION: *When draining the coolant, keep in mind that cats and dogs are attracted by the ethylene glycol antifreeze, and are quite likely to drink any that is left in an uncovered container or in puddles on the ground. This will prove fatal in sufficient quantity. Always drain the coolant into a sealable container. Coolant should be reused unless it is contaminated or several years old.*

2. Remove the intake manifold and gasket and the front and rear intake manifold seals. Refer to the intake manifold removal and installation procedure. Remove the oil pump drive assembly on the V6.

3. Remove the balancer pulley and the balancer. See Caution under V8 diesel engine front cover removal and installation, above, for V8 engine. Remove the engine front cover using the appropriate procedure. Rotate the engine so that the timing marks align on V6s.

4. Remove the valve covers. Remove the rocker arms, pushrods and valve lifters; see the procedure earlier in this section. Be sure to keep the parts in order so that they may be returned to their original positions.

5. On V8s, if equipped with air conditioning, the condenser must be discharged and removed from the car.

CAUTION: *Compressed refrigerant expands (boils) into the atmosphere at a temperature of -21°F or less. It will freeze any surface it contacts, including you skin or eyes.*

6. Remove the camshaft sprocket retaining bolt, and remove the timing chain and sprockets, using the procedure outlined earlier.

7. On V6s, remove the front camshaft bearing retainer bolt and the retainer, then remove the camshaft sprocket key and the injection pump drive gear.

8. Position the camshaft dowel pin at the 3 o'clock position on the V8.

9. On V8s, push the camshaft rearward and hold it there, being careful not to dislodge the oil gallery plug at the rear of the engine. Remove the fuel injection pump drive gear by sliding it from the camshaft while rocking the pump driven gear.

10. To remove the fuel injection pump driven gear, remove the injection pump intermediate pump adapter (V6s) and the pump adapter (All), remove the snapring, and remove the selective washer. Remove the driven gear and spring.

11. Remove the camshaft by sliding it out the front of the engine. Be extremely careful not to allow the cam lobes to contact any of the bearings, or the journals to dislodge the bearings during camshaft removal. Do not force the camshaft, or bearing damage will result.

Camshaft Bearings

263 V6 Engine

REMOVAL AND INSTALLATION

The front camshaft bearing may be replaced separately but numbers 2, 3, and 4 must be replaced as a completed set. This is because it is necessary to remove the forward bearings to gain access to the rearward bearings.

Camshaft Bearing Remover and Installer Set BT-6409 and camshaft bearing pilot spacer; BT-7817 are available tools.

This set can be used to remove cam bearings with the engine either in or out of the car. To replace the bearings with engine in car, proceed as follows:

1. To remove the front (No. 1) camshaft bearing, support the retainer in a vise and drive the bearing out using BT-6409-2 with driver BT-6409-7.

2. To install the bearing use the same tools but make certain that the oil hole in the bearing is in alignment with the oil hole in the retainer.

3. Install tool BT-6409-2 on handle BT-6409-7 and drive out No. 2 cam bearing.

4. Remove the No. 3 bearing in the same manner using BT-6409-3 handle BT-6409-7.

5. Remove the No. 4 bearing using puller BT-6409-8

NOTE: *To aid aligning the bearings with the oil passages, place each bearing in the front of the bore with tapered edge toward the block and align the oil hole in the bearing with the center of the oil slot in the bore. Mark bottom of bearing. When installing the bearings, the mark will act as a guide.*

Using pilot BT-6409-1 will aid in installing the No. 4 and 3 bearings by preventing cocking of the bearings.

6. Install No. 4 bearing using tool BT-6409-4.

NOTE: *Drive the bearing in carefully, stopping to make certain that the oil holes are in alignment otherwise it is possible to drive the bearing in beyond the oil passage opening. Use a piece of $3/32$" brass rod with a 90 degree bend at the end to check the oil hole opening.*

7. Install the No. 3 bearing using tool Bt-6409-3 carefully until the oil holes are in alignment.

8. Install the No. 2 bearing using tool BT-6409-2 carefully until the oil holes are in alignment.

9. Use a piece of $3/32$" brass rod with a 90 degree bend at the end to check all oil hole openings. Wire must enter hole or the bearing will not receive sufficient lubrication.

350 V8 ENGINE
REMOVAL AND INSTALLATION

The camshaft bearings must be replaced in complete sets. All bearings must be removed before any can be installed. No. 1 bearing must be removed before any can be installed. No. 1 bearing must be removed first, then No. 2, then 3, 4, and 5. When installing the bearings, No. 5 must be installed first, then 4, 3, 2, and 1. Camshaft Bearing Remover and Installer Set J-25262 is an available tool.

This set can be used to remove cam bearings with the engine either in or out of the car. To replace bearings with engine in car, proceed as follows:

The number one camshaft bearing is different than used on the gasoline engine.

1. Remove camshaft and engine oil pan.
2. Install No. 1 Cam Bearing Remover and Installer J-25262-1 on handle J-25262-7 and drive out front cam bearing.
3. Place Pilot J-25262-6 on driver J-25262-7 and install No. 2 Cam Bearing Tool J-25262-2 on driver and drive out No. 2 bearing.
4. Remove No. 3 and 4 bearings in the same manner, using J-25262-3 and J-25262-4 removers.

Each cam bearing is a different diameter and the correct sequence must be used both for removal and installation.

5. To remove No. 5 bearing with engine in car, use puller J-25262-8.
6. To remove the injection pump driven gear bushings, drive both bushings at the same time from the rear to the front of the block using tool J-28439-2 and driver handle J-25262-7.

NOTE: *To aid aligning bearings with oil passages, place each bearing in the front bore with tapered edge toward block and align the oil hole in the bearing with the center of the oil slot in the bore. Mark bottom of bearing. When installing the bearings, the mark will act as a guide. Failure to align oil hole could result in engine damage.*

7. Slide bearing pilot spacer on bearing pilot J-25262-6. For bearings 5, 4, 3, 2 put the driver J-25262-7 through the pilot J-25262-6, the screw the installer on the driver. Install the bearings as follows:
8. Place new No. 5 bearing on J25262-5 and drive the bearing in until the last white line on the driver is flush with the front face of the pilot.
9. Use a piece of $^3/_{32}$" brass rod with a 90 degree bend at the end to check the oil hole opening as shown in Figure 6A3-82.
10. Remove J-25262-5 Installer and install

J-25262-4. Place No. 4 bearing on installer and drive in until the next to last white line on driver is flush with pilot.

11. Follow the same procedure to install No. 3 and No. 2.
12. Install Tool J-25262-1 on Handle J-25262-7 and place No. 1 bearing on installer. Drive bearing in until it is flush with front face of block.
13. To install the injection pump bushings, align the holes in the bushings with the holes in the block. Install both bushings from the front; driving the rear bushing first, using the long end of tool J-28439-1 and driver handle J-8092. Drive the front bushing with the short end of J-28439-1.
14. Use a piece of $^3/_{32}$" brass rod with a 90 degree bend at the end to check all oil hole openings. Wire must enter hole or the bearing will not receive sufficient lubrication.

Camshaft

263, 350 Diesel Engines
INSTALLATION

1. If either the injection pump drive or driven gears are to be replaced, replace both gears. make certain the marks (0) are in alignment on both gears before inserting the cam gear key on the V6.
2. Coat the camshaft and the cam bearings with GM lubricant No. 1052365 or the equivalent.
3. Carefully slide the camshaft into position in the engine.
4. Fit the crankshaft and camshaft sprockets, aligning the timing marks as shown in the timing chain removal and installation procedure, above. Remove the sprockets without distributing the timing.
5. Install the injection pump driven gear, spring, shim, and snapring. Check the gear end play. If the end play is not within 0.002-0.006" on V8s through 1979 and V6s, and 0.002" to 0.015" in 1980 and later V8s, replace the shim to obtain the specified clearance. Shims are available in 0.003" increments, from 0.080" to 0.115"
6. On V8s position the camshaft dowel pin at the 3 o'clock position. Align the zero marks on the pump drive gear and pump driven gear. Hold the camshaft in the rearward position and slide the pump drive gear onto the camshaft. On the V6, align the zero marks on the injection pump drive and driven gears, then install the camshaft sprocket key. Install the camshaft bearing retainer.
7. Install the timing chain and sprockets, making sure the timing marks are aligned.

8. Install the lifters, pushrods and rocker arms. See Rocker Arm Replacement, Diesel Engine for lifter bleed down procedures. Failure to bleed down the lifters could bend valves when the engine is turned over.

9. Install the injection pump adapter and injection pump. See the appropriate sections under Fuel System in Chapter 4 for procedures.

10. Install the remaining components in the reverse order of removal.

Pistons and Connecting Rods

REMOVAL AND INSTALLATION

All Engines

Before removing the pistons, the top of the cylinder bore must be examined for a ridge. A ridge at the top of the bore is the result of normal cylinder wear, caused by the piston rings only traveling so far up the bore in the course of the piston stroke. The ridge can be felt by hand; it must be removed before the pistons are removed.

A ridge reamer is necessary for this operation. Place the piston at the bottom of its stroke, and cover it with a rag. Cut the ridge away with the ridge reamer, using extreme care to avoid cutting too deeply. Remove the rag, and remove the cuttings that remain on

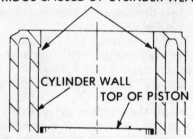

Cylinder bore ridge

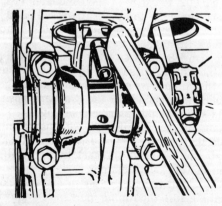

Push the piston out with a hammer handle

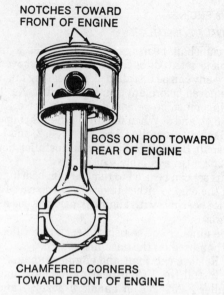

LEFT NO. 1-3-5

Piston and connecting rod assembly—(left bank)—V6 Buick built engines

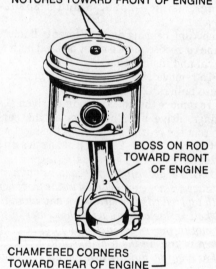

RIGHT NO. 2-4-6

Piston and connecting rod assembly—(right bank)—V6 Buick built engines

the piston with a magnet and a rag soaked in clean oil.

NOTE: *Make sure the piston top and cylinder bore are absolutely clean before moving the piston.*

1. Remove intake manifold and cylinder head and heads.

2. Remove the oil pan.

3. Remove oil pump assembly if necessary.

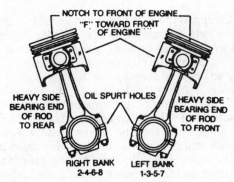

Piston and connecting rod assembly—Chevrolet built engines

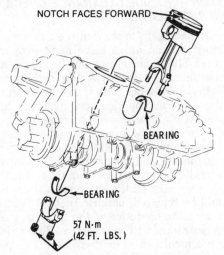

Piston and connecting rod assembly—Oldsmobile built engines

4. Match-mark the connecting rod cap to the connecting rod with a scribe; each cap must be reinstalled on its proper rod in the proper direction. Remove the connecting rod bearing cap and the rod bearing. Number the top of each piston with silver paint or a felt-tip pen for later assembly.

5. Cut lengths of ⅜" diameter hose to use as rod bolt guides. Install the hose over the threads of the rod bolts, to prevent the bolt threads from damaging the crankshaft journals and cylinder walls when the piston is removed.

6. Squirt some clean engine oil onto the cylinder wall from above, until the wall is coated. Carefully push the piston and rod assembly up and out of the cylinder by tapping on the bottom of the connecting rod with a wooden hammer handle.

7. Place the rod bearing and cap back on the connecting rod, and install the nuts temporarily. Using a number stamp or punch, stamp the cylinder number on the side of the connecting

rod and cap; this will help keep the proper piston and rod assembly on the proper cylinder.

NOTE: *On V6 engines, starting at the front the cylinders are numbered 2-4-6 on the right bank and 1-3-5 on the left. On all V8s, starting at the front the right bank, cylinders are 2-4-6-8 and the left bank 1-3-5-7.*

8. Remove remaining pistons in similar manner.

On all engines, the notch on the piston will face the front of the engine for assembly. The chamfered corners of the bearing caps should face toward the front of the left bank and toward the rear of the right bank. The boss on the connecting rod should face toward the front of the engine for the right bank and to the rear of the engine on the left bank. On some Pontiac-built engines, the rods have three dimples on one side of the rod and a single dimple on the rod cap. The dimples must face to the rear on the right bank and forward on the left.

On various engines, the piston compression rings are marked with a dimple, a letter **T**, a letter **O**, **GM** or the word **TOP** to identify the side of the ring which must face toward the top of the piston.

PISTON RING AND WRIST PIN REMOVAL

Some of the engines covered in this guide utilize pistons with pressed-in wrist pins; these must be removed by a special press designed for this purpose. Other pistons have their wrist pins secured by snaprings, which are easily removed with snapring pliers. Separate the piston from the connecting rod.

A piston ring expander is necessary for removing piston rings without damaging them; any other method (screwdriver blades, pliers, etc.) usually results in the rings being bent, scratched or distorted, or the piston itself being damaged. When the rings are removed, clean the ring grooves using an appropriate ring groove cleaning tool, using care not to cut too deeply. Thoroughly clean all carbon and varnish from the piston with solvent.

CAUTION: *Do not use a wire brush or caustic solvent (acids, etc.) on pistons.*

Inspect the pistons for scuffing, scoring, cracks, pitting, or excessive ring groove wear. If these are evident, the piston must be replaced.

The piston should also be checked in relation to the cylinder diameter. Using a telescoping gauge and micrometer, or a dial gauge, measure the cylinder bore diameter perpendicular (90 degrees) to the piston pin, 2½" below the cylinder block deck (surface where the block mates with the heads). Then, with the micrometer, measure the piston perpendicular to its wrist pin on the skirt. The difference between the two measurements is the piston clearance. If the clearance is within specifications or slightly below (after the cylinders have been bored or honed), finish honing is all that is necessary. If the clearance is excessive, try to obtain a slightly larger piston to bring clearance to within specifications. If this is not possible, obtain the first oversize piston and hone (or if necessary, bore) the cylinder to size. Generally, if the cylinder bore is tapered 0.005″ or more, or cut out of round 0.003″ or more, it is advisable to rebore for the smallest possible oversize piston and ring.

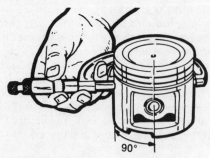

Measuring the piston

After measuring, mark pistons with a felt tip pen for reference and assembly.

NOTE: *Cylinder honing and/or boring should be performed by a reputable, professional mechanic with the proper equipment. In some cases, clean-up honing can be done with the cylinder block in the car but most excessive honing and all cylinder boring must be done with the block removed from the car.*

PISTON RING END GAP

Piston ring end gap should be checked while the rings are removed from the pistons. Incorrect end gap indicates that the wrong size rings are being used; ring breakage could occur.

Compress the piston rings to be used in a cylinder, one at a time, into that cylinder. Squirt clean oil into the cylinder, so that the rings and the top 2 inches of cylinder wall are coated. Using an inverted piston, press the rings approximately 1″ below the deck of the block (on diesels, measure ring gap clearance with the ring positioned at the bottom of ring travel in the bore). Measure the ring end gap with a feeler gauge, and compare to the Ring Gap chart in this chapter. Carefully pull the ring out of the cylinder and file the ends squarely with a fine file to obtain the proper clearance.

PISTON RING SIDE CLEARANCE CHECK AND INSTALLATION

Check the pistons to see that the ring grooves and oil return holes have been properly cleaned. Slide a piston ring into its groove, and check the side clearance with a feeler gauge. ON gasoline engines, make sure you insert the gauge between the ring and its lower land (lower edge of the groove), because any wear that occurs forms a stop at the inner portion of the lower land. On diesels, insert the gauge between the ring and the upper land. If the piston grooves have worn to the extent that relatively high steps exist on the lower land, the piston should be replaced, because these will interfere with the operation of the new rings and ring clearances will be excessive. Piston rings are not furnished in oversize widths to compensate for ring groove wear.

Install the rings on the piston. lowest ring first, using a piston ring expander. There is a high risk of breaking or distorting the rings, or scratching the piston, if the rings are installed by hand or other means.

Position the rings on the piston as illustrated; spacing of the various piston ring gaps is crucial to proper oil retention and even cylinder wear. When installing new rings, refer to the installation diagram in the furnished with the new parts.

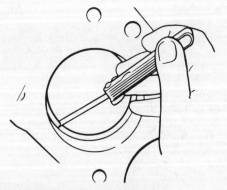

Checking the piston ring end gap

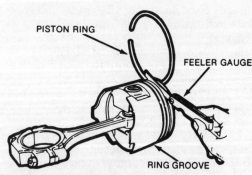

PISTON RING

FEELER GAUGE

RING GROOVE

Checking the piston ring side clearance

CONNECTING ROD BEARINGS

Connecting rod bearings for the engines covered in this guide consists of two halves or shells which are interchangable in the rod and cap

When the shells are placed in position, the ends extend slightly beyond the rod and cap surfaces so that when the rod bolts are torqued the shells will be clamped tightly in place to insure positive seating and to prevent turning. A tang hold the shells in place.

NOTE: *The ends of the bearing shells must never be filed flush with the mating surface of the rod and cap.*

If a rod bearing becomes noisy or is worn so that its clearance on the crank journal is sloppy, a new bearing of the correct undersize must be selected and installed since there is no provision for adjustment.

CAUTION: *Under no circumstances should the rod end or cap be filed to adjust the bearing clearance, nor should shims of any kink be used.*

Inspect the rod bearings while the rod assemblies are out of the engine. If the shells are scored or show flaking, they should be replaced. If they are in good shape check for proper clearance on the crank journal (see below). Any scoring or ridges on the crank journal means the crankshaft must be replaced, or reground and fitted with undersized bearings.

NOTE: *If turbo V6 crank journals are scored or ridged the crankshaft must be replaced, as regrinding will reduce the durability of the crankshaft.*

Checking Bearing Clearance and Replacing Bearings

Replacement bearings are available in standard size, and in undersizes for reground crankshaft. Connecting rod-to-crankshaft bearing clearance is checked using Plastigage® at either the top or bottom of each crank journal. The Plastigage® has a range of 0.001″ to 0.003″

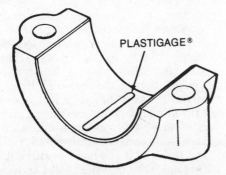

Plastigage® installed on the lower bearing shell

NOTE: *Make sure connecting rods and their caps are kept together, and that the caps are installed in the proper direction.*

1. Remove the rod cap with the bearing shell. Completely clean the bearing shell and the crank journal, and blow any oil from the oil hole in the crankshaft; Plastigage® is soluble in oil.

2. Place a piece of Plastigage® lengthwise along the bottom center of the lower bearing shell, then install the cap with shell and torque the bolt or nuts to specification. DO NOT turn the crankshaft with Plastigage® in the bearing.

3. Remove the bearing cap with the shell. The flattened Plastigage® will be found sticking to either the bearing shell or crank journal. Do not remove it yet.

4. Use the scale printed on the Plastigage® envelope to measure the flattened material at its widest point. The number within the scale which most closely corresponds to the width of the Plastigage® indicates bearing clearance in thousandths of an inch.

5. Check the specifications chart in this chapter for the desired clearance. It is advisable to install a new bearing if clearance exceeds 0.003″, however, if the bearing is in good condition and is not being checked because of bearing noise, bearing replacement is not necessary.

6. If you are installing new bearings, try a standard size, then each undersize in order until one is found that is within the specified limits when checked for clearance with Plastigage®. Each undersize shell has its size stamped on it.

7. When the proper size shell is found, clean off the Plastigage®, oil the bearing thoroughly, reinstall the cap with its shell and torque the rod bolt nuts to specification.

NOTE: *With the proper bearing selected and the nuts torqued, it should be possible to move the connecting rod back and forth freely on the crank journal as allowed by the specified connecting rod end clearance. If the rod cannot be moved, either the rod bearing is too far undersize or the rod is misaligned.*

PISTON AND CONNECTING ROD ASSEMBLY AND INSTALLATION

Install the connecting rod to the piston, making sure piston installation notches and any marks on the rod are in proper relation to one another. Lubricate the wrist pin with clean engine oil, and install the pin into the rod and piston assembly, either by hand or by using a wrist pin press as required. Install snaprings if equipped, and rotate them n their grooves to

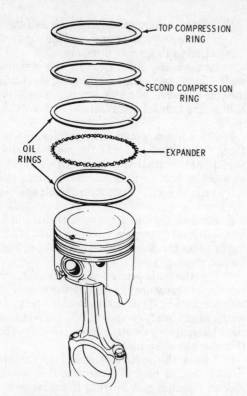

TOP COMPRESSION RING

SECOND COMPRESSION RING

OIL RINGS

EXPANDER

For detailed instructions and specifications for installation of the piston rings refer to the instructions furnished with the parts package

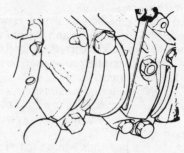

RING COMPRESSOR

Install the piston using a ring compressor

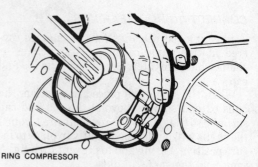

Check the connecting rod side clearance with a feeler gauge

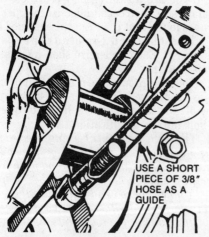

USE A SHORT PIECE OF 3/8" HOSE AS A GUIDE

Use lengths of vacuum hose or rubber tubing to protect the crankshaft journals and cylinder walls during piston installation

make sure they are seated. To install the piston and connecting rod assembly:

1. Make sure connecting rod big-end bearings (including end cap) are of the correct size and properly installed.

2. Fit rubber hoses over the connecting rod bolts to protect the crankshaft journals, as in the Piston Removal procedure. Coat the rod bearings with clean oil.

3. Using the proper ring compressor, insert the piston assembly into the cylinder so that the notch in the top of the piston faces the front of the engine (this assumes that the dimple(s) or other markings on the connecting rods are in correct relation to the piston notch(s).

4. From beneath the engine, coat each crank journal with clean oil. Pull the connecting rod, with the bearing shell in place, into position against the crank journal.

5. Remove the rubber hoses. Install the bearing cap and cap nuts and torque to specification.

NOTE: *When more than one rod and piston assembly is being installed, the connecting rod cap attaching nuts should only be tightened enough to keep each rod in position until all have been installed. This will ease the installation of the remaining piston assemblies.*

6. Check the clearance between the sides of the connecting rods and the crankshaft using a feeler gauge. Spread the rods slightly with a screwdriver to insert the gauge. If clearance is below the minimum tolerance, the rod may be machined to provide adequate clearance. If clearance is excessive, substitute an unworn rod, and recheck. If clearance is still outside specifications, the crankshaft must be welded and reground, or replaced.

7. Replace the oil pump if removed and the oil pan.

8. Install the cylinder head(s) and intake manifold.

Crankshaft and Main Bearings

CRANKSHAFT REMOVAL

All Engines

1. Drain the engine oil and remove the engine from the car. Mount the engine on a work stand in a suitable working area. Invert the engine, so the oil pan is facing up.

2. Remove the engine front (timing) cover.

3. Remove the time chain and gears.

4. Remove the oil pan.

5. Remove the oil pump.

6. Stamp the cylinder number on the machined surfaces of the bolt bosses of the connecting rods and caps for identification when reinstalling. If the pistons are to be removed eventually from the connecting rod, mark the cylinder number on the pistons with silver paint or felt-tip pen for proper cylinder identification and cap-to-rod location.

7. Remove the connecting rod caps. Install lengths of rubber hose on each of the connecting rod bolts, to protect the crank journals when the crank is removed.

8. Mark the main bearing caps with a number punch or punch so that they can be reinstalled in their original positions.

9. Remove all main bearing caps.

10. Note the position of the keyway in the crankshaft so it can be installed in the same position.

11. Install rubber bands between a bolt on each connecting rod and oil pan bolts that have been reinstalled in the block. This will keep the rods from banging on the block when the cranks is removed.

12. Carefully lift the crankshaft out of the block. The rods will pivot to the center of the engine when the crank is removed.

MAIN BEARING INSPECTION AND REPLACEMENT

Like connecting rod big-end bearings, the crankshaft main bearings are shell-type inserts that do not utilize shims and cannot be adjusted. The bearings are available in various standard and undersizes; if main bearing clearance is found to be too sloppy, a new bearing (both upper and lower halves) is required.

NOTE: *Factory-undersized crankshafts are marked, sometimes with a 9 and/or a large spot of light green paint; the bearing caps also will have the paint on each side of the undersized journal.*

Generally, the lower half of the bearing shell (except No. 1 bearing) shows greater wear and fatigue. If the lower half only shows the effects of normal wear (no heavy scoring or discoloration), it can usually be assumed that the upper half is also in good shape; conversely, if the lower half is heavily worn or damaged, both halves should be replaced. Never replace one bearing half without replacing the other.

CHECKING CLEARANCE

Main bearing clearance can be checked both with the crankshaft in the car and with the engine out of the car. If the engine block is still in the car, the crankshaft should be supported both front and rear (by the damper and to remove clearance from the upper bearing). Total clearance can then be measured between the lower bearing and journal. If the block has been removed from the car, and is inverted, the crank will rest on the upper bearings and the total clearance can be measured between the lower bearing and journal. Clearance is checked in the same manner as the connecting rod bearings, with Plastigage®.

NOTE: *Crankshaft bearing caps and bearing shells should NEVER be filed flush with the cap-to-block mating surface to adjust for wear in the old bearings. Always install new bearings.*

1. If the crankshaft has been removed, install it (block removed from car). If the block is still in the car, remove the oil pan and oil pump. Starting with the rear bearing cap, remove the cap and wipe all oil from the crank journal and bearing cap.

2. Place a strip of Plastigage® the full width of the bearing, (parallel to the crankshaft), on the journal.

CAUTION: *Do not rotate the crankshaft while the gauging material is between the bearing and the journal.*

3. Install the bearing cap and evenly torque the cap bolts to specification.

4. Remove the bearing cap. The flattened Plastigage® should be sticking to either the bearing shell or the crank journal.

5. Use the graduated scale on the Plastigage® envelope to measure the material at its widest point.

NOTE: *If the flattened Plastigage® tapers towards the middle or ends, there is a difference in clearance indicating the bearing or journal has a taper, low spot or other irregularity. If this is indicated, measure the crank journal with a micrometer.*

6. If bearing clearance is within specifications, the bearing insert is in good shape. Replace the insert if the clearance is not within specifications. Always replace both upper and lower inserts as a unit.

7. Standard, 0.001″ or 0.002″ undersize bearings should produce the proper clearance. If these sizes still produce too sloppy a fit, the crankshaft must be reground for use with the next undersize bearing. Recheck all clearances after installing new bearings.

NOTE: *Any regrinding of crankshaft journals should be performed by a competent machine shop.*

8. Replace the rest of the bearings in the same manner. After all bearings have been checked, rotate the crankshaft to make sure there is no excessive drag. When checking the No. 1 main bearing, loosen the accessory drive belts (engine in car) to prevent a tapered reading with the Plastigage®.

MAIN BEARING REPLACEMENT

Engine Out of Car

1. Remove and inspect the crankshaft.
2. Remove the main bearings from the bearing saddles in the cylinder block and main bearing caps.
3. Coat the bearing surfaces of the new, correct size main bearings with clean engine oil and install them in the bearing saddles in the block and in the main bearing caps.
4. Install the crankshaft. See Crankshaft Installation.

Engine In Car

1. With the oil pan, oil pump and spark plugs removed, remove the cap from the main bearing needing replacement and remove the bearing from the cap.
2. Made a bearing roll-out pin, using a bent cotter pin as shown in the illustration. Install the end of the pin in the oil hole in the crankshaft journal.
3. Rotate the crankshaft clockwise as viewed from the front of the engine. This will roll the upper bearing out of the block.
4. Lube the new upper bearing with clean engine oil and insert the plain (unnotched) end between the crankshaft and the indented or notched side of the block. Roll the bearing into

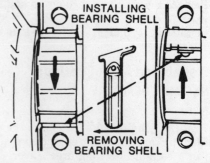

Remove or install the upper bearing insert using a roll-out pin

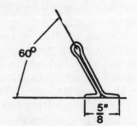

Home-made bearing roll-out pin

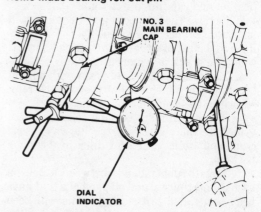

Check the crankshaft end-play with a dial indicator

place, making sure that the oil holes are aligned. Remove the roll pin from the oil hole.

5. Lube the new lower bearing and install the main bearing cap. Install the main bearing cap, making sure it is positioned in proper direction with the matchmarks in alignment.

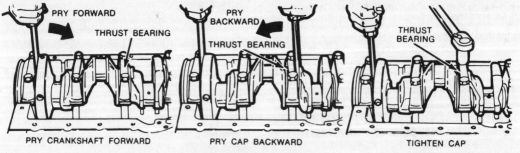

Aligning the thrust bearing

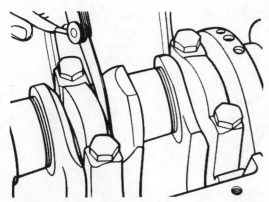

Checking the crankshaft end-play using a feeler gauge

6. Torque the main bearing cap bolts to specification.

NOTE: *See Crankshaft Installation for thrust bearing.*

CRANKSHAFT END PLAY AND INSTALLATION

When main bearing clearance has been checked, bearings examined and/or replaced, the crankshaft can be installed. Thoroughly clean the upper and lower bearing surfaces, and lube them with clean engine oil. Install the crankshaft and main bearing caps.

Dip all main bearing cap bolts in clean oil, and torque all main bearing caps, excluding the thrust bearing cap, to specifications (see the crankshaft and Connecting Rod chart in this chapter to determine which bearing is the thrust bearing). Tighten the thrust bearing bolts finger tight. To align the thrust bearing, pry the crankshaft the extent of its axial travel several times, holding the last movement toward the front of the engine. Add thrust washers if required for proper alignment. Torque the thrust bearing cap to specifications.

To check crankshaft end-play, pry the crankshaft to the extreme rear of its axial travel, then to the extreme front of its travel. Using a feeler gauge, measure the end-play at the front of the rear main bearing. End play may also be measured at the thrust bearing. Install a new rear main bearing oil seal in the cylinder block and main bearing cap. Continue to reassemble the engine.

Rear Main Oil Seal

REMOVAL AND INSTALLATION

L-6 Engine

The rear main bearing oil seal is of molded design, and both halves can be replaced without removal of the crankshaft.

1. Remove the oil pan and the oil pump.
2. Remove the rear main bearing cap.
3. Remove the oil seal from the groove by lifting the end tab, then clean the seal groove.
4. Lubricate the lip and outside diameter of the new seal with engine oil. Keep oil off the parting line surface.
5. Insert the new seal into the cap and roll it into place with you fingers. Use only light pressure on the seal to avoid cutting the outside diameter of the seal with the sharp edges of the groove. make sure the tabs of the seal are properly located in the cross grooves.
6. To remove the upper half of the seal, tap one end of the sea with a brass punch until the other end protrudes far enough to be grasped with a pair of pliers.
7. Lubricate the lip and outside diameter of a new seal with engine oil Roll the new seal into place by gradually pushing with a hammer handle while turning the crankshaft.
8. Install the rear main cap. Install the oil pan.

Buick Built Engines

LOWER HALF

1. Remove the oil pan and rear main bearing cap.
2. Remove the old seal from the bearing cap and place a new seal in the groove with both ends projecting above the parting surface of the cap.

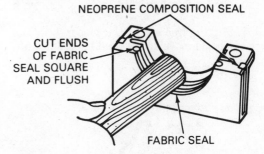

NEOPRENE COMPOSITION SEAL
CUT ENDS OF FABRIC SEAL SQUARE AND FLUSH
FABRIC SEAL

Installing rear bearing cap oil seals—Buick built engines

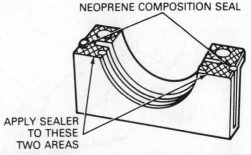

NEOPRENE COMPOSITION SEAL
APPLY SEALER TO THESE TWO AREAS

Apply a small amount of sealer to split line—Buick built engines

3. Force the seal into the groove by rubbing down with a hammer handle or smooth tool, until the seal projects above the groove not more than $\frac{1}{16}$" Cut the end off flush with the surface of the cap. Use a razor blade.

4. On the 231, 252, and 350, place new neoprene seals in the grooves in the sides of the bearing cap after soaking the seals in kerosene for a minute or two.

NOTE: *The neoprene composition seals will swell up once exposed to the oil and heat. It is normal for the seals for leak for a short time, until they become properly seated. The seals must not be cut to fit.*

5. To install, reverse the above. Use a small amount of sealer on the bearing cap mating surface. The engine must be operated at low rpm when first started, after a new seal is installed.

UPPER HALF

NOTE: *Although the factory recommends removing the crankshaft to replace the top half of the oil seal, the following procedure can be used without removing the crankshaft.*

1. Remove the oil pan and rear main bearing cap.

2. Loosen the rest of the crankshaft main bearings and allow the crankshaft to drop about $\frac{1}{16}$"

3. Remove the old upper half of the oil seal.

4. Wrap some soft copper wire around the end of the new seal and leave about 12" on the end. Generously lubricate the new seal with oil.

5. Slip the free end of the copper wire into the oil seal groove and around the crankshaft.

Pull the wire until the seal protrudes an equal amount on each side. Rotate the crankshaft as the seal if pulled into place.

6. Remove the wire. Push any excess seal that may be protruding back into the groove.

7. Before tightening the crankshaft bearing caps, visually check the bearings to make sure they are in place. Torque the bearing cap bolts to specifications. Make sure there is no oil on the parting surfaces.

8. Replace the oil pan. Run the engine slowly for the first few minutes of operation.

V8 Chevrolet Built Engines

The rear main bearing seal may be replaced without removing the crankshaft. Seals should only be replaced as a pair. The seal lips should face the front of the engine when properly installed.

1. Remove the oil pan, and pump as previously outlined, and remove the rear main bearing cap.

2. Pry the lower seal out of the bearing cap with a screwdriver, being careful not to gouge the cap surface.

3. Remove the upper seal by lightly tapping

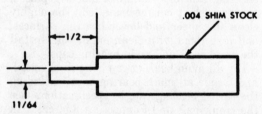

Fabricate an oil seal tool—Chevrolet and Oldsmobile built engines

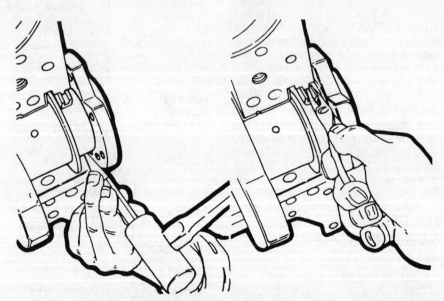

Removing the upper half of the oil seal—Chevrolet built engines and Oldsmobile built engines

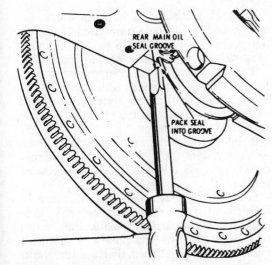

Pack the old seal into the groove—Chevrolet and Oldsmobile engines

on one end with a brass pin punch until the other end can be grasped and pulled out with pliers.

4. Clean the bearing cap, cylinder block, and crankshaft mating surfaces with solvent. Inspect all these surfaces for gouges, nicks, and burrs.

5. Apply light engine oil on the seal lips and bead, but keep the seal ends clean.

6. Insert the top of the installation tool between the crankshaft and the seal of the cylinder block. Place the seal between the tip of the tool and the crankshaft, so that the bead contacts the tip of the tool.

7. Be sure that the seal lip if facing the front of the engine, and work the seal around the crankshaft using the installation tool to protect the seal from the corner of the cylinder block.

NOTE: *Do not remove the tool until the opposite end of the seal is flush with the cylinder block surface.*

8. Remove the installation tool, being careful not to pull the seal out at the same time.

9. Using the same procedure, install the lower seal into the bearing cap. Use you finger and thumb to lever the seal into the cap.

10. Apply sealer to the cylinder block only where the cap mates to the surface. Do not apply sealer to the seal ends.

11. Install the rear cap and torque the bolt to specifications. Install the oil pan and pump as previously described.

V8 Oldsmobile Built Engines

The crankshaft need not be removed to replace the rear main bearing upper oil seal.

1. Drain the crankcase and remove the oil pan and rear main bearing cap.

2. Using a blunt-ended tool, drive the upper seal into its groove on each side until it is tightly packed. This is usually ¼-¾″

3. Cut pieces of new seal $\frac{1}{16}$″ longer than required to fill the grooves and install, packing into place.

4. Carefully trim any protruding seal, being sure not to scratch or damage the bearing surface.

5. Install a new seal in the bearing cap and install cap, tightening bolts to 120 ft.lb. (107 ft.lb. on V6 diesel). Install the oil pan.

Flywheel Or Ring Gear
REMOVAL AND INSTALLATION
Manual Transmission

1. Remove transmission and clutch assembly, being certain to mark clutch cover and flywheel so clutch may be reinstalled in original position. (See Chapter 6 for transmission removal.)

2. Remove flywheel. Flywheel is attached by unevenly spaced bolts.

3. If ring gear is to be replaced, drill a hole between two teeth and split gear with a cold chisel.

4. Heat and shrink a new gear in place as follows:

    a. Polish several spots on ring with emery cloth.

    b. Use a hot plate or slowly moving torch to heat the ring until the polished spots turn blue (approximately 600 degrees F). Heating the ring in excess of (800 degrees F) will destroy the heat treatment.

    c. Quickly place ring in position against shoulder of flywheel with chamfered inner shoulder of flywheel with chamfered inner edge of ring gear toward flywheel shoulder. Allow ring to cool slowly until it contracts and is firmly held in place.

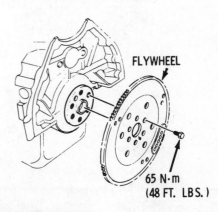

Flywheel installation

5. Make certain the flywheel and crankshaft flange are free from burrs that would cause run-out. Install flywheel.

Automatic Transmission

1. Remove transmission (refer to Chapter 6).

2. Remove six bolts attaching flywheel to crankshaft flange.

3. Inspect flywheel; if cracked, badly worn or it has broken teeth, replace flywheel.

4. Inspect crankshaft flange and flywheel for burrs. Remove any burrs with a mill file.

5. Install flywheel. Bolt holes are unevenly spaced so all flywheel bolts can be installed with flywheel in correct position. Install bolts and torque to specifications.

6. Mount dial indicator on engine block and check flywheel run-out at three attaching bosses. Run-out should not exceed 0.015". The crankshaft end play must be held in one direction during this check.

7. If run-out exceeds 0.015", attempt to correct by tapping high side with mallet. If this does not correct, remove flywheel and check for burrs between flywheel and crankshaft mounting flange.

EXHAUST SYSTEM

Whenever working on the exhaust system please observe the following:

1. Check the complete exhaust system for open seams, holes loose connections, or other deterioration which could permit exhaust fumes to seep into the passenger compartment.

2. The exhaust system is supported by free-hanging rubber mountings which permit some movement of the exhaust system, but do not permit transfer of noise and vibration into the passenger compartment.

3. Before removing any component of the exhaust system, ALWAYS squirt a liquid rust dissolving agent onto the fasteners for ease of removal.

4. Annoying rattles and noise vibrations in the exhaust system are usually caused by misalignment of the parts. When aligning the system, leave all bolts and nuts loose until all parts are properly aligned, then tighten, working from front to rear.

5. When replacing a muffler and/or resonator, the tailpipe(s) should also be replaced.

6. When installing exhaust system parts, make sure there is enough clearance between the hot exhaust parts and pipes , and hoses that would be adversely affected by excessive heat. Also make sure there is adequate clearance from the floor pan to avoid possible overheating of the floor.

7. Exhaust pipe sealers should be used at all slip joint connections except at the catalytic convertor. Do not use any sealers at the convertor as the sealer will not withstand convertor temperatures.

Emission Controls and Fuel System

4

GASOLINE ENGINE EMISSION CONTROLS

Positive Crankcase Ventilation System

All engines are equipped with a positive crankcase ventilation (PCV) system to control crankcase blow-by vapors. The system functions as follows:

When the engine is running, a small portion of the gases which are formed in the combustion chamber leak by the piston rings and enter the crankcase. Since these gases are under pressure, they tend to escape from the crankcase and enter the atmosphere. If these gases are allowed to remain in the crankcase for any period of time, they contaminate the engine oil and cause sludge to build up in the crankcase. If the gases are allowed to escape into the atmosphere, they pollute the air with unburned hydrocarbons. The job of the crankcase emission control equipment is to recycle these gases back into the engine combustion chamber where they are reburned.

The crankcase (blow-by) gases are recycled in the following way: as the engine is running, clean, filtered air is drawn through the air filter and into the crankcase. As the air passes through the crankcase, it picks up the combustion gases and carries them out of the crankcase, through the oil separator, through the PCV valve, and into the induction system. As they enter the intake manifold, they are drawn into the combustion chamber where they are reburned.

The most critical component in the system is the PCV valve. This valve controls the amount of gases which are recycled into the combustion chamber. At low engine speeds, the valve is partially closed, limiting the flow of the gases into the intake manifold. As engine speed increases, the valve opens to admit greater quantities of the gases into the intake manifold. If the valve should become blocked or plugged, the gases will be prevented from escaping from the crankcase by the normal route. Since these gases are under pressure, they will find their own way out of the crankcase. This alternate route is usually a weak oil seal or gasket in the engine. As the gas escapes by the gasket, it also creates an oil leak. Besides causing oil leaks, a clogged PCV valve also allows these gases to remain in the crankcase for an extended period of time, promoting the formation of sludge in the engine. See Chapter 1 for PCV valve replacement intervals.

SERVICE

1. Remove the PCV system components, filler cap, PCV valve, hoses, fittings, etc. from the engine.

2. Clean all the hoses with solvent and a brush if necessary. Wash the breather cap in solvent, and shake it dry. Do not blow it dry with compressed air. Damage will result.

3. PCV valves cannot be cleaned. Install a new PCV valve, and reinstall all the hoses and fittings removed earlier.

Evaporative Emission Control System

OPERATION

This system which was introduced on California cars in 1970, and other cars in 1971, reduces the amount of escaping gasoline vapors. Float bowl emissions are controlled by internal carburetor modifications. Redesigned bowl vents, reduced bowl capacity, heat shields, and improved intake manifold-to-carburetor insulation reduce vapor loss into the atmosphere. The venting of fuel tank vapors into the air has been stopped by means of the carbon canister storage method. This method transfer fuel vapors to an activated carbon storage device which absorbs and stores the vapor that is emitted from the engine's induction system while the engine is not running. When the engine is running, the stored vapor is purged from the carbon storage device by the intake air flow and then consumed in the normal combustion process. As the manifold vacuum reaches a certain point, it opens a purge control valve atop the charcoal storage canister. This allows air to be drawn into the canister, thus forcing the existing fuel vapors back into the engine to be burned normally.

In 1981, the purge function on the 231 V6 engine is electronically controlled by a purge solenoid in the line which is itself controlled by the Electronic Control Module (ECM). When the system is in the Open Loop mode, the solenoid valve is energized, blocking all vacuum to the purge valve. When the system is in the Closed Loop mode, the solenoid is de-energized, thus allowing existing vacuum to operate the purge valve. This releases the trapped fuel vapor and it is forced into the induction system.

Most carbon canisters used are of the Open design, meaning that air is drawn in through the bottom (filter) of the canister. Some (1981 and later 231 V6) canisters are of the Closed design which means that the incoming air is drawn directly from the air cleaner.

SERVICE

The only service required is the periodic replacement of the canister filter (if so equipped).

If the fuel tank cap on you car ever requires replacement, make sure that it is of the same type as the original.

Thermostatic Air Cleaner

This system is designed to warm the air entering the carburetor when underhood temperatures are low, and to maintain a controlled air temperature into the carburetor at all times. By allowing preheated air to enter the carburetor, the amount of time the choke is on is reduced, resulting in better fuel economy and lower emissions. Engine warm-up time is also reduced.

The Thermac system is composed of the air cleaner body, a filter, sensor unit, vacuum diaphragm, damper door, and associated hoses and connections. Heat radiating from the exhaust manifold is trapped by a heat stove and is ducted to the air cleaner to supply heated air to the carburetor. A movable door is the air cleaner case snorkel allows air to be drawn in from the heat stove (cold operation) or from underhood air (warm operation). The door position is controlled by the vacuum motor, which receives intake manifold vacuum as modulated by the temperature sensor.

SYSTEM CHECKS

1. Check the vacuum hoses for leaks, kinks, breaks, or improper connections and correct any defects.
2. With the engine off, check the position of the damper door within the snorkel. A mirror

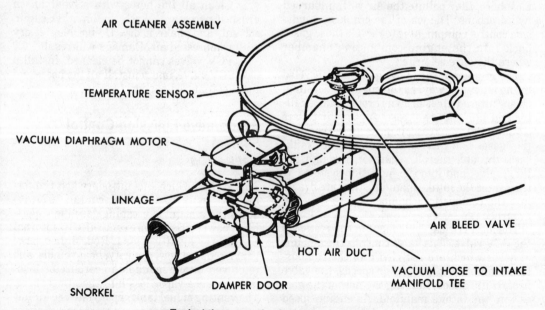

Typical thermostatic air cleaner assembly

can be used to make this job easier. The damper door should be open to admit outside air.

3. Apply at least 7 in.Hg of vacuum to the damper diaphragm unit. The door should close. If it doesn't, check the diaphragm linkage for binding and correct hookup.

4. With vacuum still applied and the door closed, clamp the tube to trap the vacuum. If the door doesn't remain closed, there is a leak in the diaphragm assembly.

Air Injection Reactor System (A.I.R.) through 1980

The AIR system injects compressed air into the exhaust system, near enough to the exhaust valves to continue the burning of the normally unburned segment of the exhaust gases. To do this it employs an air injection pump and a system of hoses, valves, tubes, etc., necessary to carry the compressed air from the pump to the exhaust manifold. Carburetors and distributors for AIR engines have specific modifications to adapt them to the air injection system; those components should not be interchanged with those intended for use on engines that do not have the system.

A diverter valve is used to prevent backfiring. The valve senses sudden increases in manifold vacuum and ceases the injection of air during fuel-rich periods. During coasting, this valve diverts the entire air flow through the pump muffler and during high engine speeds, expels it through a relief valve. Check valves in the system prevent exhaust gases from entering the pump.

NOTE: *The AIR system on the 231 V6 engine is slightly different, but its purpose remains the same.*

SERVICE

The AIR system's effectiveness depends on correct engine idle speed, ignition timing, and dwell. These settings should be strictly adhered to and checked frequently. All hoses and fittings should be inspected for condition and tightness of connections. Check the drive belt for wear and tension every 12 months or 12,000 miles.

COMPONENT REMOVAL

Air Pump

CAUTION: *Do not pry on the pump housing or clamp the pump in a vise: the housing is soft and may become distorted.*

1. Disconnect the air hoses at the pump.
2. Hold the pump pulley from turning and loosen the pulley bolts.
3. Loosen the pump mounting bolt and adjustment bracket bolt. Remove the drive belt.

4. Remove the mounting bolts, and then remove the pump.
5. Install the pump using a reverse of the removal procedure.

Diverter (Anti-afterburn) Valve

1. Detach the vacuum sensing line from the valve.
2. Remove the other hose(s) from the valve.
3. Unfasten the diverter valve from the elbow or the pump body.
4. Installation is performed in the reverse order of removal. Always use a new gasket. Tighten the valve securing bolts to 85 in.lb.

Air Management System-1981 and Later

The Air Management System is used to provide additional oxygen to continue the combustion process after the exhaust gases leave the combustion chamber; much the same as the AIR system described earlier in this chapter. Air is injected into either the exhaust port(s), the exhaust manifold(s) or the catalytic converter by an engine driven air pump. The system is in operation at all times and will by-pass air only momentarily during deceleration and at high speeds. The bypass function is performed by the Air Management Valve, while the check valve protects the air pump by preventing any backflow of exhaust gases.

The AIR system helps to reduce HC and CO content in the exhaust gases by injecting air into the exhaust ports during cold engine operation. This air injection also helps the catalytic converter to reach the proper temperature quicker during warm-up. When the engine is warm (closed loop), the AIR system injects air into the beds of a three-way converter to lower the HC and CO content in the exhaust.

The Air Management System utilizes the following components:

1. An engine driven air pump
2. Air management valves (Air Control and Air Switching)
3. Air flow and control hoses
4. Check valves
5. A dual-bed, three-way catalytic converter

The belt driven, vane-type air pump is located at the front of the engine and supplies clean air to the system for purposes already stated. When the engine is cold, the Electronic Control Module (ECM) energizes an air control solenoid. This allows air to flow to the air switching valve. The air switching valve is then energized to direct air into the exhaust ports.

When the engine is warm, the ECM de-engergizes the air switching valve, thus directing the air between the beds of the catalytic converter. This then provides additional oxygen for the oxidizing catalyst in the second bed to decrease HC and CO levels, while at the same time keeping oxygen levels low in the first bed, enabling the reducing catalyst to effectively decrease the levels of NOx.

If the air control valve detects a rapid increase in manifold vacuum (deceleration), certain operating modes (wide open throttle, etc.) or if the ECM self-diagnostic system detects any problems in the system, air is diverted to the air cleaner or directly into the atmosphere.

The primary purpose of the ECM's divert mode is to prevent backfiring. Throttle closure at the beginning of deceleration will temporarily create air/fuel mixtures which are too rich to burn completely. These mixtures will become burnable when they reach the exhaust if they are combined with injection air. The next firing of the engine will ignite the mixture causing an exhaust backfire. Momentary diverting of the injection air from the exhaust prevents this.

The Air Management System check valves and hoses should be checked periodically for any leaks, cracks or deterioration.

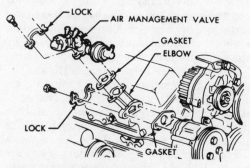

Typical Air Management Valve

REMOVAL AND INSTALLATION

Air Pump

1. Remove the valves and/or adapter at the air pump.

2. Loosen the air pump adjustment bolt and remove the drive belt.

3. Unscrew the three mounting bolts and then remove the pump pulley.

4. Unscrew the pump mounting bolts and then remove the pump.

5. Installation is in the reverse order of removal. Be sure to adjust the drive belt tension after installing it.

Check Valve

1. Release the clamp and disconnect the air hoses from the valve.

2. Unscrew the check valve from the air injection pipe.

3. Installation is in the reverse order of removal.

Air Management Valve

1. Disconnect the negative battery cable.

2. Remove the air cleaner.

3. Tag and disconnect the vacuum hose from the valve.

4. Tag and disconnect the air outlet hoses from the valve.

5. Bend back the lock tabs and then remove the bolts holding the elbow to the valve.

6. Tag and disconnect any electrical connections at the valve and then remove the valve from the elbow.

7. Installation is in the reverse order of removal.

Thermal Vacuum Switch

This switch was introduced in 1973 V8 engines. Vacuum hoses from the carburetor, intake manifold and distributor connect to this switch which is controlled by engine coolant temperature. During normal engine operation, vacuum from the carburetor passes through the TVS to the distributor. If the engine should overheat while idling, the TVS connects intake manifold vacuum to the distributor which lowers coolant temperature.

Thermal Check and Delay Valve

1973 and later 350 and 455 4-bbl. engines (except 350 cu. in manual transmission models) have a thermal check and delay valve. This valve is in the vacuum line which runs between the carburetor spark port and the TVS.

When the underhood (or engine block) temperature is below 50° F., full vacuum is supplied to the distributor. Above 50° F, the valve blocks full vacuum for up to 40 seconds. If ported vacuum drops, the valve opens, causing the distributor vacuum advance to be retarded. As vacuum increases, the valve closes, blocking full vacuum again.

Cars made after 15 March 1973 have a cover over the valve so that it is ore dependent upon engine block temperature.

Distributor Vacuum Valve

In 1974, the distributor vacuum valve (DVV) was introduced in 350 and 455 cu. in. engines sold in California and on some 455 cu. in. engines sold in the other 40 states.

The DVV switches the distributor vacuum advance unit's vacuum source from the carburetor spark port to the EGR port. Below 7 in.Hg, the vacuum unit operates from the spark port. Above 7 in.Hg the vacuum supply is switched by the SVV from the spark port to the EGR port.

SYSTEM TEST-THERMAL VACUUM SWITCH

1. Start the engine and allow it to reach normal operating temperature.

2. With the engine idling, disconnect the distributor hose at the D (top) port on the TVS.

3. Connect a vacuum gauge to the switch. There should be 2-5 in.Hg of vacuum at idle. If this is not the case, the hoses are unobstructed and connected to the proper ports, the switch is defective and must be replaced.

SYSTEM TEST-DISTRIBUTOR VACUUM TEST

1. Start the engine and allow it to reach normal operating temperature. Remove the air cleaner and plug the manifold vacuum fitting.

2. Remove the hose from the "D" port of the TVS and attach a vacuum gauge to the port. Using a "T" fitting, attach the vacuum gauge to the hose at the carburetor EGR port.

3. Gradually increase the engine speed. The first gauge should rise to 8 in.Hg and remain there, and then the second gauge should rise to 8 in.Hg and remain.
NOTE: *If the engine is a California version, the readings will be 7 in.Hg.*

4. If the above conditions are not met, replace the DVV valve.

SYSTEM TEST-THERMAL CHECK AND DELAY VALVE

1. Start the engine and allow it to reach operating temperature. Underhood temperature must be at least 50 degrees F.

2. Connect the vacuum gauge to the TVS port of the valve, and a hand-operated vacuum pump to the "CARB" port.

3. Operate the pump to create a vacuum. The vacuum gauge on the TVS side should show a slight hesitation before registering.

4. The gauge reading on the pump should drop slightly, taking 3-4 seconds for it to balance with the reading on the other gauge.

5. If steps three and four are negative, replace the valve.

6. Cover the TVS port on the valve with your fingers and operate the pump to create a vacuum of 15 in.Hg.

7. The reading on the gauge should remain steady. If the gauge reading drops, replace the valve.

8. Remove your finger. The reading on the gauge should drop slowly. If the reading goes to zero rapidly, replace the valve.

Dual Vacuum Break Choke

A dual vacuum break choke is used on inline six and some 4 bbl. V8 engines, starting in 1975.

Once the engine has reached a specified temperature, the secondary vacuum break pulls the choke to almost wide-open position. Vacuum to the secondary break is controlled by a coolant temperature operated vacuum valve on V8, and by an electrical thermoswitch and solenoid on inline sixes.

SOLENOID TEST

1. The solenoid is located next to the choke vacuum diaphragm. Remove the connector from the solenoid.

2. Connect one of the solenoid terminals to the battery and ground the other terminal. If the solenoid doesn't click when the connection is made, the solenoid is defective and must be replaced.

3. Leaving the solenoid connected as in step two, disconnect the hose from the secondary vacuum break and connect a vacuum gauge to it.

4. With the engine running and the solenoid energized, the gauge should read zero.

5. Disconnect the jumper wires and the gauge should read full manifold vacuum.

6. If these conditions are not met, the solenoid is defective.

Thermostatic Air Cleaner Thermal Valve

The TAC thermal valve was introduced in 1975 and is located on the air cleaner housing. When the engine is cold, the valve restricts the vacuum supplied to the air cleaner door vacuum motor, which slows the operation of the door down. Under wide-open throttle conditions, the door does not jump to the full cold air position, thus eliminating the flat spot that occurs during cold engine acceleration.

Early Fuel Evaporation System (EFE)

1975 and later models are equipped with this system to reduce engine warm-up time, improve driveability, and reduce emissions. On start-up, a vacuum motor acts to close a heat riser passages. Incoming fuel mixture is then heated and more complete duel evaporation is provided during warm-up.

The system consists of a Thermal Vacuum Switch, and an Exhaust Heat Valve and actuator. The Thermal Vacuum Switch is located on the coolant outlet housing on V8s, and on the block on in-line six cylinder engines. When the engine is cold, the TVS conducts manifold vac-

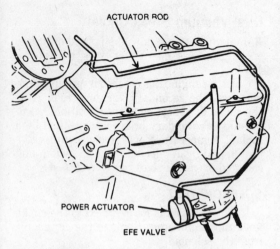

Typical EFE Valve—Buick built V6 engines

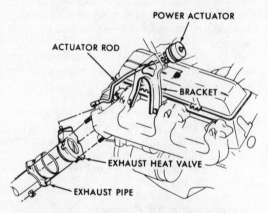

Typical EFE Valve—Chevrolet built V8 engines

uum to the actuator to close the valve. When engine coolant or, on 6 cylinder engines, oil warms up, vacuum in interrupted and the actuator should open the valve.

NOTE: *On 1981 and later models with the 231 V6 engine, the EFE system is controlled by the ECM.*

CHECKING THE EFE SYSTEM

1. With the engine overnight cold, have someone start the engine while you observe the Exhaust Heat Valve. The valve should snap to the closed position.

2. Watch the valve as the engine warms up. Be the time coolant starts circulating through the radiator the valve should snap open.

3. If the valve does not close, immediately disconnect the hose at the actuator, and check for vacuum by placing you finger over the end of the hose, or with a vacuum gauge. If there is vacuum, replace the actuator. If there is no vacuum, immediately disconnect the hose

leading to the TVS from the manifold at the TVS. If there is vacuum here, but not at the actuator, replace the TVS. If vacuum does not exist at the hose going to the TVS, check that the vacuum hose is free of cracks or breaks and tightly connected at the manifold, and that the manifold port is clear.

4. If the valve does not open when the engine coolant warms up, disconnect the hose at the actuator, and check for vacuum by placing your finger over the end of the hose or using a vacuum gauge. If there is vacuum, replace the TVS. If there is no vacuum, replace the actuator.

TVS REMOVAL AND INSTALLATION

Drain coolant until the level is below the coolant outlet housing. Apply sealer to threads. Note that the valve must be installed until just snug (120 in.lb.) and then turned by hand just far enough to line up the fittings for hose connection.

Exhaust Gas Recirculation (EGR)

All 1973 and later engines are equipped with exhaust gas recirculation (EGR). This system consists of a metering valve, a vacuum line to the carburetor, and cast-in exhaust gas passages in the intake manifold. The EGR valve is controlled by carburetor vacuum, and accordingly opens and closes to admit exhaust gases into the fuel/air mixture. The exhaust gases lower the combustion temperature, and reduce the amount of oxides and nitrogen (NOx) produced. The valve is closed at idle between the two extreme throttle positions.

In most installations, vacuum to the EGR valve is controlled by a thermal vacuum switch (TVS); the switch, which is installed into the engine block, shuts off vacuum to the EGR valve until the engine is hot. This prevents the stalling and bumpy idle which would result if EGR occurred when the engine was cold.

As the car accelerates, the carburetor throttle plate uncovers the vacuum port for the EGR valve. At 3-5 in.Hg, the EGR valve opens and then some of the exhaust gases are allowed to flow into the air/fuel mixture to lower the combustion temperature. At full-throttle the valve closes again.

Some California engines are equipped with a dual diaphragm EGR valve. this valve further limits the exhaust gas opening (compared to the single diaphragm EGR valve) during high intake manifold vacuum periods, such as high-speed cruising, and provides more exhaust gas recirculation during acceleration when manifold vacuum is low. In addition to

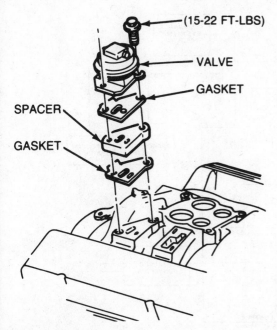

Typical EGR valve mounting location

(15-22 FT-LBS)

VALVE

GASKET

SPACER

GASKET

the hose running to the thermal vacuum switch, a second hose is connected directly to the intake manifold.

For 1977, all California models are cars delivered in areas above 4000 ft. are equipped with back pressure EGR valves. This valve is also used on all 1978-81 models. The EGR valve receives exhaust back pressure through its hollow shaft. This exerts a force on the bottom of the control valve diaphragm, opposed by a light spring. Under low exhaust pressure (low engine load and partial throttle), the EGR signal is reduced by an air bleed. Under conditions of high exhaust pressure (high engine load and large throttle opening), the air bleed is closed and the EGR valve responds to an unmodified vacuum signal. At wide open throttle, the EGR flow is reduced in proportion to the amount of vacuum signal available.

1979 and later models have a ported signal vacuum EGR valve. The valve opening is controlled by the amount of vacuum obtained from a ported vacuum source on the carburetor and the amount of backpressure in the exhaust system.

EGR VALVE REMOVAL AND INSTALLATION

1. Detach the vacuum lines from the EGR valve.
2. Unfasten the two bolts or bolt and clamp which attach the valve to the manifold. Withdraw the valve.
3. Installation is the reverse of removal. Always use a new gasket between the valve and

the manifold. On dual diaphragm valves, attach the carburetor vacuum line to the tube at the top of the valve, and the manifold vacuum line to the tube at the center of the valve.

TVS SWITCH REMOVAL AND INSTALLATION

1. Drain the radiator.
2. Disconnect the vacuum lines from the switch noting their locations. Remove the switch.
3. Apply sealer to the threaded portion of the new switch, and install it, torquing to 15 ft. lb.
4. Rotate the head of the switch to a position that will permit easy hookup of vacuum hoses. Then install the vacuum hoses to the proper connectors.

Catalytic Converter

All 1975 and later models are equipped with a catalytic converter. The converter is located midway in the exhaust system. Stainless steel exhaust pipes are used ahead of the converter. The converter is stainless steel with an aluminized steely cover and a ceramic felt blanket to insulate the converter from the floor-pan. The catalyst pellet bed inside the converter consists of noble metals which cause a reaction that converts hydrocarbons and carbon monoxide into water and carbon dioxide. No adjustments or repairs are possible.

On these models, lead-free fuel must be used exclusively in order to prevent the converter from being coated with lead particles, rendering it ineffective. However, there are many other precautions which should be taken to prevent a large amount of unburned hydrocarbons from reaching the converter. Should a sufficient amount of HC reach the converter, the unit could overheat, possibly damaging the converter, nearby mechanical components, or cause a fire hazard. Therefore, when working on your car, the following conditions should be avoided:

1. The use of fuel system cleaning agents and additives.
2. Operating the car with an inoperative (closed) choke, or submerged carburetor float.
3. Extended periods of engine rung-on (dieseling).
4. Turning off the ignition with the car in motion.
5. Ignition or charging system failure.
6. Misfiring of one or more spark plugs.
7. Disconnecting a spark plug wire while testing for bad wire, plug, or poor compression in one cylinder.
8. Push or jump starting the car, especially when hot.

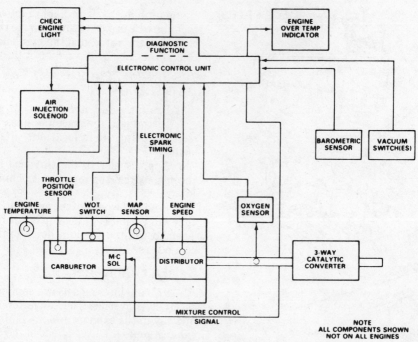

Computer Controlled Catalytic Converter (C-4) system schematic

9. Pumping the gas pedal when attempting to start a hot engine.

General Motors Computer Controlled Catalytic Converter (C-4) System, and Computer Command Control (CCC) System
INTRODUCTION

The GM designed Computer Controlled Catalytic Converter System (C-4 System), introduced in 1979 and used on GM cars through 1980, is a revised version of the 1978-79 Electronic Fuel Control System (although parts are not interchangeable between the systems). The C-4 System primarily maintains the ideal air/fuel ratio at which the catalytic converter is most effective. Some versions of the system also control ignition timing of the distributor.

The Computer Command Control System (CCC System), introduced on some 1980 California models and used on all 1981 and later carbureted car lines, is an expansion of the C-4 System. The CCC System monitors up to fifteen engine/vehicle operating conditions which it uses to control up to none engine and emission control systems. In addition to maintaining the ideal air/fuel ratio for the catalytic converter and adjusting ignition timing, the CCC System also controls the Air Management System so that the Catalytic converter can operate at the highest efficiency possible.

The system also controls the lockup on the transmission torque converter clutch (certain automatic transmission models only), adjusts idle speed over a wide range of conditions, purges the evaporative emissions charcoal canister, controls the EGR valve operation and operates the early fuel evaporative (EFE) system. Not all engines use all the above subsystems.

There are two operation modes for both the C-4 System and the CCC System: closed loop and open loop fuel control. Closed loop fuel control means the oxygen sensor is controlling the carburetor's air/fuel mixture ratio. Under open loop fuel control operating conditions (wide open throttle, engine and/or oxygen sensor cold), the oxygen sensor has not effect on the air/fuel mixture.

NOTE: *On some engines, the oxygen sensor will cool off while the engine is idling, putting the system into open loop operation. To restore closed loop operation, run the engine at part throttle and accelerate from idle to part throttle a few times.*

Computer Controlled Catalytic Converter (C-4) System
OPERATION

Major components of the system include an Electronic Control Module (ECM), an oxygen sensor, and electronically controlled variable-mixture carburetor, and a three-way oxidation-reduction catalytic converter.

The oxygen sensor generates a voltage which varies with exhaust gas oxygen content. Lean mixtures (more oxygen) reduce voltage; rich mixtures (less Oxygen) increase voltage. Voltage output is sent to the ECM.

An engine temperature sensor installed in the engine coolant outlet monitors coolant temperatures. Vacuum control switches and throttle position sensors also monitor engine conditions and supply signals to the ECM.

The Electronic Control Module (ECM) monitors the voltage input of the oxygen sensor along with information from other input signals. It processes these signals and generates a control signal sent to the carburetor. The control signal cycles between ON (lean commend) and OFF (rich command). The amount of ON and OFF time is a function of the input voltage sent to the ECM by the oxygen sensor. The ECM has a calibration unit called a PROM (Programmable Read Only Memory) which contains the specific instructions for a given engine application. In other words, the PROM unit is specifically programmed or "tailor made" for the system in which it is installed. The PROM assembly is a replaceable component which plugs into a socket on the ECM and requires a special tool for removal and installation.

On some 231 cu. in. V6 engines, the ECM controls the Electronic Spark Timing System (EST), AIR control system and the EGR valve control. ON some 350 V8 engines, the ECM controls the electronic module retard (EMR) system, which retards the engine timing 10 degrees during certain engine operations to reduce the exhaust emissions.

NOTE: *Electronic Spark Timing (EST) allows continuous spark timing adjustments to be made by the ECM. Engines with EST can easily be identified by the absence of vacuum and mechanical spark advance mechanisms on the distributor. Engines with EMR systems may be recognized by the presence of five connectors, instead of the HEI module's usual four.*

To maintain good idle and driveability under all conditions, other input signals used to modify the ECM output signal. Besides the sensors and switches already mentioned, these input signals include the manifold absolute pressure (MAP or vacuum sensors and the barometric pressure (BARO) sensor. The MAP or vacuum sensors sense changes in manifold vacuum, while the BARO sensor senses changes in barometric pressure. One important function of the BARO sensor is the maintenance of good engine performance at various altitudes. These sensors act as throttle position sensors on some engines. See the following paragraph for description.

A Rochester Dualjet carburetor is used with the C-4 system. It may be an E2SE, E2ME, E4MC or E4ME models, depending on engine application. An electronically operated mixture control solenoid is installed in the carburetor float bowl. The solenoid controls the air/fuel mixture metered to the idle and main metering systems. Air metering to the idle system is controlled by an idle air bleed valve. It follows the movement of the mixture solenoid to control the amount of air bled into the idle

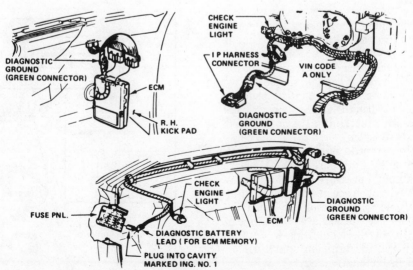

Typical C-4 system harness layouts. The location of the test lead will depend on the position of the ECM computer

system enriching or leaning out the mixture as appropriate. Air/fuel mixture enrichment occurs when the fuel valve is open and the air bleed is closed. All cycling of this system, which occurs ten times per second, is controlled by the ECM. A throttle position switch informs the ECM of open or closed throttle operation. A number of different switches are used, varying with application. The V6 engines use two pressure sensors-MAP (Manifold Absolute Pressure) and BARO (Barometric Pressure) as well as a throttle-actuated wide open throttle switch mounted in a bracket on the side of the float bowl. V8 engines use a throttle position sensor mounted in the carburetor bowl cover under the accelerator pump arm. When the ECM receives a signal from the throttle switch, indicating a change in position, it immediately searches its memory for the last set of operating conditions that resulted in an ideal air/fuel ratio, and shifts to that set of conditions. The memory is continually updated during normal operation.

Many C-4 equipped engines with AIR systems (Air Injection Reaction systems) have an AIR system diverted solenoid controlled by the ECM. These systems are similar in function to the Air Management system used in the CCC System. See below for information. Most C-4 Systems include a maintenance reminder flag connected to the odometer which becomes visible in the instrument cluster at regular intervals, signaling the need for oxygen sensor replacement.

Computer Command Control (CCC) System

OPERATION

The CCC has many components in common with the C-4 system (although they should probably not be interchanged between systems). These include the Electronic Control Module (ECM), which is capable of monitoring and adjusting more sensors and components than the ECM used on the C-4 System, an oxygen sensor, an electronically controlled variable-mixture carburetor, a three way catalytic converter, throttle position and coolant sensors, a barometric pressure (BARO) sensor, a manifold absolute pressure (MAP) sensor, a "check engine" light on the instrument cluster, and an Electronic Spark Timing (EST) distributor, which on some (turbocharged) engines is equipped with an Electronic Spark Control (ESC) which retards ignition spark under some conditions (detonation, etc.)

Components used almost exclusively by the CCC System include the Air Injection Reaction

(AIR) Management System, charcoal canister purge solenoid, EGR valve controls a vehicle speed sensor (located transmission models only), idle speed control, and early fuel evaporative (EFE) system.

See the operation descriptions under C-4 System for those components (except the ECM) the CCC System shares with the C-4 System.

The CCC System ECM, in addition to monitoring sensors and sending a control signal to the carburetor, also control the following components or sub-systems; charcoal canister purge, AIR Management System, idle speed control, automatic transmission converter lockup, distributor ignition timing, EGR valve control, EGR control, and the air conditioner compressor clutch operation. The CCC ECM is equipped with a PROM assembly similar to one used in the C-4 ECM. See above for description.

The AIR Management System is an emission control which provides additional oxygen either to the catalyst or the cylinder head ports (in some cases exhaust manifold). An AIR Management System, composed of an air switching valve and/or an air control valve, controls the air pump flow and is itself controlled by the ECM. A complete description of the AIR system is given elsewhere in this unit repair section. The major difference between the CCC AIR System and the systems used on other cars is that the flow of air from the air pump is controlled electrically by the ECM, rather than by vacuum signal.

The charcoal canister purge control is an electrically operated solenoid valve controlled by the ECM. When energized, the purge control solenoid blocks vacuum from reaching the

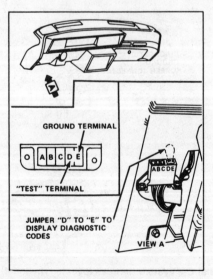

GROUND TERMINAL

"TEST" TERMINAL

JUMPER "D" TO "E" TO DISPLAY DIAGNOSTIC CODES

VIEW A

Typical 1981 and later CCC test terminal

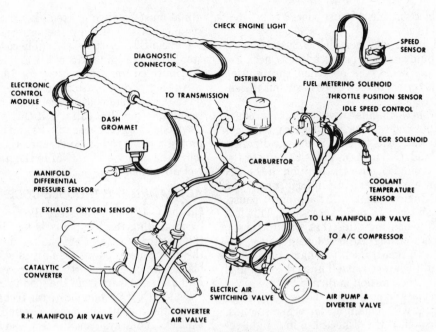

Computer Command Control (CCC) system schematic

canister purge valve. When the ECM de-energizes the purge control solenoid, vacuum is allowed to reach the canister and operate the purge valve. This releases the fuel vapors collected in the canister into the induction system.

The EGR valve control solenoid is activated by the ECM in similar fashion to the canister purge solenoid. When the engine is cold, the ECM energizes the solenoid, which blocks the vacuum signal to the EGR valve. Then the engine is warm, the ECM de-energizes the solenoid and the vacuum signal is allowed to reach and activate the EGR valve.

The Transmission Converter Clutch (TCC) lock is controlled by the ECM through an electrical solenoid in the automatic transmission. When the vehicle speed sensor in the instrument panel signals the ECM that the vehicle has reached the correct speed, the ECM energizes the solenoid which allows the torque converter to mechanically couple the engine to the transmission. When the brake pedal is pushed or during deceleration, passing, etc., the ECM returns the transmission to fluid drive.

The idle speed control adjusts the idle speed to lead conditions, and will lower the idle speed under no-load or low-load conditions to conserve gasoline.

The Early Fuel Evaporative (EFE) system is used on some engines to provide rapid heat to the engine induction system to promote smooth start-up and operation. There are two types of system: vacuum servo and electrically heated. They use different means to achieve the same end, which is to pre-heat the incoming air/fuel mixture. They are controlled by the ECM.

BASIC TROUBLESHOOTING

NOTE: *The following explains how to activate the Trouble Code signal light in the instrument cluster and gives an explanation of what each code means. This is not a full C-4 or CCC System troubleshooting and isolation procedure.*

Before suspecting the C-4 or CCC System or any of its components as faulty, check the ignition system including distributor, timing, spark plugs and wires. Check the engine compression, air cleaner, and emission control components not controlled by the ECM. Also check the intake manifold, vacuum hoses and hose connectors for leaks and carburetor bolts for tightness.

The following symptoms could indicate a possible problem with the C-4 or CCC System.

1. Detonation
2. Stalls or rough idle-cold
3. Stalls or rough idle-hot
4. Missing
5. Hesitation
6. Surges
7. Poor gasoline mileage
8. Sluggish or spongy performance
9. Hard starting-cold
10. Hard starting-hot

11. Objectionable exhaust odors
12. Cuts out
13. Improper idle speed (CCC System)

As a bulb and system check, the "Check Engine" light will come on when the ignition switch is turned to the ON position but the engine is not started.

The "Check Engine" light will also produce the trouble code or codes by a series of flashes which translate as follows. When the diagnostic test lead (C-4) or terminal (CCC) under the dash is grounded, with the ignition in the ON position and the engine not running, the "Check Engine" light will flash once, pause, then flash twice in rapid succession. This is a code 12, which indicates that the diagnostic system is working. After a longer pause, the code 12 will repeat itself two more times. The cycle will then repeat itself until the engine is started or the ignition is turned off.

When the engine is started, the "Check Engine" light will remain on for a few seconds, then turn off. If the "Check Engine" light remains on, the self-diagnostic system has detected a problem. If the test lead (C-4) or test terminal (CCC) is then grounded, the trouble code will flash three times. If more than one problem is found, each trouble code will flash thee times. Trouble codes will flash in numerical order (lowest code number to highest). The trouble codes series will repeat as long as the text lead or terminal is grounded.

A trouble code indicates a problem with a given circuit. For example, trouble code 14 indicates a problem in the cooling sensor circuit. This includes the coolant sensor, its electrical harness, and the Electronic Control Module (ECM).

Since the self-diagnostic system cannot diagnose every possible fault in the system, the absence of a trouble code does not mean the system is trouble-free. To determine problems within the system which do not activate even thought the "Check Engine" light is not on, the trouble code must be evaluated. It must be determined if the fault is intermittent or if the engine must be at certain operating conditions (under load, etc.) before the "Check Engine" light will come on. Some trouble codes will not be recorded in the ECM until the engine has been operated at part throttle for about 5 to 19 minutes.

On the C-4 System, the ECM erases all trouble codes every time the ignition is turned off. In the case of intermittent faults, a long term memory is desirable. This can be produced by connecting the orange connector/lead from terminal "S" of the ECM directly to the battery (or to a "HOT" fuse panel terminal). This terminal must be disconnected after diagnosis is complete or it will drain the battery.

On the CCC System, a trouble code will be stored until terminal "R" of the ECM has been disconnected from the battery for 10 seconds.

An easy way to erase the computer memory on the CCC System is to disconnect the battery terminals from the battery. If this method is used, don't forget to reset clocks and electronic programmable radios. Another method is to remove the fuse marked ECM in the fuse panel. Not all models have such a fuse.

ACTIVATING THE TROUBLE CODE

On the C-4 System, activate the trouble code by grounding the trouble code test lead. Use the illustrations to locate the test lead under the instrument panel (usually a white and black wire or a wire with a green connector). Run a jumper wire from the lead to ground.

On the CCC System locate the test terminal under the instrument panel. Ground the test lead. ON many systems, the test lead is situated side by side with a ground terminal. In addition, on some models, the partition between the test terminal and the ground terminal has a cut out section so that a spade terminal can be used to connect the two terminals.

NOTE: *Ground the test lead or terminal according to the instructions given in "Basic Troubleshooting", above.*

DIESEL ENGINE EMISSION CONTROLS

Exhaust Gas Recirculation (EGR)

To lower the formation of nitrogen oxides (NOx) it is necessary to reduce combustion temperatures. This is done by introducing exhaust gases into the cylinders.

FUNCTIONAL TESTS OF COMPONENTS

Vacuum Regulator Valve (VRV)

The Vacuum Regulator Valve is attached to the side of the injection pump and regulates vacuum in proportion to throttle angle. Vacuum from the vacuum pump is supplied to port A and vacuum at port B is reduced as the throttle is opened. At closed throttle, the vacuum is 15 inches; at half throttle-6 inches; at wide open throttle there is zero vacuum.

Exhaust Gas Recirculation (EGR) Valve V8

Apply vacuum to vacuum port. The valve should be fully open at 10.5 in.Hg and closed below 6 in.Hg

Explanation of Trouble Codes
GM C-4 and CCC Systems

Ground test lead or terminal AFTER engine is running.

Trouble Code	Applicable System	Notes	Possible Problem Area
12	C-4, CCC		No tachometer or reference signal to computer (ECM). This code will only be present while a fault exists, and will not be stored if the problem is intermittent.
13	C-4, CCC		Oxygen sensor circuit. The engine must run for about five minutes (eighteen on C-4 equipped 231 cu in. V6) at part throttle (and under road load—CCC equipped cars) before this code will show.
13 & 14 (at same time)	C-4		See code 43.
14	C-4, CCC		Shorted coolant sensor circuit. The engine has to run 2 minutes before this code will show.
15	C-4, CCC		Open coolant sensor circuit. The engine has to operate for about five minutes (18 minutes for C-4 equipped 231 cu in. V6) at part throttle (some models) before this code will show.
21	C-4		Shorted wide open throttle switch and/or open closed-throttle switch circuit (when used).
	C-4, CCC		Throttle position sensor circuit. The engine must be run up to 10 seconds (25 seconds—CCC System) below 800 rpm before this code will show.
21 & 22 (at same time)	C-4		Grounded wide open throttle switch circuit (231 cu in. V6).
22	C-4		Grounded closed throttle or wide open throttle switch circuit (231 cu in. V6).
23	C-4, CCC		Open or grounded carburetor mixture control (M/C) solenoid circuit.
24	CCC		Vehicle speed sensor (VSS) circuit. The car must operate up to five minutes at road speed before this code will show.
32	C-4, CCC		Barometric pressure sensor (BARO) circuit output low.
32 & 55 (at same time)	C-4		Grounded +8V terminal or V(REF) terminal for barometric pressure sensor (BARO), or faulty ECM computer.
34	C-4		Manifold absolute pressure (MAP) sensor output high (after ten seconds and below 800 rpm).
34	CCC		Manifold absolute pressure (MAP) sensor circuit or vacuum sensor circuit. The engine must run up to five minutes below 800 RPM before this code will set.
35	CCC		Idle speed control (ISC) switch circuit shorted (over ½ throttle for over two seconds).
41	CCC		No distributor reference pulses to the ECM at specified engine vacuum. This code will store in memory.
42	CCC		Electronic spark timing (EST) bypass circuit grounded.

Explanation of Trouble Codes
GM C-4 and CCC Systems (cont.)
Ground test lead or terminal AFTER engine is running.

Trouble Code	Applicable System	Notes	Possible Problem Area
43	C-4		Throttle position sensor adjustment (on some models, engine must run at part throttle up to ten seconds before this code will set).
44	C-4, CCC		Lean oxygen sensor indication. The engine must run up to five minutes in closed loop (oxygen sensor adjusting carburetor mixture), as part throttle and under road load (drive car) before this code will set.
44 & 55 (at same time)	C-4, CCC		Faulty oxygen sensor circuit.
45	C-4, CCC	Restricted air cleaner can cause code 45	Rich oxygen sensor system indication. The engine must run up to five minutes in closed loop (oxygen sensor adjusting carburetor mixture), at part throttle under road load before this code will set.
51	C-4, CCC		Faulty calibration unit (PROM) or improper PROM installation in electronic control module (ECM). It takes up to thirty seconds for this code to set.
52 & 53	C-4		"Check Engine" light off: Intermittent ECM computer problem. "Check Engine" light on: Faulty ECM computer (replace).
52	C-4, CCC		Faulty ECM computer.
53	CCC		Faulty ECM computer.
54	C-4, CCC		Faulty mixture control solenoid circuit and/or faulty ECM computer.
55	C-4		Faulty oxygen sensor, open manifold absolute pressure sensor or faulty ECM computer (231 cu in. V6).
55			Faulty throttle position sensor or ECM computer (except 231 cu in. V6).
55	CCC	Including 1980 260 cu in.	Grounded +8 volt supply (terminal 19 of ECM computer connector), grounded 5 volt reference (terminal 21 of ECM computer connector), faulty oxygen sensor circuit or faulty ECM computer.

Exhaust Gas Recirculation (EGR) Valve V6

Apply vacuum to vacuum port. The valve should be fully open at 12 inches and closed below 6 inches.

Response Vacuum Reducer (RVR)

Connect a vacuum gauge to the port marked "To EGR valve or T.C.C. solenoid". Connect a hand operated vacuum pump to the VRV port. Draw a 50.66 kPa (15 inch) vacuum on the pump and the reading on the vacuum gauge should be lower than the vacuum pump reading as follows:

- 75" Except High Altitude V8
- High Altitude V8

Torque Converter Clutch Operated Solenoid

When the Torque converter clutch is engaged, an electrical signal energizes the solenoid allowing ports 1 and 2 to be interconnected. When the solenoid is not energized, port 1 is closed and ports 2 and 3 are interconnected.

Solenoid Energized

- Ports 1 and 3 are connected

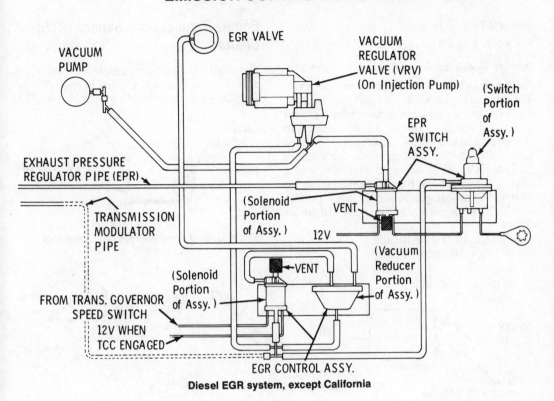

Diesel EGR system, except California

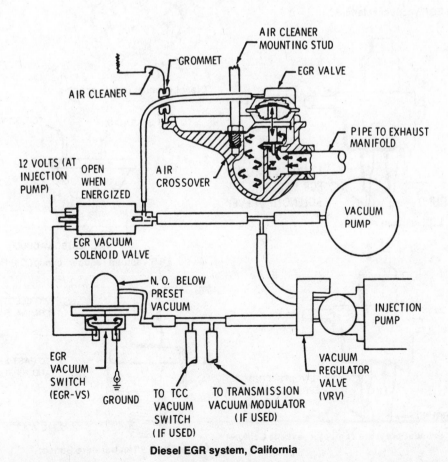

Diesel EGR system, California

Solenoid De-Energized

• Ports 2 and 3 are connected.

Vacuum Modulator Valve (VMV) V6

To test the VMV, block the drive wheels, apply the parking brake, with the shift lever in Park, start the engine and run at slow idle. Connect a vacuum gauge to the hose that connects to the port marked MAN. There should be at least 14″ of vacuum. If not, check the Vacuum pump, VRV, RVR, solenoid and connecting hoses. Reconnect the hose to the "Man" port. Connect a vacuum gauge to the "DIST" port on VMV. The vacuum reading should be as follows:

• 12″ Except High Altitude
• 9″ High Altitude

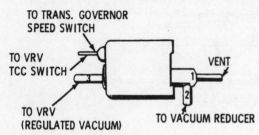

Diesel EGR vacuum solenoid

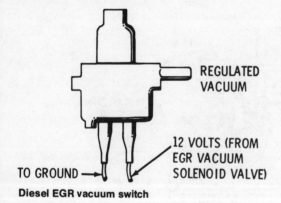

Diesel EGR vacuum switch

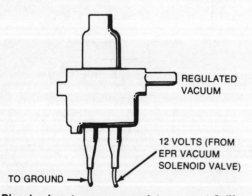

Diesel exhaust pressure regulator, except California

Engine Temperature Sensor (ETS)
OPERATION

The engine temperature sensor has two terminals. Twelve volts are applied to one terminal and the wire from the other terminal leads to

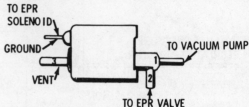

Diesel exhaust pressure regulator, California

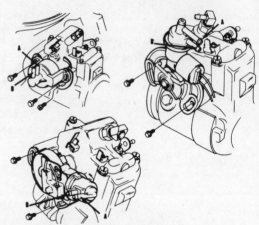

Diesel vacuum regulator valve

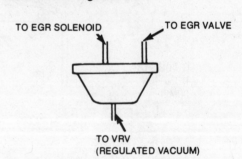

Diesel EGR vacuum reducer, except California

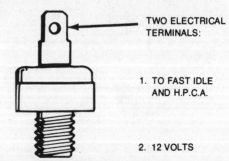

Diesel Engine Temperature Sensor

the fast idle solenoid and Housing Pressure Cold Advance solenoid that is part of the injection pump.

The switch contacts are closed below 125 degrees F. At the calibration point, the contacts are open which turns off the solenoid.

Above Calibration

- Closed circuit

Below Calibration

- Closed circuit

Crankcase Ventilation

A Crankcase Depression Regulator Valve is used to regulate (meter) the flow of crankcase gases back into the engine. The Crankcase Depression Regulator Valve (C.D.R.V.) is designed to limit vacuum in the crankcase as the gases are drawn from the valve cover(s) through the C.D.R.V. and into the intake manifold (air crossover).

Fresh air enters the engine through the combination filter, check valve and oil fill cap. The fresh air mixes with blow-by gases and enters both (V8), or one (V6) valve cover. The gases pass through a filter installed on the valve cover(s) and are drawn into connecting tubing.

Intake manifold vacuum acts against a spring loaded diaphragm to control the flow of crankcase gases. Higher intake vacuum levels pull the diaphragm closer to the top of the out-

EGR System Diagnosis—Diesel Engine

Condition	Possible Causes	Correction
EGR valve will not open.	Binding or stuck EGR valve. No vacuum to EGR valve.	Replace EGR valve. Check VRV,RVR, solenoid, T.C.C. operation, vacuum pump, VMV (V6) and connecting hoses.
EGR valve will not close. (Heavy smoke on acceleration).	Binding or stuck EGR valve. Constant high vacuum to EGR valve.	Replace EGR valve. Check VRV, RVR, solenoid, VMV (V6) and connecting hoses.
EGR valve opens partially.	Binding EGR valve. Low vacuum at EGR valve.	Replace EGR valve. Check VRV, RVR, solenoid, vacuum pump, VMV (V6) and connecting hoses.

Troubleshooting Basic Fuel System Problems

Problem	Cause	Solution
Engine cranks, but won't start (or is hard to start) when cold	• Empty fuel tank • Incorrect starting procedure • Defective fuel pump • No fuel in carburetor • Clogged fuel filter • Engine flooded • Defective choke	• Check for fuel in tank • Follow correct procedure • Check pump output • Check for fuel in the carburetor • Replace fuel filter • Wait 15 minutes; try again • Check choke plate
Engine cranks, but is hard to start (or does not start) when hot— (presence of fuel is assumed)	• Defective choke	• Check choke plate
Rough idle or engine runs rough	• Dirt or moisture in fuel • Clogged air filter • Faulty fuel pump	• Replace fuel filter • Replace air filter • Check fuel pump output
Engine stalls or hesitates on acceleration	• Dirt or moisture in the fuel • Dirty carburetor • Defective fuel pump • Incorrect float level, defective accelerator pump	• Replace fuel filter • Clean the carburetor • Check fuel pump output • Check carburetor
Poor gas mileage	• Clogged air filter • Dirty carburetor • Defective choke, faulty carburetor adjustment	• Replace air filter • Clean carburetor • Check carburetor
Engine is flooded (won't start accompanied by smell of raw fuel)	• Improperly adjusted choke or carburetor	• Wait 15 minutes and try again, without pumping gas pedal • If it won't start, check carburetor

let tube. This reduces the amount of gases being drawn from the crankcase and decreases the vacuum level in the crankcase. As the intake vacuum decrease, the spring pushes the diaphragm away from the top of the outlet tube allowing more gases to flow to the intake manifold.

NOTE: *Do not allow any solvent to come in contact with the diaphragm of the Crankcase Depression Regulator Valve because the diaphragm will fail.*

GASOLINE ENGINE FUEL SYSTEM

Fuel Pump

Fuel pumps used on all engines are of the single-action mechanical type. The fuel pump rocker arm is held in constant engagement with the eccentric on the camshaft by the rocker arm spring. As the end of the rocker arm which is in contact with the eccentric moves upward, the fuel link pulls the fuel diaphragm downward. The action of the diaphragm enlarges the fuel chamber, drawing fuel from the tank. Fuel flows to the carburetor only when the pressure in the outlet line is less than the pressure maintained by the diaphragm spring. The fuel pumps on all engines are not serviceable and must be replaced is defective.

REMOVAL AND INSTALLATION

1. Locate the fuel pump and disconnect the fuel lines.
2. Remove the two pump mounting bolts.
3. Remove the pump and the gasket.
4. Use a new gasket when installing the pump.
5. Install the fuel lines, start the engine and check for leaks.

TESTING

The fuel line from the tank to the pump is the suction side of the system and the line from the pump to the carburetor is the pressure side of the system. A leak on the pressure side, therefore, would be made apparent by dripping fuel, but a leak on the suction side would not be apparent except for the reduction of the volume of fuel on the pressure side.

1. Tighten any loose line connections and look for bends or kinks.
2. Disconnect the fuel pipe at the carburetor. Disconnect the distributor-to-coil primary wire so that the engine can be cranked without firing. Place a container at the end of the pipe and crank the engine a few revolutions. If little or no gasoline flows from the open end of the pipe, the fuel pipe is clogged or the pump is defective.

3. If fuel flows from the pump in good volume from the pipe at the carburetor, check fuel pressure to be certain that the pump is operating within specified limits as follows:

a. Attach a fuel pump pressure test gauge to the disconnected end of the pipe.

b. Run the engine at approximately 450 to 1,000 rpm (on gasoline in the carburetor bowl) and note the reading on the pressure gauge.

c. If the pump is operating properly the pressure will be within the specifications listed in the "Tune-UP Specifications" chart found in Chapter 2.

5. The pressure will remain constant between speeds of 450 to 1,000 rpm. If the pressure is too low or too high at different speeds, the pump should be replaced.

Carburetor

REMOVAL AND INSTALLATION

1. Remove the air cleaner.
2. Disconnect the fuel and vacuum lines from the carburetor. Disconnect the throttle linkage.
3. On automatic transmission cars, disconnect the downshift linkage.
4. If the car is equipped with an idle solenoid, disconnect the wiring.
5. Remove the carburetor attaching nuts and remove the carburetor.
6. Installation is in the reverse order of removal.

IDENTIFICATION

General Motors Rochester carburetors are identified by their model code. The first number indicates the number of barrels, while one of the last letters indicates the type of choke used. These are V for the manifold mounted choke coil, C for the choke coil mounted in the carburetor body, and E for electric choke, also mounted on the carburetor. Model codes ending in A indicate an altitude-compensating carburetor.

REMOVAL AND INSTALLATION

All Carburetors

1. Remove the air cleaner and its gasket.
2. Disconnect the fuel and vacuum lines from the carburetor.
3. Disconnect the choke coil rod, heated air line tube, or electrical connector.
4. Disconnect the throttle linkage.
5. On automatic transmission cars, disconnect the throttle valve linkage if so equipped.
6. If CEC equipped remove the CEC valve vacuum hose and electrical connector. Disconnect the EGR line, if so equipped.

7. Remove the idle stop solenoid, if so equipped.

8. Remove the carburetor attaching nuts and/or bolts, gasket or insulator, and remove the carburetor.

9. Install the carburetor using the reverse of the removal procedure. Use a new gasket and fill the float bowl with gasoline to ease starting the engine.

OVERHAUL

All Types

Efficient carburetion depends greatly on careful cleaning and inspection during overhaul, since dirt, gum, water, or varnish in or on the carburetor parts are often responsible for poor performance.

Overhaul your carburetor in a clean, dust free area. Carefully disassemble the carburetor, referring often to the exploded views and directions packaged with the rebuilding kit. Keep all similar and look-alike parts segregated during disassembly and cleaning to avoid accidental interchange during assembly. Make a note of all jet sizes.

When the carburetor is disassembled, wash all parts (except diaphragms, electric choke units, pump plunger, and any other plastic, leather, fiber, or rubber parts) in clean carburetor solvent. Do not leave parts in the solvent any longer then is necessary to sufficiently loosen the deposits. Excessive cleaning may remove the special finish from the float bowl and choke valve bodies, leaving these parts unfit for service. Rinse all parts in clean solvent and blow them dry with compressed air or allow them to air dry. Wipe clean all cork, plastic, leather, and fiber parts with a clean, lint-free cloth.

Blow out all passages and jets with compressed air and be sure that there are no restrictions or blockages. Never use wire or similar tools to clean jets, fuel passages, or air bleeds. Clean all jets and valves separately to avoid accidental interchange.

Check all parts for wear or damage. If wear or damage is found, replace the defective parts. Especially check the following:

1. Check the float needle and seat for wear. If wear is found, replace the complete assembly.

2. Check the float hinge pin for wear and the float(s) for dents or distortion. Replace the float if fuel has leaked into it.

3. Check the throttle an choke shaft bores for wear or an out-of-round conditions. Damage or wear to the throttle arm, shaft, or shaft bore will often require replacement of the throttle body. These parts require a close toler-

ance of fit; wear may allow air leakage, which could affect starting and idling.

NOTE: *Throttle shafts and bushings are not included in overhaul kits. They can be purchased separately.*

4. Inspect the idle mixture adjusting needles for burrs or grooves. Any such condition requires replacement of the needle, since you will not be able to obtain a satisfactory idle.

5. Test the accelerator pump check valves. They should pass air one way but not the other. Test for proper seating by blowing and sucking on the valve. Replace the valve check ball and spring as necessary. If the valve is satisfactory, wash the valve parts again to remove breath moisture.

6. Check the bowl cover for warped surfaces with a straightedge.

7. Closely inspect the accelerator pump plunger wear and damage, replacing as necessary.

8. After the carburetor is assembled, check the choke valve for freedom of operation.

NOTE: *Carburetor overhaul kits are recommended for each overhaul. These kits contain all gaskets and new parts to replace those which deteriorate most rapidly. Failure to replace all parts supplied with the kit (especially gaskets) can result in poor performance later.*

Some carburetor manufacturers supply overhaul kits of three basic types: minor repair; major repair; and gasket kits. Basically, they contain the following:

Minor Repair Kits:
- All gaskets
- Float needle valve
- All diagrams
- Spring for the pump diaphragm

Major Repair Kits:
- All jets and gaskets
- All diaphragms
- Float needle valve
- Pump ball valve
- Float
- Complete intermediate rod
- Intermediate pump lever
- Some cover hold-down screws and washers

Gasket Kits:
- All gaskets

After cleaning and checking all components, reassembly the carburetor, using new parts and referring to the exploded view. When reassembling, make sure that all screws and jets are tight in their seats, but do not overtighten as the tips will be distorted. Tighten all screws gradually, in rotation. do not tighten needle valves into their seats; uneven jetting will result. Always use new gaskets. Be sure to adjust the float level when reassembling.

PRELIMINARY CHECKS (ALL CARBURETORS)

The following should be observed before attempting any adjustments.

1. Thoroughly warm the engine. If the engine is cold, be sure that it reaches operating temperature.

2. Check the torque of all carburetor mounting nuts and assembly screws. Always check the intake manifold-to-cylinder head bolts. If air is leaking at any of these points, any attempts at adjustment will inevitably lead to frustration.

3. Check the manifold heat control valve (if used) to be sure that it is free.

4. Check and adjust the choke as necessary.

5. Adjust the idle speed and mixture. If the mixture screws are capped, don't adjust them unless all other causes of rough idle have been eliminated. If any adjustments are performed that might possibly change the idle speed or mixture, adjust the idle and mixture again when you are finished.

Before you make any carburetor adjustments make sure that the engine is in turn. Many problems which are thought to be carburetor-related can be traced to an engine which is simply out-of-tune. Any trouble in these areas will have symptoms like those of carburetor problems.

MODEL MV CARBURETOR ADJUSTMENTS

Float Level

1. Remove the top of the carburetor if you have not done so already.

2. Hold the float retainer in place and the float arm against the top of the float needle by pushing down on the top of the float arm at the outer end toward the float bowl casting.

3. Using an adjustable T-scale, measure the distance from the top of the float to the float bowl gasket surface. See the specifications chart for the proper measurement.

NOTE: *The float bowl gasket should be removed and the gauge held on the index point of the float for accurate measurement.*

4. Adjust the float level by bending the float arm up or down at the float arm junction.

Fast Idle

1. The fast idle adjustment is made with the transmission in neutral. On 1976-77 models, disconnect and plug the distributor vacuum line.

2. Make sure the engine is fully warmed up, and the choke is in the wide-open position.

3. Place the fast idle lever on the high step of the fast idle cam.

4. To adjust, bend the fast idle lever until the specified fast idle speed if obtained.

Choke Coil Lever

1. Place the fast idle speed screw on the highest step of the fast idle cam.

2. Hold the choke plate fully closed.

3. Insert a 0.120″ gauge through the hole in the arm on the choke housing and into the hole in the casting.

4. Bend the link to adjust.

Automatic Choke

1. Place the fast idle cam follower on the high step of the cam.

2. Loosen the three retaining screws and rotate the cover counterclockwise until the choke plate just closes.

3. Align the index mark on the cover with the specified housing mark. Tighten the three screws.

Unloader

1. Hold the throttle valve wide open.

2. Hold down the choke plate with your fingers and insert the specified gauge between the upper edge of the choke plate and the airhorn wall.

3. Bend the linkage tang to adjust.

Vacuum break

1. On vehicles equipped with TAC air cleaners (1975 and later), plug the sensor's vacuum take-off port after removing the air cleaner.

2. Using an external vacuum source, apply vacuum to the vacuum break diaphragm until the plunger is fully seated.

3. After the plunger is seated, push the choke plate fully closed.

4. Holding the choke plate in this position, place the specified gauge between the lower edge (upper edge in 1976-80) of the choke valve and the air horn wall.

5. If the measurement is not correct, bend the vacuum break rod.

Metering Rod

1. Remove the top of the carburetor.

2. Back out the idle stop solenoid and rotate the fast idle cam so that the fast idle screw does not contact the cam.

3. With the throttle plate completely closed, make sure the power piston is all the way up.

4. Remove the gasket from the bowl gasket surface. Measure the distance between the bowl gasket surface and the lower surface of the metering rod holder, next to the metering rod.

5. To adjust, carefully bend the metering rod holder.

CHILTON'S
FUEL ECONOMY
& TUNE-UP TIPS

Tune-up • Spark Plug Diagnosis • Emission Controls

Fuel System • Cooling System • Tires and Wheels

General Maintenance

CHILTON'S FUEL ECONOMY & TUNE-UP TIPS

Fuel economy is important to everyone, no matter what kind of vehicle you drive. The maintenance-minded motorist can save both money and fuel using these tips and the periodic maintenance and tune-up procedures in this Repair and Tune-Up Guide.

There are more than 130,000,000 cars and trucks registered for private use in the United States. Each travels an average of 10-12,000 miles per year, and, and in total they consume close to 70 billion gallons of fuel each year. This represents nearly ⅔ of the oil imported by the United States each year. The Federal government's goal is to reduce consumption 10% by 1985. A variety of methods are either already in use or under serious consideration, and they all affect you driving and the cars you will drive. In addition to "down-sizing", the auto industry is using or investigating the use of electronic fuel delivery, electronic engine controls and alternative engines for use in smaller and lighter vehicles, among other alternatives to meet the federally mandated Corporate Average Fuel Economy (CAFE) of 27.5 mpg by 1985. The government, for its part, is considering rationing, mandatory driving curtailments and tax increases on motor vehicle fuel in an effort to reduce consumption. The government's goal of a 10% reduction could be realized — and further government regulation avoided — if every private vehicle could use just 1 less gallon of fuel per week.

How Much Can You Save?

Tests have proven that almost anyone can make at least a 10% reduction in fuel consumption through regular maintenance and tune-ups. When a major manufacturer of spark plugs sur-

TUNE-UP

1. Check the cylinder compression to be sure the engine will really benefit from a tune-up and that it is capable of producing good fuel economy. A tune-up will be wasted on an engine in poor mechanical condition.

2. Replace spark plugs regularly. New spark plugs alone can increase fuel economy 3%.

3. Be sure the spark plugs are the correct type (heat range) for your vehicle. See the Tune-Up Specifications.

Heat range refers to the spark plug's ability to conduct heat away from the firing end. It must conduct the heat away in an even pattern to avoid becoming a source of pre-ignition, yet it must also operate hot enough to burn off conductive deposits that could cause misfiring.

The heat range is usually indicated by a number on the spark plug, part of the manufacturer's designation for each individual spark plug. The numbers in bold-face indicate the heat range in each manufacturer's identification system.

Periodically, check the spark plugs to be sure they are firing efficiently. They are excellent indicators of the internal condition of your engine.

Manufacturer	Typical Designation
AC	R **45** TS
Bosch (old)	WA **145** T30
Bosch (new)	HR **8** Y
Champion	RBL **15** Y
Fram/Autolite	4**15**
Mopar	P-**62** PR
Motorcraft	BRF-**42**
NGK	BP **5** ES-15
Nippondenso	W **16** EP
Prestolite	14GR **5** 2A

On AC, Bosch (new), Champion, Fram/Autolite, Mopar, Motorcraft and Prestolite, a higher number indicates a hotter plug. On Bosch (old), NGK and Nippondenso, a higher number indicates a colder plug.

4. Make sure the spark plugs are properly gapped. See the Tune-Up Specifications in this book.

5. Be sure the spark plugs are firing efficiently. The illustrations on the next 2 pages show you how to "read" the firing end of the spark plug.

6. Check the ignition timing and set it to specifications. Tests show that almost all cars have incorrect ignition timing by more than 2°.

veyed over 6,000 cars nationwide, they found that a tune-up, on cars that needed one, increased fuel economy over 11%. Replacing worn plugs alone, accounted for a 3% increase. The same test also revealed that 8 out of every 10 vehicles will have some maintenance deficiency that will directly affect fuel economy, emissions or performance. Most of this mileage-robbing neglect could be prevented with regular maintenance.

Modern engines require that all of the functioning systems operate properly for maximum efficiency. A malfunction anywhere wastes fuel. You can keep your vehicle running as efficiently and economically as possible, by being aware of your vehicle's operating and performance characteristics. If your vehicle suddenly develops performance or fuel economy problems it could be due to one or more of the following:

PROBLEM	POSSIBLE CAUSE
Engine Idles Rough	Ignition timing, idle mixture, vacuum leak or something amiss in the emission control system.
Hesitates on Acceleration	Dirty carburetor or fuel filter, improper accelerator pump setting, ignition timing or fouled spark plugs.
Starts Hard or Fails to Start	Worn spark plugs, improperly set automatic choke, ice (or water) in fuel system.
Stalls Frequently	Automatic choke improperly adjusted and possible dirty air filter or fuel filter.
Performs Sluggishly	Worn spark plugs, dirty fuel or air filter, ignition timing or automatic choke out of adjustment.

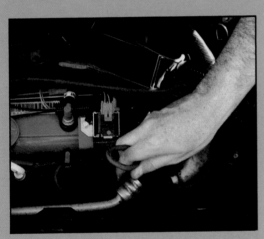

Check spark plug wires on conventional point type ignition for cracks by bending them in a loop around your finger.

Be sure that spark plug wires leading to adjacent cylinders do not run too close together. (Photo courtesy Champion Spark Plug Co.)

7. If your vehicle does not have electronic ignition, check the points, rotor and cap as specified.

8. Check the spark plug wires (used with conventional point-type ignitions) for cracks and burned or broken insulation by bending them in a loop around your finger. Cracked wires decrease fuel efficiency by failing to deliver full voltage to the spark plugs. One misfiring spark plug can cost you as much as 2 mpg.

9. Check the routing of the plug wires. Misfiring can be the result of spark plug leads to adjacent cylinders running parallel to each other and too close together. One wire tends to pick up voltage from the other causing it to fire "out of time".

10. Check all electrical and ignition circuits for voltage drop and resistance.

11. Check the distributor mechanical and/or vacuum advance mechanisms for proper functioning. The vacuum advance can be checked by twisting the distributor plate in the opposite direction of rotation. It should spring back when released.

12. Check and adjust the valve clearance on engines with mechanical lifters. The clearance should be slightly loose rather than too tight.

SPARK PLUG DIAGNOSIS

Normal

APPEARANCE: This plug is typical of one operating normally. The insulator nose varies from a light tan to grayish color with slight electrode wear. The presence of slight deposits is normal on used plugs and will have no adverse effect on engine performance. The spark plug heat range is correct for the engine and the engine is running normally.

CAUSE: Properly running engine.

RECOMMENDATION: Before reinstalling this plug, the electrodes should be cleaned and filed square. Set the gap to specifications. If the plug has been in service for more than 10-12,000 miles, the entire set should probably be replaced with a fresh set of the same heat range.

Oil Deposits

APPEARANCE: The firing end of the plug is covered with a wet, oily coating.

CAUSE: The problem is poor oil control. On high mileage engines, oil is leaking past the rings or valve guides into the combustion chamber. A common cause is also a plugged PCV valve, and a ruptured fuel pump diaphragm can also cause this condition. Oil fouled plugs such as these are often found in new or recently overhauled engines, before normal oil control is achieved, and can be cleaned and reinstalled.

RECOMMENDATION: A hotter spark plug may temporarily relieve the problem, but the engine is probably in need of work.

Incorrect Heat Range

APPEARANCE: The effects of high temperature on a spark plug are indicated by clean white, often blistered insulator. This can also be accompanied by excessive wear of the electrode, and the absence of deposits.

CAUSE: Check for the correct spark plug heat range. A plug which is too hot for the engine can result in overheating. A car operated mostly at high speeds can require a colder plug. Also check ignition timing, cooling system level, fuel mixture and leaking intake manifold.

RECOMMENDATION: If all ignition and engine adjustments are known to be correct, and no other malfunction exists, install spark plugs one heat range colder.

Photos Courtesy Fram Corporation

Carbon Deposits

APPEARANCE: Carbon fouling is easily identified by the presence of dry, soft, black, sooty deposits.

CAUSE: Changing the heat range can often lead to carbon fouling, as can prolonged slow, stop-and-start driving. If the heat range is correct, carbon fouling can be attributed to a rich fuel mixture, sticking choke, clogged air cleaner, worn breaker points, retarded timing or low compression. If only one or two plugs are carbon fouled, check for corroded or cracked wires on the affected plugs. Also look for cracks in the distributor cap between the towers of affected cylinders.

RECOMMENDATION: After the problem is corrected, these plugs can be cleaned and reinstalled if not worn severely.

MMT Fouled

APPEARANCE: Spark plugs fouled by MMT (Methycyclopentadienyl Maganese Tricarbonyl) have reddish, rusty appearance on the insulator and side electrode.

CAUSE: MMT is an anti-knock additive in gasoline used to replace lead. During the combustion process, the MMT leaves a reddish deposit on the insulator and side electrode.

RECOMMENDATION: No engine malfunction is indicated and the deposits will not affect plug performance any more than lead deposits (see Ash Deposits). MMT fouled plugs can be cleaned, regapped and reinstalled.

High Speed Glazing

APPEARANCE: Glazing appears as shiny coating on the plug, either yellow or tan in color.

CAUSE: During hard, fast acceleration, plug temperatures rise suddenly. Deposits from normal combustion have no chance to fluff-off; instead, they melt on the insulator forming an electrically conductive coating which causes misfiring.

RECOMMENDATION: Glazed plugs are not easily cleaned. They should be replaced with a fresh set of plugs of the correct heat range. If the condition recurs, using plugs with a heat range one step colder may cure the problem.

Ash (Lead) Deposits

APPEARANCE: Ash deposits are characterized by light brown or white colored deposits crusted on the side or center electrodes. In some cases it may give the plug a rusty appearance.

CAUSE: Ash deposits are normally derived from oil or fuel additives burned during normal combustion. Normally they are harmless, though excessive amounts can cause misfiring. If deposits are excessive in short mileage, the valve guides may be worn.

RECOMMENDATION: Ash-fouled plugs can be cleaned, gapped and reinstalled.

Detonation

APPEARANCE: Detonation is usually characterized by a broken plug insulator.

CAUSE: A portion of the fuel charge will begin to burn spontaneously, from the increased heat following ignition. The explosion that results applies extreme pressure to engine components, frequently damaging spark plugs and pistons.

Detonation can result by over-advanced ignition timing, inferior gasoline (low octane) lean air/fuel mixture, poor carburetion, engine lugging or an increase in compression ratio due to combustion chamber deposits or engine modification.

RECOMMENDATION: Replace the plugs after correcting the problem.

Photos Courtesy Champion Spark Plug Co.

EMISSION CONTROLS

13. Be aware of the general condition of the emission control system. It contributes to reduced pollution and should be serviced regularly to maintain efficient engine operation.

14. Check all vacuum lines for dried, cracked or brittle conditions. Something as simple as a leaking vacuum hose can cause poor performance and loss of economy.

15. Avoid tampering with the emission control system. Attempting to improve fuel econ-

FUEL SYSTEM

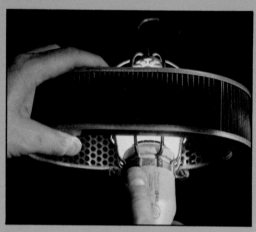

Check the air filter with a light behind it. If you can see light through the filter it can be reused.

Extremely clogged filters should be discarded and replaced with a new one.

18. Replace the air filter regularly. A dirty air filter richens the air/fuel mixture and can increase fuel consumption as much as 10%. Tests show that ⅓ of all vehicles have air filters in need of replacement.

19. Replace the fuel filter at least as often as recommended.

20. Set the idle speed and carburetor mixture to specifications.

21. Check the automatic choke. A sticking or malfunctioning choke wastes gas.

22. During the summer months, adjust the automatic choke for a leaner mixture which will produce faster engine warm-ups.

COOLING SYSTEM

29. Be sure all accessory drive belts are in good condition. Check for cracks or wear.

30. Adjust all accessory drive belts to proper tension.

31. Check all hoses for swollen areas, worn spots, or loose clamps.

32. Check coolant level in the radiator or expansion tank.

33. Be sure the thermostat is operating properly. A stuck thermostat delays engine warm-up and a cold engine uses nearly twice as much fuel as a warm engine.

34. Drain and replace the engine coolant at least as often as recommended. Rust and scale

TIRES & WHEELS

38. Check the tire pressure often with a pencil type gauge. Tests by a major tire manufacturer show that 90% of all vehicles have at least 1 tire improperly inflated. Better mileage can be achieved by over-inflating tires, but never exceed the maximum inflation pressure on the side of the tire.

39. If possible, install radial tires. Radial tires deliver as much as ½ mpg more than bias belted tires.

40. Avoid installing super-wide tires. They only create extra rolling resistance and decrease fuel mileage. Stick to the manufacturer's recommendations.

41. Have the wheels properly balanced.

omy by tampering with emission controls is more likely to worsen fuel economy than improve it. Emission control changes on modern engines are not readily reversible.

16. Clean (or replace) the EGR valve and lines as recommended.

17. Be sure that all vacuum lines and hoses are reconnected properly after working under the hood. An unconnected or misrouted vacuum line can wreak havoc with engine performance.

---

23. Check for fuel leaks at the carburetor, fuel pump, fuel lines and fuel tank. Be sure all lines and connections are tight.

24. Periodically check the tightness of the carburetor and intake manifold attaching nuts and bolts. These are a common place for vacuum leaks to occur.

25. Clean the carburetor periodically and lubricate the linkage.

26. The condition of the tailpipe can be an excellent indicator of proper engine combustion. After a long drive at highway speeds, the inside of the tailpipe should be a light grey in color. Black or soot on the insides indicates an overly rich mixture.

27. Check the fuel pump pressure. The fuel pump may be supplying more fuel than the engine needs.

28. Use the proper grade of gasoline for your engine. Don't try to compensate for knocking or "pinging" by advancing the ignition timing. This practice will only increase plug temperature and the chances of detonation or pre-ignition with relatively little performance gain.

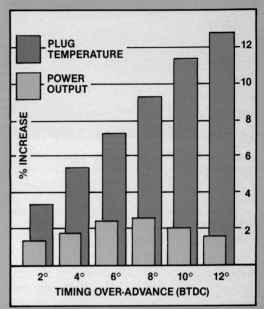

Increasing ignition timing past the specified setting results in a drastic increase in spark plug temperature with increased chance of detonation or preignition. Performance increase is considerably less. (Photo courtesy Champion Spark Plug Co.)

---

that form in the engine should be flushed out to allow the engine to operate at peak efficiency.

35. Clean the radiator of debris that can decrease cooling efficiency.

36. Install a flex-type or electric cooling fan, if you don't have a clutch type fan. Flex fans use curved plastic blades to push more air at low speeds when more cooling is needed; at high speeds the blades flatten out for less resistance. Electric fans only run when the engine temperature reaches a predetermined level.

37. Check the radiator cap for a worn or cracked gasket. If the cap does not seal properly, the cooling system will not function properly.

---

42. Be sure the front end is correctly aligned. A misaligned front end actually has wheels going in differed directions. The increased drag can reduce fuel economy by .3 mpg.

43. Correctly adjust the wheel bearings. Wheel bearings that are adjusted too tight increase rolling resistance.

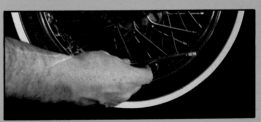

Check tire pressures regularly with a reliable pocket type gauge. Be sure to check the pressure on a cold tire.

GENERAL MAINTENANCE

Check the fluid levels (particularly engine oil) on a regular basis. Be sure to check the oil for grit, water or other contamination.

A vacuum gauge is another excellent indicator of internal engine condition and can also be installed in the dash as a mileage indicator.

44. Periodically check the fluid levels in the engine, power steering pump, master cylinder, automatic transmission and drive axle.

45. Change the oil at the recommended interval and change the filter at every oil change. Dirty oil is thick and causes extra friction between moving parts, cutting efficiency and increasing wear. A worn engine requires more frequent tune-ups and gets progressively worse fuel economy. In general, use the lightest viscosity oil for the driving conditions you will encounter.

46. Use the recommended viscosity fluids in the transmission and axle.

47. Be sure the battery is fully charged for fast starts. A slow starting engine wastes fuel.

48. Be sure battery terminals are clean and tight.

49. Check the battery electrolyte level and add distilled water if necessary.

50. Check the exhaust system for crushed pipes, blockages and leaks.

51. Adjust the brakes. Dragging brakes or brakes that are not releasing create increased drag on the engine.

52. Install a vacuum gauge or miles-per-gallon gauge. These gauges visually indicate engine vacuum in the intake manifold. High vacuum = good mileage and low vacuum = poorer mileage. The gauge can also be an excellent indicator of internal engine conditions.

53. Be sure the clutch is properly adjusted. A slipping clutch wastes fuel.

54. Check and periodically lubricate the heat control valve in the exhaust manifold. A sticking or inoperative valve prevents engine warm-up and wastes gas.

55. Keep accurate records to check fuel economy over a period of time. A sudden drop in fuel economy may signal a need for tune-up or other maintenance.

MODEL 2GC, 2GV, 2GE CARBURETOR ADJUSTMENTS

Fast Idle Speed Adjustment

The fast idle is set automatically when the curb idle and mixture is set.

Choke Rod (Fast Idle Cam)

1. Turn in the idle cam stop screw, if any, until it just contacts the bottom step of the fast idle cam. Then turn the screw one full turn.

2. Place the idle screw on the second step of the fast idle cam against the shoulder of the high step.

3. Hold the choke valve closed and check the clearance between the upper edge of the choke valve and the air horn wall.

4. Adjust the clearance by bending the tang on the choke lever.

2GC, 2GE Intermediate Choke Rod (Choke Coil Lever) Adjustment

1. Remove the thermostatic cover coil, gasket, and inside baffle plate assembly.

2. Place the idle speed screw on the highest step of the fast idle cam.

3. Close the choke valve by pushing up on the intermediate choke lever.

4. The idle of the coil lever inside the choke housing must line up with the edge of a 0.120" drill bit inserted into the hole inside the choke housing.

5. Adjust by bending the intermediate choke rod at the first bend from the bottom of the rod.

Vacuum Break Adjustment

1. Remove the air cleaner. Vehicles with a Thermac air cleaner should have the sensor's vacuum take-off port plugged.

2. Using an external vacuum source, apply vacuum to the vacuum break diaphragm until the plunger is fully seated. If the diaphragm has a bleed hole, tape it over.

3. When the plunger is seated, push the choke valve toward the closed position. For 1976 and older models, place the idle speed screw on the high step of the fast idle cam.

4. Holding the choke valve in the closed position, place the specified size gauge between the upper idle of the choke valve and the air horn wall.

5. If the measurement is not correct, bend the vacuum break rod.

Auxiliary Vacuum Break

1. Seat the auxiliary vacuum diaphragm by applying an outside source of vacuum. Tape over the vacuum bleed hole so the vacuum will not bleed down.

2. Place the idle speed screw on the high step of the fast idle cam.

3. Hold the choke toward the closed choke position.

4. Measure the distance between the upper edge of the choke valve and the air horn wall.

5. Adjust by bending the auxiliary vacuum break rod at the bottom of the U-shaped bend. Remove the piece of tape from the auxiliary vacuum diaphragm.

Choke Unloader Adjustment

1. Hold the throttle valves wide open.

2. Close the choke valve.

3. Bend the unloader tang to obtain the proper clearance between the upper edge of the choke valve and air horn wall.

2GV Choke Coil Rod Adjustment

1. Hold the choke valve completely open.

2. Disconnect the coil rod from the upper lever and push down on the rod to the end of its travel.

3. When the rod is all the way down, the top of the rod should line up with the bottom of the slotted hold in the choke valve linkage.

4. Adjust by bending the lever.

Float Level

With the air horn assembly upside down, measure the distance from the air horn gasket to the lip at the toe of the float. Bend the float arm to adjust to specifications.

Float Drop

Holding the air horn assembly upright, measure the distance from the gasket to the lip or notch at the toe of the float. If correction is necessary, bend the float tang at the rear, next to the needle and seat.

Accelerator Pump Rod

1. Back out the idle speed screw and completely close the throttle valves.

2. Place the pump gauge across the sir horn ring.

3. With the T-scale set to the specified height, the lower leg of the gauge should just touch the top of the accelerator pump rod.

4. Bend the pump rod to adjust.

NOTE: *Check and adjust, if necessary, the pump rod clearance and curb idle speed before adjusting the bowl vent valve.*

1. Remove the two bowl vent valve cover attaching screws in the top of the air horn and remove the cover and gasket. Remove the bowl vent valve spring.

2. Place the idle speed screw on the second step of the fast idle cam next to the highest

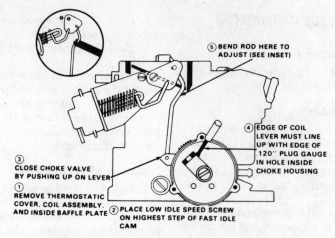

Intermediate choke rod adjustment—2GV, 2GC, 2GE

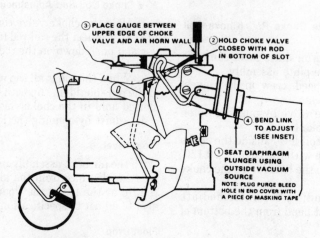

Primary vacuum break adjustment—2GV, 2GC, 2GE

step. In this position, the bowl vent valve should just be closed.

3. If the vent valve is just closed with the idle the fast idle cam, rotate the fast idle cam

so that the idle speed screw is on the next lower step. In this position, the vent valve should just begin to open.

4. If it is necessary to adjust the bowl vent

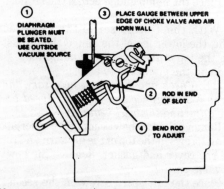

Vacuum break adjustment—2GV, 2GC, 2GE

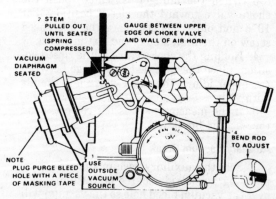

Auxillary vacuum break adjustment—2GV, 2GE, 2GC

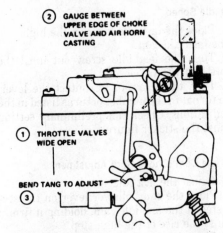

Choke unloader adjustment—2GV, 2GC, 2GE

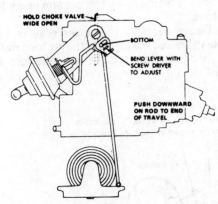

Choke coil rod adjustment—2GV, 2GC, 2GE

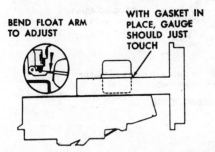

Float level measurement (metal float)—2GV, 2GC, 2GE

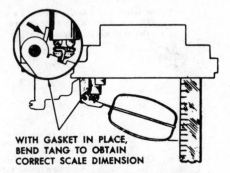

Float drop (metal float)—2GV, 2GC, 2GE

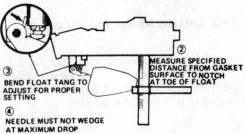

Float drop (plastic float)—2GV, 2GC, 2GE

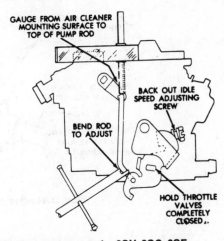

Accelerator pump rod—2GV, 2GC, 2GE

valve, turn the adjustment screw in the top of the valve, to obtain the conditions mentioned in Steps 2 and 3.

Model 2MC, M2MC, M2ME, E2ME Carburetor Adjustments

Float Level Adjustment

See the illustration for float level adjustment for all carburetors. The E2ME procedure is the same except for adjustment (step 4 in the figure). For the E2ME only, if the float level is too high, hold the retainer firmly in place and push down on the center of the float to adjust.

If the float level is too low on the E2ME, lift out the metering rods. Remove the solenoid connector screws. Turn the lean mixture solenoid screw in clockwise, counting the exact number of turns until the screw is lightly bottomed in the bowl. Then turn the screw out counterclockwise and remove it. Lift out the solenoid and connector. Remove the float and

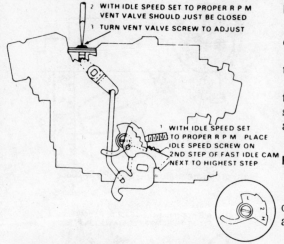

2 WITH IDLE SPEED SET TO PROPER R P M VENT VALVE SHOULD JUST BE CLOSED
3 TURN VENT VALVE SCREW TO ADJUST

1 WITH IDLE SPEED SET TO PROPER R P M PLACE IDLE SPEED SCREW ON 2ND STEP OF FAST IDLE CAM NEXT TO HIGHEST STEP

Bowel vent valve adjustment—2GV, 2GC, 2GE

bend and arm up to adjust. Install the parts, installing the mixture solenoid screw in until the lightly bottomed, then turning it out the exact number of turns counted earlier.

Fast Idle Speed

1. Place the fast idle lever on the high step of the fast idle cam.
2. Turn the fast idle screw out until the throttle valves are closed.
3. Turn the screw in to contact the lever, then turn it in the number of turns listed in the specifications. Check this preliminary setting against the sticker figure.

Fast Idle Cam (Choke Rod) Adjustment

1. Adjust the fast idle speed.
2. Place the cam follower lever on the second step of the fast idle cam, holding it firmly against the rise of the high step.
3. Close the choke valve by pushing upward on the choke coil level inside the choke housing, or by pushing up on the vacuum break lever tang.
4. Gauge between the upper edge of the choke valve and the inside of the air horn wall.
5. Bend the tang on the fast idle cam to adjust.

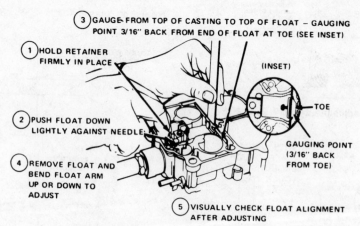

3 GAUGE FROM TOP OF CASTING TO TOP OF FLOAT — GAUGING POINT 3/16" BACK FROM END OF FLOAT AT TOE (SEE INSET)

1 HOLD RETAINER FIRMLY IN PLACE

2 PUSH FLOAT DOWN LIGHTLY AGAINST NEEDLE

4 REMOVE FLOAT AND BEND FLOAT ARM UP OR DOWN TO ADJUST

(INSET)

TOE

GAUGING POINT (3/16" BACK FROM TOE)

5 VISUALLY CHECK FLOAT ALIGNMENT AFTER ADJUSTING

Float level adjustment, 2MC, M2MC, E2ME

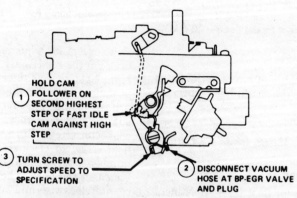

1 HOLD CAM FOLLOWER ON SECOND HIGHEST STEP OF FAST IDLE CAM AGAINST HIGH STEP

3 TURN SCREW TO ADJUST SPEED TO SPECIFICATION

2 DISCONNECT VACUUM HOSE AT BP-EGR VALVE AND PLUG

Fast idle speed adjustment, 2MC, M2MC, E2ME

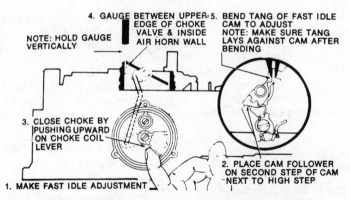

Fast idle cam (choke rod adjustment), 2MC, M2MC, E2ME

Pump Adjustment

This adjustment is not required on E2ME carburetors used in conjunction with the computer controlled system.

1. With the fast idle cam follower off the steps of the fast idle cam, back out the idle speed screw until the throttle valves are completely closed.

2. Place the pump rod in the proper hole of the lever.

3. Measure from the top of the choke valve wall, next to the vent stack, to the top of the pump stem.

4. Bend the pump lever to adjust.

Choke Coil Lever Adjustment

1. Remove the choke cover and thermostatic coil from the choke housing. On models with a fixed choke cover, drill out the rivets and re-

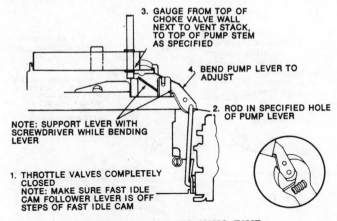

Pump adjustment, 2MC, M2MC, E2ME

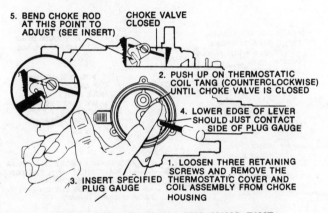

Choke coil rod adjustment, 2MC, M2MC, E2ME

move the cover. A thermostat cover kit will be required for assembly.

2. Push up on the coil tank (counterclockwise) until the choke is closed. The top of the choke rod should be at the bottom of the slot in the choke valve lever. Place the fast idle cam follower on the high step of the cam.

3. Insert a 0.120″ plug gauge in the hole in the choke housing.

4. The lower edge of the choke coil lever should just contact the side of the plug gauge.

5. Bend the choke rod to adjust.

2MC Lean/Rich Vacuum Break Adjustment

1. Place the cam follower on the highest step of the fast idle cam.

2. Seat the vacuum break diaphragm by using an outside vacuum source. Tape over the bleed hole, if any, under the rubber cover on the diaphragm.

3. Remove the choke cover and thermostatic coil and push up on the coil lever inside the choke housing until the tang on the vacuum break lever contacts the tang on the vacuum break plunger stem. Do not compress the bucking spring for lean adjustment. Compress the bucking spring for rich adjustment.

4. With the choke rod in the bottom of the slot in the choke lever, gauge between the upper edge of the choke valve and the inside wall of the air horn.

5. Bend the link rod at the vacuum break plunger stem to adjust the rich setting. Bend the link rod at the opposite end of the diaphragm to adjust the lean setting.

Front/Rear Vacuum Break Adjustment

MODELS THROUGH 1980

1. Seat the front diaphragm, using an outside vacuum source. If there is an air bleed hole in the diaphragm, tape over it.

2. Remove the choke cover and coil. Rotate the inside coil lever counter-clockwise. On models with a fixed choke cover (riveted), push up on the vacuum break lever tang and hold it in position with a rubber band.

3. Check that the specified gap is present between the top of the choke valve and the air horn wall.

4. Turn the front vacuum break adjusting screw to adjust.

5. To adjust the rear vacuum break diaphragm, perform Steps 1-3 on the rear dia-

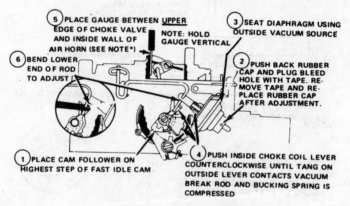

2MC rich vacuum break setting

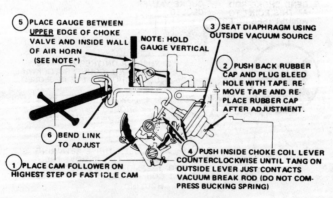

2MC lean vacuum break setting

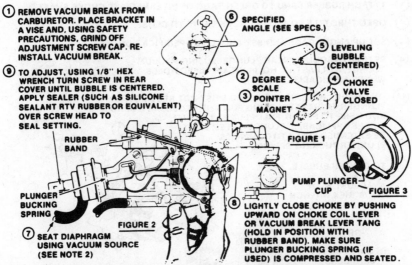

① REMOVE VACUUM BREAK FROM CARBURETOR. PLACE BRACKET IN A VISE AND, USING SAFETY PRECAUTIONS, GRIND OFF ADJUSTMENT SCREW CAP. RE-INSTALL VACUUM BREAK.

⑨ TO ADJUST, USING 1/8" HEX WRENCH TURN SCREW IN REAR COVER UNTIL BUBBLE IS CENTERED. APPLY SEALER (SUCH AS SILICONE SEALANT RTV RUBBER OR EQUIVALENT) OVER SCREW HEAD TO SEAL SETTING.

RUBBER BAND

PLUNGER BUCKING SPRING

⑦ SEAT DIAPHRAGM USING VACUUM SOURCE (SEE NOTE 2)

FIGURE 2

⑥ SPECIFIED ANGLE (SEE SPECS.)

⑤ LEVELING BUBBLE (CENTERED)

② DEGREE SCALE

③ POINTER MAGNET

④ CHOKE VALVE CLOSED

FIGURE 1

PUMP PLUNGER CUP   FIGURE 3

⑧ LIGHTLY CLOSE CHOKE BY PUSHING UPWARD ON CHOKE COIL LEVER OR VACUUM BREAK LEVER TANG (HOLD IN POSITION WITH RUBBER BAND). MAKE SURE PLUNGER BUCKING SPRING (IF USED) IS COMPRESSED AND SEATED.

NOTE 2: ON DELAY MODELS, PLUG END COVER USING AN ACCELERATOR PUMP PLUNGER CUP - 2G TYPE (FIGURE 3) OR EQUIVALENT. SEAT VACUUM DIAPHRAGM MAKING SURE VACUUM IS ABOVE 5" Hg WHEN READING GAUGE (STEP 9). REMOVE CUP AFTER ADJUSTMENT.

NOTE 1: MAKE CHOKE COIL LEVER ADJUSTMENT AND FAST IDLE ADJUSTMENT. DO NOT REMOVE RIVETS AND CHOKE COVER TO PERFORM THIS ADJUSTMENT. USE RUBBER BAND ON VACUUM BREAK LEVER TANG TO HOLD CHOKE VALVE CLOSED (STEP 8).

E2ME rear vacuum break adjustment, 1981–82

phragm, but make sure that the plunger bucking spring is compressed and seated in Step 2. Adjust by bending the link at the bend nearest the diaphragm.

1981 AND LATER

On these models a choke valve measuring gauge J-26701 or equivalent is used to mea-sure angle (degrees instead of inches). See illustration for procedure.

Unloader Adjustment

1. With the choke valve completely closed, hold the throttle valves wide open.
2. Measure between the upper edge of the choke valve and air horn wall.

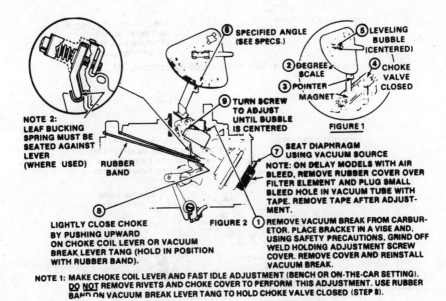

⑥ SPECIFIED ANGLE (SEE SPECS.)

⑤ LEVELING BUBBLE (CENTERED)

② DEGREE SCALE

③ POINTER MAGNET

④ CHOKE VALVE CLOSED

⑨ TURN SCREW TO ADJUST UNTIL BUBBLE IS CENTERED

FIGURE 1

NOTE 2: LEAF BUCKING SPRING MUST BE SEATED AGAINST LEVER (WHERE USED)

RUBBER BAND

⑦ SEAT DIAPHRAGM USING VACUUM SOURCE

NOTE: ON DELAY MODELS WITH AIR BLEED, REMOVE RUBBER COVER OVER FILTER ELEMENT AND PLUG SMALL BLEED HOLE IN VACUUM TUBE WITH TAPE. REMOVE TAPE AFTER ADJUST-MENT.

① REMOVE VACUUM BREAK FROM CARBUR-ETOR. PLACE BRACKET IN A VISE AND, USING SAFETY PRECAUTIONS, GRIND OFF WELD HOLDING ADJUSTMENT SCREW COVER. REMOVE COVER AND REINSTALL VACUUM BREAK.

⑧ LIGHTLY CLOSE CHOKE BY PUSHING UPWARD ON CHOKE COIL LEVER OR VACUUM BREAK LEVER TANG (HOLD IN POSITION WITH RUBBER BAND).

FIGURE 2

NOTE 1: MAKE CHOKE COIL LEVER AND FAST IDLE ADJUSTMENT (BENCH OR ON-THE-CAR SETTING). DO NOT REMOVE RIVETS AND CHOKE COVER TO PERFORM THIS ADJUSTMENT. USE RUBBER BAND ON VACUUM BREAK LEVER TANG TO HOLD CHOKE VALVE CLOSED (STEP 8).

E2ME front vacuum break adjustment, 1981–82

① ATTACH RUBBER BAND TO GREEN TANG OF INTERMEDIATE CHOKE SHAFT.

② OPEN THROTTLE TO ALLOW CHOKE VALVE TO CLOSE.

③ SET UP ANGLE GAGE AND SET ANGLE TO SPECIFICATION.

④ RETRACT VACUUM BREAK PLUNGER, USING VACUUM SOURCE, AT LEAST 18" HG. PLUG AIR BLEED HOLES WHERE APPLICABLE.

④A ON QUADRAJETS, AIR VALVE ROD MUST NOT RESTRICT PLUNGER FROM RETRACTING FULLY. IF NECESSARY BEND ROD HERE TO PERMIT FULL PLUNGER TRAVEL. WHERE APPLICABLE, PLUNGER STEM MUST BE EXTENDED FULLY TO COMPRESS PLUNGER BUCKING SPRING.

⑤ TO CENTER BUBBLE, EITHER:
A. ADJUST WITH 1/8" HEX WRENCH (VACUUM STILL APPLIED)

-OR-

B. SUPPORT AT "S" AND BEND VACUUM BREAK ROD (VACUUM STILL APPLIED)

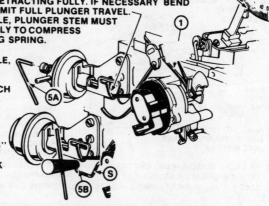

E2ME rear vacuum break adjustment, 1983 and later

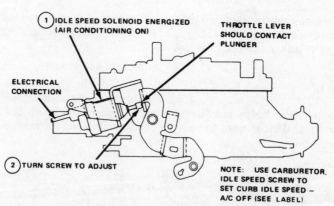

① IDLE SPEED SOLENOID ENERGIZED (AIR CONDITIONING ON)

THROTTLE LEVER SHOULD CONTACT PLUNGER

ELECTRICAL CONNECTION

② TURN SCREW TO ADJUST

NOTE: USE CARBURETOR IDLE SPEED SCREW TO SET CURB IDLE SPEED — A/C OFF (SEE LABEL)

Air conditioning idle speed-up solenoid adjustment, 2MC, M2MC

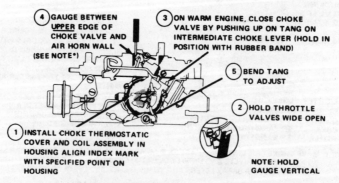

④ GAUGE BETWEEN UPPER EDGE OF CHOKE VALVE AND AIR HORN WALL (SEE NOTE*)

③ ON WARM ENGINE, CLOSE CHOKE VALVE BY PUSHING UP ON TANG ON INTERMEDIATE CHOKE LEVER (HOLD IN POSITION WITH RUBBER BAND)

⑤ BEND TANG TO ADJUST

② HOLD THROTTLE VALVES WIDE OPEN

① INSTALL CHOKE THERMOSTATIC COVER AND COIL ASSEMBLY IN HOUSING ALIGN INDEX MARK WITH SPECIFIED POINT ON HOUSING

NOTE: HOLD GAUGE VERTICAL

Unloader adjustment, 2MC, M2MC

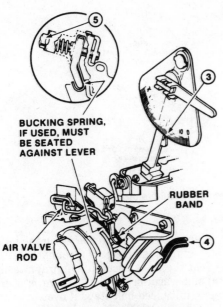

BUCKING SPRING,
IF USED, MUST
BE SEATED
AGAINST LEVER

RUBBER
BAND

AIR VALVE
ROD

① ATTACH RUBBER BAND TO GREEN
  TANG OF INTERMEDIATE CHOKE
  SHAFT

② OPEN THROTTLE TO ALLOW CHOKE
  VALVE TO CLOSE

③ SET UP ANGLE GAGE AND SET TO
  SPECIFICATION

④ RETRACT VACUUM BREAK PLUNGER
  USING VACUUM SOURCE, AT LEAST
  18" HG. PLUG AIR BLEED HOLES
  WHERE APPLICABLE
  ON QUADRAJETS, AIR VALVE ROD
  MUST NOT RESTRICT PLUNGER
  FROM RETRACTING FULLY. IF
  NECESSARY, BEND ROD (SEE
  ARROW) TO PERMIT FULL PLUNGER
  TRAVEL. FINAL ROD CLEARANCE
  MUST BE SET AFTER VACUUM
  BREAK SETTING HAS BEEN MADE.

⑤ WITH AT LEAST 18" HG STILL
  APPLIED, ADJUST SCREW TO
  CENTER BUBBLE

E2ME front vacuum break adjustment, 1983 and later

3. Bend the tang on the fast idle lever to obtain the proper measurement.

Air Conditioning Idle Speed-Up Solenoid Adjustment

1. With the engine at normal operating temperature and the air conditioning turned on but the compressor clutch lead disconnected, the solenoid should be electrically energized (plunger stem extended). Open the throttle slightly to allow the solenoid plunger to fully extend.

2. Adjust the plunger screw to obtain the specified idle speed.

3. Turn off the air conditioner. The solenoid plunger should move away from the tang on the throttle lever.

4. Adjust the curb idle speed with the idle speed screw, if necessary.

NOTE: *Do not adjust if carburetor is computer controlled.*

QUADRAJET CARBURETOR ADJUSTMENTS

The Rochester Quadrajet carburetor is a two stage, four-barrel downdraft carburetor. It has been built in many variations designated as 4MC, 4MV, M4MC, M4MCA, M4ME, M4MEA, E4MC, and E4ME. See the beginning of the Rochester section for an explanation of these designations.

The primary side for the carburetor is equipped with two primary bores and a triple venturi with plain tube nozzles. During off idle and part throttle operation, the fuel is metered through tapered metering rods operating in specially designed jets positioned by a manifold vacuum responsive piston.

The secondary side of the carburetor contains two secondary bores. An air valve is used on the secondary side for metering control and supplements the primary bore.

The secondary air valve operates tapered metering rods which regulate the fuel in constant proportion to the air being supplied.

Fast Idle Speed

1. Position the fast idle lever on the high step of the fast idle cam.

2. Be sure that the choke is wide open and the engine warm. Plug the EGR vacuum hose. Disconnect the vacuum hose to the front vacuum break unit, if there is one.

3. Make a preliminary adjustment by turning the fast idle screw out until the throttle valves are closed, then screwing it in the specified number of turns after it contacts the lever (see the carburetor specifications).

4. Use the fast idle screw to adjust the fast idle to the speed, and under the conditions, specified on the engine compartment sticker or in the specifications chart.

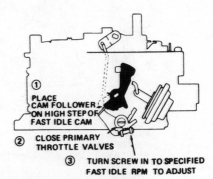

① PLACE
  CAM FOLLOWER
  ON HIGH STEP OF
  FAST IDLE CAM

② CLOSE PRIMARY
  THROTTLE VALVES

③ TURN SCREW IN TO SPECIFIED
  FAST IDLE RPM TO ADJUST

Fast idle adjustment—Quadrajet

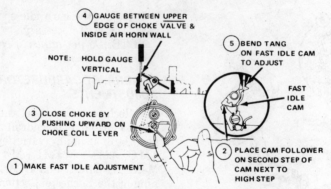

Choke rod (fast idle cam) adjustment—Quadrajet

Choke Rod (Fast Idle Cam)

1. Adjust the fast idle and place the cam follower on the second step of the fast idle cam against the shoulder of the high step.

2. Close the choke valve by exerting counter-clockwise pressure on the external choke lever. Remove the coil assembly from the choke housing and push upon the choke coil lever.

3. Insert a gauge of the proper size between the upper edge of the choke valve and the inside air horn wall.

4. To adjust, bend the tang on the fast idle cam. Be sure that the tang rests against the cam after bending.

Primary (Front) Vacuum Break Adjustment
THROUGH 1981

1. Loosen the three retaining screws and remove the thermostatic cover and coil assembly from the choke housing through 1979.

2. Place the cam follower lever on the highest step of the fast idle cam through 1977.

3. Seat the front vacuum diaphragm using an outside vacuum source. If there is a diaphragm unit bleed hole, tape it over.

4. Push up on the inside choke coil lever until the tang on the vacuum break lever contacts the tang on the vacuum break plunger. On models with a fixed choke coil cover, push up on the vacuum break lever tang.

5. Place the proper size gauge between the upper edge of the choke valve and the inside of the air horn wall.

6. To adjust, turn the adjustment screw on the vacuum break plunger lever.

7. Install the vacuum hose to the vacuum break unit.

1982-AND LATER

On these models a choke valve measuring gauge J-26701 or equivalent is used to measure angle (degrees instead of inches). See illustration for procedure.

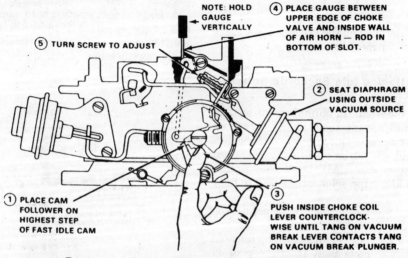

Front vacuum break adjustment, Quadrajet through 1981

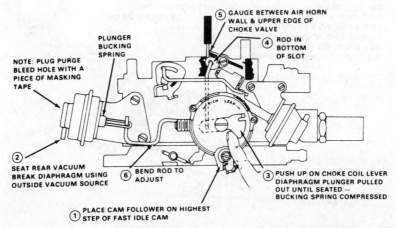

1. **ATTACH RUBBER BAND TO GREEN TANG OF INTERMEDIATE CHOKE SHAFT**

2. **OPEN THROTTLE TO ALLOW CHOKE VALVE TO CLOSE**

3. **SET UP ANGLE GAGE AND SET TO SPECIFICATION**

4. **RETRACT VACUUM BREAK PLUNGER USING VACUUM SOURCE, AT LEAST 18" HG. PLUG AIR BLEED HOLES WHERE APPLICABLE**

   ON QUADRAJETS, AIR VALVE ROD MUST NOT RESTRICT PLUNGER FROM RETRACTING FULLY. IF NECESSARY, BEND ROD (SEE ARROW) TO PERMIT FULL PLUNGER TRAVEL. FINAL ROD CLEARANCE MUST BE SET AFTER VACUUM BREAK SETTING HAS BEEN MADE.

5. **WITH AT LEAST 18" HG STILL APPLIED, ADJUST SCREW TO CENTER BUBBLE**

BUCKING SPRING, IF USED, MUST BE SEATED AGAINST LEVER

RUBBER BAND

AIR VALVE ROD

Quadrajet front vacuum break adjustment, 1982 and later

Secondary (Rear) Vacuum Break Adjustment

THROUGH 1980

1. Remove the thermostatic cover and coil assembly from the choke housing through 1979.
2. Place the cam follower on the highest step of the fast idle cam through 1977.
3. Tape over the bleed hole in the rear vacuum break diaphragm and seat the diaphragm using an outside vacuum source. Make sure the diaphragm plunger bucking spring, if any is compressed. On delay models (1980), plug the end cover with a pump plunger cup or equivalent and remove after adjustment.
4. Close the choke by pushing up on the choke coil lever inside the choke housing. ON models with a fixed choke coil cover, push up on the vacuum break lever tang and use a rubber band to hold in place.
5. With the choke rod in the bottom of the slot in the choke lever, measure between the upper edge of the choke valve and the air horn wall with a wire type gauge.
6. To adjust, bend the vacuum break rod at the first bend near the diaphragm except on 1980 models with the screw at the rear of the diaphragm; on those models, turn the screw to adjust.
7. Remove the tape covering the bleed hole of the diaphragm and connect the vacuum hose.

1981 AND LATER

On these models a choke valve measuring gauge J-26701 or equivalent is used to mea-

PLUNGER BUCKING SPRING

NOTE: PLUG PURGE BLEED HOLE WITH A PIECE OF MASKING TAPE

5. **GAUGE BETWEEN AIR HORN WALL & UPPER EDGE OF CHOKE VALVE**

4. **ROD IN BOTTOM OF SLOT**

2. **SEAT REAR VACUUM BREAK DIAPHRAGM USING OUTSIDE VACUUM SOURCE**

6. **BEND ROD TO ADJUST**

3. **PUSH UP ON CHOKE COIL LEVER DIAPHRAGM PLUNGER PULLED OUT UNTIL SEATED — BUCKING SPRING COMPRESSED**

1. **PLACE CAM FOLLOWER ON HIGHEST STEP OF FAST IDLE CAM**

Rear vacuum break adjustment (without adjustment screw), Quadrajet through 1980

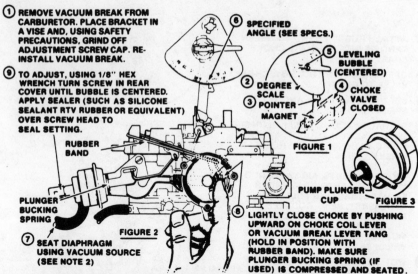

① REMOVE VACUUM BREAK FROM CARBURETOR. PLACE BRACKET IN A VISE AND, USING SAFETY PRECAUTIONS, GRIND OFF ADJUSTMENT SCREW CAP. RE-INSTALL VACUUM BREAK.

⑨ TO ADJUST, USING 1/8" HEX WRENCH TURN SCREW IN REAR COVER UNTIL BUBBLE IS CENTERED. APPLY SEALER (SUCH AS SILICONE SEALANT RTV RUBBER OR EQUIVALENT) OVER SCREW HEAD TO SEAL SETTING.

⑥ SPECIFIED ANGLE (SEE SPECS.)

⑤ LEVELING BUBBLE (CENTERED)

② DEGREE SCALE

③ POINTER MAGNET

④ CHOKE VALVE CLOSED

FIGURE 1

RUBBER BAND

PLUNGER BUCKING SPRING

⑦ SEAT DIAPHRAGM USING VACUUM SOURCE (SEE NOTE 2)

FIGURE 2

PUMP PLUNGER CUP

FIGURE 3

⑧ LIGHTLY CLOSE CHOKE BY PUSHING UPWARD ON CHOKE COIL LEVER OR VACUUM BREAK LEVER TANG (HOLD IN POSITION WITH RUBBER BAND). MAKE SURE PLUNGER BUCKING SPRING (IF USED) IS COMPRESSED AND SEATED.

NOTE 2: ON DELAY MODELS, PLUG END COVER USING AN ACCELERATOR PUMP PLUNGER CUP - 2G TYPE (FIGURE 3) OR EQUIVALENT. SEAT VACUUM DIAPHRAGM MAKING SURE VACUUM IS ABOVE 5" Hg WHEN READING GAUGE (STEP 9). REMOVE CUP AFTER ADJUSTMENT.

NOTE 1: MAKE CHOKE COIL LEVER ADJUSTMENT AND FAST IDLE ADJUSTMENT. DO NOT REMOVE RIVETS AND CHOKE COVER TO PERFORM THIS ADJUSTMENT. USE RUBBER BAND ON VACUUM BREAK LEVER TANG TO HOLD CHOKE VALVE CLOSED (STEP 8).

Quadrajet rear vacuum break adjustment, 1981–82

sure angle (degrees instead of inches). See illustration for procedure.

Choke Unloader

1. Push up on the vacuum break lever to close the choke valve, and fully open the throttle valves.

2. Measure the distance from the upper edge of the choke valve to the air horn wall.

3. To adjust, bend the tang on the fast idle lever.

4MV Choke Coil Rod

1. Close the choke valve by rotating the choke coil lever counter-clockwise.

2. Disconnect the thermostatic coil rod from the upper lever.

① ATTACH RUBBER BAND TO GREEN TANG OF INTERMEDIATE CHOKE SHAFT.

② OPEN THROTTLE TO ALLOW CHOKE VALVE TO CLOSE.

③ SET UP ANGLE GAGE AND SET ANGLE TO SPECIFICATION.

④ RETRACT VACUUM BREAK PLUNGER, USING VACUUM SOURCE, AT LEAST 18" HG. PLUG AIR BLEED HOLES WHERE APPLICABLE.

④A ON QUADRAJETS, AIR VALVE ROD MUST NOT RESTRICT PLUNGER FROM RETRACTING FULLY. IF NECESSARY, BEND ROD HERE TO PERMIT FULL PLUNGER TRAVEL. WHERE APPLICABLE, PLUNGER STEM MUST BE EXTENDED FULLY TO COMPRESS PLUNGER BUCKING SPRING.

⑤ TO CENTER BUBBLE, EITHER:
A. ADJUST WITH 1/8" HEX WRENCH (VACUUM STILL APPLIED)

-OR-

B. SUPPORT AT "S" AND BEND VACUUM BREAK ROD (VACUUM STILL APPLIED)

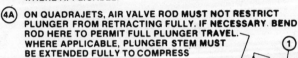

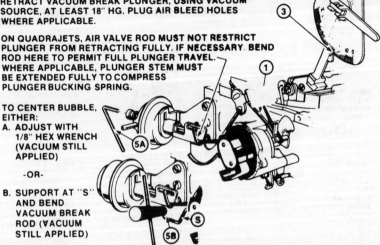

Quadrajet rear vacuum break adjustment, typical 1983 and later

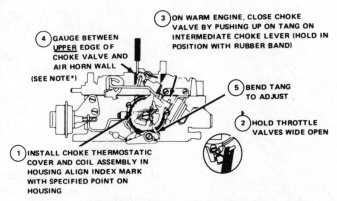

Unloader adjustment—Quadrajet

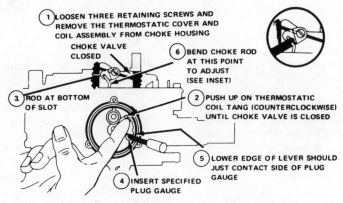

Choke coil lever adjustment—Quadrajet (MC, ME)

3. Push down on the rod until it contacts the bracket of the coil.

4. The rod must fit in the notch of the upper lever.

5. If it does not, it must be bent on the curved portion just below the upper lever.

MC, ME Choke Coil Lever Adjustment

1. remove the choke cover and thermostatic coil from the choke housing. On models with a fixed (riveted) choke cover, the rivets must be drilled out. A choke-stat kit is necessary for assembly. Place the fast idle cam follower on the high step.

2. Push up on the coil tank (counter-clockwise) until the choke valve is closed. The top of the choke rod should be at the bottom of the slot in the choke valve lever.

3. Insert a 0.120″ drill bit in the hole in the choke housing.

4. The lower edge of the choke coil lever should just contact the side of the plug gauge.

5. Bend the choke rod at the top angle to adjust.

Secondary Closing Adjustment

This adjustment assures proper closing of the secondary throttle plates.

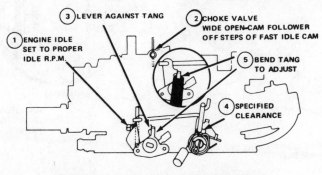

Secondary closing adjustment—Quadrajet

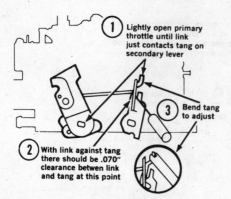

Secondary opening adjustment (three point linkage), Quadrajet

1. Set the slow idle as per instructions in the appropriate car section. Make sure that the fast idle cam follower is not resting on the fast idle cam and the choke valve is wide open.

2. There should be 0.020″ clearance between the secondary throttle actuating rod and the front of the slot on the secondary throttle lever with the closing tang on the throttle lever resting against the actuating lever.

3. Bend the secondary closing tang on the primary throttle actuating rod or lever to adjust.

Secondary Opening Adjustment

1. Open the primary throttle valves until the actuating link contacts the upper tang on the secondary lever.

2. With two point linkage, the bottom of the link should be in the center of the secondary lever slot.

3. With three point linkage, there should be 0.070″ clearance between the link and the middle tang.

4. Bend the upper tang on the secondary lever to adjust as necessary.

Float Level

With the air horn assembly removed, measure the distance from the air horn gasket surface (gasket removed) to the top of the float at the two ($\frac{1}{16}$″ back from the toe on 1975 models; $\frac{3}{16}$″ back on 1976 and later models).

NOTE: *Make sure the retaining pin is firmly held in place and that the tang of the float is lightly held against the needle and seat assembly.*

Remove the float and bend the float arm to adjust except on carburetors used with the C-4 system (E4MC and E4ME). For those carburetors, if the float level is too high, hold the retainer firmly in place and push down on the center of the float to adjust. If the float level is too low on C-4 models, lift out the metering rods. Remove the solenoid connector screw. Turn the lean mixture solenoid screw in clockwise, counting and recording the exact number of turns until the screw is lightly bottomed in the bowl. Then turn the screw out clockwise and remove. Lift out the solenoid and connector. Remove the float and bend the arm up to adjust. Install the parts, turning the mixture solenoid screw in until it is lightly bottomed,

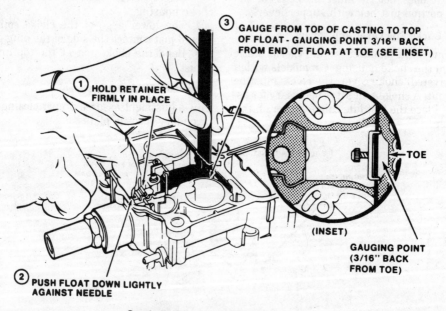

Quadrajet float level adjustment, typical

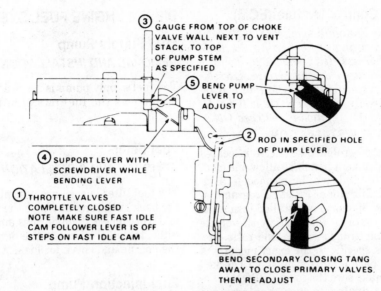

③ GAUGE FROM TOP OF CHOKE VALVE WALL. NEXT TO VENT STACK. TO TOP OF PUMP STEM AS SPECIFIED

⑤ BEND PUMP LEVER TO ADJUST

② ROD IN SPECIFIED HOLE OF PUMP LEVER

④ SUPPORT LEVER WITH SCREWDRIVER WHILE BENDING LEVER

① THROTTLE VALVES COMPLETELY CLOSED NOTE MAKE SURE FAST IDLE CAM FOLLOWER LEVER IS OFF STEPS ON FAST IDLE CAM

BEND SECONDARY CLOSING TANG AWAY TO CLOSE PRIMARY VALVES. THEN RE-ADJUST

Accelerator pump rod adjustment—Quadrajet

then unscrewing it the exact number of turns counted earlier.

Accelerator Pump

The accelerator pump is not adjustable on C-4 carburetors (E4MC and E4ME).

1. Close the primary throttle valves by backing out the slow idle screw and making sure that the fast idle cam follower is off the steps of the fast idle cam.

2. Bend the secondary throttle closing tang away from the primary throttle lever, if necessary, to insure that the throttle lever, if necessary, to insure the primary throttle valves are fully closed.

3. With the pump in the appropriate hole in the pump lever, measure from the top of the choke valve wall to the top of the pump stem.

4. To adjust, bend the pump lever.

5. After adjusting, readjust the secondary throttle tang and the slow idle screw.

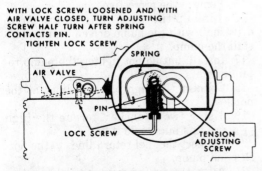

WITH LOCK SCREW LOOSENED AND WITH AIR VALVE CLOSED, TURN ADJUSTING SCREW HALF TURN AFTER SPRING CONTACTS PIN. TIGHTEN LOCK SCREW

SPRING

AIR VALVE

PIN

LOCK SCREW

TENSION ADJUSTING SCREW

Air valve spring adjustment—Quadrajet

Air Valve Spring Adjustment

To adjust the air valve spring windup, loosen the Allen head lockscrew and turn the adjusting screw counter-clockwise to remove all spring tension. With the air valve closed, turn the adjusting screw clockwise the specified number of turns after the torsion spring contacts the pin on the shaft. Hold the adjusting screw in this position and tighten the lockscrew.

Oxygen Sensor
REMOVAL AND INSTALLATION

NOTE: *The oxygen sensor uses a permanently attached pigtail and connector. This pigtail should not be removed from the oxygen sensor. Damage or removal of the pigtail or connector could affect proper operation of the oxygen sensor.*

The oxygen sensor is installed in the exhaust manifold and is removed in the same manner as a spark plug. The sensor may be difficult to remove when the engine temperature is below 120 deg. F (48 deg. C) and excessive force may damage threads in the exhaust manifold or exhaust pipe. Exercise care when handling the oxygen sensor; the electrical connector and louvered end must be kept free of grease, dirt, or other contaminants. Avoid using cleaning solvents of any kind and don't drop or roughly handle the sensor. A special anti-seize compound is used on the oxygen sensor threads when installing and care should be used NOT to get compound on the sensor itself. Disconnect the negative battery cable when servicing the oxygen sensor and torque to 30 ft. lbs. (41 Nm) when installing.

Electronic Control Module (ECM)

CAUTION: *The ignition must be OFF whenever disconnecting or connecting the ECM electrical harness. It is possible to install a PROM backwards during service. Exercise care when replacing the PROM that it is installed correctly, or the PROM will be destroyed when the ignition is switched ON.*

REMOVAL AND INSTALLATION

The electronic control module (ECM) is located under the instrument panel. To allow one model of ECM to be used on different models, a device called a calibrator or PROM (Programmable Read Only Memory) is installed inside the ECM which contains information on vehicle weight, engine, transmission, axle ratio, etc. The PROM is specific to the exact model and replacement part numbers must be checked carefully to make sure the correct PROM is being installed during service. Replacement ECM units (called Controllers) are supplied WITHOUT a PROM. The PROM from the old ECM must be carefully removed and installed in the replacement unit during service. Another device called a CALPAK is used to allow fuel delivery if other parts of the ECM are damaged (the "limp home" mode). The CALPAK is similar in appearance to the PROM and is located in the same place in the ECM, under an access cover. Like the PROM, the CALPAK must be removed and transferred to the new ECM unit being installed.

NOTE: *If the diagnosis indicates a faulty ECM unit, the PROM should be checked to see if they are the correct parts. Trouble code 51 indicates that the PROM is installed incorrectly. When replacing the production ECM with a new part, it is important to transfer the Broadcast code and production ECM number to the new part label. Do not record on the ECM cover.*

To remove the ECM, first disconnect the battery. Remove the wiring harness and mounting hardware, then remove the ECM from the passenger compartment. The PROM and CALPAK are located under the access cover on the top of the control unit. Using the rocker type PROM removal tool, or equivalent, engage one end of the PROM carrier with the hook end of the tool. Press on the vertical bar end of the tool and rock the engaged end of the PROM carrier up as far as possible. Engage the opposite end of the PROM carrier in the same manner and rock this end up as far as possible. Repeat this process until the PROM carrier and PROM are free of the socket. The PROM carrier should only be removed with the removal tool or damage to the PROM or PROM socket may occur.

DIESEL ENGINE FUEL SYSTEM

Fuel Supply Pump

REMOVAL AND INSTALLATION

The fuel supply pump is serviced in the same manner as the fuel pump on the gasoline engine.

Fuel Filter

REMOVAL AND INSTALLATION

The fuel filter is a square assembly located at the back of the engine above the intake manifold. Disconnect the fuel lines and remove the filter. Install the lines to the new filter. Start the engine and check for leaks.

Fuel Injection Pump

REMOVAL AND INSTALLATION

1. Remove the air cleaner.
2. Remove the filters and pipes from the valve covers and air crossover.
3. Remove the air crossover and cap and intake manifold with screened cover (tool J-26996-1).
4. Disconnect the throttle and transmission cables from the intake manifold brackets.
7. Disconnect the fuel lines from the filter and remove the filter.
8. Disconnect the fuel inlet line at the pump.
9. Remove the rear A/C compressor brace and remove the fuel line.
10. Disconnect the fuel return line from the injection pump.
11. Remove the clamps and pull the fuel return lines from each injection nozzle.
12. Using two wrenches, disconnect the high pressure lines at the nozzles.
13. Remove the three injection pump retaining nuts with tool J-26987 or its equivalent.
14. Remove the pump and cap all lines and nozzles.
To install:
15. Remove the protective caps.
16. Line up the offset tang on the pump driveshaft with the pump driven gear and install the pump.
17. Install, but do not tighten the pump retaining nuts.
18. Connect the high pressure lines at the nozzles.
19. Using two wrenches, torque the high pressure line nuts to 25 ft.lb.
20. Connect the fuel return lines to the nozzles and pump.
21. Align the timing mark on the injection

pump with the line on the timing mark adaptor and torque the mounting knots to 35 ft.lb.

NOTE: *A ¾" open end wrench on the boss at the front of the injection pump will aid in rotating the pump to align the marks.*

22. Adjust the throttle rod:

a. Remove the clip from the cruise control rod and remove the rod from the bellcrank.

b. Loosen the locknut on the throttle rod a few turns, then shorten the rod several turns.

c. Rotate the bellcrank to the full throttle stop, then lengthen the throttle rod until the injection pump lever contacts the injection pump full throttle stop, then release the bellcrank.

d. Tighen the throttle rod locknut.

23. Install the fuel inlet line between the transfer pump and the filter.

24. Install the rear A/C compressor brace.

25. Install the bellcrank and clip.

26. Connect the throttle rod and return spring.

27. Adjust the transmission cable:

a. Push the snap-lock to the disengaged position.

b. Rotate the injection pump lever to the full throttle stop and hold it there.

c. Push in the snap-lock until it is flush.

d. Release the injection pump lever.

28. Start the engine and check for fuel leaks.

29. Remove the screened covers and install the air crossover.

30. Install the tubes in the air flow control valve in the air crossover and install the ventilation filter in the valve cover.

31. Install the air cleaner.

32. Start the engine and allow it to run for two minutes. Stop the engine, let it stand for two minutes, then restart. This permits the air to bleed off within the pump.

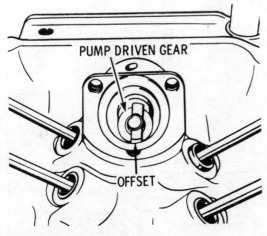

PUMP DRIVEN GEAR

OFFSET

Offset on the pump driven gear

Slow Idle Speed Adjustment

1. Run the engine to normal operating temperature.

2. Insert the probe of a magnetic pickup tachometer into the timing indicator hole.

3. Set the parking brake and block the drive wheels.

4. Place the transmission in Drive and turn the A/C Off.

5. Turn the slow idle screw on the injection pump to obtain the idle specification on the emission control label.

Fast Idle Solenoid Adjustment

1978-79

1. Set the parking brake and block the drive wheels.

2. Run the engine to normal operating temperature.

3. Place the transmission in Drive and disconnect the compressor clutch wire. Turn the A/C On. On cars without A/C, disconnect the solenoid wire, and connect jumper wires to the solenoid terminals. Ground one of the wires and connect the other to a 12 volt battery to activate the solenoid.

4. Adjust the fast idle solenoid plunger to obtain 650 rpm.

1980 AND LATER

1. With the ignition off, disconnect the single green wire from the fast idle relay located on the front of the firewall.

2. Set the parking brake and block the drive wheels.

3. Start the engine and adjust the solenoid (energized) to the specifications on underhood emission control label.

4. Turn off the engine and reconnect the green wire.

Cruise Control Servo Relay Rod Adjustment

1. Turn the engine Off.

2. Adjust the rod to minimum slack then put the clip in the first free hole closest to the bellcrank, but within the servo ball.

Injection Timing Adjustment

For the engine to be properly timed, the lines on the top of the injection pump adapter and the flange of the injection pump must be aligned.

1. The engine must be off for resetting the timing.

2. Loosen the three pump retaining nuts with J-26987 on V8's or J-25304 on V6's, an in-

jection pump intake manifold wrench, or its equivalent.

3. Align the timing marks and torque the pump retaining nuts to 35 ft.lb.

NOTE: *The use of a ¾" open end wrench on the boss at the front of the pump will aid in rotating the pump to align the marks.*

4. Adjust the throttle rod. (See Fuel Injection Pump Removal and Installation, Step 22).

Injection Nozzle

REMOVAL AND INSTALLATION

1978-79

1. Remove the fuel return line from the nozzle.

2. Remove the nozzle hold-down clamp and spacer using tool J-26952.

3. Cap the high pressure line and nozzle tip.

NOTE: *The nozzle tip is highly susceptible to damage and must be protected at all times.*

4. If an old nozzle is to be reinstalled, a new compression seal and carbon stop seal must be installed after removal of the used seals.

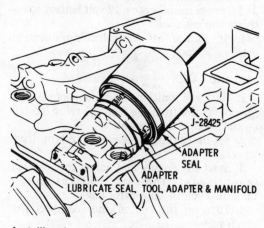

Installing the adapter seal

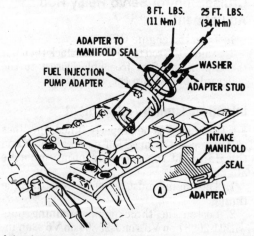

Injection pump adapter bolts

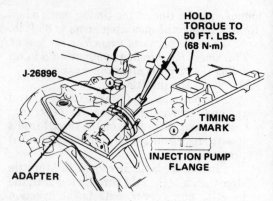

Marking the injection pump adapter

5. Remove the caps and install the nozzle, spacer and clamp. Torque to 25 ft.lb.

6. Replace the return line, start the engine and check for leaks.

1980 and Later

The injection nozzles on these engines are simply unbolted from the cylinder head, after the fuel lines are removed, in similar fashion to a spark plug. Be careful not to damage the nozzle end and make sure you remove the copper nozzle gasket from the cylinder head if it does not come off the nozzle.

Clean the carbon off the tip of the nozzle

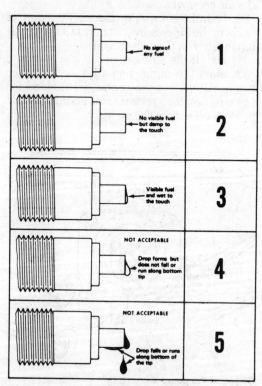

Injection nozzle seat tightness check

MV Carburetor Specifications

Year	Carburetor Identification [1]	Float Level (in.)	Metering Rod (in.)	Pump Rod	Idle Vent (in.)	Vacuum Break (in.)	Auxiliary Vacuum Break (in.)	Fast Idle Off Car (in.)	Choke Rod (in.)	Choke Unloader (in.)	Fast Idle Speed (rpm)
1970	7040014	1/4	0.070	—	—	0.200	—	—	0.170	0.350	900 [3]
	7040017	1/4	0.070	—	—	0.225	—	—	0.190	0.350	750 [3]
1971	7041014	1/4	0.070	—	—	0.200	—	—	0.160	0.350	900 [3]
	7041019	1/4	0.070	—	—	0.225	—	—	0.180	0.350	750 [3]
1975	Manual	11/32	0.080	—	—	0.350	0.312	—	0.275	0.275	1800 [2]
	Automatic	11/32	0.080	—	—	0.200	0.215	—	0.160	0.275	1800 [2]
1976	17056012	11/32	—	—	—	0.140	0.265	—	0.100	0.265	—
	17056013	11/32	—	—	—	0.165	0.320	—	0.140	0.265	—
	17056014	11/32	—	—	—	0.140	0.265	—	0.100	0.265	—
	17056015	11/32	—	—	—	0.165	0.320	—	0.140	0.265	—
	17056018	11/32	—	—	—	0.140	0.260	—	0.100	0.265	—
	17056314	11/32	—	—	—	0.165	0.320	—	0.135	0.265	—

[1] The carburetor identification number is stamped on the float bowl, next to the fuel inlet nut
[2] Preset   [3] Low step of cam

2GC-GE-GV Carburetor Specifications

Year	Carburetor Identification [1]	Float Level (in.)	Float Drop (in.)	Pump Rod (in.)	Primary Vacuum Break (in.)	Secondary Vacuum Break (in.)	Automatic Choke (notches)	Choke Rod (in.)	Choke Unloader (in.)	Fast Idle Speed (rpm)
1970	7040154	9/16	1 3/8	1 11/32	0.160	—	Index	0.140	0.170	—
	7040155	9/16	1 3/8	1 11/32	0.160	—	1 Lean	0.140	0.170	—
	7040156	9/16	1 3/8	1 11/32	0.160	—	Index	0.140	0.170	—
	7040158	9/16	1 3/8	1 11/32	0.160	—	Index	0.140	0.170	—
	7040159	9/16	1 3/8	1 11/32	0.160	—	Index	0.140	0.170	—
1971	7041155	9/16	1 3/8	1 11/32	0.200	—	1 Lean	0.140	0.170	—
	7041156	9/16	1 3/8	1 11/32	0.200	—	Index	0.140	0.170	—
	8041159	9/16	1 3/8	1 11/32	0.215	—	Index	0.140	0.170	—
1972	7042155	17/32	1 3/8	1 3/8	0.200	—	1 Lean	0.160	0.170	—
	7042156	17/32	1 3/8	1 3/8	0.200	—	Index	0.160	0.170	—
1973	All	15/32	1 9/32	1 11/32	0.200	—	Index	0.160	0.250	—
1975	7045143	15/32	1 9/32	1 19/32	0.140	0.120	1 Rich	0.080	0.080	Preset
	7045147	7/16	1 9/32	1 19/32	0.120	0.120	1 Lean	0.080	0.140	1800 [2]
	7045149	7/16	1 9/32	1 19/32	0.120	0.120	1 Rich	0.080	0.140	1800 [2]
	7045160	9/16	1 7/32	1 11/32	0.145	0.265	1 Rich	0.085	.0180	Preset
	7045161	9/16	1 7/32	1 11/32	0.145	0.265	1 Rich	0.085	0.180	Preset
	7045449	7/16	1 9/32	1 19/32	0.120	0.120	1 Lean	0.080	0.140	Preset
1976–77	17056143	15/32	1 5/32	1 11/32	0.140	0.100	1 Rich	0.080	0.180	—
	17056145	7/16	1 5/32	1 19/32	0.110	0.100	1 Rich	0.080	0.140	—
	17056447	7/16	1 5/32	1 19/32	0.130	0.110	1 Rich	0.080	0.140	—
	17056449	7/16	1 5/32	1 19/32	0.130	0.110	1 Rich	0.080	0.140	—

2GC-GE-GV Carburetor Specifications (cont.)

Year	Carburetor Identification ①	Float Level (in.)	Float Drop (in.)	Pump Rod (in.)	Primary Vacuum Break (in.)	Secondary Vacuum Break (in.)	Automatic Choke (notches)	Choke Rod (in.)	Choke Unloader (in.)	Fast Idle Speed (rpm)
1976–77	17057104	7/16	1 9/32	1 21/32	0.130	—	Index	0.260	0.325	—
	17057105	7/16	1 9/32	1 21/32	0.130	—	Index	0.260	0.325	—
	17057107	7/16	1 9/32	1 5/8	0.130	—	Index	0.260	0.325	—
	17057112	19/32	1 9/32	1 21/32	0.130	—	Index	0.260	0.325	—
	17057113	19/32	1 9/32	1 5/8	0.130	—	Index	0.260	0.325	—
	17057114	19/32	1 9/32	1 21/32	0.130	—	Index	0.260	0.325	—
	17057123	19/32	1 9/32	1 5/8	0.130	—	Index	0.260	0.325	—
	17057404	1/2	1 9/32	1 21/32	0.140	—	1 Lean	0.260	0.325	—
	17057405	1/2	1 9/32	1 5/8	0.140	—	1 Lean	0.260	0.325	—
1978	17058102	15/32	1 9/32	1 17/32	0.130	—	Index	0.260	0.325	—
	17058103	15/32	1 9/32	1 17/32	0.130	—	Index	0.260	0.325	—
	17058104	15/32	1 9/32	1 21/32	0.130	—	Index	0.260	0.325	—
	17058105	15/32	1 9/32	1 21/32	0.130	—	Index	0.260	0.325	—
	17058107	15/32	1 9/32	1 17/32	0.130	—	Index	0.260	0.325	—
	17058108	19/32	1 9/32	1 21/32	0.130	—	Index	0.260	0.325	—
	17058109	15/32	1 9/32	1 17/32	0.130	—	Index	0.260	0.325	—
	17058110	19/32	1 9/32	1 21/32	0.130	—	Index	0.260	0.325	—
	17058111	19/32	1 9/32	1 17/32	0.130	—	Index	0.260	0.325	—
	17058113	19/32	1 9/32	1 17/32	0.130	—	Index	0.260	0.325	—
	17058121	19/32	1 9/32	1 17/32	0.130	—	Index	0.260	0.325	—
	17058123	19/32	1 9/32	1 17/32	0.130	—	Index	0.260	0.325	—
	17058126	19/32	1 9/32	1 17/32	0.130	—	Index	0.260	0.325	—
	17058128	19/32	1 9/32	1 17/32	0.130	—	Index	0.260	0.325	—
	17058140	7/16	1 5/32	1 19/32	0.070	0.110	1 Rich	0.080	0.140	—
	17058145	7/16	1 5/32	1 19/32	0.060	0.110	1 Rich	0.080	0.160	—
	17058147	7/16	1 5/32	1 19/32	0.100	0.140	1 Rich	0.080	0.140	—
	17058182	7/16	1 5/32	1 19/32	0.080	0.110	1 Rich	0.080	0.140	—
	17058183	7/16	1 5/32	1 19/32	0.080	0.110	1 Rich	0.080	0.140	—
	17058185	7/16	1 5/32	1 19/32	0.050	0.110	1 Rich	0.080	0.140	—
	17058187	7/16	1 5/32	1 19/32	0.080	0.110	1 Rich	0.080	0.140	—
	17058189	7/16	1 5/32	1 19/32	0.080	0.110	1 Rich	0.080	0.140	—
	17058404	1/2	1 9/32	1 21/32	0.140	—	1/2 Lean	0.260	0.325	—
	17058405	1/2	1 9/32	1 21/32	0.140	—	1/2 Lean	0.260	0.325	—
	17058408	21/32	1 9/32	1 21/32	0.140	—	1/2 Lean	0.260	0.325	—
	17058410	21/32	1 9/32	1 21/32	0.140	—	1/2 Lean	0.260	0.325	—
	17058444	7/16	1 5/32	1 19/32	0.100	0.140	1 Rich	0.080	0.140	—
	17058446	7/16	1 5/32	1 19/32	0.110	0.130	1 Rich	0.080	0.140	—
	17058447	7/16	1 5/32	1 19/32	0.110	0.150	1 Rich	0.080	0.140	—
	17058448	7/16	1 5/32	1 9/16	0.100	0.140	1 Rich	0.080	0.140	—

① The carburetor identification number is stamped on the float bowl, next to the fuel inlet nut
② In Park

2MC, M2MC, M2ME, E2ME, E2MC Carburetor Specifications

Year	Carburetor Identification	Float Level (in.)	Choke Rod (deg./in.)	Choke Unloader (deg./in.)	Vacuum Break Lean or Front (deg./in.)	Vacuum Break Rich or Rear (deg./.)	Pump Rod (in.)	Choke Coil Lever (in.)	Automatic Choke (notches)
1975	7045297	3/16	0.130	.0300	0.300	0.150	9/32 ②	0.120	1 Rich
	7045354	3/16	0.130	.0300	0.300	0.150	5/16 ③	0.120	1 Rich
	7045358	3/16	0.130	.0300	0.300	0.150	5/16 ③	0.120	1 Rich
	7045156	5/32	0.130	.0300	0.300	0.150	9/32 ②	0.120	1 Rich
	7045598	5/32	0.130	.0300	0.300	0.150	3/16 ②	0.120	Index
	7045298	5/32	0.130	.0300	0.300	0.150	3/16 ②	0.120	1 Rich
	7045356	5/32	0.130	.0300	0.300	0.150	3/16 ②	0.120	Index
1976	17056156	1/8	0.105	0.210	0.175	0.110	9/32 ②	0.120	1 Rich
	17056157	1/8	0.105	0.210	0.175	0.110	3/16 ③	0.120	1 Rich
	17056158	1/8	0.105	0.210	0.175	0.110	9/32 ②	0.120	1 Rich
	17056454	1/8	0.105	0.210	0.210	0.110	3/16 ②	0.120	1 Rich
	17056455	1/8	0.120	0.210	0.210	0.130	9/32 ②	0.120	1 Rich
	17056456	1/8	0.105	0.210	0.210	0.110	3/16 ③	0.120	Index
	17056457	1/8	0.105	0.210	0.245	0.110	3/16 ③	0.120	Index
	17056458	1/8	0.105	0.210	0.210	0.110	3/16 ③	0.120	1 Rich
	17056459	1/8	0.105	0.210	0.210	0.110	3/16 ③	0.120	Index
1977	17057150, 17057151	1/8	0.085	0.190	0.160	0.090	11/32 ③	0.120	2 Rich
	17057157	1/8	0.090	0.190	0.190	0.100	3/8 ③	0.120	1 Rich
	17057156, 17057158	1/8	0.085	0.190	0.160	0.090	11/32 ③	0.120	1 Rich
1978	17058150	3/8	0.065	0.203	0.203	0.133	1/4 ②	0.120	2 Rich
	17058151	3/8	0.065	0.203	0.229	0.133	11/32 ③	0.120	2 Rich
	17058152	3/8	0.065	0.203	0.203	0.133	1/4 ②	0.120	2 Rich
	17058154	3/8	0.065	0.203	0.146	0.245	11/32 ③	0.120	2 Rich
	17058155	3/8	0.065	0.203	0.146	0.245	11/32 ③	0.120	2 Rich
	17058156	3/8	0.065	0.230	0.229	0.133	11/32 ③	0.120	2 Rich
	17058158	3/8	0.065	0.203	0.229	0.133	11/32 ③	0.120	2 Rich
	17058450	3/8	0.065	0.203	0.146	0.289	11/32 ③	0.120	2 Rich
1979–80	17059134	15/32	0.243	0.243	0.157	—	1/4 ②	0.120	1 Lean
	17059135	15/32	0.243	0.243	0.157	—	1/4 ②	0.120	1 Lean
	17059136	15/32	0.243	0.243	0.157	—	1/4 ②	0.120	1 Lean
	17059137	15/32	0.243	0.243	0.157	—	1/4 ②	0.120	1 Lean
	17059150	3/8	0.071	0.220	0.195	0.129	1/4 ②	0.120	2 Rich
	17059151	3/8	0.071	0.220	0.243	0.142	11/32 ③	0.120	2 Rich
	17059152	3/8	0.071	0.220	0.195	0.129	1/4 ②	0.120	2 Rich
	17059154	3/8	0.071	0.220	0.157	0.260	11/32 ③	0.120	2 Rich
	17059160	11/32	0.110	0.195	0.129	0.187	1/4 ②	0.120	2 Rich
	17059430	9/32	0.243	0.243	0.157	—	9/32	0.120	1 Lean
	17059432	9/32	0.243	0.243	0.157	—	9/32	0.120	1 Lean

2MC, M2MC, M2ME, E2ME, E2MC Carburetor Specifications (cont.)

Year	Carburetor Identification	Float Level (in.)	Choke Rod (deg./in.)	Choke Unloader (deg./in.)	Vacuum Break Lean or Front (deg./in.)	Vacuum Break Rich or Rear (deg./.)	Pump Rod (in.)	Choke Coil Lever (in.)	Automatic Choke (notches)
1979–80	17059450	3/8	0.071	0.220	0.157	—	11/32 ③	0.120	2 Rich
	17059180	11/32	0.039	0.243	0.103	0.090	1/4 ②	0.120	2 Rich
	17059190	11/32	0.039	0.243	0.103	0.090	1/4 ②	0.120	2 Rich
	17059191	11/32	0.039	0.243	0.103	0.090	9/32 ②	0.120	2 Rich
	17059196	11/32	0.039	0.277	0.129	0.117	1/4 ②	0.120	1 Rich
	17059491	11/32	0.039	0.277	0.129	0.117	9/32 ②	0.120	1 Rich
	17059492	11/32	0.039	0.277	0.129	0.117	9/32 ②	0.120	1 Rich
	17059498	11/32	0.039	0.277	0.129	0.117	9/32 ②	0.120	2 Rich
1981	17081191	5/16	24.5°	38°	28°	24°	—	0.120	—
	17081192	3/8	18°	38°	28°	24°	—	0.120	—
	17081994	3/8	18°	38°	28°	24°	—	0.120	—
	17081196	5/16	24.5°	38°	28°	24°	—	0.120	—
	17081197	3/8	18°	38°	28°	24°	—	0.120	—
	17081198	3/8	18°	38°	28°	24°	—	0.120	—
	17081199	3/8	18°	38°	28°	24°	—	0.120	—
	17081150	13/32	14°	35°	24°	36°	—	0.120	—
	17081152	13/32	14°	35°	24°	36°	—	0.120	—
	17080191	11/32	24.5°	38°	18°	18°	1/4	0.120	—
	17081492	9/32	24.5°	38°	17°	19°	1/4	0.120	—
	17081493	9/32	24.5°	38°	17°	19°	1/4	0.120	—
	17081170	13/32	20°	38°	25°	—	1/4	0.120	—
	17081171	13/32	20°	38°	25°	—	1/4	0.120	—
	17081174	9/32	20°	38°	25°	—	1/4	0.120	—
	17081175	9/32	20°	38°	25°	—	1/4	0.120	—
1982	17082130	3/8	20°	38°	27°	—	—	—	—
	17082132	3/8	20°	38°	27°	—	—	—	—
	17082138	3/8	20°	38°	27°	—	—	—	—
	17082140	3/8	20°	38°	27°	—	—	—	—
	17082150	13/32	14°	35°	24°	38°	—	—	—
	17082150	13/32	14°	35°	24°	40°	—	—	—
	17082182	5/16	18°	32°	28°	24°	—	—	—
	17082184	5/16	18°	32°	28°	24°	—	—	—
	17082186	5/16	18°	27°	21°	19°	—	—	—
	17082192	5/16	18°	32°	28°	24°	—	—	—
	17082194	5/16	18°	32°	28°	24°	—	—	—
	17082196	5/16	18°	27°	21°	19°	—	—	—
1983	17082130, 132	3/8	.110	.243	27/.157	—	④	.120	Fixed
	17083190, 192	5/16	.096	.195	28/.164	24/.136	④	.120	Fixed
	17083193	5/16	.090	.157	23/.129	28/.164	④	.120	Fixed
	17083194	5/16	.090	.220	27/.157	25/.142	④	.120	Fixed

2MC, M2MC, M2ME, E2ME, E2MC Carburetor Specifications (cont.)

Year	Carburetor Identification	Float Level (in.)	Choke Rod (deg./in.)	Choke Unloader (deg./in.)	Vacuum Break Lean or Front (deg./in.)	Vacuum Break Rich or Rear (deg./.)	Pump Rod (in.)	Choke Coil Lever (in.)	Automatic Choke (notches)
1984	17082130	⅜	.110	.243	27/.157	None	④	.120	Fixed
	17082132	⅜	.110	.243	27/.157	None	④	.120	Fixed
	17084191	5⁄16	.096	.195	28/.164	24/.136	④	.120	Fixed
	17084193	5⁄16	.090	.220	27/.157	25/.142	④	.120	Fixed
	17084194	5⁄16	.090	.220	27/.157	25/.142	④	.120	Fixed
	17084195	5⁄16	.090	.220	27/.157	25/.142	④	.120	Fixed
1985	17085190	10⁄32	.096	.195	28/.164	24/.146	④	.120	Fixed
	17085192	11⁄32	.090	.220	27/.157	25/.142	④	.120	Fixed
	17085194	11⁄32	.090	.220	27/.157	25/.142	④	.120	Fixed
1986	17086190	10⁄32	.096	.195	28/.164	24/.136	④	.120	Fixed
				CANADIAN SPECIFICATIONS					
1981	17080191	11⁄32	0.139	0.243	0.096	0.096	¼ ②	0.120	Fixed
	17081492	9⁄32	0.139	0.243	0.090	0.103	¼ ②	0.120	Fixed
	17081493	9⁄32	0.139	0.243	0.090	0.103	¼ ②	0.120	Fixed
	17081170	13⁄32	0.110	0.243	0.142	—	¼ ②	0.120	Fixed
	17081171	13⁄32	0.110	0.243	0.142	—	¼ ②	0.120	Fixed
	17081174	9⁄32	0.110	0.243	0.142	—	¼ ②	0.120	Fixed
	17081175	9⁄32	0.110	0.243	0.142	—	¼ ④	0.120	Fixed
1982	17082174	9⁄32	0.110	0.243	0.142	—	5⁄16 ②	0.120	Fixed
	17082175	9⁄32	0.110	0.243	0.142	—	5⁄16 ②	0.120	Fixed
	17082492	9⁄32	0.139	0.243	0.090	0.103	¼ ②	0.120	Fixed
	17082172	13⁄32	0.110	0.243	0.142	—	5⁄16 ②	0.120	Fixed
	17082173	9⁄32	0.110	0.243	0.142	—	5⁄16 ②	0.120	Fixed
1983–1984	17083172	9⁄32	.139	0.243	17/.090	19/.103	¼ ②	0.120	Fixed
1985	17085170	9⁄32	.139	0.243	17/.090	19/.103	9⁄32 ②	0.120	Fixed
1986	17086170	9⁄32	.139	0.243	17/.090	19/.103	9⁄32 ②	0.120	Fixed

NOTE: New model year carburetor specifications are not released by the manufacuturers until well after the press date for this book.
① The carburetor identification number is stamped on the float bowl, next to the fuel inlet nut.
② Inner hole
③ Outer hole
④ Not Adjustable

M4MC, E4ME, E4MC Carburetor Specifications

Year	Carburetor Identification ①	Float Level (in.)	Air Valve Spring (turn)	Pump Rod (in.)	Primary Vacuum Break (in. or deg.)	Secondary Vacuum Break (in.)	Secondary Opening (in.)	Choke Rod (in. or deg.)	Choke Unloader (in.)	Fast idle Speed (rpm)
1970	7040250	¼	½	⅜	0.200	—	—	0.120	0.200	—
	7040251	¼	¾	⅜	0.200	—	—	0.120	0.200	—
	7040252	¼	¾	⅜	0.200	—	—	0.120	0.200	—
	7040253	¼	¾	⅜	0.275	—	—	0.120	0.200	—

M4MC, E4ME, E4MC Carburetor Specifications (cont.)

Year	Carburetor Identification ①	Float Level (in.)	Air Valve Spring (turn)	Pump Rod (in.)	Primary Vacuum Break (in. or deg.)	Secondary Vacuum Break (in.)	Secondary Opening (in.)	Choke Rod (in. or deg.)	Choke Unloader (in.)	Fast idle Speed (rpm)
1970	7040255	¼	¾	⅜	.0325	—	—	0.120	0.200	—
	7040256	¼	¾	⅜	0.325	—	—	0.120	0.200	—
	7040257	¼	¾	⅜	0.200	—	—	0.120	0.200	—
	7040258	¼	¾	⅜	0.200	—	—	0.120	0.200	—
1971	7041250	¼	½	⅜	0.200	—	—	0.120	0.200	—
	7041251	¼	¾	⅜	0.200	—	—	0.120	0.200	—
	7041252	¼	¾	⅜	0.200	—	—	0.120	0.200	—
	7041253	¼	¾	⅜	0.200	—	—	0.120	0.200	—
	7041257	¼	¾	⅜	0.200	—	—	0.120	0.200	—
1972	7042250	¼	½	⅜	0.230	—	—	0.120	0.200	—
	7042251	¼	¾	⅜	0.215	—	—	0.120	0.200	—
	7042252	¼	¾	⅜	0.215	—	—	0.120	0.200	—
	7042953	¼	¾	⅜	0.275	—	—	0.120	0.200	—
1973	7043256	¼	¾	—	0.200	—	—	0.120	0.300	—
	7043257	¼	½	—	0.200	—	—	0.120	0.300	—
	7043255	¼	¾	—	0.200	—	—	0.120	0.300	—
	7043251	¼	¾	—	0.200	—	—	0.120	0.300	—
	7043253	¼	¾	—	0.275	—	—	0.120	0.300	—
	7043252	¼	¾	—	0.200	—	—	0.120	0.300	—
	7043259	¼	¾	—	0.215	—	—	0.120	0.300	—
1974	7043250	¼	½	⅜	0.200	—	0.070	0.120	0.300	1000 ②
	7043251	¼	¾	⅜	0.200	—	0.070	0.120	0.300	1000 ②
	7043252	¼	¾	⅜	0.200	—	0.070	0.120	0.300	1000 ②
	7043254	¼	¾	⅜	0.275	—	0.070	0.120	0.300	1000 ②
	7043255	¼	½	⅜	0.200	—	0.070	0.120	0.300	1000 ②
	7043256	¼	½	⅜	0.200	—	0.070	0.120	0.300	1000 ②
	7043259	¼	¾	⅜	0.215	—	0.070	0.120	0.300	1000 ②
	7043282	¼	¾	⅜	0.215	—	0.070	0.120	0.300	1000 ②
	7044557	¼	¾	⅜	0.200	—	0.070	0.120	0.300	1000 ②
	7044558	¼	¾	⅜	0.200	—	0.070	0.120	0.300	1000 ②
	7044559	¼	¾	⅜	0.275	—	0.070	0.120	0.300	1000 ②
1975	7045183	⅜	⅛	9/32	0.190	0.140	—	0.135	0.235	③
	7045250	⅜	½	9/32	0.250	0.180	—	0.170	0.300	③
	7045483	⅜	½	9/32	0.275	0.180	—	0.135	0.235	③
	7045550	⅜	½	9/32	0.275	0.180	—	0.135	0.235	③
	7045264	17/32	½	9/32	0.150	0.260	—	0.130	0.235	③
	7045184	⅜	¾	9/32	0.190	0.140	—	0.135	0.235	③
	7045185	⅜	¾	9/32	0.275	0.140	—	0.135	0.235	③
	7045251	⅜	¾	9/32	0.190	0.140	—	0.135	0.235	③

M4MC, E4ME, E4MC Carburetor Specifications (cont.)

Year	Carburetor Identification ①	Float Level (in.)	Air Valve Spring (turn)	Pump Rod (in.)	Primary Vacuum Break (in. or deg.)	Secondary Vacuum Break (in.)	Secondary Opening (in.)	Choke Rod (in. or deg.)	Choke Unloader (in.)	Fast idle Speed (rpm)
1975	7045484	3/8	3/4	9/32	0.190	0.140	—	0.135	0.235	③
	7045485	3/8	3/4	9/32	0.190	0.180	—	0.160	0.235	③
	7045551	3/8	3/4	9/32	0.190	0.140	—	0.135	0.235	③
	7045246	5/16	3/4	3/8	0.130	0.115	—	0.095	0.240	③
	7045546	5/16	3/4	3/8	0.145	0.130	—	0.095	0.240	③
1976–77	17056246	5/16	3/4	3/8	0.130	0.120	—	0.095	0.250	—
	17056250	13/32	1/2	9/32	0.190	0.140	—	0.130	0.230	—
	17056251	13/32	3/4	9/32	0.190	0.140	—	0.130	0.230	—
	17056252	13/32	3/4	9/32	0.190	0.140	—	0.130	0.230	—
	17056253	13/32	1/2	9/32	0.190	0.140	—	0.130	0.230	—
	17056255	13/32	3/4	9/32	0.190	0.140	—	0.130	0.230	—
	17056256	13/32	3/4	9/32	0.190	0.140	—	0.130	0.230	—
	17056257	13/32	3/4	9/32	0.190	0.140	—	0.130	0.230	—
	17056258	13/32	1/2	9/32	0.190	0.140	—	0.130	0.230	—
	17056259	13/32	1/2	9/32	0.190	0.140	—	0.130	0.230	—
	17056546	5/16	3/4	3/8	0.130	0.130	—	0.095	0.250	—
	17056550	13/32	1/2	9/32	0.190	0.140	—	0.130	0.230	—
	17056551	13/32	3/4	9/32	0.190	0.140	—	0.130	0.230	—
	17056552	13/32	3/4	9/32	0.200	0.140	—	0.130	0.230	—
	17056553	13/32	1/2	9/32	0.190	0.140	—	0.130	0.230	—
	17056556	13/32	3/4	9/32	0.190	0.140	—	0.130	0.230	—
	17057202	15/32	7/8	9/32	0.160	—	—	0.325	0.280	—
	17057204	15/32	7/8	9/32	0.160	—	—	0.325	0.280	—
	17057502	15/32	7/8	9/32	0.175	—	—	0.325	0.285	—
	17057504	15/32	7/8	9/32	0.175	—	—	0.325	0.285	—
	17057582	15/32	7/8	9/32	0.175	—	—	0.325	0.285	—
	17057584	15/32	7/8	9/32	0.175	—	—	0.325	0.285	—
1981	17081245	3/8	5/8	—	28	24	—	24.5	38	—
	17081247	3/8	5/8	—	28	24	—	24.5	38	—
	17081248	3/8	5/8	—	28	24	—	24.5	38	—
	17081249	3/8	5/8	—	28	24	—	24.5	38	—
	17081289	13/32	5/8	—	28	24	—	24.5	38	—
	17081253	15/32	1/2	—	25	36	—	14	35	—
	17081254	15/32	1/2	—	25	36	—	14	35	—
	17080201	15/32	7/8	9/32	—	23	—	46	42	—
	17080205	15/32	7/8	9/32	—	23	—	46	42	—
	17080206	15/32	7/8	9/32	—	23	—	46	42	—
	17080290	15/32	7/8	9/32	—	26	—	46	42	—
	17080291	15/32	7/8	9/32	—	26	—	46	42	—

M4MC, E4ME, E4MC Carburetor Specifications (cont.)

Year	Carburetor Identification ①	Float Level (in.)	Air Valve Spring (turn)	Pump Rod (in.)	Primary Vacuum Break (in. or deg.)	Secondary Vacuum Break (in.)	Secondary Opening (in.)	Choke Rod (in. or deg.)	Choke Unloader (in.)	Fast idle Speed (rpm)
1981	17080292	15/32	7/8	9/32	—	26	—	46	42	—
	17080213	3/8	1	9/32	23	30	—	37	40	—
	17080215	3/8	1	9/32	23	30	—	37	40	—
	17080298	3/8	1	9/32	23	30	—	37	40	—
	17080507	3/8	1	9/32	23	30	—	37	40	—
	17080513	3/8	1	9/32	23	30	—	37	40	—
	17081250	13/32	1/2	9/32	26	34	—	17	35	—
	17080260	13/32	1/2	9/32	26	34	—	17	35	—
	17081286	13/32	1/2	9/32	18	34	—	15	35	—
	17081287	13/32	1/2	9/32	18	34	—	15	35	—
	17081276	15/32	5/8	5/16	20	28	—	16	33	—
	17081282	3/8	7/8	9/32	25	—	—	20	38	—
	17081283	3/8	7/8	9/32	25	—	—	20	38	—
	17081284	1/2	7/8	9/32	25	—	—	20	38	—
	17081285	1/2	7/8	9/32	25	—	—	20	38	—
	17080243	3/16	9/16	9/32	16	16	—	14.5	30	—
	17081295	13/32	9/16	9/32	15	13	—	14.5	35	—
	17081294	5/16	5/8	9/32	18	14	—	24.5	38	—
	17081290	13/32	7/8	9/32	—	24	—	46	42	—
	17081291	13/32	7/8	9/32	—	24	—	46	42	—
	17081292	13/32	7/8	9/32	—	24	—	46	42	—
	17081506	13/32	7/8	9/32	23	36	—	46	36	—
	17081508	13/32	7/8	9/32	23	36	—	46	36	—
	17080202	7/16	7/8	1/4	27	—	—	20	38	—
	17080204	7/16	7/8	1/4	27	—	—	20	38	—
	17080207	7/16	7/8	1/4	27	—	—	20	38	—
1982	17082202	11/32	—	38	20	20	—	—	—	—
	17082204	11/32	—	38	20	20	—	—	—	—
	17082244	7/16	—	24.5	32	21	16	—	—	—
	17082245	3/8	—	24.5	32	26	26	—	—	—
	17082246	3/8	—	24.5	32	26	26	—	—	—
	17082247	13/32	—	24.5	38	28	24	—	—	—
	17082248	13/32	—	24.5	38	28	24	—	—	—
	17082251	15/32	—	14	35	25	45	—	—	—
	17082253	15/32	—	14	35	25	36	—	—	—
	17082264	7/16	—	24.5	32	21	16	—	—	—
	17082265	3/8	—	24.5	32	26	26	—	—	—
	17082266	3/8	—	24.5	32	26	26	—	—	—
	17082267	3/8	—	24.5	38	28	24	—	—	—
	17082268	13/32	—	24.5	38	28	24	—	—	—

M4MC, E4ME, E4MC Carburetor Specifications (cont.)

Year	Carburetor Identification ①	Float Level (in.)	Air Valve Spring (turn)	Pump Rod (in.)	Primary Vacuum Break (in. or deg.)	Secondary Vacuum Break (in.)	Secondary Opening (in.)	Choke Rod (in. or deg.)	Choke Unloader (in.)	Fast idle Speed (rpm)
1983	17082265	⅜	⅝	Fixed	0.149/26	0.149/26	④	0.139	0.195	⑤
	17082266	⅜	⅝	Fixed	0.149/26	0.149/26	④	0.139	0.195	⑤
	17082267	⅜	⅝	Fixed	0.149/26	0.149/26	④	0.096	0.195	⑤
	17082268	⅜	⅝	Fixed	0.149/26	0.149/26	④	0.096	0.195	⑤
	17083242	9/32	9/16	Fixed	0.110/20	—	④	0.139	0.243	⑤
	17083244	¼	9/16	Fixed	0.117/21	0.083/16	④	0.139	0.195	⑤
	17083248	⅜	⅝	Fixed	0.149/26	0.149/26	④	0.139	0.195	⑤
	17083250	7/16	½	Fixed	0.157/27	0.271/42	④	0.071	0.220	⑤
	17083253	7/16	½	Fixed	0.151/27	0.269/41	④	0.071	0.220	⑤
	17083553	7/16	½	Fixed	0.157/27	0.269/41	④	0.071	0.220	⑤
1984	17084201	11/32	⅞	Fixed	0.157/27	—	④	0.110	0.243	⑤
	17084205	11/32	⅞	Fixed	0.157/27	—	④	0.243	0.243	⑤
	17084208	11/32	⅞	Fixed	0.157/27	—	④	0.110	0.243	⑤
	17084209	11/32	⅞	Fixed	0.157/27	—	④	0.243	0.243	⑤
	17084210	11/32	⅞	Fixed	0.157/27	—	④	0.110	0.243	⑤
	17084240	5/16	1	Fixed	0.136/24	—	④	—	0.195	⑤
	17084244	5/16	1	Fixed	0.136/24	—	④	—	0.195	⑤
	17084246	5/16	1	Fixed	0.123/22	0.136/24	④	—	0.195	⑤
	17084248	5/16	1	Fixed	0.136/24	—	④	—	0.195	⑤
	17084252	7/16	½	Fixed	0.157/27	0.269/41	④	—	0.220	⑤
	17084254	7/16	½	Fixed	0.157/27	0.269/41	④	—	0.220	⑤
1985	17084282	11/32	½	9/32	0.142/25	0.278/43	④	0.110	0.220	⑤
	17085554	14/32	½	9/32	0.157/27	0.269/41	④	0.110	0.220	⑤
1986	17086008	11/32	½	Fixed	0.142/25	0.287/43	④	0.171	0.220	⑤
	17086009	14/32	½	Fixed	0.142/25	0.287/43	④	0.171	0.220	⑤

NOTE: New model year carburetor specifications are not released by the manufacturers until well after the press date for this book.
① The carburetor identification number is stamped on the float bowl, next to the secondary throttle lever
② On low step
③ 900 rpm with the fast idle cam follower on the lowest step of the fast idle cam
④ No adjustment necessary: See text
⑤ See underhood decal

Quadrajet Carburetor Specifications
All Canadian Models

Note: New model year carburetor specifications are not released by the manufacturers until well after the press date for this book.

Year	Carburetor Identification ①	Float Level (in.)	Air Valve Spring (turn)	Pump Rod (in.)	Primary Vacuum Break (deg./in.)	Secondary Vacuum Break (deg./in.)	Secondary Opening (in.)	Choke Rod (in.)	Choke Unloader (in.)	Fast Idle Speed (rpm)
1981	17080201	15/32	⅞	9/32 ②	—	23/0.129	④	0.314	0.277	⑤
	17080205	15/32	⅞	9/32 ②	—	23/0.129	④	0.314	0.277	⑤
	17080206	15/32	⅞	9/32 ②	—	23/0.129	④	0.314	0.277	⑤

Quadrajet Carburetor Specifications
All Canadian Models (cont.)

Note: New model year carburetor specifications are not released by the manufacturers until well after the press date for this book.

Year	Carburetor Identification ①	Float Level (in.)	Air Valve Spring (turn)	Pump Rod (in.)	Primary Vacuum Break (deg./in.)	Secondary Vacuum Break (deg./in.)	Secondary Opening (in.)	Choke Rod (in.)	Choke Unloader (in.)	Fast Idle Speed (rpm)
1981	17080201	¹⁵⁄₃₂	⁷⁄₈	⁹⁄₃₂ ②	—	23/0.129	④	0.314	0.277	⑤
	17080291	¹⁵⁄₃₂	⁷⁄₈	⁹⁄₃₂ ②	—	26/0.149	④	0.314	0.277	⑤
	17080292	¹⁵⁄₃₂	⁷⁄₈	⁹⁄₃₂ ②	—	26/0.149	④	0.314	0.277	⑤
	17080213	³⁄₈	1	⁹⁄₃₂ ②	23/0.129	30/0.179	④	0.234	0.260	⑤
	17080215	³⁄₈	1	⁹⁄₃₂ ②	23/0.129	30/0.179	④	0.234	0.260	⑤
	17080298	³⁄₈	1	⁹⁄₃₂ ②	23/0.129	30/0.179	④	0.234	0.260	⑤
	17080507	³⁄₈	1	⁹⁄₃₂ ②	23/0.129	30/0.179	④	0.234	0.260	⑤
	17080513	³⁄₈	1	⁹⁄₃₂ ②	23/0.129	30/0.179	④	0.234	0.260	⑤
	17081250	¹³⁄₃₂	½	⁹⁄₃₂ ②	26/0.149	34/0.211	④	0.090	0.220	⑤
	17080260	¹³⁄₃₂	½	⁹⁄₃₂ ②	26/0.149	34/0.211	④	0.090	0.220	⑤
	17081276	¹⁵⁄₃₂	⅝	⁵⁄₁₆ ②	20/0.110	28/0.164	④	0.083	0.203	⑤
	17081286	¹³⁄₃₂	½	⁹⁄₃₂ ②	18/0.096	34/0.211	④	0.077	0.220	⑤
	17081287	¹³⁄₃₂	½	⁹⁄₃₂ ②	18/0.096	34/0.211	④	0.077	0.220	⑤
	17081282	³⁄₈	⅝	⁹⁄₃₂ ②	20/0.110	—	④	0.110	0.243	⑤
	17081283	³⁄₈	⁷⁄₈	⁹⁄₃₂ ②	20/0.110	—	④	0.110	0.243	⑤
	17081284	½	⁷⁄₈	⁹⁄₃₂ ②	20/0.110	—	④	0.110	0.243	⑤
	17081285	½	⁷⁄₈	⁹⁄₃₂ ②	20/0.110	—	④	0.110	0.243	⑤
	17080243	³⁄₁₆	⁹⁄₁₆	⁹⁄₃₂ ②	14.5/0.075	16/0.083	④	0.075	0.179	⑤
	17081295	¹³⁄₃₂	⁹⁄₁₆	⁹⁄₃₂ ②	14.5/0.075	13/0.066	④	0.075	0.220	⑤
	17081294	⁵⁄₁₆	⅝	⁹⁄₃₂ ②	24.5/0.139	14/0.071	④	0.139	0.243	⑤
	17081290	¹³⁄₃₂	⁷⁄₈	⁹⁄₃₂ ②	46/0.314	24/0.136	④	0.314	0.277	⑤
	17081291	¹³⁄₃₂	⁷⁄₈	⁹⁄₃₂ ②	46/0.314	24/0.136	④	0.314	0.277	⑤
	17081292	¹³⁄₃₂	⁷⁄₈	⁹⁄₃₂ ②	46/0.314	24/0.136	④	0.314	0.277	⑤
	17081506	¹³⁄₃₂	⁷⁄₈	⁹⁄₃₂ ②	46/0.314	36/0.227	④	0.314	0.227	⑤
	17081508	¹³⁄₃₂	⁷⁄₈	⁹⁄₃₂ ②	40/0.314	36/0.227	④	0.314	0.227	⑤
	17080202	⁷⁄₁₆	⁷⁄₈	¼ ②	20/0.110	—	④	0.110	0.243	⑤
	17080204	⁷⁄₁₆	⁷⁄₈	¼ ②	20/0.110	—	④	0.110	0.243	⑤
	17080207	⁷⁄₁₆	⁷⁄₈	¼ ②	20/0.110	—	④	0.110	0.243	⑤
1982	17082280	³⁄₈	⁷⁄₈	⁹⁄₃₂ ②	25/0.142	—	④	0.110	0.243	⑤
	17082281	³⁄₈	⁷⁄₈	⁹⁄₃₂ ②	25/0.142	—	④	0.110	0.243	⑤
	17082282	³⁄₈	⁷⁄₈	⁹⁄₃₂ ②	25/0.142	—	④	0.110	0.243	⑤
	17082283	³⁄₈	⁷⁄₈	⁹⁄₃₂ ②	25/0.142	—	④	0.110	0.243	⑤
	17082286	¹³⁄₃₂	½	⁹⁄₃₂ ②	22/0.123	34/0.211	④	0.077	0.243	⑤
	17082287	¹³⁄₃₂	½	⁹⁄₃₂ ②	22/0.123	34/0.211	④	0.077	0.243	⑤
	17082288	³⁄₈	⁷⁄₈	⁹⁄₃₂ ②	25/0.142	—	④	0.110	0.243	⑤
	17082289	³⁄₈	⁷⁄₈	⁹⁄₃₂ ②	25/0.142	—	④	0.110	0.243	⑤
	17082296	½	⁷⁄₈	⁹⁄₃₂ ②	25/0.142	—	④	0.110	0.243	⑤
	17082297	½	⁷⁄₈	⁹⁄₃₂ ②	25/0.142	—	④	0.110	0.243	⑤

Quadrajet Carburetor Specifications
All Canadian Models (cont.)

Note: New model year carburetor specifications are not released by the manufacturers until well after the press date for this book.

Year	Carburetor Identification ①	Float Level (in.)	Air Valve Spring (turn)	Pump Rod (in.)	Primary Vacuum Break (deg./in.)	Secondary Vacuum Break (deg./in.)	Secondary Opening (in.)	Choke Rod (in.)	Choke Unloader (in.)	Fast Idle Speed (rpm)
1983	17080213	³⁄₈	1	⁹⁄₃₂	23/.129	30/.179	④	0.234	0.260	⑤
	17082213	⁹⁄₃₂	1	⁹⁄₃₂	23/.129	30/.179	④	0.234	0.260	⑤
	17082282	³⁄₈	⁷⁄₈	⁹⁄₃₂	25/.142	—	④	0.110	0.243	⑤
	17082283	³⁄₈	⁷⁄₈	⁹⁄₃₂	25/.142	—	④	0.110	0.243	⑤
	17082286	¹³⁄₃₂	½	⁹⁄₃₂	23/.129	34/.211	④	0.107	0.220	⑤
	17082287	¹³⁄₃₂	½	⁹⁄₃₂	23/.129	34/.211	④	0.107	0.220	⑤
	17082296	½	⁷⁄₈	⁹⁄₃₂	25/0.142	—	④	0.110	0.243	⑤
	17082297	½	⁷⁄₈	⁹⁄₃₂	25/0.142	—	④	0.110	0.243	⑤
	17083280	³⁄₈	⁷⁄₈	⁹⁄₃₂	25/0.142	—	④	0.110	0.243	⑤
	17083281	³⁄₈	⁷⁄₈	⁹⁄₃₂	25/0.142	—	④	0.110	0.243	⑤
	17083282	³⁄₈	⁷⁄₈	⁹⁄₃₂	25/0.142	—	④	0.110	0.243	⑤
	17083283	³⁄₈	⁷⁄₈	⁹⁄₃₂	25/0.142	—	④	0.110	0.243	⑤
	17083290	¹³⁄₃₂	⁷⁄₈	⁹⁄₃₂	—	24/.136	④	0.314	0.251	⑤
	17083292	¹³⁄₃₂	⁷⁄₈	⁹⁄₃₂	—	24/.136	④	0.314	0.251	⑤
	17083298	³⁄₈	1	⁹⁄₃₂	23/.129	30/.179	④	0.234	0.260	⑤
1984	17084280	³⁄₈	⁷⁄₈	⁹⁄₃₂ ②	23/.129	—	④	0.110	0.243	⑤
	17084281	³⁄₈	⁷⁄₈	⁹⁄₃₂ ②	23/.129	—	④	0.110	0.243	⑤
	17084282	³⁄₈	⁷⁄₈	⁹⁄₃₂ ②	23/.129	—	④	0.110	0.243	⑤
	17084283	³⁄₈	⁷⁄₈	⁹⁄₃₂ ②	23/.129	—	④	0.110	0.243	⑤
	17084284	³⁄₈	⁷⁄₈	⁹⁄₃₂ ②	23/.129	—	④	0.110	0.243	⑤
	17084285	³⁄₈	⁷⁄₈	⁹⁄₃₂ ②	23/.129	—	④	0.110	0.243	⑤
	17084286	¹³⁄₃₂	½	⁹⁄₃₂ ②	23/.129	34/.211	④	0.107	0.220	⑤
	17084287	¹³⁄₃₂	½	⁹⁄₃₂ ②	23/.129	34/.211	④	0.107	0.220	⑤
	17084288	³⁄₈	⁷⁄₈	⁹⁄₃₂ ②	23/.129	—	④	0.110	0.243	⑤
	17084289	³⁄₈	⁷⁄₈	⁹⁄₃₂ ②	23/.129	—	④	0.110	0.243	⑤
	17084296	½	⁷⁄₈	⁹⁄₃₂ ②	23/.129	—	④	0.110	0.243	⑤
	17084297	½	⁷⁄₈	⁹⁄₃₂ ②	23/.129	—	④	0.110	0.243	⑤
1985	17080213	³⁄₈	1	⁹⁄₃₂ ②	23/.129	30/0.179	④	0.234	40/0.260	⑤
	17080298	³⁄₈	1	⁹⁄₃₂ ②	23/.129	30/0.179	④	0.234	40/0.260	⑤
	17082213	³⁄₈	1	⁹⁄₃₂ ②	23/.129	30/0.179	④	0.234	40/0.260	⑤
	17083298	³⁄₈	1	⁹⁄₃₂ ②	23/.129	30/0.179	④	0.234	40/0.260	⑤
	17085247	¹³⁄₃₂	⁷⁄₈	⁹⁄₃₂ ②	20/0.110	—	④	0.096	30/0.179	⑤
	17085246	¹³⁄₃₂	⁷⁄₈	⁹⁄₃₂ ②	20/0.110	—	④	0.096	30/0.179	⑤
	17085249	¹³⁄₃₂	⁷⁄₈	⁹⁄₃₂ ②	20/0.110	—	④	0.096	30/0.179	⑤
	17085248	¹³⁄₃₂	⁷⁄₈	⁹⁄₃₂ ②	20/0.110	—	④	0.096	30/0.179	⑤
	17085580	³⁄₈	⁷⁄₈	⁹⁄₃₂ ②	21/0.117	—	④	0.077	30/0.179	⑤
	17085582	³⁄₈	⁷⁄₈	⁹⁄₃₂ ②	21/0.117	—	④	0.077	30/0.179	⑤
	17085581	³⁄₈	⁷⁄₈	⁹⁄₃₂ ②	21/0.117	—	④	0.077	30/0.179	⑤

Quadrajet Carburetor Specifications
All Canadian Models (cont.)

Note: New model year carburetor specifications are not released by the manufacturers until well after the press date for this book.

Year	Carburetor Identification ①	Float Level (in.)	Air Valve Spring (turn)	Pump Rod (in.)	Primary Vacuum Break (deg./in.)	Secondary Vacuum Break (deg./in.)	Secondary Opening (in.)	Choke Rod (in.)	Choke Unloader (in.)	Fast Idle Speed (rpm)
1985	17085583	⅜	⅞	9/32 ②	21/0.117	—	④	0.077	30/0.179	⑤
	17085584	⅜	⅞	9/32 ②	21/0.117	—	④	0.077	30/0.179	⑤
	17085586	⅜	⅞	9/32 ②	21/0.117	—	④	0.077	30/0.179	⑤
	17085592	13/32	½	9/32 ②	21/0.117	34/.211	④	0.077	35/0.220	⑤
	17085594	13/32	½	9/32 ②	21/0.117	34/.211	④	0.077	28/0.164	⑤
	17085588	⅜	⅞	9/32 ②	21/0.117	—	④	0.077	30/0.179	⑤
	17085590	⅜	⅞	9/32 ②	21/0.117	—	④	0.077	30/0.179	⑤
	17085596	½	⅞	9/32 ②	23/0.129	—	④	0.077	38/.243	⑤
	17085598	½	⅞	9/32 ②	23/0.129	—	④	0.077	38/0.243	⑤
1986	17086246	13/32	⅞	9/32 ②	20/0.110	—	④	0.096	30/0.179	⑤
	17086247	13/32	⅞	9/32 ②	20/0.110	—	④	0.096	30/0.179	⑤
	17086248	13/32	⅞	9/32 ②	20/0.110	—	④	0.096	30/0.179	⑤
	17086249	13/32	⅞	9/32 ②	20/0.110	—	④	0.096	30/0.179	⑤
	17086580	12/32	⅞	9/32 ②	21/0.117	—	④	0.077	30/0.179	⑤
	17086581	12/32	⅞	9/32 ②	21/0.117	—	④	0.077	30/0.179	⑤
	17086582	12/32	⅞	9/32 ②	21/0.117	—	④	0.077	30/0.179	⑤
	17086583	12/32	⅞	9/32 ②	21/0.117	—	④	0.077	30/0.179	⑤
	17086584	12/32	⅞	9/32 ②	21/0.117	—	④	0.077	30/0.179	⑤
	17086586	12/32	⅞	9/32 ②	21/0.117	—	④	0.077	30/0.179	⑤
	17086588	12/32	⅞	9/32 ②	21/0.117	—	④	0.077	30/0.179	⑤
	17086590	12/32	⅞	9/32 ②	21/0.117	—	④	0.077	30/0.179	⑤
	17086596	16/32	⅞	9/32 ②	21/0.117	—	④	0.077	30/0.179	⑤
	17086598	16/32	⅞	9/32 ②	21/0.117	—	④	0.077	30/0.179	⑤

① The carburetor indentification number is stamped on the float bowl, near the secondary throttle lever.
② Inner hole ④ No measurement necessary on two point linkage; see text
③ Outer hole ⑤ See underhood decal.

with a soft brass wire brush and install the nozzles, with gaskets.

NOTE: 1981 and later models use two type of injectors, CAV Lucas and Diesel Equipment. When installing the inlet fittings, torque the Diesel Equipment injector fitting to 45 ft.lb. and the CAV Lucas to 25 ft.lb.

Injection Pump Adapter, Adapter Seal, and New Adapter Timing Mark

REMOVAL AND INSTALLATION

NOTE: *Skip steps 4 and 9 if a new adapter is not being installed.*

1. Remove injection pump and lines as described earlier.
2. Remove the injection pump adapter.
3. Remove the seal from the adapter.
4. File the timing mark from the adapter. Do not file the mark off the pump.
5. Position the engine at TDC of No. 1 cylinder. Align the mark on the balancer with the zero mark on the indicator. The index is offset to the right when No. 1 is at TDC.
6. Apply chassis lube to the seal areas. Install, but do not tighten the injection pump.
7. Install the new seal on the adapter using tool J-28425, or its equivalent.

INLET FITTING TO BODY TORQUE
DIESEL EQUIPMENT – 45 FT. LBS. (60 N·m)
C.A.V. LUCAS – 25 FT. LBS. (34 N·m)

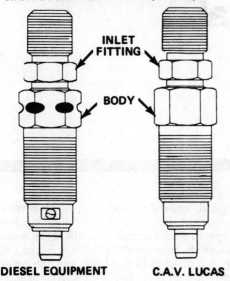

DIESEL EQUIPMENT   **C.A.V. LUCAS**

Injection nozzles

8. Torque the adapter bolts to 25 ft.lb.

9. Install timing tool J-26896 into the injection pump adapter. Torque the tool, toward No. 1 cylinder, to 50 ft.lb. Mark the injection pump adapter. Remove the tool.

10. Install the injection pump.

Glow Plugs

There are two types of glow plugs used on General Motors Corp. diesels; the "fast glow" type and the "slow glow" type. The fast glow type use pulsing current applied to 6 volt glow plugs while the slow glow type use continuous current applied to 12 volt glow plugs.

An easy way to tell the plugs apart is that the fast flow (6 volt) plugs have a $5/16$" wide electrical connector plug while the slow flow (12 volt) connector plug is $1/4$" wide. Do not attempt to interchange any parts of these two glow plug systems.

Chassis Electrical

5

UNDERSTANDING BASIC ELECTRICITY

Understanding the basic theory of electricity makes electrical trouble-shooting much easier. Several gauges are used in electrical trouble-shooting to see inside the circuit being tested. Without a basic understanding, it will be difficult to understand testing procedures.

Electricity is the flow of electrons — hypothetical particles thought to constitute the basic stuff of electricity. In a comparison with water flowing in a pipe, the electrons would be the water. As the flow of water can be measured, the flow of electricity can be measured. The unit of measurement is amperes, frequently abbreviated amps. An ammeter will measure the actual amount of current flowing in the circuit.

Just as the water pressure is measured in units such as pounds per square inch, electrical pressure is measured in volts. When a voltmeter's two probes are placed on two live portions of an electrical circuit with different electrical pressures, current will flow through the voltmeter and produce a reading which indicates the difference in electrical pressure between the two parts of the circuit.

While increasing the voltage in a circuit will increase the flow of current, the actual flow depends not only on voltage, but on the resistance of the circuit. The standard unit for measuring circuit resistance is an ohm, measured by an ohmmeter. The ohmmeter is somewhat similar to an ammeter, but incorporates its own source of power so that a standard voltage is always present.

An actual electric circuit consists of four basic parts. These are: the power source, such as a generator or battery; a hot wire, which conducts the electricity under a relatively high voltage to the component supplied by the circuit; the load, such as a lamp, motor, resistor or relay coil; and the ground wire, which carries the current back to the source under very low voltage. In such a circuit the bulk of the resistance exists between the point where the hot wire is connected to the load, and the point where the load is grounded. In an automobile, the vehicle's frame, which is made of steel, is used as a part of the ground circuit for many of the electrical devices.

Remember that, in electrical testing, the voltmeter is connected in parallel with the circuit being tested (without disconnecting any wires) and measures the difference in voltage between the locations of the two probes; that the ammeter is connected in series with the load (the circuit is separated at one point and the ammeter inserted so it becomes a part of the circuit); and the ohmmeter is self-powered, so that all the power in the circuit should be off and the portion of the circuit to be measured contacted at either end by one of the probes of the meter.

For any electrical system to operate, it must make a complete circuit. This simply means that the power flow from the battery must make a complete circle. When an electrical component is operating, power flows from the battery to the component, passes through the component causing it to perform it to function (lighting a light bulb) and then returns to the battery through the ground of the circuit. This ground is usually (but not always) the metal part of the car on which the electrical component is mounted.

Perhaps the easiest way to visualize this is to think of connecting a light bulb with two wires attached to it to you car battery. The battery in your car has two posts (negative and positive). If one of the two wires attached to the light bulb was attached to the negative post of the battery and the other wire was attached to the positive post of the battery, you would have a complete circuit. Current from the battery would flow out one post, through the wire attached to it and then to the light bulb, where it would pass through causing it to light. It would then leave the light bulb, travel through the other wire, and return to the other post of the battery.

The normal automotive circuit differs from this simple example in two ways. First, instead of having a return wire from the bulb to the battery, the light bulb return the current to the battery through the chassis of the vehicle. Since the negative battery cable is attached to the chassis and the chassis is made of electrically conductive metal, the chassis of the vehicle can serve as a ground wire to complete the circuit. Secondly, most automotive circuits contain switches to turn components on and off when it is turned off.

Some electrical components which require a large amount of current to operate also have a relay in their circuit. Since these circuits carry a large amount of current, the thickness of the wire in the circuit (gauge size) is also greater. If this large wire were connected from the component to the control switch on the instrument panel, and then back to the component, a voltage drop would occur in the circuit. To prevent this potential drop in voltage, an electromagnetic switch (relay) is used. The large wires in the circuit are connected from the car battery to one side of the relay, and from the opposite side of the relay to the component. The relay is normally open, preventing current from passing through the circuit. An additional, smaller wire is connected from the relay to the control switch for the circuit. When the control switch is turned on, it grounds the smaller wire from the relay and complete the circuit. When the control switch is turned on, it grounds the smaller wire from the relay and complete the circuit. When the control switch is turned on, it grounds the smaller wire from the relay. If you were to disconnect the light bulb (from the previous example of a light-bulb being connected to the battery by two wires) from the wires and touch the two wires together (please take our word for this; don't try it), the result will be a shower of sparks. A similar thing happens (on a smaller scale) when the power supply wire to a component or the electrical component itself becomes grounded before the normal ground connection for the circuit. To prevent damage to the system, the fuse for the circuit blows to interrupt the circuit-protecting the components from damage. Because grounding a wire from a power source makes a complete circuit-less the required component to use the power-the phenomenon is called a short circuit. The most common causes of short circuits are: the rubber

insulation on a wire breaking or rubbing through to expose the current carrying core of the wire to a metal part of the car, or a shorted switch.

Some electrical systems on the car are protected by a circuit breaker which is, basically, a self-repairing fuse. When either of the above-described events takes place in a system which is protected by a circuit breaker, the circuit breaker opens the circuit the same way a fuse does. However, when either the short is removed from the circuit or the surge subsides, the circuit breaker resets itself and does not have to be replaced as a fuse does.

The final protective device in the chassis electrical system is a fuse link. A fuse link is a wire that acts as a fuse. It is connected between the starter relay and the main wiring harness for the car. This connection is under the hook, very near a similar fuse link which protects the engine electrical system. Since the fuse link protects all the chassis electrical components, it is the probably cause of trouble when none of the electrical components function, unless the battery is disconnected or dead.

Electrical problems generally fall into one of three areas:

1. The component that is not functioning is not receiving current.

2. The component itself is not functioning.

3. The component is not properly grounded.

Problems that fall into the first category are by far the most complicated. It is the current supply system to the component which contains all the switches, relay, fuses, etc.

The electrical system can be checked with a test light and a jumper wire. A test light is a device that looks like a pointed screwdriver with a wire attached to it. It has a light bulb in its handle. A jumper wire is a piece of insulated wire with an alligator clip attached to each end.

If a light bulb is not working, you must follow a systematic plan to determine which of the three causes is the villain.

1. Turn on the switch that controls the inoperable bulb.

2. Disconnect the power supply wire from the bulb.

3. Attach the ground wire to the test light to a good metal ground.

4. Touch the probe end of the test light to the end of the power supply wire that was disconnected from the bulb. If the bulb is receiving current, the test light will go on.

NOTE: *If the bulb is one which works only when the ignition key is turned on (turn signal), make sure the key is turned on.*

If the test light does not go on, then the problem is in the circuit between the battery and the bulb. As mentioned before, this includes all the switches, fuses, and relays in the system. Turn to the wiring diagram and find the bulb on the diagram. Follow the wire that runs back to the battery. The problem is an open circuit between the battery and the bulb. If the fuse is blown and, when replaced, immediately blows again, there is a short circuit in the system which must be located and repaired. If there is a switch in the system, bypass it with a jumper wire. This is done by connecting one end of the jumper wire to the power supply wire into the switch and the other end of the jumper wire to the wire coming out of the switch. Again, consult the wiring diagram. If the test light lights with the jumper wire installed, the switch or whatever was bypassed is defective.

NOTE:Never substitute the jumper wire for the bulb, as the bulb is the component required to use the power from the power source.

5. If the bulb in the test light goes on, then the current is getting to the bulb that is not working in the car. This eliminates the first of the three possible causes. Connect the power supply wire and connect a jumper wire from the bulb to a good metal ground. Do this with the switch which controls the bulb works with jumper wire installed, then it has a bad ground. This is usually caused by the metal area on which the bulb mounts to the car being coated with some type of foreign matter.

6. If neither test located the source of the trouble, then the light bulb itself is defective.

The above test procedure can be applied to any of the components of the chassis electrical system by substituting the component that is not working for the light bulb. Remember that for any electrical system to work, all connections must be clean and tight.

NOTE: *A new upper speedometer cable was released during the 1982 model year. This cable offers improved lubrication, grease retention, and noise suppression however, this cable should not be used on any models older than 1981. This cable can be identified by a longer ferrule at the speedometer end.*

SEATBELT/STARTER INTERLOCK SYSTEM

1974-75

As required by law, all 1974 and some 1975 Buick passenger cars cannot be started until the front seat occupants are seated and have fastened their seat belts. If the proper sequence is not followed, the engine cannot be started.

If, after the car is started, the seat belts are unfastened, a warning buzzer and light will be activated.

The shoulder harness and lap belt are permanently fastened together, so that they both must be worn. The shoulder harness uses an inertia-lock reel to allow freedom of movement under normal driving conditions.

NOTE: *This type of reel locks up when the car decelerates rapidly, as during a crash.*

The switches for the interlock system have been removed from the lap belt retractors and placed in the belt buckles.

For ease of service, the car may be started from outside, by reaching in the turning the key, but without depressing the seat sensors.

In case of system failure, an over-ride switch is located under the hood. This is a one start switch and it must be reset each time it is used.

DISABLING THE INTERLOCK SYSTEM

Since the requirement for the interlock system was dropped during the 1975 model year, those systems installed on cars built earlier may now be legally disabled. The seat belt warning light is still required.

1. Disconnect the negative battery cable.
2. Locate the interlock harness connector under the left side of the instrument panel on or near the fuse block. It has orange, yellow, and green leads.
3. Cut and tape the ends of the green wire on the body side of the connector.
4. Remove the buzzer from the fuse block or connector.

HEATER

Blower

REMOVAL AND INSTALLATION

1. Disconnect the blower motor wire.
2. Remove the blower motor attaching screws and the motor.
3. Installation is the reverse of removal.

Core

REMOVAL AND INSTALLATION

Without A/C

THROUGH 1977

1. Drain the radiator and disconnect the heater inlet and outlet hoses at the dash. Remove the blower inlet to firewall screws, remove the blower inlet, motor and wheel as an assembly.
2. Disconnect the control wires from the de-

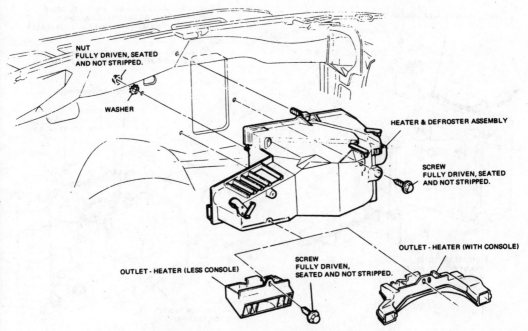

Heater and defroster assembly—through 1977

froster door and vacuum hose diverter door actuator diaphragm and control cable from the temperature door lever.

3. Remove the four nuts securing the heater assembly to the dash.

4. Remove the screw securing the defroster outlet tab to the heater assembly.

5. Remove the heater from the car.

6. Reverse the above steps to install.

1978 AND LATER

1. Disconnect the heater hoses at the core tubes. Place the hoses in an up position to prevent excess coolant loss.

2. Disconnect all electrical connectors at the module case.

3. Remove the front case from the module on 1978-79 models and the top module cover on 1980-83 models.

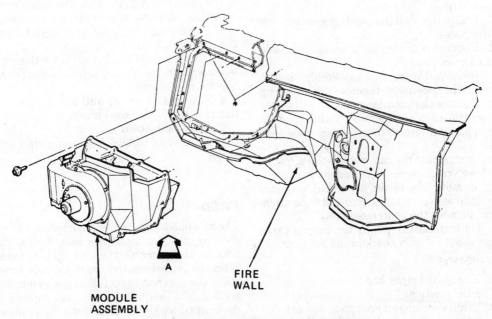

Heater module assembly—1978 and later

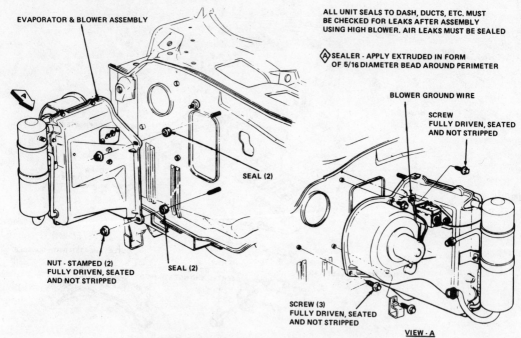

EVAPORATOR & BLOWER ASSEMBLY

ALL UNIT SEALS TO DASH, DUCTS, ETC. MUST BE CHECKED FOR LEAKS AFTER ASSEMBLY USING HIGH BLOWER. AIR LEAKS MUST BE SEALED

Ⓐ SEALER - APPLY EXTRUDED IN FORM OF 5/16 DIAMETER BEAD AROUND PERIMETER

BLOWER GROUND WIRE

SCREW
FULLY DRIVEN, SEATED AND NOT STRIPPED

SEAL (2)

NUT - STAMPED (2)
FULLY DRIVEN, SEATED AND NOT STRIPPED

SEAL (2)

SCREW (3)
FULLY DRIVEN, SEATED AND NOT STRIPPED

VIEW - A

Evaporator and blower assembly—through 1977

4. Remove the core. On later models, remove core bracket and ground screws to gain access.

5. Reverse the above for installation. Replace any damaged sealer.

With A/C

THROUGH 1979

NOTE: *Includes removal of Heater assembly.*

1. Drain the radiator and disconnect the heater hoses.

2. Disconnect the temperature control cable and vacuum hoses.

3. Remove the resistor assembly. Reach through the opening and remove the attaching nut. Remove the attaching nut directly over the transmission and the two attaching nuts to the upper and lower inboard evaporator case half.

4. From inside the car, remove the screw in the lower right corner of the passenger side.

5. Remove the lower attaching outlets. Work the assembly to the rear until the studs clear. Remove the heater assembly.

6. On installation, adjust the control cable to get about ⅛″ springback in the hot position.

1980 AND LATER

1. Engage the right head wiper arm so it is in the UP position.

2. Drain the radiator enough so you can disconnect the heater core hoses, then disconnect the hoses and plug them. Disconnect the battery ground cable.

3. Pull off the trim seal and remove the screens from the assembly. Mark and remove any electrical connections in the way.

4. Loosen and move up the lower windshield trim. Remove the windshield molding cowl brackets.

5. Tape a strip of wood below the lower edge of the windshield glass near the module for protection. Remove all module cover screws.

6. Cut through the sealing material along the cowl with a knife.

7. Pry the module cover off from the side, not down from the top, to insure you don't damage the windshield.

8. Lift the cover off and away from the flange of the fender-cowl brace.

9. Remove the core.

10. Reverse to install. Use new strip caulk sealer.

Radio

The antenna trim must be adjusted on AM radios, when major repair has been done to the unit or the antenna changed. The trimmer screw is located behind the right side knob. Raise the antenna to its full height. Tune to a weak station around 1400 and turn the volume down until barely audible. Turn the trimmer screw until the maximum volume is achieved.

REMOVAL AND INSTALLATION

1970-72

1. Disconnect the battery.

2. If equipped with air conditioning, remove the cool air manifold, if necessary.

3. Remove the defroster manifold, if necessary.

4. Remove the radio knobs washers or rear speaker control.

5. Remove the radio attaching nuts or escucheons.

6. Disconnect the wiring including the antenna lead-in.

7. Remove the radio support bracket attaching screw (s), if applicable.

8. Remove the radio from the rear of the instrument panel.

9. Installation is the reverse of removal.

1973-77

1. Disconnect the battery cable.

2. Remove the four screws which secure the steering column cover and separate it from the instrument panel.

3. Pull the knobs off of the front of the radio and remove the retaining nuts.

4. Remove the four retaining screws, then pull the right hand control panel up and out.

5. Unfasten the radio support bracket screw.

6. Remove the four ash tray housing screws and take the housing off the tie bar.

7. Disconnect the antenna and speaker wire from the radio.

8. Remove the radio from behind the instrument panel.

9. Installation is the reverse of removal.

1978 and Later

1. Disconnect the negative battery cable and remove the radio knobs.

2. Pull the lower trim cover outward, off the retaining clips.

3. Remove the four mounting plate screws and the screw from the radio support bracket on the lower tie bar.

4. Pull the radio out and detach the wiring and the antenna lead.

5. Installation is the reverse of removal.

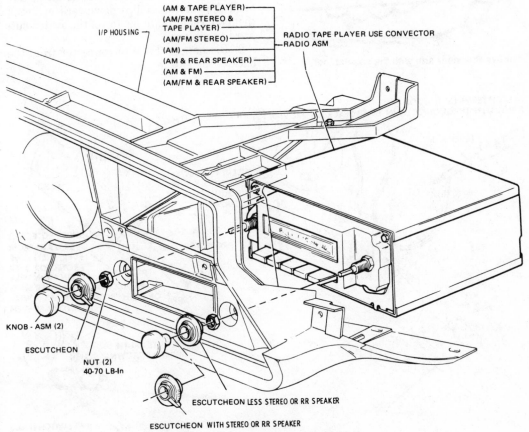

(AM & TAPE PLAYER)
(AM/FM STEREO & TAPE PLAYER)
(AM/FM STEREO)
(AM)
(AM & REAR SPEAKER)
(AM & FM)
(AM/FM & REAR SPEAKER)

I/P HOUSING

RADIO TAPE PLAYER USE CONVECTOR
RADIO ASM

KNOB - ASM (2)

ESCUTCHEON

NUT (2)
40-70 LB-In

ESCUTCHEON LESS STEREO OR RR SPEAKER

ESCUTCHEON WITH STEREO OR RR SPEAKER

Typical radio installation—through 1977

WINDSHIELD WIPERS

Blade and Arm

REPLACEMENT

If the wiper assembly has a press type release tab at the center, simply depress the tab and remove the blade. If the blade has no release tab, use a screwdriver to depress the spring at the center. This will release the assembly. To install the assembly, position the blade over the pin at the tip of the arm and press until the spring retainer engages the groove in the pin.

To remove the element, either depress the release button or squeeze the spring type retainer clip at the outer end together, and slide

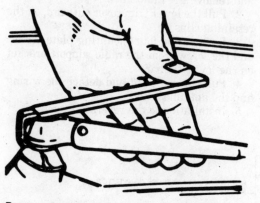

Remove the wiper arm with the special tool

the blade element out. Just slide the new element in until it latches.

Removal of the wiper arms requires the use of a special tool, G.M. J8966 or its equivalent. Versions of this tool are generally available in auto parts stores.

1. Insert the tool under the wiper arm and lever the arm off the shaft.

NOTE: *Raising the hood on most later models will facilitate easier wiper arm removal.*

2. Disconnect the washer hose from the arm (if so equipped). Remove the arm.

3. Installation is in the reverse order of removal. The proper park position for the arms is with the blades approximate 2″ (50 mm) above the lower molding of the windshield. Be sure that the motor is in the park position before installing the arms.

Wiper Switch

REPLACEMENT

Through 1977

1. If the wiper switch is found to be defective, insert one or two narrow bladed screw drivers into each of the two slots within the switch face immediately above the knobs and bend the retaining clips downward or break them off, then rotate the top of the switch outward to remove.

2. Disconnect the wire connector from the back of the switch.

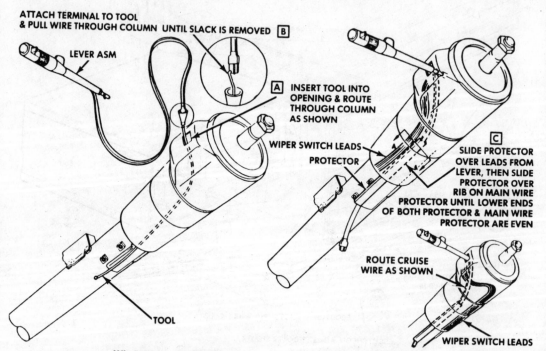

Windshield wiper switch removal and installation—1982 and later

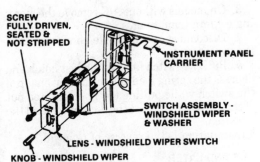

SCREW
FULLY DRIVEN,
SEATED &
NOT STRIPPED

INSTRUMENT PANEL
CARRIER

SWITCH ASSEMBLY -
WINDSHIELD WIPER
& WASHER

LENS - WINDSHIELD WIPER SWITCH

KNOB - WINDSHIELD WIPER

Washer and wiper switch—1978–81

3. After connecting the wire to the back of the new switch, simply align and press the switch into place.

1978-81

1. Remove the headlight switch knob and escutcheon.
2. Remove the trim plate.
3. Remove the two retaining screws and remove the switch.
4. Installation is the reverse of removal.

1982 and Later

All 1982 and later models use the multi-function lever on the steering column.

1. Disconnect the turn signal electrical connector at the base of the steering column jacket.
2. Remove the wiring protector on the bottom of the column to ease the wiring harness removal.
3. Grasp the lever and pull straight out.
4. See Illustration to install.

Wiper Motor
REMOVAL AND INSTALLATION

1970

1. Remove the three cowl screen attaching screws from the left side of the cowl screen and lift the screen.
2. Loosen the two nuts securing the linkage crankarm to the pivot arm, through the cowl opening.
3. Disconnect the wiring and the washer hoses.
4. Remove the three screws which secure the motor and, guiding the crankarm through the hole in the dash, remove the motor.
5. Installation is in the reverse order of removal.

1971 and Later

1. Remove the cowl screen.
2. Loosen the linkage drive link-to-crank

arm attaching nuts, and remove the link from the arm.
3. Disconnect the wiring and the washer hoses.
4. Remove the three motor attaching screw, guide the crankarm through the hole in the dash, and remove the motor.
5. Installation is the reverse order of removal.

Wiper Transmission
REMOVAL AND INSTALLATION

1. Make sure the wipers are in the fully parked position.
2. Remove the cowl vent screen. On later models, it is necessary to raise the hood.
3. Remove the wiper arm and blade assemblies.
4. Loosen the nuts which attach the transmission drive links to the motor crank arm.
5. Disconnect the transmission drive links from the motor crank arm.
6. Remove the screws which attach the transmission to the body.
7. Remove the transmission and linkage assembly by guiding it through the plenum chamber opening.
8. To install, position the assembly in the plenum chamber through the opening. Loosely install the attaching screws.
9. Install the drive links on the motor crank arm and tighten the attaching nuts.
NOTE: *Wiper motor must be in the park position.*
10. Align the transmissions, and tighten the attaching screws.
11. Reinstall the wiper arms and blades.

Instrument Cluster
REMOVAL AND INSTALLATION

1970-77

The instrument cluster on these models is not removed as a unit, instead each gauge is removed individually once the cluster bezel and lens are removed.

When removing the speedometer it's necessary to disconnect the shift indicator cable from the steering column on most models.
NOTE: *Always disconnect the battery before removal of any electrical gauges.*

1978 AND LATER

1. Disconnect the battery.
2. Disconnect the speedometer at the transducer on models equipped with air conditioning.
3. Remove the instrument cluster pad assembly.
4. Remove the steering column trim cover.

5. Remove the indicator clip from the steering column shift bowl.

6. Remove the four screws holding the instrument cluster to the panel adapter.

7. Pull the instrument cluster assembly rearward far enough to reach behind the cluster and disconnect the speedometer cable.

8. Disconnect the vehicle speed sensor, if so equipped.

9. Remove the instrument cluster.

10. Installation is the reverse of removal.

Speedometer Cable

REPLACEMENT

1. Reach up underneath the instrument panel and disconnect the cable housing from the cluster housing. On some models you might first have to remove the left air conditioning duct.

2. Carefully pull the cable housing down and pull out the cable.

3. Hold the cable vertically and turn it slowly between you fingers. If it is kinked, you will notice it flopping around. Replace any kinked cable.

4. If the cable is broken, raise and support the car. Disconnect the cable housing from the transmission, remove the gear and pull the cable from the cable housing.

5. Install the new cable in the cable housing after thoroughly lubricating it.

LIGHTING

Headlights

REMOVAL AND INSTALLATION

1. Unscrew the four retaining screws and remove the headlight bezel.

2. Remove the headlight bulb retaining screws. These are the screws which hold the retaining ring for the bulb to the front of the car. Do not touch the two headlight aiming screws, at the top of the side of the retaining ring (these screws will have different heads), or the headlight aim will have to be re-adjusted.

3. Pull the bulb and ring forward and then separate them. Unplug the electrical connector from the rear of the bulb.

4. Plug the new bulb into the electrical connector. Install the bulb into the retaining ring and then install the ring and the bulb. Install the headlight bezel.

Headlight Switch

REMOVAL AND INSTALLATION

1970-77

1. Disconnect the battery.

2. On A/C equipped models remove the L.H. control panel.

3. On models without A/C remove the steering column trim cover.

4. Disconnect the multiple connector from the switch.

5. Pull the switch knob to the last notch and depress the spring loaded latch button on top of the switch while pulling the knob and rod out of the switch. 6.Remove the escutcheon and the switch.

5. Installation is the reverse of removal.

1978 AND LATER

1. Disconnect the negative battery cable.

2. Remove the cluster pad assembly.

3. Remove the two headlamp switch retaining screws.

4. Pull the switch away from the panel adapter to remove.

CIRCUIT PROTECTION

Fusible Links

All models are equipped with fusible links. These links are attached to the lower ends of the main supply wires and connect to the starter solenoid. One of the main wires is a No. 12 red wire which supplies the headlight circuit and the other is a No. 10 red wire which supplies all electrical units except the headlights. The links consist of wire which is several gages smaller than the supply wires they are connected to and function as additional protection to the wiring in the event of an overloaded or short circuited condition in that they will melt before the wiring insulation is damaged elsewhere in the circuit. A burned out fusible link would be indicated by: All the electrical accessories dead except the headlights or, headlights dead but all other electrical units operative.

REPLACEMENT

1. Disconnect the battery ground cable.

2. Disconnect the fusible link from the junction block or starter solenoid.

3. Cut the harness directly behind the connector to remove the damaged fusible link.

4. Strip the harness wire approximately ½".

5. Connect the new fusible link to the harness wire using a crimp on connector. Solder the connection using resin core solder.

6. Tape all exposed wires with plastic electrical tape.

7. Connect the fusible link to the junction block or starter solenoid and reconnect the battery ground cable.

Fuses and Flashers

The fuse block on all models is located under the left hand side of the instrument panel. All

REMOVE EXISTING VINYL TUBE SHIELDING
REINSTALL OVER FUSE LINK BEFORE CRIMPING
FUSE LINK TO WIRE ENDS

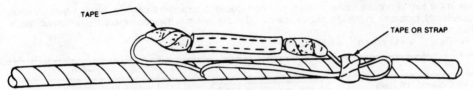

TAPE

TAPE OR STRAP

TYPICAL REPAIR USING THE SPECIAL #17 GA. (9.00" LONG-YELLOW) FUSE LINK REQUIRED FOR THE AIR/COND.
CIRCUITS (2) #687E and #261A LOCATED IN THE ENGINE COMPARTMENT

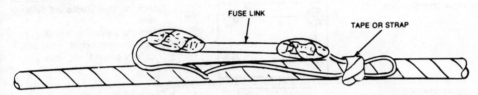

FUSE LINK

TAPE OR STRAP

TYPICAL REPAIR FOR ANY IN-LINE FUSE LINK USING THE SPECIFIED GAUGE FUSE LINK FOR THE SPECIFIC CIRCUIT

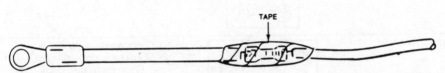

TAPE

TYPICAL REPAIR USING THE EYELET TERMINAL FUSE LINK OF THE SPECIFIED GAUGE FOR ATTACHMENT TO A CIRCUIT WIRE END

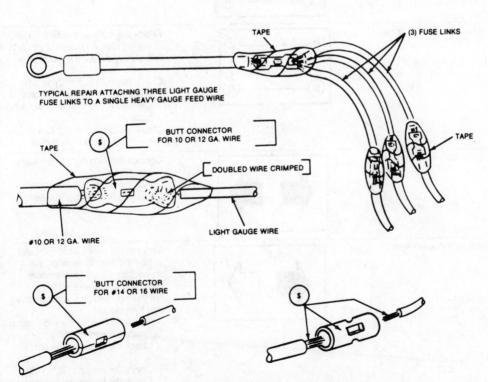

TAPE

(3) FUSE LINKS

TYPICAL REPAIR ATTACHING THREE LIGHT GAUGE
FUSE LINKS TO A SINGLE HEAVY GAUGE FEED WIRE

BUTT CONNECTOR
FOR 10 OR 12 GA. WIRE

$

TAPE

DOUBLED WIRE CRIMPED

TAPE

#10 OR 12 GA. WIRE

LIGHT GAUGE WIRE

'BUTT CONNECTOR
FOR #14 OR 16 WIRE

$

$

FUSIBLE LINK REPAIR PROCEDURE

General fuse link repair procedure

Troubleshooting Basic Turn Signal and Flasher Problems

Most problems in the turn signals or flasher system, can be reduced to defective flashers or bulbs, which are easily replaced. Occasionally, problems in the turn signals are traced to the switch in the steering column, which will require professional service.

F = Front   R = Rear   ● = Lights off   o = Lights on

Problem		Solution
Turn signals light, but do not flash		• Replace the flasher
No turn signals light on either side		• Check the fuse. Replace if defective. • Check the flasher by substitution • Check for open circuit, short circuit or poor ground
Both turn signals on one side don't work		• Check for bad bulbs • Check for bad ground in both housings
One turn signal light on one side doesn't work		• Check and/or replace bulb • Check for corrosion in socket. Clean contacts. • Check for poor ground at socket
Turn signal flashes too fast or too slow		• Check any bulb on the side flashing too fast. A heavy-duty bulb is probably installed in place of a regular bulb. • Check the bulb flashing too slow. A standard bulb was probably installed in place of a heavy-duty bulb. • Check for loose connections or corrosion at the bulb socket
Indicator lights don't work in either direction		• Check if the turn signals are working • Check the dash indicator lights • Check the flasher by substitution

One indicator light doesn't light		• On systems with 1 dash indicator: See if the lights work on the same side. Often the filaments have been reversed in systems combining stoplights with taillights and turn signals.
		  Check the flasher by substitution
		• On systems with 2 indicators: Check the bulbs on the same side
		  Check the indicator light bulb
		  Check the flasher by substitution

Troubleshooting Basic Lighting Problems

Problem	Cause	Solution
Lights		
One or more lights don't work, but others do	• Defective bulb(s) • Blown fuse(s) • Dirty fuse clips or light sockets • Poor ground circuit	• Replace bulb(s) • Replace fuse(s) • Clean connections • Run ground wire from light socket housing to car frame
Lights burn out quickly	• Incorrect voltage regulator setting or defective regulator • Poor battery/alternator connections	• Replace voltage regulator • Check battery/alternator connections
Lights go dim	• Low/discharged battery • Alternator not charging • Corroded sockets or connections • Low voltage output	• Check battery • Check drive belt tension; repair or replace alternator • Clean bulb and socket contacts and connections • Replace voltage regulator
Lights flicker	• Loose connection • Poor ground • Circuit breaker operating (short circuit)	• Tighten all connections • Run ground wire from light housing to car frame • Check connections and look for bare wires
Lights "flare"—Some flare is normal on acceleration—if excessive, see "Lights Burn Out Quickly"	• High voltage setting	• Replace voltage regulator
Lights glare—approaching drivers are blinded	• Lights adjusted too high • Rear springs or shocks sagging • Rear tires soft	• Have headlights aimed • Check rear springs/shocks • Check/correct rear tire pressure
Turn Signals		
Turn signals don't work in either direction	• Blown fuse • Defective flasher • Loose connection	• Replace fuse • Replace flasher • Check/tighten all connections
Right (or left) turn signal only won't work	• Bulb burned out • Right (or left) indicator bulb burned out • Short circuit	• Replace bulb • Check/replace indicator bulb • Check/repair wiring
Flasher rate too slow or too fast	• Incorrect wattage bulb • Incorrect flasher	• Flasher bulb • Replace flasher (use a variable load flasher if you pull a trailer)
Indicator lights do not flash (burn steadily)	• Burned out bulb • Defective flasher	• Replace bulb • Replace flasher
Indicator lights do not light at all	• Burned out indicator bulb • Defective flasher	• Replace indicator bulb • Replace flasher

Troubleshooting Basic Dash Gauge Problems

Problem	Cause	Solution
Coolant Temperature Gauge		
Gauge reads erratically or not at all	• Loose or dirty connections • Defective sending unit	• Clean/tighten connections • Bi-metal gauge: remove the wire from the sending unit. Ground the wire for an instant. If the gauge registers, replace the sending unit.

Troubleshooting Basic Dash Gauge Problems (cont.)

Problem	Cause	Solution
Coolant Temperature Gauge		
Gauge reads erratically or not at all	• Defective gauge	• Magnetic gauge: disconnect the wire at the sending unit. With ignition ON gauge should register COLD. Ground the wire; gauge should register HOT.
Ammeter Gauge—Turn Headlights ON (do not start engine). Note reaction		
Ammeter shows charge	• Connections reversed on gauge	• Reinstall connections
Ammeter shows discharge	• Ammeter is OK	• Nothing
Ammeter does not move	• Loose connections or faulty wiring	• Check/correct wiring
	• Defective gauge	• Replace gauge
Oil Pressure Gauge		
Gauge does not register or is inaccurate	• On mechanical gauge, Bourdon tube may be bent or kinked	• Check tube for kinks or bends preventing oil from reaching the gauge
	• Low oil pressure	• Remove sending unit. Idle the engine briefly. If no oil flows from sending unit hole, problem is in engine.
	• Defective gauge	• Remove the wire from the sending unit and ground it for an instant with the ignition ON. A good gauge will go to the top of the scale.
	• Defective wiring	• Check the wiring to the gauge. If it's OK and the gauge doesn't register when grounded, replace the gauge.
	• Defective sending unit	• If the wiring is OK and the gauge functions when grounded, replace the sending unit
All Gauges		
All gauges do not operate	• Blown fuse	• Replace fuse
	• Defective instrument regulator	• Replace instrument voltage regulator
All gauges read low or erratically	• Defective or dirty instrument voltage regulator	• Clean contacts or replace
All gauges pegged	• Loss of ground between instrument voltage regulator and car	• Check ground
	• Defective instrument regulator	• Replace regulator
Warning Lights		
Light(s) do not come on when ignition is ON, but engine is not started	• Defective bulb	• Replace bulb
	• Defective wire	• Check wire from light to sending unit
	• Defective sending unit	• Disconnect the wire from the sending unit and ground it. Replace the sending unit if the light comes on with the ignition ON.
Light comes on with engine running	• Problem in individual system	• Check system
	• Defective sending unit	• Check sending unit (see above)

flashers are mounted on the fuse block. Each fuse is marked on the fuse block as to which circuit it is protecting. Some early models also use an in-line 30 amp. fuse for the air conditioning hi blower, located at the cowl relay and an in-line 10 amp. fuse for power antennas.

To determine whether a fuse is blow, remove the suspect fuse and check to see if the element is broken. If so replace the fuse with one of equal amperage value.

Circuit Breakers.

Circuit breakers are also located in the fuse block. A circuit breaker is an electrical switch which breaks the circuit during an electrical overload. The circuit breaker will remain open

Troubleshooting the Heater

Problem	Cause	Solution
Blower motor will not turn at any speed	• Blown fuse • Loose connection • Defective ground • Faulty switch • Faulty motor • Faulty resistor	• Replace fuse • Inspect and tighten • Clean and tighten • Replace switch • Replace motor • Replace resistor
Blower motor turns at one speed only	• Faulty switch • Faulty resistor	• Replace switch • Replace resistor
Blower motor turns but does not circulate air	• Intake blocked • Fan not secured to the motor shaft	• Clean intake • Tighten security
Heater will not heat	• Coolant does not reach proper temperature • Heater core blocked internally • Heater core air-bound • Blend-air door not in proper position	• Check and replace thermostat if necessary • Flush or replace core if necessary • Purge air from core • Adjust cable
Heater will not defrost	• Control cable adjustment incorrect • Defroster hose damaged	• Adjust control cable • Replace defroster hose

Troubleshooting Basic Windshield Wiper Problems

Problem	Cause	Solution
Electric Wipers		
Wipers do not operate— Wiper motor heats up or hums	• Internal motor defect • Bent or damaged linkage • Arms improperly installed on linking pivots	• Replace motor • Repair or replace linkage • Position linkage in park and reinstall wiper arms
Wipers do not operate— No current to motor	• Fuse or circuit breaker blown • Loose, open or broken wiring • Defective switch • Defective or corroded terminals • No ground circuit for motor or switch	• Replace fuse or circuit breaker • Repair wiring and connections • Replace switch • Replace or clean terminals • Repair ground circuits
Wipers do not operate— Motor runs	• Linkage disconnected or broken	• Connect wiper linkage or replace broken linkage
Vacuum Wipers		
Wipers do not operate	• Control switch or cable inoperative • Loss of engine vacuum to wiper motor (broken hoses, low engine vacuum, defective vacuum/fuel pump) • Linkage broken or disconnected • Defective wiper motor	• Repair or replace switch or cable • Check vacuum lines, engine vacuum and fuel pump • Repair linkage • Replace wiper motor
Wipers stop on engine acceleration	• Leaking vacuum hoses • Dry windshield • Oversize wiper blades • Defective vacuum/fuel pump	• Repair or replace hoses • Wet windshield with washers • Replace with proper size wiper blades • Replace pump

until the short or overload condition in the circuit is corrected.

WIRING DIAGRAMS

Wiring diagrams have been left out of this book. As cars have become more complex, and available with longer and longer option lists, wiring diagrams have grown in size and complexity also. It has become virtually impossible to provide a readable reproduction in a reasonable number of pages. Information on ordering wiring diagrams from the vehicle manufacturer can be found in the owner's manual.

Drive Train

+6

MANUAL TRANSMISSION

The 3-speed transmission is the Saginaw unit. The standard 4-speed transmission in all models is also a Saginaw unit. The optional heavy-duty 4-speed offered in the Cutlass through 1973 is the Muncie transmission. On the Saginaw, all three shift rods go to levers on the side cover, while on the Muncie, one rod (reverse) goes to a lever on the case extension housing. The 5-speed transmission is the Warner T-50 unit. There is no shift linkage adjustment necessary or possible on the GM 70 mm 4-speed or the Warner T-50 5-speed.

See the Capacities Table for manual transmission refill capacities.
No manual transmission was offered in 1982.

Linkage

ADJUSTMENT

3-Speed Column Shift 1970-77

1. Place the transmission in reverse.
2. Raise the car in the air and support it with jackstands.
3. Loosen the swivel bolts on the shift rods at the transmission. Make sure the shift rods are free to move in the swivels.

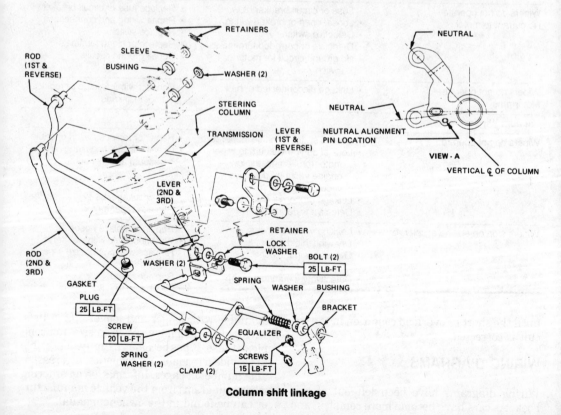

Column shift linkage

4. Push up on the reverse shift rod until the detent in the column is felt and tighten the swivel bolt for the first/reversed rod.

5. Place the transmission in neutral and insert a $\frac{3}{16}$" rod through the 2-3 shift lever and into the alignment hole. Tighten the swivel bolt at the transmission.

6. Lower the car. Check the shifter operation. Place the shifter in reverse, and the ignition switch in the lock position. Make sure the ignition key can be removed and that the steering wheel will not turn.

3-Speed Column Shift From 1978

1. Turn the ignition switch to Off.
2. Raise and support the car.
3. Remove the retainer from the shift rods.
4. Place the transmission levers in Neutral.
5. Align the control levers and place a ¼" gauge pin into the levers and brackets, with the shift handle in Neutral.
6. Loosen the nuts on the shift rods and adjust the trunnion and pin assembly on First/Reverse, then tighten the nuts and install the shift rod and retainer.
7. Loosen the shift rod nut and adjust the trunnion and pin assembly on Second/Third, then tighten the nuts and install the shift rod and retainer.
8. Remove the gauge pin from the control lever assembly and check the operation of the control lever. Readjust as required.
9. Lower the car.

3-Speed Floor Shift

1. Place the transmission in reverse, and the ignition switch in the lock position.
2. Raise the car in the air and support it with jackstands.

NOTE: *Do not place the shifter in reverse from below.*

3. Loosen the swivel bolt on the back drive rod at the equalizer. Make sure the rod moves freely in the swivel.
4. Pull down lightly on the back drive rod until a stop is felt. Tighten the swivel bolt.
5. Place the shifter in neutral, and loosen the jam nuts at the shifter assembly.
6. Insert a ¼" pin through the shift lever brackets and levers as shown in the illustration. Adjust the swivels to obtain a "free pin" fit at the levers.
7. Tighten the jam nuts.
8. Lower the car and check the shifter operation.

4-Speed Floor Shift 1978-80

1. Turn the ignition switch to the Off position.
2. Raise and support the car.
3. Loosen the lock nuts at the swivels on the shift rods.
4. Set the transmission levers in Neutral.
5. Place the shifter in Neutral.
6. Align the control levers and place a ¼" gauge pin into the levers and brackets.

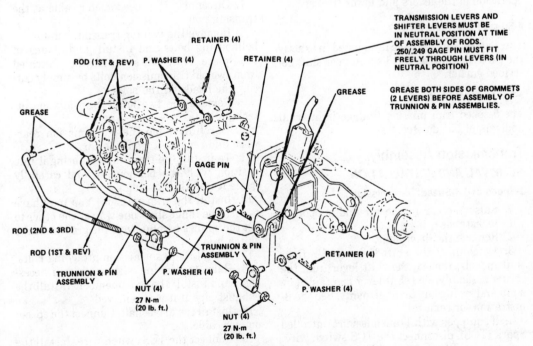

TRANSMISSION LEVERS AND SHIFTER LEVERS MUST BE IN NEUTRAL POSITION AT TIME OF ASSEMBLY OF RODS. .250/.249 GAGE PIN MUST FIT FREELY THROUGH LEVERS (IN NEUTRAL POSITION)

GREASE BOTH SIDES OF GROMMETS (2 LEVERS) BEFORE ASSEMBLY OF TRUNNION & PIN ASSEMBLIES.

RETAINER (4)
ROD (1ST & REV)
P. WASHER (4)
RETAINER (4)
GREASE
GREASE
GAGE PIN
ROD (2ND & 3RD)
ROD (1ST & REV)
TRUNNION & PIN ASSEMBLY
TRUNNION & PIN ASSEMBLY
P. WASHER (4)
RETAINER (4)
NUT (4)
27 N·m
(20 lb. ft.)
P. WASHER (4)
NUT (4)
27 N·m
(20 lb. ft.)

Three-speed floorshift linkage

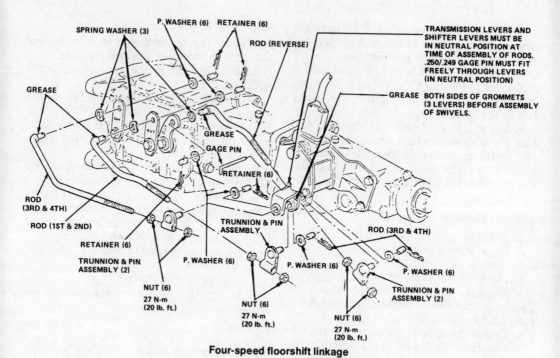

SPRING WASHER (3)   P. WASHER (6)   RETAINER (6)

ROD (REVERSE)

TRANSMISSION LEVERS AND SHIFTER LEVERS MUST BE IN NEUTRAL POSITION AT TIME OF ASSEMBLY OF RODS. .250/.249 GAGE PIN MUST FIT FREELY THROUGH LEVERS (IN NEUTRAL POSITION)

GREASE

GREASE BOTH SIDES OF GROMMETS (3 LEVERS) BEFORE ASSEMBLY OF SWIVELS.

GREASE

GAGE PIN

RETAINER (6)

ROD (3RD & 4TH)

ROD (1ST & 2ND)

RETAINER (6)

TRUNNION & PIN ASSEMBLY

ROD (3RD & 4TH)

TRUNNION & PIN ASSEMBLY (2)

P. WASHER (6)

P. WASHER (6)

P. WASHER (6)

NUT (6) 27 N·m (20 lb. ft.)

NUT (6) 27 N·m (20 lb. ft.)

NUT (6) 27 N·m (20 lb. ft.)

TRUNNION & PIN ASSEMBLY (2)

Four-speed floorshift linkage

7. Tighten the First/Second shift rod nut against the swivel. Torque to 10 ft.lb.

8. Tighten the Third/Fourth shift rod nut against the swivel. Torque to 10 ft.lb.

9. Tighten the reverse shift control rod nut to 10 ft.lb.

10. Remove the gauge pin, check for proper operation of the levers and lower the car.

4-Speed Floor Shift 1970-77

The 4-speed shift linkage is adjusted in exactly the same manner as the 3-speed floor shift described earlier.

5-Speed Floor Shift

The 5-speed transmission linkage is internal and cannot be adjusted.

Transmission Assembly

REMOVAL AND INSTALLATION

3-Speed and 4-Speed Transmission

1. Raise the car in the air and support it with jackstands.

2. Remove the driveshaft.

3. Disconnect the shift linkage. On floor shift models, remove the shift lever from the shifter assembly. The shift lever is retained by a pin and spring clip arrangements. See the illustration for removal.

4. If equipped with Transmission Controlled Spark (TCS), disconnect the TCS switch wire.

5. Support the engine with a jack. Remove the bolts which attach the crossmember to the transmission.

6. Disconnect the parking brake cable, and unbolt the transmission crossmember from the frame. On dual exhaust models, if may be necessary to disconnect the left hand exhaust pipe at exhaust manifold to provide clearance.

7. Disconnect the speedometer cable at the transmission.

8. Remove the two top transmission-to-bellhousing bolts and install guide studs in their place. The guide studs may be fabricated from two old transmission bolts by simply cutting the heads off the bolts.

9. Remove the two lower transmission attaching bolts.

10. Carefully slide the transmission rearward and remove it from the car.

11. To install the transmission, bring it into position with the bellhousing and carefully guide it into the housing.

12. Install the transmission. You may have to turn the input shaft one way or the other to get the splines to mate with the grooves in the clutch hub.

13. Install the transmission attaching bolts.

14. Raise the engine with the jack if necessary, and install the crossmember. Install the exhaust pipe if it was removed.

15. Install the driveshaft. Connect the speedometer cable.

16. Connect the TCS switch wire. Install the shift lever or shift linkage.

5-Speed Transmission

1. Remove the shift control knob, the shift boot retainer, shift boot, and insulator.

2. Pull back the edge of the carpeting and remove the bolts that attach the shifter assembly and remove the assembly.

3. Raise the car in the air and support it with jackstands.

4. Remove the driveshaft.

5. Disconnect the speedometer cable. Remove the catalytic converter support bracket.

6. Support the engine with a jack and remove the bolts which attach the crossmember to the transmission. Unbolt the crossmember from the frame and remove it from the car.

7. Remove the two upper bolts which attach the transmission to the bellhousing. Install guide pins in their place. These may be made from a pair of old transmission bolts with the heads cut off. Guide pins are necessary to prevent distortion of the clutch plate when the two lower bolts are removed. If no guide pins are available, support the transmission in some way before removing the two lower bolts.

8. Remove the two lower bolts and slide the transmission out of the bellhousing.

9. To install the transmission, bring it into position with the bellhousing and carefully guide it into the housing. It will probably be necessary to turn the input shaft one way or the other to get the splines to mate with the grooves in the clutch hub.

10. Reinstall the crossmember.

11. Install the driveshaft and the speedometer cable. Reinstall the catalytic converter support bracket.

12. Install the shifter.

CLUTCH

A single plate dry disc-type clutch is used on all cars. The only exception to this are the early 4-4-2-models which could be ordered with a dual disc clutch assembly. The clutch pressure plate is of the disc spring type. There is an overcenter effect inherent in the action of the disc spring itself, eliminating the need for an overcenter assist spring. Pressure plate spring pressure forces the clutch driven plate against the flywheel, thereby coupling the engine to the transmission.

The clutch linkage mechanism consists of a clutch release bearing, and the appropriate linkage to manually connect the bearing release arm to the clutch pedal.

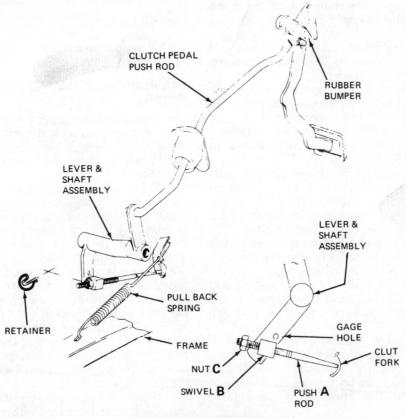

Clutch linkage adjustment

FREE PLAY ADJUSTMENT

1. Total clutch pedal free play should be between ¾″ and 1″. The free play is adjusted by means of a threaded rod which rides in the outer end of the throwout bearing arm.

2. To adjust the free play, first remove the pedal return spring.

3. Loosen the locknut on the equalizer rod (the threaded rod).

4. Adjust the rod length by turning the rod. When the release bearing (throwout bearing) is just lightly resting on the fingers of the pressure plate, the adjustment should be just about right.

5. Check the clutch pedal free play. There should be no more than one inch of free play before resistance is encountered. If there is too much free play, the clutch will not engage fully. If there is too little, the pressure plate will ride against the clutch all the time and the clutch will wear out quickly.

6. Tighten the lock rod nut and install the return spring.

REMOVAL AND INSTALLATION

1. Remove the transmission as previously outlined.

2. Disconnect the clutch return spring and the clutch rod assembly. Remove the throwout bearing.

3. Remove the bellhousing. The starter does not have to be removed. The clutch release arm can stay in the housing.

4. Scribe an **X** mark on the flywheel opposite the mark on the pressure plate cover. The marks are there for balance purposes.

5. Remove the pressure plate attaching bolts, and remove the pressure plate and the clutch assembly.

6. To install the clutch and pressure plate assembly, you will need a clutch alignment tool or an old input shaft. During installation, be very careful not to get grease on the clutch disc, the flywheel or the pressure plate.

7. Install the clutch disc and pressure plate assembly, being careful to align the **X** marks. Install the attaching bolts loosely.

8. Align the clutch disc using an alignment tool or an old input shaft. Leave the alignment tool in place while you tighten the attaching bolts.

9. Tighten the attaching bolts using the illustration as a guide. Tighten the three bolts marked **L** first. Tighten all the bolts to 30 ft.lb.

10. Reinstall the bellhousing.

11. Install the throwout bearing (release bearing).

12. Install the transmission.

Dual-Disc Clutch Assembly

Removal and Installation of the dual-disc clutch assembly is the same as that of the single disc clutch. However, during disassembly, be careful to note which way the two driven plates and the front pressure plate are installed, as it is possible to install them backwards.

AUTOMATIC TRANSMISSION

Identification

Many different automatic transmission have been used in rear wheel drive models. Basically, all of the transmission used fall into 3 basic groups, as follows:

• **THM-200 GROUP**	
THM-200	3S-standard duty
THM-200-C	3S-LTC
THM-200-4R	4S-LTC
• **THM-350 GROUP**	
THM-250	3S-light duty
THM-350	3S-standard duty
THM-350-C	3S-LTC
THM-375-B	3S-heavy duty
• **THM-400 GROUP**	
THM-400	3S-heavy duty

3S-3 speed
4S-4 speed
LTC-Locking torque convertor

PAN REMOVAL, FLUID AND FILTER CHANGE

The fluid should be changed with the engine and transmission at normal operating temperature. If the car is raised, the transmission should be level. Be careful when draining, because the fluid will be hot.

1. Raise and safely support the vehicle.

2. On some models, it may be necessary to remove the transmission supporting crossmember in order to gain access to all of the pan bolts. Support the transmission with a jack before removing the crossmember.

3. Place a large pan underneath the transmission to catch the fluid. Loosen all the pan screws, then pull down one corner to drain most of the fluid. Be careful, the fluid will be hot. Do not pry between the pan and the transmission with a screwdriver or the like to remove the pan, as this will damage the mating surfaces. The pan can be tapped with a rubber mallet to loosen its grip.

4. Remove the pan screws and empty out the pan. The pan can be cleaned with solvent but it must be air dried thoroughly before replace-

ment. Be very careful not to leave any lint or threads from rags in the pan.

NOTE: *It is normal to find a SMALL amount of metal shavings in the pan. An excessive amount of metal shavings indicates transmission damage which must be professionally investigated.*

5. Remove the filter or strainer retaining bolt (two on the Turbo Hydra-Matic 200, 250 and 350). A reuseable strainer is used on the Turbo Hydra-Matic, 200 and 250. The strainer may be cleaned in solvent and thoroughly air dried. Filters are to be replace. On the 400, Turbo Hydra-Matic, remove the filter retaining bolt(s), filter, and intake pipe O-ring (or gasket).

6. Install the new filter or cleaned strainer with a new gasket (or O-ring). Tighten the screws to 12 ft.lb. On the 400 install a new intake pipe O-ring and a new filter, tightening the retaining bolts to 10 ft.lb.

7. Install the pan with a new gasket. Tighten the bolts evenly in a crisscross pattern to 12 ft.lb.

8. Replace the crossmember if removed.

9. Lower the car. Add DEXRON®II fluid through the dipstick tube.

10. Start the engine and let it idle. Do not race the engine. Shift into each lever position,

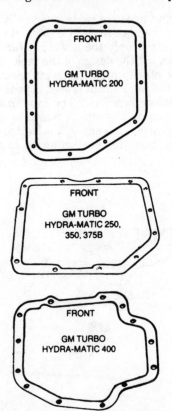

FRONT

GM TURBO
HYDRA-MATIC 200

FRONT

GM TURBO
HYDRA-MATIC 250,
350, 375B

FRONT

GM TURBO
HYDRA-MATIC 400

Identifying automatic transmission by pan gasket

holding the brakes. Check the fluid level with the engine idling in park. The level should be between the two dimples on the dipstick, about ¼" below the ADD mark. Add fluid as necessary.

11. Check the fluid level after the car has been driven enough to thoroughly warm up the transmission. The level should be at the FULL mark on the dipstick. If the transmission is overfilled, the excess must be drained off. Overfilling causes aerated fluid, resulting in transmission slippage and probable damage.

INTERMEDIATE BAND ADJUSTMENT

Only the THM250 has an externally adjustable band. Band adjustments are not externally possible on other transmissions. The intermediate band must be adjusted with every required fluid change or whenever there is slippage.

1. Position the shift lever in Neutral.

2. Loosen the locknut on the right side of the transmission. Tighten the adjusting screw to 30 in.lb.

3. Back the screw out three turns and then tighten the locknut to 15 ft.lb.

NEUTRAL SAFETY SWITCH ADJUSTMENT

The neutral safety switch prevents the engine from being started in any transmission position except Neutral or Park. The switch is located on the upper side of the steering column under the instrument panel on column shift cars and inside the shift console on floor shift models.

Colunm-Mounted Switch

1. Place the shifter in Neutral.

2. Loosen the screws which secure the switch.

3. Fit a 0.090" gauge pin into the outer hole on the switch cover.

4. Move the switch until the gauge pin drops into the alignment hole on the inner slide. Tighten the switch securing screws. Remove the gauge pin.

Console-Mounted Switch

1. Place the shifter in Park.

2. Remove the center console.

3. Loosen the switch securing screws.

4. Fit a 0.090" gauge pin into the outer hole on the switch cover.

5. Move the switch until the gauge pin drops into the alignment hole on the inner slide. Tighten the switch securing screws.

6. Remove the gauge pin. Check to make sure the car will only start in Neutral or Park.

SHIFT LINKAGE ADJUSTMENT

Column Shift

1. Place the shift lever in Neutral.

2. Loosen the shift rod clamp screw and make sure the lever on the transmission is in the Neutral position. Have someone move the shift lever through the gears while you watch the lever on the transmission, if you are unsure as to which position is the Neutral position.

3. With the lever on the transmission in the Neutral position and the shift lever on the column being held against the Neutral stop (do not raise the lever), tighten the shift rod clamp screw to 23 ft.lb.

4. Check the operation of the shifter.

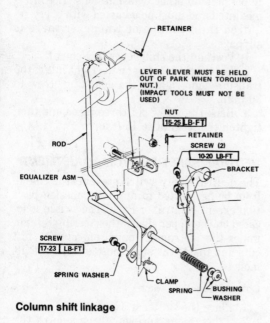

Column shift linkage

Console Shift

1. Place the shift lever in the Park position.

2. The ignition key must be in the Lock position.

3. Make sure the lever on the transmission is in the Park position.

4. Loosen the shift rod clamp screw. See the illustration.

5. Loosen the pin in the lever on the transmission.

6. Pull the shift rod lightly against the lock stop at the shifter and tighten the clamp screw.

7. Adjust the pin at the transmission lever for a "free pin" fit, and tighten the attaching nut.

8. Check the operation of the shifter.

THROTTLE VALVE (TV) OR DETENT CABLE ADJUSTMENT

Gas Engine Models Only

On all transmissions except the THM250, THM350 and THM400 models, a TV cable is used to control hydraulic pressures, shift points, shift feel, and downshifting. The THM250 and THM350 use a detent cable.

NOTE: *THM400 models use an electrical detent (downshift) switch. Adjustment of this switch is covered separately, after cable adjustment.*

Though the detent cable is virtually identical in appearance to the TV cable, the detent cable controls only the downshift function of the cable, not the design of the cable itself.

Before attempting adjustment, identify the style of the cable which is used in your vehicle (Type One or Type Two). The Type One Cable uses a snap-lock assembly which is integral with the cable. The snap-lock is located next to the cable mounting bracket at the engine. In

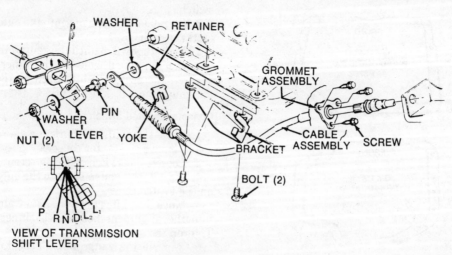

Console shift linkage

its normal position, the snap-lock is pushed fully downward (locked) so that it is flush with the snap-lock assembly. Adjustment is made with the snap lock in the raised (unlocked) position, as outlined in the Type One adjustment procedure.

The Type Two cable uses a different type of locking mechanism. Though it is located in the same position as the Type One snaplock, the Type Two lock tab is set when released (upward) and adjusted when pushed downward (unlocked). On 1981 and earlier models, the Type Two cable can be easily identified by the presence of a spring, visible beneath the lock tab. The spring is not exposed on 1982 and later cable assemblies. Refer to the Type Two adjusting procedure to adjust the cable.

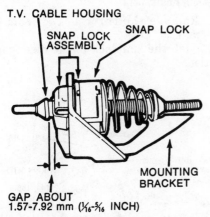

T.V. CABLE HOUSING

SNAP LOCK ASSEMBLY

SNAP LOCK

MOUNTING BRACKET

GAP ABOUT 1.57-7.92 mm (1/16-5/16 INCH)

Turbo Hydra-Matic 200 throttle valve adjustment

TYPE ONE

1. Remove the engine air cleaner assembly.
2. Push up on the bottom of the snaplock at the cable bracket. Make sure that the cable is free to slide through the snaplock.
3. Move the carburetor lever to the wide open throttle position and hold it there.
4. Push the snap-lock flush and let the lever return to the closed position.
5. If the adjustment does not correct late shifting or no part throttle downshift, a transmission fluid pressure test should be made by a qualified mechanic.

TYPE TWO

1. Depress and hold the metal lock tab on the TV cable.
2. Move the slider back through the fitting in the direction away from the throttle body until the slider stops against fitting.
3. Release the metal lock tab.
4. Open the throttle lever to full throttle stop position. This will automatically adjust the slider on the cable to the correct setting.

DETENT SWITCH ADJUSTMENT

Turbo Hydra-Matic 400 transmissions are equipped with an electrical detent, or downshift switch operated by the throttle linkage.

1. Pull the detent switch driver rearward until the hole in the switch body aligns with the hole in the driver. Insert a 0.092″ diameter pin through the aligned holes to hold the driver in position.
2. Loosen the switch plunger as far forward

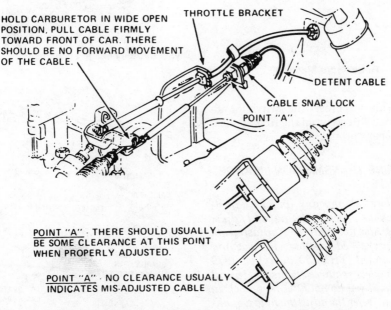

HOLD CARBURETOR IN WIDE OPEN POSITION, PULL CABLE FIRMLY TOWARD FRONT OF CAR. THERE SHOULD BE NO FORWARD MOVEMENT OF THE CABLE.

THROTTLE BRACKET

DETENT CABLE

CABLE SNAP LOCK

POINT "A"

POINT "A" - THERE SHOULD USUALLY BE SOME CLEARANCE AT THIS POINT WHEN PROPERLY ADJUSTED.

POINT "A" - NO CLEARANCE USUALLY INDICATES MIS-ADJUSTED CABLE

Typical downshift cable adjustment—Turbo Hydra-Matic 200

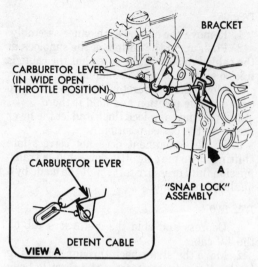

Typical detent cable adjustment—Turbo Hydra-Matic 200, 250, and 350

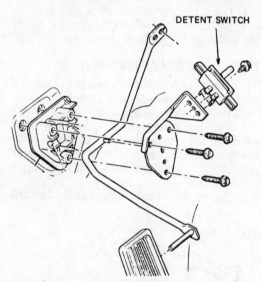

Detent switch—Turbo Hydra-Matic 400

as possible. This will preset the switch for adjustment, which will occur on the first application of wide open throttle.

DIESEL ENGINE TRANSMISSION LINKAGE ADJUSTMENTS

NOTE: *Before making any linkage adjustments, check the injection timing, and adjust if necessary. Also note that these adjustments should be performed together. The vacuum valve adjustment (THM350's only) on 1979 and later models requires the use of several special tools. If you do not have these tools at your disposal, refer the adjustment to a qualified, professional technician.*

Throttle Rod Adjustment

1. If equipped with cruise control, remove the clip from the control rod, then remove the rod from the bellcrank.

2. Remove the throttle valve cable (THM200) or detent cable (THM350) from the bellcrank.

3. Loosen the locknut on the throttle rod, then shorten the rod several turns.

4. Rotate the bellcrank to the full throttle stop, then lengthen the throttle rod until the injection pump lever contacts the injection pump full throttle stop. Release the bell-crank.

5. Tighten the throttle rod locknut.

6. Connect the throttle valve or detent cable and cruise control rod to the bellcrank. Adjust if necessary.

Throttle Valve Cable (THM200) or Detent Cable (THM350) Adjustment

1. Remove the throttle rod from the bell-crank.

2. Push the snaplock to the disengaged position.

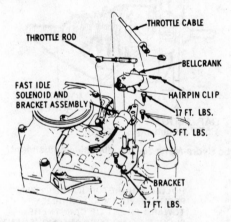

Diesel throttle linkage adjustment

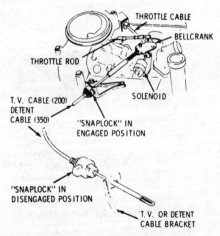

Diesel throttle valve cable adjustment

3. Rotate the bellcrank to the full throttle stop and hold it there.

4. Push in the snaplock until it is flush with the cable end fitting. Release the bellcrank.

5. Reconnect the throttle.

Transmission Vacuum Valve Adjustment

1981 AND LATER MODELS

1. Remove the air cleaner assembly.

2. Remove the air intake crossover from the intake manifold. Cover the intake manifold passages to prevent foreign material from entering the engine.

3. Disconnect the throttle rod from the injection pump throttle lever.

4. Loosen the transmission vacuum valve-to-injection pump bolts.

5. Mark and disconnect the vacuum lines from the vacuum valve.

6. Attach a carburetor angle gauge adapter (Kent-Moore tool J-26701-15 or its equivalent)

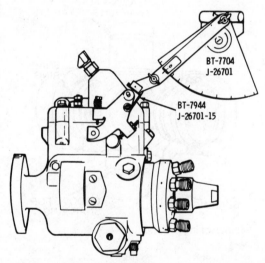

Vacuum regulator valve with an angle gauge attached and set to zero degrees

to the injection pump throttle lever. Attach an angle gauge (J-26701 or its equivalent) to the gauge adapter.

NOTE: *To service the V6 diesel, it may be necessary to file the gauge adapter in order for it to fit the thicker throttle lever of the V6 injection pump.*

7. Turn the throttle lever to the wide open throttle position. Set the angle gauge to zero degrees.

8. Center the bubble in the gauge level.

9. Set the angle gauge to one of the following setting, according to the year and type of engine:

Year	Engine	Setting
1981	V8—Calif.	49–50°
1981	V8—non-Calif.	58°
1982–83	V8	58°
All	V6	49°

10. Tighten the vacuum valve retaining bolts.

11. Reconnect the original vacuum lines to the vacuum valve.

12. Remove the angle gauge and adapter.

13. Connect the throttle rod to the throttle lever.

14. Install the air intake crossover, using new gaskets.

15. Install the air cleaner assembly.

TRANSMISSION REMOVAL AND INSTALLATION

1. Disconnect the negative battery cable at the battery.

2. If so equipped, disconnect the detent/downshift cable at its upper end (accelerator pedal or carburetor).

3. Raise the vehicle and support it safely with jackstands. Preferably, the front AND rear of the vehicle should be raised to provide adequate clearance for transmission removal.

4. Disconnect the exhaust crossover pipe at the manifold, if exhaust system-to-transmission interference is obvious. It may be necessary to remove the catalytic converter, exhaust pipe, or just the brackets in order to clear the transmission.

CAUTION: *Exhaust system services must be performed while all components are COLD.*

5. Remove the transmission inspection cover.

6. Remove the torque converter-to-flywheel bolts. The relationship between the flywheel and converter must be marked so that proper balance is maintained after installation.

7. Matchmark the propeller shaft and the rear yoke (for reinstallation purposes). With a drain pan positioned under the front yoke, unbolt and remove the propeller shaft.

8. Mark and disconnect the vacuum lines, wiring, and speedometer cable from the transmission, as required.

9. Place a transmission jack (carefully) up against the transmission oil pan, then secure the transmission to the jack.

10. Remove the transmission mounting pad bolt(s), then carefully raise the transmission just enough to take the weight of the transmission off of the supporting crossmember.

CAUTION: *Exercise extreme care to avoid damage to the underhood components while raising or lowering the transmission.*

11. Unbolt and remove the transmission crossmember, complete with the mount. It may be necessary to raise or lower the transmission a small amount to remove the crossmember.

12. Remove the transmission dipstick, then unbolt and remove the filler tube.

13. Disconnect the shift linkage (or cable on floor shift-equipped models) and oil cooler lines from the transmission.

14. Support the engine using a jackstand placed beneath the engine oil pan. Be sure to put a block of wood between the jackstand and the oil pan, to prevent damage to the pan.

15. Securely wire the torque converter to the transmission case.

16. Remove the transmission-to-engine mounting bolts, then carefully move the transmission rearward, downward, and out from beneath the vehicle.

CAUTION: *If interference is encountered with the cable(s), cooler lines, etc., remove the components(s), before finally lowering the transmission.*

Refer to the Automatic Transmission segment of the Unit Repair Section for further information.

Installation is basically the reverse of the previous steps. Note the following points during and after installation.

1. Torque the transmission-to-engine mounting bolts to 30-40 ft.lb.

2. Align the matchmarks of the propeller shaft with the marks of the rear yoke before installing the joint straps and bolts.

3. Align the convertor and flywheel markings before installing the convertor bolts.

4. Add the proper type and quantity of transmission fluid. If the convertor was replaced, an additional 4 pints (approx.) should be added. NEVER overfill the transmission.

5. Adjust the shift linkage (or cable) and the detent/downshift cable.

6. Make sure that the vacuum lines, electrical connections, and oil cooler line connections are secure before driving the vehicle.

7. Check for fluid leakage, then after the transmission is hot, recheck the fluid level.

DRIVELINE

Driveshaft and U-Joints

REMOVAL AND INSTALLATION

1. Raise the vehicle in the air and support it with jackstands.

2. Mark the relationship of the driveshaft to the differential flange so that they can be reassembled in the same position.

3. Disconnect the rear U-joint by removing the U-bolts or retaining straps.

4. To prevent the loss of the needle bearings,

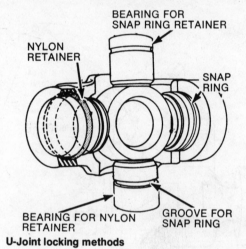

U-Joint locking methods

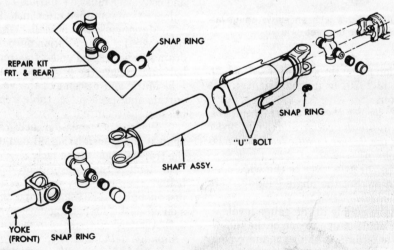

Typical driveshaft and U-Joints

tape the bearing caps in place. If you are re-placing the U-joint, this is not necessary.

5. Remove the driveshaft from the transmission by sliding it rearward. There will be some oil leakage from the rear of the transmission. It can be contained by placing a small plastic bag over the rear of the transmission and holding it in place with a rubber band.

6. To install the driveshaft, insert the front yoke into the transmission so that the drive-shaft splines mesh with the transmission splines.

7. Using the reference marks made earlier, align the driveshaft with the differential flange and secure it with the U-bolts or retaining straps.

U-JOINT OVERHAUL

1. Remove the driveshaft as explained above and remove the snaprings from the end of the bearing cup.

2. After removing the snaprings, place the driveshaft on the floor and place a large diameter socket under one of the bearing cups. Using a hammer and a drift, tap on the bearing opposite this one. This will push the trunnion through the yoke enough to force the bearing cup out of the yoke and into the socket. Repeat this procedure for the other cups. If a hammer doesn't loosen the cups, they will have to be pressed out.

NOTE: *A Saginaw design driveshaft secures its U-joints in a different manner than the conventional snaprings of the Dana and Cleveland designs. Nylon material is injected*

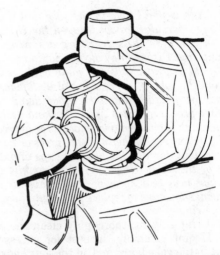

Press the bearing cup into the yoke, then install the cross

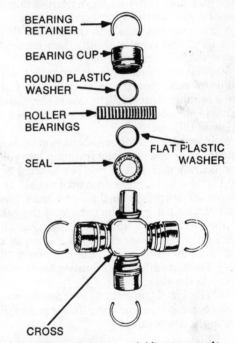

BEARING RETAINER

BEARING CUP

ROUND PLASTIC WASHER

ROLLER BEARINGS

SEAL

FLAT PLASTIC WASHER

CROSS

Plastic retainer U-Joint repair kit components

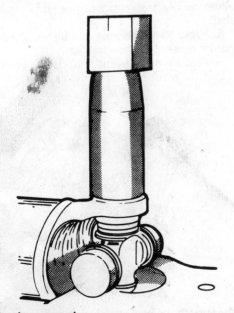

Bearing removal

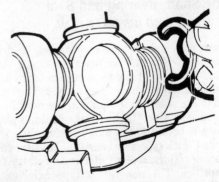

Service snap rings are installed inside the yoke

through a small hole in the yoke and flows along a circular groove between the U-joint and the yoke thus creating a synthetic snapring. Disassemlby of this Saginaw-type U-joint requires that the joint be recessed from the yoke. If a press is not available, it may be carefully hammered out using the same procedure (Step 2) as the Dana design although it may requirer more force to break the nylon ring. Either method, press or hammer, will damage the bearing cups and destroy the nylon rings. Replacement kits include new bearing cups and conventional metal snaprings to replace the original nylon type rings.

3. Using solvent, thoroughly clean the entire U-joint assembly. Inspect for excessive wear in the yoke bores and on the four ends of the trunnion. The needle bearings should not be scored, broken, or loose in their cups. Bearings cups may suffer slight distortion during removal and should be replaced.

4. Pack the bearings with chassis lube (lithium base) and completely fill each trunnion end with the same lubricant.

5. Place new dust seals on trunnions with cavity of seal toward end of trunnion. Care must be taken to avoid distortion of the seat. A suitable size socket and a vise can be used to press on the seal.

6. Insert one bearing cup about ¼ of the way into the yoke and place the trunnion into yoke and bearing cup. Install another bearing cup and press both cups in and install the snaprings. snaprings on the Dana and Cleveland shaft must go on the outside of the yoke while the Saginaw shaft requires that the rings go on the inside of the yoke. The gap in the Saginaw ring must face in toward the yoke. Once installed, the trunnion must move freely in the yoke.

NOTE: *The Saginaw shaft uses two different size bearing cups (the one with the groove) fit into the driveshaft yoke.*

Axle Shaft, Bearing and Seal
REMOVAL AND INSTALLATION

These cars use two different types of drive axle, the C-lock and the non C-lock type. Axle shaft in the C-lock type are retained by C-shaped licks, which fit grooves at the inner end of the shaft. Axle shafts in the non C-lock type are retained by the brake backing plate, which is bolted to the axle housing. Bearings in the C-lock type axle consist of an outer race, bearing rollers, and a roller cage, retained by snaprings. The non C-lock type axle uses a unit roller bearing (inner race, rolers and out-

er race), which is pressed onto the shaft up to a shoulder. It is imperative to determine the axle type before attempting any service.

The axle identification number is stamped on the front of the passenger side axle tube next to the differential carrier on all models except those with an 8½″ ring gear. These models have the I.D. on a tag under one of the differential rear cover bolts.

Non C-Lock Type

CAUTION: *Before attempting any service to the drive axle or axle shafts, remove the differential carrier cover and visually determine if the axle shafts are retained by C-shaped locks at the inner end, or by the brake backing plate at the outer end. If the shafts are not retained by C-locks, proceed as follows.*

Design allows for maximum axle shaft end-play of 0.022″, which can be measured with a dial indicator. If end-play is found to be excessive, the bearing should be replaced. Shimming the bearing is not recommended as this ignores end-play of the bearing itself and could result in improper seating of the bearing.

1. Remove the wheel, tire and brake drum.

2. Remove the nuts holding the retainer plate to the backing plate. Disconnect the brake line.

3. Remove the retainer and install the two lower nuts fingertight, to prevent the brake backing plate from being dislodged.

4. Pull out the axle shaft and bearing assembly, using a slide hammer.

5. Using a chisel, nick the bearing retainer in three or four places. The retainer does not have to be cut, merely collapsed sufficiently to allow the bearing retainer to be slid from the shaft.

6. Press off the bearing and install the new one by pressing it into position.

NOTE: *Do not attempt to press the bearing and the retainer on at the same time.*

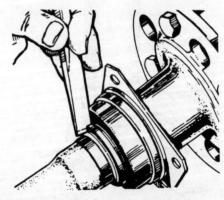

Breaking the bearing retainer with a chisel

Troubleshooting the Manual Transmission and Transfer Case

Problem	Cause	Solution
Transmission shifts hard	• Clutch adjustment incorrect • Clutch linkage or cable binding • Shift rail binding	• Adjust clutch • Lubricate or repair as necessary • Check for mispositioned selector arm roll pin, loose cover bolts, worn shift rail bores, worn shift rail, distorted oil seal, or extension housing not aligned with case. Repair as necessary.
	• Internal bind in transmission caused by shift forks, selector plates, or synchronizer assemblies • Clutch housing misalignment • Incorrect lubricant • Block rings and/or cone seats worn	• Remove, dissemble and inspect transmission. Replace worn or damaged components as necessary. • Check runout at rear face of clutch housing • Drain and refill transmission • Blocking ring to gear clutch tooth face clearance must be 0.030 inch or greater. If clearance is correct it may still be necessary to inspect blocking rings and cone seats for excessive wear. Repair as necessary.
Gear clash when shifting from one gear to another	• Clutch adjustment incorrect • Clutch linkage or cable binding • Clutch housing misalignment • Lubricant level low or incorrect lubricant • Gearshift components, or synchronizer assemblies worn or damaged	• Adjust clutch • Lubricate or repair as necessary • Check runout at rear of clutch housing • Drain and refill transmission and check for lubricant leaks if level was low. Repair as necessary. • Remove, disassemble and inspect transmission. Replace worn or damaged components as necessary.
Transmission noisy	• Lubricant level low or incorrect lubricant • Clutch housing-to-engine, or transmission-to-clutch housing bolts loose • Dirt, chips, foreign material in transmission • Gearshift mechanism, transmission gears, or bearing components worn or damaged • Clutch housing misalignment	• Drain and refill transmission. If lubricant level was low, check for leaks and repair as necessary. • Check and correct bolt torque as necessary • Drain, flush, and refill transmission • Remove, disassemble and inspect transmission. Replace worn or damaged components as necessary. • Check runout at rear face of clutch housing
Jumps out of gear	• Clutch housing misalignment • Gearshift lever loose • Offset lever nylon insert worn or lever attaching nut loose • Gearshift mechanism, shift forks, selector plates, interlock plate, selector arm, shift rail, detent plugs, springs or shift cover worn or damaged • Clutch shaft or roller bearings worn or damaged	• Check runout at rear face of clutch housing • Check lever for worn fork. Tighten loose attaching bolts. • Remove gearshift lever and check for loose offset lever nut or worn insert. Repair or replace as necessary. • Remove, disassemble and inspect transmission cover assembly. Replace worn or damaged components as necessary. • Replace clutch shaft or roller bearings as necessary

Troubleshooting the Manual Transmission and Transfer Case (cont.)

Problem	Cause	Solution
Jumps out of gear (cont.)	• Gear teeth worn or tapered, synchronizer assemblies worn or damaged, excessive end play caused by worn thrust washers or output shaft gears • Pilot bushing worn	• Remove, disassemble, and inspect transmission. Replace worn or damaged components as necessary. • Replace pilot bushing
Will not shift into one gear	• Gearshift selector plates, interlock plate, or selector arm, worn, damaged, or incorrectly assembled • Shift rail detent plunger worn, spring broken, or plug loose • Gearshift lever worn or damaged • Synchronizer sleeves or hubs, damaged or worn	• Remove, disassemble, and inspect transmission cover assembly. Repair or replace components as necessary. • Tighten plug or replace worn or damaged components as necessary • Replace gearshift lever • Remove, disassemble and inspect transmission. Replace worn or damaged components.
Locked in one gear—cannot be shifted out	• Shift rail(s) worn or broken, shifter fork bent, setscrew loose, center detent plug missing or worn • Broken gear teeth on countershaft gear, clutch shaft, or reverse idler gear Gearshift lever broken or worn, shift mechanism in cover incorrectly assembled or broken, worn damaged gear train components	• Inspect and replace worn or damaged parts • Inspect and replace damaged part • Disassemble transmission. Replace damaged parts or assemble correctly.
Transfer case difficult to shift or will not shift into desired range	• Vehicle speed too great to permit shifting • If vehicle was operated for extended period in 4H mode on dry paved surface, driveline torque load may cause difficult shifting • Transfer case external shift linkage binding • Insufficient or incorrect lubricant • Internal components binding, worn, or damaged	• Stop vehicle and shift into desired range. Or reduce speed to 3–4 km/h (2–3 mph) before attempting to shift. • Stop vehicle, shift transmission to neutral, shift transfer case to 2H mode and operate vehicle in 2H on dry paved surfaces • Lubricate or repair or replace linkage, or tighten loose components as necessary • Drain and refill to edge of fill hole with SAE 85W-90 gear lubricant only • Disassemble unit and replace worn or damaged components as necessary
Transfer case noisy in all drive modes	• Insufficient or incorrect lubricant	• Drain and refill to edge of fill hole with SAE 85W-90 gear lubricant only. Check for leaks and repair if necessary. Note: If unit is still noisy after drain and refill, disassembly and inspection may be required to locate source of noise.
Noisy in—or jumps out of four wheel drive low range	• Transfer case not completely engaged in 4L position • Shift linkage loose or binding • Shift fork cracked, inserts worn, or fork is binding on shift rail	• Stop vehicle, shift transfer case in Neutral, then shift back into 4L position • Tighten, lubricate, or repair linkage as necessary • Disassemble unit and repair as necessary
Lubricant leaking from output shaft seals or from vent	• Transfer case overfilled • Vent closed or restricted	• Drain to correct level • Clear or replace vent if necessary

Troubleshooting the Manual Transmission and Transfer Case (cont.)

Problem	Cause	Solution
Lubricant leaking from output shaft seals or from vent (cont.)	• Output shaft seals damaged or installed incorrectly	• Replace seals. Be sure seal lip faces interior of case when installed. Also be sure yoke seal surfaces are not scored or nicked. Remove scores, nicks with fine sandpaper or replace yoke(s) if necessary.
Abnormal tire wear	• Extended operation on dry hard surface (paved) roads in 4H range	• Operate in 2H on hard surface (paved) roads

Troubleshooting Basic Clutch Problems

Problem	Cause
Excessive clutch noise	Throwout bearing noises are more audible at the lower end of pedal travel. The usual causes are: • Riding the clutch • Too little pedal free-play • Lack of bearing lubrication A bad clutch shaft pilot bearing will make a high pitched squeal, when the clutch is disengaged and the transmission is in gear or within the first 2″ of pedal travel. The bearing must be replaced. Noise from the clutch linkage is a clicking or snapping that can be heard or felt as the pedal is moved completely up or down. This usually requires lubrication. Transmitted engine noises are amplified by the clutch housing and heard in the passenger compartment. They are usually the result of insufficient pedal free-play and can be changed by manipulating the clutch pedal.
Clutch slips (the car does not move as it should when the clutch is engaged)	This is usually most noticeable when pulling away from a standing start. A severe test is to start the engine, apply the brakes, shift into high gear and SLOWLY release the clutch pedal. A healthy clutch will stall the engine. If it slips it may be due to: • A worn pressure plate or clutch plate • Oil soaked clutch plate • Insufficient pedal free-play
Clutch drags or fails to release	The clutch disc and some transmission gears spin briefly after clutch disengagement. Under normal conditions in average temperatures, 3 seconds is maximum spin-time. Failure to release properly can be caused by: • Too light transmission lubricant or low lubricant level • Improperly adjusted clutch linkage
Low clutch life	Low clutch life is usually a result of poor driving habits or heavy duty use. Riding the clutch, pulling heavy loads, holding the car on a grade with the clutch instead of the brakes and rapid clutch engagement all contribute to low clutch life.

Troubleshooting Basic Automatic Transmission Problems

Problem	Cause	Solution
Fluid leakage	• Defective pan gasket	• Replace gasket or tighten pan bolts
	• Loose filler tube	• Tighten tube nut
	• Loose extension housing to transmission case	• Tighten bolts
	• Converter housing area leakage	• Have transmission checked professionally

Troubleshooting Basic Automatic Transmission Problems (cont.)

Problem	Cause	Solution
Fluid flows out the oil filler tube	• High fluid level • Breather vent clogged • Clogged oil filter or screen • Internal fluid leakage	• Check and correct fluid level • Open breather vent • Replace filter or clean screen (change fluid also) • Have transmission checked professionally
Transmission overheats (this is usually accompanied by a strong burned odor to the fluid)	• Low fluid level • Fluid cooler lines clogged • Heavy pulling or hauling with insufficient cooling • Faulty oil pump, internal slippage	• Check and correct fluid level • Drain and refill transmission. If this doesn't cure the problem, have cooler lines cleared or replaced. • Install a transmission oil cooler • Have transmission checked professionally
Buzzing or whining noise	• Low fluid level • Defective torque converter, scored gears	• Check and correct fluid level • Have transmission checked professionally
No forward or reverse gears or slippage in one or more gears	• Low fluid level • Defective vacuum or linkage controls, internal clutch or band failure	• Check and correct fluid level • Have unit checked professionally
Delayed or erratic shift	• Low fluid level • Broken vacuum lines • Internal malfunction	• Check and correct fluid level • Repair or replace lines • Have transmission checked professionally

Lockup Torque Converter Service Diagnosis

Problem	Cause	Solution

No lockup	• Faulty oil pump
	• Sticking governor valve
	• Valve body malfunction
	  (a) Stuck switch valve
	  (b) Stuck lockup valve
	  (c) Stuck fail-safe valve
	• Failed locking clutch
	• Leaking turbine hub seal
	• Faulty input shaft or seal ring
		• Replace oil pump
		• Repair or replace as necessary
		• Repair or replace valve body or its internal components as necessary
		
		• Replace torque converter
		• Replace torque converter
		• Repair or replace as necessary

Will not unlock	• Sticking governor valve
	• Valve body malfunction
	  (a) Stuck switch valve
	  (b) Stuck lockup valve
	  (c) Stuck fail-safe valve
		• Repair or replace as necessary
		• Repair or replace valve body or its internal components as necessary

Stays locked up at too low a speed in direct	• Sticking governor valve
	• Valve body malfunction
	  (a) Stuck switch valve
	  (b) Stuck lockup valve
	  (c) Stuck fail-safe valve
		• Repair or replace as necessary
		• Repair or replace valve body or its internal components as necessary

Locks up or drags in low or second	• Faulty oil pump
	• Valve body malfunction
	  (a) Stuck switch valve
	  (b) Stuck fail-safe valve
		• Replace oil pump
		• Repair or replace valve body or its internal components as necessary

Sluggish or stalls in reverse	• Faulty oil pump
	• Plugged cooler, cooler lines or fittings
	• Valve body malfunction
	  (a) Stuck switch valve
	  (b) Faulty input shaft or seal ring
		• Replace oil pump as necessary
		• Flush or replace cooler and flush lines and fittings
		• Repair or replace valve body or its internal components as necessary

Lockup Torque Converter Service Diagnosis (cont.)

Problem	Cause	Solution
Loud chatter during lockup engagement (cold)	• Faulty torque converter • Failed locking clutch • Leaking turbine hub seal	• Replace torque converter • Replace torque converter • Replace torque converter
Vibration or shudder during lockup engagement	• Faulty oil pump • Valve body malfunction • Faulty torque converter • Engine needs tune-up	• Repair or replace oil pump as necessary • Repair or replace valve body or its internal components as necessary • Replace torque converter • Tune engine
Vibration after lockup engagement	• Faulty torque converter • Exhaust system strikes underbody • Engine needs tune-up • Throttle linkage misadjusted	• Replace torque converter • Align exhaust system • Tune engine • Adjust throttle linkage
Vibration when revved in neutral Overheating: oil blows out of dip stick tube or pump seal	• Torque converter out of balance • Plugged cooler, cooler lines or fittings • Stuck switch valve	• Replace torque converter • Flush or replace cooler and flush lines and fittings • Repair switch valve in valve body or replace valve body
Shudder after lockup engagement	• Faulty oil pump • Plugged cooler, cooler lines or fittings • Valve body malfunction • Faulty torque converter • Fail locking clutch • Exhaust system strikes underbody • Engine needs tune-up • Throttle linkage misadjusted	• Replace oil pump • Flush or replace cooler and flush lines and fittings • Repair or replace valve body or its internal components as necessary • Replace torque converter • Replace torque converter • Align exhaust system • Tune engine • Adjust throttle linkage

Transmission Fluid Indications

The appearance and odor of the transmission fluid can give valuable clues to the overall condition of the transmission. Always note the appearance of the fluid when you check the fluid level or change the fluid. Rub a small amount of fluid between your fingers to feel for grit and smell the fluid on the dipstick.

If the fluid appears:	It indicates:
Clear and red colored	• Normal operation
Discolored (extremely dark red or brownish) or smells burned	• Band or clutch pack failure, usually caused by an overheated transmission. Hauling very heavy loads with insufficient power or failure to change the fluid, often result in overheating. Do not confuse this appearance with newer fluids that have a darker red color and a strong odor (though not a burned odor).
Foamy or aerated (light in color and full of bubbles)	• The level is too high (gear train is churning oil) • An internal air leak (air is mixing with the fluid). Have the transmission checked professionally.
Solid residue in the fluid	• Defective bands, clutch pack or bearings. Bits of band material or metal abrasives are clinging to the dipstick. Have the transmission checked professionally.
Varnish coating on the dipstick	• The transmission fluid is overheating

7. Assemble the shaft and bearing in the housing, being sure that the bearing is seated properly in the housing.

8. Install the retainer, drum, wheel and tire. Bleed the brakes.

C-Lock Type

CAUTION: *Before attempting any service to the drive axle or axle shafts, remove the carrier cover and visually determine if the axle shaft(s) are retained by C-shaped locks at the*

Troubleshooting Basic Driveshaft and Rear Axle Problems

When abnormal vibrations or noises are detected in the driveshaft area, this chart can be used to help diagnose possible causes. Remember that other components such as wheels, tires, rear axle and suspension can also produce similar conditions.

BASIC DRIVESHAFT PROBLEMS

Problem	Cause	Solution
Shudder as car accelerates from stop or low speed	• Loose U-joint • Defective center bearing	• Replace U-joint • Replace center bearing
Loud clunk in driveshaft when shifting gears	• Worn U-joints	• Replace U-joints
Roughness or vibration at any speed	• Out-of-balance, bent or dented driveshaft • Worn U-joints • U-joint clamp bolts loose	• Balance or replace driveshaft • Replace U-joints • Tighten U-joint clamp bolts
Squeaking noise at low speeds	• Lack of U-joint lubrication	• Lubricate U-joint; if problem persists, replace U-joint
Knock or clicking noise	• U-joint or driveshaft hitting frame tunnel • Worn CV joint	• Correct overloaded condition • Replace CV joint

BASIC REAR AXLE PROBLEMS

First, determine when the noise is most noticeable.

Drive Noise: Produced under vehicle acceleration.

Coast Noise: Produced while the car coasts with a closed throttle.

Float Noise: Occurs while maintaining constant car speed (just enough to keep speed constant) on a level road.

Road Noise

Brick or rough surfaced concrete roads produce noises that seem to come from the rear axle. Road noise is usually identical in Drive or Coast and driving on a different type of road will tell whether the road is the problem.

Tire Noise

Tire noises are often mistaken for rear axle problems. Snow treads or unevenly worn tires produce vibrations seeming to originate elsewhere. **Temporarily** inflating the tires to 40 lbs will significantly alter tire noise, but will have no effect on rear axle noises (which normally cease below about 30 mph).

Engine/Transmission Noise

Determine at what speed the noise is most pronounced, then stop the car in a quiet place. With the transmission in Neutral, run the engine through speeds corresponding to road speeds where the noise was noticed. Noises produced with the car standing still are coming from the engine or transmission.

Front Wheel Bearings

While holding the car speed steady, lightly apply the footbrake; this will often decease bearing noise, as some of the load is taken from the bearing.

Rear Axle Noises

Eliminating other possible sources can narrow the cause to the rear axle, which normally produces noise from worn gears or bearings. Gear noises tend to peak in a narrow speed range, while bearing noises will usually vary in pitch with engine speeds.

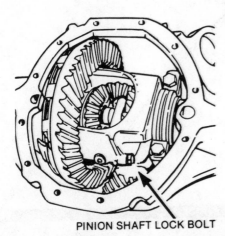

PINION SHAFT LOCK BOLT

Removing the pinion shaft lock bolt from the differential

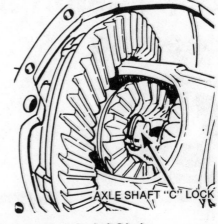

AXLE SHAFT "C" LOCK

Removing the axle shaft C lock

inner ends or by a brake backing plate at the outer end. If they are retained by C-shaped locks, proceed as follows.

1. Raise the vehicle and remove the wheels.

2. The differential cover has already been removed (see Caution above). Remove the differential pinion shaft lockscrew and the differential pinion shaft.

3. Push the flanged end of the axle shaft toward the center of the vehicle and remove the C-lock from the end of the shaft.

4. Remove the axle shaft from the housing, being careful not to damage the oil seal.

5. Remove the oil seal by inserting the button end of the axle shaft behind the steel case of the oil seal. Pry the seal loose from the bore.

6. Seat the legs of a bearing puller behind the bearing. Seat a washer against the bearing and hold it in place with a nut. Use a slide hammer to pull the bearing.

7. Pack the cavity between the seal lips with wheel bearing lubricant and lubricate a new wheel bearing with same.

8. Use a suitable driver and install the bearing until it bottoms against a tube. Install the oil seal.

9. Slide the axle shaft into place. Be sure that the splines on the shaft do not damage the oil seal. Make sure that the splines engage the differential side gear.

10. Install the axle shaft C-lock on the inner end of the axle shaft and push the shaft outward so that the C-lock seats in the differential side gear counterbore.

11. Position the differential pinion shaft through the case and pinions, aligning the hole in the case with the hole in the lockscrew.

12. Install the pinion shaft lockscrew.

13. Use a new gasket and install the carrier cover. Be sure that the gasket surfaces are clean before installing the gasket and cover.

14. Fill the axle with lubricant to the bottom of the filler hole.

15. Install the brake drum and wheels and lower the car. Check for leaks and road test the car.

Suspension and Steering

FRONT SUSPENSION
Ball Joint Inspection
LOWER BALL JOINT

All 1975 and later cars have visual wear indicators on the lower ball joints. The lower ball joint grease plug screws into the wear indicator which protrudes from the bottom of the ball joint housing. As long as the wear indicator extends out of the ball joint housing, the ball joint is not worn. If the tip of the wear indicator is parallel with, or recessed into the ball joint housing, the ball joint is defective.

UPPER BALL JOINT

1. Place a jack under each lower control arm between the suspension spring pocket and the ball joint and raise the car.
2. Grasp the wheel at the 6 and 12 o'clock position and shake the top of the wheel in and out. Observe the steering knuckle for any movement relative to the control arm. If the ball joint is loose, it must be replaced.

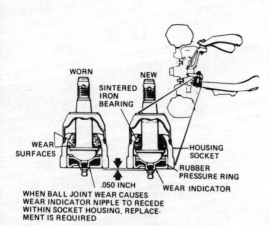

WORN NEW
SINTERED IRON BEARING
WEAR SURFACES
HOUSING SOCKET
RUBBER PRESSURE RING
.050 INCH
WEAR INDICATOR
WHEN BALL JOINT WEAR CAUSES WEAR INDICATOR NIPPLE TO RECEDE WITHIN SOCKET HOUSING, REPLACEMENT IS REQUIRED

Lower ball joint wear indicator

Upper Control Arm And/Or Ball joint
REMOVAL AND INSTALLATION

1. Raise the car and place a jack under the frame. Remove the wheel and tire.
2. With another jack, support the car weight under the outer edge of the lower control arm. Raise the jack enough to free the upper control arm from the upper ball stud.
3. Remove the cotter pin from the upper ball joint stud.
4. Loosen, but do not remove, the nut.
CAUTION: *If the nut is removed, the full force of the coil spring could be released.*
   Use a ball joint removal tool to free the stud from the knuckle.
5. Wire the brake and knuckle in place to prevent brake hose damage, then lift the upper arm from the knuckle.
NOTE: *If only the ball joints are to be replaced, stop at this point. Center punch and drill out the four rivets, then chisel off their heads. Remove the old ball joint. The new joint comes with four specially hardened bolts which must be torqued to 8 ft.lb. The nut goes on top.*
6. Remove the upper control arm shaft-to-bracket nuts and lock washers. Carefully note the number, thickness, and location of the adjusting shims. Remove the control arm assembly.
7. Reverse the above steps to install. Observe the following torque figures.
Upper control arm-to-frame nuts: 46 ft.lb.
Ball joint stud nut: 60-65 ft.lb.
Upper control arm bushing nuts:
   55 rear; 90 front through 1978
   45 front; 55 rear for 1979
   85 front and rear for 1980-87
The upper control arm bushing nuts must be torqued with the weight of the car on the wheels.
CAUTION: *When installing the cotter pin,*

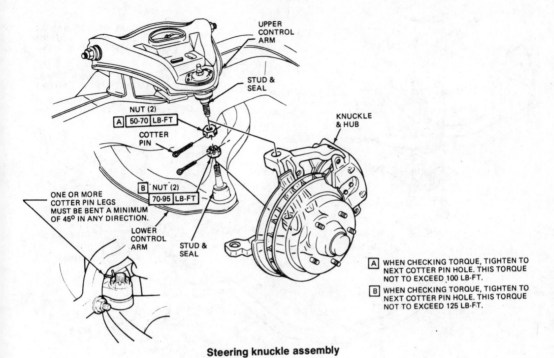

UPPER
CONTROL
ARM

STUD &
SEAL

NUT (2)
[A] 50-70 LB-FT

COTTER
PIN

KNUCKLE
& HUB

ONE OR MORE
COTTER PIN LEGS
MUST BE BENT A MINIMUM
OF 45° IN ANY DIRECTION.

[B] NUT (2)
70-95 LB-FT

LOWER
CONTROL
ARM

STUD &
SEAL

[A] WHEN CHECKING TORQUE, TIGHTEN TO
NEXT COTTER PIN HOLE. THIS TORQUE
NOT TO EXCEED 100 LB-FT.

[B] WHEN CHECKING TORQUE, TIGHTEN TO
NEXT COTTER PIN HOLE. THIS TORQUE
NOT TO EXCEED 125 LB-FT.

Steering knuckle assembly

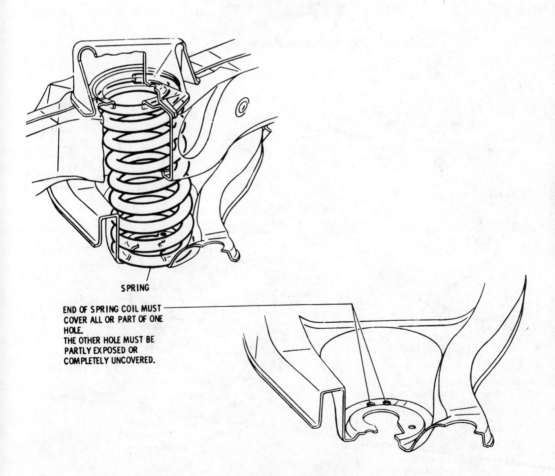

SPRING

END OF SPRING COIL MUST
COVER ALL OR PART OF ONE
HOLE.
THE OTHER HOLE MUST BE
PARTLY EXPOSED OR
COMPLETELY UNCOVERED.

Front spring installation

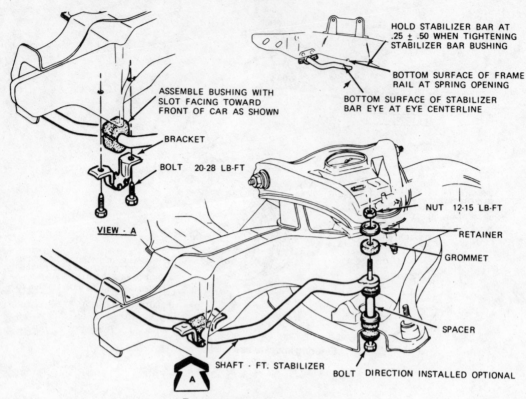

ASSEMBLE BUSHING WITH SLOT FACING TOWARD FRONT OF CAR AS SHOWN

HOLD STABILIZER BAR AT .25 ± .50 WHEN TIGHTENING STABILIZER BAR BUSHING

BOTTOM SURFACE OF FRAME RAIL AT SPRING OPENING

BOTTOM SURFACE OF STABILIZER BAR EYE AT EYE CENTERLINE

BRACKET

BOLT   20-28 LB-FT

VIEW - A

NUT   12-15 LB-FT

RETAINER

GROMMET

SPACER

SHAFT - FT. STABILIZER

BOLT   DIRECTION INSTALLED OPTIONAL

Front stabilizer shaft installation

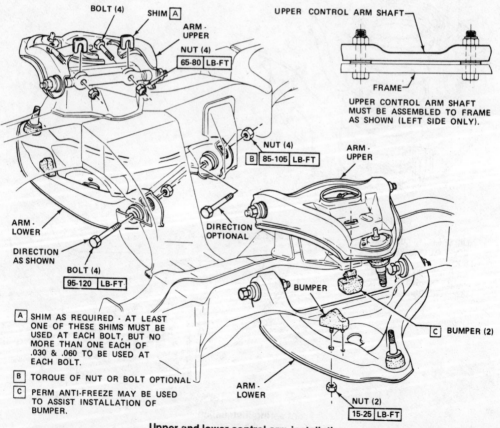

BOLT (4)

SHIM A

ARM - UPPER

NUT (4)   65-80 LB-FT

UPPER CONTROL ARM SHAFT

FRAME

UPPER CONTROL ARM SHAFT MUST BE ASSEMBLED TO FRAME AS SHOWN (LEFT SIDE ONLY).

NUT (4)   B   85-105 LB-FT

ARM - UPPER

ARM - LOWER

DIRECTION OPTIONAL

DIRECTION AS SHOWN

BOLT (4)   95-120 LB-FT

BUMPER

C   BUMPER (2)

ARM - LOWER

NUT (2)   15-25 LB-FT

A   SHIM AS REQUIRED - AT LEAST ONE OF THESE SHIMS MUST BE USED AT EACH BOLT, BUT NO MORE THAN ONE EACH OF .030 & .060 TO BE USED AT EACH BOLT.

B   TORQUE OF NUT OR BOLT OPTIONAL

C   PERM ANTI-FREEZE MAY BE USED TO ASSIST INSTALLATION OF BUMPER.

Upper and lower control arm installation

never loosen the nut to align the cotter pin holes. Always tighten the nut to the next slot that lines up with the hole.

Lower Control Arm Or Spring
REMOVAL AND INSTALLATION

1. Raise the front of the car and remove the wheel.
2. Disconnect and remove the shock absorber.
3. Remove the front stabilizer rod link from the lower control arm.
4. Disconnect the brake reaction rod from the lower control arm.
5. As a safety precaution and to gain maximum leverage, place a jack about ½" below the lower ball joint stud. Now, remove the ball stud cotter pin and loosen the nut about ⅛". Do not remove the nut.
CAUTION: *If the nut is removed, the full force of the coil spring could be released.*
6. Rap the steering knuckle in the area of the stud or use a ball joint removal tool to separate the stud from the knuckle.
7. After the stud has broken loose from the knuckle, raise the jack against the control arm. Remove the nut and separate the steering knuckle from the tapered stud.
8. Carefully lower the jack under the control arm and release the spring. With the jack entirely lowered, it may be necessary to pry the spring off its seat on the lower control arm with a pry bar.
9. After the spring is removed, the lower control arm may be removed by removing the lock nut which attaches the control arm to the frame.
10. Reverse to install. Torque the control arm to frame bolts, with the car on the ground, to the following settings:
 • through 1976–90 ft.lb.
 • 1977–125 ft.lb.
 • 1978 and later–95 ft.lb.

Lower Ball Joint
REMOVAL AND INSTALLATION

1. Refer to steps 1-7 of the lower control arm procedure.
2. Install a ball joint remover and tighten the tool to force the ball joint out of the lower control arm.
3. Reverse the above to install. Tighten the castellated nut to 85-90 ft.lb. Always tighten the castellated nut to the next slot if necessary to align the cotter pin.

Shock Absorber
TESTING

Visually inspect the shock absorber. If there is evidence of leakage and the shock absorber is covered with oil, the shock is defective and should be replaced.

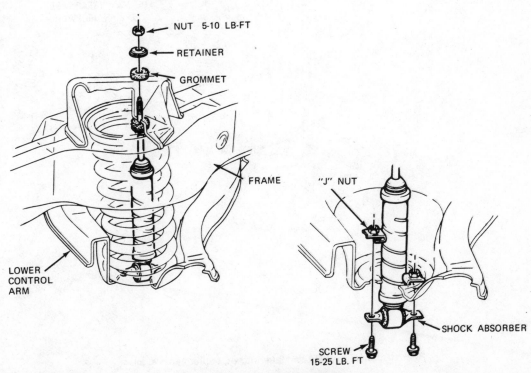

Front shock absorber installation

If there is no sign of excessive leakage (a small amount of weeping is normal) bounce the car at one corner by pressing down on the fender or bumper and releasing. When you have the car bouncing as much as you can, release the fender or bumper. The car should stop bouncing after the first rebound. If the bouncing continues past the center point of the bounce more than once, the shock absorbers are worn and should be replaced.

REMOVAL AND INSTALLATION

1. Remove the upper shock absorber attaching nut, grommet retainer, and grommet.
2. Remove the lower retaining screws. Lower the shock through the hole in the lower control arm.

NOTE: *Purge new shocks of air by repeatedly extending them in their normal position and compressing them while inverted.*

3. Reverse the above steps to install. Tighten the upper nut to 8 ft.lb.; the lower bolts to 20 ft.lb.

Front End Alignment

CASTER AND CAMBER ADJUSTMENT

Caster and camber are controlled by shims between the frame bracket and the upper suspension arm pivot shaft.

To adjust caster, remove shims from the front bolt and replace them at the rear bolt, or vice versa. To adjust camber, add or remove the same number of shims from each bolt.

Keep in mind when loosening the bolts that the upper suspension arm is supporting the weight of the vehicle. Loosen the bolts only a sufficient amount to remove the shims.

TOE-IN ADJUSTMENT

Adjust toe-in by loosening the clamps on the sleeves at the outer ends of the tie-rod, and turning the sleeves an equal amount in the opposite direction, to maintain steering wheel spoke alignment while adjusting toe-in.

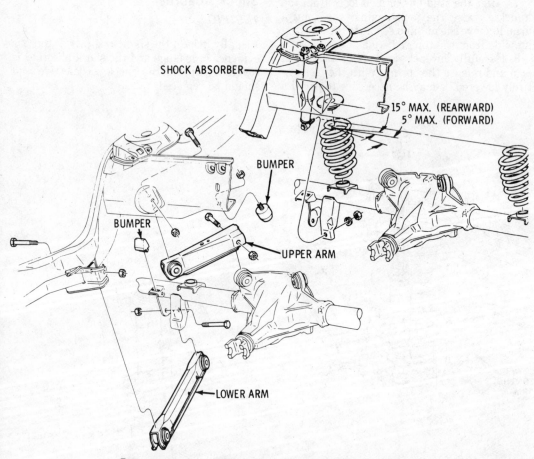

SHOCK ABSORBER

15° MAX. (REARWARD)
5° MAX. (FORWARD)

BUMPER

BUMPER

UPPER ARM

LOWER ARM

Rear suspension—1978 and later shown, earlier years similar

REAR SUSPENSION

Coil Spring
REPLACEMENT

1. Jack up the back of the car and support both sides on jackstands on the frame, in front of the rear axle. Support the rear axle with an adjustable lifting device. Disconnect the shock absorber.

2. Detach the upper control arm at the differential.

3. Disconnect the stabilizer bar, if so equipped.

4. Remove any brake hose supports but disconnect the brake hose, only if necessary.

5. Carefully lower the axle until the tension is released from the coil spring. Be careful not to stretch the brake hose. Remove the spring. Note the direction in which the end of the last coil is pointing. Install the spring in the same position.

6. When starting a new coil spring, make certain that the bottom of the coil is properly inserted into the socket in the frame and into the form plate on the trailing arm.

7. Jack the axle into place and reinstall the control arm bolt. Tighten the bolts with the car's weight on the springs.

Shock Absorber
REMOVAL AND INSTALLATION

NOTE: *Purge new shocks of air by repeatedly extending them in their normal position and compressing them while inverted.*

1. Raise the car at the axle housing.

2. Remove the nut, retainer, and grommet, or nut and lockwasher, as equipped, which attaches the lower end of the shock absorber. to its mounting.

3. Remove the two shock absorber upper attaching screws and remove the shock absorber.

4. Reverse the removal procedures to install. Tighten the upper bolts to 18-20 ft.lb. for all models. The nuts that lock the upper bolts on some 1977 and later models are torqued to 12 ft.lb. Tighten the lower nut to 65 ft.lb.

STEERING

Steering Wheel
REMOVAL AND INSTALLATION

Except Tilt and Telescope Column

1. Disconnect the battery ground and unplug the horn wire connector from the steering column.

Wheel Alignment Specifications

Year	Model	Caster Range (deg)	Caster Pref Setting (deg)	Camber Range (deg)	Camber Pref Setting (deg)	Toe-in (in.)	Steering Axis Inclination (deg)	Wheel Pivot Ratio Inner Wheel	Wheel Pivot Ratio Outer Wheel
'70	All	½N to 2N	1½N ①	¼N to ½P	⅛	⅛ to ³⁄₁₆	9	20	18⅗
'71–'72	All	¾N to 1¾N	1¼N	¾N to ¾P*	¼P*	¹⁄₁₆N to ¹⁄₁₆P	8	20	19②
'73	All	¾N to 1¾N	1¼N	⑤	⑤	¹⁄₁₆	10½	20	19②
'74	exc. Salon	1N to 1P	0	⑥	⑥	0 to ⅛	10½	20	19②
	Salon	1P to 3P	2P	⑥	⑥	0 to ⅛	10½	20	19②
'76–'77	All	1P to 3P	2P	⑨	⑩	0 to ⅛	10½	20	19②
'78–'80	pwr. str.	2½P to 3½	3P	0 to 1P	½	¹⁄₁₆ to ³⁄₁₆	—	—	—
	man. str.	½P to 1½	1P	0 to 1P	½	¹⁄₁₆ to ³⁄₁₆	—	—	—
'81–'85	All	2½P to 3½P	3P	0 to 1P	½P	¹⁄₁₆ to ³⁄₁₆	—	—	—
'86–'87	All	1¹³⁄₁₆P to 3¹³⁄₁₆P	2¹³⁄₁₆P	0 to 1⅝P	¹³⁄₁₆	¹⁄₁₆ to ¼	—	—	—

*Left side chamber to be ½° more positive than right side
① Power steering—¾N
② Power steering—18
⑤ 1°P—LH; ½°N—RH: ± ¾°
⑥ 1P ± ½—LH; ½P ± ½—RH
⑨ ¼P to 1¾P—LH, ¼N to 1¼P—RH
⑩ 1P—LH, ¼P—RH
—Not specified
N Negative   P Positive

2. On cars with a standard wheel or optional wood-rim wheel, pull off the cap, remove the three screws and the contact, insulator, and spring. On cars with the bar type horn actuator, remove the screws securing the actuator from the underside of the steering wheel, unhook the lead connector plug, and remove the actuator assembly.

3. Loosen the steering wheel nut.

4. Apply the steering wheel puller and pull the wheel up to the nut. Now remove the puller, nut and steering wheel.

CAUTION: *Don't pound on the steering wheel in either direction or the collapsible steering column will collapse, requiring replacement.*

On installaton:

NOTE: *Location marks are provided on the steering wheel and shaft to simplify proper indexing at the time of installation.*

1. Install wheel with the location mark aligned with that of the shaft.

2. Install the wheel nut and torque to 30 ft.lb.

3. Reinstall horn button or actuator assembly.

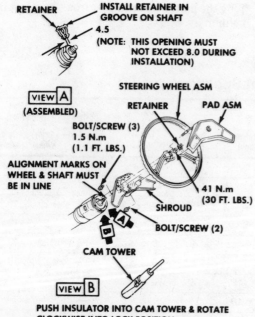

INSTALL RETAINER IN GROOVE ON SHAFT

RETAINER

4.5 (NOTE: THIS OPENING MUST NOT EXCEED 8.0 DURING INSTALLATION)

VIEW A (ASSEMBLED)

STEERING WHEEL ASM

RETAINER   PAD ASM

BOLT/SCREW (3) 1.5 N.m (1.1 FT. LBS.)

ALIGNMENT MARKS ON WHEEL & SHAFT MUST BE IN LINE

41 N.m (30 FT. LBS.)

SHROUD

BOLT/SCREW (2)

CAM TOWER

VIEW B

PUSH INSULATOR INTO CAM TOWER & ROTATE CLOCKWISE INTO LOCK POSITION

Typical standard steering wheel installation

Tilt and Telescope Column

1. Disconnect the battery ground.

2. Remove the attaching screws and lift the pad from the column.

3. Disconnect the horn wire by pushing in the connector and turning it counterclockwise.

4. Push the locking lever counterclockwise until full release if obtained.

5. Mark the lock plate-to-locking lever position and remove the plate and lever.

6. Remove the steering wheel retaining nut and remove the wheel with a puller.

7. Install a $5/16''$ x 18 set screw into the upper shaft at the fully extended position and lock it.

8. Install the steering wheel, observing the aligning mark on the hub and the slash mark on the end of the shaft. Make certain that the unattached end of the horn upper contact assembly is seated flush against the top of the horn contact carrier button.

9. Install the nut on the upper steering shaft and torque to 30 ft.lb.

10. Remove the set screw installed in Step 7.

11. Install the plate assembly finger tight.

12. Position the locking lever in the vertical position and move it counterclockwise until the holes in the plate align with the holes in the lever. Install the attaching screws.

13. Align the pad assembly with the holes in the steering wheel and install the retaining screws.

14. Connect the battery.

15. Make certain that the locking lever securely locks the wheel travel and that the wheel travel is free in the unlocked position.

Special Procedure for Cars with A.C.R.S. (Air Bags)

Some 1976 models have an air cushion, or air bag, restraint system. One of the elements of this complex system is an air cushion module in the top of the steering wheel. The steering wheel can be removed in the normal manner after the module has been removed.

To remove the module:

1. Turn the ignition lock to the LOCK position.

2. Disconnect the battery ground cable and tape the end to prevent any possibility of a complete circuit.

3. Remove the 4 module-to-steering wheel screws. A special tool is available to do this.

4. Lift up the module and disconnect the horn wire.

5. Disconnect the module wire connector. A special tool is available to do this, too.

CAUTION: *The driver air cushion module should always be carried with the vinyl cover away from all parts of one's body and should always be laid on a flat surface with the vinyl side up. This is necessary so that a free space is provided to allow the air cushion to expand in the case of accidental deployment.*

Do not attempt to repair any portion of the module. The module must be serviced as a unit. Attempting repairs such as soldering wires, changing covers, etc. may cause accidental inflation or impair operation of the driver module and cause serious injury.

Do not dispose of a module in any way. The highly inflammable material in the module can cause serious burns if ignited. Modules must be exchanged at an authorized dealer's parts department.

To install the module:

6. Hold the module with the emblem in the lower right corner.

7. Loop the air cushion harness clockwise from the 11 o'clock position to the 6 o'clock position.

8. Install the module connector by pushing it onto the column circuit firmly.

9. Install the horn wire.

10. Position the module, making sure that the wiring is still in place, and install the 4 screws. Torque them to 40 in.lb.

11. Reconnect the battery ground cable.

12. Turn the ignition lock to any position other than LOCK and check that the restraint indicator light operates correctly.

Turn Signal Switch

REMOVAL AND INSTALLATION

Except Tilt and Telescope Column, Except A.C.R.S.

NOTE: *The steering wheel must always be supported. Use extreme care not to bend the steering column.*

1. Remove the steering wheel.

2. Remove the three cover screws and the cover. All 1976 and later steering columns have a redesigned lock plate which is removed by inserting a screwdriver in the cover slot and prying out. This is done in at least two of the slots to avoid breaking the plate.

3. Depress the lock plate and remove the snapring. Remove the lock plate.

4. Remove the spring and horn contact signal cancelling cam. Remove the thrust washer.

5. Place the turn signal lever in the right turn position, remove the attaching screw and remove the turn signal lever. On models with the dimmer switch mounted on the column, remove the actuator arm screw and the actuator arm. Pull the turn signal lever straight out to remove. Depress the hazard warning knob, and remove the knob. Some models have a screw in the end of the knob which must be removed.

6. Remove the three turn signal switch mounting screws.

7. Remove the instrument panel lower trim panel and disconnect the turn signal connector from the harness.

8. Remove the four bracket attaching screws and remove the bracket.

9. On 1977 and later models with automatic transmissions, loosen the shift indicator needle attaching screw and remove the needle.

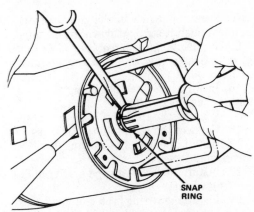

Using the special steering wheel lockplate compressing tool and removing the snap-ring

10. On 1977 and later models, remove the two steering column supporting bolts while supporting the column. Do not allow the column to drop suddenly.

11. Remove the bracket and wiring from the column. Loosely reinstall the column supporting bolts, if removed.

12. Pull the switch straight up with the wire protector and wire harness.

13. Reverse the above steps to install.

Tilt and Telescope Column, Except A.C.R.S.

1. Disconnect the battery ground.

2. Remove the steering wheel and lock plate as previously described.

3. Remove the upper bearing preload spring.

4. Position the turn signal lever in the right turn position and remove the lever and screw.

5. With column mounted dimmer switches, remove the actuator arm and screw, then remove the turn signal arm by pulling it straight out.

6. Push in on the warning hazard knob, then remove the retaining screw and knob.

7. Position the column in the center position and remove the three turn signal switch attaching screws.

8. Remove the instrument panel lower trim pad and disconnect the turn signal harness connector. Lift the connector from the mounting bracket on the right side of the jacket.

9. Remove the toe pan bolts.

10. Remove the four bolts attaching the bracket assembly to the jacket.

11. Remove the shift indicator retaining clip.

12. Support the column and remove the bracket assembly. Remove the wire protector from the turn signal wiring. Pull the turn signal switch and wiring from the column.

13. Prior to installation, coat all moving parts with lithium based grease.

14. Insert switch wiring into the column.

15. Place the switch in the right turn position and push it straight down until seated.
CAUTION: *Angling or cocking of the switch can cause damage to the buzzer terminal or tangs.*
16. Install the switch attaching screws and torque them to 25 ft.lb.
17. Position the turn signal in the center.
18. Connect the wiring to the harness.
19. Install the hazard warning knob and turn signal lever.
20. Install the lockplate and carrier and the steering wheel.
21. Install the wiring protector and bracket. Torque the bracket bolts to 18 ft.lbs. and the nuts to 24 ft.lb.
22. Install the shift indicator needle or clip.
23. Position the harness connector in the bracket on the right side of the jacket.
24. Install the instrument panel lower trim pad and connect the battery ground.

1976 With A.C.R.S. (Air Bags)

Follow the procedure for removing the steering wheel and air cushion module which appears previously under "Steering Wheel Removal and Installation, Special Procedure for Cars with A.C.R.S."
1. Remove the 3 screws from the retainer and cover. Carefully lift the cover and retainer from the column.
2. Carefully insert a screwdriver blade into the locking tab at the side and lift the slip ring from the column.
3. Proceed with the Turn Signal Switch Replacement procedure, beginning with Step 3.
4. To replace the slip ring, align the slip ring locating tab with the slot in the bowl and push the slip ring into position. Make sure that all 3 locking tabs are securely positioned.
5. Install the cover and retainer, aligning the cover over the locating tab. Torque the screws to 15 in.lb.

Ignition Switch Lock Cylinder
REMOVAL AND INSTALLATION

1. Refer to the Turn Signal Switch Replacement procedure, Steps 1-6.
2. Disconnect the turn signal connector from the harness and pull out the turn signal switch. Allow it to hang.
3. With the lock cylinder in the RUN position, insert a small screwdriver or steel strip into the slot next to the turn signal switch mounting screw boss (right-hand slot), depress the spring latch and remove the key lock. On 1979 and later models remove the retaining screw and cock cylinder.
4. Pull the buzzer switch straight out, depressing the switch clip with pliers.

5. Place the ignition switch in the OFF-UNLOCKED position by pulling up on the connecting rod until there is a definite stop or detent felt.
6. Remove the two attaching screws and the ignition switch.
7. Assembly is the reverse of the above. However, note the following steps before proceeding with the reassembly.
8. To install the steering lock, hold the lock cylinder sleeve and rotate the knob clockwise against the stop. Insert the cylinder into the cover bore with the key on the cylinder sleeve aligned with the keyway in the housing. Then push the cylinder in until it bottoms. Maintaining a light inward pressure, rotate the knob counterclockwise until the drive section of the cylinder mates with the drive shaft. Push in until the snapring pops into the groove and the lock cylinder is secured in the cover. Check for free rotation.
9. Move the switch slider to the extreme left position (ACC), then two detents to the right, to the OFF-LOCKED position. Fit the actuator rod into the hole and attach the switch to the column.
10. The neutral start switch is adjusted with the shift lever in the Drive position.

Tilt Column

1. Refer to the Turn Signal Switch Replacement procedure for tilt and telescopic columns, Steps 1-6.
2. Position the tilt column in the center position and remove the three turn signal switch screws. Tape the wires to the wire shift bowl in Low. Pull the switch straight up and out, allowing it to hang.
3. Insert a small screwdriver or steel strip into the slot next to the turn signal switch mounting screw boss (right-hand slot), depress the spring latch and remove the key lock. On 1979 and later models, remove the retaining screw and the lock cylinder.

SMALL STEEL STRIP

CYLINDER

Depress the spring latch to remove the lock cylinder on models through 1978

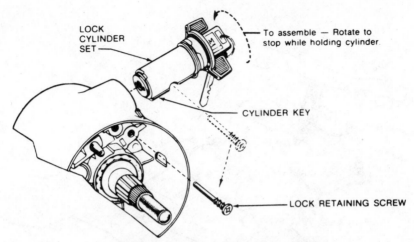

LOCK
CYLINDER
SET

To assemble — Rotate to
stop while holding cylinder.

CYLINDER KEY

LOCK RETAINING SCREW

Ignition lock removal—1979 and later models

4. Remove the buzzer switch straight out, depressing the switch clip with pliers.

5. Remove the three housing cover screws and cover.

6. Install the tilt release lever and place column in full UP position.

7. Place a screwdriver in the slot of the tilt spring retainer, press in about $\frac{3}{16}''$ and turn counterclockwise. Remove the spring and guide.

NOTE: *The spring is very strong-be careful.*

8. Push the column in neutral position, push in on the upper steering shaft, remove the inner race seat and race.

9. Remove the upper flange pinch bolt, place the ignition switch in the accessory position, remove the two switch mounting screws and switch.

NOTE: *The neutral start switch can be removed at this time, if necessary.*

10. Assembly is the reverse of the above. However, note the following steps before proceeding with the reassembly.

11. To install the steering lock, hold the lock cylinder sleeve and rotate the knob clockwise against the stop. Insert the cylinder into the cover bore with the key on the cylinder sleeve aligned with the keyway in the housing. Push the cylinder in until it bottoms. Maintaining a light inward pressure, rotate the knob counterclockwise until the drive section of the cylinder mates with the drive shaft. Push in until the snapring pops into the groove and the lock cylinder is secured in the cover. Check for free rotation.

12. When installing the ignition switch, be sure the lock cylinder is in the LOCK position. Put the shift bowl or shroud in the PARK position. Make sure the ignition switch is in the LOCK position. Insert the actuator rod into the switch and assemble the switch to the column.

13. The neutral start switch is adjusted with the shift lever in the drive position.

Tie Rod End
REMOVAL AND INSTALLATION

1. Raise and support the car. Loosen the tie rod adjuster sleeve clamp nuts.

2. Remove the tie rod stud nut cotter pin and nut.

3. Remove the tie rod stud from the steering arm or intermediate rod. This is a taper fit. Removal is accomplished using a ball joint removal tool or by hitting the steering arm sharply with a hammer, while using a heavy hammer as a backup. If the joint is to be reused, the removal joint must be used.

4. Unthread the tie rod from the adjusted sleeve. Outer tie rods have right-hand threads and inner tie rods have left-hand threads. Count the number of turns the tie rod must be rotated to remove it from the adjusting sleeve. This will allow a reasonably accurate realignment upon reassembly.

NOTE: *If a turning force of more than 7 ft.lb. is needed for end removal, after break-away, the nuts and bolts should be replaced.*

5. Reverse the removal procedures to install. Clean rust and dirt from the threads. Observe the following torque specifications: steering arm-to-tie rod end nut, 35 ft.lb.; tie rod clamp nuts, 11-14 ft.lb.; tie rod-to-intermediate nut, 40 ft.lb. Check the alignment and adjust as necessary.

Power Steering Pump
REMOVAL AND INSTALLATION

1. Remove the hoses at the pump and tape the openings shut to prevent contamination. Position the disconnected lines in a raised position to prevent leakage.

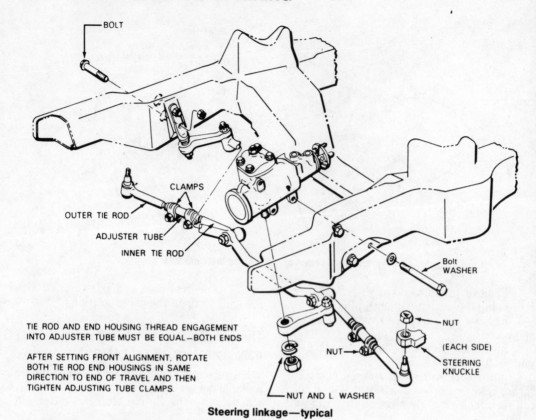

TIE ROD AND END HOUSING THREAD ENGAGEMENT INTO ADJUSTER TUBE MUST BE EQUAL—BOTH ENDS

AFTER SETTING FRONT ALIGNMENT, ROTATE BOTH TIE ROD END HOUSINGS IN SAME DIRECTION TO END OF TRAVEL AND THEN TIGHTEN ADJUSTING TUBE CLAMPS.

Steering linkage—typical

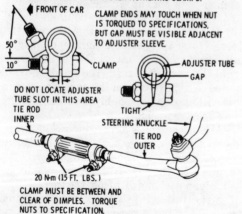

BOLTS MUST BE INSTALLED IN DIRECTION SHOWN, ROTATE BOTH INNER AND OUTER TIE ROD HOUSINGS REARWARD TO THE LIMIT OF BALL JOINT TRAVEL BEFORE TIGHTENING CLAMPS. WITH THIS SAME REARWARD ROTATION ALL BOLT CENTERLINES MUST BE BETWEEN ANGLES SHOWN AFTER TIGHTENING CLAMPS.

CLAMP ENDS MAY TOUCH WHEN NUT IS TORQUED TO SPECIFICATIONS, BUT GAP MUST BE VISIBLE ADJACENT TO ADJUSTER SLEEVE.

DO NOT LOCATE ADJUSTER TUBE SLOT IN THIS AREA

20 N·m (15 FT. LBS.)

CLAMP MUST BE BETWEEN AND CLEAR OF DIMPLES. TORQUE NUTS TO SPECIFICATION.

Tie rod clamp and sleeve positioning

2. Remove the pump belt.

3. Loosen the retaining bolts and any braces, and remove the pump.

4. Install the pump on the engine with the retaining bolts hand-tight.

5. Connect and tighten the hose fittings.

6. Refill the pump with fluid and bleed by turning the pulley counterclockwise (viewed from the front). Stop the bleeding when air bubbles no longer appear.

7. Install the pump belt on the pulley and adjust the tension.

BLEEDING

1. Fill the pump reservoir to the proper level. See the steering index page for fluid recommendations. Operate the engine and turn the steering wheel fully to the left and right without hitting the stops until the power steering fluid reaches normal operating temperature (165-175°F), then stop the engine.

2. Raise the front of the vehicle off the ground and support it on jack stands. Failure to raise the front end off the ground could cause flat spots to be worn into the tires during the bleeding procedure.

3. Turn the wheels to full left turn position and add power steering fluid to the COLD mark on the dipstick, if necessary.

4. Bleed the system by turning the wheels, with the engine running, from side to side without hitting hard against the stops. Maintain the fluid level at the COLD mark on the dipstick. Fluid with air in it will have a milky appearance. Air must be eliminated from the fluid before normal steering action can be ob-

tained. Continue turning the wheels back and forth until all of the air is bled from the system.

5. Return the wheels to center position and operate the engine for an additional 2-3 minutes, then stop the engine.

6. Road test the car to make sure the steering functions normally and is free of noise. Check the fluid level. All fluid to the HOT mark.

PRELIMINARY TESTS

NOTE: *The following tests are generally applicable to most power steering systems.*

Turning Effort

Check the effort required to turn the steering wheel after aligning the front wheels and inflating the tires to the proper pressure.

1. With the vehicle on dry pavement and the front wheels straight ahead, set the parking brake and turn the engine on.

2. After a short warm-up period turn the steering wheel back and forth several times to warm the steering fluid.

3. Attach a spring scale to the steering wheel rim and measure the pull required to turn the steering wheel one complete revolution in each direction.

NOTE: *This test may be done with torque wrench on the steering wheel nut. See the section on Manual Steering for a discussion of this test.*

Checking the Fluid Flow and Pressure Relief Valve in the Pump Assembly

When the wheels are turned hard right or hard left, against the stops, the fluid flow and pressure relief valves come into action. If these valves are working, there should be a slight buzzing noise. Do not hold the wheels in the extreme position for over three or four seconds because, if the pressure relief valve is not working, the pressure could get high enough to damage the system.

Manual Steering Gear
REMOVAL AND INSTALLATION

1. Disconnect the steering shaft coupling.
2. Remove the pitman arm with a puller after marking the arm-to-shaft relationship.
3. Remove the steering gear-to-frame mounting bolts and remove the steering gear.
4. Reverse the removal steps to install the steering gear. Tighten the frame mounting bolts to 70 ft.lb. Tighten the pitman shaft nut to 180 ft.lb. and the steering coupling nuts to 20 ft.lb.

Power Steering Gear
REMOVAL AND INSTALLATION

Installation and removal of power steering gears is the same as that described for manual steering gears above, with the addition of disconnecting and reconnecting the hydraulic lines. Cap both hoses and steering gear outlets to prevent foreign material from entering the system.

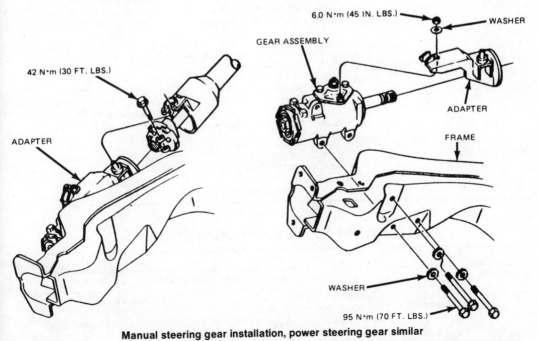

Manual steering gear installation, power steering gear similar

Noise Diagnosis

The Noise Is	Most Probably Produced By
• Identical under Drive or Coast	• Road surface, tires or front wheel bearings
• Different depending on road surface	• Road surface or tires
• Lower as the car speed is lowered	• Tires
• Similar with car standing or moving	• Engine or transmission
• A vibration	• Unbalanced tires, rear wheel bearing, unbalanced driveshaft or worn U-joint
• A knock or click about every 2 tire revolutions	• Rear wheel bearing
• Most pronounced on turns	• Damaged differential gears
• A steady low-pitched whirring or scraping, starting at low speeds	• Damaged or worn pinion bearing
• A chattering vibration on turns	• Wrong differential lubricant or worn clutch plates (limited slip rear axle)
• Noticed only in Drive, Coast or Float conditions	• Worn ring gear and/or pinion gear

Troubleshooting Basic Steering and Suspension Problems

Problem	Cause	Solution
Hard steering (steering wheel is hard to turn)	• Low or uneven tire pressure	• Inflate tires to correct pressure
	• Loose power steering pump drive belt	• Adjust belt
	• Low or incorrect power steering fluid	• Add fluid as necessary
	• Incorrect front end alignment	• Have front end alignment checked/adjusted
	• Defective power steering pump	• Check pump
	• Bent or poorly lubricated front end parts	• Lubricate and/or replace defective parts
Loose steering (too much play in the steering wheel)	• Loose wheel bearings	• Adjust wheel bearings
	• Loose or worn steering linkage	• Replace worn parts
	• Faulty shocks	• Replace shocks
	• Worn ball joints	• Replace ball joints
Car veers or wanders (car pulls to one side with hands off the steering wheel)	• Incorrect tire pressure	• Inflate tires to correct pressure
	• Improper front end alignment	• Have front end alignment checked/adjusted
	• Loose wheel bearings	• Adjust wheel bearings
	• Loose or bent front end components	• Replace worn components
	• Faulty shocks	• Replace shocks
Wheel oscillation or vibration transmitted through steering wheel	• Improper tire pressures	• Inflate tires to correct pressure
	• Tires out of balance	• Have tires balanced
	• Loose wheel bearings	• Adjust wheel bearings
	• Improper front end alignment	• Have front end alignment checked/adjusted
	• Worn or bent front end components	• Replace worn parts
Uneven tire wear	• Incorrect tire pressure	• Inflate tires to correct pressure
	• Front end out of alignment	• Have front end alignment checked/adjusted
	• Tires out of balance	• Have tires balanced

Troubleshooting the Steering Column

Problem	Cause	Solution
Will not lock	• Lockbolt spring broken or defective	• Replace lock bolt spring
High effort (required to turn ignition key and lock cylinder)	• Lock cylinder defective	• Replace lock cylinder
	• Ignition switch defective	• Replace ignition switch
	• Rack preload spring broken or deformed	• Replace preload spring

Troubleshooting the Steering Column (cont.)

Problem	Cause	Solution
High effort (required to turn ignition key and lock cylinder)	• Burr on lock sector, lock rack, housing, support or remote rod coupling	• Remove burr
	• Bent sector shaft	• Replace shaft
	• Defective lock rack	• Replace lock rack
	• Remote rod bent, deformed	• Replace rod
	• Ignition switch mounting bracket bent	• Straighten or replace
	• Distorted coupling slot in lock rack (tilt column)	• Replace lock rack
Will stick in "start"	• Remote rod deformed	• Straighten or replace
	• Ignition switch mounting bracket bent	• Straighten or replace
Key cannot be removed in "off-lock"	• Ignition switch is not adjusted correctly	• Adjust switch
	• Defective lock cylinder	• Replace lock cylinder
Lock cylinder can be removed without depressing retainer	• Lock cylinder with defective retainer	• Replace lock cylinder
	• Burr over retainer slot in housing cover or on cylinder retainer	• Remove burr
High effort on lock cylinder between "off" and "off-lock"	• Distorted lock rack	• Replace lock rack
	• Burr on tang of shift gate (automatic column)	• Remove burr
	• Gearshift linkage not adjusted	• Adjust linkage
Noise in column	• One click when in "off-lock" position and the steering wheel is moved (all except automatic column)	• Normal—lock bolt is seating
	• Coupling bolts not tightened	• Tighten pinch bolts
	• Lack of grease on bearings or bearing surfaces	• Lubricate with chassis grease
	• Upper shaft bearing worn or broken	• Replace bearing assembly
	• Lower shaft bearing worn or broken	• Replace bearing. Check shaft and replace if scored.
	• Column not correctly aligned	• Align column
	• Coupling pulled apart	• Replace coupling
	• Broken coupling lower joint	• Repair or replace joint and align column
	• Steering shaft snap ring not seated	• Replace ring. Check for proper seating in groove.
	• Shroud loose on shift bowl. Housing loose on jacket—will be noticed with ignition in "off-lock" and when torque is applied to steering wheel.	• Position shroud over lugs on shift bowl. Tighten mounting screws.
High steering shaft effort	• Column misaligned	• Align column
	• Defective upper or lower bearing	• Replace as required
	• Tight steering shaft universal joint	• Repair or replace
	• Flash on I.D. of shift tube at plastic joint (tilt column only)	• Replace shift tube
	• Upper or lower bearing seized	• Replace bearings
Lash in mounted column assembly	• Column mounting bracket bolts loose	• Tighten bolts
	• Broken weld nuts on column jacket	• Replace column jacket
	• Column capsule bracket sheared	• Replace bracket assembly
	• Column bracket to column jacket mounting bolts loose	• Tighten to specified torque
	• Loose lock shoes in housing (tilt column only)	• Replace shoes
	• Loose pivot pins (tilt column only)	• Replace pivot pins and support

Troubleshooting the Steering Column (cont.)

Problem	Cause	Solution
Lash in mounted column assembly (cont.)	• Loose lock shoe pin (tilt column only)	• Replace pin and housing
	• Loose support screws (tilt column only)	• Tighten screws
Housing loose (tilt column only)	• Excessive clearance between holes in support or housing and pivot pin diameters	• Replace pivot pins and support
	• Housing support-screws loose	• Tighten screws
Steering wheel loose—every other tilt position (tilt column only)	• Loose fit between lock shoe and lock shoe pivot pin	• Replace lock shoes and pivot pin
Steering column not locking in any tilt position (tilt column only)	• Lock shoe seized on pivot pin	• Replace lock shoes and pin
	• Lock shoe grooves have burrs or are filled with foreign material	• Clean or replace lock shoes
	• Lock shoe springs weak or broken	• Replace springs
Noise when tilting column (tilt column only)	• Upper tilt bumpers worn	• Replace tilt bumper
	• Tilt spring rubbing in housing	• Lubricate with chassis grease
One click when in "off-lock" position and the steering wheel is moved	• Seating of lock bolt	• None. Click is normal characteristic sound produced by lock bolt as it seats.
High shift effort (automatic and tilt column only)	• Column not correctly aligned	• Align column
	• Lower bearing not aligned correctly	• Assemble correctly
	• Lack of grease on seal or lower bearing areas	• Lubricate with chassis grease
Improper transmission shifting— automatic and tilt column only	• Sheared shift tube joint	• Replace shift tube
	• Improper transmission gearshift linkage adjustment	• Adjust linkage
	• Loose lower shift lever	• Replace shift tube

Troubleshooting the Ignition Switch

Problem	Cause	Solution
Ignition switch electrically inoperative	• Loose or defective switch connector	• Tighten or replace connector
	• Feed wire open (fusible link)	• Repair or replace
	• Defective ignition switch	• Replace ignition switch
Engine will not crank	• Ignition switch not adjusted properly	• Adjust switch
Ignition switch wil not actuate mechanically	• Defective ignition switch	• Replace switch
	• Defective lock sector	• Replace lock sector
	• Defective remote rod	• Replace remote rod
Ignition switch cannot be adjusted correctly	• Remote rod deformed	• Repair, straighten or replace

Troubleshooting the Turn Signal Switch

Problem	Cause	Solution
Turn signal will not cancel	• Loose switch mounting screws	• Tighten screws
	• Switch or anchor bosses broken	• Replace switch
	• Broken, missing or out of position detent, or cancelling spring	• Reposition springs or replace switch as required
Turn signal difficult to operate	• Turn signal lever loose	• Tighten mounting screws
	• Switch yoke broken or distorted	• Replace switch
	• Loose or misplaced springs	• Reposition springs or replace switch

Troubleshooting the Turn Signal Switch (cont.)

Problem	Cause	Solution
Turn signal difficult to operate (cont.)	• Foreign parts and/or materials in switch • Switch mounted loosely	• Remove foreign parts and/or material • Tighten mounting screws
Turn signal will not indicate lane change	• Broken lane change pressure pad or spring hanger • Broken, missing or misplaced lane change spring • Jammed wires	• Replace switch • Replace or reposition as required • Loosen mounting screws, reposition wires and retighten screws
Turn signal will not stay in turn position	• Foreign material or loose parts impeding movement of switch yoke • Defective switch	• Remove material and/or parts • Replace switch
Hazard switch cannot be pulled out	• Foreign material between hazard support cancelling leg and yoke	• Remove foreign material. No foreign material impeding function of hazard switch—replace turn signal switch.
No turn signal lights	• Inoperative turn signal flasher • Defective or blown fuse • Loose chassis to column harness connector • Disconnect column to chassis connector. Connect new switch to chassis and operate switch by hand. If vehicle lights now operate normally, signal switch is inoperative • If vehicle lights do not operate, check chassis wiring for opens, grounds, etc.	• Replace turn signal flasher • Replace fuse • Connect securely • Replace signal switch • Repair chassis wiring as required
Instrument panel turn indicator lights on but not flashing	• Burned out or damaged front or rear turn signal bulb • If vehicle lights do not operate, check light sockets for high resistance connections, the chassis wiring for opens, grounds, etc. • Inoperative flasher • Loose chassis to column harness connection • Inoperative turn signal switch • To determine if turn signal switch is defective, substitute new switch into circuit and operate switch by hand. If the vehicle's lights operate normally, signal switch is inoperative.	• Replace bulb • Repair chassis wiring as required • Replace flasher • Connect securely • Replace turn signal switch • Replace turn signal switch
Stop light not on when turn indicated	• Loose column to chassis connection • Disconnect column to chassis connector. Connect new switch into system without removing old. Operate switch by hand. If brake lights work with switch in the turn position, signal switch is defective. • If brake lights do not work, check connector to stop light sockets for grounds, opens, etc.	• Connect securely • Replace signal switch • Repair connector to stop light circuits using service manual as guide

Troubleshooting the Turn Signal Switch (cont.)

Problem	Cause	Solution
Turn indicator panel lights not flashing	• Burned out bulbs • High resistance to ground at bulb socket • Opens, ground in wiring harness from front turn signal bulb socket to indicator lights	• Replace bulbs • Replace socket • Locate and repair as required
Turn signal lights flash very slowly	• High resistance ground at light sockets • Incorrect capacity turn signal flasher or bulb • If flashing rate is still extremely slow, check chassis wiring harness from the connector to light sockets for high resistance • Loose chassis to column harness connection • Disconnect column to chassis connector. Connect new switch into system without removing old. Operate switch by hand. If flashing occurs at normal rate, the signal switch is defective.	• Repair high resistance grounds at light sockets • Replace turn signal flasher or bulb • Locate and repair as required • Connect securely • Replace turn signal switch
Hazard signal lights will not flash—turn signal functions normally	• Blow fuse • Inoperative hazard warning flasher • Loose chassis-to-column harness connection • Disconnect column to chassis connector. Connect new switch into system without removing old. Depress the hazard warning lights. If they now work normally, turn signal switch is defective. • If lights do not flash, check wiring harness "K" lead for open between hazard flasher and connector. If open, fuse block is defective	• Replace fuse • Replace hazard warning flasher in fuse panel • Conect securely • Replace turn signal switch • Repair or replace brown wire or connector as required

Troubleshooting the Manual Steering Gear

Problem	Cause	Solution
Hard or erratic steering	• Incorrect tire pressure • Insufficient or incorrect lubrication • Suspension, or steering linkage parts damaged or misaligned • Improper front wheel alignment • Incorrect steering gear adjustment • Sagging springs	• Inflate tires to recommended pressures • Lubricate as required (refer to Maintenance Section) • Repair or replace parts as necessary • Adjust incorrect wheel alignment angles • Adjust steering gear • Replace springs
Play or looseness in steering	• Steering wheel loose • Steering linkage or attaching parts loose or worn • Pitman arm loose	• Inspect shaft spines and repair as necessary. Tighten attaching nut and stake in place. • Tighten, adjust, or replace faulty components • Inspect shaft splines and repair as necessary. Tighten attaching nut and stake in place

Troubleshooting the Manual Steering Gear (cont.)

Problem	Cause	Solution
Play or looseness in steering	• Steering gear attaching bolts loose • Loose or worn wheel bearings • Steering gear adjustment incorrect or parts badly worn	• Tighten bolts • Adjust or replace bearings • Adjust gear or replace defective parts
Wheel shimmy or tramp	• Improper tire pressure • Wheels, tires, or brake rotors out-of-balance or out-of-round • Inoperative, worn, or loose shock absorbers or mounting parts • Loose or worn steering or suspension parts • Loose or worn wheel bearings • Incorrect steering gear adjustments • Incorrect front wheel alignment	• Inflate tires to recommended pressures • Inspect and replace or balance parts • Repair or replace shocks or mountings • Tighten or replace as necessary • Adjust or replace bearings • Adjust steering gear • Correct front wheel alignment
Tire wear	• Improper tire pressure • Failure to rotate tires • Brakes grabbing • Incorrect front wheel alignment • Broken or damaged steering and suspension parts • Wheel runout • Excessive speed on turns	• Inflate tires to recommended pressures • Rotate tires • Adjust or repair brakes • Align incorrect angles • Repair or replace defective parts • Replace faulty wheel • Make driver aware of conditions
Vehicle leads to one side	• Improper tire pressures • Front tires with uneven tread depth, wear pattern, or different cord design (i.e., one bias ply and one belted or radial tire on front wheels) • Incorrect front wheel alignment • Brakes dragging • Pulling due to uneven tire construction	• Inflate tires to recommended pressures • Install tires of same cord construction and reasonably even tread depth, design, and wear pattern • Align incorrect angles • Adjust or repair brakes • Replace faulty tire

Troubleshooting the Power Steering Gear

Problem	Cause	Solution
Hissing noise in steering gear	• There is some noise in all power steering systems. One of the most common is a hissing sound most evident at standstill parking. There is no relationship between this noise and performance of the steering. Hiss may be expected when steering wheel is at end of travel or when slowly turning at standstill.	• Slight hiss is normal and in no way affects steering. Do not replace valve unless hiss is extremely objectionable. A replacement valve will also exhibit slight noise and is not always a cure. Investigate clearance around flexible coupling rivets. Be sure steering shaft and gear are aligned so flexible coupling rotates in a flat plane and is not distorted as shaft rotates. Any metal-to-metal contacts through flexible coupling will transmit valve hiss into passenger compartment through the steering column.
Rattle or chuckle noise in steering gear	• Gear loose on frame	• Check gear-to-frame mounting screws. Tighten screws to 88 N·m (65 foot pounds) torque.

Troubleshooting the Power Steering Gear (cont.)

Problem	Cause	Solution
Rattle or chuckle noise in steering gear (cont.)	• Steering linkage looseness • Pressure hose touching other parts of car • Loose pitman shaft over center adjustment **NOTE:** A slight rattle may occur on turns because of increased clearance off the "high point." This is normal and clearance must not be reduced below specified limits to eliminate this slight rattle. • Loose pitman arm	• Check linkage pivot points for wear. Replace if necessary. • Adjust hose position. Do not bend tubing by hand. • Adjust to specifications • Tighten pitman arm nut to specifications
Squawk noise in steering gear when turning or recovering from a turn	• Damper O-ring on valve spool cut	• Replace damper O-ring
Poor return of steering wheel to center	• Tires not properly inflated • Lack of lubrication in linkage and ball joints • Lower coupling flange rubbing against steering gear adjuster plug • Steering gear to column misalignment • Improper front wheel alignment • Steering linkage binding • Ball joints binding • Steering wheel rubbing against housing • Tight or frozen steering shaft bearings • Sticking or plugged valve spool • Steering gear adjustments over specifications • Kink in return hose	• Inflate to specified pressure • Lube linkage and ball joints • Loosen pinch bolt and assemble properly • Align steering column • Check and adjust as necessary • Replace pivots • Replace ball joints • Align housing • Replace bearings • Remove and clean or replace valve • Check adjustment with gear out of car. Adjust as required. • Replace hose
Car leads to one side or the other (keep in mind road condition and wind. Test car in both directions on flat road)	• Front end misaligned • Unbalanced steering gear valve **NOTE:** If this is cause, steering effort will be very light in direction of lead and normal or heavier in opposite direction	• Adjust to specifications • Replace valve
Momentary increase in effort when turning wheel fast to right or left	• Low oil level • Pump belt slipping • High internal leakage	• Add power steering fluid as required • Tighten or replace belt • Check pump pressure. (See pressure test)
Steering wheel surges or jerks when turning with engine running especially during parking	• Low oil level • Loose pump belt • Steering linkage hitting engine oil pan at full turn • Insufficient pump pressure • Pump flow control valve sticking	• Fill as required • Adjust tension to specification • Correct clearance • Check pump pressure. (See pressure test). Replace relief valve if defective. • Inspect for varnish or damage, replace if necessary
Excessive wheel kickback or loose steering	• Air in system	• Add oil to pump reservoir and bleed by operating steering. Check hose connectors for proper torque and adjust as required.

Troubleshooting the Power Steering Gear (cont.)

Problem	Cause	Solution
Excessive wheel kickback or loose steering (cont.)	• Steering gear loose on frame • Steering linkage joints worn enough to be loose • Worn poppet valve • Loose thrust bearing preload adjustment • Excessive overcenter lash	• Tighten attaching screws to specified torque • Replace loose pivots • Replace poppet valve • Adjust to specification with gear out of vehicle • Adjust to specification with gear out of car
Hard steering or lack of assist	• Loose pump belt • Low oil level **NOTE:** Low oil level will also result in excessive pump noise • Steering gear to column misalignment • Lower coupling flange rubbing against steering gear adjuster plug • Tires not properly inflated	• Adjust belt tension to specification • Fill to proper level. If excessively low, check all lines and joints for evidence of external leakage. Tighten loose connectors. • Align steering column • Loosen pinch bolt and assemble properly • Inflate to recommended pressure
Foamy milky power steering fluid, low fluid level and possible low pressure	• Air in the fluid, and loss of fluid due to internal pump leakage causing overflow	• Check for leak and correct. Bleed system. Extremely cold temperatures will cause system aeriation should the oil level be low. If oil level is correct and pump still foams, remove pump from vehicle and separate reservoir from housing. Check welsh plug and housing for cracks. If plug is loose or housing is cracked, replace housing.
Low pressure due to steering pump	• Flow control valve stuck or inoperative • Pressure plate not flat against cam ring	• Remove burrs or dirt or replace. Flush system. • Correct
Low pressure due to steering gear	• Pressure loss in cylinder due to worn piston ring or badly worn housing bore • Leakage at valve rings, valve body-to-worm seal	• Remove gear from car for disassembly and inspection of ring and housing bore • Remove gear from car for disassembly and replace seals

Troubleshooting the Power Steering Pump

Problem	Cause	Solution
Chirp noise in steering pump	• Loose belt	• Adjust belt tension to specification
Belt squeal (particularly noticeable at full wheel travel and stand still parking)	• Loose belt	• Adjust belt tension to specification
Growl noise in steering pump	• Excessive back pressure in hoses or steering gear caused by restriction	• Locate restriction and correct. Replace part if necessary.
Growl noise in steering pump (particularly noticeable at stand still parking)	• Scored pressure plates, thrust plate or rotor • Extreme wear of cam ring	• Replace parts and flush system • Replace parts
Groan noise in steering pump	• Low oil level • Air in the oil. Poor pressure hose connection.	• Fill reservoir to proper level • Tighten connector to specified torque. Bleed system by operating steering from right to left—full turn.

Troubleshooting the Power Steering Pump (cont.)

Problem	Cause	Solution
Rattle noise in steering pump	• Vanes not installed properly • Vanes sticking in rotor slots	• Install properly • Free up by removing burrs, varnish, or dirt
Swish noise in steering pump	• Defective flow control valve	• Replace part
Whine noise in steering pump	• Pump shaft bearing scored	• Replace housing and shaft. Flush system.
Hard steering or lack of assist	• Loose pump belt • Low oil level in reservoir **NOTE:** Low oil level will also result in excessive pump noise • Steering gear to column misalignment • Lower coupling flange rubbing against steering gear adjuster plug • Tires not properly inflated	• Adjust belt tension to specification • Fill to proper level. If excessively low, check all lines and joints for evidence of external leakage. Tighten loose connectors. • Align steering column • Loosen pinch bolt and assemble properly • Inflate to recommended pressure
Foaming milky power steering fluid, low fluid level and possible low pressure	• Air in the fluid, and loss of fluid due to internal pump leakage causing overflow	• Check for leaks and correct. Bleed system. Extremely cold temperatures will cause system aeration should the oil level be low. If oil level is correct and pump still foams, remove pump from vehicle and separate reservoir from body. Check welsh plug and body for cracks. If plug is loose or body is cracked, replace body.
Low pump pressure	• Flow control valve stuck or inoperative • Pressure plate not flat against cam ring	• Remove burrs or dirt or replace. Flush system. • Correct
Momentary increase in effort when turning wheel fast to right or left	• Low oil level in pump • Pump belt slipping • High internal leakage	• Add power steering fluid as required • Tighten or replace belt • Check pump pressure. (See pressure test)
Steering wheel surges or jerks when turning with engine running especially during parking	• Low oil level • Loose pump belt • Steering linkage hitting engine oil pan at full turn • Insufficient pump pressure • Sticking flow control valve	• Fill as required • Adjust tension to specification • Correct clearance • Check pump pressure. (See pressure test). Replace flow control valve if defective. • Inspect for varnish or damage, replace if necessary
Excessive wheel kickback or loose steering	• Air in system	• Add oil to pump reservoir and bleed by operating steering. Check hose connectors for proper torque and adjust as required.
Low pump pressure	• Extreme wear of cam ring • Scored pressure plate, thrust plate, or rotor • Vanes not installed properly • Vanes sticking in rotor slots • Cracked or broken thrust or pressure plate	• Replace parts. Flush system. • Replace parts. Flush system. • Install properly • Freeup by removing burrs, varnish, or dirt • Replace part

Brakes

8

BRAKE SYSTEM

1970 through 1972 models were equipped with front drum brakes as standard equipment, with front disc brakes as an option. On 1973 and later models front disc brakes are standard.

The standard drum brakes are of the conventional, internally expanding type which have been in use on American cars for decades. Unless they have been replace, the brake shoe linings will be of the bonded type. Replacement linings may be either bonded or riveted. Front disc brakes are of the single piston floating caliper type.

Dual reservoir master cylinders are used on all models.

ADJUSTMENT

Adjustment procedures are given here for drum brakes only. No adjustment is possible on disc brakes since they are inherently self-adjusting type. All drum brakes are of the self-adjusting type, also. All that is normally required to adjust the brakes is to stop the car moderately hard several times while backing up. If more adjustment is required, however, or if the brakes have been replace, use the following procedure:

1. Raise the car and support it with safety stands.

2. Remove the rubber plug from the adjusting slot on the backing plate.

3. Insert a brake adjusting spoon into the slot and engage the lowest possible tooth on the starwheel. Move the end of the brake spoon downward to move the starwheel upward and expand the adjusting screw. Repeat this operation until the brakes lock the wheel.

4. Insert a small screwdriver or piece of firm wire (coat-hanger wire) into the adjusting slot and push the automatic adjuster lever out and free of the starwheel on the adjusting screw.

5. Holding the adjusting lever out of the way, engage the topmost tooth possible on the starwheel with a brake adjusting spoon. Move the end of the adjusting spoon upward to move the adjusting screw starwheel downward and contract the adjusting screw. Back off the adjusting screw starwheel until the wheel springs freely with a minimum of drag. Keep track of the number of turns the starwheel is backed off.

6. Repeat this operation for the other side. When backing off the brakes on the other side, the adjusting lever must be backed off the same number of turns to prevent side-to-side brake pull.

7. Repeat this operation on the other set of brakes.

8. When all brakes are adjusted, make several stops, while backing the car, to equalize all of the wheels.

9. Road-test the car.

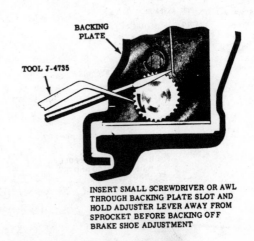

INSERT SMALL SCREWDRIVER OR AWL THROUGH BACKING PLATE SLOT AND HOLD ADJUSTER LEVER AWAY FROM SPROCKET BEFORE BACKING OFF BRAKE SHOE ADJUSTMENT

Drum brake adjustment

Master Cylinder

REMOVAL AND INSTALLATION

On cars with power brakes, the master cylinder can be removed without removing the vacuum booster from the car.

1. Disconnect the hydraulic lines from the master cylinder. Cap the lines to prevent leakage or contamination of the brake fluid.

2. If the car is equipped with non-power brakes, disconnect the push-rod from the brake pedal by removing the clevis pin.

3. Remove the master cylinder attaching nuts and remove the master cylinder.

4. To install a non-power master cylinder, position the cylinder against the firewall with the pushrod inserted into the driver's compartment.

5. Torque the master cylinder attaching nuts to 28 ft.lb. Attach the pushrod to the brake pedal with the clevis pin.

6. On power brake systems, position the master cylinder over the pushrod and torque the nuts to 28 ft.lb.

7. Install the hydraulic lines.

8. Bleed the brake system as outlined in this chapter.

OVERHAUL

Either a Bendix or a Delco-Moraine master cylinder is used. The repair kits may differ slightly, but procedures are the same. Pay particular attention to the instructions that come with the kit.

1. Remove the master cylinder from the car.

2. Remove the mounting gasket and boot, and the main cover, and purge the unit of its fluid.

3. Secure the cylinder in a vise and remove the pushrod retainer and secondary piston stop bolt found inside the forward reservoir.

4. Compress the retaining ring and extract it along with the primary piston assembly.

5. Blow compressed air into the piston stop screw hole to force the secondary piston, spring, and retainer from the bore of the cylinder. An alternative method is to use hooked wire to snap and extract the secondary piston.

6. Check the brass tube fitting inserts and if they are damaged, remove them. Leave undamaged inserts in place.

7. If replacement is necessary, thread a 6-3 x 5/8" self-tapping screw into the insert. Hook the end of the screw with a claw hammer and pry the insert free.

8. An alternative way to remove the inserts is to first drill the outlet holes to 13/64" and thread them with a 1/4"-20 tap. Position a thick washer over the hole to serve as a spacer, and then thread a 1/4"-20 x 3/4" hex head bolt into the insert and tighten the bolt until the insert is freed.

9. Use denatured alcohol and compressed

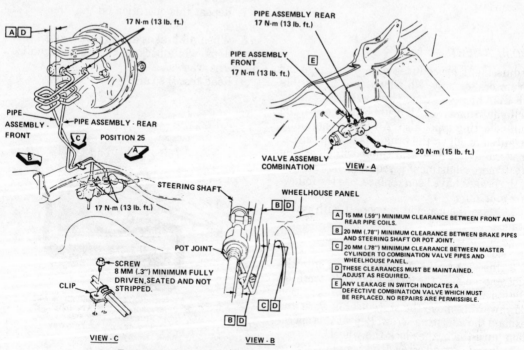

Typical master cylinder and combination valve mounting

air to clean the parts. Slight rust may be removed with crocus cloth.

10. Replace the brass tube inserts by positioning them in their holes and threading a brake line tube nut into the outlet hole. Turn down the nut until the insert is seated.

11. Check the piston assemblies for correct identification and, when satisfied, position the replacement secondary seals in the twin grooves of the secondary piston.

12. The outside seal is correctly placed when its lips face the flat end of the piston.

13. Slip the primary seal and its protector over the end of the secondary piston opposite the secondary seals. The flat side of this seal should face the piston's compensating hole flange.

14. Replace the primary piston assembly with assembled pieces in the overhaul kit.

15. Moisten the cylinder bore and the secondary piston's inner and outer seals with brake fluid. Assemble the secondary piston spring to its retainer and position them over the end of the primary seal.

16. Insert the combined spring and piston assembly into the cylinder and use a small wooden dowel or pencil to seal the spring against the end of the bore.

17. Moisten the primary piston seals with brake fluid and push it, pushrod receptacle end out, into the cylinder.

18. Keep the piston pushed in and snap the retaining ring into place.

19. Relax the pressure on the pistons and allow them to seek their static positions.

20. Replace the secondary piston stop screw and torque it to 25-40 in.lb.

21. Replace the reservoir diaphragm and cover.

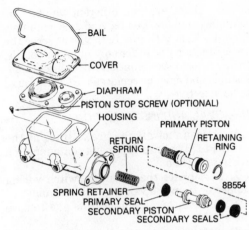

Disassembled view of master cylinder—Diesel V8

NOTE: *Overhaul of the main cylinder portion of power master cylinders is the same as that for manual master cylinders.*

Power Booster

REMOVAL AND INSTALLATION

1. Disconnect the booster pushrod from the brake pedal arm by removing the retaining clip, and sliding the eyelet end of the pushrod off of the pin on the brake arm.

2. Disconnect the master cylinder from the booster.

3. Remove the attaching nuts and remove the booster from the firewall.

4. Installation is the reverse of removal. Tighten the booster-to-firewall attaching nuts to 22-33 ft.lb.

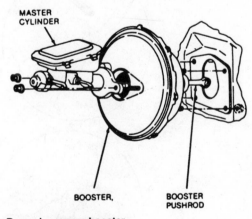

Removing power booster

Combination Valve

The combination valve used in a three-function valve. It serves as a metering valve, balance valve, and brake warning

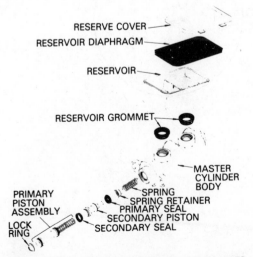

Typical disassembled view of master cylinder, 1978 and later shown, other years similar

switch. There are two different valves, one manufactured by Bendix and one manufactured by Kelsey-Hayes. Both valves serve the same function and differ only in minor details. In any case, all combination valves are non-adjustable and must be replaced if they are found to be defective.

REMOVAL AND INSTALLATION

1. Disconnect all the brake lines at the valve. Plug the lines to prevent contamination and loss of fluid.

2. Disconnect the warning switch wiring connector from the valve switch terminal.

3. Remove the attaching bolts and remove the valve.

4. Install the valve in the reverse order of removal.

5. Bleed the entire brake system after valve installation.

Brake Bleeding

The hydraulic brake system must be bled any time one of the brake lines is disconnected or air enters the system. There are two ways to bleed the system; pressure bleeding or manual bleeding. Both procedures will be given here, although pressure bleeding requires the use of some fairly expensive equipment (a pressure tank) and is seldom used. Both methods are equally effective.

The correct bleeding sequence is: left rear wheel cylinder, right rear, right front, and left front.

PRESSURE BLEEDING

1. Clean the top of the master cylinder, remove the cover, and attach the pressure bleeding adapter.

2. The spring-loaded plunger on the front of the proportioning valve must be depressed while bleeding. Wire or tape can be wrapped around the valve to hold the plunger in.

3. Check the pressure bleeder reservoir for correct pressure and fluid level, then open the release valve.

4. Fasten a bleeder hose to the wheel cylinder or caliper bleeder nipple and submerge the free end of the hose in a transparent receptacle. The receptacle should contain enough brake fluid to cover the open end of the hose.

5. Open the wheel cylinder or caliper bleeder nipple and allow the fluid to flow until all bubbles disappear and an uncontaminated flow exists.

6. Close the nipple, remove the bleeder hose and repeat the procedure on the other wheel cylinders according to the sequence.

MANUAL BLEEDING

An alternative to the pressure method of bleeding requires two people to perform; one to depress the brake pedal and the other to open the bleeder nipples.

1. Clean the top of the master cylinder, and then remove the cover and fill the reservoir.

2. The spring-loaded plunger on the front of the proportioning valve must be depressed

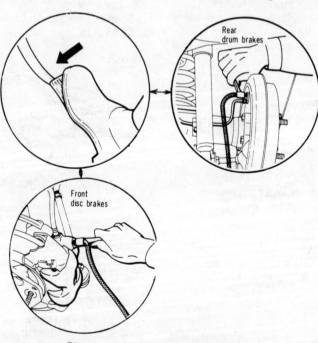

Bleeding the hydraulic brake system

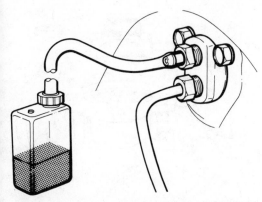

Bleeder hose attachment—rear drum brakes

while bleeding. Wire or tape can be wrapped around the valve to hold the plunger in.

3. Attach a bleeder hose and a clear container as in the pressure bleeding procedure.

4. Have the assistant depress the brake pedal to the floor, and then pause until the fluid stops and the bleeder nipple is closed.

5. Allow the pedal to return and repeat the procedure until a steady, bubble-free flow is seen.

6. Tighten the nipple and move on to the other wheels in sequence.

7. Frequently check the master cylinder level during this procedure. If the reservoir runs dry, air will enter the system and the bleeding will have to be repeated.

FRONT DISC BRAKES

Front disc brakes on all models are of the single piston floating-caliper type. This type of brake is constructed of a large single casting with the piston in the inboard section of the casting. The caliper assembly is mounted directly to the steering knuckle with two allen head bolts. The caliper is free to slide on the sleeves at the inboard ears and at the bolt at the outboard ears.

Disc Brake Pads

INSPECTION

The pads can be inspected for wear by removing the wheel and inspecting the pads through the opening in the top of the caliper. Later models have a wear sensor which squeals when the brakes are worn beyond their limits.

REMOVAL AND INSTALLATION

1. Siphon off ⅔ of the brake fluid from the master cylinder.

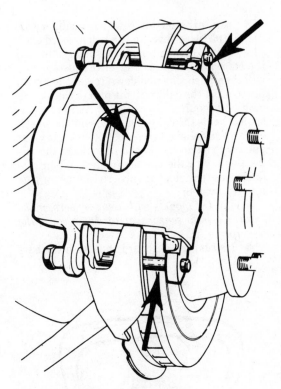

Lining inspection—front disc brakes

NOTE: *The insertion of the thicker replacement pads will push the caliper piston back into its bore and will cause a full master cylinder to overflow.*

2. Jack the car up and support it with jackstands. Remove the wheel(s).

3. Install a C-clamp on the caliper so that the solid side of the clamp rests against the back of the caliper and the screw end rests against the metal part of the outboard pad.

4. Tighten the clamp until the caliper moves enough to bottom the piston in its bore. Remove the clamp.

5. Remove the two allen head caliper mounting bolts enough to allow the caliper to be pulled off the disc.

6. Remove the inboard pad and dislodge the outboard pad. Place the caliper where it won't be supported by the brake hose. Make a wire hook and suspend it from the spring.

7. Remove the pad support spring clip from the piston.

8. Remove the two bolt ear sleeves and the four rubber bushings from the ears.

9. Brake pads should be replaced when they are worn to within $\frac{1}{32}$″ of the rivet heads.

10. Check the inside of the caliper for leakage and the condition of the piston dust boot.

11. Lubricate the two new sleeves and four bushings with a silicone spray.

12. Install the bushings in each caliper ear. Install the two sleeves in the two inboard ears.

13. Install the pad support spring clip and the old pad into the center of the piston. You will then push this pad down to get the piston flat against the caliper. This part of the job is a pain and requires an assistant. While the assistant holds the caliper and loosens the bleeder valve to relieve pressure, you get a pry bar and try to force the old pad in to make the piston flush with the caliper surface. When it is flush, close the bleeder valve so that no air gets into the system.

NOTE: *On models with wear sensors, make sure the wear sensor is toward the rear of the caliper.*

14. Position the outboard shoe with the ears

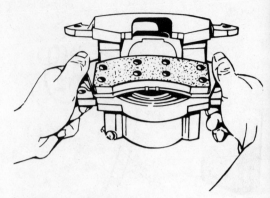

Installing the inboard shoe

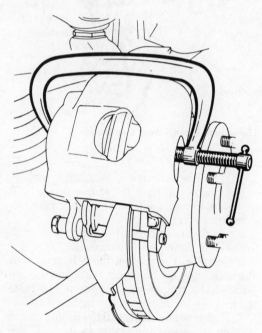

Bottom the piston in its bore with the use of a C-clamp

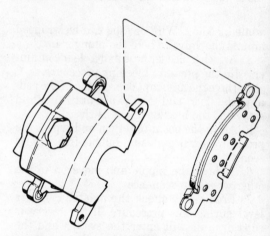

Installing the outboard shoe

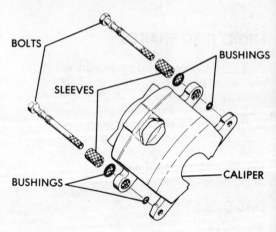

⊠ LUBRICATE AREAS INDICATED

Lubricate the sleeves and bushings

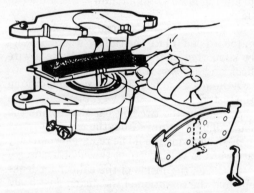

Installing the shoe support spring on the inboard spring

of the shoes over the caliper ears and the tab at the bottom engaged in the caliper cutout. Cinch the upper ears of the outer shoes by positioning channel lock pliers with one jaw on top of the upper ear and one jaw in the notch on the bottom of the shoe opposite the upper ear.

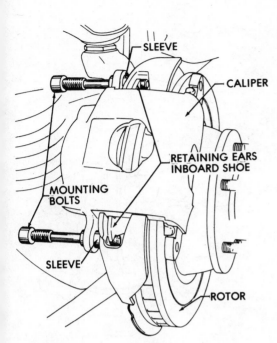

Installation of mounting bolts

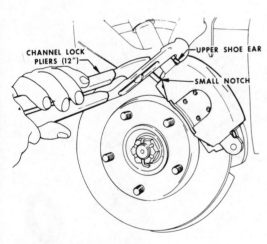

Cinching the outboard shoe

15. With the two shoes in position, place the caliper over the brake disc and align the holes in the caliper with those of the mounting bracket.

CAUTION: *Make certain that the brake hose is not twisted or kinked.*

16. Install the mounting bracket bolts through the sleeves in the inboard caliper ears and through the mounting bracket, making sure that the ends of the bolts pass under the retaining ears on the inboard shoe.

17. Tighten the bolts into the bracket and tighten to 35 ft.lb. Bend over the outer pad ears.

18. Install the front wheel and lower the car.

19. Add fluid to the master cylinder reservoirs so that they are ¼" from the top.

20. Test the brake pedal by pumping it to obtain a "hard" pedal. Check the fluid level again and add fluid as necessary. Do not move the vehicle until a "hard" pedal is obtained. Bleed the brakes if necessary.

Disc Brake Calipers

REMOVAL, INSTALLATION AND OVERHAUL

1. Perform the removal steps for pad replacement.

2. Disconnect the brake hose and plug the line.

3. Remove the U-shaped retainer from the fitting.

4. Pull the hose from the frame bracket and remove the caliper with the hose attached.

5. Clean the outside of the caliper with denatured alcohol.

6. Remove the brake hose and discard the copper gasket.

7. Remove the brake fluid from the caliper.

8. Place clean rags inside the caliper opening to catch the piston when it is released.

9. Apply compressed air to the caliper fluid inlet hole and force the piston out of its bore. Do not blow the piston out, but use just enough pressure to ease it out.

CAUTION: *Do not place your fingers in front of the piston in an attempt to catch or protect it when applying compressed air. This could result in serious injury.*

10. Use a screwdriver to pry the boot out of the caliper. Avoid scratching the bore.

11. Remove the piston seal from its groove in the caliper bore. Do not use a metal tool of any type for this operation.

12. Blow out all passages in the caliper and bleeder valve. Clean the piston and piston bore with fresh brake fluid.

13. Examine the piston for scoring, scratches or corrosion. If any of these conditions exist the piston must be replace, as it is plated and cannot be refinished.

14. Examine the bore for the same defects. Light rough spots may be removed by rotating crocus cloth, using finer pressure, in the bore. Do not polish with an in and out motion or use any other abrasive.

15. Lubricate the piston bore and the new rubber parts with fresh brake fluid. Position the seal in the piston bore groove.

16. Lubricate the piston with brake fluid and assemble the boot into the piston groove so that the fold faces the open end of the piston.

17. Insert the piston into the bore, taking care not to unseat the seal.

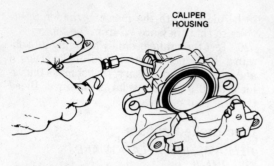

Removing the piston from its bore

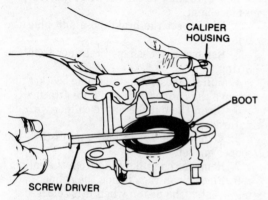

Removing the dust boot from the bore

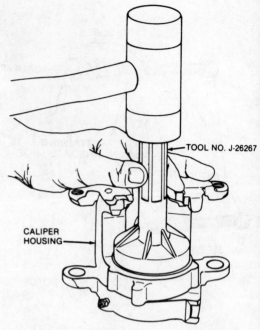

Seat the boot lip around the caliper counterbore

18. Force the piston to the bottom of the bore. (This will require a force of 50-100 lbs.). Seat the boot lip around the caliper counterbore. Proper seating of the boot is very important for sealing out contaminants.

19. Install the brake hose into the caliper using a new copper gasket.

20. Lubricate the new sleeves and rubber bushings. Install the bushings in the caliper ears. Install the sleeves so that the end toward the disc pad is flush with the machined surface.

NOTE: *Lubrication of the sleeves and bushings is essential to ensure the proper operation of the sliding caliper design.*

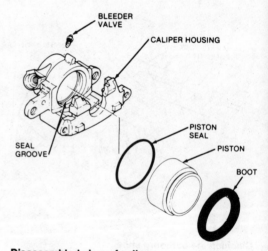

Disassembled view of caliper

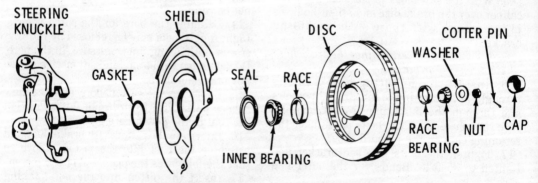

Exploded view of knuckle and hub assembly

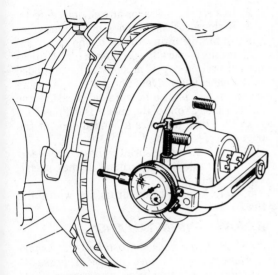

Checking the rotor for lateral runout using a dial indicator

21. Follow steps 13 through 17 of "Disc Brake Pad" installation outlined earlier.

22. Reconnect the brake hose to the steel brake line. Install the retainer clip. Bleed the brakes (see Brake Bleeding).

23. Replace the wheels, check the brake fluid level, check the brake pedal travel, and road-test the vehicle.

Brake Disc

REMOVAL AND INSTALLATION

1. Raise the car, support it with jack stands, and remove the wheel and tire assembly.

2. Remove the brake caliper as previously outlined.

3. Remove the dust cap and remove the wheel bearing nut after removing the cotter pin.

4. Remove the wheel bearing, hub, and disc assembly from the spindle.

5. Installation is in the reverse order of removal. Adjust the wheel bearing.

INSPECTION

1. Check the disc for any obvious defects such as excessive rust, chipping, or deep scoring. Light scoring is normal on disc brakes.

2. Make sure there is no wheel bearing play and then check the disc for runout as follows:

3. Install a dial indicator on the caliper so that its feeler will contact the disc about one inch below its outer edge.

4. Turn the disc and observe the runout reading. If the reading exceeds 0.002″, the disc should be replaced.

5. Check the caliper thickness with a verni-er caliper or other appropriate tool. Minimum thickness dimensions are cast into the disc.

Wheel Bearings

ADJUSTMENT

1. Jack the car up and support it at the lower arm.

2. Remove the hub dust cover, spindle cotter pin, and spindle nut.

3. While spinning the wheel, snug the nut down to seat the bearings. Do not exert over 12 ft.lb. of force on the nut.

4. Back the nut off ¼-½ a turn. Line up the cotter pin hole in the spindle with a hole in the nut.

5. Insert the cotter pin. End-play should be between 0.001″ and 0.005″. If play exceeds this tolerance, the wheel bearings should be replaced.

REMOVAL, INSTALLATION AND PACKING

1. Jack up the car and support it. Remove the wheel and tire assembly.

2. On disc brake cars, remove the hub and disc as an assembly. Remove the caliper mounting bolts and wire the caliper out of the way.

3. On drum brake cars, remove the outer wheel bearing nut and remove the brake drum.

4. Remove the outer bearing from the hub. The inner bearing assembly will remain in the hub and may be removed after prying out the inner seal. Discard the seal.

5. Clean all the parts in solvent, air dry them, and check them for excessive wear or damage.

6. To replace the outer or inner bearing race, first knock out the old race with a hammer and a brass drift. new races must be installed squarely and evenly to avoid damage. Use a short piece of two-by-four or something similar.

7. Pack the bearings with wheel bearing grease. It is important that the bearings be fully packed, and not simply coated with lubricant. Immerse the bearing completely in the lubricant and work the grease into the bearing with your hand. You'll get greasy hands, but your wheel bearings will last.

8. Lightly grease the steering spindle and the inside of the hub.

9. Place the inner bearing in the hub race and install a new grease seal.

10. Install the hub and rotor assembly (or hub and drum assembly) on the spindle.

11. Install the outer wheel bearing. Adjust the wheel bearing as outlined earlier.

12. Reinstall the caliper assembly on disc brake models.

13. Install the dust cap, wheel and tire assembly, and lower the car.

FRONT DRUM BRAKES

Brake Drums

REMOVAL AND INSTALLATION

1. Raise the front of the car and support it with jackstands.

2. Remove the wheel and tire assembly.

3. Remove the dust cap. Remove the cotter pin from the wheel bearing nut.

4. Remove the outer wheel bearing. Don't drop it.

5. The drum can now be pulled off the spindle, provided the adjustment is not too tight. If it is, back off the brake adjuster until the drum can be removed.

6. Installation is in the reverse order of removal. Adjust the wheel bearing after installing the drum.

7. Adjust the brakes as outlined earlier.

8. Reinstall the wheel and tire and lower the car.

INSPECTION

With the drum off the car, inspect it for any cracks, scores, grooves, or an out-of-round condition. If the drum is cracked, replace it. Light scoring can be removed with emery cloth or fine sandpaper. If the scoring is extensive, have the drum turned. Never have a drum turned more than 0.060″.

Brake Shoes

INSPECTION

1. Remove the brake drum as outlined earlier.

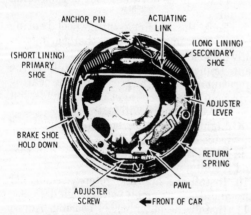

Brake shoe assembly

2. Inspect the hoses for any obvious defects.

3. If there are no obvious defect, measure the remaining lining to see of the shoes are still usable. Generally specking, a lining thickness of around $3/32$″ is acceptable for a bonded brake shoe. On a riveted brake shoe, a lining depth of $3/32$″ is also acceptable. Measure the riveted shoe at one of the rivets. Don't measure it at the edge. Measure a bonded shoe at the edge.

4. Check to make sure the hoses are wearing evenly all the way around. If they aren't, replace them.

5. Reinstall the brake drum and wheel and tire.

REMOVAL AND INSTALLATION

NOTE: *If you have not installed brake shoes before, it is a good idea to leave the brake assembly on one side intact as a reference.*

1. Jack up the car and remove the tire and wheel.

2. Remove the brake drum as outlined earlier.

3. Free the brake shoe return spring, holddown pins and springs, and adjuster assembly. Special tools are available at auto supply stores to ease spring and anchor pin removal, but the job may still be done with common hand tools. Be careful removing the springs, as they are under considerable tension.

4. Remove the shoes from the drum once the springs and pins are removed.

5. Clean all the brake shoes attaching parts with gasoline or a solvent. Special brake cleaning solvent is available, though not strictly necessary. Clean the backing plate, also.

6. Check the wheel cylinders for leakage. If you suspect any leakage, replace the cylinders.

7. Reinstall the new brake shoes. Install the anchor pins first to hold them in place. It will then be possible to install the return springs.

8. A pair of vise grips is handy for installing the return spring. If you don't remember what went where, refer to the other side, providing the other side is still intact. Once the brake shoes are installed, install the brake drum.

9. Install the wheel bearing and adjust it.

10. Install the wheel and tire and adjust the brakes.

Wheel Cylinders

The procedures given here are for both front and rear wheel cylinders.

REMOVAL AND INSTALLATION

1. Remove the brake shoes.

2. On rear brakes, loosen the brake line on the rear of the cylinder but do not pull the line away from the cylinder or it may bent.

3. On front brakes, disconnect the metal brake line from the rubber brake hose where they join in the wheel well. Pull off the horseshoe clip that attaches the rubber brake hose to the underbody of the car. Loosen the hose at the cylinder, then turn the whole brake hose to remove it from the wheel cylinder.

4. Remove the bolts and lockwashers or retaining clip (1978 and later) that attach the wheel cylinder to the backing plate and remove the cylinder.

5. Position the new wheel cylinder on the backing plate and install the cylinder attaching bolts and lockwashers or retainer clip.

6. Attach the metal brake line or rubber hose by reversing the procedure given in Steps 2 or 3.

7. Install the brakes.

OVERHAUL

Since the travel of the pistons i the wheel cylinder changes when new brake shoes are installed, it is possible for previously good wheel cylinders to start leaking after new brakes are installed. Therefore, to save yourself the expense of having to replace new brakes that become saturated with brake fluid and the aggravation of having to take everything apart again, it is strongly recommended that wheel cylinders be rebuilt every time new brake shoes are installed. This is especially true on high-mileage cars.

1. Remove the brakes.

2. Place a bucket or old newspapers under the brake backing plate to catch the brake fluid that will run out of the wheel cylinder.

3. Remove the boots from the end of the wheel cylinder.

4. Push one piston toward the center of the cylinder to force the opposite piston and cup out the other end of the cylinder. Reach in the open end of the cylinder and push the spring, cup, and piston out of the cylinder.

5. Remove the bleeder screw from the rear of the cylinder, on the back of the backing plate.

6. Inspect the inside of the wheel cylinder. If it is scored in any way, the cylinder must be honed with a wheel cylinder hone or fine emery paper, and finished with crocus cloth if emery paper is used. If the inside of the cylinder is excessively worn, the cylinder will have to be replace, as only 0.003" of material can be removed from the cylinder walls. When honing or cleaning the wheel cylinders, keep a small amount of brake fluid in the cylinder to serve as a lubricant.

7. Clean any foreign matter from the pistons. The sides of the pistons must be smooth for the wheel cylinders to operate properly.

8. Clean the cylinder bore with alcohol and lint-free rag. Pull the rag through the bore several times to remove all foreign matter and dry the cylinder.

9. Install the bleeder screw and the return spring in the cylinder.

10. Coat new cylinder cups with new brake fluid and install them in the cylinder. Make sure that they are square in the bore or they will leak.

11. Install the pistons in the cylinder after coating them with new brake fluid.

12. Coat the inside of the boots with new brake fluid and install them on the cylinder. Install the brakes.

REAR DRUM BRAKES

Brake Drums

REMOVAL AND INSTALLATION

1. Raise the rear of the car in the air and support it with jackstands.

2. Remove the wheel and tire assemblies.

3. Make sure the parking brake is not on.

4. It may be necessary to back off the brake adjustment to remove the brake drum. The drum is held in place by the wheel and can be removed by simply sliding it off the wheel studs. If the drum is stubborn and you have backed the brake adjustment off, tap the drum with a hammer in several places. Don't beat on it. Just tap it.

5. Installation is in the reverse order of removal. Adjust the brakes after installation.

INSPECTION

With the drum off the car, inspect it for any cracks, scores, grooves, or an out-of-round condition. If the drum is cracked, replace it. Light scoring can be removed with emery cloth or fine sandpaper. If the scoring is extensive, have the drum turned. Never have a drum turned more than 0.060".

Brake Shoes

INSPECTION

1. Remove the brake drum as outlined earlier.

2. Inspect the shoes for any obvious defects.

3. If there are no obvious defects, measure the remaining lining to see if the shoes are still usable. Generally speaking, a lining thickness of around $3/32$" is acceptable for a bonded brake shoe. On a riveted brake shoe, a lining depth of $3/32$" is also acceptable. Measure a riveted shoe at one of the rivets. don't measure it at the edge. Measure a bonded shoe at the edge.

4. Check to make sure the shoes are wearing evenly all the way around. If they aren't, replace them.

5. Reinstall the brake drum and wheel and tire.

REMOVAL AND INSTALLATION

NOTE: *If you have not installed brake shoes before, it is a good idea to leave one set of brake shoes intact as a reference.*

1. Remove the wheel and tire. Remove the brake drum.

2. Free the brake shoe return springs, and the actuating link and guide.

3. Remove the brake shoe hold-down springs, the adjuster lever and return spring and the parking brake lever strut and spring.

4. Spread the shoes to clear the end of the wheel cylinder, then remove the brake shoes as an assembly.

5. Disconnect the parking brake cable from the operating lever.

6. To install, first connect the parking brake cable to the lever.

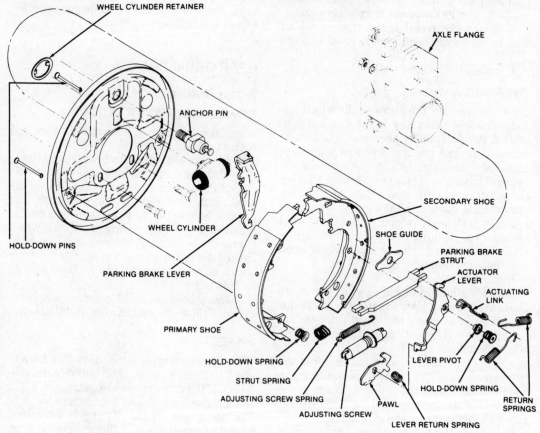

Drum brake assembly, 1978 and later (1985–87 models have pawl part of the actuator)

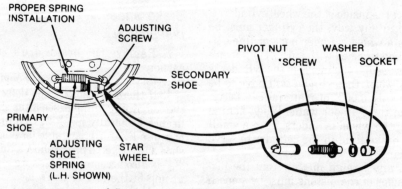

Adjusting screw—disassembled view

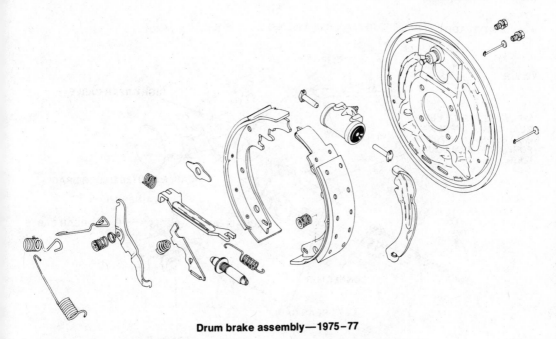

Drum brake assembly—1975–77

7. Position the shoe assemblies on the backing plate. Install the hold-down pins and springs.

8. Install the adjuster and the primary-to-secondary shoe spring and the actuating link.

9. Install the shoe return springs.

10. Once the brake shoes are installed, install the brake drum. Install the tire and wheel and adjust the brakes.

PARKING BRAKE

Cable

Adjustment

NOTE: *Be sure that the parking brake does not drag. An overtightened, dragging parking brake on a car with automatic brake adjusters will result in an extremely short life for rear brake linings.*

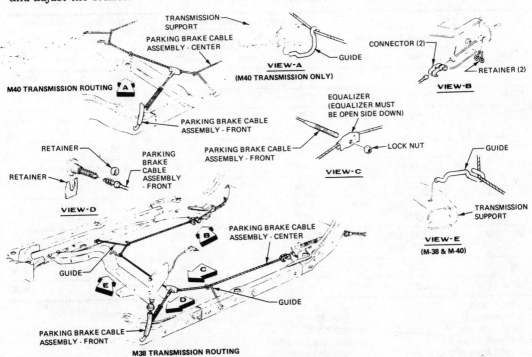

Parking brake cables—through 1977

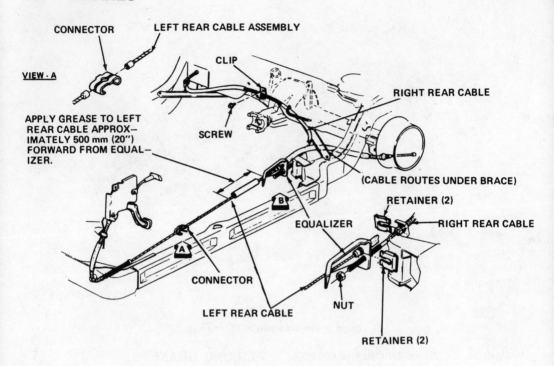

VIEW - A

CONNECTOR

LEFT REAR CABLE ASSEMBLY

CLIP

RIGHT REAR CABLE

SCREW

APPLY GREASE TO LEFT REAR CABLE APPROX— IMATELY 500 mm (20") FORWARD FROM EQUAL— IZER.

(CABLE ROUTES UNDER BRACE)

RETAINER (2)

RIGHT REAR CABLE

EQUALIZER

CONNECTOR

LEFT REAR CABLE

NUT

RETAINER (2)

VIEW - B

Parking brake cables—1978 and later

Brake Specifications
(measurements in inches)

Year	Master Cylinder Bore		Caliper/Wheel Cylinder Bore			Brake Disc or Drum Diameter		
				Drum		Front		
	Disc	Drum	Disc	Front	Rear	Disc	Drum	Rear Drum
1970	1⅛	1.0	2¹⁵⁄₁₆	1⅛	⅞	10.88	9.5	9.5
1971	1⅛	1.0	2¹⁵⁄₁₆	1⅛	⅞	10.88	9.5	9.5
1972	1.12	1.0	2.94	1.125	1.0 ① .875 ②	11.74	9.5	9.5
1973	1.12	N/A	2.94	N/A	.875	10.88	N/A	9.5
1974	1.12	N/A	2.94	N/A	.875	10.88	N/A	9.5
1975	1.12	N/A	2.94	N/A	.875	10.88	N/A	9.5
1976	1.12 ③ .94 ④	N/A	2.94	N/A	.94 ③	10.88	N/A	9.5
1977–80	1.12 ③⑤ .94 ④⑥	N/A	2.94 ⑦	N/A	.94 ③⑧ 1.0 ④⑧	10.88 ⑨	N/A	9.5
1981	.875	N/A	2.50	N/A	.750	11.000	N/A	9.50
1982–87	1.0 ⑩	N/A	2.50	N/A	.750	10.500	N/A	9.50

① Front discs
② Front drums
③ Power brake
④ Manual brake
⑤ 1980 Manual brakes: ¹³⁄₁₆"
⑥ 1980 Power brakes: ⅞"
⑦ 1980: 2.5
⑧ 1980: .75
⑨ 1980: 11.00
⑩ Quick Take-Up: ¹⁵⁄₁₆
   Hydro-Boost: 1¹⁄₁₆

Troubleshooting the Brake System

Problem	Cause	Solution
Low brake pedal (excessive pedal travel required for braking action.)	• Excessive clearance between rear linings and drums caused by inoperative automatic adjusters	• Make 10 to 15 alternate forward and reverse brake stops to adjust brakes. If brake pedal does not come up, repair or replace adjuster parts as necessary.
	• Worn rear brakelining	• Inspect and replace lining if worn beyond minimum thickness specification
	• Bent, distorted brakeshoes, front or rear	• Replace brakeshoes in axle sets
	• Air in hydraulic system	• Remove air from system. Refer to Brake Bleeding.
Low brake pedal (pedal may go to floor with steady pressure applied.)	• Fluid leak in hydraulic system	• Fill master cylinder to fill line; have helper apply brakes and check calipers, wheel cylinders, differential valve tubes, hoses and fittings for leaks. Repair or replace as necessary.
	• Air in hydraulic system	• Remove air from system. Refer to Brake Bleeding.
	• Incorrect or non-recommended brake fluid (fluid evaporates at below normal temp).	• Flush hydraulic system with clean brake fluid. Refill with correct-type fluid.
	• Master cylinder piston seals worn, or master cylinder bore is scored, worn or corroded	• Repair or replace master cylinder
Low brake pedal (pedal goes to floor on first application—o.k. on subsequent applications.)	• Disc brake pads sticking on abutment surfaces of anchor plate. Caused by a build-up of dirt, rust, or corrosion on abutment surfaces	• Clean abutment surfaces
Fading brake pedal (pedal height decreases with steady pressure applied.)	• Fluid leak in hydraulic system	• Fill master cylinder reservoirs to fill mark, have helper apply brakes, check calipers, wheel cylinders, differential valve, tubes, hoses, and fittings for fluid leaks. Repair or replace parts as necessary.
	• Master cylinder piston seals worn, or master cylinder bore is scored, worn or corroded	• Repair or replace master cylinder
Decreasing brake pedal travel (pedal travel required for braking action decreases and may be accompanied by a hard pedal.)	• Caliper or wheel cylinder pistons sticking or seized	• Repair or replace the calipers, or wheel cylinders
	• Master cylinder compensator ports blocked (preventing fluid return to reservoirs) or pistons sticking or seized in master cylinder bore	• Repair or replace the master cylinder
	• Power brake unit binding internally	• Test unit according to the following procedure: (a) Shift transmission into neutral and start engine (b) Increase engine speed to 1500 rpm, close throttle and fully depress brake pedal (c) Slow release brake pedal and stop engine (d) Have helper remove vacuum check valve and hose from power unit. Observe for backward movement of brake pedal. (e) If the pedal moves backward, the power unit has an internal bind—replace power unit

Troubleshooting the Brake System (cont.)

Problem	Cause	Solution
Spongy brake pedal (pedal has abnormally soft, springy, spongy feel when depressed.)	• Air in hydraulic system • Brakeshoes bent or distorted • Brakelining not yet seated with drums and rotors • Rear drum brakes not properly adjusted	• Remove air from system. Refer to Brake Bleeding. • Replace brakeshoes • Burnish brakes • Adjust brakes
Hard brake pedal (excessive pedal pressure required to stop vehicle. May be accompanied by brake fade.)	• Loose or leaking power brake unit vacuum hose • Incorrect or poor quality brakelining • Bent, broken, distorted brakeshoes • Calipers binding or dragging on mounting pins. Rear brakeshoes dragging on support plate. • Caliper, wheel cylinder, or master cylinder pistons sticking or seized • Power brake unit vacuum check valve malfunction • Power brake unit has internal bind • Master cylinder compensator ports (at bottom of reservoirs) blocked by dirt, scale, rust, or have small burrs (blocked ports prevent fluid return to reservoirs). • Brake hoses, tubes, fittings clogged or restricted • Brake fluid contaminated with improper fluids (motor oil, transmission fluid, causing rubber components to swell and stick in bores • Low engine vacuum	• Tighten connections or replace leaking hose • Replace with lining in axle sets • Replace brakeshoes • Replace mounting pins and bushings. Clean rust or burrs from rear brake support plate ledges and lubricate ledges with molydisulfide grease. **NOTE:** If ledges are deeply grooved or scored, do not attempt to sand or grind them smooth—replace support plate. • Repair or replace parts as necessary • Test valve according to the following procedure: (a) Start engine, increase engine speed to 1500 rpm, close throttle and immediately stop engine (b) Wait at least 90 seconds then depress brake pedal (c) If brakes are not vacuum assisted for 2 or more applications, check valve is faulty • Test unit according to the following procedure: (a) With engine stopped, apply brakes several times to exhaust all vacuum in system (b) Shift transmission into neutral, depress brake pedal and start engine (c) If pedal height decreases with foot pressure and less pressure is required to hold pedal in applied position, power unit vacuum system is operating normally. Test power unit. If power unit exhibits a bind condition, replace the power unit. • Repair or replace master cylinder **CAUTION:** Do not attempt to clean blocked ports with wire, pencils, or similar implements. Use compressed air only. • Use compressed air to check or unclog parts. Replace any damaged parts. • Replace all rubber components, combination valve and hoses. Flush entire brake system with DOT 3 brake fluid or equivalent. • Adjust or repair engine

Troubleshooting the Brake System (cont.)

Problem	Cause	Solution
Grabbing brakes (severe reaction to brake pedal pressure.)	• Brakelining(s) contaminated by grease or brake fluid	• Determine and correct cause of contamination and replace brakeshoes in axle sets
	• Parking brake cables incorrectly adjusted or seized	• Adjust cables. Replace seized cables.
	• Incorrect brakelining or lining loose on brakeshoes	• Replace brakeshoes in axle sets
	• Caliper anchor plate bolts loose	• Tighten bolts
	• Rear brakeshoes binding on support plate ledges	• Clean and lubricate ledges. Replace support plate(s) if ledges are deeply grooved. Do not attempt to smooth ledges by grinding.
	• Incorrect or missing power brake reaction disc	• Install correct disc
	• Rear brake support plates loose	• Tighten mounting bolts
Dragging brakes (slow or incomplete release of brakes)	• Brake pedal binding at pivot	• Loosen and lubricate
	• Power brake unit has internal bind	• Inspect for internal bind. Replace unit if internal bind exists.
	• Parking brake cables incorrrectly adjusted or seized	• Adjust cables. Replace seized cables.
	• Rear brakeshoe return springs weak or broken	• Replace return springs. Replace brakeshoe if necessary in axle sets.
	• Automatic adjusters malfunctioning	• Repair or replace adjuster parts as required
	• Caliper, wheel cylinder or master cylinder pistons sticking or seized	• Repair or replace parts as necessary
	• Master cylinder compensating ports blocked (fluid does not return to reservoirs).	• Use compressed air to clear ports. Do not use wire, pencils, or similar objects to open blocked ports.
Vehicle moves to one side when brakes are applied	• Incorrect front tire pressure	• Inflate to recommended cold (reduced load) inflation pressure
	• Worn or damaged wheel bearings	• Replace worn or damaged bearings
	• Brakelining on one side contaminated	• Determine and correct cause of contamination and replace brakelining in axle sets
	• Brakeshoes on one side bent, distorted, or lining loose on shoe	• Replace brakeshoes in axle sets
	• Support plate bent or loose on one side	• Tighten or replace support plate
	• Brakelining not yet seated with drums or rotors	• Burnish brakelining
	• Caliper anchor plate loose on one side	• Tighten anchor plate bolts
	• Caliper piston sticking or seized	• Repair or replace caliper
	• Brakelinings water soaked	• Drive vehicle with brakes lightly applied to dry linings
	• Loose suspension component attaching or mounting bolts	• Tighten suspension bolts. Replace worn suspension components.
	• Brake combination valve failure	• Replace combination valve
Chatter or shudder when brakes are applied (pedal pulsation and roughness may also occur.)	• Brakeshoes distorted, bent, contaminated, or worn	• Replace brakeshoes in axle sets
	• Caliper anchor plate or support plate loose	• Tighten mounting bolts
	• Excessive thickness variation of rotor(s)	• Refinish or replace rotors in axle sets
Noisy brakes (squealing, clicking, scraping sound when brakes are applied.)	• Bent, broken, distorted brakeshoes	• Replace brakeshoes in axle sets
	• Excessive rust on outer edge of rotor braking surface	• Remove rust

Troubleshooting the Brake System (cont.)

Problem	Cause	Solution
Noisy brakes (squealing, clicking, scraping sound when brakes are applied.) (cont.)	• Brakelining worn out—shoes contacting drum of rotor	• Replace brakeshoes and lining in axle sets. Refinish or replace drums or rotors.
	• Broken or loose holdown or return springs	• Replace parts as necessary
	• Rough or dry drum brake support plate ledges	• Lubricate support plate ledges
	• Cracked, grooved, or scored rotor(s) or drum(s)	• Replace rotor(s) or drum(s). Replace brakeshoes and lining in axle sets if necessary.
	• Incorrect brakelining and/or shoes (front or rear).	• Install specified shoe and lining assemblies
Pulsating brake pedal	• Out of round drums or excessive lateral runout in disc brake rotor(s)	• Refinish or replace drums, re-index rotors or replace

Adjustment of the parking brake is necessary whenever the rear brake cables have been disconnected or the parking brake pedal can be depressed more than eight ratchet clicks under heavy foot pressure. The car should first be raised on a lift.

1. Make sure that the service brakes are properly adjusted.

2. Depress the parking brake pedal two ratchet clicks, or three clicks on handle types.

3. Loosen the jam nut on the equalizer adjusting nut. Tighten the adjusting nut until the rear wheel can just be turned rearward by hand, but not forward.

4. Release the ratchet one click; the rear wheel should rotate rear ward freely and forward with a slight drag.

5. Release the ratchet fully; rear wheel should turn freely in either direction.

REMOVAL AND INSTALLATION

1. Raise the car in the air and support it.

2. Remove the adjusting nut from the equalizer underneath the car.

3. Remove the retainer clip which attaches the cable to the frame.

4. Disconnect the cable from the pedal assembly.

5. Remove the front brake cable.

6. Installation is the reverse of removal.

EXTERIOR

Doors

REMOVAL AND INSTALLATION

NOTE: *When removing the door only, it is recommended that the door be removed from the hinges because of easier access to the door side hinge bolts.*

1. Before loosening any hinge bolts, mark the position of the hinge on the door to ease adjustment when reinstalling the door on the hinge.

2. On doors equipped with power operated components, remove the trim panel and detach the inner panel water panel water deflector enough to disconnect the wiring harness from the components. Detach the rubber conduit from the door and remove the wiring harness from the door.

3. With the aid of a helper, support the door in the open position and remove the upper and lower hinge-to-door hinge pillar attaching bolts.

4. Installation is the reverse of removal. Adjust the door as outlined later and tighten the hinge attaching bolts to 15-21 ft.lb.

ADJUSTMENT

Door adjustments are provided through the use of floating anchor plates in the door and front body hinge pillars. When checking the door for alignment and prior to making any adjustments, mark the location and remove the door lock striker from the body to allow the door to hang freely on its hinges

1. Adjust the door up and down and/or fore and aft at the body hinge pillar attachments. If rearward adjustment of either front door is made, replace the jamb switch.

2. Adjust the door in and out at the door hinge pillar attachments.

3. After adjustments, tighten the attaching bolts to 20 to 29 ft.lb.

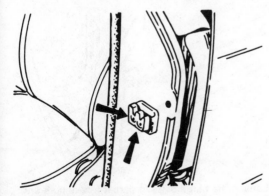

Adjusting the door striker

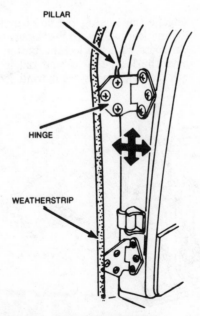

Adjusting the door hinge position

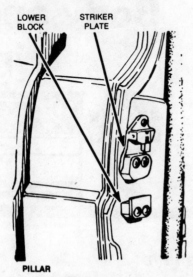

Adjusting the striker plate and lower block

Door Locks

REMOVAL AND INSTALLATION

1. Remove all the door trim to gain access to the lock.

2. On the front door on sedan models, remove the inner panel cam for easier access.

3. On rear doors, remove the stationary window and ventilator assembly.

4. Disengage the inside handle and power lock connecting rods as required. On front doors with electric locks, remove the electric lock actuator as required. On some styles it may be necessary to remove the inside handle and then remove the lock and connecting rod as a unit.

5. Disengage the locking rod on rear door locks and front door locks with the remote lock button. On doors with the locking button directly above the lock, the locking rod is removed with the lock. On the sedan front doors,

disengage the lock cylinder to lock connecting rod and outside handle to the lock connecting rod.

6. Remove the lock attaching screws and remove the lock through the access hole.

7. To install, first install the spring clips to the lock assembly, then reverse the removal procedure. Tighten the retaining screws to 80 to 100 in.lb.

Hood

REMOVAL AND INSTALLATION

1. Raise the hood and install some kind of protective coverings over the fender areas to prevent damage to the paint and moldings during removal and installation of the hood.

2. Disconnect the underhood lamp wiring, if so equipped.

3. Mark the position of the hinge on the hood to facilitate alignment during installation.

4. While supporting the hood, remove the hinge to hood retaining screws on both sides and with the aid of an assistant remove the hood.

5. Installation is the reverse of removal.

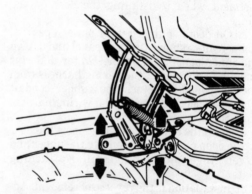

The height of the hood at the rear is adjusted by loosening the hinge-to-body bolts and moving the hood up and down

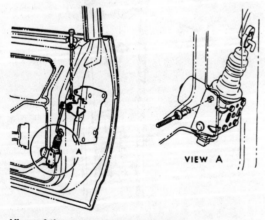

View of the power door lock actuator

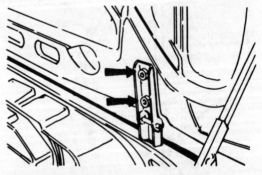

Loosen the hinge bolts to permit fore-and-aft and horizontal adjustment

ALIGNMENT

The mounting holes in the hood hinge bracket are enlarged to provide slight fore and aft adjustment of the hood panel.

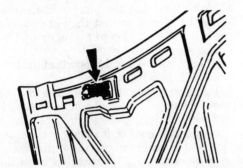

The hood pin can be adjusted for proper lock engagement

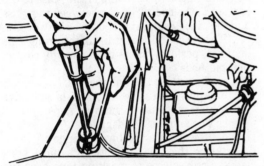

The hood is adjusted vertically by stop screws at the front and/or rear

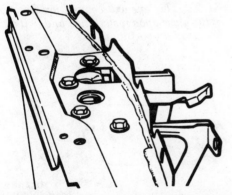

The base of the hood lock can also be repositioned slightly to give more positive lock engagement

Trunk Lid

REMOVAL AND INSTALLATION

1. Prop the lid open and place protective coverings along the edges of the rear compartment opening to prevent damage to the painted surfaces.

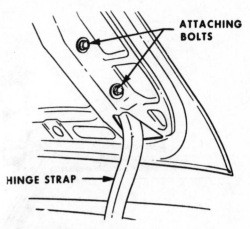

View of the trunk lid-to-hinge bolts

2. Mark the location of the hinge strap attaching bolts to the lid and disconnect the electrical wiring harness from the lid, if so equipped.
3. With the aid of a helper, support the lid, remove the hinge attaching bolts and remove the lid.
4. Installation is the reverse of removal.

ADJUSTMENTS

To adjust the lid, loosen the hinge-to-lid attaching bolts and shift the lid to the desired position; then tighten the bolts. Some styles have rubber bumpers at the rear outboard corners of the lid. These bumpers can be adjusted to lower or raise the rear corners of the lid.

Windshield

NOTE: *The bonded windshield requires special tools and expertise. We recommend that replacement procedures be left to professional installers.*

REMOVAL

1. Place protective coverings over the hood.
2. Remove the windshield wiper arms and windshield trim.
3. If equipped with a radio antenna built into the windshield, disconnect the antenna's lead from the lower end of the windshield and tape the lead onto the outer surface of the windshield to protect it from damage.
4. Using a utility knife and the edge of a windshield as a guide, cut through the adhesive material around the entire perimeter.
5. Using a Hot Knife tool No. J-24709-1 and a cold knife, completely cut through the urethane adhesive.
6. With the help of an assistant, remove the windshield from the vehicle.

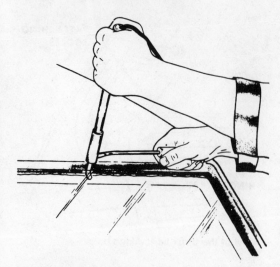

Using an electric knife to cut the window seal

7. If reinstalling the windshield, perform the following procedures:

a. Place the windshield onto a protective bench or holding fixture.

b. Using a razor blade or a sharp scraper, remove the excessive adhesive from the perimeter of the windshield.

c. Using denatured alcohol or lacquer thinner with a cloth, remove all traces of the adhesive from the perimeter of the windshield.

INSTALLATION

Short Method

NOTE: *This method is used when no other adhesive materials are used in the installation procedures. When using a new windshield for installation, DO NOT use kerosene or gasoline as a solvent, for film is left which will prevent adhesion of the sealing material. When using a volatile cleaner, avoid contacting the plastic laminate material (around the edge of the glass) for discoloration and/or deterioration may occur.*

1. To prepare the windshield frame for glass installation, perform the following procedures:

a. Using a sharp scraper or a chisel, clean the excess sealing material from the windshield frame.

NOTE: *It is not necessary to remove all traces of the original material; there should be no mounds or loose pieces remaining. If, while removing the old material, the metal surface has been exposed, cover the area with black primer.*

b. Inspect the reveal molding retaining clip(s); if the upper end of the clip(s) is bent (more than $1/16''$) away from the body metal, replace the clip(s)

NOTE: *When using weatherstrip adhesive, apply enough material to obtain a water tight seal beneath the spacer; DO NOT allow the material to squeeze out excessively.*

c. Cement the flat rubber spacers to the window opening at the pinchweld flanges; locate the spacers so that they are equally spaced around the perimeter of the windshield.

d. Reinstall the metal supports at the lower edge of the windshield glass.

2. Using an assistant, lift the glass into the window opening; the windhield can be positioned without the use of suction cups. Check the position of the glass, it should not overlap the pinchweld flange (around the entire perimeter) by more than $3/16''$. The overlap across the top of the windshield can be corrected by readjusting the lower metal support spacers.

3. Check the relationship of the glass to the contour of the body. The gap between the glass and the pinchweld frame should be between $1/8$-$1/4''$. If there is difficulty in maintaining this distance, perform one of the following correction methods:

a. Reposition the flat spacers.

b. Apply excessive amounts of adhesive caulking material to the wide gaps.

c. Try another windshield.

d. Rework the pinchweld flange

4. After the final adjustments have been made, apply pieces of masking tape over the edges of the glass and the body, then slit the tape between the glass and the body. Remove the glass from the opening.

NOTE: *The tape will be used for alignment of the glass upon installation and will aid in the clean up operation.*

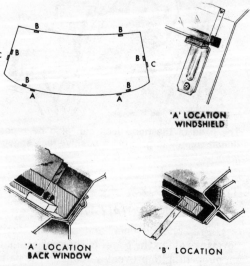

'A' LOCATION
WINDSHIELD

'A' LOCATION
BACK WINDOW

'B' LOCATION

View of the glass spacer installation

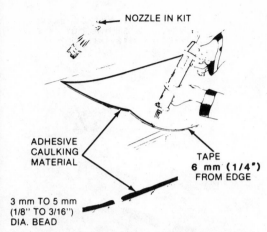

NOZZLE IN KIT

ADHESIVE
CAULKING
MATERIAL

TAPE
6 mm (1/4")
FROM EDGE

3 mm TO 5 mm
(1/8" TO 3/16")
DIA. BEAD

Applying adhesive to the window—short method

GUIDE GLASS ALONG REAR
EDGE OF FRONT FENDER

PIGTAIL LEAD
TAPED TO GLASS

Installing the windshield

5. If, desired apply masking to the inboard edge of the windshield; the tape should be placed ¼" (from the outer edge) around the top and sides (NOT the bottom) of the glass.

6. Using alcohol and a clean cloth, clean the inner perimeter of the glass and allow it to air dry.

7. Using the Urethane Adhesive Kit No. 9636067 (two primers are provided), apply primer using the following procedures:

    a. Apply the clear primer around the entire perimeter of the glass. Allow the primer to dry for 5 minutes.

    b. If refinishing or painting operations are needed for any portions of the glass opening apply the black primer to these portions. Allow the primer to dry for 5 minutes.

8. Using a caulking gun and an adhesive cartridge, apply a smooth continuous bead ⅜" wide around the entire perimeter of the glass.

9. Reposition the glass to the window opening using the tape as the installation guide. Apply light hand pressure to the glass to ensure a bond to the body opening. Using a small brush or a flat bladed tool, paddle the bonding material around the edge of the glass to ensure a water tight seal.

10. Using a soft , warm water spray, allow the water to spill over the edges of the glass to detect water leaks. If a water leak is encoun-

tered, paddle additional material around the leak.

11. Cement rubber spacers between the right and left sides of the windshield and the frame, to keep the glass centered during the installation procedures.

12. Install the windshield molding strips. Remove the masking tape from the inner perimeter of the windshield; pull the tape toward the center.

13. Complete the installation by replacing all of the removed parts.

NOTE: *After the windshield installation, the vehicle must remain at room temperature for 6 hours.*

Extended Method

NOTE: *This method is used in conjunction with unknown adhesive materials such as butyl strips. When using a new windshield for installation, DO NOT use kerosene or gasoline as a solvent, for film is left which will prevent adhesion of the sealing material. When using a volatile cleaner, avoid contacting the plastic laminate material (around the edge of the glass) for discoloration and/or deterioration may occur.*

1. To prepare the windshield frame for glass installation, perform the following procedures:

    a. Using a sharp scraper or a chisel, clean the excess sealing material from the windshield frame.

NOTE: *If using Butyl tape or unknown material to install the windshield, it is necessary to remove all traces of the original material.*

If using a Urethane sealing material, it is not necessary to remove all traces of the original material; there should be no mounds or loose pieces remaining. If while removing the old material, the metal surface has been exposed, cover the area with black primer.

    b. Inspect the reveal molding retaining clip(s); if the upper end of the clip(s) is bent (more than $\frac{1}{16}$") away from the body metal, replace the clip(s)

NOTE: *If using weatherstrip adhesive, apply enough material to obtain a water tight seal beneath the spacer; DO NOT allow the material to squeeze out excessively. Weatherstrip material is not compatible with other replacement adhesives; leaks may develop where the two dissimilar materials are joined.*

    c. Cement the flat rubber spacers to the window opening at the pinchweld flanges; locate the spacers so that they are equally spaced around the perimeter of the windshield.

    d. Reinstall the metal supports at the lower edge of the windshield glass.

2. Using an assistant, lift the glass into the

window opening; the windshield can be positioned without the use of suction cups. Check the position of the glass, it should not overlap the pinchweld flange (around the entire perimeter) by more than $\frac{3}{16}$". The overlap across the top of the windshield can be corrected by readjusting the lower metal support spacers.

3. Check the relationship of the glass to the contour of the body. The gap between the glass and the pinchweld frame should be between $\frac{1}{8}$-$\frac{1}{4}$". If there is difficulty in maintaining this distance, perform one of the following correction methods:

    a. Reposition the flat spacers.

    b. Apply excessive amounts of adhesive caulking material to the wide gaps.

    c. Try another windshield.

    d. Rework the pinchweld flange

4. After the final adjustments have been made, apply pieces of masking tape over the edges of the glass and the body, then slit the tape between the glass and the body. Remove the glass from the opening.

NOTE: *The tape will be used for alignment of the glass upon installation and will aid in the clean up operation.*

5. If, desired apply masking to the inboard edge of the windshield; the tape should be placed $\frac{1}{4}$" (from the outer edge) around the top and sides (NOT the bottom) of the glass.

6. If equipped with an embedded antenna, apply an 8" butyl filler strip to the bottom inner center surface of the windshield. If not equipped with an embedded windshield antenna the butyl strip is not necessary.

7. Using alcohol and a clean cloth, clean the inner perimeter of the glass and allow it to air dry.

8. Using the Urethane Adhesive Kit No. 9636067 (two primers are provided), apply primer using the following procedures:

    a. If equipped with an embedded windshield antenna, apply the clear primer around the entire perimeter (except at the location of the filler strip); If not equipped with an embedded windshield antenna, apply the clear primer around the entire perimeter of the glass. Allow the primer to dry for 5 minutes.

    b. If refinishing or painting operations are needed for any portions of the glass opening apply the black primer to these portions. Allow the primer to dry for 5 minutes.

9. Using a caulking gun and an adhesive cartridge, apply a smooth continuous bead $\frac{3}{8}$" wide around the entire perimeter of the glass.

10. Reposition the glass to the window opening using the tape as the installation guide. Apply light hand pressure to the glass to ensure a bond to the body opening. Using a small

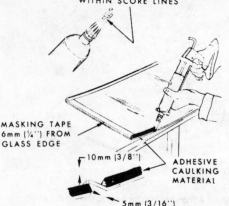

FOR EXTENDED METHOD, ENLARGE NOZZLE BY CUTTING OUT MATERIAL WITHIN SCORE LINES

MASKING TAPE 6mm (¼") FROM GLASS EDGE

10mm (3/8")

ADHESIVE CAULKING MATERIAL

5mm (3/16")

Applying adhesive to the window—extended method

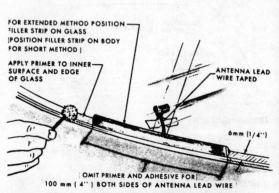

FOR EXTENDED METHOD POSITION FILLER STRIP ON GLASS (POSITION FILLER STRIP ON BODY FOR SHORT METHOD)

APPLY PRIMER TO INNER SURFACE AND EDGE OF GLASS

ANTENNA LEAD WIRE TAPED

6mm (1/4")

(OMIT PRIMER AND ADHESIVE FOR) 100 mm (4") BOTH SIDES OF ANTENNA LEAD WIRE

Preparing an embedded antenna windshield for installation—extended method

brush or a flat bladed tool, paddle the bonding material around the edge of the glass to ensure a water tight seal.

NOTE: *If equipped with an embedded antenna, paddle additional material at the edges of the butyl strip; avoid the area near the antenna pigtail.*

11. Using a soft , warm water spray, allow the water to spill over the edges of the glass to detect water leaks. If a water leak is encountered, paddle additional material around the leak.

12. Cement rubber spacers between the right and left sides of the windshield and the frame, to keep the glass centered during the installation procedures.

13. Install the windshield molding strips. Remove the masking tape from the inner perimeter of the windshield; pull the tape toward the center.

14. Complete the installation by replacing all of the removed parts.

NOTE: *After the windshield installation, the*

vehicle must remain at room temperature for 6 hours.

Rear Window Glass

NOTE: *The bonded rear window requires special tools and procedures.*

REMOVAL

1. Place protective coverings over the hood.
2. Remove the trim and molding from around the glass.
3. If equipped with a rear window electric grid defogger (built into the glass) disconnect the wiring harness connectors from the glass and tape the leads onto the outer surface of the window to protect it from damage.
4. Using a utility knife and the edge of a window as a guide, cut through the adhesive material around the entire perimeter.
5. Using a Hot Knife tool No. J-24709-1 and a cold knife, completely cut through the urethane adhesive.
6. With the help of an assistant, remove the window from the vehicle.
7. If reinstalling the window, perform the following procedures:

   a. Place the window onto a protective bench or holding fixture.

   b. Using a razor blade or a sharp scraper, remove the excessive adhesive from the perimeter of the window.

   c. Using denatured alcohol or lacquer thinner with a cloth, remove all traces of the adhesive from the perimeter of the window.

INSTALLATION

Short Method

NOTE: *This method is used when no other adhesive materials are used in the installation procedures. When using a new window for installation, DO NOT use kerosene or gasoline as a solvent, for film is left which will prevent adhesion of the sealing material. When using a volatile cleaner, avoid contacting the plastic laminate material (around the edge of the glass) for discoloration and/or deterioration may occur.*

1. To prepare the window frame for glass installation, perform the following procedures:

   a. Using a sharp scraper or a chisel, clean the excess sealing material from the window frame.

   NOTE: *It is not necessary to remove all traces of the original material; there should be no mounds or loose pieces remaining. If while removing the old material, the metal surface has been exposed, cover the area with black primer.*

   b. Inspect the reveal molding retaining

clip(s); if the upper end of the clip(s) is bent (more than $\frac{1}{16}''$) away from the body metal, replace the clip(s)

NOTE: *When using weatherstrip adhesive, apply enough material to obtain a water tight seal beneath the spacer; DO NOT allow the material to squeeze out excessively.*

   c. Cement the flat rubber spacers to the window opening at the pinchweld flanges; locate the spacers so that they are equally spaced around the perimeter of the window.

   d. Reinstall the metal supports at the lower edge of the windshield glass.

2. Using an assistant, lift the glass into the window opening; the windshield can be positioned without the use of suction cups. Check the position of the glass, it should not overlap the pinchweld flange (around the entire perimeter) by more than $\frac{3}{16}''$. The overlap across the top of the window can be corrected by readjusting the lower metal support spacers.
3. Check the relationship of the glass to the contour of the body. The gap between the glass and the pinchweld frame should be between $\frac{1}{8}$-$\frac{1}{4}''$. If there is difficulty in maintaining this distance, perform one of the following correction methods:

   a. Reposition the flat spacers.

   b. Apply excessive amounts of adhesive caulking material to the wide gaps.

   c. Try another window.

   d. Rework the pinchweld flange

4. After the final adjustments have been made, apply pieces of masking tape over the edges of the glass and the body, then slit the tape between the glass and the body. Remove the glass from the opening.

NOTE: *The tape will be used for alignment of the glass upon installation and will aid in the clean up operation.*

5. If, desired apply masking to the inboard edge of the window; the tape should be placed $\frac{1}{4}''$ (from the outer edge) around the top and sides (NOT the bottom) of the glass.
6. Using alcohol and a clean cloth, clean the inner perimeter of the glass and allow it to air dry.
7. Using the Urethane Adhesive Kit No. 9636067 (two primers are provided), apply primer using the following procedures:

   a. Apply the clear primer around the entire perimeter of the glass. Allow the primer to dry for 5 minutes.

   b. If refinishing or painting operations are needed for any portions of the glass opening apply the black primer to these portions. Allow the primer to dry for 5 minutes.

8. Using a caulking gun and an adhesive cartridge, apply a smooth continuous bead $\frac{3}{8}''$ wide around the entire perimeter of the glass.

9. Reposition the glass to the window opening using the tape as the installation guide. Apply light hand pressure to the glass to ensure a bond to the body opening. Using a small brush or a flat bladed tool, paddle the bonding material around the edge of the glass to ensure a water tight seal.

10. Using a soft , warm water spray, allow the water to spill over the edges of the glass to detect water leaks. If a water leak is encountered, paddle additional material around the leak.

11. Cement rubber spacers between the right and left sides of the window and the frame, to keep the glass centered during the installation procedures.

12. Install the window molding strips. Remove the masking tape from the inner perimeter of the window; pull the tape toward the center.

13. Complete the installation by replacing all of the removed parts.

NOTE: *After the window installation, the vehicle must remain at room temperature for 6 hours.*

Extended Method

NOTE: *This method is used in conjunction with unknown adhesive materials such as butyl strips. When using a new window for installation, DO NOT use kerosene or gasoline as a solvent, for film is left which will prevent adhesion of the sealing material. When using a volatile cleaner, avoid contacting the plastic laminate material (around the edge of the glass) for discoloration and/or deterioration may occur.*

1. To prepare the window frame for glass installation, perform the following procedures:

a. Using a sharp scraper or a chisel, clean the excess sealing material from the windshield frame.

NOTE: *If using Butyl tape or unknown material to install the window, it is necessary to remove all traces of the original material.*

If using a Urethane sealing material, it is not necessary to remove all traces of the original material; there should be no mounds or loose pieces remaining. If while removing the old material, the metal surface has been exposed, cover the area with black primer.

b. Inspect the reveal molding retaining clip(s); if the upper end of the clip(s) is bent (more than $1/16''$) away from the body metal, replace the clip(s)

NOTE: *If using weatherstrip adhesive, apply enough material to obtain a water tight seal beneath the spacer; DO NOT allow the material to squeeze out excessively. Weatherstrip material is not compatible with other replace-*

ment adhesives; leaks may develop where the two dissimilar materials are joined.

c. Cement the flat rubber spacers to the window opening at the pinchweld flanges; locate the spacers so that they are equally spaced around the perimeter of the window.

d. Reinstall the metal supports at the lower edge of the window glass.

2. Using an assistant, lift the glass into the window opening; the window can be positioned without the use of suction cups. Check the position of the glass, it should not overlap the pinchweld flange (around the entire perimeter) by more than $3/16''$. The overlap across the top of the window can be corrected by readjusting the lower metal support spacers.

3. Check the relationship of the glass to the contour of the body. The gap between the glass and the pinchweld frame should be between $1/8$-$1/4''$. If there is difficulty in maintaining this distance, perform one of the following correction methods:

a. Reposition the flat spacers.

b. Apply excessive amounts of adhesive caulking material to the wide gaps.

c. Try another window.

d. Rework the pinchweld flange

4. After the final adjustments have been made, apply pieces of masking tape over the edges of the glass and the body, then slit the tape between the glass and the body. Remove the glass from the opening.

NOTE: *The tape will be used for alignment of the glass upon installation and will aid in the clean up operation.*

5. If, desired apply masking to the inboard edge of the window; the tape should be placed $1/4''$ (from the outer edge) around the top and sides (NOT the bottom) of the glass.

6. If equipped with an electric defogger, apply an $8''$ butyl filler strip to the bottom inner center surface of the glass. If not equipped with an electric defogger the butyl strip is not necessary.

7. Using alcohol and a clean cloth, clean the inner perimeter of the glass and allow it to air dry.

8. Using the Urethane Adhesive Kit No. 9636067 (two primers are provided), apply primer using the following procedures:

a. If equipped with an defogger, apply the clear primer around the entire perimeter (except at the location of the filler strip); If not equipped with a defogger, apply the clear primer around the entire perimeter of the glass. Allow the primer to dry for 5 minutes.

b. If refinishing or painting operations are needed for any portions of the glass opening apply the black primer to these portions. Allow the primer to dry for 5 minutes. Apply

CHILTON'S
AUTO BODY REPAIR TIPS

Tools and Materials • Step-by-Step Illustrated Procedures
How To Repair Dents, Scratches and Rust Holes
Spray Painting and Refinishing Tips

With a little practice, basic body repair procedures can be mastered by any do-it-yourself mechanic. The step-by-step repairs shown here can be applied to almost any type of auto body repair.

TOOLS & MATERIALS

You may already have basic tools, such as hammers and electric drills. Other tools unique to body repair — body hammers, grinding attachments, sanding blocks, dent puller, half-round plastic file and plastic spreaders — are relatively inexpensive and can be obtained wherever auto parts or auto body repair parts are sold. Portable air compressors and paint spray guns can be purchased or rented.

Auto Body Repair Kits

The best and most often used products are available to the do-it-yourselfer in kit form, from major manufacturers of auto body repair products. The same manufacturers also merchandise the individual products for use by pros.

Kits are available to make a wide variety of repairs, including holes, dents and scratches and fiberglass, and offer the advantage of buying the materials you'll need for the job. There is little waste or chance of materials going bad from not being used. Many kits may also contain basic body-working tools such as body files, sanding blocks and spreaders. Check the contents of the kit before buying your tools.

BODY REPAIR TIPS

Safety

Many of the products associated with auto body repair and refinishing contain toxic chemicals. Read all labels before opening containers and store them in a safe place and manner.

• Wear eye protection (safety goggles) when using power tools or when performing any operation that involves the removal of any type of material.

• Wear lung protection (disposable mask or respirator) when grinding, sanding or painting.

Sanding

1 Sand off paint before using a dent puller. When using a non-adhesive sanding disc, cover the back of the disc with an overlapping layer or two of masking tape and trim the edges. The disc will last considerably longer.

2 Use the circular motion of the sanding disc to grind *into* the edge of the repair. Grinding or sanding away from the jagged edge will only tear the sandpaper.

3 Use the palm of your hand flat on the panel to detect high and low spots. Do not use your fingertips. Slide your hand slowly back and forth.

WORKING WITH BODY FILLER

Mixing The Filler

Cleanliness and proper mixing and application are extremely important. Use a clean piece of plastic or glass or a disposable artist's palette to mix body filler.

1 Allow plenty of time and follow directions. No useful purpose will be served by adding more hardener to make it cure (set-up) faster. Less hardener means more curing time, but the mixture dries harder; more hardener means less curing time but a softer mixture.

2 Both the hardener and the filler should be thoroughly kneaded or stirred before mixing. Hardener should be a solid paste and dispense like thin toothpaste. Body filler should be smooth, and free of lumps or thick spots.

Getting the proper amount of hardener in the filler is the trickiest part of preparing the filler. Use the same amount of hardener in cold or warm weather. For contour filler (thick coats), a bead of hardener twice the diameter of the filler is about right. There's about a 15% margin on either side, but, if in doubt use less hardener.

3 Mix the body filler and hardener by wiping across the mixing surface, picking the mixture up and wiping it again. Colder weather requires longer mixing times. Do not mix in a circular motion; this will trap air bubbles which will become holes in the cured filler.

Applying The Filler

1 For best results, filler should not be applied over ¼″ thick.

Apply the filler in several coats. Build it up to above the level of the repair surface so that it can be sanded or grated down.

The first coat of filler must be pressed on with a firm wiping motion.

Apply the filler in one direction only. Working the filler back and forth will either pull it off the metal or trap air bubbles.

REPAIRING DENTS

Before you start, take a few minutes to study the damaged area. Try to visualize the shape of the panel before it was damaged. If the damage is on the left fender, look at the right fender and use it as a guide. If there is access to the panel from behind, you can reshape it with a body hammer. If not, you'll have to use a dent puller. Go slowly and work the metal a little at a time. Get the panel as straight as possible before applying filler.

1 This dent is typical of one that can be pulled out or hammered out from behind. Remove the headlight cover, headlight assembly and turn signal housing.

2 Drill a series of holes ½ the size of the end of the dent puller along the stress line. Make some trial pulls and assess the results. If necessary, drill more holes and try again. Do not hurry.

3 If possible, use a body hammer and block to shape the metal back to its original contours. Get the metal back as close to its original shape as possible. Don't depend on body filler to fill dents.

4 Using an 80-grit grinding disc on an electric drill, grind the paint from the surrounding area down to bare metal. Use a new grinding pad to prevent heat buildup that will warp metal.

5 The area should look like this when you're finished grinding. Knock the drill holes in and tape over small openings to keep plastic filler out.

6 Mix the body filler (see Body Repair Tips). Spread the body filler evenly over the entire area (see Body Repair Tips). Be sure to cover the area completely.

7 Let the body filler dry until the surface can just be scratched with your fingernail. Knock the high spots from the body filler with a body file ("Cheese-grater"). Check frequently with the palm of your hand for high and low spots.

8 Check to be sure that trim pieces that will be installed later will fit exactly. Sand the area with 40-grit paper.

9 If you wind up with low spots, you may have to apply another layer of filler.

10 Knock the high spots off with 40-grit paper. When you are satisfied with the contours of the repair, apply a thin coat of filler to cover pin holes and scratches.

11 Block sand the area with 40-grit paper to a smooth finish. Pay particular attention to body lines and ridges that must be well-defined.

12 Sand the area with 400 paper and then finish with a scuff pad. The finished repair is ready for priming and painting (see Painting Tips).

Materials and photos courtesy of Ritt Jones Auto Body, Prospect Park, PA.

REPAIRING RUST HOLES

There are many ways to repair rust holes. The fiberglass cloth kit shown here is one of the most cost efficient for the owner because it provides a strong repair that resists cracking and moisture and is relatively easy to use. It can be used on large and small holes (with or without backing) and can be applied over contoured areas. Remember, however, that short of replacing an entire panel, no repair is a guarantee that the rust will not return.

1 Remove any trim that will be in the way. Clean away all loose debris. Cut away all the rusted metal. But be sure to leave enough metal to retain the contour or body shape.

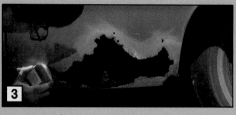

2 Grind away all traces of rust with a 24-grit grinding disc. Be sure to grind back 3-4 inches from the edge of the hole down to bare metal and be sure all traces of paint, primer and rust are removed.

3 Block sand the area with 80 or 100 grit sandpaper to get a clear, shiny surface and feathered paint edge. Tap the edges of the hole inward with a ball peen hammer.

4 If you are going to use release film, cut a piece about 2-3" larger than the area you have sanded. Place the film over the repair and mark the sanded area on the film. Avoid any unnecessary wrinkling of the film.

5 Cut 2 pieces of fiberglass matte to match the shape of the repair. One piece should be about 1" smaller than the sanded area and the second piece should be 1" smaller than the first. Mix enough filler and hardener to saturate the fiberglass material (see Body Repair Tips).

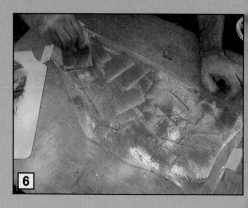

6 Lay the release sheet on a flat surface and spread an even layer of filler, large enough to cover the repair. Lay the smaller piece of fiberglass cloth in the center of the sheet and spread another layer of filler over the fiberglass cloth. Repeat the operation for the larger piece of cloth.

7 Place the repair material over the repair area, with the release film facing outward. Use a spreader and work from the center outward to smooth the material, following the body contours. Be sure to remove all air bubbles.

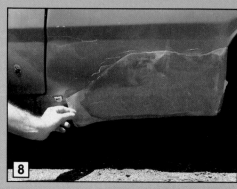

8 Wait until the repair has dried tack-free and peel off the release sheet. The ideal working temperature is 60°-90° F. Cooler or warmer temperatures or high humidity may require additional curing time. Wait longer, if in doubt.

9 Sand and feather-edge the entire area. The initial sanding can be done with a sanding disc on an electric drill if care is used. Finish the sanding with a block sander. Low spots can be filled with body filler; this may require several applications.

10 When the filler can just be scratched with a fingernail, knock the high spots down with a body file and smooth the entire area with 80-grit. Feather the filled areas into the surrounding areas.

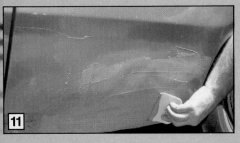

11 When the area is sanded smooth, mix some topcoat and hardener and apply it directly with a spreader. This will give a smooth finish and prevent the glass matte from showing through the paint.

12 Block sand the topcoat smooth with finishing sandpaper (200 grit), and 400 grit. The repair is ready for masking, priming and painting (see Painting Tips).

Materials and photos courtesy Marson Corporation, Chelsea, Massachusetts

PAINTING TIPS

Preparation

1 SANDING — Use a 400 or 600 grit wet or dry sandpaper. Wet-sand the area with a 1/4 sheet of sandpaper soaked in clean water. Keep the paper wet while sanding. Sand the area until the repaired area tapers into the original finish.

2 CLEANING — Wash the area to be painted thoroughly with water and a clean rag. Rinse it thoroughly and wipe the surface dry until you're sure it's completely free of dirt, dust, fingerprints, wax, detergent or other foreign matter.

3 MASKING — Protect any areas you don't want to overspray by covering them with masking tape and newspaper. Be careful not get fingerprints on the area to be painted.

4 PRIMING — All exposed metal should be primed before painting. Primer protects the metal and provides an excellent surface for paint adhesion. When the primer is dry, wet-sand the area again with 600 grit wet-sandpaper. Clean the area again after sanding.

Painting Techniques

P aint applied from either a spray gun or a spray can (for small areas) will provide good results. Experiment on an old piece of metal to get the right combination before you begin painting.

SPRAYING VISCOSITY (SPRAY GUN ONLY) — Paint should be thinned to spraying viscosity according to the directions on the can. Use only the recommended thinner or reducer and the same amount of reduction regardless of temperature.

AIR PRESSURE (SPRAY GUN ONLY) — This is extremely important. Be sure you are using the proper recommended pressure.

TEMPERATURE — The surface to be painted should be approximately the same temperature as the surrounding air. Applying warm paint to a cold surface, or vice versa, will completely upset the paint characteristics.

THICKNESS — Spray with smooth strokes. In general, the thicker the coat of paint, the longer the drying time. Apply several thin coats about 30 seconds apart. The paint should remain wet long enough to flow out and no longer; heavier coats will only produce sags or wrinkles. Spray a light (fog) coat, followed by heavier color coats.

DISTANCE — The ideal spraying distance is 8"-12" from the gun or can to the surface. Shorter distances will produce ripples, while greater distances will result in orange peel, dry film and poor color match and loss of material due to overspray.

OVERLAPPING — The gun or can should be kept at right angles to the surface at all times. Work to a wet edge at an even speed, using a 50% overlap and direct the center of the spray at the lower or nearest edge of the previous stroke.

RUBBING OUT (BLENDING) FRESH PAINT — Let the paint dry thoroughly. Runs or imperfections can be sanded out, primed and repainted.

Don't be in too big a hurry to remove the masking. This only produces paint ridges. When the finish has dried for at least a week, apply a small amount of fine grade rubbing compound with a clean, wet cloth. Use lots of water and blend the new paint with the surrounding area.

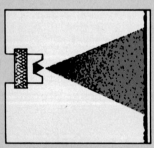

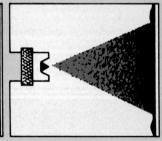

WRONG	CORRECT	WRONG
Thin coat. Stroke too fast, not enough overlap, gun too far away.	*Medium coat. Proper distance, good stroke, proper overlap.*	*Heavy coat. Stroke too slow, too much overlap, gun too close.*

the clear primer around the entireperimeter of the glass. Allow the primer to dry for 5 minutes.

c. If refinishing or painting operations are needed for any portions of the glass opening apply the black primer to these portions. Allow the primer to dry for 5 minutes.

9. Using a caulking gun and an adhesive cartridge, apply a smooth continuous bead ⅜" wide around the entire perimeter of the glass.

10. Reposition the glass to the window opening using the tape as the installation guide. Apply light hand pressure to the glass to ensure a bond to the body opening. Using a small brush or a flat bladed tool, paddle the bonding material around the edge of the glass to ensure a water tight seal.

NOTE: *If equipped with an electric defogger, paddle additional material at the edges of the butyl strip; avoid the area near the electrical harness.*

11. Using a soft , warm water spray, allow the water to spill over the edges of the glass to detect water leaks. If a water leak is encountered, paddle additional material around the leak.

12. Cement rubber spacers between the right and left sides of the window and the frame, to keep the glass centered during the installation procedures.

13. Install the window molding strips. Remove the masking tape from the inner perimeter of the window; pull the tape toward the center.

14. Complete the installation by replacing all of the removed parts.

NOTE: *After the window installation, the vehicle must remain at room temperature.*

INTERIOR

Front Door Panels
REMOVAL AND INSTALLATION

1. Remove the door handles and locking knobs from inside of the doors.

NOTE: *If equipped with door pull handles, remove the screws through the handle into the door inner panel.*

2. If equipped with remote control mirrors, remove the remote mirror escutcheon, then disengage the end of the mirror control cable from the escutcheon.

3. If equipped with a switch cover plate in the door armrest, remove the cover plate screws, then disconnect. The switches and the cigar lighter (if equipped) from the electrical harness.

4. If equipped with an integral armrest, re-

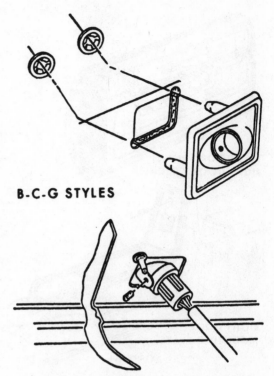

B-C-G STYLES

View of the remote mirror cable and escutcheon

move the screws inserted through the pull cup into the armrest hanger support. if equipped with an armrest applied after the trim panel installation, remove the armrest-to-inner panel screws.

5. If equipped with two piece trim panels, disengage the retainer clips from the front and rear of the upper trim panel, using tool No. BT-7323A, then lift the upper door trim and slide it slightly rearward to disengage it from the door inner panel at the beltline.

NOTE: *If equipped with electric switches in the door trim panel, disconnect the electrical connectors from the switch assembly.*

6. Along the upper edge of the lower trim panel, remove the mounting screws. At the lower edge of the panel, insert tool No. BT-2323A between the inner panel and the trim panel, then disengage the retaining clips from around the outer perimeter. To remove the lower panel, push the panel down and outward to disengage it from the door.

NOTE: *If equipped with courtesy lights, disconnect the wiring harness.*

7. If equipped with an insulator pad glued to the door inner panel, remove the pad (with a putty knife) by separating it from the inner panel.

8. Installation is the reverse of removal.

NOTE: *If replacing the inner pad to the door*

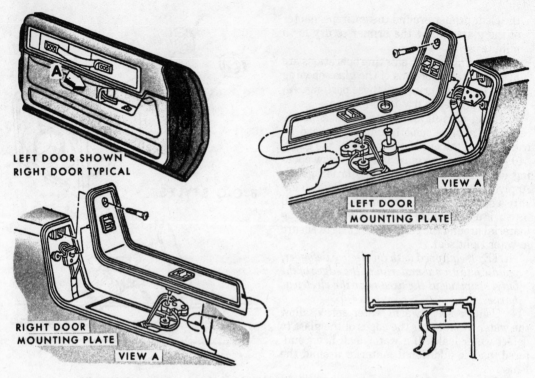

LEFT DOOR SHOWN
RIGHT DOOR TYPICAL

VIEW A

LEFT DOOR
MOUNTING PLATE

RIGHT DOOR
MOUNTING PLATE

VIEW A

View of the armrest switch cover plate and remote mirror cable attachment

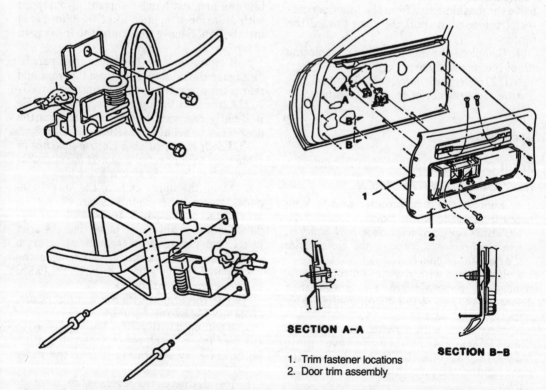

SECTION A-A

SECTION B-B

1. Trim fastener locations
2. Door trim assembly

View of the door lock remote control handle

Exploded view of the door trim panel

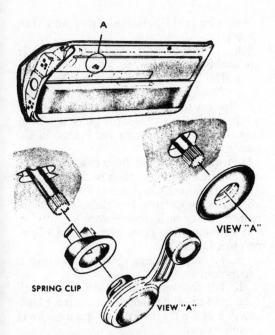

VIEW "A"

SPRING CLIP

VIEW "A"

View of the window regulator handle

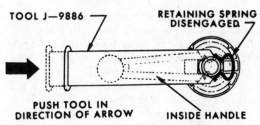

TOOL J—9886

RETAINING SPRING
DISENGAGED

PUSH TOOL IN
DIRECTION OF ARROW

INSIDE HANDLE

Removing the clip from inside the door handle

NOTE: *If equipped with door pull handles, remove the screws through the handle into the door inner panel.*

2. If equipped with a switch cover plate in the door armrest, remove the cover plate screws, then disconnect. the switches and the cigar lighter (if equipped) from the electrical harness.

3. If equipped with an integral armrest, remove the screws inserted through the pull cup into the armrest hanger support. if equipped with an armrest applied after the trim panel installation, remove the armrest-to-inner panel screws.

4. If equipped with two piece trim panels, disengage the retainer clips from the front and rear of the upper trim panel, using tool No. BT-7323A, then lift the upper door trim and slide it slightly rearward to disengage it from the door inner panel at the beltline.

5. Along the upper edge of the lower trim

inner panel, use 3M General Trim Adhesive No. 8080 to glue it to the panel.

Rear Door Panels

REMOVAL AND INSTALLATION

1. Remove the door handles and locking knobs from inside of the doors.

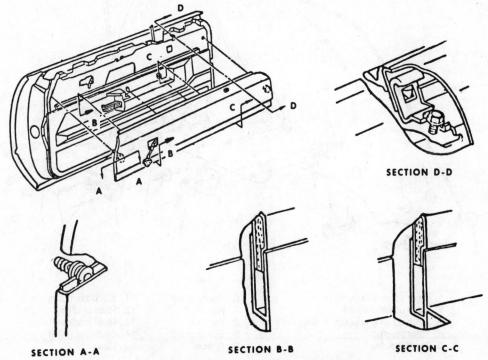

SECTION D-D

SECTION A-A

SECTION B-B

SECTION C-C

Exploded view of the two-piece door trim

panel, remove the mounting screws. At the lower edge of the panel, insert tool No. BT-2323A between the inner panel and the trim panel, then disengage the retaining clips from around the outer perimeter. To remove the lower panel, push the panel down and outward to disengage it from the door.

NOTE: *If equipped with courtesy lights, disconnect the wiring harness.*

6. If equipped with an insulator pad glued to the door inner panel, remove the pad (with a putty knife) by separating it from the inner panel.

7. Installation is the reverse of removal.

NOTE: *If replacing the inner pad to the door inner panel, use 3M General Trim Adhesive No. 8080 to glue it to the panel.*

Front Door Glass

REMOVAL AND INSTALLATION

Coupes

1. Remove the door trim panel(s) as outlined earlier in this chapter.

2. With the glass in the half raised position, mark the location of the mounting screws, then remove the following components:

a. The front belt stabilizer and trim retainer.

b. The rear belt stabilizer and pin assembly.

c. The front up-travel stop (on the glass).

d. The rear up-travel stop (on the glass).

3. Remove the vertical guide upper and lower screws, then disengage the guide assembly from the roller and lay in the bottom of the door.

4. Position the glass to expose the lower sash channel cam nuts, then remove the nuts through the inner panel access hole.

5. While supporting the glass, separate it from the lower sash channel cam.

6. To remove the glass, perform the following procedures:

a. Raise the glass slowly and slide it rearward.

b. Tilt the top of the glass inboard until the front up-step roller clears the front loading hole at the inner panel belt reinforcement.

c. Rotate the glass rearward 45°, then raise it slowly to clear the glass attaching screws through the belt loading holes.

d. To install reverse the removal proce-

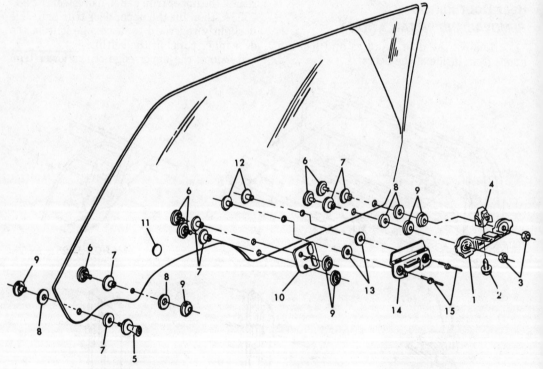

1. Rear up-stop support	6. Spanner bolt	11. Stabilizer button
2. Rear up-stop screw	7. Bushing	12. Rivet bushing
3. Rear up-stop support to glass nuts	8. Washer	13. Rivet retainer
4. Rear up-stop	9. Spanner nut	14. Stabilizer guide
5. Front up-stop	10. Spacer	15. Rivet

Exploded view of the door window assembly—stabilizer guide riveted to glass

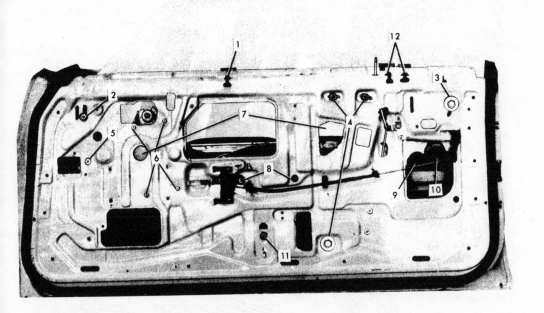

1. Front belt stabilizer and trim retainer screw
2. Front up-travel stop screw (on inner panel)
3. Rear up-travel stop screw (on inner panel)
4. Vertical guide upper and lower screws
5. Glass stabilizer rivet
6. Window regulator rivets (manual window)
7. Access holes–lower sash channel cam to glass attaching nuts

8. Inner panel cam screws
9. Rear up-stop support to glass attaching nut
10. Rear up-stop attaching screw
11. Down-travel stop screw
12. Rear belt stabilizer pin assembly screws

View of the front door hardware attachments, coupe models

dure. Adjust the window glass. Torque the hardware fasteners to 90-125 in.lb.

Sedans

1. Remove the door trim panel(s) as outlined earlier in this chapter.

2. To disengage the rear roller, lower the glass to ¾ of the way down, tip the nose of the glass down and slide it backward.

3. To disengage the front roller, raise the nose of the glass 45° and slide it rearward.

4. Lift the outboard of the upper frame to remove the glass.

5. To install reverse the removal procedure. Torque the the fasteners to 90-125 inch lbs.

ADJUSTMENT

Coupe

1. Remove the door panel(s) as outlined earlier.

2. To rotate the window, loosen the front and rear up-stops, adjust the inner panel cam and the up-stops, then tighten the screws.

3. To adjust the window's upper inboard and outboard edge, perform the following procedures:

a. Position the window in the partially down position.

b. Loosen the vertical guide upper support (lower) screws, which are accessible through the inner panel access holes.

c. Loosen the pin assembly screws, the rear up-stop screw and the front belt stabilizer screw.

d. Adjust the vertical guide upper support and pin assembly (in or out) as required, then tighten the screws. Adjust and tighten the other components.

NOTE: *When adjusting the glass, make sure it remains inboard of the blow-out clip, when cycled.*

4. If the window is too far forward or rearward, position the window partially down, loosen the vertical guide (upper and lower) screws, then adjust as required.

5. If the window is too high or low in its UP

position, adjust the front and rear up travel stop.

6. If the window is too high or low in its DOWN position, adjust the down travel stop.

7. If the window binds during the up and down operations, adjust the front and/or rear belt stabilizer pin assemblies.

Sedan

1. Remove the door panel(s) as outlined earlier.

2. If the window is rotated, loosen the inner panel cam adjusting screws, position the glass and tighten the screws.

3. If the window is too high or low in the

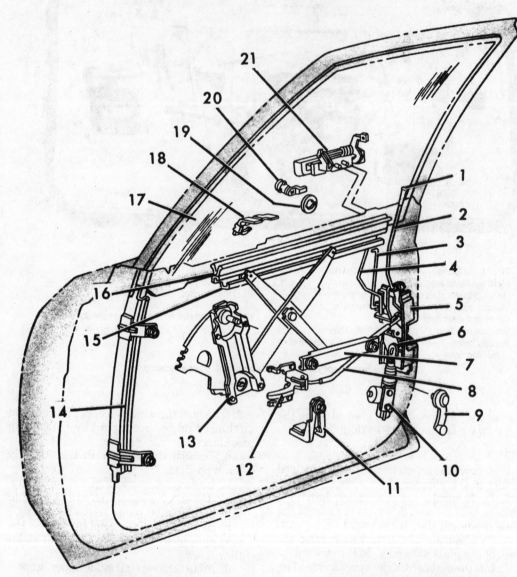

1. Inside locking rod knob
2. Inside locking rod
3. Lock cylinder to lock connecting rod
4. Outside handle to lock connecting rod
5. Door lock
6. Inside locking rod to electric actuator connecting rod
7. Inner panel cam
8. Inside remote handle to lock connecting rod
9. Manual window regulator handle
10. Power door lock actuator
11. Down-travel stop

12. Inside remote handle
13. Manual window regulator
14. Glass run channel retainer
15. Lower sash channel cam
16. Lower sash channel
17. Window glass
18. Lock cylinder retainer
19. Lock cylinder gasket
20. Lock cylinder assembly
21. Outside handle assembly

View of the front door hardware attachments, sedan models

down position, loosen the down-travel stop screws, position the glass, position the down-stop and tighten the screws.

Front Door Regulator
REMOVAL AND INSTALLATION
Coupe

1. Remove the door panel(s) as outlined earlier.

2. Prop the window in the half way-position by inserting rubber wedges between the window and the inner panel (at the belt) at the front and rear of the window.

NOTE: *If rubber stops are not available, remove the window.*

3. Mark (locate) and remove the inner panel cam and the vertical guide screws. Remove the vertical guide through the large access hole.

4. Using a center punch and a ¼″ drill bit, drive out the center pins and drill out the rivets of the regulator.

5. Remove the lower sash channel cam-to-glass rear nut, then slide the regulator rearward and disengage the rollers from the lower sash channel cam.

6. Remove the regulator through the largest inner panel access hole.

7. To install, reverse the removal procedure. Use ¼-20 x ½″ nuts to mount the regulator.

Sedan

1. Remove the door panel(s) as outlined earlier.

2. Position the window in the Full-Up position and tape the glass to the frame.

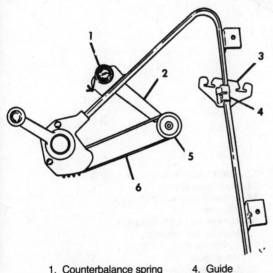

1. Counterbalance spring
2. Assist arm
3. Sash
4. Guide
5. Roller
6. Tape

View of the tape drive regulator assembly

3. Locate and remove the inner panel cam screws and the cam.

4. Remove the remote handle-to-lock connecting rod.

5. Using a center punch and a ¼″ drill bit, drive out the center pins and drill out the rivets of the regulator.

6. Disengage the rollers from the lower sash channel cam.

7. Remove the regulator through the largest inner panel access hole.

8. To install, reverse the removal procedure. Use ¼-20 x ½″ nuts to mount the regulator.

Electric Window Motor - Front Door
REMOVAL AND INSTALLATION
Coupe

1. Remove the door panel(s) as outlined earlier.

2. Prop the window in the half way-position by inserting rubber wedges between the window and the inner panel (at the belt) at the front and rear of the window.

NOTE: *If rubber stops are not available, remove the window.*

3. Mark (locate) and remove the inner panel cam and the vertical guide screws. Remove the vertical guide through the large access hole. Disconnect the electrical connector from the window regulator motor.

4. Using a center punch and a ¼″ drill bit, drive out the center pins and drill out the rivets of the regulator.

5. Remove the lower sash channel cam-to-glass rear nut, then slide the regulator rearward and disengage the rollers from the lower sash channel cam.

6. Remove the regulator and motor through the largest inner panel access hole.

7. To install, reverse the removal procedure. Use ¼-20 x ½″ nuts to mount the regulator.

Sedan

1. Remove the door panel(s) as outlined earlier.

2. Position the window in the Full-Up position and tape the glass to the frame.

3. Locate and remove the inner panel cam screws and the cam.

4. Remove the remote handle-to-lock connecting rod. Disconnect the wiring harness connector at the window regulator motor.

5. Using a center punch and a ¼″ drill bit, drive out the center pins and drill out the rivets of the regulator.

6. Disengage the rollers from the lower sash channel cam.

7. Remove the regulator and motor through the largest inner panel access hole.

8. To install, reverse the removal procedure. Use ¼-20 x ½" nuts to mount the regulator.

Rear Door Glass
REMOVAL AND INSTALLATION
Sedan

NOTE: *The rear door window is a frameless, solid, safety plate glass window which is retained by two beltline support clips; the window remains in a fixed position.*

1. Remove the rear door panel as outlined earlier.
2. Remove the beltline support clips and the trim support retainer.
3. With the use of suction cups, slide the glass down and remove it from the inboard side of the door.
4. To install, lubricate the glass channel with silicone spray or liquid soap, then reverse the removal procedures.

Rear Door Operating Vent Window Assembly

The rear doors have a movable vent window which can be either manual or electric operated. The window is held in place by mounting screws in the upper door frame and the door belt return flange.

The manual vent window has a latch handle which locks or opens the window

The electric vent window is operated by an electric motor and a drive cable assembly. It is controlled by a master switch on the left front-armrest or on a switch on the rear door trim panel.

REMOVAL AND INSTALLATION
Manual

1. Remove the rear door glass as outlined earlier.
2. Remove the frame and the belt mounting screws, then pull the top of the vent assembly

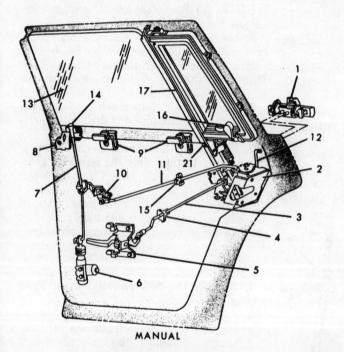

MANUAL

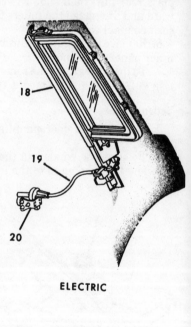

ELECTRIC

1. Outside handle assembly
2. Door lock
3. Inside handle to lock connecting rod
4. Shoe
5. Inside remote handle
6. Power door lock actuator
7. Inside locking rod
8. Trim support retainer
9. Glass support clips
10. Bell crank
11. Bell crank to lock connecting rod

12. Outside handle to lock connecting rod
13. Door glass (stationary)
14. Inside locking rod knob
15. Silencer
16. Manual vent latch assembly
17. Manual vent assembly
18. Electric vent assembly
19. Drive cable
20. Motor assembly–electric vent
21. Belt screw

View of the rear door hardware

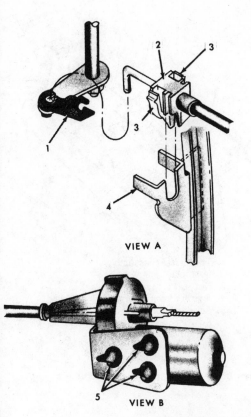

VIEW A

VIEW B

1. Retaining clip–actuator rod to actuator lever
2. Retaining clip–drive cable to retainer
3. Tabs–drive cable retaining clip
4. Retainer
5. Grommets–motor assembly to rear door inner panel

View of the door electric vent window—rear door

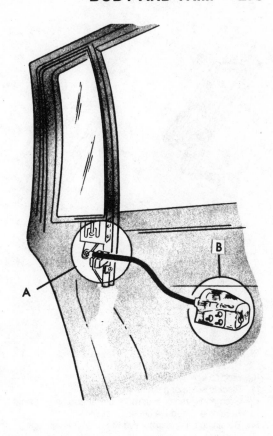

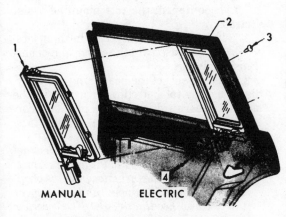

MANUAL   ELECTRIC

1. Manual vent window
2. Electric vent window
3. Upper frame attaching screw
4. Belt attaching screw

Installing the rear door vent window

forward and remove it from the inside of the door.

3. To install, lubricate the glass channel with silicone spray or liquid soap, then reverse the removal procedures.

Electric

1. Remove the rear door glass as outlined earlier.

2. Disconnect the actuator rod-to-actuator lever plastic clip, by rotating the clip inward with a suitable tool.

3. To remove the drive cable plastic retaining clip, depress the tabs and push up.

4. Remove the upper frame screws and the belt screw.

5. Pull the top of the vent assembly forward and remove it from the inside of the door.

6. To install, lubricate the glass channel with silicone spray or liquid soap, then reverse the removal procedures.

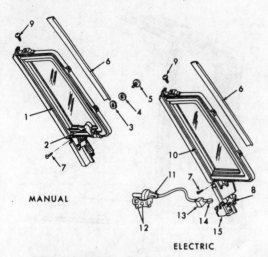

MANUAL

ELECTRIC

1. Manual vent window assembly
2. Manual latch handle
3. Washer (inboard of glass)
4. Spacer (outboard of glass)
5. Support screw
6. Reveal molding
7. Belt attaching screw
8. Actuator lever
9. Upper frame attaching screw
10. Electric vent window assembly
11. Electric actuator assembly
12. Grommets–motor assembly to rear door inner panel
13. Retaining clip–drive cable to retainer
14. Retaining clip–actuator rod to actuator lever
15. Retainer

Exploded view of the rear door hardware—vent window

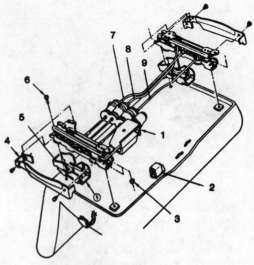

1. Transmission assembly
2. Seat relay
3. Nut
4. Adjuster track lower cover
5. Adjuster track upper cover
6. Adjuster-to-seat frame attaching bolts
7. Horizontal drive cable
8. Rear vertical drive cable
9. Front vertical drive cable

View of the six-way power seat adjusters

Power Seat Motor

REMOVAL AND INSTALLATION

1. Disconnect the electrical harness connector and remove the seat from the vehicle. Place the seat upside down on a protected workbench.

2. Disconnect the motor feed wires from the motor control relay.

3. Remove the motor mounting screws and the transmission-to-motor screws, then move the motor away to disengage it from the rubber coupling.

4. To install, reverse the removal procedure.
NOTE: *When installing the motor, make sure that the rubber coupling is properly engaged at the motor and transmission.*

Headliner

REMOVAL AND INSTALLATION

1. Remove the following items:
   a. Courtesy lamps.
   b. Sunshade support brackets.
   c. Coat hooks.
   d. Upper corner trim finishing panels.
   e. Roof side rail moldings.
   f. Windshield and rear window garnish moldings.
   g. Windshield side garnish moldings.
   h. Shoulder strap retainers and covers.
   i. If equipped, the roof mounted assist straps.
   j. If equipped, sun roof trim finishing lace.
   k. If equipped, twin lift-off panel roof garnish moldings.

2. On each side of the headlining assembly, disengage the tabs or clips, then remove the assembly rearward enough (to provide clearance) for the front portion of the assembly to be removed through the front door opening.
NOTE: *If the replacement headliner does not have an insulator glued to the upper surface, carefully remove the insulator from the original headlining (if equipped) and spot cement it to the new headlining. DO NOT overflex the headlining, for it can become easily damaged.*

3. To install reverse the removal procedure.
NOTE: *DO NOT attach the roof hardware until the headlining has been completely installed.*

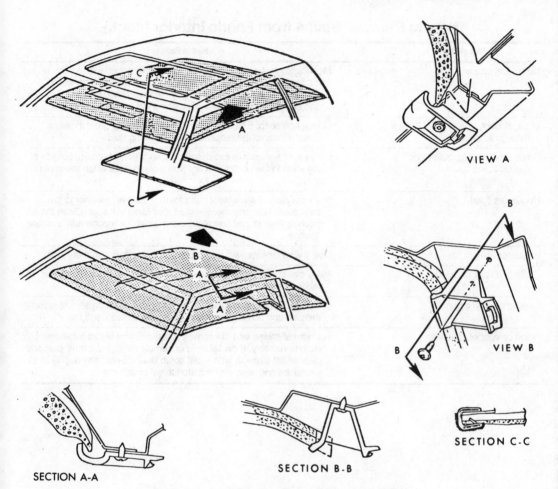

Exploded view of the headliner—others are similar

How to Remove Stains from Fabric Interior

For rest results, spots and stains should be removed as soon as possible. Never use gasoline, lacquer thinner, acetone, nail polish remover or bleach. Use a 3' x 3" piece of cheesecloth. Squeeze most of the liquid from the fabric and wipe the stained fabric from the outside of the stain toward the center with a lifting motion. Turn the cheesecloth as soon as one side becomes soiled. When using water to remove a stain, be sure to wash the entire section after the spot has been removed to avoid water stains. Encrusted spots can be broken up with a dull knife and vacuumed before removing the stain.

Type of Stain	How to Remove It
Surface spots	Brush the spots out with a small hand brush or use a commercial preparation such as K2R to lift the stain.
Mildew	Clean around the mildew with warm suds. Rinse in cold water and soak the mildew area in a solution of 1 part table salt and 2 parts water. Wash with upholstery cleaner.
Water stains	Water stains in fabric materials can be removed with a solution made from 1 cup of table salt dissolved in 1 quart of water. Vigorously scrub the solution into the stain and rinse with clear water. Water stains in nylon or other synthetic fabrics should be removed with a commercial type spot remover.
Chewing gum, tar, crayons, shoe polish (greasy stains)	Do not use a cleaner that will soften gum or tar. Harden the deposit with an ice cube and scrape away as much as possible with a dull knife. Moisten the remainder with cleaning fluid and scrub clean.

How to Remove Stains from Fabric Interior (cont.)

Type of Stain	How to Remove It
Ice cream, candy	Most candy has a sugar base and can be removed with a cloth wrung out in warm water. Oily candy, after cleaning with warm water, should be cleaned with upholstery cleaner. Rinse with warm water and clean the remainder with cleaning fluid.
Wine, alcohol, egg, milk, soft drink (non-greasy stains)	Do not use soap. Scrub the stain with a cloth wrung out in warm water. Remove the remainder with cleaning fluid.
Grease, oil, lipstick, butter and related stains	Use a spot remover to avoid leaving a ring. Work from the outisde of the stain to the center and dry with a clean cloth when the spot is gone.
Headliners (cloth)	Mix a solution of warm water and foam upholstery cleaner to give thick suds. Use only foam—liquid may streak or spot. Clean the entire headliner in one operation using a circular motion with a natural sponge.
Headliner (vinyl)	Use a vinyl cleaner with a sponge and wipe clean with a dry cloth.
Seats and door panels	Mix 1 pint upholstery cleaner in 1 gallon of water. Do not soak the fabric around the buttons.
Leather or vinyl fabric	Use a multi-purpose cleaner full strength and a stiff brush. Let stand 2 minutes and scrub thoroughly. Wipe with a clean, soft rag.
Nylon or synthetic fabrics	For normal stains, use the same procedures you would for washing cloth upholstery. If the fabric is extremely dirty, use a multi-purpose cleaner full strength with a stiff scrub brush. Scrub thoroughly in all directions and wipe with a cotton towel or soft rag.

Mechanic's Data

General Conversion Table

Multiply By	To Convert	To	
		LENGTH	
2.54	Inches	Centimeters	.3937
25.4	Inches	Millimeters	.03937
30.48	Feet	Centimeters	.0328
.304	Feet	Meters	3.28
.914	Yards	Meters	1.094
1.609	Miles	Kilometers	.621
		VOLUME	
.473	Pints	Liters	2.11
.946	Quarts	Liters	1.06
3.785	Gallons	Liters	.264
.016	Cubic inches	Liters	61.02
16.39	Cubic inches	Cubic cms.	.061
28.3	Cubic feet	Liters	.0353
		MASS (Weight)	
28.35	Ounces	Grams	.035
.4536	Pounds	Kilograms	2.20
—	To obtain	From	Multiply by

Multiply By	To Convert	To	
		AREA	
.645	Square inches	Square cms.	.155
.836	Square yds.	Square meters	1.196
		FORCE	
4.448	Pounds	Newtons	.225
.138	Ft./lbs.	Kilogram/meters	7.23
1.36	Ft./lbs.	Newton-meters	.737
.112	In./lbs.	Newton-meters	8.844
		PRESSURE	
.068	Psi	Atmospheres	14.7
6.89	Psi	Kilopascals	.145
		OTHER	
1.104	Horsepower (DIN)	Horsepower (SAE)	.9861
.746	Horsepower (SAE)	Kilowatts (KW)	1.34
1.60	Mph	Km/h	.625
.425	Mpg	Km/1	2.35
—	To obtain	From	Multiply by

Tap Drill Sizes

National Coarse or U.S.S.

Screw & Tap Size	Threads Per Inch	Use Drill Number
No. 5	40	39
No. 6	32	36
No. 8	32	29
No. 10	24	25
No. 12	24	17
1/4	20	8
5/16	18	F
3/8	16	5/16
7/16	14	U
1/2	13	27/64
9/16	12	31/64
5/8	11	17/32
3/4	10	21/32
7/8	9	49/64

National Coarse or U.S.S.

Screw & Tap Size	Threads Per Inch	Use Drill Number
1	8	7/8
1 1/8	7	63/64
1 1/4	7	1 7/64
1 1/2	6	1 11/32

National Fine or S.A.E.

Screw & Tap Size	Threads Per Inch	Use Drill Number
No. 5	44	37
No. 6	40	33
No. 8	36	29
No. 10	32	21

National Fine or S.A.E.

Screw & Tap Size	Threads Per Inch	Use Drill Number
No. 12	28	15
1/4	28	3
6/16	24	1
3/8	24	Q
7/16	20	W
1/2	20	29/64
9/16	18	33/64
5/8	18	37/64
3/4	16	11/16
7/8	14	13/16
1 1/8	12	1 3/64
1 1/4	12	1 11/64
1 1/2	12	1 27/64

Drill Sizes In Decimal Equivalents

Inch	Decimal	Wire	mm	Inch	Decimal	Wire	mm	Inch	Decimal	Wire & Letter	mm	Inch	Decimal	Letter	mm	Inch	Decimal	mm
1/64	.0156		.39		.0730	49			.1614		4.1		.2717		6.9		.4331	11.0
	.0157		.4		.0748		1.9		.1654		4.2		.2720	I		7/16	.4375	11.11
	.0160	78			.0760	48			.1660	19			.2756		7.0		.4528	11.5
	.0165		.42		.0768		1.95		.1673		4.25		.2770	J		29/64	.4531	11.51
	.0173		.44	5/64	.0781		1.98		.1693		4.3		.2795		7.1	15/32	.4688	11.90
	.0177		.45		.0785	47			.1695	18			.2810	K			.4724	12.0
	.0180	77			.0787		2.0	11/64	.1719		4.36	9/32	.2812		7.14	31/64	.4844	12.30
	.0181		.46		.0807		2.05		.1730	17			.2835		7.2		.4921	12.5
	.0189		.48		.0810	46			.1732		4.4		.2854		7.25	1/2	.5000	12.70
	.0197		.5		.0820	45			.1770	16			.2874		7.3		.5118	13.0
	.0200	76			.0827		2.1		.1772		4.5		.2900	L		33/64	.5156	13.09
	.0210	75			.0846		2.15		.1800	15			.2913		7.4	17/32	.5312	13.49
	.0217		.55		.0860	44			.1811		4.6		.2950	M			.5315	13.5
	.0225	74			.0866		2.2		.1820	14			.2953		7.5	35/64	.5469	13.89
	.0236		.6		.0886		2.25		.1850	13		19/64	.2969		7.54		.5512	14.0
	.0240	73			.0890	43			.1850		4.7		.2992		7.6	9/16	.5625	14.28
	.0250	72			.0906		2.3		.1870		4.75		.3020	N			.5709	14.5
	.0256		.65		.0925		2.35	3/16	.1875		4.76		.3031		7.7	37/64	.5781	14.68
	.0260	71			.0935	42			.1890		4.8		.3051		7.75		.5906	15.0
	.0276		.7	3/32	.0938		2.38		.1890	12			.3071		7.8	19/32	.5938	15.08
	.0280	70			.0945		2.4		.1910	11			.3110		7.9	39/64	.6094	15.47
	.0292	69			.0960	41			.1929		4.9	5/16	.3125		7.93		.6102	15.5
	.0295		.75		.0965		2.45		.1935	10			.3150		8.0	5/8	.6250	15.87
	.0310	68			.0980	40			.1960	9			.3160	O			.6299	16.0
1/32	.0312		.79		.0981		2.5		.1969		5.0		.3189		8.1	41/64	.6406	16.27
	.0315		.8		.0995	39			.1990	8			.3228		8.2		.6496	16.5
	.0320	67			.1015	38			.2008		5.1		.3230	P		21/32	.6562	16.66
	.0330	66			.1024		2.6		.2010	7			.3248		8.25		.6693	17.0
	.0335		.85		.1040	37		13/64	.2031		5.16		.3268		8.3	43/64	.6719	17.06
	.0350	65			.1063		2.7		.2040	6		21/64	.3281		8.33	11/16	.6875	17.46
	.0354		.9		.1065	36			.2047		5.2		.3307		8.4		.6890	17.5
	.0360	64			.1083		2.75		.2055	5			.3320	Q		45/64	.7031	17.85
	.0370	63		7/64	.1094		2.77		.2067		5.25		.3346		8.5		.7087	18.0
	.0374		.95		.1100	35			.2087		5.3		.3386		8.6	23/32	.7188	18.25
	.0380	62			.1102		2.8		.2090	4			.3390	R			.7283	18.5
	.0390	61			.1110	34			.2126		5.4		.3425		8.7	47/64	.7344	18.65
	.0394		1.0		.1130	33			.2130	3		11/32	.3438		8.73		.7480	19.0
	.0400	60			.1142		2.9		.2165		5.5		.3445		8.75	3/4	.7500	19.05
	.0410	59			.1160	32		7/32	.2188		5.55		.3465		8.8	49/64	.7656	19.44
	.0413		1.05		.1181		3.0		.2205		5.6		.3480	S			.7677	19.5
	.0420	58			.1200	31			.2210	2			.3504		8.9	25/32	.7812	19.84
	.0430	57			.1220		3.1		.2244		5.7		.3543		9.0		.7874	20.0
	.0433		1.1	1/8	.1250		3.17		.2264		5.75		.3580	T		51/64	.7969	20.24
	.0453		1.15		.1260		3.2		.2280	1			.3583		9.1		.8071	20.5
3/64	.0465	56			.1280		3.25		.2283		5.8	23/64	.3594		9.12	13/16	.8125	20.63
	.0469		1.19		.1285	30			.2323		5.9		.3622		9.2		.8268	21.0
	.0472		1.2		.1299		3.3		.2340	A			.3642		9.25	53/64	.8281	21.03
	.0492		1.25		.1339		3.4	15/64	.2344		5.95		.3661		9.3	27/32	.8438	21.43
	.0512		1.3		.1360	29			.2362		6.0		.3680	U			.8465	21.5
	.0520	55			.1378		3.5		.2380	B			.3701		9.4	55/64	.8594	21.82
	.0531		1.35		.1405	28			.2402		6.1		.3740		9.5		.8661	22.0
	.0550	54		9/64	.1406		3.57		.2420	C		3/8	.3750		9.52	7/8	.8750	22.22
	.0551		1.4		.1417		3.6		.2441		6.2		.3770	V			.8858	22.5
	.0571		1.45		.1440	27			.2460	D			.3780		9.6	57/64	.8906	22.62
	.0591		1.5		.1457		3.7		.2461		6.25		.3819		9.7		.9055	23.0
	.0595	53			.1470	26			.2480		6.3		.3839		9.75	29/32	.9062	23.01
	.0610		1.55		.1476		3.75	1/4	.2500	E	6.35		.3858		9.8	59/64	.9219	23.41
1/16	.0625		1.59		.1495	25			.2520		6.		.3860	W			.9252	23.5
	.0630		1.6		.1496		3.8		.2559		6.5		.3898		9.9	15/16	.9375	23.81
	.0635	52			.1520	24			.2570	F		25/64	.3906		9.92		.9449	24.0
	.0650		1.65		.1535		3.9		.2598		6.6		.3937		10.0	61/64	.9531	24.2
	.0669		1.7		.1540	23			.2610	G			.3970	X			.9646	24.5
	.0670	51		5/32	.1562		3.96		.2638		6.7		.4040	Y		31/32	.9688	24.6
	.0689		1.75		.1570	22		17/64	.2656		6.74	13/32	.4062		10.31		.9843	25.0
	.0700	50			.1575		4.0		.2657		6.75		.4130	Z		63/64	.9844	25.0
	.0709		1.8		.1590	21			.2660	H			.4134		10.5	1	1.0000	25.4
	.0728		1.85		.1610	20			.2677		6.8	27/64	.4219		10.71			

AIR/FUEL RATIO: The ratio of air to gasoline by weight in the fuel mixture drawn into the engine.

AIR INJECTION: One method of reducing harmful exhaust emissions by injecting air into each of the exhaust ports of an engine. The fresh air entering the hot exhaust manifold causes any remaining fuel to be burned before it can exit the tailpipe.

ALTERNATOR: A device used for converting mechanical energy into electrical energy.

AMMETER: An instrument, calibrated in amperes, used to measure the flow of an electrical current in a circuit. Ammeters are always connected in series with the circuit being tested.

AMPERE: The rate of flow of electrical current present when one volt of electrical pressure is applied against one ohm of electrical resistance.

ANALOG COMPUTER: Any microprocessor that uses similar (analogous) electrical signals to make its calculations.

ARMATURE: A laminated, soft iron core wrapped by a wire that converts electrical energy to mechanical energy as in a motor or relay. When rotated in a magnetic field, it changes mechanical energy into electrical energy as in a generator.

ATMOSPHERIC PRESSURE: The pressure on the Earth's surface caused by the weight of the air in the atmosphere. At sea level, this pressure is 14.7 psi at 32°F (101 kPa at 0°C).

ATOMIZATION: The breaking down of a liquid into a fine mist that can be suspended in air.

AXIAL PLAY: Movement parallel to a shaft or bearing bore.

BACKFIRE: The sudden combustion of gases in the intake or exhaust system that results in a loud explosion.

BACKLASH: The clearance or play between two parts, such as meshed gears.

BACKPRESSURE: Restrictions in the exhaust system that slow the exit of exhaust gases from the combustion chamber.

BAKELITE: A heat resistant, plastic insulator material commonly used in printed circuit boards and transistorized components.

BALL BEARING: A bearing made up of hardened inner and outer races between which hardened steel ball roll.

BALLAST RESISTOR: A resistor in the primary ignition circuit that lowers voltage after the engine is started to reduce wear on ignition components.

BEARING: A friction reducing, supportive device usually located between a stationary part and a moving part.

BIMETAL TEMPERATURE SENSOR: Any sensor or switch made of two dissimilar types of metal that bend when heated or cooled due to the different expansion rates of the alloys. These types of sensors usually function as an on/off switch.

BLOWBY: Combustion gases, composed of water vapor and unburned fuel, that leak past the piston rings into the crankcase during normal engine operation. These gases are removed by the PCV system to prevent the build-up of harmful acids in the crankcase.

BRAKE PAD: A brake shoe and lining assembly used with disc brakes.

BRAKE SHOE: The backing for the brake lining. The term is, however, usually applied to the assembly of the brake backing and lining.

BUSHING: A liner, usually removable, for a bearing; an anti-friction liner used in place of a bearing.

BYPASS: System used to bypass ballast resistor during engine cranking to increase voltage supplied to the coil.

CALIPER: A hydraulically activated device in a disc brake system, which is mounted straddling the brake rotor (disc). The caliper contains at least one piston and two brake pads. Hydraulic pressure on the piston(s) forces the pads against the rotor.

CAMSHAFT: A shaft in the engine on which are the lobes (cams) which operate the valves. The camshaft is driven by the crankshaft, via a belt, chain or gears, at one half the crankshaft speed.

CAPACITOR: A device which stores an electrical charge.

CARBON MONOXIDE (CO): a colorless, odorless gas given off as a normal byproduct of combustion. It is poisonous and extremely dangerous in confined areas, building up slowly to toxic levels without warning if adequate ventilation is not available.

CARBURETOR: A device, usually mounted on the intake manifold of an engine, which mixes the air and fuel in the proper proportion to allow even combustion.

CATALYTIC CONVERTER: A device installed in the exhaust system, like a muffler, that converts harmful byproducts of combustion into carbon dioxide and water vapor by means of a heat-producing chemical reaction.

CENTRIFUGAL ADVANCE: A mechanical method of advancing the spark timing by using flyweights in the distributor that react to centrifugal force generated by the distributor shaft rotation.

CHECK VALVE: Any one-way valve installed to permit the flow of air, fuel or vacuum in one direction only.

CHOKE: A device, usually a moveable valve, placed in the intake path of a carburetor to restrict the flow of air.

CIRCUIT: Any unbroken path through which an electrical current can flow. Also used to describe fuel flow in some instances.

CIRCUIT BREAKER: A switch which protects an electrical circuit from overload by opening the circuit when the current flow exceeds a predetermined level. Some circuit breakers must be reset manually, while other reset automatically

COIL (IGNITION): A transformer in the ignition circuit which steps of the voltage provided to the spark plugs.

COMBINATION MANIFOLD: An assembly which includes both the intake and exhaust manifolds in one casting.

COMBINATION VALVE: A device used in some fuel systems that routes fuel vapors to a charcoal storage canister instead of venting them into the atmosphere. The valve relieves fuel tank pressure and allows fresh air into the tank as fuel level drops to prevent a vapor lock situation.

COMPRESSION RATIO: The comparison of the total volume of the cylinder and combustion chamber with the piston at BDC and the piston at TDC.

CONDENSER: 1. An electrical device which acts to store an electrical charge, preventing voltage surges.
2. A radiator-like device in the air conditioning system in which refrigerant gas condenses into a liquid, giving off heat.

CONDUCTOR: Any material through which an electrical current can be transmitted easily.

CONTINUITY: Continuous or complete circuit. Can be checked with an ohmmeter.

COUNTERSHAFT: An intermediate shaft which is rotated by a mainshaft and transmits, in turn, that rotation to a working part.

CRANKCASE: The lower part of an engine in which the crankshaft and related parts operate.

CRANKSHAFT: The main driving shaft of an engine which receives reciprocating motion from the pistons and converts it to rotary motion.

CYLINDER: In an engine, the round hole in the engine block in which the piston(s) ride.

CYLINDER BLOCK: The main structural member of an engine in which is found the cylinders, crankshaft and other principal parts.

CYLINDER HEAD: The detachable portion of the engine, fastened, usually, to the top of the cylinder block, containing all or most of the combustion chambers. On overhead valve engines, it contains the valves and their operating parts. On overhead cam engines, it contains the camshaft as well.

DEAD CENTER: The extreme top or bottom of the piston stroke.

DETONATION: An unwanted explosion of the air fuel mixture in the combustion chamber caused by excess heat and compression, advanced timing, or an overly lean mixture. Also referred to as "ping".

DIAPHRAGM: A thin, flexible wall separating two cavities, such as in a vacuum advance unit.

DIESELING: A condition in which hot spots in the combustion chamber cause the engine to run on after the key is turned off.

DIFFERENTIAL: A geared assembly which allows the transmission of motion between drive axles, giving one axle the ability to turn faster than the other.

DIODE: An electrical device that will allow current to flow in one direction only.

DISC BRAKE: A hydraulic braking assembly consisting of a brake disc, or rotor, mounted on an axle, and a caliper assembly containing, usually two brake pads which are activated by hydraulic pressure. The pads are forced against the sides of the disc, creating friction which slows the vehicle.

DISTRIBUTOR: A mechanically driven device on an engine which is responsible for electrically firing the spark plug at a predetermined point of the piston stroke.

DOWEL PIN: A pin, inserted in mating holes in two different parts allowing those parts to maintain a fixed relationship.

DRUM BRAKE: A braking system which consists of two brake shoes and one or two wheel cylinders, mounted on a fixed backing plate, and a brake drum, mounted on an axle, which revolves around the assembly. Hydraulic action applied to the wheel cylinders forces the shoes outward against the drum, creating friction and slowing the vehicle.

DWELL: The rate, measured in degrees of shaft rotation, at which an electrical circuit cycles on and off.

ELECTRONIC CONTROL UNIT (ECU): Ignition module, module, amplifier or igniter. See Module for definition.

ELECTRONIC IGNITION: A system in which the timing and firing of the spark plugs is controlled by an electronic control unit, usually called a module. These systems have not points or condenser.

ENDPLAY: The measured amount of axial movement in a shaft.

ENGINE: A device that converts heat into mechanical energy.

EXHAUST MANIFOLD: A set of cast passages or pipes which conduct exhaust gases from the engine.

FEELER GAUGE: A blade, usually metal, of precisely predetermined thickness, used to measure the clearance between two parts. These blades usually are available in sets of assorted thicknesses.

F-Head: An engine configuration in which the intake valves are in the cylinder head, while the camshaft and exhaust valves are located in the cylinder block. The camshaft operates the intake valves via lifters and pushrods, while it operates the exhaust valves directly.

FIRING ORDER: The order in which combustion occurs in the cylinders of an engine. Also the order in which spark is distributed to the plugs by the distributor.

FLATHEAD: An engine configuration in which the camshaft and all the valves are located in the cylinder block.

FLOODING: The presence of too much fuel in the intake manifold and combustion chamber which prevents the air/fuel mixture from firing, thereby causing a no-start situation.

FLYWHEEL: A disc shaped part bolted to the rear end of the crankshaft. Around the outer perimeter is affixed the ring gear. The starter drive engages the ring gear, turning the flywheel, which rotates the crankshaft, imparting the initial starting motion to the engine.

FOOT POUND (ft.lb. or sometimes, ft. lbs.): The amount of energy or work needed to raise an item weighing one pound, a distance of one foot.

FUSE: A protective device in a circuit which prevents circuit overload by breaking the circuit when a specific amperage is present. The device is constructed around a strip or wire of a lower amperage rating than the circuit it is designed to protect. When an amperage higher than that stamped on the fuse is present in the circuit, the strip or wire melts, opening the circuit.

GEAR RATIO: The ratio between the number of teeth on meshing gears.

GENERATOR: A device which converts mechanical energy into electrical energy.

HEAT RANGE: The measure of a spark plug's ability to dissipate heat from its firing end. The higher the heat range, the hotter the plug fires.

HUB: The center part of a wheel or gear.

HYDROCARBON (HC): Any chemical compound made up of hydrogen and carbon. A major pollutant formed by the engine as a byproduct of combustion.

HYDROMETER: An instrument used to measure the specific gravity of a solution.

INCH POUND (in.lb. or sometimes, in. lbs.): One twelfth of a foot pound.

INDUCTION: A means of transferring electrical energy in the form of a magnetic field. Principle used in the ignition coil to increase voltage.

INJECTION PUMP· A device, usually mechanically operated, which meters and delivers fuel under pressure to the fuel injector.

INJECTOR: A device which receives metered fuel under relatively low pressure and is activated to inject the fuel into the engine under relatively high pressure at a predetermined time.

INPUT SHAFT: The shaft to which torque is applied, usually carrying the driving gear or gears.

INTAKE MANIFOLD: A casting of passages or pipes used to conduct air or a fuel/air mixture to the cylinders.

JOURNAL: The bearing surface within which a shaft operates.

KEY: A small block usually fitted in a notch between a shaft and a hub to prevent slippage of the two parts.

MANIFOLD: A casting of passages or set of pipes which connect the cylinders to an inlet or outlet source.

MANIFOLD VACUUM: Low pressure in an engine intake manifold formed just below the throttle plates. Manifold vacuum is highest at idle and drops under acceleration.

MASTER CYLINDER: The primary fluid pressurizing device in a hydraulic system. In automotive use, it is found in brake and hydraulic clutch systems and is pedal activated, either directly or, in a power brake system, through the power booster.

MODULE: Electronic control unit, amplifier or igniter of solid state or integrated design which controls the current flow in the ignition primary circuit based on input from the pickup coil. When the module opens the primary circuit, the high secondary voltage is induced in the coil.

NEEDLE BEARING: A bearing which consists of a number (usually a large number) of long, thin rollers.

OHM: (Ω) The unit used to measure the resistance of conductor to electrical flow. One ohm is the amount of resistance that limits current flow to one ampere in a circuit with one volt of pressure.

OHMMETER: An instrument used for measuring the resistance, in ohms, in an electrical circuit.

OUTPUT SHAFT: The shaft which transmits torque from a device, such as a transmission.

OVERDRIVE: A gear assembly which produces more shaft revolutions than that transmitted to it.

OVERHEAD CAMSHAFT (OHC): An engine configuration in which the camshaft is mounted on top of the cylinder head and operates the valve either directly or by means of rocker arms.

OVERHEAD VALVE (OHV): An engine configuration in which all of the valves are located in the cylinder head and the camshaft is located in the cylinder block. The camshaft operates the valves via lifters and pushrods.

OXIDES OF NITROGEN (NOx): Chemical compounds of nitrogen produced as a byproduct of combustion. They combine with hydrocarbons to produce smog.

OXYGEN SENSOR: Used with the feedback system to sense the presence of oxygen in the exhaust gas and signal the computer which can reference the voltage signal to an air/fuel ratio.

PINION: The smaller of two meshing gears.

PISTON RING: An open ended ring which fits into a groove on the outer diameter of the piston. Its chief function is to form a seal between the piston and cylinder wall. Most automotive pistons have three rings: two for compression sealing; one for oil sealing.

PRELOAD: A predetermined load placed on a bearing during assembly or by adjustment.

PRIMARY CIRCUIT: Is the low voltage side of the ignition system which consists of the ignition switch, ballast resistor or resistance wire, bypass, coil, electronic control unit and pick-up coil as well as the connecting wires and harnesses.

PRESS FIT: The mating of two parts under pressure, due to the inner diameter of one being smaller than the outer diameter of the other, or vice versa; an interference fit.

RACE: The surface on the inner or outer ring of a bearing on which the balls, needles or rollers move.

REGULATOR: A device which maintains the amperage and/or voltage levels of a circuit at predetermined values.

RELAY: A switch which automatically opens and/or closes a circuit.

RESISTANCE: The opposition to the flow of current through a circuit or electrical device, and is measured in ohms. Resistance is equal to the voltage divided by the amperage.

RESISTOR: A device, usually made of wire, which offers a preset amount of resistance in an electrical circuit.

RING GEAR: The name given to a ring-shaped gear attached to a differential case, or affixed to a flywheel or as part a planetary gear set.

ROLLER BEARING: A bearing made up of hardened inner and outer races between which hardened steel rollers move.

ROTOR: 1. The disc-shaped part of a disc brake assembly, upon which the brake pads bear; also called, brake disc.
2. The device mounted atop the distributor shaft, which passes current to the distributor cap tower contacts.

SECONDARY CIRCUIT: The high voltage side of the ignition system, usually above 20.000 volts. The secondary includes the ignition coil, coil wire, distributor cap and rotor, spark plug wires and spark plugs.

SENDING UNIT: A mechanical, electrical, hydraulic or electromagnetic device which transmits information to a gauge.

SENSOR: Any device designed to measure engine operating conditions or ambient pressures and temperatures. Usually electronic in nature and designed to send a voltage signal to an on-board computer, some sensors may operate as a simple on/off switch or they may provide a variable voltage signal (like a potentiometer) as conditions or measured parameters change.

SHIM: Spacers of precise, predetermined thickness used between parts to establish a proper working relationship.

SLAVE CYLINDER: In automotive use, a device in the hydraulic clutch system which is activated by hydraulic force, disengaging the clutch.

SOLENOID: A coil used to produce a magnetic field, the effect of which is produce work.

SPARK PLUG: A device screwed into the combustion chamber of a spark ignition engine. The basic construction is a conductive core inside of a ceramic insulator, mounted in an outer conductive base. An electrical charge from the spark plug wire travels along the conductive core and jumps a preset air gap to a grounding point or points at the end of the conductive base. The resultant spark ignites the fuel/air mixture in the combustion chamber.

SPLINES: Ridges machined or cast onto the outer diameter of a shaft or inner diameter of a bore to enable parts to mate without rotation.

TACHOMETER: A device used to measure the rotary speed of an engine, shaft, gear, etc., usually in rotations per minute.

THERMOSTAT: A valve, located in the cooling system of an engine, which is closed when cold and opens gradually in response to engine heating, controlling the temperature of the coolant and rate of coolant flow.

TOP DEAD CENTER (TDC): The point at which the piston reaches the top of its travel on the compression stroke.

TORQUE: The twisting force applied to an object.

TORQUE CONVERTER: A turbine used to transmit power from a driving member to a driven member via hydraulic action, providing changes in drive ratio and torque. In automotive use, it links the driveplate at the rear of the engine to the automatic transmission.

TRANSDUCER: A device used to change a force into an electrical signal.

TRANSISTOR: A semi-conductor component which can be actuated by a small voltage to perform an electrical switching function.

TUNE-UP: A regular maintenance function, usually associated with the replacement and adjustment of parts and components in the electrical and fuel systems of a vehicle for the purpose of attaining optimum performance.

TURBOCHARGER: An exhaust driven pump which compresses intake air and forces it into the combustion chambers at higher than atmospheric pressures. The increased air pressure allows more fuel to be burned and results in increased horsepower being produced.

VACUUM ADVANCE: A device which advances the ignition timing in response to increased engine vacuum.

VACUUM GAUGE: An instrument used to measure the presence of vacuum in a chamber.

VALVE: A device which control the pressure, direction of flow or rate of flow of a liquid or gas.

VALVE CLEARANCE: The measured gap between the end of the valve stem and the rocker arm, cam lobe or follower that activates the valve.

VISCOSITY: The rating of a liquid's internal resistance to flow.

VOLTMETER: An instrument used for measuring electrical force in units called volts. Voltmeters are always connected parallel with the circuit being tested.

WHEEL CYLINDER: Found in the automotive drum brake assembly, it is a device, actuated by hydraulic pressure, which, through internal pistons, pushes the brake shoes outward against the drums.

ABBREVIATIONS AND SYMBOLS

A: Ampere

AC: Alternating current

A/C: Air conditioning

A-h: Ampere hour

AT: Automatic transmission

ATDC: After top dead center

μA: Microampere

bbl: Barrel

BDC: Bottom dead center

bhp: Brake horsepower

BTDC: Before top dead center

BTU: British thermal unit

C: Celsius (Centigrade)

CCA: Cold cranking amps

cd: Candela

cm^2: Square centimeter

cm^3, cc: Cubic centimeter

CO: Carbon monoxide

CO_2: Carbon dioxide

cu.in., in^3: Cubic inch

CV: Constant velocity

Cyl.: Cylinder

DC: Direct current

ECM: Electronic control module

EFE: Early fuel evaporation

EFI: Electronic fuel injection

EGR: Exhaust gas recirculation

Exh.: Exhaust

F: Fahrenheit

F: Farad

pF: Picofarad

μF: Microfarad

FI: Fuel injection

ft.lb., ft. lb., ft. lbs.: foot pound(s)

gal: Gallon

g: Gram

HC: Hydrocarbon

HEI: High energy ignition

HO: High output

hp: Horsepower

Hyd.: Hydraulic

Hz: Hertz

ID: Inside diameter

in.lb.; in. lb.; in. lbs: inch pound(s)

Int.: Intake

K: Kelvin

kg: Kilogram

kHz: Kilohertz

km: Kilometer

km/h: Kilometers per hour

kΩ: Kilohm

kPa: Kilopascal

kV: Kilovolt

kW: Kilowatt

l: Liter

l/s: Liters per second

m: Meter

mA: Milliampere

mg: Milligram

mHz: Megahertz

mm: Millimeter

mm^2: Square millimeter

m^3: Cubic meter

MΩ: Megohm

m/s: Meters per second

MT: Manual transmission

mV: Millivolt

μm: Micrometer

N: Newton

N-m: Newton meter

NOx: Nitrous oxide

OD: Outside diameter

OHC: Over head camshaft

OHV: Over head valve

Ω: Ohm

PCV: Positive crankcase ventilation

psi: Pounds per square inch

pts: Pints

qts: Quarts

rpm: Rotations per minute

rps: Rotations per second

R-12: A refrigerant gas (Freon)

SAE: Society of Automotive Engineers

SO$_2$: Sulfur dioxide

T: Ton

t: Megagram

TBI: Throttle Body Injection

TPS: Throttle Position Sensor

V: 1. Volt; 2. Venturi

μV: Microvolt

W: Watt

∝: Infinity

‹: Less than

›: Greater than

Index

A

Air cleaner, 8
Air conditioning inspection, 14
Air pump, 138
Alternator, 68
Automatic transmission
  Adjustments, 206
  Filter change, 204
  Pan removal, 204
  Removal and installation, 209
Axle
  Axle shaft, bearings and seals, 212
  Identification, 212
  Lubricant level, 219

B

Ball joints, 220
Battery
  Fluid level, 10
  Jump starting, 30
  Removal and installation, 11
Belts, 11
Brakes
  Adjustment, 241
  Bleeding, 244
  Disc brakes
    Caliper, 247
    Pads, 245
    Rotor (Disc), 249
  Drum brakes
    Drum, 250, 251
    Shoes, 250, 251
    Wheel cylinder, 250
  Fluid level, 28
  Master cylinder, 242
  Parking brake, 253
  Power booster, 243
  Proportioning (combination) valve, 243

C

Calipers, 247
Camber, 224
Camshaft and bearings, 117
Capacities, 32
Carburetor
  Adjustments, 154
  Overhaul, 153
  Removal and Installation, 152
  Specifications, 173
Caster, 224
Chassis lubrication, 28
Catalytic Converter, 141
Charging system, 64
Circuit protection, 194
Clutch
  Adjustment, 204
  Removal and installation, 204
Combination valve, 243

Combination switch, 243
Compression testing, 76
Condenser, 49
Connecting rods and bearings, 124
Control arm
  Upper, 220
  Lower, 223
Cooling system, 27, 99
Crankcase ventilation valve, 9
Crankshaft, 129
Cylinder head
  Inspection, 103
  Rebuilding, 103
  Removal and installation, 100

D

Diesel fuel system
  Injection lines, 171
  Injection pump, 184
  Injection timing, 171
  Injectors, 171
Disc brakes, 245
Distributor
  Breaker points, 49
  Condenser, 49
  Removal and installation, 67
Door glass, 265, 270
Door locks, 260
Doors, 259
Drive axle
  Identification, 212
Driveshaft, 210
Drum brakes, 250, 251
Dwell angle, 52

E

EGR valve, 140
Electric window motor, 273
Electrical
  Chassis, 186
  Engine, 64
Electronic Ignition, 52
Emission controls, 135
Engine
  Camshaft, 117
  Connecting rods and bearings, 124
  Crankshaft, 129
  Cylinder head, 100
  Exhaust manifold, 97
  Fluids and lubricants, 24
  Flywheel, 133
  Front (timing) cover, 111
  Front seal, 111
  Identification, 6
  Intake manifold, 95
  Main bearings, 129
  Oil pan, 108
  Oil pump, 110

Engine (*continued*)
  Overhaul tips, 74
  Pistons, 124
  Rear main seal, 131
  Removal and installation, 73
  Rings, 125
  Rocker arms and/or shafts, 83, 93
  Specifications, 78
  Thermostat, 95
  Timing chain, 111
  Timing gears, 111
  Valve guides, 105
  Valves, 105
  Valve springs, 105
  Water pump, 99
Evaporative canister, 10, 136
Exhaust Manifold, 97
Exhaust System, 134

F

Firing orders, 49
Flashers, 194
Fluids and lubricants
  Automatic transmission, 26
  Battery, 10
  Chassis greasing, 28
  Coolant, 27
  Engine oil, 24
  Manual transmission, 26
    Brake, 28
  Power steering pump, 28
Flywheel and ring gear, 133
Front brakes, 245, 250
Front hubs, 249
Front suspension
  Ball joints, 220
  Lower control arm, 223
  Shock absorbers, 223
  Springs, 223
  Upper control arm, 220
  Wheel alignment, 224
Front wheel bearings, 249
Fuel filter, 22
Fuel pump, 152
Fuel system
  Diesel, 170
  Gasoline, 152
Fuses and circuit breakers, 194
Fusible links, 194

G

Gearshift linkage adjustment
  Automatic, 206
  Manual, 200

H

Headlights, 194
Headliner, 276
Heater
  Blower, 188
  Core, 188

Hood, 260
Hoses, 14

I

Identification
  Axle, 6
  Engine, 6
  Transmission, 6, 200, 204
  Vehicle, 4
Idle speed and mixture adjustment, 59
Ignition lock cylinder, 228
Ignition module, 57
Ignition switch, 228
Ignition timing, 57
Injection pump, 170
Injection timing, 170
Instrument cluster, 193
Intake manifold, 97

J

Jacking points, 29
Jump starting, 30

L

Lower control arm, 223
Lubrication
  Chassis, 28
  Engine, 24
  Transmission, 26

M

Main bearing, 129
Maintenance intervals, 31
Mainfolds
  Intake, 95
  Exhaust, 97
Manual transmission, 200
Master cylinder
  Brake, 242
Mechanic's data, 279
Model identification, 4

N

Neutral safety switch, 205

O

Oil and fuel recommendations, 23, 24
Oil and filter change (engine), 25
Oil level check
  Engine, 24
  Transmission, 26
Oil pan, 108
Oil pump, 110

P

Parking brake, 253
Pistons, 124

PCV valve, 9
Points, 49
Power brake booster, 243
Power seat motor, 276
Power steering pump, 229
Power window motor, 273
Pushing, 29

R

Radiator, 99
Radio, 190
Rear axle, 212
Rear brakes, 251
Rear main oil seal, 131
Rear suspension
  Shock absorbers, 225
  Springs, 225
Rear wheel bearings, 212
Regulator, 70
Rings, 125
Rocker arms or shaft, 83, 93
Routine maintenance, 8

S

Safety notice, ii
Serial number location, 5
Shock absorbers
  Front, 223
  Rear, 225
Spark plugs, 39
Special tools, 4
Specifications
  Brakes, 254
  Capacities, 32
  Carburetor, 173
  Crankshaft and connecting rod, 84
  General engine, 78
  Piston and ring, 86
  Torque, 87
  Tune-up, 40, 44
  Valves, 80
  Wheel alignment, 225
Speedometer cable, 194
Springs
  Front, 223
  Rear, 225
Starter, 70
Steering gear
  Manual, 231
  Power, 231
Steering linkage, 229

Steering wheel, 225
Stripped threads, 75

T

Thermostat, 95
Tie rod ends, 229
Timing
  Ignition, 57
  Injection, 170
Timing chain, 111
Timing gears, 111
Tires, 19
Tools, 2
Towing, 34
Transmission
  Automatic, 204
  Manual, 200
  Routine maintenance, 26
Trunk lid, 261
Tune-up
  Procedures, 39
  Specifications, 40, 44
Turn signal switch, 227

U

U-joints, 210
Upper control arm, 220

V

Valve guides, 105
Valves
  Adjustment, 59, 105
  Service, 105
  Specifications, 80
Valve seats, 106
Valve springs, 106
Vehicle identification, 4

W

Water pump, 99
Wheel alignment, 224
Wheel bearings, 249
Wheel cylinders, 250
Window glass, 265, 270
Windshield, 261
Windshield wipers
  Arm, 192
  Blade, 18, 192
  Linkage, 193
  Motor, 193
  Switch, 192

Chilton's Repair & Tune-Up Guides

The Complete line covers domestic cars, imports, trucks, vans, RV's and 4-wheel drive vehicles.

RTUG Title	Part No.
AMC 1975-82	7199
Covers all U.S. and Canadian models	
Aspen/Volare 1976-80	6637
Covers all U.S. and Canadian models	
Audi 1970-73	5902
Covers all U.S. and Canadian models.	
Audi 4000/5000 1978-81	7028
Covers all U.S. and Canadian models including turbocharged and diesel engines	
Barracuda/Challenger 1965-72	5807
Covers all U.S. and Canadian models	
Blazer/Jimmy 1969-82	6931
Covers all U.S. and Canadian 2- and 4-wheel drive models, including diesel engines	
BMW 1970-82	6844
Covers U.S. and Canadian models	
Buick/Olds/Pontiac 1975-85	7308
Covers all U.S. and Canadian full size rear wheel drive models	
Cadillac 1967-84	7462
Covers all U.S. and Canadian rear wheel drive models	
Camaro 1967-81	6735
Covers all U.S. and Canadian models	
Camaro 1982-85	7317
Covers all U.S. and Canadian models	
Capri 1970-77	6695
Covers all U.S. and Canadian models	
Caravan/Voyager 1984-85	7482
Covers all U.S. and Canadian models	
Century/Regal 1975-85	7307
Covers all U.S. and Canadian rear wheel drive models, including turbocharged engines	
Champ/Arrow/Sapporo 1978-83	7041
Covers all U.S. and Canadian models	
Chevette/1000 1976-86	6836
Covers all U.S. and Canadian models	
Chevrolet 1968-85	7135
Covers all U.S. and Canadian models	
Chevrolet 1968-79 Spanish	7082
Chevrolet/GMC Pick-Ups 1970-82 Spanish	7468
Chevrolet/GMC Pick-Ups and Suburban 1970-86	6936
Covers all U.S. and Canadian 1/2, 3/4 and 1 ton models, including 4-wheel drive and diesel engines	
Chevrolet LUV 1972-81	6815
Covers all U.S. and Canadian models	
Chevrolet Mid-Size 1964-86	6840
Covers all U.S. and Canadian models of 1964-77 Chevelle, Malibu and Malibu SS; 1974-77 Laguna; 1978-85 Malibu; 1970-86 Monte Carlo; 1964-84 El Camino, including diesel engines	
Chevrolet Nova 1986	7658
Covers all U.S. and Canadian models	
Chevy/GMC Vans 1967-84	6930
Covers all U.S. and Canadian models of 1/2, 3/4, and 1 ton vans, cutaways, and motor home chassis, including diesel engines	
Chevy S-10 Blazer/GMC S-15 Jimmy 1982-85	7383
Covers all U.S. and Canadian models	
Chevy S-10/GMC S-15 Pick-Ups 1982-85	7310
Covers all U.S. and Canadian models	
Chevy II/Nova 1962-79	6841
Covers all U.S. and Canadian models	
Chrysler K- and E-Car 1981-85	7163
Covers all U.S. and Canadian front wheel drive models	
Colt/Challenger/Vista/Conquest 1971-85	7037
Covers all U.S. and Canadian models	
Corolla/Carina/Tercel/Starlet 1970-85	7036
Covers all U.S. and Canadian models	
Corona/Cressida/Crown/Mk.II/Camry/Van 1970-84	7044
Covers all U.S. and Canadian models	

RTUG Title	Part No.
Corvair 1960-69	6691
Covers all U.S. and Canadian models	
Corvette 1953-62	6576
Covers all U.S. and Canadian models	
Corvette 1963-84	6843
Covers all U.S. and Canadian models	
Cutlass 1970-85	6933
Covers all U.S. and Canadian models	
Dart/Demon 1968-76	6324
Covers all U.S. and Canadian models	
Datsun 1961-72	5790
Covers all U.S. and Canadian models of Nissan Patrol; 1500, 1600 and 2000 sports cars; Pick-Ups; 410, 411, 510, 1200 and 240Z	
Datsun 1973-80 Spanish	7083
Datsun/Nissan F-10, 310, Stanza, Pulsar 1977-86	7196
Covers all U.S. and Canadian models	
Datsun/Nissan Pick-Ups 1970-84	6816
Covers all U.S and Canadian models	
Datsun/Nissan Z & ZX 1970-86	6932
Covers all U.S. and Canadian models	
Datsun/Nissan 1200, 210, Sentra 1973-86	7197
Covers all U.S. and Canadian models	
Datsun/Nissan 200SX, 510, 610, 710, 810, Maxima 1973-84	7170
Covers all U.S. and Canadian models	
Dodge 1968-77	6554
Covers all U.S. and Canadian models	
Dodge Charger 1967-70	6486
Covers all U.S. and Canadian models	
Dodge/Plymouth Trucks 1967-84	7459
Covers all 1/2, 3/4, and 1 ton 2- and 4-wheel drive U.S. and Canadian models, including diesel engines	
Dodge/Plymouth Vans 1967-84	6934
Covers all 1/2, 3/4, and 1 ton U.S. and Canadian models of vans, cutaways and motor home chassis	
D-50/Arrow Pick-Up 1979-81	7032
Covers all U.S. and Canadian models	
Fairlane/Torino 1962-75	6320
Covers all U.S. and Canadian models	
Fairmont/Zephyr 1978-83	6965
Covers all U.S. and Canadian models	
Fiat 1969-81	7042
Covers all U.S. and Canadian models	
Fiesta 1978-80	6846
Covers all U.S. and Canadian models	
Firebird 1967-81	5996
Covers all U.S. and Canadian models	
Firebird 1982-85	7345
Covers all U.S. and Canadian models	
Ford 1968-79 Spanish	7084
Ford Bronco 1966-83	7140
Covers all U.S. and Canadian models	
Ford Bronco II 1984	7408
Covers all U.S. and Canadian models	
Ford Courier 1972-82	6983
Covers all U.S. and Canadian models	
Ford/Mercury Front Wheel Drive 1981-85	7055
Covers all U.S. and Canadian models Escort, EXP, Tempo, Lynx, LN-7 and Topaz	
Ford/Mercury/Lincoln 1968-85	6842
Covers all U.S. and Canadian models of FORD Country Sedan, Country Squire, Crown Victoria, Custom, Custom 500, Galaxie 500, LTD through 1982, Ranch Wagon, and XL; MERCURY Colony Park, Commuter, Marquis through 1982, Gran Marquis, Monterey and Park Lane; LINCOLN Continental and Towne Car	
Ford/Mercury/Lincoln Mid-Size 1971-85	6696
Covers all U.S. and Canadian models of FORD Elite, 1983-85 LTD, 1977-79 LTD II, Ranchero, Torino, Gran Torino, 1977-85 Thunderbird; MERCURY 1972-85 Cougar,	

continued on next page

RTUG Title	Part No.	RTUG Title	Part No.
1983-85 Marquis, Montego, 1980-85 XR-7; LINCOLN 1982-85 Continental, 1984-85 Mark VII, 1978-80 Versailles		**Mercedes-Benz 1974-84** Covers all U.S. and Canadian models	6809
Ford Pick-Ups 1965-86 Covers all ½, ¾ and 1 ton, 2- and 4-wheel drive U.S. and Canadian pick-up, chassis cab and camper models, including diesel engines	6913	**Mitsubishi, Cordia, Tredia, Starion, Galant 1983-85** Covers all U.S. and Canadian models	7583
		MG 1961-81 Covers all U.S. and Canadian models	6780
Ford Pick-Ups 1965-82 Spanish	7469	**Mustang/Capri/Merkur 1979-85** Covers all U.S. and Canadian models	6963
Ford Ranger 1983-84 Covers all U.S. and Canadian models	7338	**Mustang/Cougar 1965-73** Covers all U.S. and Canadian models	6542
Ford Vans 1961-86 Covers all U.S. and Canadian ½, ¾ and 1 ton van and cutaway chassis models, including diesel engines	6849	**Mustang II 1974-78** Covers all U.S. and Canadian models	6812
		Omni/Horizon/Rampage 1978-84 Covers all U.S. and Canadian models of DODGE omni, Miser, 024, Charger 2.2; PLYMOUTH Horizon, Miser, TC3, TC3 Tourismo; Rampage	6845
GM A-Body 1982-85 Covers all front wheel drive U.S. and Canadian models of BUICK Century, CHEVROLET Celebrity, OLDSMOBILE Cutlass Ciera and PONTIAC 6000	7309		
		Opel 1971-75 Covers all U.S. and Canadian models	6575
GM C-Body 1985 Covers all front wheel drive U.S. and Canadian models of BUICK Electra Park Avenue and Electra T-Type, CADILLAC Fleetwood and deVille, OLDSMOBILE 98 Regency and Regency Brougham	7587	**Peugeot 1970-74** Covers all U.S. and Canadian models	5982
		Pinto/Bobcat 1971-80 Covers all U.S. and Canadian models	7027
		Plymouth 1968-76 Covers all U.S. and Canadian models	6552
		Pontiac Fiero 1984-85 Covers all U.S. and Canadian models	7571
GM J-Car 1982-85 Covers all U.S. and Canadian models of BUICK Skyhawk, CHEVROLET Cavalier, CADILLAC Cimarron, OLDSMOBILE Firenza and PONTIAC 2000 and Sunbird	7059	**Pontiac Mid-Size 1974-83** Covers all U.S. and Canadian models of Ventura, Grand Am, LeMans, Grand LeMans, GTO, Phoenix, and Grand Prix	7346
		Porsche 924/928 1976-81 Covers all U.S. and Canadian models	7048
GM N-Body 1985-86 Covers all U.S. and Canadian models of front wheel drive BUICK Somerset and Skylark, OLDSMOBILE Calais, and PONTIAC Grand Am	7657	**Renault 1975-85** Covers all U.S. and Canadian models	7165
		Roadrunner/Satellite/Belvedere/GTX 1968-73 Covers all U.S. and Canadian models	5821
GM X-Body 1980-85 Covers all U.S. and Canadian models of BUICK Skylark, CHEVROLET Citation, OLDSMOBILE Omega and PONTIAC Phoenix	7049	**RX-7 1979-81** Covers all U.S. and Canadian models	7031
		SAAB 99 1969-75 Covers all U.S. and Canadian models	5988
GM Subcompact 1971-80 Covers all U.S. and Canadian models of BUICK Skyhawk (1975-80), CHEVROLET Vega and Monza, OLDSMOBILE Starfire, and PONTIAC Astre and 1975-80 Sunbird	6935	**SAAB 900 1979-85** Covers all U.S. and Canadian models	7572
		Snowmobiles 1976-80 Covers Arctic Cat, John Deere, Kawasaki, Polaris, Ski-Doo and Yamaha	6978
Granada/Monarch 1975-82 Covers all U.S. and Canadian models	6937	**Subaru 1970-84** Covers all U.S. and Canadian models	6982
Honda 1973-84 Covers all U.S. and Canadian models	6980	**Tempest/GTO/LeMans 1968-73** Covers all U.S. and Canadian models	5905
International Scout 1967-73 Covers all U.S. and Canadian models	5912	**Toyota 1966-70** Covers all U.S. and Canadian models of Corona, MkII, Corolla, Crown, Land Cruiser, Stout and Hi-Lux	5795
Jeep 1945-87 Covers all U.S. and Canadian CJ-2A, CJ-3A, CJ-3B, CJ-5, CJ-6, CJ-7, Scrambler and Wrangler models	6817		
		Toyota 1970-79 Spanish	7467
Jeep Wagoneer, Commando, Cherokee, Truck 1957-86 Covers all U.S. and Canadian models of Wagoneer, Cherokee, Grand Wagoneer, Jeepster, Jeepster Commando, J-100, J-200, J-300, J-10, J20, FC-150 and FC-170	6739	**Toyota Celica/Supra 1971-85** Covers all U.S. and Canadian models	7043
		Toyota Trucks 1970-85 Covers all U.S. and Canadian models of pick-ups, Land Cruiser and 4Runner	7035
		Valiant/Duster 1968-76 Covers all U.S. and Canadian models	6326
Laser/Daytona 1984-85 Covers all U.S. and Canadian models	7563	**Volvo 1956-69** Covers all U.S. and Canadian models	6529
Maverick/Comet 1970-77 Covers all U.S. and Canadian models	6634	**Volvo 1970-83** Covers all U.S. and Canadian models	7040
Mazda 1971-84 Covers all U.S. and Canadian models of RX-2, RX-3, RX-4, 808, 1300, 1600, Cosmo, GLC and 626	6981	**VW Front Wheel Drive 1974-85** Covers all U.S. and Canadian models	6962
		VW 1949-71 Covers all U.S. and Canadian models	5796
Mazda Pick-Ups 1972-86 Covers all U.S. and Canadian models	7659	**VW 1970-79 Spanish**	7081
Mercedes-Benz 1959-70 Covers all U.S. and Canadian models	6065	**VW 1970-81** Covers all U.S. and Canadian Beetles, Karmann Ghia, Fastback, Squareback, Vans, 411 and 412	6837
Mereceds-Benz 1968-73 Covers all U.S. and Canadian models	5907		

Chilton's Repair & Tune-Up Guides are available at your local retailer or by mailing a check or money order for **$13.50** plus **$2.50** to cover postage and handling to:

Chilton Book Company
Dept. DM
Radnor, PA 19089

NOTE: When ordering be sure to include your name & address, book part No. & title.